The Nahuas

After the Conquest

The Nahuas
After the Conquest

—◆—

A Social and Cultural History of the

Indians of Central Mexico,

Sixteenth Through Eighteenth Centuries

James Lockhart

Stanford University Press, Stanford, California

Stanford University Press
Stanford, California
© 1992 by the Board of Trustees of the
Leland Stanford Junior University
Printed in the
United States of America
CIP data appear at the end of the book

Published with the support of the
National Endowment for the Humanities,
an independent federal agency

Stanford University Press publications are
distributed exclusively by Stanford
University Press within the United States,
Canada, Mexico, and Central America;
they are distributed exclusively by Cambridge
University Press throughout the rest of the world.

Original Printing 1992
Last figure below indicates year of this printing:
05   04   03   02   01   00   99   98   97   96

To the memory of

Ned Lockhart and Bertha VanFossen Lockhart, my parents

and

to Arthur J. O. Anderson

Contents

Tables

Figures

Abbreviations

AGN	Archivo General de la Nación, Mexico City
ANS	*The Art of Nahuatl Speech: The Bancroft Dialogues*, ed. Karttunen and Lockhart
AZ	*Aztekischer Zensus*, ed. Hinz et al.
BC	*Beyond the Codices*, by Anderson, Berdan, and Lockhart
CA	Codex Aubin (*Historia de la nación mexicana*, ed. Dibble)
CAN	Colección Antigua in MNAH AH
CDC	*Colección de documentos sobre Coyoacán*, ed. Carrasco and Monjarás-Ruiz
CFP	"De la Cruz family papers," Tepemaxalco (Calimaya), MNAH AH, GO 186
CH	*Die Relationen Chimalpahin's zur Geschichte Mexico's*, ed. Zimmermann
FC	*Florentine Codex: General History of the Things of New Spain*, by Sahagún, tr. Anderson and Dibble
GO	Gómez de Orozco Collection in MNAH AH
HJ	Hospital de Jesús, a section in AGN
HTC	*Historia tolteca-chichimeca*, ed. Kirchhoff, Güemes, and Reyes García
MNAH AH	Archivo Histórico of the Museo Nacional de Antropología e Historia, Mexico City
Molina	*Vocabulario castellano y mexicano y mexicano y castellano*, by fray Alonso de Molina (1571), 1970 edition
NAC	Newberry Library, Ayer Collection
NMY	*Nahuatl in the Middle Years*, by Karttunen and Lockhart
N&S	*Nahuas and Spaniards*, by Lockhart
RA	*Treatise on the Heathen Superstitions*, by Ruiz de Alarcón, ed. Andrews and Hassig
TA	*The Tlaxcalan Actas*, by Lockhart, Berdan, and Anderson

TC	*Testaments of Culhuacan*, ed. Cline and León-Portilla
TCB	Tula Cofradía Book, in Lilly Library, Indiana University, section Latin American Mss.—Mexico
TN	*Teatro náhuatl*, by Horcasitas
UCLA TC	UCLA Research Library Special Collections, Tulancingo Collection
ZM	The annals of don Juan Buenaventura Zapata y Mendoza, Bibliothèque Nationale, Paris, Mexican ms. 212

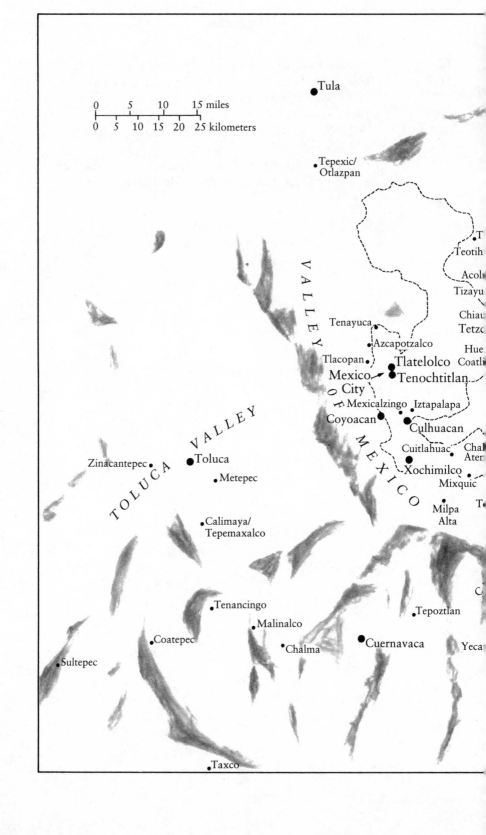

Tula

0   5   10   15 miles

0   5   10   15   20   25 kilometers

Tepexic/
Otlazpan

VALLEY

T

Teotih

Acol

Tizayu

Chiau
Tetzc

Tenayuca

Azcapotzalco

Hue

Tlacopan

Tlatelolco

Coatli

Mexico
City

Tenochtitlan

Mexicalzingo

Iztapalapa

O F

Coyoacan

Culhuacan

M
E
X
I
C
O

VALLEY

TOLUCA

Cuitlahuac

Cha

Aten

Zinacantepec

Toluca

Xochimilco

Metepec

Mixquic

Milpa
Alta

T

Calimaya/
Tepemaxalco

C

Tenancingo

Tepoztlan

Malinalco

Coatepec

Chalma

Cuernavaca

Yeca

Sultepec

Taxco

. Acatlan   . Acaxochitlan

● Tulancingo

ımba

aoztoc

TEPETICPAC

QUIAHUIZTLAN   ●   TIÇATLA   .Huamantla
Tlaxcala

OCOTELOLCO

nanalco
naquemecan
mecameca)
ʒo
tzingo
auhtlan
nalhuacan
pan

● Huejotzingo

.Calpan
●Cholula

●Puebla

●Cuauhtinchan

N

The Nahuas
After the Conquest

I

Introduction

SPEAKERS OF THE so-called Uto-Aztecan languages can be found scattered across a vast area stretching from the western United States through the entire northwest of Mexico and on into the heart of the country, with a few enclaves located as far south as Nicaragua. The southernmost major branch of the Uto-Aztecan family is Nahuatl, which by the fifteenth and sixteenth centuries was the language of the majority of the people living in the core regions of central Mexico. Divided into a large number of separate, often warring regional states, each with a sense of unique ethnic origin, sometimes living under the partial dominance of imperial confederations and sometimes not, the central Mexicans at the time of European contact were united, to the extent that they were, not by politics or even by an assertive consciousness of unity, but by a shared culture carried in the vocabulary of their common language.

These people I call the Nahuas, a name they sometimes used themselves and the one that has become current today in Mexico, in preference to Aztecs. The latter term has several decisive disadvantages: it implies a kind of quasi-national unity that did not exist, it directs attention to an ephemeral imperial agglomeration, it is attached specifically to the preconquest period, and by the standards of the time, its use for anyone other than the Mexica (the inhabitants of the imperial capital, Tenochtitlan) would have been improper even if it had been the Mexica's primary designation, which it was not.

Simply put, the purpose of the present book is to throw light on the history of Nahua society and culture through the use of records in Nahuatl, concentrating on the time when the bulk of the extant documents were written, between about 1540–50 and the late eighteenth century. At the same time, the earliest records are full of implications for the very first years after contact, and ultimately for the preconquest epoch as well, both of which are touched on here in ways that are more than introductory or ancillary.

Views of Postconquest Nahua History

It is not unnatural that until recently the historical literature relating to
the Indians of Mexico (and other Spanish American areas) in the time after
European contact should have turned on the imagined relative position of
Indians and Spaniards. The matter has two interconnected dimensions, the
actual roles postulated for the two groups and the Spanish sources used at
various points, which provided the primary perspective on the Indians and
hence went far toward determining the putative roles.

Successive generations of historians have viewed the interaction of Spaniards and Nahuas in very different ways.[1] The first wave, of whom William
Prescott is foremost, followed the Spanish chronicles in writing narrative histories of the sixteenth-century conquest; they emphasized the simple military
clash, the victories and defeats of the opposing sides. Conflict was the main
interpretive framework. But even though everyone has realized all along that
the military struggle was soon over in central Mexico (as opposed to peripheral areas), and it has since been shown that disturbances in the following
centuries were sporadic and limited, initiated by restricted local entities in
defense of their autonomy within the already existing scheme of things,[2] conflict and resistance have long continued to shape scholars' notions of Spanish-
Indian relations.

Those who followed the epic historians, approaching the topic of the development of Spanish American civilization largely through the avenue of
formal institutions, added a new general interpretive notion, displacement, to
that of clash. They, and above all the greatest of them, Robert Ricard, tended
to see the quick replacement of indigenous elements or structures by European equivalents, or indeed, the introduction of things European into a relative vacuum. This view arose straightforwardly, or if you will naïvely, from
the early institutionalists' main source, the reports of officials and priests to
the crown. Although officials in America did have a fair grasp of how crucial
indigenous structures were for the success of the measures they took, it was
not in their interest, in reporting on progress to their superiors, to talk much
about this aspect. If they had done so, their steps would have seemed obvious,
almost inevitable, with the outcome determined largely by the nature of indigenous society (as was in fact the case). Instead, they painted pictures of
the vast revolutions they were bringing about in indigenous life and how well
their introductions were being received.

Perhaps the most formidable and accessible body of relevant official documents was that produced by the mendicant friars of Mexico in the aftermath
of the conquest—voluminous correspondence and chronicles written above
all by Franciscans, and secondarily by Dominicans and Augustinians. This

literature tells how the mendicants converted the Indians of Mexico by the millions and introduced the full panoply of Christian pomp and ceremony among them, to the point that only a few piteous tatters of preconquest belief and practice were left. At the same time, the mendicants, according to themselves, brought the Indians the elements of European culture more generally, concentrating the scattered natives in new urban foundations, introducing European-style governance, teaching them European skills from agriculture to the crafts to music and other arts, with the most splendid and immediate results. The mendicants' version of events, as ably synthesized by Ricard,[3] long served as the basic model for interpreting cultural interaction in Mexico and all of Spanish America.

The displacement model never held the stage undisputed, however. A counterview pointed to the isolation of the Indians from the social-economic centers of Hispanic life in cities and mines, with the consequent wholesale survival of indigenous elements untouched by outside influence. Supporting such notions were two kinds of evidence. First, institutional historians found in Spanish law a well-developed doctrine of two separate commonwealths: one for Spaniards, centered in the newly created Spanish cities; the other for Indians, consisting of towns and villages dotting the cities' hinterlands. The illusion of two entirely separate spheres was augmented by the fact that, in order to throw their own activity into higher relief, friars and others wrote as little as possible about the role of competing agencies or of the Spanish civil population that almost immediately began to spill out of the cities. An apparently compatible message was delivered by twentieth-century ethnographers. Interested from the outset in continuities reaching back to the preconquest period, these scholars found (usually in relatively isolated areas) irrefutable evidence of survivals in diverse matters, including religious beliefs, kinship, medicinal practices, and material culture. The impression arising was that of communities turned in upon themselves, frozen internally and resisting all change from the outside.[4]

A breakthrough in the direction of giving more weight to the Indian side in shaping Spanish-indigenous interaction came with the work of Charles Gibson. First, Gibson showed that in the important central Mexican province of Tlaxcala, Hispanic-style municipal government was introduced and flourished in the sixteenth century not merely by Spanish design or fiat, or entirely on the Spanish model; rather it was extensively adapted to the local indigenous situation and took hold in part because of the Tlaxcalans' perception that it could serve their interests. Then in his pivotal *Aztecs Under Spanish Rule*, Gibson gave an entirely different perspective to the history of Spanish-Indian interaction and hence to postconquest Indian history.[5] He showed that the local indigenous states of the Valley of Mexico survived long into the

postconquest period with their territories and many of their internal mechanisms essentially intact, giving the basis for all the structures the Spaniards
implanted in the countryside. The *encomienda* (for newcomers to the field, a
grant of Indian tribute and originally labor to a Spaniard, the foundation of
the largest Spanish estates in the first decades after the conquest), the rural
parish, and the Spanish-style Indian town followed the borders of the indigenous states and functioned through their already existing mechanisms. Administrative districts in the countryside (*corregimientos*) were collections of
these Indian units, relying on them for collecting taxes, keeping the peace,
and much else.

The error of the Ricardian view now became fully apparent. The friars
had stepped into a situation already made for them (and for the governmental
officials to whom they had given less than full credit). The extent of their
success depended precisely upon the acceptance and retention of indigenous
elements and patterns that in many respects were strikingly close to those of
Europe. Relatively few of the friars' innovations were entirely new to the
Mesoamericans. It was because of such things as their own crafts and writing
systems, their tradition of sumptuous temples as the symbol of the state and
the ethnic group, their well-developed calendar of religious festivities and
processions, their relatively high degree of stability and nucleation of settlement, that they could quickly take to similar aspects of the Spanish heritage.

As to the notion of isolation shared by the institutionalists and the anthropologists, post-Gibsonian scholarship has cut into it deeply. The encomienda has been seen to involve a whole staff of Europeans, Africans, and
Indians in permanent Spanish employ. Communities of humble Hispanic
people, including small agriculturalists and stockmen, petty traders, and muleteers, soon grew up inside many Indian towns.[6] Over time, Spanish influence on indigenous patterns of alcohol use and homicide was appreciable,
especially in those areas with the largest Spanish populations and most opportunities for personal interaction.[7]

As things now stand, then, it has become apparent that straightforward
clash, simple displacement, and indigenous survival through isolation are
modes more characteristic of areas on the fringe, where Spanish immigrants
were few and indigenous people less than fully sedentary, than of a core region such as central Mexico. It is true that even there those modes came into
play to some extent. But in any case, the crucial factor is not so much the
particular modality of contact as the simple degree of contact, measured in
distance, frequency, or hours spent, as the vehicle for interaction, regardless
of whether that contact is construed as hostile or friendly, harmful or benign.
The presence of Europeans among Indians unleashed a long series of vast
epidemics that had nothing to do with the intentions of either party, but

resulted from the combination of the historical attributes of both sides. Likewise, in the cultural sphere, the degree of contact between the two populations helped shape centuries-long processes combining gradual transformation with deep continuities, depending on the relative attributes of the two. Wherever human beings come into touch, there will be both conflict and cooperation, both congregation and avoidance; some things on both sides will be strongly affected, others less so. In the central areas, contact was relatively close from the beginning, and with a quickly and steadily expanding Hispanic sector, it grew ever closer in a cumulative trend covering centuries.

Another important defining characteristic of the Spanish American central areas as opposed to the periphery is the widespread interaction of indigenous and intrusive cultures on the basis of coincidences that allowed the quick, large-scale implantation among the indigenous people of European forms, or what appeared on the face of it to be such. Only in areas resembling central Mexico were large and lucrative encomiendas possible, only there could hundreds of rural parishes be set up and independent Indian municipalities on the Spanish model be made to function. In many ways, the Europeans and indigenous peoples of the central areas had more in common than either did with the other peoples of the hemisphere.

The coincidences, however, though real, were inevitably and invariably imperfect, leading to mixed forms. Absolutely unaltered survival and total displacement are equally rare in the history of cultural contact in central Mexico. In the early stages, what one typically finds is the preliminary identification of intrusive and indigenous elements, allowing an indigenous concept or practice to operate in a familiar manner under a Spanish-Christian overlay. Over the centuries, stable composite forms and patterns took shape, owing some traits to one donor, some to the other, and some to both. By the late eighteenth century, almost nothing in the entire indigenous cultural ensemble was left untouched, yet at the same time almost everything went back in some form or other to a preconquest antecedent.

Uses of Language

The Franciscan friars of the sixteenth century remain unsurpassed in the importance they gave to language—recorded as well as spoken—in understanding the indigenous population of Mexico. Trained in the methods of humanistic philology, the Franciscans and their Nahua aides produced one indispensable work after another. By the late 1540's, fray Andrés de Olmos had completed a sophisticated grammar of Nahuatl, accompanied by a list of idiomatic expressions and a set of sample speeches by informants. In the next decade, fray Alonso de Molina published a Spanish-Nahuatl dictionary, greatly expanded in an edition of 1571; Molina went far beyond utilitarian basics to include a vast range of vocabulary, making many subtle semantic and grammatical distinctions. From the 1540's forward, fray Bernardino de Sahagún and a team of Nahuas worked for decades on an encyclopedic corpus; it was provisionally complete by the late 1570's, covering every aspect of preconquest Nahua life in Nahuatl texts written down by the indigenous aides and only later translated into Spanish. Sahagún himself saw much of the potential usefulness of his work in its illustration of the meaning of special indigenous vocabulary as employed in actual texts.[8]

A by-product of the indigenist philology done under Spanish auspices proved to be as significant as the movement itself, and in some ways more so. The Franciscans, other ecclesiastics, and possibly some literate Spanish laymen taught enough Nahuas how to write their own language in the Roman alphabet that the art became self-perpetuating among writing specialists throughout the Nahua world, serving as the normal medium for record-keeping of all kinds. The practice continued generation after generation for most of the time up to Mexican independence, creating a large and varied corpus with remarkable time depth and uninterrupted continuity. Much of the material once preserved in local centers across the central Mexican countryside—indeed, apparently most of it—has been lost, but a great deal reached Mexico City through litigation and is still to be found in various sections of the Mexican national archive, not to speak of special caches in repositories in Mexico, this country, and elsewhere.

Yet it was to be a long road to the exploitation of these unique records for the history of the people who wrote them. The gods of the disciplines seemed to have decreed that historians should study Indians indirectly, leaving it to others, mainly anthropologists, to approach them through their own language. From William Prescott through Robert Ricard and Lewis Hanke, historians gave no small amount of attention to the Indians of Mexico, but always through Spanish eyes, using Spanish accounts and concepts. In his *Tlaxcala in the Sixteenth Century* (1952), Charles Gibson took a most meaningful step forward in his use of Nahuatl cabildo records along with more traditional sources, but in *The Aztecs* (1964), he reverted to almost exclusive reliance on Spanish records.

Meanwhile, serious scholarship on Nahuatl-language materials had been in progress for two generations or more, but the postconquest period failed to get its due, partly because anthropologists and others were primarily interested in the Indians before European contact, and partly because they turned first to the most spectacular and accessible documents, many of which were devoted to recounting preconquest events or recapturing preconquest culture.[9] The largest project of this type was Anderson and Dibble's complete translation of the Nahuatl in Sahagún's Florentine Codex. Nonanthropologists entering this area were Angel María Garibay and on his heels Miguel León-Portilla, concentrating on Nahuatl song as well as the Florentine Codex and similar texts in an effort to reconstruct and analyze preconquest intellectual life.[10] The only clearly postconquest phenomenon receiving attention was the corpus of Nahuatl religious plays, some of which were published many years ago by Francisco del Paso y Troncoso; other scholars, notably J. H. Cornyn, continued the process, leading finally to the appearance of a large collection by Fernando Horcasitas in recent years.[11] Since themes, plots, and perhaps more originated with Spanish ecclesiastics, however, the genre is so rarefied and in a sense artificial that it produced relatively little understanding until the material could be put in a broader context of Nahua writing.

By the 1970's, scholars in both Mexico and this country were finally ready to turn to the more mundane documentation in Nahuatl. Some of it had been catalogued for decades, so the mere fact of its existence was not, properly speaking, a surprise. But the extent, richness, and variety of the corpus surprised and continue to surprise those involved in opening it up. Done by Nahuas for Nahua eyes and for the purposes of everyday life, these documents, though most of them are ostensibly in Spanish genres, are not only more individual in their language, conventions, and content than the Spanish counterparts, but more complex in belonging to two traditions rather than one. They are both more difficult and potentially richer (that is, per item) than Spanish records. A realization of their nature has called forth a New Philology to render them understandable and available and put them in their true context. In the wake of the philological activity, often inextricably bound up with it or indistinguishable from it, have come dissertations, articles, and monographs using the new sources for substantive analysis of aspects of Nahua social or cultural history.[12] The present work is one of these.

I need not belabor the advantage of using records produced in the mother tongue by the subjects of a given historical study. Wherever native-language materials have been available, they have been used as the primary source for writing a people's history. In the present case, certain considerations make the language question even more critical than normal. Much of the vitality in recent early Latin American history has come from an approach that goes beyond aggregate statistics to find meaning and pattern in a series of individual lives, even and perhaps especially in the lives of quite humble people. But the extant record of the Nahuas, whether in Spanish or Nahuatl, only rarely allows us to track a single person through a variety of documents. Largely deprived of seeing the pattern in a succession of actions, we must fall back on the other aspect of the career-pattern approach, a close attention to the categories that the person and his peers used to classify himself and his thoughts and actions, as well as the phenomena surrounding him, thus studying concepts borne in a person's language rather than patterns manifested in the person's life. Only in the original language can the categories be detected, for in a translation one sees the categories of the translator's language instead. Moreover, at present the interests of the field are turning ever more, naturally and laudably so, to the cultural side of history. We begin to be interested in the categories of thought in and of themselves.

Let me make the point more concretely. Spanish documents, and even Spanish translations of Nahuatl documents, make repeated use of the term Indian (*indio*), but rarely do we find it in Nahuatl documents, not even in the very ones whose translations use the word. The significant subject of the evolution of indigenous corporate self-definition must be worked out exclusively from Nahuatl-language sources.[13] To take an equally basic matter, Spanish sources speak of indigenous political entities in terms of head towns and subject hamlets, but in Nahuatl sources we find only terms for the entire entity and its constituent parts, a fact with profound implications and the key to the discovery of a general Nahua mode of organization (see Chapter 2).

Another reason why it is so important to have materials on the Nahuas in the original language is that language itself turns out to be an irreplaceable vehicle for determining the nature and rate of general cultural evolution. Perhaps the same could be said for any human situation, but the special conditions of research in this field have led to the discovery that the language used at any particular juncture is the best and often only way to place a given phenomenon on a stepped continuum of Nahua adaptation to the Spanish presence. A Spanish translation will give a brute fact well enough, but it will not tell us if a loanword was used or how it was handled grammatically. It will not distinguish between *iteachcauh*, "his older brother or cousin," the original Nahuatl expression current in the first half of the colonial period, and *iprimo hermano*, "his male first cousin," taken from Spanish and characteristic of a later time. It will give identical translations of *oquifirmayoti* and *oquifirmaro*; both mean "he signed," but the first is nominally based and indicative of an earlier stage than the second, which incorporates a Spanish verb.

This is not to say that sources in Spanish lack value for Nahua history. Rarely does one find in the archives a whole dossier in Nahuatl. Rather a dossier with Nahuatl documentation usually contains one, two, or at most a few items in Nahuatl, presented as primary evidence, whereas the whole lawsuit with its explanatory apparatus is in Spanish. It would be self-defeating not to take advantage of the context, and I have done so as far as I could, without poring over the Spanish as closely as the Nahuatl. I have not explored extensively in files containing no Nahuatl, because, in all truth, I have had my hands full. I have no doubt, however, that the history of Nahuas can profit greatly from further research in relevant purely Spanish sources. The sheer bulk of extant Nahuatl documentation greatly exceeds my original expectations; since 1976, when the first systematic survey of an already extensive corpus was carried out,[14] it has doubled or tripled, with no end in sight. Yet a laborious process of exploration, cataloging, and other steps is required to make this difficult and scattered material accessible and usable. Furthermore, though no specific cap can be predicted for the growth of the corpus, clearly at its maximum it will still be only a fraction of the archival material in Spanish related to central Mexican Indians, and whole aspects will be treated only in Spanish (it is also true, of course, that whole aspects are treated only in Nahuatl). Future ethnohistorical researchers must surely be prepared to consider material in either language according to the case, hopefully not forgetting that the Nahua concepts and special vocabulary of which Nahuatl texts have given us a grasp can serve as a key to open up the meaning of documents in Spanish in a way that would not have been possible before.

Some Dimensions and Attributes of the Book

I have already said that the purpose of this study is to describe and analyze the postconquest Nahua world using sources coming directly from the Nahuas themselves. The materials may strike the scholarly public, including even connoisseurs of early Spanish American history, as quite exotic, and to make things more difficult, I have taken a broad view of my task. Lest the reader despair at having entered a dark and impenetrable forest, let me provide a few guidelines.

I have always believed that though cultures are fluid and miscellaneous rather than truly organic, everything in a given society, or simply in a given group of people in contact with each other, affects everything else, and some phenomena are pervasive, so that to achieve the greatest insight one should proceed on a broad front, seeing many elements in relation to each other. As my work with the Nahuas progressed, I was struck by the existence of parallel modes of organization in many different branches of life and parallel movements in evolution across time. The eight core chapters of the book seek to show these themes in all those domains of Nahua society (including political and economic life) and culture (which I take to be the common lore of the society and hence inseparable from it) for which Nahuatl sources yield systematic information. Between the earlier chapters, which the reader may find more social, and the later ones, which may seem more cultural—though in my own mind there is little difference—a great variety of topics are broached, not all of which a given reader may be able to muster an interest in. Indeed, in a sense the eight chapters are like sketches of eight separate books, on quite broad topics themselves, waiting to be written. Realizing that particular readers will want or need to go to certain chapters or even portions thereof, I have tried to make each quite independent within the common thematics and have divided each into titled sections amounting to subchapters.[15] Nevertheless, I wish the sources had allowed the thorough exploration of even more dimensions, especially music, dance, markets, material culture, crafts, the technical side of agriculture, and gender roles. Perhaps avenues of more direct entry into these topics will yet be found.

The temporal and spatial limits of the study are those dictated by the Nahuatl documents that have appeared to date, whether found by myself and my colleagues and associates or published by others. Temporally, the records are distributed across the years from about 1545 to at least 1770 in such a way that no decades and few years are missing, and a certain number of texts from after 1770 provide a glimpse into the very late era as well. Spatial distribution is more problematic. Presently known material tends to come from places scattered unevenly across central Mexico, one or two items at a time. Certain subregions give the appearance of being endowed with a coherent corpus (Tlaxcala, Cuauhtinchan, Coyoacan, Culhuacan, the south-central Toluca Valley, for example), but on examination that turns out to be the case only for a limited time period or for a certain type of record. Except perhaps for sociopolitical organization and land tenure, it would be impossible to find examples of each of the phenomena of interest in each subregion across the whole time span. The only known thoroughgoing local Nahuatl census was done in the Cuernavaca region around 1540; the only sodality book containing lists of members and officers over a substantial time period, as well as discussions of crises and countermeasures, is from Tula; the only set of municipal council records is from sixteenth-century Tlaxcala; the only set of family papers maintained consistently over a long period of time is from the Toluca Valley in the seventeenth and eighteenth centuries.[16]

I have, therefore, for the most part treated the material as a unit, carefully spotting each example geographically in the Notes, but using it in relation to patterns in the Nahua world more generally. A general approach seemed appropriate in view of the nature of the whole enterprise and the nascent condition of postconquest Nahuatl studies. But as I proceeded with the work, I became convinced that the Nahua world was in fact a unit in many respects, before and after the conquest. No other conclusion could be drawn, given the use of the same terminology and concepts in politics, kinship, and land tenure in random attestations across the whole region, and the appearance of similar Spanish loan particles and verbs at roughly the same time in texts spread from

Sultepec in the southwest of the Nahua region to Tulancingo in the extreme northeast. Where subregional differentiation has come to my attention, I have discussed it, as with the apparently different conception of lordly houses in the eastern and western halves of the Nahua world (Chapter 4), or the possible role of Mexico City and environs as the point of origin of linguistic innovations that spread out from there (Chapter 7).

In general, however, I speak of patterns and trends for the whole central Nahuatl speech area, leaving future research to establish the doubtless significant subregional distinctions. I am by no means unaware of the necessity of accounting exhaustively for the spatial distribution of phenomena, and I also understand, if anyone does, the unique value of intensive microsituational research as a laboratory. I have been able to adopt my present procedure because of the extensive mapping of indigenous units carried out by Gibson in *The Aztecs*, supplemented by the even more thorough mapping of a specific region, Coyoacan, by Rebecca Horn, plus a series of subregional studies of various kinds (by Pedro Carrasco, S. L. Cline, Robert Haskett, Horn, Frances Krug, Ursula Dyckerhoff and Hanns Prem, Luis Reyes García, Susan Schroeder, and Stephanie Wood), all of which make it possible to proceed with confidence at the macroregional level.

For those who know Nahuatl, and for the swelling group of scholars interested in Mexico who are studying the language, I will explain my practices and conventions in reproducing Nahuatl words and passages.

All longer passages, as well as some shorter ones and some individual words, are reproduced in a system closely following the original orthography. Given the often erratic and hard-to-determine original spacing, and the difficulty that even relative experts experience in understanding utterances in that form, they are respaced here according to current grammatical norms. For convenience, overbars are resolved as *n* or *m*, and the lines associated with *q* are reproduced as the corresponding vowels. No punctuation is added, and the passages are otherwise left exactly as in the original manuscript.

When I rewrite Nahuatl words and phrases, representing generalized usage rather than that of a specific individual, the orthography I employ as standard is that of the grammarian Horacio Carochi, minus diacritics, since, though a bit idealized, it seems to me to correspond better to what was actually written in the late sixteenth and early seventeenth centuries than any other single consistent system. I generally write Nahuatl toponyms (more properly the names of sociopolitical units) in the same orthography, but where the name is well known in present-day Mexico, I use the current form instead (e.g., Tlaxcala rather than Tlaxcallan).

Because I consider it extremely important to have the Nahuatl open to examination, I strive to give in the Notes the original of all Nahuatl passages

I have translated in the body of the book, except in a few cases where the "original" is itself a garbled copy that would only mislead the reader. To save space, however, I do not reproduce the original whenever a transcription has already been published, instead referring to that version in a note.

Passages from original texts (sometimes as short as a single word) are understood to represent the original orthography if reproduced in quotes, whereas italicized words and passages have been rewritten in the standard form. Full as the body of the book is of Nahuatl terminology, I have worked to prevent it from becoming a forest of italics. Nahuatl terms are italicized only on first appearance, or perhaps on reappearance after a long interval if the term is not a basic one within the book's framework. If in the body a Nahuatl term is highlighted or used as a linguistic or conceptual example, it is placed in quotes. In the Notes I have proceeded differently, and in view of the linguistic nature of much of the discussion there, the same word may be italicized repeatedly when it is being used as an example.

Debts and Affinities

Although I appear as author of the present work and indeed organized it and wrote it, the entire process that led to it was a collective effort, so that a separate acknowledgments section, with implications of distance between the product and those thanked, could not do justice to the situation.* Without actually collaborating with them, I have profited greatly from the work of J. Richard Andrews, John Bierhorst, Forrest and Jean G. Brewer, Pedro Carrasco, Charles E. Dibble, Eike Hinz, Fernando Horcasitas, Harold and Mary Ritchie Key, Thelma D. Sullivan, Günter Zimmermann, and most especially, Charles Gibson. Some close colleagues and collaborators have worked with me in the analysis of Nahuatl materials to the point that it becomes difficult to decide who is responsible for what; among these I count Arthur J. O. Anderson, Frances Berdan, S. L. Cline, and Frances Karttunen. A large number of people, including the just named, some of them having been at some point my students, have generously shared their own research materials with me, without which the present work could hardly have become what it is: Robert S. Haskett, Rebecca Horn, Frances M. Krug, Dana Leibsohn, Miguel León-Portilla, Mary Ann Lockhart, Juan López y Magaña, Andrea Martínez de Assadourian, Leslie Scott Offutt, Jeanette F. Peterson, Luis Reyes García,

* In the realm of simple thanks, I am grateful to the Guggenheim Foundation, the American Council of Learned Societies, the Institute for Advanced Study, the UCLA Humanities Foundation and research committees, and the Institute of Latin American Studies of La Trobe University for financial and fellowship support. I also thank Barbara Mnookin, who copy edited this volume for Stanford University Press.

Susan Schroeder, Barry David Sell, William Taylor, and Stephanie G. Wood.

Some of these connections are embodied in specific works of a philological nature that I have used repeatedly in the preparation of this book: Horcasitas's *Teatro náhuatl* (TN), Cline and León-Portilla's *Testaments of Culhuacan* (TC), *Beyond the Codices* (BC) and *The Tlaxcalan Actas* (TA), by Anderson, Berdan, and myself, and *Nahuatl in the Middle Years* (NMY), by Karttunen and myself. Many other publications of this general type have played an important part as well, as the Notes will show, but these five works, along with the Zimmermann edition of Chimalpahin (CH), have entered so deeply as almost to become a part of the book. They have with time acquired personalities, and I feel about them almost as I do about the people who have helped me. Those who study this book deeply will doubtless want to seek out these items and become well acquainted with their contents.[17] I have also published a series of smaller items, some more philological, some more monographic, some more accessible and some more technical, during the years that I was engaged in the present project. Though I have frequently drawn on these works here, readers will find in them much additional useful information on various special topics. The material has been gathered, together with some previously unpublished pieces, and published in a supplementary volume *Nahuas and Spaniards* (N&S).

2

Altepetl

AT THE HEART OF the organization of the Nahua world, both before the Spaniards came and long after, lay the *altepetl* or ethnic state. Indigenous people thought of the entire countryside of central Mexico in terms of such entities. We find it said of a preconquest spectacle that "the whole land assembled, the altepetl inhabitants from all around came to behold."[1] In a sixteenth-century Nahuatl history, the indigenous inhabitants of the Valley of Mexico in preconquest times are described as "the people in the altepetl."[2]

The word itself is a slightly altered form of the metaphorical doublet *in atl, in tepetl*, "the water(s), the mountain(s)," and thus it refers in the first instance to territory, but what is meant is primarily an organization of people holding sway over a given territory.[3] A sovereign or potentially sovereign entity of any size whatever could be considered an altepetl, and on occasion the wide-ranging Nahuatl annalist Chimalpahin actually puts Japan, Peru, and the Moluccas into that classification.[4] In central Mexican conditions, though, the altepetl was perhaps comparable in size to the early Mediterranean city-states. In the smallest, such as Huitzilopochco (Churubusco), just south of Mexico City, the territory might be measured in terms of a few thousand yards. The largest entities to be called altepetl, such as the great power of Tlaxcala, occupying most of today's Mexican state of that name, were actually confederations lacking a single head, and everything again came back to their constituent altepetl, which shared all duties and benefits among themselves. Preconquest empires were conglomerations in which some altepetl were dominant and some subordinated, but the unit either giving or receiving tribute was always the altepetl. While empires and even large ethnic confederations came and went, the smaller constituent states tended to survive in some form through the centuries. After the conquest, the altepetl if anything gained in importance. Everything the Spaniards organized outside their own settlements in the sixteenth century—the encomienda, the rural parishes, Indian municipalities, the initial administrative jurisdictions—was built solidly upon individual, already existing altepetl.[5]

In his dictionary of 1571, the great Franciscan lexicographer fray Alonso de Molina defines altepetl as "pueblo," and in fact that is the word Spaniards were already using for Indian polities and settlements of any size. "Town" or "city" is often the best English translation in a given case. When speaking of altepetl, however, the Spaniards did not normally use their standard terminology for urban entities: *ciudad* or city for the highest rank, *villa* or town for the second, and *aldea* or village for smaller dependencies.[6] "Pueblo" means "people," and in that sense the Spanish term was perfect, for each altepetl imagined itself a radically separate people. It does not appear that "pueblo" as used in sixteenth-century New World Spanish implied a particularly small unit, a "village." That connotation was to arise with changed conditions in later times. Perhaps "pueblo" was preferred as a term not implying as much urban nucleation as the normal Spanish vocabulary did. Like the altepetl, a Spanish municipality stretched over a large territory and was not confined to a strictly urban center, but in the Spanish entity everything did point in toward the urban core, from which dominance in all spheres of life spread out into the relatively undifferentiated surrounding territory. Among the Nahuas, although nucleation was a significant factor, it was not central to the modes of sociopolitical organization.

Basic Principles of Altepetl Organization

The Nahua manner of creating larger constructs, whether in politics, society, economy, or art, tended to place emphasis on a series of relatively equal, relatively separate and self-contained constituent parts of the whole, the unity of which consisted in the symmetrical numerical arrangement of the parts, their identical relationship to a common reference point, and their orderly, cyclical rotation.[7] This mode of organization can be termed cellular or modular as opposed to hierarchical, but it is by no means incapable of producing real, cohesive, lasting larger units.

As the principal container of Nahua life, the altepetl was fully within the general tradition, both in its simpler forms and in more complex agglomerations. Let us look first at altepetl organization in its simplest manifestation and perhaps somewhat abstractly, for it now begins to appear that a considerable degree of complexity and conglomeration was the general rule in central Mexico by the time the Spaniards arrived. The minimum requirements for an altepetl as the Nahuas mainly used the word (in reference, that is, to preconquest times) are a territory; a set (usually a fixed canonical number) of named constituent parts; and a dynastic ruler or *tlatoani* (pl. *tlatoque*). In central Mexico, virtually all altepetl maintained the tradition of having been established in their sixteenth-century form by migrants (most often refugees from the breakup of legendary Tula or the hunting-gathering people from the north known under the cover term Chichimeca). Such groups were imagined to have had an ethnic unity going back into unremembered times, and even during their travels they had a set of named subgroups and (at least usually) a special god of their own. Some traveled under the leadership of a tlatoani, while others acquired one at the time of the acquisition of their territory and the formal establishment of the altepetl. An established altepetl would have a main temple, symbol of its sovereignty (and apparently always the abode of its special ethnic god, though the topic is not fully studied), as well as some sort of central market.[8]

As to the constituent parts of the altepetl, they are well known under the name of *calpolli*, a term meaning literally "big house."* At one time, the calpolli was confidently spoken of as an egalitarian kin group looking back to a common ancestor.[9] More recent scholars have reexamined the sources and found quite a different picture, beginning with the fact that the calpolli plays a very small role in Nahuatl documents, compared with the altepetl (which earlier scholars nevertheless tended to ignore in favor of attention to the "Aztec" empire). The notion of semi-independent subgroups of the alte-petl is found everywhere, but the word calpolli itself is much less common than *tlaxilacalli*, a term of obscure etymology.[10] Some texts use calpolli more for the migratory phase, tlaxilacalli for a group with a fixed territory.[11] Since "calpolli" does not disappear entirely from colonial Nahuatl texts, and the term is readily recognized, I will continue to use it at times in referring to the subunits of the altepetl.

Whatever we call them, the calpolli were not typically miscellaneous in number. Some ethnic groups appear to have fancied seven parts, probably associated with the Seven Caves of the origin legend, but most preferred symmetry. Four, six, and eight parts were common (four relating readily to a persistent dualism, as well as coinciding with the cardinal directions and fitting neatly into the Mesoamerican numerical system, and eight being the result of doubling that number). Each part often had its own god.[12] Each had a distinctive name remaining the same over long periods of time, most often referring to geographical features or ethnic affiliation. Each had its own leader (called by some *teuctlatoani*) with a distinctive title or *teuctocaitl* ("lordly name");[13] whether or not such leaders were dynastic, even after the

*This is most often written in English and Spanish as *calpulli*, but there is no reason not to use the normal Nahuatl form. Perhaps the different spelling can serve to underline the difference between the unit as we understand it today and the clan imagined by earlier scholars. In Nahuatl, "calpolli" in the sense of the organization, as an inanimate noun, does not show a plural, so as with "altepetl" I use the same form for singular and plural. The form *calpoltin* with an overt plural, which is indeed seen in Nahuatl texts, means "members of a calpolli or of various calpolli," not "various calpolli."

groups were settled, is not yet established, but in well-developed situations they very likely were. And each held a portion of the altepetl territory, exclusively for the use of its own members. To what extent these subterritories were contiguous solid blocks, to what extent interspersed with each other, is not known. Probably at origin the territories tended to be blocks, with complications arising later.[14] The even numbers typical of calpolli sets and the close association between the larger group and the calpolli names (which were often retained as a set even when the altepetl suffered a schism or created a colony) make one think that calpolli arose from a process of division of an earlier unitary group of people. On the other hand, some calpolli names imply foreign ethnicity, and doubtless many subgroups indeed originated as outsiders joining the main group. In any case, the ethnic pride so characteristic of the altepetl is seen at the calpolli level too. Nor was the calpolli thoroughly exogamous like a kin group; members married outside it, but apparently more often within.[15]

Thus the constituent calpolli were in many respects microcosms of the altepetl. They in their turn were divided into what may be called wards (no indigenous term emerges) of (roughly) twenty, forty, eighty, or a hundred households, each ward having a leader responsible for land allocation, tax collection, and the like. From the little that is known, organization at this level seems to have been relatively flexible, ad hoc, and without the long-term stability of the parent calpolli units. Wards lacked names as distinctive as those of calpolli; some appear in Nahuatl census lists unnamed, and others may at times have taken on some of the innumerable toponyms that blanketed the Nahua countryside, sometimes with the result that each field had its separate name.[16]

As equal and separate entities, the calpolli would contribute separately and more or less equally to common obligations of the altepetl; each would separately deliver its part of a general levy in maize or other products to the designated common place of collection; in time of war, each contributed a fighting unit under its own leadership. For ongoing altepetl duties, however, involving either draft labor or the delivery of products throughout the year, a scheme of rotation was necessary. The fixed order of rotation of the calpolli was the life thread of the altepetl. Once in operation, the important thing about it was the sequence, since it repeated on itself indefinitely and could be halted and restarted at any point. A rotation order, however, was not merely cyclical. It was at the same time a ranking and order of precedence from first to last. Nahuatl lists of constituent parts of entities show great regularity in always beginning with the same name and proceeding in invariant order until the last listed, and the ordinal numbers play a prominent role: first, second, third, and so forth.

It happens that the sources tell us more about ranking in composite alte-petl than among calpolli sets. At the higher level, we know that ranking at times reflected historical evolution, that is, that the first to join or be founded ranked first, the second second, and so on; but at the same time, in some cases, one can see an apparent preoccupation with an orderly movement in relation to the cardinal directions.[17] We do, at least, have some examples of calpolli sets listed in unchanging order in reference to both preconquest and postconquest periods.[18]

Rotational order manifested itself above all in duties performed for the tlatoani or king, the primary reference point of all the calpolli and the em-bodiment of the altepetl. A prominent view both before and after the con-quest was that an altepetl existed where and only where there was a tlatoani. Yet despite standing above the various calpolli as their common reference point, the tlatoani was himself usually (and perhaps always) based in an in-dividual calpolli, the highest ranking, where he in effect served as teuctlatoani of the smaller entity as well as being general ruler of the whole. Like the teuctlatoque, he bore a polity-specific title handed down from one generation to the next.[19] In many cases, his position may have originated historically in an exaltation of the leadership of the first-ranked calpolli. Even so, taxes and labor duties from all over the altepetl went in the first instance directly to the tlatoani. Nobles from all the calpolli resorted to his *tecpan* or palace to pay court, and calpolli commoners rotated in service there. The rulership was dynastic, hereditary within a given line, but the rules of inheritance varied greatly from one kingdom to the next, much flexibility was the practice, and rulerships repeatedly survived dynastic breaks. Once established, a given polity could be said to possess a given *tlatocayotl* or rulership whether it was occupied by a dynastic tlatoani at the moment or not.

Other focal points for the calpolli sets were the market and the temple of the principal god. The market was closely associated with the tlatoani, who taxed and regulated it; rather than rotation, the principle here was the simultaneous congregation of representatives of all the calpolli to trade com-plementary specialties.[20] All the calpolli alike looked to the temple and its god in the same way as they looked to the tlatoani (the altepetl deity may often have grown out of the deity of the senior calpolli, as the tlatoani may have grown out of its leadership). A priesthood consisting of high nobles often closely related to the tlatoani was in charge of the temple, and though we know few details, it appears that the calpolli rotated in duties to the temple and the performance of rites and festivities, as they did in duties to the tlatoani.

Palace, temple, and market would ordinarily be located near to one an-other, representing a considerable force toward nucleation. During the preconquest centuries, a formidable degree of urban nucleation in fact existed in central Mexico, and not only in the famous great cities of Tenochtitlan and Tetzcoco.[21] Yet a dominant central city was not really compatible with the principles of altepetl organization. The notion of a city separate from the altepetl did not enter into the vocabulary in the form of any distinct word. It appears that when Nahuas spoke of Xochimilco, Azcapotzalco, or Culhuacan, they may have sometimes meant the largest urban settlement, and sometimes the whole altepetl, but it is nearly impossible to be sure in a given instance that only the urban part is meant. Never does one find a central nucleated settlement in an altepetl with any other name than that of the altepetl as a whole. There were words that meant the built-up part of the polity, where houses crowded together, but these terms hardly occur in documents bearing on political life.[22]

In a Nahua altepetl, any central urban cluster that might exist would not constitute a separate jurisdiction, but would fall into the areas of some of the constituent calpolli, so that it was the calpolli each separately and as a part of the overall rotation, not some "city," that contributed to and benefitted from altepetl operations. Figure 2.1 illustrates a hypothetical, idealized altepetl whose territory is divided symmetrically among eight calpolli. The four outward ones have hamlet-like settlement clusters central to their respective territories, whereas the settlement clusters in the inner four are pushed in

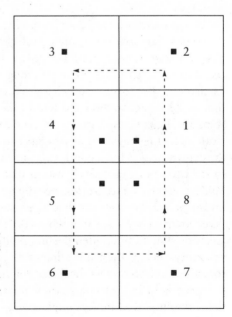

Fig. 2.1. Cellular organization and nucleation in a hypothetical altepetl. In this figure and the similar one that follows, the dotted lines show the direction of rotation and the numbers show the order of precedence.

toward one another, creating an agglomeration that might in many respects resemble a "city," but in other respects belongs to four different parts of an eight-part structure.

To the Spaniards, thinking in terms of city and countryside, dominant and subordinated entities, a very different picture would present itself. They would see a capital city ruling outlying subjected hamlets; they were to call the concentrated group of inner calpolli the *cabecera* ("head town") and the outlying calpolli *sujetos* ("subjects"). Although the Spaniards thus profoundly misunderstood the altepetl, there was little on the surface to tell them that they were wrong, and in time their conception and their terminology were to have important effects on the Nahuas themselves.

Complex Altepetl

Just as symmetrical cellular organization extended downward and inward to a host of little-understood subdivisions of the calpolli, so it extended upward and outward to encompass configurations larger and more complex than the simple or one-tlatoani altepetl. Indeed, the simple form may have been characteristic above all of earlier times, recent creations, and marginal cases, and complexity may have been the norm among the polities the Spaniards found in the sixteenth century. Surely it seems that whenever the sources allow us to penetrate very deeply into a central Mexican state, it proves complex.

Larger entities retained an ethnic character. They might arise through the progressive subdivision or hiving off of an originally unitary group, as with Tlaxcala and Tenochtitlan/Tlatelolco; or a common historical experience could mold a sense of ethnicity among an originally diverse group, as with Chalco and Tetzcoco; or ethnicities retaining a sharp sense of ethnic distinction could be accommodated within the state, as with Cuauhtinchan. Constant among entities of this type, even those of common descent, were fierce rivalries and feelings of independence and superiority on the part of each of the constituents.[23] Indeed, schism, splitting off in dissatisfaction, was as basic to the process of growth as was conglomeration. Such organizations could hold together over centuries, becoming so deeply entwined (as with Xochimilco or Amaquemecan) that after the conquest they could no longer be taken apart. They were in a sense confederations, but they should be distinguished from ad hoc, often fleeting political confederations with little ethnic solidarity, such as the triple alliance of Tenochtitlan, Tetzcoco, and Tlacopan sometimes referred to as the Aztec empire.

Essentially, in a complex ethnic state whole altepetl played the same role that calpolli played in the simple state; in other words, a set of altepetl, numerically and if possible symmetrically arranged, equal and separate, yet ranked in order of precedence and rotation, constituted the larger state, which was considered and called an altepetl itself. In some situations, notably Tlaxcala, there was no known terminological distinction between the constituent and the overarching entities. The historian Chimalpahin, however, introduces the useful word *tlayacatl* for constituent altepetl of a tightly knit composite state,[24] and I will at times follow his terminology. When the Spaniards became aware of these sovereign units within larger states, they were often to call them *parcialidades* or *partes*.

Although the composite state was at root an enlargement of the simple altepetl, it differed in lacking a single tlatoani for the whole. The only heads were the tlatoque of the constituent parts; each ruler received all the tribute of his own subjects and none from the other constituents. The tlatoani of the highest-ranked tlayacatl might function to an extent as ceremonial head for the whole, and it appears that in each generation one of the four tlatoque of preconquest Tlaxcala was designated titular representative for his lifetime.[25] The composite state thus needed reinforcement of its unity if it was to continue to exist as such, and it was always in danger of becoming a mere alliance, as happened with greater Chalco.[26] One important way such unity was attained was through repeated dynastic intermarrying, with the result that the various tlatoque of a composite altepetl were often close blood relatives, and a person might succeed in a tlayacatl other than the one in which he was born. In Amaquemecan, the web grew so thick that one person might be a candidate for several of the rulerships and even advance in the course of his lifetime from a lower-ranked to a higher-ranked position, treating the entire composite state as a single stepped system.[27]

Let us look for a moment at a few examples. Best known is that of Tlaxcala, which consisted of four altepetl distributed in four pie-shaped territories converging on a central point (see Fig. 2.2).[28] The seats of the respective tlatoque, rather than being deep within each territory, were close together at the center (though not so close as to merge or even be in sight of each other; the unified City of Tlaxcala was an innovation of the postconquest period). By Tlaxcalan tradition, Tepeticpac was the first kingdom founded, with Ocotelolco, Tiçatla, and Quiahuiztlan branching off in that order; the order of foundation then became the order of precedence and rotation, as reported by some writers of the sixteenth and seventeenth centuries.[29] As time passed, the balance of real power among the four shifted to the point that Tepeticpac was left the weakest and least populous. The order of rotation was so important to the whole, however, that the Tlaxcalans did not abandon it; they retained the same sequence and changed only the starting point, with Ocotelolco first and Tepeticpac hence last (which would have been entirely unnoticeable with

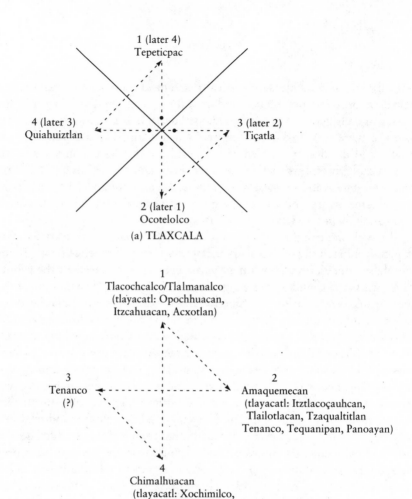

1 (later 4)
Tepeticpac

4 (later 3)
Quiahuiztlan

3 (later 2)
Tiçatla

2 (later 1)
Ocotelolco

(a) TLAXCALA

1
Tlacochcalco/Tlalmanalco
(tlayacatl: Opochhuacan,
Itzcahuacan, Acxotlan)

3
Tenanco
(?)

2
Amaquemecan
(tlayacatl: Itztlacoçauhcan,
Tlailotlacan, Tzaqualtitlan
Tenanco, Tequanipan, Panoayan)

4
Chimalhuacan
(tlayacatl: Xochimilco,
Tepetlixpan)

(b) CHALCO

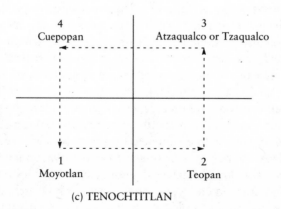

4
Cuepopan

3
Atzaqualco or Tzaqualco

1
Moyotlan

2
Teopan

(c) TENOCHTITLAN

Fig. 2.2 Organization of Tlaxcala, Chalco, and Tenochtitlan

any ongoing rotations). So things stood when the Spaniards arrived, and for a long time thereafter.

The internal organization of each of the four constituent altepetl of Tlaxcala is not presently well understood. A Nahuatl census of the mid-sixteenth century divides each altepetl into four to six numbered and ordered but not named groupings called *tequitl* (in this context, "slices" or "sections"). Each tequitl in turn contained several named settlements. No clear geographical, numerical, or ethnic criteria have yet been recognized in the formation of the tequitl, and since the term (in this meaning) appears in no other early Tlaxcalan records, it may be that the units were ad hoc aggregations disguising a more complex and permanent organization. From records of the postconquest Tlaxcalan municipal council or *cabildo*, each altepetl appears to have had a settlement located in the interior of the jurisdiction, well away from the seat of the tlatoani, that from an early time was made the headquarters of a lieutenant in charge of keeping the peace in the countryside; the same places often became the site of ambitious church-building projects.[30] One is led to wonder if in preconquest times each of the altepetl had some form of dual organization and two tlatoque rather than one. Indeed, greater Tlaxcala was so large, populous, and diverse that it could easily have contained a full set of tlayacatl and tlatoque within each of the four constituent altepetl.[31] Perhaps the especially strong development in the Tlaxcalan region of *teccalli* (noble lineages with a titular lord possessing their own lands and dependents) worked against the multiplication of rulerships and sovereign entities.[32] At any rate, by the sixteenth century each of the four altepetl did have a single clearly dominant tlatoani with authority over the whole.[33]

In the case of Chalco, the organization of complex kingdoms can be discussed with greater than usual clarity, mainly because of the work of the Chalco historian Chimalpahin.[34] According to Chimalpahin, a series of migratory groups arriving in succession in what was to be the Chalco region, most but not all of them "Chichimeca" and by no means all related to each other, established in the course of the thirteenth and fourteenth centuries a set of kingdoms that by the end of the process had a two-tiered numerical organization and ranking (see Fig. 2.2). All the peoples were considered Chalca, and Chimalpahin calls the entire structure an altepetl, Chalco or Chalcayotl ("collective entity of the Chalca"). The four parts were ranked in the order Tlalmanalco, Amaquemecan, Tenanco, and Chimalhuacan, which was the same as the chronological order of their foundation, although the first-ranking, Tlalmanalco, incorporated more recent arrivals as well as the original fountainhead of the Chalca, Acxotlan. Note that though this ranking starts in the north like the original order in Tlaxcala, the sequence varies thereafter; it seems likely that chronology was more central to the rationale than the cardinal directions.

The four parts of Chalco, unlike those of Tlaxcala, lacked unitary tla-toque but were instead composite altepetl themselves. Greater Chalco was a very loose entity, hardly more than a regional defense alliance stiffened by some sense of common ethnicity and historical experience. Each of the four parts consisted of a number of constituent altepetl, which, as already mentioned, Chimalpahin calls tlayacatl, each with its own specially titled ruler and rulership. For only one of the four parts, his own Amaquemecan, does Chimalpahin provide fairly complete information on the evolution and structure of the tlayacatl. By the time of the conquest, Amaquemecan had five tlayacatl, the odd fifth having arisen through a schism in the first; the ranking was chronological by order of arrival in the area and constitution as a kingdom, except that the splinter group of the first ranked second instead of last. How the five tlayacatl were allocated across Amaquemecan's jurisdiction is nowhere specified, but each did have its own territory, whether contiguous or not. Each also had, as we would expect, a ranked set of constituent calpolli or tlaxilacalli.[35]

Cuauhtinchan, located east of Puebla, is a preconquest composite state that bears a strong resemblance to Tlaxcala and Chalco in certain respects but seems to deviate sharply in others.[36] By the sixteenth century, there were seven distinct titled rulerships, some bearing the same titles as counterparts in Chalco; the number seven may have represented an ideal based on group legend, but it also appears to have been a way of accommodating two originally very distinct ethnicities, the Nahuas and the Pinome, since the rulerships were divided between them, with the normal four held by one group, and the rest by the other. The fixed ranking is not known, but since allocations were made differentially, there is reason to believe that one existed. Nor is the geographical distribution of the rulerships established; their lands appear to have been interspersed to a considerable extent. The surprising thing is that the seven units, as far as is presently understood, were called teccalli, not altepetl or tlayacatl.[37] Nothing is said about any subdivisions within them, and the entities in Cuauhtinchan called calpolli were few, outside the teccalli, and peripheral to the state's overall organization. It may be that the difference is largely a question of terminology alone, or it may be that powerful noble houses subverted and replaced the usual elements of altepetl structure (though in the end functioning very similarly themselves).[38]

Organization of the type I have been describing was characteristic of the "imperial" powers as well. The Mexica origin legend, as is well known, speaks of a typical wandering calpolli set.[39] Less frequently discussed is the Mexica reorganization after the establishment of Mexico Tenochtitlan on its permanent site. By that time, in the early fourteenth century, there were according to the Mexica historian Tezozomoc fifteen calpolli, each with its own divinity, plus the general ethnic divinity Huitzilopochtli (based no doubt in a calpolli of his own, making sixteen in all). Shortly after the foundation of Tenochtitlan, it was said, Huitzilopochtli told the Mexica to divide themselves into four parts and name the parts. That done, the calpolli gods were allocated accordingly.[40] The resulting configuration can be seen in Figure 2.2. Tezozomoc gives the four parts as "Moyotlan, now called San Juan; Teopan, now called San Pablo; Tzaqualco, now called San Sebastián, and Cuepopan, now called Santa María la Redonda." The order given by Tezozomoc is the same one still functioning in the sixteenth and seventeenth centuries.[41] It follows the general Mesoamerican preference for a counterclockwise movement around the four directions, though it differs from the norm in not starting to the east. Possibly it had undergone adjustment at some point, as in Tlaxcala, and it certainly was not established at the command of Huitzilopochtli, but the Mexica clearly saw the four-part supra-calpolli organization and sequence as an ancient and basic facet of their polity. Within each part, there was probably a ranking of four constituent calpolli, and as Tenochtitlan grew, one would expect these to have been subdivided in turn.[42] Each unit no doubt had a leader with a polity-specific title, and it would be natural to expect a dynasty of tlatoque in each of the four parts, one of them being the "emperor." The Mexica rewrote their history so thoroughly for political purposes, emphasizing unity and the strength of the principal ruler, that little trace is left of any set of rulerships in the constituent parts, but certain hints exist.[43]

As to Tetzcoco, its principal historian, Ixtlilxochitl, came relatively late in time, was far less well informed than Chimalpahin and Tezozomoc, and obscured things further by writing in Spanish; he expressed himself in terms of kings and vast empires, with rulers "giving" regions to their subordinates and allies. Ixtlilxochitl paid little attention to and even perhaps had little grasp of the polity-specific nature of central Mexican rulership or of the importance of a fixed complex of constituent parts. Nevertheless, it can be discerned that Tetzcoco in the narrower sense consisted of six constituents named after various ethnicities. In some postconquest sources these are referred to as tlaxilacalli or barrios, but they may once have been tlayacatl.[44]

A specific form of complexity in central Mexican polities of all sizes was dual organization. The frequency of fours, sixes, and eights is closely related to the pervasiveness of an underlying duality. Whether an altepetl was relatively simple or enormously complex, its units might fall into two quite distinct parallel sets, each with a separate head, though one set for historical or other reasons might constitute an upper moiety, and its ruler might represent the whole in some ways. In Tulancingo (north of Tlaxcala), the two halves, each with many constituents spread over a large territory, differed in language

and ethnicity, Tlatocan in the south part of the region apparently going back
to Nahuatl-speaking conquerors, Tlaixpan in the northern part originating in
the Otomi-speaking conquered population. The two halves of Azcapotzalco
(near Mexico City), Mexicapan and Tepanecapan, seem to have been somewhat similar. The basis for the two halves of Coyoacan (just southwest of
Mexico City), Acohuic and Tlalnahuac, is not known except that they constituted separate geographical districts and mean "upper" and "lower." Two
separate contiguous territorial blocks may have been the most usual type of
dual arrangement, but there appear to have been other possibilities. Fragmentary data hint that Calimaya and Tepemaxalco (in the Toluca Valley) may
have been interspersed across the same general territory, each constituent
consisting of a larger Calimaya part on the north and a smaller Tepemaxalco
part on the south.[45]

If many dual entities arose from the combination of disparate parts,
moiety-like arrangements also arose through splitting previously more unitary groups. The Tlacochcalca, who eventually became the dominant party
in Tlalmanalco, had been six constituents under one tlatoani, then divided
into two groups of three; both had a tlatoani of the original royal line. It
seems that there was no entity too small to have moieties and a second ruler.
Though Chimalpahin's Tzaqualtitlan Tenanco was only the third-ranking
tlayacatl in Amaquemecan, which was itself one of the four parts of Chalco,
it had two tlatoque, a senior one based in the calpolli Tlailotlacan and a
junior one based in the calpolli Atlauhtlan. The status of the second ruler was
precarious, and he eventually fell to the rank of teuctlatoani or calpolli head;
yet after the conquest, in the early seventeenth century, Atlauhtlan was to
attain independence of the rest.[46] The tiny town of Sula (Çollan), probably
part of Tlalmanalco in preconquest times and too small to merit mention by
Chimalpahin, retained the legend of a pair of primordial leaders, of whom
the secondary was partly foreign and suspect.[47]

Looking across the totality of reasonably well-documented preconquest
central Mexican polities, it is clear that they all operated along the same
general lines, but that they also varied a great deal in size, complexity, terminology, and the relative weight given to certain structures and mechanisms
compared to others. Nor were they static. There was nothing to prevent the
simplest form of altepetl from growing through natural increase or the absorption of migrants and becoming complex, with one or more former calpolli heads transformed into tlatoque. Conversely, there was nothing to prevent a composite form from being collapsed into a simpler and more unified
one, which might happen either because the entire group suffered reverses
such as population loss and military defeat or because one constituent part
outgrew the others.[48]

When the Spaniards came to central Mexico and conquered it, they would need, as everywhere in Spanish America, to operate in a great many respects through existing sociopolitical units. The "empire" was not a viable unit for this purpose. Although great economic and demographic concentrations had arisen at Tenochtitlan and Tetzcoco, and although these two and Tlacopan had established certain enclaves and areas of direct dominance throughout much of the region, the individual altepetl were left essentially intact and self-contained, fully aware of their heritage and eager to cast off tribute obligations and other ties at the first opportunity. Within a few miles of Tetzcoco and in its area of dominance were entities such as Huexotla, Coatlichan, and Chiauhtla, altepetl of considerable complexity that cherished larger memories and ambitions of their own. Around Tenochtitlan, the situation was even more exaggerated; former imperial powers like Azcapotzalco and Culhuacan were at the very doorstep, and the Mexica did not lie unduly when they told Cortés "we have no lands, no fields." [49] Once the Spaniards had emerged as the new military and economic power in the region, there was nothing to keep the imperial conglomeration from falling apart into its constituent ethnic altepetl, as it in fact largely did in the course of the Spanish conquest itself. Getting rid of imperial obligations was a large part of the reason why so many central Mexican groups ran so quickly into the arms of the invaders. By the time the Spaniards were well installed, an indigenous imperial structure through which they could have worked essentially no longer existed. Like the Triple Alliance before them, they would have to deal directly with the altepetl.

Nevertheless, the Spaniards still had a certain degree of flexibility, for as we have seen, the altepetl were evolving structures with inner tensions, and the Nahuas were by no means always unanimous among themselves on the size and nature of their own entities. After the conquest, feelings of pride and solidarity, economic interdependence, and extensive dynastic intermarriage all still worked to hold large units together, but the strongest adhesive, the urgent need to combine for self-defense or aggrandizement, was now lacking, and the always existing forces in the direction of fragmentation could assert themselves more freely. Microethnicity was perhaps the strongest such force. Despite the growth of a dominant Nahua culture throughout the region, cultural minorities persisted, especially the Otomi. Even when local conquered groups and intrusive migrants were no longer discernibly distinct in language and culture, they retained a tradition of separate origin. Not only such large and diverse realms as Tulancingo and Cuauhtinchan recognized ethnicity in their organization; even the smallest and apparently most homogeneous altepetl was in a sense a confederation of distinct and competing ethnic groups. The general principle of cellular organization itself meant that constituent parts at each level were relatively complete, rounded entities capable of maintaining an independent existence.

In effect, the Spaniards had two options: attempting to retain and work through large entities on the order of Tlaxcala, Coyoacan, Xochimilco, and Tulancingo or dividing them into their more obvious parts such as halves or tlayacatl. Depending on the conditions, they were sometimes to take one course, sometimes the other. Relatively small and unified altepetl were ordinarily left unchanged. Rarely would the Spaniards attempt to divide an indigenous unit in a way not following already existing lines of subdivision, and seldom indeed would they try to create an independent unit in the absence of a recognized tlatoani commanding the allegiance of a well-defined calpolli set. Yet in the few cases when they appear to have taken such steps, the new unit proved viable. The splinter group would accept its new independence only too gladly; invariably it had at least one titled leader who could be made to pass for a tlatoani, and by generally understood principles, it could soon achieve an order of rotation among its constituents.

The Sixteenth-Century Reorganization

After the Spanish conquest—to which if their own and other accounts are to be believed, nearly all the altepetl of central Mexico contributed men and logistical support[50]—the first major organizational act of the conquerors was to create and bestow encomiendas on individual Spaniards in reward for their part in the conquest. In most aspects, the institution had already taken shape on the Caribbean islands whence the conquerors came. The intention, and indeed the only possibility, was to rely initially on indigenous units however they happened to be constituted in a given area. In the Antilles, the Spaniards had not always been able to discern sociopolitical units as such. They had therefore normally based an encomienda grant on a *cacique* and the Indians under him, the powers of the cacique or indigenous ruler in any case being crucial to the organization and channeling of the encomienda's benefits. In central Mexico, the Spaniards immediately took the tlatoque to be caciques and to a large extent shaped encomiendas around them. At the same time, they could not but become aware of the elaborately organized, strongly territorial, prominently named altepetl units, so that they increasingly issued encomiendas in terms of them, denominated "pueblos" as discussed above.

On the heels of the creation of encomiendas in the 1520's came the establishment of *doctrinas* or Indian parishes. A few vast encomienda units were to be divided into more than one parish, and in some cases, one parish encompassed two closely associated encomiendas. But generally the parish was simply a function of the encomienda, depending on it for financial and other support and relying on the same indigenous units and authorities. In the 1530's, Spanish officials began the process of reshaping indigenous government on the model of Spanish-style municipalities. Once again, the units were largely the same.

Essentially, then, the altepetl survived into postconquest times as the basis for all the most important institutional forms affecting life in the indigenous countryside, away from Spanish cities. A simple altepetl could expect to become, with unchanged borders and constituent parts, first an encomienda, then (in addition) a parish, then also a Spanish-style municipal organization. Such cases (taking into consideration that a fully studied altepetl rarely turns out to be truly simple) are, in the south of the Valley of Mexico, Mixquic, Cuitlahuac, and Huitzilopochco, and in the north of the same valley, Xilotzinco, Tizayuca, and Tecama.[51]

In multiple-tlatoani altepetl, too, the principle of building on the indigenous units remained the same, but the forms of adaptation could become very complex. Other things being equal, Spaniards in America tended to opt for the largest encomiendas the indigenous structure could support, that is, to retain the largest viable indigenous units.[52] Beyond a certain point, however, and in Mexico that point was quickly reached, pressures built up in the opposite direction, not only because of the search for more encomiendas for eligible candidates, but above all because of the unwillingness of the bulk of the encomenderos to let any one of their number enjoy such disproportionate riches as would accrue, say, from the possession of all Tlaxcala or all Chalco in encomienda.

Thus a large altepetl with sharply defined moieties and two principal tlatoque might be made into two encomiendas. Each half of Tulancingo became an encomienda, and in the wake of that, two separate municipal corporations arose, although they shared a common parish.[53] Without an explanation of the Spanish rationale in a case like this, we cannot be sure that the main reason for the arrangement was to create more encomiendas or deprive someone of too great a plum. It may be rather that the moieties were so separate that they could not readily be made into a single tribute-paying unit. In the Toluca Valley, the intertwined Calimaya and Tepemaxalco became separate encomiendas and municipal organizations (again sharing a parish, with a patron saint for each) even though the same Spaniard held both encomiendas.[54]

Often, however, a unit of considerable size and complexity had a good chance to be left unaltered. Several of the very largest entities were so valuable that they were never put in encomienda at all, or were encomiendas for only a few years after the conquest; thus they remained under direct crown jurisdiction, and the ordinary pressures for subdivision were less strong. Xochimilco, with three tlatoque and three tlayacatl, became and long remained one parish and one municipal corporation, as did Coyoacan, which despite the existence of a single dominant tlatoani was sharply divided into halves.[55] Tlaxcala, the outstanding case of large-unit retention, became one municipality and for a time one parish, even though it could easily have been divided into its four altepetl, which already had entirely distinct rulers and territories.[56] But unity was not always the result even under favorable conditions. Having originally treated Chalco as a unit, Spanish officials seem in time to have understood its true nature better, creating four corporations and parishes and before long recognizing subdivisions even of those. In the Acolhua region, the area closely associated with Tetzcoco (not to speak of former imperial dependencies such as Teotihuacan and Otumba), no fewer than four independent corporations and parishes arose in addition to Tetzcoco proper.[57] Ordinarily, the constituent attaining recognition would have lobbied long and hard for it, with the senior constituent of the larger entity stiffly resisting.[58]

Governorship

The campaign to create Hispanic-style municipal governments in the central Mexican altepetl stretched over much of the middle part of the sixteenth century, typically affecting the largest and most prominent entities first. Nor did the entire cabildo (municipal council) normally spring into being all at the same time in any one place. It seems, rather, that often the higher offices were instituted first and the lower ones filled in progressively. Since the first stages are naturally enough the least well documented, it is often not known whether a full cabildo was planned from the beginning or not. In any event, the office of "governor" (Spanish *gobernador*, becoming a loanword in Nahuatl by midcentury) in many cases preceded the rest by a decade or more.

It is symptomatic of the whole process of rapprochement of Hispanic and indigenous government that the title gobernador was not a standard part of the terminology of Spanish municipal office. In sixteenth-century Spain, a large city with a full cabildo would be expected to have as its presiding officer a *corregidor*, a person from the outside appointed by the crown and representing the interests of the central government as well as those of the municipality. More a counterweight to the cabildo than a part of it, he usually held office for only a few years before being replaced, lest he become either too powerful on the local scene or too subservient to local interests. The central Mexican indigenous governor of the postconquest period, on the other hand, was to be, in general, a permanent member of the unit over which he presided. Usually, in fact, he was to be in the first instance the sole or premier tlatoani of the altepetl being reorganized as a municipality. Spanish officials were not, we will see, necessarily reconciled to the locally born governor as a permanent feature of the system, though in the end that solution was to prevail, but at first they had little choice in the matter. Even if there had been enough Spanish candidates available to supervise each and every Indian town, they would not have been knowledgeable enough to act as presiding officers in any meaningful way. Nor would it have made sense to send Nahuas into foreign and hostile altepetl to help introduce a system they had yet to learn themselves.

Beginning with the tlatoani, the fulcrum of the altepetl, was an obvious way to proceed, perhaps the only realistic possibility. Spanish manipulation of the tlatoque had begun immediately, during the conquest itself, and at the same time tlatoque and rivals for their rulership had tried to maneuver the Spaniards into supporting the claims of some candidates over others. Such dealings were new to neither side. All over the Indies, the Spaniards, particularly in the conquest years, removed recalcitrant rulers in favor of pretenders who promised greater cooperation. The Nahuas were already familiar with similar interventions by the imperial altepetl Tenochtitlan and Tetzcoco (though generally associated with the politics of dynastic intermarriage). The rulers of the imperial cities had exercised the power of confirmation of tlatoque in office across broad areas of central Mexico (as had the rulers of Cholula and others before them), and rival factions in individual altepetl had not failed to carry on intrigues with the imperial rulers in the hope of gaining leverage in the battle for succession.[59]

Often, it seems, the Spaniards in the early stages had an unconscious impact on altepetl organization and succession in that, all unaware of such things as multiple tlatoque, tlayacatl, or moieties, they took the most visible leader to be the out-and-out ruler of the whole entity and dealt with him alone. For example, they apparently considered Maxixcatzin, tlatoani of Tlaxcala's ranking tlayacatl Ocotelolco and perhaps indeed titular head of the larger polity, to be simply king of Tlaxcala.[60] In Coyoacan, they may have been responsible for exalting don Juan de Guzmán Itztlolinqui to a position of exclusive dominance, for Coyoacan otherwise shows many signs of dual organization and multiple tlatoque.[61]

Spaniards apparently sometimes spontaneously referred to Indian leaders as governors from a very early time.[62] But it was after 1535, in the time of Viceroy don Antonio de Mendoza, that Spanish officials systematically began naming the ranking tlatoque of important altepetl to formal governorships of their respective units, so that in Spanish the head of an Indian town was often called "cacique y gobernador" or "señor y gobernador."[63] In Nahuatl, he of course continued to be called tlatoani as well as governor, and the governor was to continue to be addressed as tlatoani long past the time when one and the same person ordinarily held both offices.* In these formative years, the governorship permanently took on a great deal of the aura, powers, and characteristics of the preconquest rulership.

---

*In Chapter 4 we will see that with time the meaning of "tlatoani" itself broadened and weakened, but even in relatively early texts, and in unambiguous contexts, non-tlatoani governors were to be called "tlatoani" in the sense of "ruler."

One characteristic that was often retained by first-generation governors was lifetime tenure in office. Because of high mortality from epidemic disease, offices turned over quite often, despite life terms, but even so Spanish officials gave serious attention to attaining regular rotation in the office. Almost immediately in some places, later in the sixteenth century in others, sporadically in yet others, governors came to be replaced after short terms, whether through ad hoc appointments or prescribed frequent reelections. This necessarily involved a separation of the governorship and the tlatocayotl, which would at least at some times have to be occupied by separate persons; consequently, many of the powers of the tlatoani would be exercised by the governor instead, and the dynastic rulership would inevitably lose some of its meaning.[64]

Thus a very considerable transformation took place in the nature of the highest political office of the altepetl in a relatively short time. Some of the change, however, was only apparent, because traditional tlatoque could continue to be decisive behind the scenes,[65] and some of it was only temporary, since principles of dynastic selection and long-term rule reasserted themselves somewhat in later years. Some of it, though real enough and owing much to Spanish pressure, also responded to indigenous patterns and needs. The holders of the governorship, while no longer always tlatoque, were most often high nobles who might have been in the running for a rulership. Succession to the throne was generally less automatic among the Nahuas than among Europeans. Each kingdom had its own variant tradition, but depending on demonstrated capability and political maneuvering, any of the former ruler's sons or brothers might succeed, or even his uncles or grandsons. A corporate body of the senior noblemen of the altepetl ratified the choice by a group "election," which was ordinarily unanimous.[66] Eventually formally recognized in many postconquest municipalities, this body of electors could and did lend legitimacy to any Nahua nobleman named to the governorship.[67]

In preconquest times, the losing candidates for the throne had represented a formidable problem. A bloodbath during or immediately after a succession was not uncommon. Surviving unsuccessful candidates often lived in exile in neighboring altepetl, hatching plots against the incumbent. Or the kings and their own ambitions sent them to wars in which they were often killed.[68] After the conquest, despite the increased mortality from disease, the decline of fratricide, exile, and war left more than enough would-be tlatoque on the scene. A rotating governorship was well adapted to the new situation, satisfying several claimants in turn rather than one for a lifetime. High nobles not succeeding to a dynastic rulership had every reason to be happy with the new arrangement, and indeed it is only the tlatoque themselves whom we see complaining.[69] A rotating governorship could also ease the inequities caused in complex altepetl by the frequent Spanish overemphasis on the leading tlaya-catl. In Amaquemecan, after a brief time in which some feared that the senior tlatoani would monopolize the governorship, it began to rotate among the tlatoque of all the tlayacatl.[70] In Tlaxcala, the Spanish preference for appoint-ing Ocotelolcans to the governorship caused serious strife and precipitated an elaborate reorganization in 1545, with all offices allocated equally among the four constituent altepetl and the governorship (no longer held by the four tlatoque) rotating among the four units in strict order.[71]

A nondynastic, less than life-term governorship had a preconquest prece-dent in the institution of the *quauhtlatoani* or interim ruler in an established tlatocayotl. Meaning literally "eagle-ruler," the term originally had the con-notation that the occupant had achieved his position through personal merit in war, not inheritance, and hence was only standing in until a dynastic heir could be agreed on or come of age. Even as late as the sixteenth century, the quauhtlatoani was often still a person of relatively humble birth, but the con-cept had expanded to include a ruler who, for whatever reason, was not laying permanent and dynastic claim to the office, so that on occasion rulers of subunits and even members of royal lineages served as quauhtlatoque. De-spite the interim nature of their appointment, many of them are said to have exercised the powers of the rulership to the fullest.[72] A postconquest non-tlatoani governor could readily imagine himself a quauhtlatoani, and be so perceived by his subjects. Some of the earliest cases of non-tlatoani governor-ship in fact arose in the primary situation calling for a quauhtlatoani, to serve as regent for a minor successor.[73] In Tenochtitlan, two quauhtlatoque held forth for five years each after 1525, filling the gap until the reestablishment of the dynastic tlatocayotl in the late 1530's (see Table 2.1). Since the new tlatoani was also the first formally appointed, the quauhtlatoque can certainly be said to have represented a transition to governorship in this case.[74]

Governors were generally first chosen locally, through some combination of election, inheritance, and rotation, with influence sometimes exercised by locally based Spanish ecclesiastics or administrators, then confirmed by the viceregal government in Mexico City. In the second half of the sixteenth cen-tury, however, the central government at times took the choice out of local hands entirely and named someone from a foreign altepetl. A priori, such appointments would seem to correspond to a general Spanish campaign over the long haul to make the governor more like the Spanish model, the corre-gidor. But there may have been more pressing reasons for the policy. The early and middle years of the sixteenth century produced their share of embroiled disputes within and between altepetl over lands, jurisdictions, and succes-sions. Unadvised Spaniards were in no position to adjudicate such matters. The best judge would be an outsider who was at once fully acquainted with

TABLE 2.1

Postconquest Rulers of Tenochtitlan

Name	Position	Background	Tenure
Don Andrés de Tapia Motelchiuhtzin	quauhtlatoani	not born nobleman	1526–30
Don Pablo Xochiquentzin	quauhtlatoani	not born nobleman	1532–36
Don Diego de Alvarado Huanitzin	tlatoani, governor	royal line	1538–41
Don Diego de San Francisco Tehuetzquititzin	tlatoani, governor	royal line	1541–54
Don Esteban de Guzmán	judge of residencia	noble from Xochimilco	1554–57
Don Cristóbal de Guzmán Cecetzin (son of Huanitzin)	tlatoani, governor	royal line	1557–62
Don Luis de Santa María Cipactzin	tlatoani, governor	royal line	1563–65
(Don) Francisco Jiménez[a]	judge-governor	noble from Tecamachalco	1568–69
Antonio Valeriano (son-in-law of Huanitzin)[b]	judge-governor	not noble, from Azcapotzalco	1573–99
Don Gerónimo López	judge-governor	mestizo from Xaltocan	1599–1608
Don Juan Bautista	judge-governor	from Malinalco	1609
Juan Pérez de Monterrey[c]	judge-governor	mestizo	1610–14ff

SOURCES: CH, 2; Gibson 1964; MNAH AH, GO 14; Tezozomoc 1949.

[a]Sometimes entitled "don," sometimes not, in both Tenochtitlan and Tecamachalco (CH).

[b]Originally not "don," but custom soon gave him the title. In 1596–99, Valeriano was failing, and don Juan Martín, mestizo, as deputy acted in his stead.

[c]Sometimes, but not usually, called "don" (that is, his naming pattern is more Spanish than Indian). A Spaniard, Francisco Sánchez, was "presidente" in the governorship between don Juan Bautista and Juan Pérez de Monterrey.

indigenous modes and knowledgeable about the Spanish system. Those most clearly qualified were Nahua noblemen with experience of Spanish-style Indian administration, and the viceregal government soon started sending them from one altepetl to another on temporary missions to judge each other's disputes.[75]

The next step was using figures of this type as judges in the periodic reviews to which Spanish governmental practice assigned a persistent role. Such a *juez de residencia*, as in the Hispanic tradition, actually took over the local government during the period of his inquiry; in other words, he acted as governor. For three years in the 1550's, the judge don Esteban de Guzmán, from Xochimilco, was the de facto governor of Tenochtitlan.[76] Outside inspectors led easily to a further stage, simply assigning the outsider the governorship for a time. It was probably because of the association with outside judges that governors from the later sixteenth century through the rest of the colonial period were often styled "judge-governor" (*juez gobernador*). Outsiders as governors became a very frequent phenomenon in the Valley of Mexico and remained so on into the early decades of the seventeenth century, when they began to fade out in favor of locals, who had probably been the large majority all along.[77] Outside governors were especially prevalent in the immediate vicinity of Mexico City, an area whose dynasties had long been so interrelated that tlatoque frequently ruled outside the altepetl where they were born, so that there may have been a partial preconquest precedent. But most governors from the outside in the postconquest did not have any dynastic affiliation with the governed group.

Much of the impetus for outside recruitment may have come from the desire to spread Spanish-style indigenous government outward from the places where it had taken root most firmly. An inordinate number of the traveling governors came from Xochimilco and Tlaxcala, two of the best-developed of the early municipal organizations. In other cases, someone would apparently demonstrate great proficiency, acquire valuable experience, and then receive such assignments again and again. At his death in 1600, the mestizo don Juan Martín was in his second term as governor of Tlatelolco and had served in the same post in five other major towns, Calimaya, Xochimilco, Cuitlahuac, Acolman, and Mexico Tenochtitlan.[78] Whatever the advantages of appointing governors from outside the altepetl, the practice proved a transitional one, and by the middle of the seventeenth century, it was again unusual for a governor to originate anywhere but in the unit he was governing. In this respect, then, the preconquest structure dominated in the long run. Once the basic elements of Spanish-Indian municipal government had spread across all central Mexico, and Spaniards and Indians in general had learned more about each other's manner of operation, it was probably no longer worth going to the trouble of maintaining a cross-regional indigenous administrative cadre and dealing with the opposition to outside governors that must have made itself felt in each case.

The Cabildo: Alcaldes and Regidores

We find some use of standard Spanish titles for municipal officeholders in central Mexican altepetl from the time when formal governorships were created in the later 1530's.[79] It is not until the 1550's, however, that one expects a full complement of officials with Spanish titles in all the more prominent altepetl. In most cases, the exact year of their first appointment is not known, nor do we have much evidence of who instigated the creation of the offices. In the relatively well-documented case of Coyoacan, an undated text shows the governor petitioning the Audiencia for permission to name two alcaldes and twelve regidores because, being so close to Mexico City, he had grasped the Spanish style of government and wanted his subjects to be properly ruled.[80] Nevertheless, generally speaking the initiative must ultimately have come from the Spaniards, bent on spreading their own system. In the fiercely competitive world of central Mexican altepetl, of course, the moment certain prominent kingdoms acquired new offices, others would clamor to do the same.

As with the governors, Nahua alcaldes and regidores were to deviate substantially from Spanish models. To appreciate the deviance, we first need to understand the model. The backbone of the cabildo of a full-fledged Spanish city, either in Spain or in the Indies, was its corps of perhaps half a dozen to a dozen regidores or councilmen. Noblemen or those with pretensions to nobility usually occupied the posts; typically, they held office for long terms or life, and even when annual rotation was the practice, holders repeated frequently, maintaining representation of the same group over the years. Essentially, the regidores were representatives of large familial-economic complexes that were based in the city proper but in some sense dominated most aspects of life throughout the whole municipal territory. The continuity of the corps of regidores gave the Spanish cabildo a strong corporate identity. Completing the cabildo were the (standardly two) alcaldes, first-instance judges who ex officio sat with the council as full voting members. Alcaldes invariably rotated annually, and this characteristic, together with the rather onerous and demanding nature of the post, meant that the recruitment pool was somewhat different. While a regidor might on occasion serve as alcalde, often the alcalde was receiving recognition as an individual rather than as a representative of a family, or he belonged to a family complex on the rise and would later become a regidor. In other words, in social terms regidor ranked rather higher than alcalde.[81] With both offices, the representation of subjurisdictions played a minimal or nonexistent role.

What equivalent machinery existed in the central Mexican altepetl? We are told that the imperial altepetl of Tenochtitlan and Tetzcoco had high councils consisting of officers with special titles who carried out different combinations of judicial and military functions. Accounts vary greatly. It is not clear whether such councils were a constitutional facet of the altepetl or ad hoc creations of the principal ruler at the time. The sources do not assign them a strong corporate role.[82] My own feeling is that the officers of this kind of high council must each have been based in a specific subunit of the altepetl. Looking away from the shadowy councils of the imperial powers, the main officers one would find in a Mexican polity would be the heads of its subunits: in a complex altepetl, the tlatoque of the constituent tlayacatl, and in a tlayacatl or simple altepetl, the teuctlatoque or calpolli heads. As people of noble rank accustomed to adjudicate and administer, they offer close parallels to Spanish municipal functionaries, but some striking differences may also be observed. Although the Nahua officials were generally representatives of lineages and in that somewhat comparable to Spanish functionaries, they above all represented geographically and jurisdictionally separate subunits of the whole, a principle alien to the Spanish system. Partly for this reason, they lacked the corporate cohesion of the cabildo, that is, they did not stand out from the rest of the altepetl structure as a closed body. No equivalent appears for the corps of regidores, long-term representatives of dominant families without regard to jurisdictions. Nahua kingdoms did have another sort of corporation that asserted itself at critical junctures, such as successions and decisions of war or peace. At these times, all the prominent or elder nobles of the realm would assemble, provide a forum for debate, and through consensus, legitimate the action taken.[83] The group of elders or electors, however, was far too large and unwieldy to meet regularly and carry on business like a Spanish cabildo. The most famous such body, in Tlaxcala, had no fewer than 220 members.[84]

Comparing the two systems, one would expect that, in the introduction of Spanish offices into the Nahua world, it would prove necessary to modify them to the extent of having each officer represent a specific subjurisdiction, and this is what seems to have happened, as far as the sources allow us to follow the process. One consequence was an early tendency, in the more complex altepetl, to multiply the alcaldes beyond the usual two, in addition to a large set of regidores. The cabildo of Tlaxcala after 1545 consisted of four alcaldes, one from each of the constituent altepetl; the four tlatoque sitting as perpetual regidores; and three annually changing regidores from each altepetl.[85] Tenochtitlan divided twelve regidores among its four tlayacatl, not always evenly in view of the predominance of San Juan Moyotlan, but each regidor always represented a specific tlayacatl and even possibly a specific subdivision within that.[86] In 1600, after a long period of rotating two alcalde posts among the four tlayacatl following the basic rotational sequence, Tenochtitlan went over to four alcaldes, one for each tlayacatl, and in 1610 the number was raised to eight, two for each (though it may be that neither of these schemes was carried out with full consistency).[87] Coyoacan petitioned for two alcaldes (one for each half?) and twelve regidores, each to be chosen from a different subunit.[88] The Coyoacan cabildo roster of 1553 in fact proves to include eight regidores plus four "*principales*," perhaps tlatoque of tlayacatl serving as permanent regidores as in Tlaxcala (see Table 2.2).[89] As in all of these cases, and as in the structure of preconquest altepetl, sets of four, eight, twelve, or sixteen predominate generally in the staffing of the postconquest municipalities. But if the altepetl through some historical process had

TABLE 2.2

Officials of Coyoacan, 1553

Office	Occupant	Number	Office	Occupant	Number
Governor[a]	Don Juan (de Guzmán)	1	Majordomos	Martín Tlacateuctli	
Alcaldes	Don Luis de San Pedro			Miguel Huecamecatl	2
	Don Luis Cortés	2	Accountants	Agustín Gallego	
Regidores	Don Luis de Santiago			Alonso Hueiteuctli	2
	Juan de San Lázaro		Notaries	Pedro de Suero	
	Miguel de la Cruz			Alonso de Benavides	2
	Pedro de Paz		Alguaciles	Miguel Huecamecatl	
	Toribio Silvestre		(constables)	Gonzalo López	
	Juan Hueiteuctli			Francisco Amiztlato	
	Bartolomé Atempanecatl			Luis Daniel	
	Don Martín de Paz	8		Miguel de la Cruz	
"Principales"	Don Antonio			Martín Tlacochcalcatl	
	Don Baltasar			Miguel Sánchez	
	Juan de Guzmán			Cristóbal Xochihua	8
	Bartolomé de León	4	Alcaide (jailer)	Alonso Tlapaltecatl	1

SOURCE: CDC, 1: 74–75.
NOTE: Unless otherwise specified, all tables give names and offices in the sources' original order.
[a] Also tlatoani.

an uneven number of constituents, the municipal offices would reflect it, as with the sets of three in Xochimilco and Tenango (Chalco region).[90]

Clearly, then, the Nahuas in a general sense equated preconquest with postconquest sociopolitical structure and officeholding, and there were significant carryovers from one period to the other.[91] The extent of the continuity, indeed, was crucial to the quick and successful establishment of independently functioning municipal governments across the whole region, something that in many parts of Spanish America happened later or never at all. Little terminological evidence exists for specific retentions and equations because of the great stress laid on the new nomenclature by the Spaniards and the high prestige it enjoyed among the Nahuas. Just as ranking noblemen over the sixteenth century abandoned Nahuatl surnames in favor of Spanish ones, so in documents any Nahuatl titles gave way immediately to "alcalde," "regidor," and so on, with retention of Nahuatl office nomenclature only below the cabildo level. This does not mean, however, that either indigenous names or indigenous office titles had really been forgotten so quickly. A document of the mid-sixteenth century from Coyoacan seems to equate teuctlatoque and alcaldes, calling the latter officials by both titles as if trying to make entirely clear what an alcalde was.[92] If we think of Chimalpahin's definition of teuctlatoani as calpolli head, then this would be a case of one-to-one identification of preconquest and postconquest office. In fact, however, usage varies in Nahuatl texts, and in some, such as Sahagún, "teuctlatoani" appears applicable to anyone acting as a judge. The term is even found in reference to the Spanish judges of the Royal Audiencia.[93]

A different sort of example comes from Huitzilopochco around the same time. In a letter to his counterpart in neighboring Coyoacan, the governor and tlatoani of Huitzilopochco steps outside the documentary genres associated with the postconquest municipality to use preconquest-style invective (and some polite language) in which the new vocabulary had no place. The Huitzilopochco official who led his side in recent transactions having to do with a border dispute is called the Tlacateccatl, and the leading official for Coyoacan is called the Mixcoatlailotlac.[94] In all likelihood, these people were members of their respective cabildos as alcalde or regidor. In any case, such titles and functions remained unforgotten, and they were still unforgotten when Chimalpahin wrote in the early seventeenth century.

Another possible sign of identification of preconquest with postconquest offices is the Nahua treatment of the office of alcalde as opposed to that of regidor. Whereas in the Spanish scheme, as just seen, regidor tended to be the more permanent and highly valued post, among the Nahuas alcalde distinctly ranked higher. Alcaldes more often bore the title "don," more often had Spanish surnames, and in general were of more illustrious lineage. Moreover, as regidores gained experience, connections, and renown, they advanced to alcalde, creating a hierarchical ranking of the two offices.[95]

Are we to presume, then, that alcalde and regidor correspond to two different preconquest functions, one higher and one lower? I believe that the reason for the Nahua divergence is to be sought rather in the lack of any close indigenous parallel to the Spanish regidor. Having once redefined both offices as representing subjurisdictions, the Nahuas may have found that the post of alcalde stood out as better reflecting the importance in preconquest office of adjudication, in addition to having greater scarcity value (regidores being more numerous). For the rest, indigenous people may have seen little difference between the two offices and little need for both of them beyond the necessity for adequate representation of subunits. It is known that alcaldes did hold court and render judgments, at least in some places, often in conjunction with the governor, but in at least one case a regidor is shown in the same role.[96] Eventually, as we will see, the corps of regidores was to fade into insignificance, in many places disappearing entirely, and even in the late sixteenth and early seventeenth centuries there were signs of the trend. Toward the end of the sixteenth century, Tlaxcala added four "provincial alcaldes" and dropped four regidores.[97] Lists of Tenochtitlan officials from the 1560's carefully specify the twelve regidores after the two alcaldes, but starting in 1600, as noted, the alcaldes doubled in number, then doubled again, and Chimalpahin's lists of this time no longer give the names of regidores.[98]

Nahuas were much less aware of the borders of the cabildo than Spaniards were. Again and again one finds joint reference to the municipal officials and the broader group of all the noblemen of the altepetl. Thus those who speak in a 1560 letter from Huexotzinco are described as "I the governor, and we alcaldes and regidores, and we lords and nobles."[99] In 1582 in the Tlaixpan half of Tulancingo, the governor, alcaldes, regidores, "and all the noblemen of Tlaixpan" took responsibility for a debt.[100] The regidores were likely to be overlooked entirely, as when Spaniards reported that they were met by a town's "governor, alcaldes, and other noblemen (principales)," or municipal accounts contain an entry detailing the expenses of a feast for "governor, alcaldes, and noblemen."[101] The Nahua cabildo was also more inclusive than the Spanish model in respect to competing hierarchies, specifically the ecclesiastical. Although a Spanish cabildo standardly put much effort into support of general religious festivities, it brooked no direct interference or participation from the personnel of church organizations. In preconquest Mesoamerica, priestly and political office had been closely associated, held by the same families and even interpenetrating. In the postconquest municipality, a second Spanish-style organization was responsible for the church and religious affairs at all levels below those requiring a Spanish priest. As we shall see in Chapter 6, this organization and the cabildo eventually grew into each other to a considerable extent, and especially the highest religious official, the *fiscal*, in some times and places and for some purposes virtually functioned as a member of the cabildo.

Notaries

A Spanish cabildo was inconceivable without its official clerk-notary (*escribano*), who kept the minutes, wrote up the cabildo's pronouncements in proper form, and as notary attested to their authenticity. The notary was not a voting member of the cabildo, but he was not exactly a lower official either. He might come from a solid middling family, or he might have pretensions to nobility; after some years in the post, he could even rise to full cabildo membership, though not nearly all did so. Preconquest Mexico also knew the official writer, the *amatlacuilo* or "painter on paper," and the role was associated with nobility. The records kept were, as far as is known, mainly religious and divinatory manuals, historical annals, censuses, land cadastrals, and tribute lists, in a form as much pictorial as glyphic.[102] The parallel may have been of a rather general kind, but the Nahuas (as well as other Mesoamericans) apparently did see some parallel, since they adapted to the post of notary quickly, successfully, and permanently, and notarial skills became self-perpetuating among them.

Thus, starting from the 1540's, when alcaldes and regidores first began to be appointed regularly, no Nahua cabildo was without its notary. The governor's petition that Coyoacan be granted a full cabildo includes a request that the alcaldes and regidores be empowered to name a notary.[103] The earliest known functioning municipal notaries are seen in 1545 (Tlaxcala) and 1548 (Coyoacan).[104] Since the documents they produced show them as full masters of their skills, it would seem that even then they had been practicing for some time. But it is unlikely that any substantial number of town clerks in the Spanish style were trained and installed before 1540. Indeed, the roughly simultaneous appearance of notaries, alcaldes, and regidores is doubtless no accident; the creation of full cabildos in advance of people who had some understanding of Spanish procedures and documentary genres would have been illusory.

Because of the unique sixteenth-century cabildo minutes of Tlaxcala, it is there that evidence on the notaries is fullest. At least six of the eight clerks appearing in those records were "electors," members of the 220-man body that contained the cream of Tlaxcala's nobility; two served at some time as regidor, and one of these as alcalde. The original functionaries, to judge by a few hints in the records, may have been trained by Franciscans at the local monastery, but by the 1560's or earlier, they seem to have begun to train younger relatives in turn. An elaborate rotation of four clerks from the four constituent altepetl gave lip service to the general procedures of complex altepetl structure, but in fact the two most capable figures did most of the writing over a period well in excess of twenty years. The most capable of all, a Diego de Soto, was a nobleman though not an elector, nor did he attain full cabildo office; he was born around 1511, witnessed the conquest as a boy of ten or twelve, must have learned how to read and write Nahuatl in his teens or later, and served as cabildo notary at least from 1545 to 1582.[105] The general profile of postconquest Nahua notaries is thus hardly distinguishable from that of their Spanish counterparts except for their closer attachment to a certain subjurisdiction of the unit they served, and in view of their relative scarcity, even that aspect was not always pronounced. Since the role and status of the preconquest amatlacuilo remain shadowy, it is hard to know to what extent the similarity rests on previous convergence.

Minor Officials

The Spanish system emphasized a sharp distinction between noble, prestigious full cabildo members and shifting, unprestigious, plebeian sub-cabildo officials like constables and attendants. Rarely if ever could a person in the second category rise to the first. As we might by now expect, no such distinction existed in preconquest central Mexico, so that here too the Indian cabildo was to have more fluid borders than its Spanish counterpart. Partly perhaps because of the lack of a separate, well-defined, restricted corporation at the head of the polity, and partly perhaps because many governmental or quasi-governmental matters involved attendance at the ruler's tecpan and consequently had a courtly aura, the association of office with nobility was much broader in the Nahua world than in the Spanish.[106]

Again Tlaxcala is our best example. The well-developed Tlaxcalan municipality of the 1550's and 1560's included provincial lieutenants (*tenientes*), urban and rural constables (*alguaciles*), city majordomos (*mayordomos*), an usher (*portero*), a jailer (*alcaide*), custodians of the tribute house, tribute overseers, and keepers of the municipal inns (*mesoneros*). A large proportion of these functionaries were electors of Tlaxcala, and turns of phrase used in the records give us reason to think that they were all noblemen (*pipiltin*). As many as a dozen are known to have sat on the cabildo at some time, usually after their service in minor office. Yet only a small fraction rose to that eminence, and the minor officials as a whole stand out in the records from cabildo members in that hardly any bore the title "don," most had Nahuatl surnames, and such Spanish surnames as they had tended to be less imposing than those of the alcaldes and regidores. Like their superiors, the sub-cabildo officials represented specific constituent altepetl and probably subdistricts within them. Some served within their home areas, but even when they were located in the city proper, they remained compartmentalized and worked with their own people. Thus the municipal treasury contained four separate funds, collected and managed by four different people.[107]

Some confirmation of the generality of certain elements in the Tlaxcalan picture comes from fragments in less fully documented situations. In the Tlaixpan half of Tulancingo at the same time, the four or sometimes more municipal tribute collectors represented four subunits and made separate collections in their own units; unlike the cabildo officers, who had fully Hispanic names, they retained indigenous surnames, but their high position can be deduced from the fact that most of the names end in the element *teuctli*, "lord."[108] The constables, accountants, and majordomos of Coyoacan in 1553 show a similar naming pattern, many using surnames that, though indigenous, were also typical preconquest titles of calpolli heads or lords of noble houses.[109] In late-sixteenth-century Culhuacan, some of the lower officials later rose to cabildo membership.[110]

In Tlaxcala and, to judge by sketchier information, apparently in Culhuacan and Coyoacan as well, frequent shifting about was a common feature of lower officialdom, with the same person appearing in a variety of apparently unrelated posts.[111] It would seem that the Nahuas viewed these as in some way the same thing and thus interchangeable. All the officials at this level were apparently deputies in the sense that they operated on authority delegated, in preconquest times, from the tlatoque and titular calpolli heads, and in postconquest times from the cabildo. They differed from ward officers in that the scope of their authority embraced larger units.[112] The Nahuatl category for the intermediate officers may have been *topile*. Although Molina translates the word as constable, and it does indeed appear in Nahuatl texts most frequently in alternation with the Spanish "alguacil," it is also used at times as an alternative description for the holders of a variety of intermediate posts, including ones in the church organization.[113] Literally, "topile" means "holder of a staff." Since the staff was the Spaniards' primary symbol of office, it may be that the word came into use after the conquest, but if so, it entered the language very early and must have replaced another common word of nearly identical meaning.

We have been discussing office at the altepetl level. The internal governance of the calpolli constitutes another level, of which far less is presently known. Some sixteenth-century Nahuatl censuses show the existence of ward-like entities arranged in groups of twenty households, forty, and so on to a hundred (these numerical definitions must be construed in the most approximate fashion).[114] Reorganization around midcentury could be carried out in terms of such units,[115] and there is reason to believe that in a general way organization by small wards with individual heads projected indefinitely into the future.

After the creation of cabildos, most of the lower officials associated with them had Spanish titles (although one does find *calpixqui*, "steward," used at times for the municipal tribute officers). These figures, who in the overall context are actually middle-level officials, were mainly directly involved in cabildo (i.e., altepetl) operations, or at least received their appointments directly from the cabildo. In both respects, they differed from the ward officers, who are perhaps better imagined as citizens with some special duties than as functionaries. It appears that in preconquest times they were commonly named after the size of the unit with which they were charged, but terms like *macuiltecpanpixqui* "keeper of a hundred," become very rare in Nahuatl documents after the 1550's. The Spanish titles *merino*, "rural constable," and *capitán* were sometimes used for ward heads in Nahuatl, mainly from a distance or in references to the officials en masse, although "merino" did gain much ground as time went on. More commonly applied to individual people, especially before the late period, were the indigenous and probably traditional words *tepixqui*, "keeper of people, one in charge of people"; *tlayacan-*

qui, teyacanqui, "leader, guide"; and *tequitlato*, "tribute-speaker." The terms appear to have varied with the function being emphasized and with the alte-petl, each developing its somewhat special terminology.[116] The office of *cihua-tepixqui*, "female person in charge of people," also existed at this level; pre-sumably, this officer, in addition to being a woman, had special responsibility for organizing or regulating women's activity, but no more is known at the present juncture.[117] Much is still to be learned about the recruitment of ward officers in general, for we have little more than secondhand Spanish accounts. In the censuses of the Cuernavaca jurisdiction and Tlaxcala, they appear very much a part of the groups they led; their naming patterns hardly differ from those of the populace at large, and considering the large number of ward heads, it is impossible to imagine that they were all or even mainly noble or acquired office by virtue of lineage.[118]

In the records of actual proceedings, the ward heads with their more spe-cific titles rarely appear as such. What one sees again and again in the au-thentication of wills, sales, and acts of possession is the appearance of an undifferentiated body of *tlaxilacaleque*, literally "holders or owners of the tlaxilacalli (calpolli unit)." The word is highly ambiguous, since it can mean "inhabitant of the tlaxilacalli" as well as "tlaxilacalli authority," and in fact in some of the cases where the tlaxilacaleque remain unnamed, the authenti-cating group seems to be a broader section of the citizenry at large.[119] Some-times, however, the word *huehuetque*, "elders," appears instead of or in ad-dition to "tlaxilacaleque," making it clear that we are dealing with authority figures of some kind.[120] Or a contemporary Spanish translation may resolve any doubt.[121] I take it that these tlaxilacaleque or elders, of whom anywhere from four or five to a dozen may be named, are the ward bosses as a group, minus the highest representative of the unit, who would normally be on the cabildo.[122]

Congregation and Corregimiento

The Spanish policy of attempting to "congregate" or "reduce" scattered indigenous populations into more compact, well-defined permanent settle-ments had appeared in the Caribbean phase and was to reappear in some form almost everywhere the Spaniards went. Since the central Mexicans were already organized in extremely well-defined, reasonably compact units and in many cases even showed a relatively high degree of urban nucleation, Spanish officials put less emphasis on congregation there than in peripheral areas or even in Peru.[123] It has been shown for the Valley of Mexico that the number of full-scale congregations ever planned was quite limited, and that of these many failed or were never put into effect at all.[124] A wave of actions called congregations apparently took place in the 1550's, since they are widely mentioned in generalizing administrative reports and gained a permanent place in the collective memory of the people of many altepetl, but little specific record seems to remain. From the general configuration of the central Mexican altepetl in the second half of the sixteenth century, it is obvious that the essential distribution of altepetl and calpolli remained untouched. Many of these "congregations" seem rather to have fallen together with or indeed to have been the same thing as the formal institution of a Spanish-style cabildo in an altepetl, with the attendant confirmation of its boundaries and those of its constituent parts. That was surely, in any case, how the Nahuas tended to remember it. Where main settlements had been located on hills for defensive purposes, they may have been relocated on level land at this time, and existing clusters may have been rearranged to the extent of establishing a grid pattern of streets, with a church and government buildings on a dominant central plaza.[125]

Sixteenth-century relocations seem to have fallen far short of moving whole subunits. In the 1540's, a new City of Tlaxcala was established at the intersection of the territories of the four altepetl as a seat for the cabildo and a base for the Franciscans in the province. Though many important noblemen built their homes there, they retained their original affiliations, and the nearby seats of the four tlatoque continued to exist as separate entities. One has no sense of a massive enforced movement of people. When, in 1560, Spanish officials proposed a series of general congregations across the whole territory of Tlaxcala, the cabildo saw nothing but disadvantages in moving the commoners, but was willing to have some noblemen settle in a more concentrated fashion around local churches. The cabildo's pleas were heard, and this sort of compromise arrangement may have been common at the time.[126]

In the early decades of the seventeenth century, another wave of congregations took place, this time of a rather different nature. After many decades of severe population loss, some of the constituent calpolli of altepetl were no longer viable units, and consolidation was called for. The normal procedure was to bring people in from an altepetl's outlying districts to the central area; it is precisely in these terms that Chimalpahin, thinking of the seventeenth century, describes a congregation.[127] It may be that at times people or subunits were relocated in altepetl other than their own,[128] but normally the reorganization would affect altepetl structure only in that the place of residence of the people in some of its constituent parts would be moved, and the smallest constituents might cease to exist separately at all, changing the ranking and rotation. Even when subunits were lost, their memory often lasted, and they might be revived at a future time.[129]

But if congregation failed to revolutionize the sociopolitical structure, it was not without its impact. At the level of social practice, it reinforced or increased the relative importance of the altepetl's central settlement cluster, which through accretions came to hold a larger proportion of the total population, including in particular a great share of the noblemen and leaders of the subunits. In addition to people encouraged or made to move as a part of the reorganization itself, congregation set up secondary movements. A good part of this, it is true, simply saw those unwillingly uprooted moving straight back to their original homes, but in the case of Tlaxcala at least, the newly established central capital attracted voluntary migrants from all over the province and beyond. The actuality thus came ever closer to the Spanish notion of a cabecera or head town. At the level of concepts, congregation made the Nahuas more aware of the terms cabecera and sujeto. Although Nahuatl documents continued to use the indigenous "altepetl" and "tlaxilacalli" for most purposes until a much later time, the act of deliberate nucleation demanded some terminology distinguishing between nucleus and outlying parts. Chimalpahin, who in his voluminous discussions of central Mexican altepetl both before and after the conquest hardly ever uses cabecera and sujeto, does resort to those terms in describing the congregation campaigns.[130]

Over the middle part of the sixteenth century, a system of Spanish provincial administration came into being which, though not a direct part of the indigenous world, was to have a certain impact on its development. The countryside was divided into a series of large districts, *corregimientos*, in each of which a Spanish official, the *corregidor*, presided as chief judge and tax collector, taking, usually, the largest indigenous settlement of the district as headquarters for himself and a small staff.[131] Like previous Spanish institutional innovations, this one too rested on the altepetl, although not always in so clear a one-to-one relationship, since in the majority of cases the corregimiento contained several Indian municipalities. Even so, the corregidor relied on them for most adjudication and tax collection, limiting himself largely to hearing certain appeals and channeling taxes to Mexico City. Moreover, in most cases, the corregimientos were not simple collections of towns that happened to be in the same general geographical region. It is true that in the Toluca Valley and the Cuernavaca region, the corregimientos came close to being miscellanies. But in the Valley of Mexico, Chalco for example became a single corregimiento (with four separate full-scale municipalities), Mexicalzingo contained four closely associated "Colhua" altepetl, and Teotihuacan and Otumba had existed as administrative districts, if not confederations, at least as early as the time of Tetzcocan imperial dominance.[132] In no small number of cases, an entire complex altepetl became a single corregimiento, the whole continuing at the same time to function as a municipal unit; such were Xochimilco, Coyoacan, Tlaxcala, and in a way Tulancingo, which after a time as two municipalities merged into one.

In a several-municipality corregimiento, the Spaniards considered the headquarters of the corregidor to be in a sense the cabecera of the whole district. The normal flow of legal and administrative business frequently brought parties from outlying towns into the corregimiento capital, adding to any preeminence it might already enjoy. Being normally the district's largest settlement as well as the seat of its Spanish authority, the cabecera of the corregimiento was likely to become the primary headquarters of any community of Spaniards residing in the area. By the late sixteenth century, Toluca and Cuernavaca had far outstripped any other communities in their respective basins as Spanish residential centers, loci of Spanish-Indian interaction, and hubs of valley-wide economic activity involving both Spaniards and Indians.* Not that the indigenous municipal governments in district capitals suffered in any obvious way; rather the cabildos there long continued, typically, to be the strongest, most active, and best developed in their regions, without at all ceasing to be authentic carriers of the principal indigenous traditions. Even so, the corregidor and his staff were likely to supervise and utilize the cabildo at the corregimiento base more than the councils in distant towns and also to attempt to exercise more influence on gubernatorial and other elections (just as, conversely, Indian factions in the cabecera were most likely to seek the corregidor's support against rivals).†

Town Government and Structure in the Later Colonial Period

It would not be wrong to say that the main lines of the mixed system of local government that had come into existence in the central Mexican countryside by 1580 or earlier lasted until the time of Mexican independence. The persistence of entities, offices, and forms of organization is striking. Yet the

---

*I do not mean to imply that the district cabecera invariably outgrew other local centers. For example, although Tlalmanalco was preeminent among the four parts of Chalco and became cabecera as one would expect, it eventually lost the lead to Amecameca (Amaquemecan), earlier the second-ranking, and even inside the Tlalmanalco jurisdiction, the weight shifted increasingly to Chalco Atenco.

†See Haskett 1985. Cuernavaca, seat of the magistrate, seems to have generated more extra-altepetl litigation and documents than any other municipality, though Tepoztlan ran a strong second. The imposition of the corregimiento brought the overall system one step closer to the Spanish model by introducing a frequently replaced higher official from the outside. Nevertheless, the indigenous governor still did much of what a corregidor would have done in a Spanish municipality, since most districts contained several Indian towns, and even when there was only one, it does not appear that the corregidor usually presided over the sessions of its cabildo. In Tlaxcala, after a breaking-in period in the late 1540's and early 1550's, when the corregidor often did attend sessions and give instructions, he was present only on ceremonial occasions and during emergencies (TA, pp. 15–16).

system had its own dynamics; the principles of microethnicity, small unit self-containedness, and the separate representation of subunits held the possibility of a progressive fragmentation that in fact began very early in the postconquest period and gained momentum in the seventeenth and eighteenth centuries. Spanish concepts continued to penetrate deeper into Nahua consciousness, or at least to gain currency, although on consideration it often appears that their function was to give a label to deviance from the Spanish norm or the resurgence of Nahua patterns. The changes are sufficiently marked and sufficiently bunched in time to justify speaking of a new period beginning around the middle decades of the seventeenth century.

Office and the Vocabulary of Office

I have mentioned above that Hispanic-style Nahua municipal officialdom in several ways constituted a more open-ended, wider, less corporate body than the Spanish cabildo. Indeed, by speaking of individual officers or the broader nobility rather than of the cabildo as such, both Spaniards and Indians showed some appreciation of this fact from an early time. Yet the word does occur in Nahuatl sources of the sixteenth century, and in the Tlaxcalan council records, it is seen on almost every page.[133] In records of succeeding centuries, apart from some rare chance occurrence, "cabildo" virtually disappears from the vocabulary of both Spaniards and Nahuas in connection with Indian town government. The term universally preferred in the later period is *oficiales de república*, "officers of the commonwealth (polity)." Presumably the terminology originated with the Spaniards, who must have seen in time that an Indian municipality was not the same thing as a Spanish one even if the officeholders bore Spanish titles. Among the Nahuas, "oficiales" sometimes refers directly to the alcaldes or governor, but more frequent are formulations such as "the governor, alcaldes, and all the oficiales de república."[134] Here as often, the term is a catchall for any position below alcalde, serving to emphasize that the real officials, worth naming individually, are the governor and alcaldes. "Oficiales de república" seems to stand for an undifferentiated larger group, much as "the nobles" did in texts of the sixteenth and early seventeenth centuries.

The language of rulership and nobility did continue to be used in connection with town officeholders, but the proportions and connotations were different. In the late period, the governor is referred to less frequently as "tlatoani," "ruler," while the officers as a whole are constantly called "tlatoque," "rulers," often with some modifier meaning "honorable" or the like.[135] But the meaning of the word by this time seems to have become very broad and attenuated, especially in the plural, where it hardly goes beyond a courtesy title that could apply to any group of respectable citizens. The words teteuctin (lords) and pipiltin (nobles), so frequently seen for sixteenth-century office-holders, become rare enough by the eighteenth century to strike one as an oddity or archaism. As far as I can recall, I have never seen "teteuctin" in eighteenth-century documents at all, and have seen "pipiltin" only once.[136]

Of all the terminological innovations of the late period, the most revealing is the use of the pair of Spanish words *actual*, "current, present," and *pasado*, "past," as modifiers for titles of office. The earliest example I have yet found is from 1654.[137] Since the Nahuatl language was making a whole series of new adaptations to Spanish around the mid-seventeenth century, the 1640's may have been the time when the terms were introduced into general use, although I expect further research to unearth at least some isolated examples from the 1620's or 1630's. At any rate, in the late seventeenth and eighteenth centuries, "actual" and "pasado" were a standard part of the vocabulary, and one will not read far in Nahuatl documents of that epoch without encountering them, especially "pasado," which is the more frequent by far. Presumably the terms came in as a result of the Spanish campaign to drive home to the Nahuas, accustomed as they were to lifetime or indefinite tenure in preconquest times, the distinction between holding office and not holding office. Once adopted, however, the words came to play a much more prominent role in the indigenous world than among the Spaniards, who for the most part used them only when distinguishing between an incumbent and a nonincumbent or speaking of their individual service history. In Nahuatl documents, a past officeholder tends to be identified as such every time he appears in the record, and it is often precisely because of that past officeholding that he makes his appearance. Also, at times the current governor and alcaldes will be designated "actuales," even when no "pasados" are mentioned, a usage one would rarely if ever see in reference to Spanish officials.[138]

"Pasado" is not found equally applied to all municipal officials, but primarily to the highest ranking, governors and alcaldes. Occasionally it may accompany the title of *fiscal*, the high-ranking quasi-municipal office in the church hierarchy.[139] Only in special circumstances is it associated with lesser offices. Thus when a certain investigation involved establishing the authenticity of a document, the past notaries of Amaquemecan were summoned and identified as such.[140] In Tepetlixpan (Chalco region) in 1791, a person claiming to descend from the town's former dynastic rulers was identified as "merino pasado" just to give him some scrap of an honorific title.[141] That more attention should have been paid to past officeholding at the upper level than at the lower is not surprising; what stands out is the lack of association of "pasado" with the office of regidor.[142] To understand this, we need to follow changes that had been going on in the municipal offices themselves.

By the mid-seventeenth century, tendencies already seen at work earlier had led in many places to the practical disappearance of regidores, in others to a lower status as auxiliaries, in effect minor officials. A corollary was the expansion of the alcaldes to the point that there was one for each major subunit. The named officials in any major act of a town government in the late period are likely to be the governor, several alcaldes, a regidor mayor, sometimes an alguacil mayor or chief constable, and the notary (compare Tables 2.3–2.5). There may have been lesser regidores in some cases, as a chief regidor implies, merely being too lowly to be named, but I suspect that often the regidor mayor was alone. To date there are few clues to his function, but the treatment accorded him in documentary protocol seems to put him at a rank comparable to that of the alcaldes.

It is entirely possible that much of the change observable in late colonial officeholding is in terminology only. That is, since both alcaldes and regidores

TABLE 2.3

Officials of Tulancingo at Two Points in the Late Period

1687	1720
Don Nicolás de San Juan y Aguiar, governor	Don Juan Maldonado, governor
Don Nicolás Josef, alcalde	Don Antonio de Galicia, regidor mayor
Don Juan de San Francisco, alcalde	Don Pedro de la Cruz, alcalde
Don Josef Gaspar, alcalde	Don Juan Ramos, alcalde
Don Francisco Josef de Galicia, regidor mayor	Don Bartolomé de la Cruz, alcalde
Don Ventura de San Juan, alcalde	Don Antonio Mejía, interim alcalde for Tlaixpan
Don Josef de la Cruz, notary	Antonio Rodríguez, notary

SOURCE: UCLA TC, folders 14 (Oct. 7, 1687), 19 (July 30, 1720).

TABLE 2.4

Some Sets of Town Officials in the Late Period

Tenayuca (Valley of Mexico), 1708	Don Antonio Juárez, alcalde, Sta. Ma. de la Asunción
Don Antonio de San Juan, governor	Don Sebastián Serrano, alcalde, Santiago
Don Bartolomé Felipe, alcalde, Iztaccalla barrio	Francisco Nicolás, regidor mayor
Baltasar Gregorio, alcalde	Don Andrés de Santiago, notary
Diego Felipe, alcalde	Calimaya (Toluca Valley), 1750
Mateo García, regidor mayor	Don Pablo de Estrada, judge-governor
Antonio Juan, alguacil mayor	Don Asenscio de la Cruz, alcalde
Gaspar Lorenzo, notary	Don Agustín de la Cruz, alcalde
Tepemaxalco (Toluca Valley), 1682	Don Francisco Javier, regidor mayor
Don Juan de la Cruz, governor	Julián Asenscio, notary
Don Lorenzo López, alcalde	
Don Nicolás Blas, alcalde, San Lucas	

SOURCES: AGN, Tierras 1805, exp. 3, f. 127; MNAH AH, GO 186, f. 16; AGN, Tierras 2541, exp. 11, f. 3.

TABLE 2.5

Witnesses to the Will of don Josef de la Cruz,
Tlapitzahuayan (Valley of Mexico), 1763

Don Lázaro Josef, alcalde actual	Don Juan Eugenio, alcalde pasado
Nicolás Hernández, fiscal mayor	Don Juan Luis, fiscal pasado
Domingo Antonio, alcalde pasado	Don Juan Francisco, alcalde pasado
Josef Joaquín, alcalde pasado	Andrés Ramírez, regidor mayor
Matías Juárez, alcalde pasado	Don Juan de la Trinidad, alguacil mayor

SOURCE: AGN, Tierras 2554, exp. 4, f. 23v.
NOTE: The "escribano de la república" who wrote the document was Pedro Hilario.

represented specific constituencies from the beginning and functioned primarily as leaders of their own units, it could be that the change merely consisted of renaming the regidores.[143] Likewise, the Tlaxcalan records document in great detail a sixteenth-century situation that I imagine to have been widespread—monopolization of the offices of governor, alcalde, and regidor by a relatively small cadre, with those who had once held office retaining great influence whether they were currently incumbents or not.[144] Once the term "pasado" came into use, the role of past officeholders is much easier to appreciate in the records, but that does not mean that associated practices were necessarily new.

At any rate, regidores were mainly out of the picture by the eighteenth century, and Nahua towns now looked not only to incumbent municipal officials, but to the corps of all living past governors (in towns that had them), alcaldes, and in some places and for some purposes, fiscales of the church for guidance, representation, and legitimation of actions. The same people might return to office again and again after short intervals, and they also held the different positions in succession. Don Pedro de Santiago Maxixcatzin of Coatepec (between Tenancingo and the mines of Sultepec, south of the Nevado de Toluca) was following a common path in serving first as master of the church choir, then alcalde, then fiscal, and finally governor.[145] Reaching the top of the ladder as governor, however, did not necessarily prevent one from repeating later as alcalde or fiscal.

Past officials joined incumbents as those most sought out as witnesses to testaments. For an ordinary will, any two or three might suffice, either present or past; in the will of a prominent person, the names of the whole corps might appear (see Table 2.5 for an example). In litigation it was primarily past officials who were called on to give testimony.[146] Petitions to higher authority often bore the signatures of past as well as present officers, and delegations sent to the corregidor or to higher Spanish officials in Mexico City were likely to include both (see, as an example, Table 2.6). I have yet to see past officials

TABLE 2.6

*Delegation Sent to Represent Tepetlixpan in Tlalmanalco, Capital
of the Corregimiento, 1724*

Don Matías Gerónimo, alcalde actual	Nicolás Salvador, notary
Don Josef de Avila, teniente de alcalde (deputy alcalde)	Don Diego Francisco, alcalde pasado
Juan Antonio, alguacil mayor	Don Salvador Pacheco, alcalde pasado
Antonio Juan, regidor	Don Domingo de la Cruz, alcalde pasado
	Don Nicolás Rodríguez, alcalde pasado

SOURCE: AGN, Tierras 2549, exp. 1, f. 41.
NOTE: Tepetlixpan does not seem to have had a governor at this time, although it had acquired one by the 1780's and 1790's (f. 50). Tepetlixpan is in the Chalco region, Valley of Mexico.

actually act independently to issue judgments, decrees, or grants in the name of the town, but they could nevertheless be drawn into such transactions quite deeply and formally. Thus in Calimaya in 1750, when a citizen applied for a grant of land, the governor called together all the past governors and alcaldes, presented the case to them, and upon their reply that the land should be given to the applicant, proceeded to take the necessary steps.[147] In nearby Santa María de la Asunción (a constituent part of Tepemaxalco) in 1781, the past alcaldes joined current officials in clarifying the status of a piece of land, and one of them actually signed the document with the others.[148]

Note that where Santa María's alcalde had been part of the Tepemaxalco government in 1682 (Table 2.4), the entity now had its own set of officials—alcalde, regidor mayor, fiscal, and notary—issuing documents on their own authority. The earlier arrangement made such a transition easy and natural. All that was required was for the alcalde to stay at home, in addition to which some tlaxilacalli functionaries already helping collect taxes and maintain the local chapel could be renamed regidor mayor, fiscal, and notary. Indeed, it appears that in some cases alcaldes may have acted part of the time with the larger unit, part of the time with the smaller ones independently, so that although formal independence may have been declared at some specific point in time, it would be hard to say when it became an effective reality.

The Evolution of Units and Unit Concepts

Surely the most striking aspect of the entire picture of indigenous central Mexican sociopolitical structure in the eighteenth century is the recognition of an increased number of independent units, most of them formerly constituent parts of larger units. As time passed, the Spanish notion of a cabecera had an impact on indigenous thought, and traces of it began to appear occasionally in Nahuatl texts even in the absence of any impelling factor such as a congregation or a direct translation of a Spanish order. The reference might be either to the cabecera of a corregimiento containing several independent altepetl or to the central cluster of a single altepetl; it might involve the use of either the actual Spanish word or a Nahuatl equivalent.[149] Even in the eighteenth century, the use of the word does not seem necessarily to imply that the speaker has gone over to the Spanish concept of a headtown ruling distinct subject hamlets. In San Francisco Centlalpan (Chalco region) in 1736, a testator declares: "I make my home (am a citizen) in the barrio of San Diego Chalcatepehuacan, and I belong in the altepetl of San Francisco, our cabecera."[150] Here, though a distinction is apparently made between the cabecera and the outlying units, those units are called barrios rather than sujetos, and their inhabitants are thought of as belonging to the cabecera after all, just as in the original indigenous concept of the all-embracing altepetl. Traces of Spanish "sujeto" are also to be found in texts of the eighteenth century, most often embodied in indigenous vocabulary implying something pulled along in the wake of something larger, so that here too indigenous and Spanish concepts may have continued to be somewhat at variance.[151]

Ever since the mid-sixteenth century, constituent parts had been successfully pulling free of larger units to be awarded the status of independent cabeceras (in their own terms, the status of full-scale altepetl not part of any larger rotation scheme). In the early period, however, the entities affected were above all what the Spaniards called *estancias*, located at a considerable distance from the main settlement cluster and in many cases not even contiguous with the rest of the altepetl territory.* Such units had arisen sometimes through conquest, sometimes through out-migration from the main group; in either case, they were likely to have attained a complex organization of their own and have developed an especially strong sense of independence, so that they were ripe for separation on all counts. A second source of pressure for independence, exerted from an early time, came from full-fledged altepetl that had been members of empire-confederations, as with Huexotla and others surrounding Tetzcoco; in such instances, de facto sepa-

---

*See Gibson 1964, pp. 53–57. I find that Gibson's terminology (followed by Gerhard) of *estancia* for a distant, separate constituent part and *barrio* for a constituent belonging to the main contiguous cluster makes an important distinction often borne out in Spanish sources, and I favor retention of this vocabulary for some purposes. It is well to be aware, however, that the Spaniards were by no means consistent in their usage; "estancia" in this sense is fairly rare, probably out of a fear of confusion with the much more common meaning "privately owned tract of land for agrarian purposes." And I have never seen "estancia" meaning a sociopolitical unit in a mundane Nahuatl document, nor does it correspond to any special term in indigenous vocabulary. I have seen it just once in Nahuatl historical writing, in the anonymous annals of Tenochtitlan during the 1560's (MNAH AH, GO 14), in an entry for 1566, where people are said to have come in for a special occasion "yn ipan Estancia yn ima altepetl," "from the estancias, the dependencies of the altepetl." As one can see, the author felt the need to explain the meaning.

ration already existed, and only a word of formal pronouncement was required.

Relatively new in the late period (though, as we have seen, the germ of it existed from an early time) was independence attained by one of the ordinary calpolli-tlaxilacalli in the core section of a simple altepetl, as in the example given just above of Santa María de la Asunción and Tepemaxalco, but by the eighteenth century it was just this type of movement that was snowballing. As mentioned earlier, it is clear that internal pressures for such a development are present in cellular structure, schemes of rotation and ranking, and ethnic differences between tlaxilacalli. The end of the Triple Alliance and of endemic warfare eliminated two of the main counterpressures in the direction of maintaining larger units. We may ask, then, why it was that minimal-unit independence did not come earlier than it did.

On the Spanish side, in the sixteenth century it was very much in the interest of Spanish individuals and officialdom to maintain large units and preserve the integrity of existing indigenous authorities. Large units meant large and lucrative encomiendas, and everything was channeled through the primary tlatoani. As cabildos succeeded tlatoque and the repartimiento succeeded the encomienda in the recruitment of temporary labor, the large altepetl remained an indispensable channeling device. The monumental church-building campaigns on which both Spanish friars and their Indian parishioners put such emphasis also required the full resources of the larger unit. But by the early decades of the seventeenth century, with the great churches built, the repartimiento in decay, Spanish enterprises honeycombing the countryside and negotiating with Indian neighbors for their services as individuals or in small groups, and more Hispanic people available and willing to man additional parishes or serve as deputies to the corregidor, the larger altepetl form no longer had a marked advantage over small units from the Spanish point of view, and there was less reason to oppose indigenous pressure for fragmentation.

On the Nahua side, the large altepetl lost only a part of its utility after the conquest. Large entities could still do better than small ones in sharing burdens and representing the community's interests before Spanish authorities. Although the Spaniards made drastic changes in the general economy by a few years after they had entered the country, the subregional markets organized by altepetl remained very meaningful to the Nahuas. Interdependencies of all kinds that had grown up over the centuries, including intermarriage patterns, did not immediately disappear. The linchpin of the altepetl, the tlatoani, to whom each subunit had a direct and equal relationship, remained in place for a time, and both the structural relationship and the sense of allegiance were successfully transferred to governors and cabildos, who enjoyed their heyday in the later sixteenth century. In this time when many Nahuas had not yet been exposed to the full force of Spanish cultural influence, individuals and small units still often had great need of the well-organized cabildo of the large altepetl as an intermediary in dealing with Spanish officials or employers. Later, with growing experience and acculturation, they would be more able to operate on their own. As already implied, it was not only the Spaniards who wanted to see a splendid monastery church built in each altepetl. Just as all the tlaxilacalli had the same relationship to the tlatoani and viewed him as their own, so too they had, in preconquest times, a common ethnic god and central temple that represented the sovereignty and power of the altepetl; not only the biased reports of approving friars but the internal logic of the situation lead to the interpretation that the people of the entire altepetl must have sympathized with the construction of a general altepetl church in the sixteenth century, and the task itself must have been a unifying factor. Once that task was finished, the construction of churches in each tlaxilacalli could proceed, helping refocus both energy and loyalties toward the smaller unit. Although there can be no doubt that in the late period many a community specifically built a church to reinforce its claims to independence,[152] the timing of separatist movements may have borne a significant relation to the natural sequence and timing of secondary church construction. By the time the labor repartimiento ended, tlaxilacalli citizens were in more direct economic contact with Spaniards; no longer being sheltered by or receiving guidance in unfamiliar places from the altepetl government, they might now begin to see it primarily in terms of the exactions it made. By mid-seventeenth century, the conditions for separatism were in a sense already fully given on both Spanish and Nahua sides; at the same time, all the trends were cumulative, so that the pressures to separate mounted with each decade to 1800 and beyond.

As the situation gradually changed, Spanish concepts and vocabulary relative to indigenous organization evolved correspondingly, and this in turn further eased the way to fragmentation and had its impact on Indian notions. As mentioned at the beginning of the chapter, even while emphasizing the cabecera and the sujeto, the Spaniards had also used the term pueblo from an early time, primarily for larger settlements, so that very often Spanish "pueblo" coincided with "altepetl," each referring to the same organization and group of people even though quite differently imagined. Yet the coincidence was never perfect; Spaniards were prepared to refer to any discernible cluster and its surroundings as a pueblo, not caring or not knowing that it was part of a larger altepetl. As early as the late sixteenth century, one can find Spaniards on inspection tours of the countryside calling cabeceras simply pueblos and using either pueblo or barrio for subunits.[153]

As time went on, "pueblo" came to dominate ordinary Spanish usage (including that of officials), diminishing the terminological distinction between "cabecera" and "sujeto," which words were now used for the most part only when the relation of altepetl parts was being called into question. In the second half of the colonial period, legislation such as that establishing a 600-*vara* land area within which an Indian town's possession could not be challenged speaks simply in terms of pueblos.[154] Any entity that could get itself recognized as a pueblo would be in line for confirmation of the 600 varas. And indeed, whereas in sixteenth-century separation campaigns a successful "sujeto" was freed of its "cabecera" and became a "cabecera" itself (i.e., in indigenous terms two independent sets of calpolli-tlaxilacalli came into existence, constituting two full-scale altepetl), the Spanish government now began to give new recognition to Indian entities simply as pueblos, independent of any others it is true, but with no implication that the pueblo contained any large or complex set of constituent parts. Similarly, the independent "formal y rigoroso pueblo" of the late seventeenth and eighteenth centuries might lack a governor, its highest official being the single alcalde it had already had as a barrio or tlaxilacalli.[155] Although it is hard to demonstrate philologically in specific cases, one cannot avoid the impression that by the eighteenth century, the entity denoted by pueblo was likely to be a small one, the same connotation the word was to bring with it into the twentieth century.

The Nahuas seem to have had a quite full grasp of the evolving Spanish term pueblo and its implications. Getting legal confirmation of the right to 600 varas was one motivation for many of the eighteenth-century movements in which barrios sought recognition as pueblos.[156] Barrios also tended to use Spanish perceptions of many small separate units among Indians to give the appearance of full independence even where it did not quite exist. In 1720, petitioners from Tequixquinahuac in the Tetzcoco region appeared in court in the corregimiento capital, led by their alcalde, complaining that the fiscal of the (apparently neighboring) town of Tezontla had been taking Tequixquinahuac land and giving it to people from his own pueblo. Only with further investigation does it turn out that Tequixquinahuac was still a barrio (in accompanying Nahuatl documents, tlaxilacalli) of Tezontla, a full pueblo (in Nahuatl called altepetl).[157]

Yet though seeming to understand and embrace the concept "pueblo," the Nahuas very rarely used the word in documents in their own language.[158] "Altepetl" continues to occur as long as Nahuatl documents are found. Not only small entities are so denominated (such as Tocuillan near Tetzcoco in 1722),[159] but even entities remaining within larger ones. In 1786, Sacaquauhtla, with only alcaldes and admitting to being the *tlatilanalli* (sujeto) of

Acaxochitlan, which itself was originally only one of the subdivisions of the northern half of Tulancingo, nevertheless appears as "the precious honored altepetl of our precious honored mother Santa María de la Natividad."[160] Examples such as this have a double implication. On the one hand, they indicate that the Nahuas brought the key term of indigenous sociopolitical organization along with them to the level of the often smaller and, to all appearances, less complex new independent unit, viewing it in the same light as they had its larger predecessor. On the other hand, it seems possible that the meaning of "altepetl" may actually have been somewhat influenced by Spanish "pueblo," even though the indigenous term and doubtless many of its connotations were retained.

Where subunits stayed together under one set of officials and shared or rotated duties as before (and a great many altepetl did so, with or without mutilations), "tlaxilacalli" remained current to the end of the colonial period,[161] but "barrio" appears as a loanword in Nahuatl with increasing frequency through the eighteenth century. Both words may be used in the same document, even in reference to the same entity, so that it is hard to detect any conceptual change involved in the introduction of the Spanish term.[162] As far as one can tell from usage in texts, the meaning of the two was identical. The sense also appears unchanged from earlier times, although in some complex altepetl the tlayacatl or sub-altepetl, originally sovereign entities with separate tlatoque, had apparently been reduced to the level of tlaxilacalli.[163] By 1746, Chimalpahin's five "tlayacatl altepetl" of Amaquemecan are being called tlaxilacalli and barrios; the only indication of a greater complexity is the occasional use of a double name, as Itztlacoçauhcan Acolhuacan, where Itztlacoçauhcan is the senior of the old tlayacatl, and Acolhuacan must have been one of the Itztlacoçauhcan tlaxilacalli, although its status as of 1746 is a subject for speculation.[164]

Eighteenth-century developments in Indian town structure should not be quickly labeled "decline." The evolution resulted in large part from vigorous, protracted campaigns by smaller units to attain their independence from larger entities that under changed conditions no longer seemed to serve their interests. And while the ever-growing Hispanic community of central Mexico, as a fact of life, was doubtless the ultimate reason for the change, the Indians had by no means simply gone over to Spanish organizational modes. Although affected by Spanish concepts to some extent, they had above all reshaped notions like cabecera and pueblo in their own minds and manipulated them as a means to attain their own ends. Their goals were indigenous rather than Spanish in inspiration, an embodiment of small-unit ambitions that had existed since remote times. What had happened was not so much "fragmentation" or "homogenization" as a decentralization that was one of the possibilities inherent in indigenous sociopolitical organization from the beginning. Nor is decentralization, in the sense of the reduction to small simple pueblos, each the same as the next, a full description of the result of the process in the late period. Many altepetl-tlaxilacalli complexes remained relatively intact by the time of Mexican independence, and even such idiosyncratic arrangements as double governments in a single territory were still extant in places.[165] Even where a formerly unified altepetl was now divided into several pueblos, in many cases there was still a distinction between the direct descendant of the altepetl government, located in the largest settlement cluster, headed by a governor, and containing a full complement of higher and lower officials, and the set of officials in former tlaxilacalli, not reaching above alcalde and very restricted in staff. A distinction also obtained in that the former tlaxilacalli were generally less populous and headed by figures of lower social rank. Ironically, despite the formal decentralization, the late-period seat of large altepetl government may have become more of a "cabecera" in a social and economic sense than ever before. Although by independence Spanish estates with their own dependent communities and Spanish clusters in the cabeceras had changed the configuration of the countryside considerably, the main outlines of the original large altepetl structures could still be discerned.*

---

*Despite the changes it introduced, Spanish society in the Indian countryside, having at first been dependent on the various altepetl, to a very large extent replicated the original structure and settlement pattern, thus perpetuating it.

3

Household

THE ORGANIZATION OF familial life and kinship ties is no less a central aspect of Nahua society than of any other. Yet looking at the many Nahuatl sources touching on family matters (above all the numerous wills), no single term for a general organizing concept, comparable to "altepetl" in the larger sociopolitical sphere, seems to emerge. The promising-looking *tlacamecayotl*, consisting of the roots "human being" and "rope," plus a nominal suffix that sometimes denotes a collective entity, apparently means simply the totality of kinship ties as seen from the vantage point of some particular individual, not any actual, functioning, independently existing unit.[1] In any case, the word is extremely rare in texts. Nor do naming patterns, either preconquest or postconquest, emphasize lineages as surnames in the Mayan region do.[2]

Terminology and Constitution of the Household Complex

Not only do any lineages tend to remain unnamed and undiscussed in Nahuatl sources;* no word appears that would have approximately the same scope as English "family." Looking in Molina's dictionary under *familia*, one finds the following collection of terms: *cenyeliztli*, "being together"; *cencalli*, "one house"; *cencaltin*, "those in one house"; *cemithualtin*, "those in one patio"; and *techan tlaca*, "people in someone's home." "Cenyeliztli" receives the alternate gloss "people who live together in a house." All the words, then, emphasize the setting in which a joint life takes place, not the origin of the relationships between those living together; as a set, the terms converge on something akin to the English notion of "household," which can therefore serve to lend a title to the present chapter.

Some of Molina's words are not unheard of in actual texts, but none is very common.[3] More frequently seen is the metaphorical doublet *in quia-huatl, in ithualli*, literally "the exit, the patio," which is like "altepetl" in

---

*The *teccalli* or "lordly house," a specific and important manifestation of the lineage, will be discussed in Chapter 4.

seeming to describe the physical aspect but actually referring to the connection between an organized group of people and a physical surrounding; the effect is very close indeed to "household."[4] In preconquest times, the household was probably the repository of certain holy objects associated with the ancestors, lands, and possessions of those who lived there. In the postconquest centuries, "quiahuatl ithualli" is often seen accompanied by reference to God, either as his possession or as something one is maintaining on his behalf. Images of saints may be mentioned in the same breath.[5] An alternative phrase for the dwelling with implications of household is "where we await the order of (obey) our lord God."[6]

An important related term is -*chan*, "home."[7] It may be that in some times and places "-chan" was the most inclusive word of all, combining and hence unifying notions close to both "household" and "family."[8] Ordinarily, however, "-chan" is limited to indicating a person's place of residence or affiliation; the word appears to have been primarily locative by origin.[9] One's home is said to be in a certain tlaxilacalli or altepetl, or one is said to be the "possessor of a home" (*chane*) there, that is, a resident or citizen.[10] Both formulations often have the connotation that the person was born in the district, and sometimes one's "-chan" is the birthplace even though one now makes one's home elsewhere.[11] Often "-chan" means the entire home altepetl rather than the specific residence.[12]

In the available sources, which are above all wills and land documents, the overwhelmingly most frequent word associated with household affairs is *calli*, "house" (primarily in the sense of the actual physical structure). Nahuatl ordinarily makes no distinction between singular and plural with inanimate nouns, so it is very hard to tell whether "calli" is being used as a collective name for the whole household complex or not, but following the details of the word's use in texts allows one to discover a great deal about household structure. Reading in Nahuatl testaments, one soon forms the impression that an extraordinarily large number of people owned more than one house; such houses are usually described only as facing in a certain direction: east ("where the sun emerges"), west ("where the sun enters"), or, for north and south, usually ad hoc expressions, "toward such and such an altepetl" lying in the proper direction. Finally it dawns on the reader that these houses are not scattered haphazardly across the landscape but are arranged around a central patio that the writers of the documents took so much for granted as to leave it unmentioned most of the time. Rather than saying a building is on the west of the patio, the Nahuas said it faces east, that is, had its door on that side, for doors always opened onto the patio, not the outside. A "calli," then, is by no means necessarily the entire abode, but may be a component part (see Fig. 3.1). Spanish translations of the time often render the word as *aposento*, which depending on context can mean "lodging," "room," or "one-room

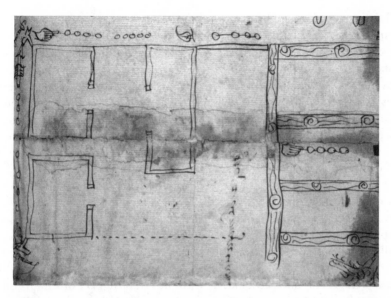

Fig. 3.1 House complex of Diego Juárez and Juliana de San Miguel, Huehuecalco district, Mexico City, 1585. One of the buildings on the east has a second story, as does the one on the west. To the west are three *chinampas* (strips of agricultural land artificially raised out of the water) belonging to the property. The measurements given are 7 brazas (*matl*) and a *mitl* ("arrow," ⅗[?] of a matl) across the front of the property, 9 brazas and a *yollotli* ("heart," ½ of a matl) along the side, with the chinampas 4 brazas, (presumably in length). Source: AGN, Tierras 1810, exp. 1, f. 4.

structure."[13] It is perhaps best to think of a calli as simply a building, the only definite expectations being, in this context, that it is primarily destined for human residence and has an independent doorway onto a patio.

Within the possibly two, three, or more calli in a single compound, the parents, grown children, and other relatives and in-laws might each maintain a partly separate establishment. At any given time, the whole complex might either be owned by one person or held separately by various relatives to whom a previous owner had left it. The Nahua household, then, with its independent calli arranged around a center, separately occupied by individual members who at the same time belonged to the whole, is another example of the principle of cellular organization and as such is comparable to the altepetl. As an ephemeral structure undergoing constant losses and increments, the household of necessity lacked formal organizational elements present in the altepetl, such as a fixed, symmetrical number of constituent parts. That the subhouseholds might have divided stores and duties among themselves, participating in some rotation scheme, with the head of the household playing a role analogous to that of the tlatoani in the altepetl, is imaginable but not documented, and the situation would have precluded a truly rigorous carrying out of such arrangements. Nor can any consistent allocation of the parts in relation to the cardinal points be discerned. It is true that most documents speak as though all buildings face in a cardinal direction, but that is most likely a convenient shorthand.[14] Where there are one or two buildings, they are perhaps most often on the west and east; where there are three, also on the north; buildings on the south are the least common, though by no means unusual. The pattern seems primarily to reflect a desire to have some sun striking the front of the building; a structure on the south would open north, and its doorway would never be in the direct sun.

I do not mean to imply that every Nahua household was multiple, either as to buildings or as to familial units. Nuclear families with a single building may have been the most common type.[15] Wills cannot answer the question of proportions. On the one hand, the presence of an undefined, unmodified "calli" does *not* necessarily mean a single building; the testator merely may have chosen not to go into detail on the complex.[16] Even when there was but one structure with one occupant, as with the establishment of Ana Justina in Mexico City in 1593 (see Fig. 3.2), the house would face on to a patio and

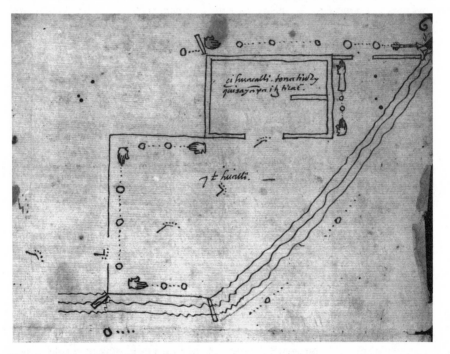

Fig. 3.2. House of Ana Justina, San Hipólito Teocaltitlan district, Mexico City, 1593. Source: AGN, Hospital de Jesús, 298: 4, f. 6.

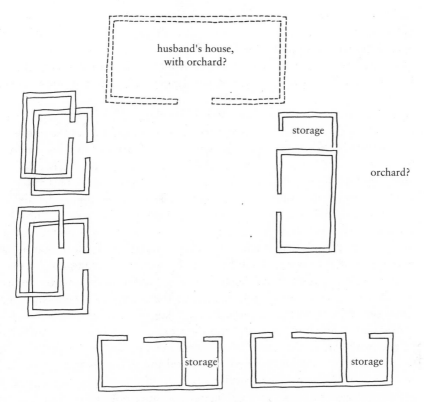

Fig. 3.3 House complex of doña Catalina de Sena, Coyoacan, 1588. Overlapping rectangles here and in the following figures indicate upper stories. Source: Arthur J. O. Anderson, Frances Berdan, and James Lockhart, *Beyond the Codices* (1976), doc. 2, p. 56.

stand, at least in principle, inside an enclosure with its own egress. More structures could readily be built against the enclosure wall or fence when needed, just as in larger compounds older buildings were frequently demolished.[17] As with altepetl of varying complexity, single and multistructure households came within one overall system of organization and obeyed the same dynamics.

The selective dismantling of individual buildings again emphasizes their separateness. With the exception of some two-story structures, calli are always illustrated in maps accompanying land documents as having separate doorways, only one apiece. It seems to have been the general practice to allow space between each calli, since relatively few are specifically said to be directly attached to another, "just sticking to it."[18] In some cases, more than one of the calli have a storage building or room (*tlecopatl*) connected with them, heightening the impression of separateness (Fig. 3.3). The general notion of

an inward-turned household with special spaces for different members was
not unique to the Nahuas, of course, but shared with, among others, the
Spaniards, who commonly used the plural "houses" in speaking of a large
dwelling.[19] But the Spanish entity was more integrated, with contiguous wings
forming solid blocks around the patio and more intercommunication between
rooms.

Occasionally, the mainly static house descriptions provide enough historical depth to allow some glimpse of processes. The evolution of the household
of Juan de San Pedro, who made his will in Culhuacan in 1581, has an archetypal quality (see Fig. 3.4). In Juan's childhood, the complex consisted of only
one building, on the north of the patio, which was the abode of his father, his
mother, himself, his younger sister, Bárbara Tiacapan, and possibly his aunt
Ana Xoco, who seems to have been his father's younger sister. When Juan
came of age but was not yet married, he built himself a house on the east side
of the patio (doubtless with the help of his father, though about that he says
nothing).[20] He then married and began to have children, continuing to live in
the house he had built. Later, he and his wife built a third house on the west
side of the patio for his sister, Bárbara, who then married.[21] There was apparently some lack of agreement on just who the third building belonged to. Juan
considered it his, but Bárbara, who died before Juan and who must have
helped with the construction (along with her husband-to-be perhaps), ordered that it should be knocked down and the materials given to various
relatives, and Juan on making his own will decided to respect her wishes.

At the death of Juan's parents, he did not move into the original building
but stayed in the second house. His aunt Ana apparently continued to live in
the first house the whole time. By the time he made his will, Juan's wife had
died, and his three young children were living elsewhere, probably under the
care of maternal relatives. He left the house of his own residence to the chil-

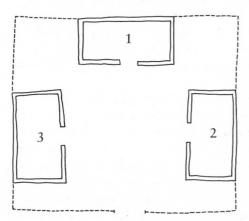

Fig. 3.4. House complex of Juan de
San Pedro, Culhuacan, 1581. 1 is
the original house, 2 the house Juan
built for himself, and 3 the house he
built for his younger sister. The enclosure borders and places of egress are
entirely speculative. Source: S. L.
Cline and Miguel León-Portilla, eds.,
The Testaments of Culhuacan (1984),
doc. 48, pp. 170–75.

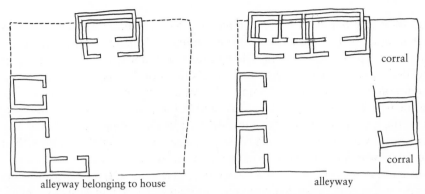

Fig. 3.5. Evolution of a house complex in San Martín Caltzallan district, Tlatelolco, 1620–69. Source: AGN, Tierras 442, exp. 5, ff. 9v, 10.

dren and the original house to Ana, apparently (though he does not say so) expecting her to look after the place until the children came of age and probably also to leave them the first house at the end of her life. Thus in one generation a single-structure complex expanded to three structures, then was reduced again to two, with the future uncertain. If the children survived, the process may well have repeated itself.

The quick dissolution of larger compounds was not an inevitable result, however. Because a property in seventeenth-century Tlatelolco changed hands more than once, we have an example of slow, steady accretion (see Fig. 3.5). In 1620, one Constantino Esteban sold his house in the San Martín Caltzallan district (tlaxilacalli) of Tlatelolco to Miguel Hernández and his wife Magdalena Angelina, from the neighboring Santa María la Redonda Tezcatzonco in Mexico City, at a price of 70 pesos. Inside the enclosure were a two-story building on the north side and two separate one-story buildings on the west, the southernmost of which had a small attached structure. Forty-nine years later, Magdalena Angelina, now a widow, sold the same property to don Juan Gallego and his wife Agustina Catarina, of another tlaxilacalli of Tlatelolco, for double the price, 140 pesos. The smallest structure was gone, but the two-story building had doubled in size, a new one-story building had been added on the east side, and two subenclosures, corrals or pens, now bordered the main patio. Magdalena Angelina's family had probably expanded and prospered, then her heirs had moved away or died prematurely, one of the most common reasons for selling houses.[22]

All in all, the impression arising from descriptions of Nahua house complexes is that of a series of similar separate structures for each of the adult residents or nuclear families, as opposed to structures specialized by function and serving all the residents in common. Nevertheless, some specialized ter-

minology for buildings in the complex existed. The most frequently seen is
cihuacalli, "woman-house," a word not found in Molina or other dictionaries. Some Spanish translations (though posterior, not strictly contemporary)
render it as "kitchen," and a modern scholar is of the opinion that it was a
common room where all manner of tasks were performed, mainly by
women.[23] Nahuatl texts so far discovered fail to provide a basis for unravel-
ling the question completely, but they do add some suggestive details. The
cihuacalli was likely to be owned by a woman, or if owned by a man then
left to a woman upon his death. In one case, the term is used for the single
structure of a property owned by a woman (see Fig. 3.2).[24] Such cases lead
one to wonder if the term did not have more to do with tenure arrangements
than with the function of the building. Yet I have never seen a case in which
a single complex had more than one cihuacalli, pointing again in the direction
of a unique common function. Also, for the linguistically comparable *oquichpan,* literally "where the men are," we have Molina's definition "large hall,"
presumably where the men sat about and socialized while women did the
chores, although in one case the building was said to be a place where everyone could go to gather around a fire for warmth. "Oquichpan" occurs only
once in known mundane documentation, and such a structure cannot be considered a standard feature except perhaps in palaces.[25] The use of the word
cihuacalli is limited, in presently known sources, to the sixteenth century, the
latest date being 1593 (Fig. 3.2). An eighteenth-century Nahuatl text has the
loanword *cocina,* "kitchen," for a building in a complex, but nothing assures
us that this is the same thing as the cihuacalli of earlier times.[26]

We will later see that when possible Nahua households contained one or
more images of saints. Though most sources do not say so, from the ones we
have we know that these images were often housed in a special structure. If
imagined simply as an oratory, this building seems unremarkable enough,
perhaps even something taken over from the Spaniards. And indeed, praying
must have gone on there. The name of the structure in an eighteenth-century
text from the Tulancingo region, however, puts things in a different light;
among the elements of the house complex of Domingo de la Cruz of Sacaquauhtla is a *santocalli,* a "saint-house."[27] In other words, just as each grown
family member or couple tended to have a separate place to be, where possible, so did the saints. The central purpose of the structure was not to carry
out observances there but to provide the saint or saints with a residence.

Consider the establishment of Baltasar Bautista, an independent baker in
seventeenth-century Mexico City (probably selling his wares in the city's marketplaces), as shown in Figure 3.6. Baltasar left the building where baking
was done, together with all the equipment, to his wife, and one of the three
residential buildings to each of his three children (two boys and a girl). The

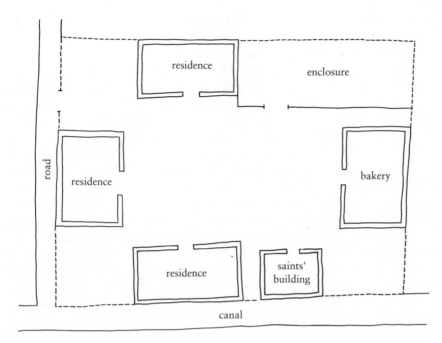

Fig. 3.6. House complex of Baltasar Bautista, San Pablo Toçanitlan district, Mexico City, 1639. Source: AGN, Bienes Nacionales 339, item 9.

small building ("caltepitzin") containing two images of the Virgin was not left specifically to anyone; the images were to remain always in their house, and Baltasar's wife was to sweep up for them.[28]

Although single-story houses were the norm, two stories were by no means unusual, as in the buildings of Figures 3.1, 3.3, and 3.5. While it may be that two-story structures were more characteristic of the residences of the noble and wealthy, as in the case of doña Catalina de Sena's establishment in Coyoacan (Fig. 3.3), they also occur in relatively small complexes owned by apparent plebeians with few lands. The word for a building of two stories, seen as a unit, was *calnepanolli*. Such a structure was sometimes said to consist of two *pantli* or "rows." The impression this may give of a large-scale unitary "house" is, however, largely illusory. The top and bottom parts were still treated separately; in Culhuacan in 1579, a testator ordered the materials of the upper part of his house to be sold and the lower part to be kept provisionally as it was.[29] Internal stairs are never drawn or mentioned; access to upper rooms must have been by ladder or by the external stairway that one occasionally finds pictured.[30] A term better reflecting the true situation was the more common *tlapancalli*, "roof house." In other words, what was built on the roof was nearly as much an independent calli as any of the other units, separately entered, separately occupied, and likely to be built later and torn down earlier than the unit over which it stood.[31]

Only rarely do wills contain any special mention of the general enclosure around a house complex, though frequent mention of an exit implies that one existed. Impermanent reed fences, reinforced by trees, bushes, and magueys, may have been the most common solution, though true walls did exist in some cases.[32] More frequently spoken of are enclosures inside the compound, *tepancalli*, literally "wall-houses"; the word is usually translated into Spanish as *corral*, "animal pen," and sometimes the loanword corral is used in the Nahuatl text itself (see Figs. 3.4 and 3.5).[33] The term tepancalli may in many cases be taken as what its constituent roots imply, a house with substantial walls and lacking only a roof that the owner may have been planning to add.[34]

In the Hispanic tradition, the household often included a garden or orchard but was not closely associated with agricultural land as such; typically, one's house was in a town or village, one's lands at some distance. Though much the same could happen in indigenous central Mexico, one's house was located, in principle, on the main piece of land from which one drew one's sustenance. This *callalli*, "house-land," might be supplemented by one or several additional plots scattered at a distance, but it retained preeminence and was the most likely to stay in the family over generations (for further discussion, see Chap. 5). As with the altepetl in a different way, the basic pattern implied a society fully sedentary but more dispersed on the land than in the Hispanic system. Even in the greatest urban concentration, Tenochtitlan itself, a house complex normally had at its side a set of *chinampas* (cultivated strips standing in water) which, though perhaps not enough to sustain the residents, represented the residue of the callalli rather than a "garden" (see Fig. 3.1).[35]

A Spanish house occupied a *solar* or lot. Although reality did not always conform, the implication of the term, and particularly in the Indies, was that the house lot was a surveyed rectangle or square of moderate size located among a series of identical lots constituting an urban cluster, each lot facing on one of the streets in a grid. The early stages of the mid-sixteenth-century reorganization of altepetl as municipalities apparently often involved some gesture toward creating a Spanish-style street-and-lot complex, particularly in the vicinity of the church and central square.[36] By 1550, the word solar had entered the Nahuatl language, where it quickly took root and has remained to this day.[37] It did not, however, necessarily mean the same thing in Nahuatl as in Spanish. Since the Nahuas pronounced the final *r* of "solar" as *l*, they often appear to have imagined that the word was a compound containing the Nahuatl root for "land."[38] In effect, they interpreted "solar" as being the same thing as "callalli," including not only the house lot in the narrower sense, but a good chunk of productive agricultural land as well.[39] Spanish influence was manifest, however, in the orchard or *huerta* (characteristically with both introduced and indigenous fruit trees) that was sometimes part of a house complex, mainly among the well-to-do.[40]

Appurtenances of the household play little role in Nahuatl documents; either they were of too little economic value to warrant mention or they were handed from one person to another following procedures so well understood that there was no need to commit anything to paper. Separate bequests of house parts—doors, lintels, wooden columns, cornerstones, and the like— imply that these were often the only items that were carefully worked or of valuable materials, the rest being subject to frequent renewal.[41] The loanword *puerta*, "door," appears by the late sixteenth century, designating a house-part of value, presumably a swinging, latchable door of wood in European fashion.[42] Windows are hardly mentioned at all; I am unsure whether this is because windows were slow to be introduced or because they were valueless.

The *cuezcomatl*, or indigenous grainbin for unshelled maize, appears quite infrequently, just enough to remind us that it probably continued to be found in most Nahua households across the postconquest centuries.[43] Even more rarely is any trace detected of the *temazcalli* (Spanish *temascal*), or sweathouse. In fact, I have as yet seen only two references to one in mundane Nahuatl documentation, from sixteenth-century Culhuacan and Mexico City.[44] An elaborate Nahua holding in Soyatzingo (Chalco region) came into litigation in 1734, and the complete inventory carried out (in Spanish; Table 3.1) also shows a temascal as part of the main building complex, as with the similar complex briefly described in the Spanish will of a nobleman of Cuauhtinchan in 1707.[45] Since the temascal has survived to this day in parts of central

TABLE 3.1

House Complex of doña Felipa de Jesús, Soyatzingo (Chalco Region), 1734

Item	Value (pesos)
House with its walls and timbers	100
Kitchen	10
Wooden granary	30
Building (aposento) next to the granary	25
Another building with oven and entryway for horses (zaguán)	35
Stable and enclosure	20
Temascal (sweathouse)	7
All items	227

SOURCE: AGN, Tierras 2555, exp. 14, f. 18.

Mexico, it must have been present during the colonial period as well. There is no reason to think that every home establishment ever had one. Those that existed may have been thought of as a common facility rather than something to be left to a single family member; the one in Culhuacan was shared by two sisters (though one claimed to own the stone).[46]

As to the actual contents of the house, these are often dismissed as "everything that is inside the house(s)," and testators generally included them with the buildings or ordered them to be sold. A term frequently appearing in this context is *cihuatlatquitl*, literally "woman-property (movable)," or "woman's things." Sometimes weaving equipment is mentioned together with the cihuatlatquitl, giving some notion of the flavor of the word, but it is often used very broadly, in the same breath as the phrase referring to everything in the house, as if to say in effect that all the general movable equipment is women's things. The possessor is usually a woman, but in one case a man speaks of "all our things that we used in our house, our cihuatlatquitl."[47] In one text, we find the rare complementary term *oquichtlatquitl*, "man's things," specified as "the boat, the chest, the jars, and the boards of my sleeping platform."[48]

One household item sometimes escaping the general anonymity was the chest or *caja* (a Spanish loanword), not the indigenous *petlacalli* made of reeds, but a wooden chest of European style with metal hinges and latch. By the late sixteenth century, many Nahua houses contained one or more such chests. Though these were a purchased item, not homemade, even people in the most modest circumstances apparently coveted them enough to shoulder the expense.[49] In the 1580's in Tulancingo, one Cristóbal, who lacked either a surname or gainful employment and was reduced to stealing turkeys from his neighbors, nevertheless had a Spanish-style chest in his house.[50] Another item frequently mentioned is the *metlatl* (Spanish *metate*), the indigenous grinding stone for maize, which usually went to female family members. Indigenous jars, *tecomatl* (Spanish *tecomate*) also make their appearance.[51] Rarely does one see a listing as specific as that of María Pascuala's dinnerware (Tezontla near Tetzcoco, 1713): "a dozen and a half plates in Puebla style; two little bowls; two large calabash vases."[52]

Most of the best descriptions of Nahua residential complexes are from the late sixteenth and early seventeenth centuries, an unremarkable fact considering that this was the golden age of writing in Nahuatl in general and that up till then written testaments (our main source of information) were mainly restricted to high nobles. Unfortunately for us, Nahuatl writings about the preconquest period are vague on such matters as the layout of households.[53] Nevertheless, the principles of organization are so congruent with those to be seen in the Nahua world generally, and the basic terminology is so well developed and undeniably indigenous, that one can safely deduce the existence of essentially the entire concatenation in late pre-Hispanic times. Here, as so often, the highly specific and authentic everyday documentation produced in the century after the conquest is the best source for unknown facets of life in the century before the conquest.

What of the later centuries, the remainder of the colonial period? The special terminology just reviewed tends to fade with time. Of all the special terms, only "callalli" ("house-land"), "cuezcomatl" ("grainbin"), the metaphor "quiahuatl ithualli" ("exit and patio") for the household, and the phrases related to the saints remain common enough to be considered part of the standard vocabulary. On the other hand, Spanish "solar" ("lot"), "corral" ("animal pen"), and "cocina" ("kitchen") gain currency. My own impression, however, is one of relatively slow and minor change. Perhaps the greatest observable trend is simply that the documents became increasingly less specific about houses as time passed. The same tendency to give less detail about normal procedures and transactions once they had become fully routine within postconquest practice can be observed in the Spaniards' record-keeping as well. The essence, the existence of separate structures likely to be separately inherited by members of the succeeding generations, remains if not literally unchanged then at least still visible in the later period.

The Spanish-language will of doña María de los Santos, notarized in 1721 in Tlatelolco, demonstrates the survival of elements of the system that late, even in the country's Spanish metropolis. Buildings were still spoken of as facing in a certain direction rather than as standing on a certain side of the complex. An "oratory" contained two saint's images (paintings). A son inherited the oratory, as well as keeping the structure that he built for himself on the patio, while one daughter received the "small house or room" perpendicular to the oratory, and a second daughter the room where her mother slept.[54]

With a general lack of information about structural details, it is hard to know when and to what extent Spanish influence affected Nahua house building. Construction techniques, building shape, and style of ornamentation could have undergone considerable change (and doubtless did, in view of the availability and use of metal hammers, nails, and saws) without a change in the basic layout. Eventually, by our days that is, Nahua building patterns were to merge with the Spanish scheme of a more integrated "house," with intercommunicating rooms or built in a solid block around a patio, but there is no way to be sure just when this happened. An unusual document shows us an eighteenth-century case in which the process had apparently begun, but there are ambiguities even here. In 1734, the will of the wealthy doña Felipa de Jesús, a resident of Soyatzingo in the Chalco jurisdiction, was contested, as a result of which Spanish officials carried out a thorough investigation and inventory, including a list and evaluation of the buildings (Table 3.1). The list shows some of the expected one-room residences around a patio and some specifically indigenous appurtenances (grainbin, sweathouse), but also a stable and a European-style built-over driveway (*zaguán*). Above all, there is what the list maker considered the "house" pure and simple, far outshadowing the other buildings in value. This house, with adobe walls and roofed with beams and shingles, was said to consist of parlor, bedroom, and another room, which would constitute a reasonable endowment for a rural Spanish home,* and the location of a kitchen in a separate building would also have been normal. Another Spaniard surveying the scene, however, considered the entire complex to be the "house," and instead of the house on the list reported an oratory (full of saints) and two rooms, which would bring the ensemble very close indeed to a traditional Nahua house complex.[55]

The Vocabulary of Kinship

If the effective minimum unit in Nahua society seems to approach "household" more than "family," the core residents of the household were nevertheless still consanguineal and affinal kin, so that the topic of the organization and evolution of Nahua kin relationships will bear discussion in this context. But as a last reminder of the pervasiveness of the Nahua emphasis on household, on the fact of being together rather than the rationale for being together, let it be said that the predominant term for "relatives" in Nahuatl is -*huanyolque*, "those who live with one."[56] Perhaps this can help explain how in preconquest times sons-in-law and persons of dubious paternity sometimes succeeded to the throne.[57] I do not mean to say that blood ties were unimportant; looking at it from the other direction, the term -huanyolque presumes that blood relatives will live together. And in fact terms existed (though seen but rarely in everyday texts) that put more emphasis on the genesis of the connection: -*tlacamecahuan*, "one's descendants" (and ascendants as well?), based on "human being" and "rope," and -*tlacayohuan*, "one's relatives," based on "human being" plus the -*yo* of inalienable possession.[58]

---

*The rooms are described as a "sala, recámara, y aposento" (AGN, Tierras 2555, exp. 14, ff. 2, 18–20). A *recámara* could be any inner private room, however. Even in this (for an Indian) impressive estate, valued at between 600 and 1,000 pesos including lands, animals, and crops on hand, there was hardly any furniture of value: a 9-vara table of ordinary wood with a bench; a smaller table; a chair; a kneading trough; a bed of ordinary wood; and a wooden chest with lock and key. The total value of these items (all Spanish in genre) was 8 pesos, 6 reales. In Spanish Mexican homes of the time, to be sure, hangings, clothing, utensils, and ornamental objects also far outweighed the furniture in value and extent, but the tendency seems to have been carried to an extreme in Nahua homes.

Even more noteworthy than the nature of Nahuatl words for "relative" is the rarity in texts of any collective term, just as any full equivalent of "family" appears to be lacking. It is true that the more common documentary types all emphasize individual bequests, grants, or claims and thus afford relatively little occasion for mentioning the collectivity. But even when the occasion arises, one is likely to see a list rather than a more general term. In Coyoacan in 1622, don Juan de Guzmán refers to the designated familial burial place in the Dominican monastery as "the place where we are buried, where my father, older brothers, and younger siblings all lie buried."[59] Again and again the Nahua kinship system seems to deemphasize larger units of any kind,[60] and look at the totality of relationships as an ordered scheme in which each relative or class of relative occupies a specific, distinct place as seen from the common center of ego. The principle is quite like that of cellular organization in state, household, and other spheres, but whereas there the result is to create relatively concrete, permanent, functioning entities, here the contents of the construct are different for each individual and in a sense have reality only for him or her.

Modern English speakers would find themselves at home with many aspects of the Nahua system, including not only its individualism and relative simplicity, but the actual definition of many relationships. Nahuatl had words equivalent to mother, father, aunt, uncle, grandmother, and grandfather, and these terms were used precisely as we use them today, except that the last two could be extended to great-aunt and great-uncle.[61] Paternal and maternal grandparents were called the same, as they are with us, and the words for aunt and uncle were no different whether the connection was through the maternal or the paternal line, through blood or marriage:[62]

One's father	-ta	One's aunt	-ahui
One's mother	-nan	One's grandfather	-col
One's uncle	-tla	One's grandmother	-ci

Other aspects of Nahua kinship terms are less familiar to us. All the categories are contingent; they are specifically predicated on the point of view of some particular person, the reference point, which is as important to the categorization as the person referred to. The importance of the reference point is seen in the fact that kinship words virtually do not appear in the free or absolutive form but instead are possessed, incorporating a possessive prefix governed by the reference point.[63] Thus in mundane documentation one will look in vain for *tatli*, "father"; instead, one will see *nota*, "my father," *ita*, "his/her father," and so on. The age and sex of the reference point can affect the term used as much as the age and sex of the person spoken of. (It is definitely the nature of the reference point or possessor that governs the choice

TABLE 3.2

Distinctions in Kin Terminology by Gender of Reference Point

Male reference point	Relationship	Female reference point
-teachcauh	one's older brother/male cousin	-ach, -oquichtiuh
-hueltiuh	one's older sister/female cousin	-pi
-tex	one's brother-in-law	-huepol
-huepol	one's sister-in-law	-huezhui
-teiccauh	one's younger sibling/cousin	-iuc
-pil[a]	one's child	-coneuh[a]
-mach	one's niece/nephew	-pillo

NOTE: The wife of a man is quite often -*cihuauh*, "one's woman," the husband of a woman less frequently -*oquichhui*, "one's man," but -*namic*, "one's spouse," a reciprocal term with differentiation only by implication, is the most common in postconquest contexts. "-Cihuauh" and "-oquichhui" distinguish gender by specifying the referent's sex rather than reference point's. (See also Table 3.5.)

[a]The contrast is not thoroughgoing. The reference point for "-pil" is frequently female, and on rarer occasions, one finds "-coneuh" with a male reference point. For "-pil" with female reference point, see UCLA TC, folder 25, March 1, 1768 (Acaxochitlan, Tulancingo area). There is also a distinction with stepchildren, the stepchild of a male being -*tlacpahuitec*, and the stepchild of a female -*chahuaconeuh* or -*chahuapil*.

TABLE 3.3

Gender Distinctions by Referent

Male		Female	
one's great-grandfather	-achton	one's great-grandmother	-pipton
one's grandfather	-col	one's grandmother	-ci
one's father	-ta	one's mother	-nan
one's uncle	-tla	one's aunt	-ahui
one's older brother/ male cousin (different for male and female reference point)	-teachcauh, -ach, -oquichtiuh	one's older sister/female cousin (different for male and female reference point)	-hueltiuh, -pi
one's (grown) son	-telpoch	one's (grown) daughter	-(i)chpoch

NOTE: All the terms for ascendants beyond the parents' generation also apply to collateral kin.

of the word, not the accident of who is speaking, as some have thought.[64]) A whole set of relationships manifests parallel double categories depending on whether the reference point is a female or a male (see Table 3.2). All of these terms describe relationships between the reference point, or ego, and people of ego's generation or the succeeding generation. As to gender distinctions of the type to which we are more accustomed, by the sex of the person referred to, these exist in Nahuatl, but nearly all concern people older than ego (see Table 3.3). With people younger than ego, for the most part no distinction was made. The two exceptions, -*telpoch*, "one's (grown) son," and -*(i)chpoch*, "one's (grown) daughter," appear to be late though preconquest modifications of a system that in its purity would have contained literally no sex distinctions for junior relatives.[65] Thus -*pil* was one's child either male or female, -*(i)xhuiuh* one's grandchild regardless of sex. There were two different terms for the offspring of one's brother or sister (see Table 3.2), but the sex of the reference point determined the choice of term, and neither made any distinction between niece and nephew. The division of all relatives into two classes based on their age relative to the reference point's age is a striking instance of the ego orientation of the Nahua system and also of the general Nahua preoccupation with sequence.

Closely related to these aspects of Nahua kinship is the feature most widely at variance with European systems, the lack of a unified category on the order of sister, brother, or sibling that would bring together all the members of ego's own generation. Rather, for both male and female egos, the categories were older brother, older sister, and younger sibling without distinction by the referent's sex (see Table 3.2).[66] There was literally no way to classify people in more than one of these categories at the same time other than by listing them,[67] nor was it possible to speak of someone's sibling without taking a position on his or her age relative to the reference point. The Nahua sibling terms also differed from European ones in that they could be extended to cousins, or rather included both cousins and siblings. It has been noted elsewhere that this feature, associated with the so-called Hawaiian system of kinship, is congruent with a situation in which related nuclear families live in the same household, or at least side by side, so that cousins are a single interacting group. Just how the terminology relating to siblings versus cousins was used in actual situations remains extremely hard to determine. On the one hand, modifiers existed to distinguish cousins from siblings (though it is not entirely clear whether these were introduced in preconquest times or in the early postconquest period).[68] On the other hand, such modifiers are totally absent in everyday documentation. Moreover, in cases where certainty can be established, the terms usually refer in fact to siblings; only a few instances can be found in which they demonstrably refer to cousins.[69]

Much the same kind of extension of terminology from lineal to collateral relatives can be found in categories for some (not all) generations other than ego. As noted, the grandparent terms can mean great-aunt and great-uncle. Likewise, "-(i)xhuiuh" can mean great-niece/great-nephew as well as grandchild, and the same applies to terms for more distant ascendants and descendants. The same problem arises as with sibling terminology, namely, that these words can hardly ever (in my experience to date never) be demonstrated to refer to other than lineal relatives in real textual situations. Yet dictionary glosses and the lack of any known separate categories for collateral kin in these generations are convincing evidence that in principle the terms embrace both lineal and collateral relatives. In the generations of ego's parents and

TABLE 3.4

Some Cross-Generational Projections and Symmetries

Terms for older kin		Related terms for younger kin	
one's great-great-grandparent	-minton[a]	one's great-great-grandchild	-minton
one's great-grandfather	-achton[b]	one's older brother/male cousin (female reference point)	-ach
one's great-grandmother	-pipton	one's older sister/female cousin (female reference point)	-pi
one's younger sibling/cousin (male reference point)	-(te)iccauh	one's great-grandchild	-iccaton[c]
one's younger sibling/cousin	-iuc	one's great-grandchild	-iucton[c]

[a]The terms for ascendants also apply to collateral kin. Though *-minton* has the *-ton* diminutive of the great-grandkin terms, it is not derived from a same-generation term, as they are, and does not distinguish gender like other terms for elders. In all other cases here, terms for distant ascendants are derived from terms for older same-generation kin, and terms for distant descendants are derived from those for younger same-generation kin.

[b]The alternate term for *-achton*, *-achcocol*, falls out of the scheme of formation of great-grandkin terms by adding *-ton* to a same-generation root.

[c]It remains unsure whether *-iccaton* and *-iucton* distinguish the gender of the reference point. In the only textual cases I have recorded, they seem to: *-iccaton* has a male reference point (CH, 2: 91), and *-iucton* (actually appearing as *-iuctzin* with the other diminutive ending) has a female reference point (TC, p. 232).

children, however, lineal and collateral relatives are distinguished, with father and mother distinct from aunt and uncle, and child distinct from niece/nephew (see Tables 3.2 and 3.3). Even so, traces of the tendency remain. "Father" and "uncle" are by origin the same word. And "-pil," "child of a man or woman," is related to "-pillo," "niece/nephew of a female."[70] Here, too, inclusiveness is emphasized over precise descent.

Nahua kin terminology shows certain other symmetries and reciprocal relationships characteristic of indigenous modes of organization. Some reciprocal terms name the relationship of two people in such a way that gender is specified, but by the reference point rather than by the term itself; this kind of reciprocity is characteristic of affinal rather than consanguineal terms. *-Huepol* means a sibling's spouse of the opposite sex (see Table 3.2). If ego is a man, it refers to a woman ("sister-in-law"); if ego is a woman, it refers to a man ("brother-in-law"). Likewise *-namic* (on which more below) means "spouse"; the referent is always of the opposite sex, with ego's gender alone specifying the referent's.[71] A different kind of symmetry is seen in the projection of terms from ego's generation onto the generations of great-grandparents and great-grandchildren, words for older siblings being transferred to ascendants and words for younger siblings to descendants (see Table 3.4).[72]

Terms for affinal kin, those connected through marriage, are in several respects similar to the European terms, though, as just mentioned in the cases of "-huepol" and "-namic," they also manifest special features such as reciprocity (see Table 3.5). In fact, all the words for siblings-in-law are recipro-

TABLE 3.5
Affinal Kin Terms

Terms for male referents		Terms for referents not distinguished by gender		Terms for female referents	
one's husband	-oquichhui[a]	one's spouse	-namic	one's wife	-cihuauh
one's father-in-law	-monta[b]	one's fellow parent-in-law	-huexiuh	one's mother-in-law	-monnan
one's brother-in-law (male reference point)	-tex	one's in-law of the same generation, opposite sex	-huepol	one's sister-in-law (female reference point)	-huezhui
one's son-in-law	-mon			one's daughter-in-law	-cihuamon
one's stepfather	-tlacpata	one's stepchild (male reference point)	-tlacpahuitec[c]	one's stepmother	-chahuanan
		one's stepchild (female reference point)	-chahuaconeuh, -chahuapil		

[a] Rare after the conquest.
[b] Terms for more distant generations, which follow the principle of adding *mon-* to a consanguineal term, are omitted.
[c] No terms for stepbrothers or stepsisters have been identified. Perhaps the children of one's stepparent were simply called by the sibling/cousin words.

TABLE 3.6
Reciprocity in Terminology for Siblings of Spouse

Relevant spouse	Relevant sibling	Term used by each for the other
Female spouse	Male spouse's sister	-huezhui
Male spouse	Female spouse's brother	-tex
Female spouse	Male spouse's brother	-huepol
Male spouse	Female spouse's sister	-huepol

cal; any two siblings-in-law would always use the same term in speaking of each other (see Table 3.6). The same is true with -*huexiuh*, one's fellow parent-in-law (English lacks such a category, but Spanish has a quite exact equivalent, *consuegro/a*, differing only in that it shows the gender of the referent).[73] This kind of reciprocity is prevented from appearing in Nahua consanguineal terminology by the insistence on differentiating consanguineal relatives by their age relative to ego's; thus in the system as the Spaniards found it in the sixteenth century, no two blood relatives would address each other by the same term.

For affinal kin of one's own generation, the age distinction was suspended, but a form of it reappears with the preceding and following generations. Just as terms for blood kin distinguish the sex of older relatives but not of younger ones, so parents-in-law and stepparents are distinguished as male or female while children-in-law and stepchildren are not, or at least not in the same way (see Table 3.5). For stepchildren there is no such distinction at all, and for children-in-law the basic word is -*mon* for both genders, but in practice the modifier *cihua*- always appears for a daughter-in-law, so that the distinction is drawn after all.[74]

As can be seen in Table 3.5, some of the affinal terms are based, as in English, on consanguineal categories, using the same word plus a modifier. This almost inherent and universal analogy, strengthened no doubt by the Nahua emphasis on the household, led to a type of extension of terminology unmentioned in Molina or the classic lists of kin terms but seen frequently in texts describing specific situations, namely, the use of unmodified consanguineal terminology for affinal kin. In-laws were thereby brought entirely into the fold. I do not mean to say that affinal terminology was entirely avoided; on the contrary, examples can be found from a great many times and places. The more one reads the documents, however, the more one senses that the affinal terms, with the exception of "-namic," "one's spouse," were rather cold in tone. They are never used metaphorically, and no extensions in domain are attested for them as for the consanguineal terms.[75] In wills, the affinal terms were often deliberately avoided; rather than refer to a son- or daughter-in-law, one would say "the spouse of my child."

Since a certain amount of triangulation is required to detect the use of consanguineal for affinal terms, demonstrable examples from texts are not numerous, but they are suggestive. In Culhuacan in 1581, Tomás Motolinia calls his daughter and his son-in-law "my children" ("nopilhuan"), though at the same time he uses the affinal term for the son-in-law in particular ("no-mon").[76] In the Tulancingo region in 1659, don Francisco de Larios likewise calls daughter and son-in-law "my children," but unlike Tomás Motolinia, he proceeds to refer to his son-in-law as "my child."[77] In both these cases, a testator is bequeathing property to a couple in which the in-law is male. Since the son-in-law will probably have much to say about managing the bequest, and is perforce being treated like a full-scale heir, he had just as well be denominated "child." Another document, however, shows Juana Martina, in Culhuacan in 1587, calling her son and her daughter-in-law "my children."[78] Apparently it was not uncommon, then, for parents to ignore the affinal term and speak of couples consisting of a child and an in-law as children regardless of the gender of the natural child.

Although examples showing parents-in-law being called by consanguineal terms have not turned up so far, the corresponding phenomenon is shown with uncles and aunts, nieces and nephews. As noted, it appears that just as with us, "uncle" terminology was normally used not only for the consanguineal kin, but also for their marriage partners. Thus one would call the wife of one's blood uncle "aunt," and she would call one "-pillo" ("niece/nephew"; see Table 3.7).[79] Special affinal terminology for the relationship between ego and the spouse of a parent's sibling, or between ego and the child

TABLE 3.7

Consanguineal and Affinal Relationships at the Level of Aunt, Uncle, and Niece/Nephew

Consanguineal		Affinal	
uncle calls niece/nephew	-mach	uncle calls niece/nephew	-mach
niece/nephew calls uncle	-tla	niece/nephew calls uncle	-tla
		uncle calls nephew-in-law	-machmon
		uncle calls niece-in-law	-cihuamachmon
		niece/nephew-in-law calls uncle	?
aunt calls niece/nephew	-pillo	aunt calls niece/nephew	-pillo
niece/nephew calls aunt	-ahui	niece/nephew calls aunt	-ahui
		aunt calls nephew-in-law	-pillomon[a]
		aunt calls niece-in-law	-cihuapillomon[a]
		niece/nephew-in-law calls aunt	?

[a]These terms are unattested but can be deduced from -*machmon* and -*cihuamachmon*.

of a spouse's sibling, is at present entirely unattested, so that this particular kind of overlapping of consanguineal and affinal terms is apparently best seen as a standard feature of the system rather than an extension. For the spouse of a nephew or niece, however, affinal terminology did exist, the equivalent of "niece/nephew-in-law" (see Table 3.7).[80] But this distinction could be ignored in texts, as when in Mexico City in 1600 Francisca Ana and her husband refer to Francisco Hernández as "our uncle" ("totlatzin"), and he calls them "my niece/nephews" ("nomachhuan").[81]

An example is even available in which a pair of sisters refer to their late sister-in-law as their younger sister, using the consanguineal term,[82] but this enters into the realm of polite conversational usage, to be discussed further below.

Unlike English, Nahuatl had a convention for incorporating into an affinal term an indication whether the person through whom the relationship was established was dead or alive. The element *micca-* (the combining form of *micqui*, "dead person") added to an in-law word meant that the relevant consanguineal kinsman of the reference point had died; thus *nomon* is "my son-in-law" and *nomiccamon* is "my son-in-law, husband of my deceased daughter." Instances of the use of this (from the point of view of European languages exotic) type of expression continue well into the postconquest period.[83] But it does not appear that the distinction was ever obligatory, and the modifier is omitted in some sixteenth-century texts even when it is stated elsewhere that the consanguineal relative had died.[84]

Central to any treatment of affinal kin is the nature of the categorization of spouses, which is a bit problematical in the sense that even the earliest accounts and examples that have come down to us may already show Spanish influence. That the kin terms and principles of organization I have been discussing are indigenous there is no reason to doubt; aside from being specifically so presented in early chronicles and being used consistently in actual sixteenth-century texts, the words in several basic respects, as we have seen, vary widely from European counterparts. "-Namic," "spouse," is a special case. True, it shows the reciprocity characteristic of some other Nahua same-generation affinal terms and to that extent definitely fits well into the Nahua system and embodies a favorite indigenous principle. But the one thing that the Spaniards almost from the beginning seriously intended to change in Nahua family life was the practice of having plural wives. Some Nahuatl annals contain entries stating boldly that "marriage began" ("opeuh nenamictiliztli") in such and such a year in the 1520's.[85] This could be taken to refer to monogamous Christian marriage, as opposed to a close indigenous counterpart, and doubtless that is in some sense the intention, but one is left wondering if the word itself might not have been a new construction.

Alternate terms did exist. As shown in Table 3.5, in addition to the genderless "-namic," Nahuatl had and to an extent continued to use -*cihuauh*, "one's wife" (literally "one's woman"), and -*oquichhui*, "one's husband" (literally "one's man"). Though "-oquichhui" is rarely found in texts after 1540, "-cihuauh" remained current throughout the colonial period.[86] Nahuatl annalists like Chimalpahin and the author of the Historia Tolteca-Chichimeca seem to prefer these terms, and verbs based on them, when the reference is to preconquest times, and "-namic" for the postconquest period. The early Cuernavaca-region censuses use virtually only -cihuauh and -oquichhui, even at times with couples married in the church.[87] Formal marriage, with lengthy celebrations and rites including the tying together of the couple's garments, was known before the conquest and is described in the Florentine Codex. But that work is inconclusive on the question of "-namic." The word does appear, but so rarely and in such contexts as to leave doubt about whether or not it is integrated into the general vocabulary; the occurrences could represent authentic preconquest usage, but they could as easily be posterior explications, even half-inadvertent anachronisms.[88]

A final ambiguous clue is the frequent use in early Nahuatl documents of *teoyotica*, "through sacrament," as a modifier of "-namic."[89] One could construe this as implying that the category already existed, the modifier merely specifying Christian as opposed to non-Christian. But "teoyotica" could just as well redundantly reinforce the newness of the arrangement or have been necessary, originally, to complete the meaning, since "-namic" by itself might mean just match, mate, or an equivalent of any kind.[90] All in all, I strongly incline to the opinion that "-namic" is a postconquest neologism.

Whether the category "spouse" was largely indigenous (affected only by connotations of monogamy) or was a new amalgam of indigenous and Spanish principles, the overall system of the early postconquest period was surely little changed from its pre-Hispanic form. But it was not therefore totally unified within itself. The "Hawaiian" principle of giving the same name to all kin of the same generation was violated blatantly by the existence of categories for uncle, aunt, and niece/nephew, and a bit more obliquely by the division of all siblings into older and younger. The general distinction between all older and all younger relatives, gender being differentiated only for relatives older than ego, ran into conflict with the tendency to differentiate gender in all adults. Kinship categorization may have been in flux for a short or a long time, and especially it may have been affected by the other Mesoamerican groups with whom the Nahuas had been in various kinds of contact for centuries, leading to a set of classifications that could strike one as miscellaneous. The system as a whole seems not to point strongly in any direction, not to preclude or dictate particular forms of social interaction, except perhaps that it might seem to imply a sharply differential treatment of one's older and younger siblings. What does stand out is the flexibility inherent in the total lack of named larger groupings. The lack of descent groups did not prevent Chimalpahin and others from keeping dynastic lists of kings through many generations, but it must have helped deemphasize automatic lineage solidarity, leaving a greater role for the less kin-oriented structure of calpolli and altepetl. All indigenous Nahuatl kinship categories are seen from ego outward in such a strict sense that the terms are not only always possessed, but keep the point of reference and the referent so separate that they can never be included within the same category at the same time. Until the penetration of Spanish influence, statements like "we are sisters" and "we are cousins" did not exist in Nahuatl, not even for the affinal terms where reciprocity is the rule.[91] Even *notlacamecayo*, "my set of consanguineal ties," does not include me myself. Everything is reconstituted for each person.

Flexible as the Nahua kinship system was, there was no apparent need for subtractions and additions in adjustment to Spanish demands in the sixteenth century, or even to the great demographic storms that swept through the indigenous population. And indeed, the borrowing of Spanish kinship terms was minimal, nearly nonexistent, until the late seventeenth century. The marital-status terms *viuda*, "widow," and *viudo*, "widower," were a standard part of the language by 1600, relating as they did to Christian marriage and the payment of taxes.[92] But these words, though they mark a status important in family life, do not define a relationship and are not kin terms properly speaking, as can be seen in the fact that the indigenous equivalents, *icnocihuatl*, "widow," and *icnooquichtli*, "widower," are always found in the absolute rather than the possessed form.[93]

It was noted above that the most striking deviation between the Nahua and Spanish systems lay in their treatment of siblings and cousins. Table 3.8 recapitulates the divergences, of which the outstanding ones have to do with Nahuatl's obligatory age distinction between the referent and the reference point, and its lack of distinction between siblings and cousins. Each system made distinctions lacking in the other, and each had six categories in common use for siblings and cousins (see Table 3.9). But if we note that Spanish had only one special distinction to Nahuatl's two, that its six terms were really only three with transparent indication of gender, and that it unified the whole generation of ego, the Spanish terminology can be considered the simpler of the two.

At any rate, given sibling and cousin terminology as the focal point of difference, one would expect changes in the Nahuatl system to concentrate there, as in fact proceeded to happen. Isolated examples of Spanish influence begin to appear in Nahuatl texts as early as the late sixteenth century. In

TABLE 3.8

Comparison of Nahuatl and Spanish Systems of Categorizing Siblings and Cousins

Diagnostic trait	Nahuatl	Spanish
Distinction of age of referent relative to reference point	yes	no
Distinction of sex of reference point	yes	no
Distinction of sex of referent	for older siblings/ cousins only	yes (except in the collective)
Distinction between siblings and cousins	no	yes
Existence of collective terms including cousins as well as siblings	yes	no
Existence of collective terms including both younger and older consanguineal kin of one's own generation	no	yes[a]

[a]Spanish has words for all siblings, all sisters, all cousins, and all female cousins. Since the masculine plural is also the collective, there is properly speaking no separate collective term for all brothers or male cousins, although in context that intention is often clear.

TABLE 3.9

Approximately Equivalent Terms in the Spanish and Nahuatl Categorization of Siblings and Cousins

Spanish	Nahuatl	
	Male reference point	Female reference point
Male referent		
hermano, brother	-teachcauh, older	-ach, older brother/
primo, cousin	brother/cousin	cousin
primo hermano, first cousin	-teiccauh, younger sibling/cousin	-iuc, younger sibling/ cousin
Female referent		
hermana, sister	-hueltiuh, older	-pi, older sister/
prima, cousin	sister/cousin	cousin
prima hermana, first cousin	-teiccauh (as above)	-iuc (as above)

Tetzcoco in 1596, the high nobleman don Miguel de Carvajal first, in the usual way, calls his cousin Juan (Bautista) de Pomar, son of a Spaniard and a Nahua noblewoman, "notiachcauh," "my older brother/cousin," but then he adds "noprimo hermano," "my first cousin," using the Spanish term. In a very similar instance a little later, referring to the year 1613 and perhaps written or rewritten in the 1620's, the historian Chimalpahin, who for the rest keeps strictly to the Nahua system, employs the terminology "iteyccauh yhermano," that is, first "his younger sibling/cousin," then "his brother" using a Spanish loan.[94] Both times the Spanish term is employed only in the manner of a coefficient to the indigenous category, in relation to people from the Spanish world, and in an attempt to report in Nahuatl something emanating from Spanish. These instances represent only the beginning of a transition, when some Nahuatl speakers were becoming cognizant of the implications of a system different from their own.

Not until the late seventeenth century does one see evidence of the Spanish terms actually displacing the Nahuatl counterparts and appearing in ordinary situations concerning Nahuas, not Spaniards. "Hermano," "brother," is presently attested as of 1672, "hermana," "sister," as of 1691, and "noyermanos noyermanas," "my brothers and sisters," as of the same year.[95] In a document of 1746 from Amecameca, the transition seems to have been completed. Several writers and witnesses discussing a matter of inheritance use "primo," "cousin," "primo hermano," "first cousin," and "hermano" as a matter of course, to the exclusion of indigenous Nahuatl sibling/cousin terms. Yet in the same text the terms for grandfather, father, uncle, and child are all indigenous.[96] How general this kind of displacement was remains to be seen.[97]

The great majority of Spanish kin terms as used in Nahuatl show the same contingency characteristic of indigenous terminology, that is, they are practically always possessed, always indicating "someone's" brother, sister, or cousin. A single instance, however, shows that even this most basic aspect of the Nahua system may have begun to yield, at least where the new Spanish loan terms are concerned. In a text from San Francisco Centlalpan in the Chalco region, dated 1736, we find the phrase "ynn ome termanos" (*yn omen tihermanos*) with the meaning "we two brothers," or in the particular context, "we, brother and sister."[98] The kin term is not possessed, and ego and another person are put in one category. Had this principle been extended to indigenous terminology, the system would have been changed profoundly, but the indigenous words have remained impervious to this day, and even kin words of Spanish origin are mainly treated as contingent.

By the eighteenth century, if not earlier, other aspects of the Nahua system that differed sharply from Spanish categories were also being affected. Nahuatl's terms for same-generation in-laws, based primarily on the distinction between same-sex and opposite-sex relationships (see Table 3.6), were quite unlike Spanish *cuñado*, "brother-in-law," and *cuñada*, "sister-in-law," and thus in a text of 1737, "noconado," "my brother-in-law," makes its appearance.[99] Likewise, in speaking of the children of siblings, Nahuatl distinguished the gender of ego, not of the referent, the opposite of Spanish, so we are not surprised to see *nosobrinos*, "my nephews," in a text of 1746.[100] It is rather surprising, however, to find the Spanish *tío*, "uncle," in eighteenth-century Nahuatl texts,[101] since there is no detectable difference in the definition of "tío" and "-tla" beyond the Nahuatl term's obligatory possession, and "tío" too appears possessed in known examples.

As far as is known, the terms for direct lineal kin—grandparents, parents, children, grandchildren—remained entirely unaffected by Spanish.[102] Of these, the words for grandparents and parents were essentially identical to the Spanish terms. Though those for offspring differed in not distinguishing the sex of the referent (with the exception of grown children, as noted earlier), they apparently resisted the influence that impinged on the niece/nephew words. As modified, the Nahua system was moving far in the direction of giving up the important distinction between relatives older than and younger than ego, as well as dual terminology by ego's gender, and was adding a more thorough distinction between lineal and collateral kin. In the absence of far better information than we are likely ever to acquire, it is impossible to know whether or not the terminological change corresponded to changes in social interaction. It is imaginable that the changes signal the abandonment of elaborate rules governing relations between older and younger siblings and between same-generation in-laws according to gender. There is, however, remarkably little firm evidence that such rules ever existed; if they did, the change of terms in itself would not have eradicated ancient practices immediately. The Nahua system remained flexible and ego-oriented, without fixed larger groupings; no such loanword as "family" has yet appeared in older Nahuatl documents. The one thing the changes definitely accomplished was to ease communication and interaction with the inhabitants of the Mexican Spanish world.

Hints of Household Interaction

One would like to know a great deal about what went on in the households and among the kin so skeletally described above, not only to appreciate Nahua humanity, but to learn how the principles of social organization worked themselves out in everyday life, which would bring in turn a better understanding of those principles, their evolution over time, and conflicts between them. The truth is that until different sources appear, we must proceed in the opposite way, using what we know of principles and structure to make deductions about behavior. Still, since even there our knowledge is sketchy and ambiguous, it is best not to push the deductions very far, and to concentrate instead on such direct glimpses as the documents may allow us.

Only a very few texts of the anecdotal, conversational kind we need have in fact come down to us, all from the time around 1580–90.[103] Each has its peculiarities, and even taken together they yield far less than a systematic view. But they are no less valuable for all that and well worth looking at in some detail.

A marvelous document written in 1583 in the small lakeside settlement of

Tocuillan, in Tetzcoco's jurisdiction, uses mainly dialogue to report how a woman named simply Ana (together with her husband and son) was granted a house site by the local authorities. One of these functionaries was a regidor (her older brother); the others may have been an alcalde and regidores, but they could have been only ward heads, for Tocuillan was probably nothing more than a minor constituent part of Tetzcoco at this time.[104] Ana and her brother Juan Miguel address each other repeatedly, constantly calling each other "my dear older brother" or "my honored younger sibling," while strictly avoiding "Ana" or "Juan Miguel."* The narrator does use the personal names, but also repeats the sibling terms again and again, far more than would be necessary for clarity of reference. In this example, then, social interaction emphasizes sibling categorization (and with it the age distinction), just as one might expect from a review of the kinship categories themselves. Indeed, the categories, with their implication of a set behavior pattern, seem to have displaced the personal identity of the actors entirely. That effect may be illusory, however, since, as we will see below, the avoidance of personal names in direct address could be a sign of politeness or deference, by no means indicating that one was neglecting the more personal characteristics of one's interlocutor.

As to the substance of relationships, the document shows Ana turning to her older brother for help and submitting herself and her husband to his authority as long as she should live under his roof. For some reason, perhaps the flooding of which the text speaks, Ana, her husband Juan, and their young son (also Juan) no longer have a satisfactory place to live; Ana asks her brother if they can live with him for a while, and he assents. Ana utters words of formal thanks and continues: "Even if I should get intoxicated, I declare that I will never act badly in the household (*quiahuatl ithualli*), but will behave respectfully, and as to my husband Juan here, if he should ever lose respect, I leave it in your hands." Juan Miguel replies that he will pick no fights if his brother-in-law "goes along behaving himself well." The implied picture is that the eldest male is the figure of authority for everyone living in the household, but that friction with resident in-laws is not unanticipated.

After a month, Ana fears that she and hers are being too much trouble, that perhaps they should request a bit of land and build their own house there. Juan Miguel immediately goes out to round up his fellow town fathers, first telling Ana to prepare tortillas for them to eat. When the dignitaries arrive, polite greetings and inquiries are exchanged, and Ana is referred to most respectfully as "lady" (*cihuapille*). Nevertheless, she retires from the

---

*Since Ana's parents are not mentioned, it is entirely possible that the regidor was Ana's cousin, not her brother. I speak here in terms of siblings for simplicity's sake and because in my experience of everyday texts in which relationships can be tested, the same-generation consanguineal terms refer to siblings far more often than to cousins.

room during the meal and returns only after it is finished to present her petition. By implication, many household functions and groupings were defined
strictly by sex; the female function, however, was not only to cook, weave,
and obey, but in this case and perhaps many others, to serve as principal
spokesperson and petitioner for the nuclear family.[105]

Without a doubt the richest extant source for Nahua conversation and
behavior in everyday contexts is another document from Tetzcoco, though it
has reached us by a very indirect route. Intended for the language instruction
of Spanish ecclesiastics, the text has come down to us as used by Jesuits in
Mexico City in the seventeenth century. Nevertheless, everything indicates that
it was composed around 1570 or 1580 in Tetzcoco by an indigenous person
drawing scenes primarily from his own experience.[106] Alongside lengthy formal speeches on the occasion of marriage, birth, and death, the writer has
included small talk taking place both in public and in the household. Language
and behavior, it seems, did not vary greatly in these two spheres; in both,
elaborate and highly conventional patterns of speech imply equally well-
defined expectations about behavior. The writer was a nobleman, and his
characters are from leading families of Tetzcoco, including some of the royal
line. No doubt, then, many of the specific formulations were appropriate to
the nobility alone; yet some of the principles involved, including the basic one
of defining social interaction through elaborate formula, probably operated
at all levels, as they do in some surviving Mesoamerican speech communities
to this day.[107]

The content of the household transactions portrayed is testimony to the
near universality of certain behavior among sedentary peoples. A woman
stops by her sister's house on the way to market, answers inquiries about the
health of her husband and children, apologizes for not visiting more frequently, and on leaving says she may stop by again after having done her
market business. A loquacious old lady goes on and on with concern over the
welfare of two boys and praise of their good progress; the flattered mother
then pretends she is having problems with them, and the old lady reassures
her. Children greet their parents in the morning and say thanks after a meal.
The manner in which such quintessentially familiar things is expressed, however, may surprise us. Here is the speech of two boys to their mother after
eating:

Our Lord has been generous, oh my noble lady: in peace the food and drink have
been consumed at your table. The goods of our Lord have been our good fortune; let
us greatly praise him for it. Thank you, oh personage, oh lady, oh my noble person.[108]

Although the translation gives something of the effect, the Nahuatl original is
even more elaborate and indirect.

For encounters both inside and outside the family, a certain protocol was maintained. The arriving party assumed the role of the supplicant; bowing very low, then standing while he spoke, he apologized for interrupting his interlocutor, keeping him from his pressing duties, and even endangering his health by making him listen to long and idle prattle. The stationary party, taking the role of the superior, might remain seated, and though respectful, was less effusive than the first person to speak. The inferior never called the superior by name or made mention of his exact relationship with him, and the superior too was likely to be indirect, but less so. In conversations in the collection, younger relatives never name the relationship with the interlocutor, but older relatives may do so on occasion. Here two boys greet their mother, the older son speaking first:

(The older.) Oh our mistress, oh lady, I kiss your hands and feet, I bow down to your dignity. How did our Lord cause you to feel on rising? Do you enjoy a bit of His health?
(The younger.) Oh my noble person, oh personage, oh lady, we do not wish to distract you; we bow down to you, we salute your ladyship and rulership. How did you enjoy your sleep, and now how are you enjoying the day? Are you enjoying a bit of the good health of the All-pervasive, the Giver of Life? [109]

By no means do the boys at any point dare say "mother." To them she replies only "Greetings, little pages"—a turn of phrase that, while not specifying the relationship, was an affectionate, mock-pejorative way of acknowledging them as junior members of the circle.

In the visit between the sisters (or possibly cousins) mentioned a moment ago, the younger calls the older only "my lady," whereas the older at least alludes to their relationship by calling the younger "my child, my dear daughter." A boy avoids specificity in making a typical inquiry into the health of his uncle:

How did you feel on rising, how did our Lord cause you to feel on rising? Are you enjoying a bit of His health? Or is He about to send some of His afflictions upon you? For we do not know how the Master of heaven and earth, the Giver of Life, is causing you to fare on His earth. [110]

The uncle then feels free to respond in open simplicity with "Thank you, my nephew," and goes on to call his own wife "your aunt" (but she was not present, and there was less restriction on naming relationships in such a case). Presumably the rules varied for different circles and situations. As we saw, Ana did not hesitate to say "my older brother" at every turn. In all cases, an elaborate texture of speech and behavioral signals seems to have reinforced the relative seniority and status of the parties involved.

In conversations reported in the Tetzcoco dialogues, kin terms are used not so much to designate relatives, those relationships being taken for granted, as in various extended senses. In the most straightforward and probably most common extension, the same kin term was applied to nonrelatives of the same age or generation relative to ego as to the primary referents, with some implication that the relationship was in some way analogous to the primary model. Thus older adults are found calling children below the age of puberty their grandchildren and referring to young adults in whom they take a friendly interest as their children. "Teachcauh," "one's older brother/cousin," and "teiccauh," "one's younger sibling/cousin," appear in the specific context of boys eating together in a group, with the meaning of older and younger male companions in general.[111] One's elder is to start eating first, and if by some chance the younger is served first, he is to move the food over to his elder and wait for him to start. That was surely the ideal of practice inside the household as well; the norm for household and kin is generalized to society. On the other hand, distinction by age was a general principle of social behavior. In the Tetzcoco dialogues, children are told to greet old people first and stand to one side as they go by. Thus general and familial principles interpenetrate and project on each other without a strong feeling of separate domains. The extension that first went beyond lineal to collateral kin then sweeps on, using the same principle of generational equation (though with subtly different effect and tone), to neighbors and acquaintances.

Another type of extension of kinship terms was their inversion in polite speech to mean the opposite, that is, a word for an older person was used for a younger (or inferior) person, and vice versa.[112] A governor or tlatoani would call his aides his fathers. More surprisingly to the English speaker, they might call him "my grandchild." Nor are such things confined to Tetzcoco. In a document of 1548 from Coyoacan, a woman calls the ruler and governor don Juan de Guzmán "noconeuh," "my child."[113] Primary inversions (such as a father calling his own child "father" or vice versa) have not yet been found and may not have existed. Indeed, the great majority of known inversions are not applied to the speaker's kin at all. The single presently attested instance was mentioned above in a different context. This was the case of the two unmarried sisters who referred to their sister-in-law as their younger sibling, since that woman, having been married, was doubtless older than they.[114] Here inversion occurs alongside extension of consanguineal vocabulary to an affinal relationship. At our remove in time and with as little context as we have, it is often impossible for us to decipher the exact intention and flavor of a Nahuatl kin term in a specific instance, but one can appreciate that an elaborate system of subtle modulations of kinship terminology was used to define distance and relative rank in social interaction generally. Extant examples of inversions are from before 1600. It may be, though it cannot be considered demonstrated, that the more elaborate metaphors went out of use in the course of the seventeenth century, at about the time Spanish terminology began to affect the system seriously.[115]

Much of the above carries the implication that each Nahua kin term was associated with very well-defined norms of behavior, for both referent and point of reference, and that a knowledge of these norms would shed much light on household interaction. We do find a statement of kinship norms, in the Florentine Codex, but it turns out to be less enlightening than one might have thought.[116] Perhaps many of the distinctions were not fully at the level of consciousness; at any rate, in this version most of the relatives end up looking very much like each other or are associated with roles that would immediately be recognized as familiar in almost any culture. The item of greatest note is the role of surrogate parent and provider (in effect, household head) assigned to an uncle or older brother on the death of the father of a minor or unmarried woman. A search among everyday Nahuatl documents for confirmation of such a function does not, however, turn up many examples.

In Coyoacan in 1568, a woman having been left alone, the governor makes three of her uncles the custodians of a house belonging to her.[117] In Culhuacan in the early 1580's, there is an instance of a man who treated his nieces as daughters and even left them a good share of his inheritance; a niece, on the other hand, disinherits her uncles (or possibly her uncle and aunt) on the grounds that they did not house and feed her when she was destitute. The same collection of documents has a classic example of an older brother who has acted as a father and now assigns portions of the inheritance to his younger siblings, expecting the oldest male to take over his role.[118] In Mexico City in 1600, an orphaned woman says that her uncle brought her up precisely because he was her uncle, and he says the same thing in reverse. He tried, however, to keep the property his niece was to inherit, until finally she brought the case to the governor and alcaldes and won possession.[119] Further illustrations do not appear. Since siblings or uncles as custodians were probably expected to hand out portions informally whenever an heir came of age, such a custodial role could have been quite standard without making much of an impact on records in which testaments are so prominent. Even if an uncle still had custody, he might not have considered a certain piece of property his own and so have mentioned it in his will.

Inheritance patterns, indeed, redefined the household in each generation. If more large blocks of testaments were available from a spread of times and places, we would probably be able to detect subtle patterns such as same-sex or opposite-sex preference in the inheritance of certain kind of property, and to trace regional and temporal trends in household composition. As things now stand, a trend that seems to emerge in the records of one region may be so roundly contradicted in those of an adjacent region as to leave one with the impression that the finding is merely the result of chance in a small sample.[120] Without the added context that we have only in those rare cases where documents cluster, individual wills often give an untrue picture of the immediate general situation. If a testator is one of three brothers who have each inherited a building in their father's compound, very likely the reader of the testament will not appreciate that more than one building was involved.

Nevertheless, some general aspects of inheritance in relation to the household (it will be necessary to return to the matter when speaking of land) can be deduced from Nahuatl documents as a whole, with no apparent difference from early to late or across regions. Female children inherited residential buildings along with male children; the basic pattern, presuming a parent in possession of a compound, was to divide the parts equally among all the children. Those who were grown assumed possession immediately, while some adults took care of the parts inherited by minors on their behalf. It is quite impossible to say how often such division led to the dissolution of the original household. Sometimes an heir would build a new fence in his part of the enclosure, break out a separate exit for himself, and destroy the unity of the compound.[121] One might also dismantle the inherited structure and set up anew elsewhere, as was actually envisioned in the case of one female heir expected to reside elsewhere after marriage.[122] Attempts to maintain the compound are also documented, as when a man, having inherited a building at home, left to live with his wife's family; he eventually bequeathed the building to his in-laws, but they never occupied it, for his blood relatives bought it back from them.[123] It is important, in any case, to recognize that formal division did not necessarily mean the breaking up of a unit, nor indeed would it, in many cases, have meant very much change at all. As seen above in the example of the home of Juan de San Pedro (Fig. 3.4), a structure was often originally built with a specific family member in mind, who may have already been occupying it for quite some time at the moment of inheriting it. With this decentralized mode as the household's normal manner of operation, it must have been possible in many cases to proceed as before, with a new titular household head.[124]

If women when children seem, on the face of it, to have inherited their fair share of residential buildings, as wives and mothers their situation was different. Whenever there were living children, what men left to their wives was practically always meant to go to the children once grown. Even when a specific statement to that effect is missing, this appears to have been the intention. Also in those cases where the wife seems to be neglected entirely, it was apparently presumed that she would continue to live in the household and manage things with the interests of the children in mind.[125] It might be specified, in fact, that if she left the household she would forfeit whatever she had been given.[126]

It is not that women were being discriminated against as women, but that inheritance was essentially a matter between consanguineal, not affinal kin. Sons-in-law and daughters-in-law were mentioned in bequests only as a function of the testator's blood kin. One might leave the home complex mainly to one's daughter and grandchildren, but also along the way mention the son-in-law who was being left in charge of it all.[127] Daughters-in-law were mentioned less frequently, especially if their husbands were still alive, but even so they might share in a bequest. They might even be the sole recipient, particularly when there was friction between parent and son and the parent trusted the daughter-in-law more.[128]

A corollary of men making bequests to their wives with their children in mind should have been women putting the same kind of condition on bequests to their husbands, but such cases are rare.[129] Exactly why this should be is hard to demonstrate rigorously, but the discrepancy seems to betray a significant gender differential after all. Although the position of the household head remains shadowy, early Nahua censuses do recognize such a figure, and in the great majority of cases he is male if the household contains an adult male at all.[130] Probably it was so clear that the responsibility for managing a minor's inheritance would fall to the father that a woman could leave property directly to her children with no thought of mentioning her husband, but procedures were less automatic in the opposite case. For another thing, a large proportion of all women issuing wills were widows, so the question did not arise. The very prevalence of such wills is a possible indication that property held by a woman alone was particularly exposed to perhaps unwelcome male management and was in special need of the formal protections of a testament.[131] Thus the long-continuing symbolic act of leaving an axe or hoe to a son, a grinding stone (metate) to a daughter,[132] may have corresponded to some differences in the management of inheritances even if not in the actual ability to inherit and bequeath.

Nahua inheritance patterns of the colonial period, with division among all heirs, both males and females inheriting from both parents, spouses acting primarily as custodians, and great male executor responsibility, are suspiciously close to the Spanish system in basic respects. On the other hand, there seems no need to posit that inheritance as we can see it in Nahuatl documents was (other than the adjustment to monogamy) the result of Spanish influence. No chronological trend such as that seen so clearly with the borrowing of kinship terms can be discerned. Everything is already present in documents of the sixteenth century and remains stable thereafter. The keynote of Nahua inheritance at all times is a flexibility not unlike that seen in the organization of households and in the use of kin terms. Inheritance is used not for the benefit of a certain household or a certain lineage, but for the welfare of certain individuals. Although it is conceivable that quite elaborate exclusionary and inclusionary principles of inheritance allocation existed and may yet be discovered, it is already certain that any such principles did not operate in a mechanical and exceptionless fashion. Rather testators were prepared to do whatever was in the interests of their children and grandchildren; this could at times involve the generous inclusion of affinal and collateral kin even though lineal descendants were the primarily intended ultimate beneficiaries. Nahuatl wills in the end do give a somewhat different impression than their Spanish counterparts. In the latter, the emphasis is overwhelmingly on one's children if there are any alive, and a good deal of attention goes to various kinds of attempts to maintain family status, whereas in Nahuatl wills, grandchildren sometimes play a large role even when children are still alive, and in general (though the assertion must be tested in future research) more kinds of kinfolk are mentioned, with more emphasis on something for everyone, in line with the general principles of ego orientation and division of any field into separate compartments.

4

Social Differentiation

SIXTEENTH-CENTURY Spaniards found in central Mexico a society remarkably like their own. Both the Spanish and the indigenous system divided the entire population between the two basic hereditary categories of noble and commoner. Furthermore, in both cases gradations and various types of special status made for a social continuum rather than two sharply separated blocks. Not only did both societies recognize different ranks of nobility and accord special titles to the heads of noble houses and lords of domains, but in both great leeway and regional variation existed in the use of noble terminology. In both, some commoners rose to be nobles, through wealth or notable deeds, while some borderline nobles were indistinguishable from commoners. In central Mexico as well as Spain, commoners varied greatly in wealth, and significant groups of merchants, retainers, and craftsmen stood out from the mass of commoner-agriculturalists in one way or another. Both societies associated nobility with high governmental office, leadership in war, and many other higher functions. As a result of this wide-ranging similarity, Spanish writers of the sixteenth century have left us more nearly adequate accounts of the indigenous system of social ranking than they have of political or familial organization.

Nothing in either the Spanish or the Nahuatl records justifies the interpretation, to which some still cling, that indigenous society was or recently had been egalitarian. From both sides of the documentation comes the same picture: that the noble-commoner distinction, modified by numerous subdistinctions, was as basic to social and political life as was altepetl structure, and probably as ancient. The Nahuatl sources also continue to overwhelm us with data on the wide variation in wealth not only among nobles but especially among commoners, demonstrating the relative autonomy and complexity of the forces of social differentiation and the limits on political redistribution. Nahua society and social categorization were neither unusually simple nor unduly rigid, but in both respects fell within the normal range for sedentary

TABLE 4.1

Some Nahua Social Categories

Term	Plural	Literal Meaning	Translation
tlatoani	tlatoque	speaker	king, ruler
teuctli	teteuctin	?	lord
pilli	pipiltin	child	nobleman
cihuapilli	cihuapipiltin	woman-child	noblewoman
macehualli	macehualtin	human being?	commoner, ordinary person, vassal, subject
tlalmaitl	—	land-hand	
temilti	temiltique	one who makes a field for someone	person specifically subordinated to a lord or noble
teixhuiuh	teixhuihuan	someone's grandchild	
-tlan nenqui	-tlan nenque*ᵃ*	someone who lives with one	household dependent
tlacotli, -tlacauh	tlatlacotin, -tlacahuan	derived from *tlacatl*, "person"?	slave (bought for a price or captured)

*ᵃ*Sometimes -tlannencahuan.

agricultural societies worldwide from ancient to early modern times. (For a list of the main categories of social rank, see Table 4.1.)

As a brief introduction to the system and its terminology, nothing can compare with the Tlaxcalan plan of 1548 for collecting the 8,000 fanegas of maize owed by the municipal corporation as its royal tribute.* At this relatively early time, neither tax exemptions nor flat per capita payments had come on the scene. Each person (actually each household head), from lowest to highest, was to pay according to his ability, an individual assessment being made in each case by members of the cabildo or other altepetl officials. A *macehualli* (commoner) who was "somewhat well off" was to give half a fanega, one who was very poor only a fourth of a fanega, and one who was very well off a whole fanega or even a fanega and a half. A *pilli* (noble) might give as little as two fanegas, or three or four, depending on his wealth. A tlatoani or ruler would contribute the most, but there were differences among Tlaxcala's four tlatoque also, with two giving seven fanegas, and two six. There were also some very rich pipiltin who were expected to approximate the amounts given by the tlatoque. Whereas only half a fanega divided the commoners from the nobles, five fanegas separated the richest nobles from the poorest. Thus not only did a continuum reach bit by bit from the poorest to the richest member of the society, the Tlaxcalans were prepared to recognize the fine gradations and give people correspondingly differentiated treatment. In the Tlaxcalan statement, "pilli" is taken as the generic term for all nobles; *teuctli*, "lord," does not appear.[1]

*A fanega is generally thought to be about a bushel and a half.

Commoners

Macehualli was a very broad and frequently used term with somewhat different connotations in different contexts.[2] Like analogous words in European languages, it could be used pejoratively. Molina has *macehuallatoa,* "to speak in a rustic manner," and *macehualquixtia,* "to belittle oneself." Similar implications can be found in mundane texts well into the postconquest period. In 1613 in Coyoacan, one Leonor Magdalena said of her daughter-in-law Petronilla, who had accosted her in public, kicked her, and ripped her clothing, that "great is her commonness" ("huel ymacehualyo").[3] The macehualli could also inspire pity and compassion; adding the normally reverential element *-tzin* (*macehualtzintli*) gave the sense "poor commoner."[4]

Although sometimes glossed as vassal, "macehualli" had that meaning only when in the possessed form: *nimomacehual,* "I am your vassal, subject, under your suzerainty," but *nimacehualli,* "I am a commoner" (an ordinary person with ordinary duties and privileges rather than those of a noble). When possessed, the term was often applied to persons of high birth as well, since nearly everyone was the subject of someone or other. Whether for this reason or because, as I tend to think, "macehualli" originally meant "human being," it by no means always had the pejorative flavor just mentioned; used in the plural, as it frequently was, it conveyed much the same as "the people" conveys in English—the ordinary people to be sure, but with the implication that they make up the bulk and norm from which others might be distinguished.[5] Thus Chimalpahin once speaks of the population of a part of China as "the macehualtin there."[6]

The use of the same term for "commoner" and "subject" is an example of the general intermingling in Nahuatl of the terminologies of social status and political role. The role of the macehualli, as understood by Spaniards of the time and by recent scholars, was to deliver tribute in kind and perform services, including heavy tasks such as burden carrying and construction work, for the authorities of calpolli and altepetl, primarily as a function of holding certain calpolli-altepetl land. It now appears that nobles too may have paid tribute in kind to higher authority, but they did not perform strenuous personal labor as a public duty; it was the macehualli as the mainstay of the *coatequitl,* or draft rotary labor, who was symbolized by the carrying frame and tumpline.[7] Whether because of the specific duties of the macehualli, or because of the lack in Spanish of any frequently used neutral term for commoner, or because of their general inclination to use other than the standard Spanish terminology for indigenous social distinctions, the Spaniards borrowed the Nahuatl word (as *macehual*) rather than using a Spanish one, and it became a staple of the Mexican Spanish vocabulary.

Starting with the sixteenth-century Spanish treatise of the jurist Zorita, much has been written about another category in the lower ranks of society, a class of people who did not hold public land or perform public duties, but instead lived on the land of a nobleman or lord and performed duties and services for him.[8] Zorita called the type a *maye* (pl. *mayeque*), considering him serflike, distinct from and lower than the macehualli, and later scholars often enlarged on this view, making the mayeque a basic and separate component of society.[9] Skepticism set in, however, as the rarity of the term in Spanish texts and its near total absence in Nahuatl documents became more apparent.[10] We have since learned that there were in fact great numbers of dependent people on the lands of nobles, in some places even constituting the majority, but that the terminology for them varied, and that rather than being something radically distinct from the macehualtin, they were a type of macehualtin.[11]

In sixteenth-century Tlaxcala, those dependent on a certain noble, lord, or ruler were for the most part called simply the macehualtin of that person (which, the form being possessed, meant "subjects of that person" without any very specific statement on their social characteristics). The same usage is found in Coyoacan around 1550.[12] Other words do appear in these regions, *tlalmaitl* ("land-hand") in Tlaxcala, *temilti* ("one who makes a field for someone") in Coyoacan, but the people to whom they are applied are macehualtin as well.[13] Indeed, in one of only two occurrences of mayeque that I have found in a Nahuatl document (Tetzcoco, 1589), the term is paired with "macehualtin": "yn macehualtzitzintin tomayecauan," "the poor macehualtin our mayeque."[14] In the Cuernavaca basin and the Puebla region, dependents are found referred to simply as -*tech pouhque*, "those who belong to a certain person."[15]

Another word used (as far as is now known, in Tlaxcala only) for special dependents was *teixhuiuh*, "someone's grandchild." To judge by the derivation alone, one would conclude that this was a higher category. Since the principal word for noble, "pilli," originally meant "child" (of an important person), the teixhuiuh might be thought to be the grandchild of such a person, perhaps more distant and subordinate, but still related to the noble members of the house. In fact, formulations can be found tying the two terms together in a suggestive manner.[16] And on one occasion the Tlaxcalan cabildo asserted in so many words that the duties of the teixhuihuan were light, much more so than those of the noblemen's fieldhands (tlalmaitl).[17] Yet for that very reason the cabildo decided to assign them to draft rotary labor for the alte-petl, something from which a nobleman would be exempted. A Spanish source speaks of "macehualtin who are called teixhuihuan."[18] The teixhui-huan of Tlaxcala (and their approximate counterparts in other regions) were

thus apparently transitional between noblemen and commoners, part of the
process whereby some nobles were falling out of the nobility while some
commoners were rising into it.[19]

The difficulty of distinguishing between dependents of noblemen and ordinary commoners, with calpolli land and duties, can be traced in large part
to the difficulty of fitting the *teccalli*, or house of a lord, into the altepetl-
calpolli structure. I will return to this topic below; let me say here that in my
view we are dealing not merely with a problem of interpretation for modern
scholars but with a point of substantive controversy in preconquest times.
A teccalli could become as large as a calpolli subdivision, or in the case of
the holdings of altepetl rulers, as large as a whole calpolli. The individual
dependent held land from the teccalli and did the same kinds of duties for its
lord as the ordinary macehualli did for the calpolli authorities. Considering
that in many instances the chief calpolli authority was the same person as
the head of the teccalli, one can see that the difference between the two
types might be minimal, resting to a large extent on an abstract and controversial definition of residual landownership and political organization. Teccalli and calpolli competed, threatening in principle to swallow each other up.[20]
Where the noble and patrimonial teccalli won out, the majority of the
population might be special dependents, as in Cuauhtinchan and parts of
Huexotzinco;[21] where the ethnic calpolli was predominant, the majority
would be ordinary macehualtin. Since a large teccalli would perforce operate
much like a calpolli, one might not have been able to tell from simple observation which of the two frameworks obtained in a given case. Indeed, the
question might have been in dispute, as it was so frequently through the
sixteenth century.

Once it is seen that the special dependents were considered macehualtin
as well as the independent commoners, that the dependents' status was not
well defined, and that transfer from one status to the other was a frequent
phenomenon, it becomes less necessary and appropriate to rank the two relative to each other. The dependents have usually been considered to stand
lower on the scale, but in the absence of good evidence, such rankings are
generally exercises in weighing the dependents' hypothetical disadvantages,
especially their apparent lack of juridical claim to the land they worked,
against possible advantages, especially their close association with powerful
lords.[22] Early postconquest cadastral records allow some more tangible comparisons. In Oztoticpac (Tetzcoco region) in 1540, the plots of independent
macehualtin were somewhat larger on the average than those of dependents,
and above all showed far greater variation.[23] In the Cuernavaca region too,
the holdings of those directly dependent on the tlatoani varied less than the
holdings of calpolli members.[24] This could be interpreted as a result of the

dependents' inability to inherit, accumulate, and subdivide lands like the cal-polli members, or of the relatively recent division or allocation of teccalli lands compared with calpolli lands, or of the relative newness or transience of the dependent population.

Of the last phenomenon there are several indications. An early Spanish writer asserts that it was general practice for lords to take in people newly arrived from other regions, and specific evidence of newcomers among the dependents is available for Huexotzinco and the Cuernavaca region.[25] In Huexotzinco, the great majority of the population in two outlying regions consisted of dependents of nobles residing in the core region;[26] apparently, then, the Huexotzinca in comparatively recent times had conquered some of their neighbors and converted them from independent calpolli members of other altepetl into dependents of their own leaders. A more subtle indication of transience among the dependents can be seen in the early Cuernavaca-region censuses. The term *tequinanamiqui*, "one who helps with the tribute," is used at times for the dependents of certain lords (teteuctin), some of them relatives and some not. Although the establishments of these lords are not called teccalli, they match the description in many respects. The lord gives each dependent some of his land, and in return the dependent performs certain services for the lord and delivers products to him. The same word and the same practice, however, are found among the ordinary commoners. A commoner might give some of his land to another, most often a younger relative, under exactly the same terms. No doubt, as is documented specifi-cally for a region of Tetzcoco at about the same time, this was in the nature of a temporary arrangement until the younger relative could get established on his own, and it may well be that many of a lord's dependents similarly hoped for something different at a later stage in life.[27]

The different types and levels of dependents of lords whom we have been discussing may or may not have headed a household, and the "tribute-help-ers" often did not; they would, however, be expected at least to reside in their own separate "calli" (in the sense explained in Chapter 3) within the com-plex. At the bottom of the society were those who lacked even that, but lived in the houses of others without fully belonging to the group. In the Cuerna-vaca-region censuses, where they are best described, these people are called -*tlan nenqui*, "one who lives with someone," or -*pal nemi*, "one who lives by means of someone." Mainly young, they were often orphans or from the outside; within the household, they swept up, carried water, and the like. They were to be found in the households of both lords and commoners. Very similar in both provenience and role were the *tlatlacotin* (sing., *tlacotli*), or slaves, who were still to be found in the Cuernavaca area at the time (1530's or 1540's). They too had usually come from a distance as children, though they differed in that merchants had brought them and sold them for a certain quantity of cloth.[28] For the rest, the two types can hardly be distinguished, and it seems appropriate that a source from Tetzcoco mentions them together: "the macehualtin who were tetlan nenque, or the tlatlacotin" (leaving us to guess whether the writer is saying that the two are literally the same thing or that one of them will serve the purpose of his statement as well as the other).[29] In preconquest times, tlatlacotin may have been quite numerous, and several subtypes may have existed. Surely foreign slaves for religious sacrifice were a standard feature of the scene.[30] But by a few years after the conquest, slaves were a minor population element barely distinguished from other menial servants and lower dependents, with whom they had probably had a great deal in common even in preconquest times.

Commoners of the two main kinds so far treated were closely associated with agricultural work.[31] But the crafts and commerce were well developed in preconquest central Mexico, and it is necessary to examine the question of where the practitioners of these activities fell within the noble-commoner scheme. In chronicles speaking of the preconquest period, they appear to have occupied a privileged position above the macehualtin and transitional between the two basic categories, if not indeed more associated with the nobles. We are told that they were exempt from draft labor and even from tribute in agricultural products, giving instead items they made or sold.[32] Merchants (*pochteca*; sing., *pochtecatl*), it is said, at times acquired a position as teuctli or married the daughter of a tlatoani.[33] In the Florentine Codex, the pochteca are seen as a prominent group with their own tight organization and their own subculture.[34] As to the crafts, even nobles are said to have practiced them. One retrospective discussion of the education of noblemen mentions that, in addition to instruction in war, music, oratory, astronomy, and religion, some "were taught the different crafts: featherwork, how feathers and plumes were arranged; also mosaic work, goldsmithery, jewel cutting, and metal polishing; and also painting, woodworking, and various other crafts."[35] Despite such words, it is likely that the nobles going into artisanry were primarily those who did not receive lands or offices.

When we turn to early postconquest sources, including censuses and individual attestations in Nahuatl texts, the picture at first looks quite different. In Huexotzinco, the best recorded situation, over 20 percent of the economically active population had a trade specialty in 1560, but the specialists are listed among the ordinary commoners and the dependents of noblemen. A Spaniard assessing the population at the same time as the indigenous census found less than a fourth as many artisans as are included in the indigenous lists. The merchants, of whom there were far fewer, lived together in certain subdivisions where they predominated but did not make up the total membership; like the artisans, they were distributed among ordinary commoners and dependents.[36] In Tlaxcala too, tradespeople were listed here and there as macehualtin, and some pochteca appeared as dependents of the ruler of one of the four altepetl.[37] In Cuauhtinchan in 1576, we find groups of carpenters, feather-workers, and sandal makers separately congregated on different pieces of land belonging to a tlatoani; apparently they were viewed as his dependents.[38]

In the Nahuatl censuses and lists, and even in Spanish descriptions of contemporary indigenous life, it is often clear that a given activity was carried on because the raw material was available locally: fishing at lakeside, woodcutting in the forest, pottery where there was good clay, mat making where there were reeds, and so on.[39] Under such conditions, though in a sense a certain trade would be a specialty of the people of a given subunit, not all local inhabitants would necessarily engage in it, and few or none might practice it full-time. They would hold and work lands, whether as calpolli members or as dependents, and perform duties as such; then at the proper time, they would produce or procure their objects of trade and take them to sell in markets of the region (generally of the altepetl). Other activities appear in the vicinity of a good market: near where noblemen were congregated, or along a highway.[40] Often involving luxury products or longer-distance trade, enterprise of this type was more likely to lead to full-time specialization. Pochteca often had little or no land and lived entirely from commerce.[41] Something similar may have happened with the finer crafts; some of the artisans located on a lord's lands may have been not dependents of the fieldhand type but "teixhuihuan" or even low-ranking nobles, in either case perhaps related in one way or another to him. Even full-time specialists seem to have called on the principles of ethnic-geographical assembly and subdivision as seen in the calpolli and the teccalli to organize themselves.*

Thus the image projected in Zorita, Ixtlilxochitl, and other writers, of whole organized districts of artisans and merchants, freed from ordinary tribute and services and in many senses impinging on the nobility, may hold true for a certain number of full-time specialists dealing in goods of high value or making very refined products, but a great deal of general production and commerce would have been carried out by people who were at the same time macehualtin and farmers. The trades were an important area intermediate

---

*The two principal words for merchants, "pochtecatl" and "oztomecatl," are both derived from the names of geopolitical units: "inhabitant of Pochtlan" and "inhabitant of Oztoman." See also Berdan 1986.

between noble and commoner, but they did not themselves provide a third category. In many contexts, a person had to be considered either a macehualli or a pilli without any other alternative.[42]

Nobles, Lords, and Rulers

In Nahua society, then, allowing for borderline cases, essentially everyone not a macehualli was a pilli, or noble. The categories applied equally to both genders (although the modifier *cihua-* was almost always added to "pilli" when reference was to a woman, yielding *cihuapilli*, "noblewoman, lady"). A lord (teuctli) or king (tlatoani) was a pilli at the same time, and the plural, pipiltin, referred collectively to nobles of all ranks. As the most general term, one would expect pilli to be the most basic as well, but that is not the case, at least not by origin. As mentioned earlier, pilli originally had the meaning "child," making the status of the person so denominated derivative from that of the parent.[43] Since the word was no longer possessed, it had acquired an independence in usage, but sources can be found asserting that pilli status was still derivative, accorded only to the children of a teuctli or lord.[44] Indeed, it is linguistically plausible that the two categories hardest to relate to a literal meaning, teuctli and macehualli, might have provided the poles of Nahua social ranking. In the strictest view, the mere grandchild of a teuctli would no longer have been a pilli. Although this agrees in a way with one interpretation of how the Tlaxcalan term teixhuiuh got its meaning (see above), such an abrupt dismissal from noble status seems intuitively unrealistic.

To approach closer to a matter on which the sources are radically insufficient, uneven, and contradictory, we must look at both "teuctli" and "pilli" in the framework of the shadowy institution that in the eastern part of the Nahua region often bore the name *teccalli*, literally "lord-house."[45] The view that emerges from material on the Puebla-Tlaxcala area is that neither the teuctli nor the pilli existed separately from the teccalli. Every teuctli was the head of such an establishment, and every pilli was a member of one; aside from some statements to this effect in Spanish writings, the Tlaxcalan cabildo minutes are explicit that this was the assumption. A nobleman who was not a lord held land only by virtue of his membership in the teccalli.[46] Here then, as one scholar has already noted, is the organization by lineage that fails to appear among the macehualtin or in Nahua kinship terminology.[47] That the noble members of the teccalli were related to the teuctli is clear from the evidence,[48] but about the rules of membership and succession practically nothing is known. It can be said, at any rate, that since some teccalli contained as many as forty pipiltin or more,[49] not all pipiltin are likely to have been the children of the current teuctli or his predecessor. Collateral relatives must have been maintained in noble status at least part of the time.[50] Very probably a crucial factor in determining whether or not relatives were considered pipiltin was the rank of their mothers. Nahua descent and inheritance were bilateral. The teuctli was nearly always male, but it may be that in the preconquest era a female sometimes succeeded for lack of an eligible male; after the conquest, there is no doubt that some teteuctin were women.[51] The female line was also used, in certain cases, to reckon descent for purposes of succession.[52] Just as intermarriage among tlatoani families was a normal procedure, and the son whose mother had the highest connections was most often the one to succeed, so there must have been teccalli intermarriage, with the children whose mothers came from important lineages given much consideration whether they inherited the lordship or not. Marriages with relatives of the altepetl's tlatoani would doubtless be most sought after, and the children of such unions most preferred.

But if pipiltin were not all children of a teuctli, it does seem to be literally true that every teuctli was the holder of a specific lordship involving subordinate nobles, dependents, and lands.[53] Above all, each lord had a title, looking essentially no different from the specific title of a tlatoani (see Chapter 2), which like the title of a tlatocayotl adhered not to him as an individual but to him as head of a given teccalli (or as head of a calpolli or calpolli subdivision, as we will see). Hiving off was possible, with a member of the parent teccalli becoming teuctli of a new one that was independent but also allied and possibly lower-ranking or subsidiary. If the new foundation was lacking in people and resources, it might be recognized only as a *pilcalli* ("nobleman-house"), another of the transitional phenomena that were typically found at the edges of Nahua social categories; a few of these appear in an early Tlaxcalan census.[54]

As to the manner of succession of teteuctin, it seems to have varied from direct descent in some situations to emphasis on brother succession in others, always depending on the capacity of the candidates and the difference in their outside connections, with the whole body of nobles of the teccalli making the final choice, at least in cases of doubt.[55] The process would thus have been hardly distinguishable from that of tlatoani succession at a higher level. It has been maintained that the tlatoque named whomever they pleased to lordships to reward allies and meritorious individuals,[56] but this seems to fly in the face of the whole principle of the teccalli as a lineage; to name an outsider head of a given teccalli would surely be as great a transgression (and impossibility) as to name someone tlatoani in an altepetl where he had no kinship ties. What went on, I think, is the kind of actions attributable to the imperial tlatoque of Tenochtitlan, Tetzcoco, and Tlacopan, and earlier the tlatoque of Cholula, when they "named" the tlatoque of other altepetl, which is to say, that they had rights of confirmation and exercised influence on the choice among already eligible candidates, working in favor of their own relatives.[57] It does appear to be true that tlatoque had the power to create new teteuctin, that is, new titles, presumably with associated lands and dependents.*

For the eastern part of the Nahua area, then, something approaching an intelligible picture of lords, nobles, and lordly houses can be discerned. For the Valley of Mexico and the whole western part of the area, things are at least superficially very different, for the word teccalli fails to appear in known Nahuatl documents of that vast subregion even a single time. Nor is it easy to find any full equivalent. In the work of Chimalpahin, which covers Chalco and other parts of the Valley in preconquest and early postconquest times and constitutes by far the most thorough extant treatment by an indigenous writer of the history and sociopolitical organization of a Nahua region, teteuctin are hardly mentioned, and there is no hint of the existence of entities like teccalli.[58] It has been suggested that *tecpan*, "palace," meant the same thing in the west as "teccalli" in the east.[59] The suggestion has merit. Linguistically, the two forms are closely related. "Tecpan" is literally "where a lord is" and means in the first instance a building or precinct, just as "teccalli" uses the metaphor of "house"; indeed, in the west, the form *tecpancalli*, combining both, is frequently found as an equivalent of tecpan.[60] Moreover, usage in the east was not entirely uniform. Often an entity that is recognizably a teccalli is given no label at all in the records. The word tecpan also occurs in the east at times, and one of the best-documented teccalli of Tlaxcala was suggestively named Ayapanco Tecpan.[61]

The largest problem with the identification of the two terms is that the tecpan of the west is primarily restricted, in the sources for that area, to the establishments (relatives, followers, buildings, lands) of altepetl tlatoque. Chimalpahin emphatically recognizes the existence of only one tecpan for each of the five sub-altepetl of Amaquemecan (there having been, it is true, at times two tecpan in the one that according to him had dual tlatoque).[62] Only a few indications of a possible wider use of "tecpan" can be found. Molina, first glossing the term as the establishment of a king, then extends it to that of a great lord. In the records of sixteenth-century Culhuacan, there are tantaliz-

---

*A large question is where in this picture to fit the "judges" we find mentioned (FC, book 8, pp. 42, 54–55; FC, book 10, pp. 15–16, chap. 4; Offner 1983, pp. 132, 137, 243, 250–53, 271; Zorita 1941, pp. 100–4). Note that though "teuctli" is translated as "judge" in FC, it is *senador* in Sahagún 1975, p. 551. Often spoken of in Spanish simply as royal officials, in Nahuatl these functionaries bore titles like "teuctli" and "teuctlatoani." I do believe that in more complex altepetl especially, such figures carried out specialized, more or less bureaucratic-governmental functions, but I think that at the same time they must have been based, at least nominally, in some subunit of the altepetl and must also have been teteuctin with something like lordly establishments in the normal way.

ing hints of the existence of a tecpan in each calpolli/tlaxilacalli, though the implied nature of the entity is quite different from the usual picture of the teccalli of the east, for apparently the tlaxilacalli citizens had some claim on the tecpan's buildings and lands, and public assembly or entertainment was part of its functions.[63] Overall, labeled lordly establishments are beyond comparison rarer in the western than in the eastern sources.

If we proceed to the level of observing actual structures, however, close parallels emerge. The best source for the west, the Cuernavaca-region census records, shows us a number of teteuctin holding substantial lands that they subdivide among relatives and other dependents. These establishments answer well to the description of the eastern teccalli, except that they have no special name and are counted as part of the calpolli structure. The teteuctin pay tribute to the altepetl; usually there is only one teuctli within a calpolli (actually calpolli subdivision; the records recognize two levels of entities as calpolli), and he governs the whole in addition to his group of dependents. His title can be based on the name of the calpolli, as in Molotlan the Molotecatl teuctli (Molotlan-inhabitant Lord).[64] The teteuctin of the Cuernavaca region, then, are exercising the same function (except for the few cases where a second teuctli with fewer dependents is found in the same subdivision) as the teuctlatoque or calpolli rulers of whom Chimalpahin speaks. Though Chimalpahin says nothing of these calpolli heads having extensive lands and dependents as in the Cuernavaca area, there is no reason to think that they did not.

Thus somewhat similar configurations, headed by teteuctin possessed of locally differentiated titles, existed in both the eastern and the western part of the Nahua area. The apparent difference lies in the different relationship of the lordly houses to the calpolli-altepetl structure. In the west, as seen in the records of the Cuernavaca region and as implied negatively by other western accounts, the lords and their holdings are quite fully integrated into that structure. Aside from heading their houses, the lords are at the same time the heads of their calpolli subdivisions in a political sense; their titles are apparently an inalienable attribute of those subdivisions, of which they are officers in the same sense that a tlatoani was an officer of an altepetl. Presumably in the same fashion as an altepetl might outlast its dynasty and refill its rulership when a dynasty died out, so too the calpolli or calpolli subdivision would renew its lord regardless of the continuance of the teuctli line. The holdings of a Cuernavaca-region teuctli appear to be calpolli land, and he and his followers constitute one of several wardlike sets of people and land within his calpolli subdivision. His relationship with his followers is no different in kind from that of commoners with the poorer relatives to whom they give some of their land in return for help with their taxes. In this system, no real line can be drawn between the ordinary commoner and the special dependent; all alike are on land belonging in the final analysis to the calpolli, and all contribute directly or indirectly to calpolli obligations.

In the east, the documents seem to say that the teccalli stood entirely outside the calpolli and even outside the framework of altepetl obligations (though not ultimately beyond ethnic and political allegiance to the altepetl). In the first place, the various teccalli held land as corporations; this is most clearly stated for Tlaxcala, but the principle also probably lies behind assertions that lords and rulers of other altepetl owned the land.[65] In any case, the documents emphatically deny that the dependents held land in any other way than as temporary recipients of lands belonging to the lords, and this even in cases where, as in Cuauhtinchan and Tecali, it appears that the vast majority of commoners were teccalli dependents, and independent calpolli members were a small minority peripheral to the organization of the altepetl. Indeed, we are told that the basic numerical subdivision of Cuauhtinchan was in terms of units called teccalli (though each was headed by a tlatoani, in the fashion of tlayacatl or sub-altepetl elsewhere).[66] If this is really true, the teccalli had virtually replaced the calpolli as the basic unit of sociopolitical organization. The second essential aspect of the extra-calpolli stance of the eastern teccalli is a relatively sharp distinction between plebeian teccalli dependents and calpolli members. Though the Tlaxcalan cabildo minutes do not use special terminology for the two in most cases, they insist on the difference between the "macehualtin of the altepetl" and those of the lords.[67] From Huexotzinco, we have an affirmation that calpolli members had land, as opposed to the dependents of lords, who did not.[68]

Nevertheless, the picture of the eastern teccalli as being divorced from the calpolli and even to an extent from the altepetl is not the entire truth of the matter. The Tlaxcalan records repeatedly document the proposition that lords and nobles paid tribute to the altepetl as a matter of course.[69] This facet of the system, deliberately obscured in the representations the lords made to Spanish authorities, brings the eastern teccalli in one basic respect very close to the manner of operation of western teteuctin as seen in the example of the Cuernavaca region.* Even if they did not use the calpolli mechanism, the

---

*The propaganda of the lords, at times abetted by Franciscan friars, led to assertions, which have often been taken at face value by modern scholars, that teteuctin and pipiltin gave no tribute either in kind or in service (see, for example, Zorita 1941, p. 144). I have seen only one statement by a Spaniard showing a full comprehension of the truth of the matter (though I have little doubt that many more grasped it). In 1564, responding to complaints by friars about "principales" and governors being counted as tributaries and their dependents being made responsible for tribute, Dr. Vasco de Puga wrote that the nobles had always been reckoned as tributaries, paying more than commoners (he gave the specific examples of Xochimilco and Tlaxcala), and that the reason the dependents did not pay tribute directly was that they were relieved of the burden by their lord's payments. (Paso y Troncoso 1939–42, 10: 34.) Despite this

lords were delivering tribute assessed on their lands in the same manner as calpolli members, and their dependents were ultimately functioning as "tribute-helpers" just as in the west (though it remains possibly true that they were normally exempted from draft labor for the altepetl). If we go beyond the level of synthetic accounts, often authored by interested parties, which is where most of the evidence for sharply separated lordly establishments in the east comes from, we find indications that many of the teccalli bore a close relationship to the calpolli after all. In Tlaxcala, the general census of the population in the 1550's ignores the teccalli, putting commoners and nobles into the various altepetl divisions and subdivisions with no distinction between altepetl subjects and teccalli dependents.[70] It is entirely possible that a good number of dependents were omitted from the census, but if the picture the nobles of the cabildo give is true—that most of the commoners of Tlaxcala belonged to a teccalli—then it must be that large numbers of them were included in the general census, counted as members of altepetl subunits.

Moreover, it has been demonstrated that some of the teccalli coincide with altepetl units. Let us return to the previously mentioned example of Ayapanco Tecpan, a teccalli in Tlaxcala's premier altepetl, Ocotelolco, of which don Julián de la Rosa was teuctli in the mid-sixteenth century. The census shows a unit named San Pedro Tecpan, with which we know (from his will) that don Julián was connected; two of San Pedro's subunits, Ayapanco and Tecpan, bear the same names that serve to identify the teccalli. Furthermore, don Julián was styled Tecpanecatl teuctli (Tecpan-inhabitant Lord), so that he, just like the Molotecatl teuctli of the Cuernavaca region, took his title from an altepetl unit. If we imagine that the two subunits Ayapanco and Tecpan constituted the core of don Julián's teccalli, the similarity in structure between Tlaxcala and the Cuernavaca area leaps to the eye. In the Tlaxcalan case, too, the teuctli is head of an altepetl branch that embraces his establishment. Nor is the example an isolated one; elsewhere in Ocotelolco, the Tezcacoacatl teuctli was connected with a subdivision Tezcacoac, the Mixcotecatl with Mixcotlan, and the Tlamaocatl with Tlamaoco, an entity of a higher order, like San Pedro Tecpan.[71] Also in the Huexotzinco census of 1560, many lords and nobles are associated with a calpolli (others are not), and though dependent commoners are distinguished from the commoners of the calpolli, to which they do not seem to belong fully, both are listed together under calpolli headings.[72]

On the other side of the matter, in the west, the multiple (and confused) categories of lands held by rulers, lords, and nobles, such as those described

basic insight, Puga was dead wrong in his belief that tribute was paid per capita rather than according to property (p. 35).

by Ixtlilxochitl for preconquest Tetzcoco, are distinguished and separated from calpolli lands in various ways, and the altepetl duties of lords and nobles are minimized. Though in Ixtlilxochitl, noblemen's lands appear to pertain primarily to offices or individuals, inheritance is also emphasized, and most of what Ixtlilxochitl says on this subject can be interpreted in the framework of corporate landholding by lineages (i.e., entities no different from eastern teccalli).[73] In the Cuernavaca region, too, one can find the inherited lands of nobles distinguished from calpolli land in such a way as to make them seem mutually exclusive categories.[74] In a word, there are strong hints to support the claim that noblemen's holdings were a world in themselves, detached from the calpolli-altepetl, in the west as well as the east.

Ultimately, though it appears undeniable that the teccalli acquired a sharper profile in the eastern part of the Nahua region than in the western, it would be wrong to take the version presented by the eastern lords at face value. In many cases (possibly all, if we knew the full truth), the lordly establishments of the east prove to be as integrated into the calpolli and altepetl framework as their western counterparts, and we have some evidence of a similar mentality among lords in both areas. The two types of description—that, for example, of Chimalpahin for the west, of the Cuauhtinchan documents for the east—could be two ways of looking at almost exactly the same thing, the western view emphasizing ethnicity, with the lords seen primarily as officers and leaders of the ethnic group, the eastern view emphasizing noble lineages, with the broader ethnic group relegated to the background and imagined as dependent on the lineages (see Fig. 4.1). Although ethnic entities and noble lineages both operated along the general Nahua lines of

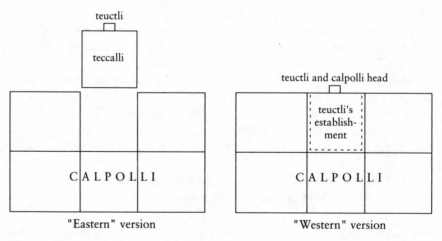

Fig. 4.1. Two standard views of the position of lords in relation to the calpolli.

subdivision into separate independent corporations, real tension did exist between the two principles of organization, leading to different configurations in different situations. Yet both would have been in evidence in almost any given situation, and regional differentiation in the actual distribution of structures may have been less striking than the opposing interpretations that different parties and interests would have put on the same situation (this being one facet of the ongoing conflicts reported in all the annals of the preconquest period).

If the concept "teuctli" is an inextricable mixture of social rank and political office, so is "tlatoani," in both respects the highest position in the Nahua world. Above I have used some analogies from tlatoani selection procedures and intermarriage patterns to illuminate the teccalli, but the major thrust of the analogy is in the other direction. In a sense nothing more needs to be said about a tlatoani than that he was a large-scale teuctli at the altepetl level. His title was at once that of the rulership (tlatocayotl) of the entire altepetl and that of his specific establishment, just as the titles of the teteuctin were often ambiguously associated with a calpolli or calpolli subdivision as well as with their teccalli. Tlatoani titles in fact included the element "teuctli"; the tlatoque of the imperial altepetl of Tenochtitlan, Tetzcoco, and Tlacopan were the Colhuateuctli, Chichimecateuctli, and Tepanecateuctli, respectively.[75] A tlatoani was at the same time a teuctli and a pilli. His establishment, tecpan or teccalli, was like a teuctli's except larger.[76] As seen in Chapter 2, the tlatoani, just like the teteuctin, had his base in a specific subdivision of the altepetl. There, as with them, his palace and core holdings would be located, although he would also, to a greater extent than other lords, have lands and dependents scattered across the entire altepetl.[77] Just as officially the tlatoani's tecpan was the focal point of altepetl tribute, socially it was the focal point of the lords and nobles of the altepetl, who paid court there and acquired both unity and individual prestige through extensive kinship ties to the tlatoani (in addition to jockeying for position with each other and even with the tlatoani in ways that we can hardly discern).

Although noble status was by and large inherited, it could (as already mentioned) sometimes be achieved, especially by military activity, or so the posterior chronicles tell us. A special term existed for the noble through merit, *quauhpilli*, literally "eagle-noble," eagle referring to martial exploits. In the usage of Chimalpahin, at least, the quauhpilli was not very highly regarded, and eyebrows rose whenever such a new nobleman or even one of his descendants attained high position. At the same time, a quauhpilli was an excellent candidate for the similarly named post of *quauhtlatoani*, or interim ruler of an altepetl, since he did not belong to a dynasty and represented little threat as far as long-term succession was concerned. Indeed, in one place

Chimalpahin seems to imply that the acquisition of quauhpilli status did not make a noble of one's children. On the other hand, he gives an example of a quauhpilli of Amaquemecan who actually became tlatoani and founded a dynasty.[78] The *yaotequihuacacalli*, "houses of leaders in war," of which a certain number are found in early postconquest Tlaxcala and Huexotzinco, may have been establishments (small compared with a teccalli) headed by quauhpipiltin.[79]

General Changes in the Postconquest Era

All the above is intended primarily to depict the system of social ranking as it existed before the Spaniards arrived. But since the best sources for this purpose are postconquest Nahuatl documents, mainly of a mundane nature, dating from the late 1530's to the early seventeenth century, the analysis also applies to the first generations after the conquest. Accordingly, rather than construct a whole new picture for the postconquest period, I will presume an overall identity and deal with changes as they occurred. Although it is theoretically possible that the types of categorization seen in postconquest documents were already changed from before the conquest, there are several good reasons for thinking that this was not the case.

First, we have seen in discussing political and familial organization that there the deeper organizing concepts of society long remained unchanged, and that especially when writing in their own language for other speakers of it, the Nahuas continued to use their own categories in an unadulterated form.

Second, the largest and most comprehensive source for understanding social differentiation, the collection of Cuernavaca-region censuses, from which alone virtually the entire system emerges, constitutes the earliest known major Nahuatl documentary corpus. A large portion of the population was not yet even baptized, and soon-to-be-banned practices like polygamy and slavery were unabashedly recorded. Parts of the census were apparently written as little as fifteen years after the end of the military phase of the conquest, in an area less directly affected by the first Spanish impact than the Valley of Mexico was.

Third, broadly congruent findings arise from sources originating in different decades and in regional societies separated by considerable distances or by mutual hostilities, without any evidence of the kind of item-by-item parallels with Spanish counterparts that one would expect if direct outside influence were at work. Prior existence of the classifications can be deduced by the principle used in historical linguistics that phenomena shared by scattered groups and distinct from those seen elsewhere are taken as characteristic of a common predecessor.

Finally, the mundane Nahuatl documents describing things then current can be combined readily with the historical literature written at the same time, in both Spanish and Nahuatl, and speaking directly of the preconquest period. In many essentials the two types are in complete agreement, and the differences point not to temporal change so much as to tendencies in the historical writings such as posterior idealization (giving a false impression of very rigid distinctions between categories and subcategories), partisan distortion (such as magnifying the power of lords and minimizing their duties), and giving specific regional variants as generally valid (as Zorita does in part).

In one sense, preconquest social categorization can be said to have survived into the early seventeenth century intact, since some people alive at that time, the writers Chimalpahin and Tezozomoc foremost among them, still used and understood the entire vocabulary. On the other hand, changes in actual conditions had the consequence, from an early time, that certain social groupings ceased to exist or certain distinctions ceased to be made. The warfare endemic in preconquest central Mexico had played a large role in social dynamics. Through war, new nobles were created, born noblemen acquired eligibility to occupy lordships and rulerships, prospective heirs to lordships were eliminated in their prime, slaves were captured, and new dependents were conquered. With the effective end of warfare, the category quauhpilli, which as we just saw described the nobleman through merit rather than birth, seems to have fallen quickly into disuse. No attestation of the term has yet been found outside historical writings. Next to disappear were the slavelike tlatlacotin. In the absence of battles, one source of supply was gone. Just as importantly, or even more so, though the Spaniards had taken slaves themselves in the course of conquest, they saw by the 1540's that Indian slavery's time of usefulness to them had passed and abolished it among sedentary peoples, relegating it to the nonsedentary fringes.[80] By the 1550's, hardly any indigenous central Mexicans were held as slaves either by Spaniards or by Indians. In the early Cuernavaca-region censuses, tlatlacotin, though not a large proportion of the population, are a persistent, standard feature, but in the Tlaxcalan census of the 1550's, only three are listed in a population of over 30,000 households.[81] After that time, Indian slaves were a negligible factor in indigenous society. However, to the extent that, as explained above, tlatlacotin were assimilated to other lesser dependents and servants, their disappearance implied no major social rearrangement.

A deeper-going change occurring across the sixteenth century was the progressive movement in the direction of erasing any distinction between ordinary commoners and the special dependents of rulers and lords, with large implications for the lordly establishments. Two complementary forces lay behind the trend: from the outside, the Spanish pressure, especially as the effects

of vast population decline made themselves felt, to maximize tribute income
and reduce exemptions;[82] from the inside, repeated and determined efforts by
the dependents themselves to make good their right to the lands they worked
and deny special obligations to the lords, or failing that, simply to go elsewhere. To first appearances, the end result, by sometime in the seventeenth
century, was in effect the extinction of the status of special dependent and the
loss of any terminology such as tlalmaitl or maye, with the result that all
macehualtin were now equally calpolli members on altepetl land as such, and
hence obliged to pay altepetl tribute directly and perform public labor. The
development did not take place quickly, however, or in a linear fashion, and
it is, in fact, extraordinarily difficult for one to discern, through the mislead-
ing verbiage surrounding the issue and the paucity of well-established facts,
just what really happened.

If we listen to Zorita, we must conclude that the lords had lost virtually
all their dependents by 1560 or before.[83] Yet the 1560 census of Huexotzinco
shows a majority of dependents over full calpolli members and is indeed the
most solid extant evidence for the prevalence of dependent status at any time
period. What Zorita says is greatly weakened by the fact that he wrote primarily in defense of a campaign by high nobles aimed at cementing their
claims to lands, dependents, and emoluments at the expense of the nascent
Spanish-style town governments (a campaign supported by some friars and
Spanish administrators who felt that dealing with fewer authorities was simpler or more efficient).[84] As I have implied above, I by no means believe all of
the nobles' claims about their rights and privileges in preconquest times. We
should not fall into the same trap as with drinking, where from having too
readily accepted idealized and self-serving posterior statements that hardly
anyone drank pulque before the conquest, we wrongly deduced an explosion
of alcoholism after the Spaniards arrived.[85] It is conceivable that nobles actually increased their hold on commoners in the immediate postconquest years.
A Spanish witness claimed in the 1560's that with the support of the Franciscans a local tlatoani was taking lands owned by macehualtin and turning the
owners into his tenants and dependents.[86] Although it is possible that we will
never know the true state of things in the time before and immediately after
the conquest, I myself think that the whole question of the status of commoners relative to lords must have already been in flux and the focus of serious
contention, and that both sides tried to use changed postconquest conditions
to their own advantage.

In the mid-sixteenth century and even later, some lords, especially altepetl
tlatoque, won impressive legal victories in the Spanish courts confirming their
exclusive rights to lands and dependents.[87] A favorable formal judgment
might be of little use, however, if the dependents refused to comply with it.

In the earliest known Nahuatl lists of a lord's holdings, those written ca. 1550 concerning don Juan de Guzmán, tlatoani and governor of Coyoacan, don Juan had already "given" lands to several sets of his dependents, probably under pressure. In Tlaxcala in 1566, the holdings of the by now familiar teuctli don Julián de la Rosa were also under attack, and the obedience of his retainers seems to have been in doubt.[88] Known lists of dependents for the later sixteenth century show a precipitous decline.[89] In Tetzcoco in 1589, a noble widow complained that her late husband's scattered lands could no longer be cultivated because none of the dependents who worked them were left; all had died.[90]

The great epidemics of the years around 1580 are the first thing to come to mind in connection with the diminution, probably rightly so. But the epidemics did not absolutely wipe out the macehualtin in general. If the dependents in preconquest times were often, as I have suggested, transients, marginal people fleeing from overcrowded situations, then the maintenance of the dependent population would require frequent renewal. Population loss must have meant less pressure on the land and hence less need for anyone to join a lord's establishment, perhaps drying up the supply; nor could the conquests of neighbors add to the numbers of dependents as in preconquest times.

Possibly the greatest difference of all in the postconquest world was that where people in these straits would once have entered the establishments of indigenous lords, they now increasingly became dependent upon Spaniards for their livelihood and protection. From their experience in the Antilles, the Spaniards knew of the status of special dependents in indigenous societies (calling them at first *naborías*, a word brought from the islands), and they consciously sought to appropriate Indians who were already in that relationship or to recruit or commandeer others in the same capacity, using them in positions requiring the skill or responsibility that came only with permanent employ. From the indigenous point of view, the fact that Spanish employers had more money than Nahua lords would hardly have gone unremarked.[91] With each generation, the new group of Indians-among-Spaniards grew in size and importance, and soon Spanish employ far outweighed the estates of indigenous lords as a safety valve for Nahua society.[92]

Later censuses of Indians no longer recognize a distinction between dependents and nondependents; this is true not only of Spanish summaries but of full local population counts and tribute lists naming every individual (though these become scarcer as time progresses).[93] Still, the lack of a distinction in bare lists and counts is not decisive evidence; the same sources also gradually drop the distinction between commoners and nobles, even though, as we will see, that distinction continued to be a basic feature of indigenous society. It is not impossible to find indications that the lord-dependent struc-

ture retained its importance in the scheme of things far into the colonial period, at least in some places. In Cuauhtinchan, as late as 1705, a local priest
writing in complaint about an administrative action described the situation
as follows: "many caciques" owned land that they allowed the macehualtin
as *terrazgueros* ("dependent renters, serfs") to use in return for a payment in
acknowledgment of their status (*reconocimiento*); the priest relied on the caciques to get people to fulfill their ecclesiastical duties and regarded the bulk
of the local municipal officers simply as personnel whom the caciques named
and supplied.[94] This highly partisan description cannot be taken literally, but
it does reveal the persistence of all the elements existing in that region in the
first postconquest generations (including the disputes, for the macehualtin
were now claiming that all land within the town's core territory belonged to
them and not to the caciques). Perhaps the lordly house with dependents
remained stronger in the eastern region, where its position had been best
defined from the beginning.

In the west (although with further investigation the same is likely to hold
true for the east as well), a new category began to emerge in the seventeenth
century that may have replaced the earlier terms for dependents to some extent. It is only a hint, but in a few instances references occur in Nahuatl texts
to the *gañán* of a high-ranking indigenous person (in the cases so far, a governor).[95] A Spanish loanword, the term was a partial successor in Mexican
Spanish to "naboría," which was disappearing by the end of the sixteenth
century. In the seventeenth and eighteenth centuries, "gañán" was used to
designate resident Indian workers on Spanish rural estates, subordinate to
more Hispanic foremen and specialists but still holding permanent and often
responsible positions.[96] Though paid in money and supplies, the gañanes were
reminiscent of preconquest dependents in that they had the use of some land
and a house on the owner's estate and often escaped direct altepetl tribute
and labor obligations. To what extent the gañanes in indigenous employ resembled those working for Spaniards, to what extent they were simply mayeque renamed, is not known, but in view of the general if partial Hispanization of Indian noblemen's enterprises, Spanish ways could be expected to
have had at least some impact. On the other hand, there can be little doubt
that indigenous relationships between lord and dependent had much to do
with the original definition of the gañán's role.

By around 1600, "macehualli" was, even more than earlier, the primary
word applied to the bulk of the indigenous population; its competitors and
modifiers had largely dropped out of sight. Perhaps for this reason, by the
early seventeenth century, the word was being used in the plural as a designation for indigenous people regardless of rank, as opposed to Spaniards,
blacks, or those of mixed descent. "Macehualli" thereby returned in a way in

the direction of what (as noted above) I take to be its basic meaning—"human being, person." Although in general all of the ethnic terms used by Spaniards in the Indies quickly became loanwords in Nahuatl, *indio*, "Indian," was a large exception.[97] No more than a couple of examples have so far been found in the voluminous Nahuatl texts of the sixteenth century, and even they seem to involve, in one case, non-Nahua Indians, and, in the other, direct translation of an entire Spanish document into Nahuatl.[98] For that matter, "indio" did not become part of the normal Nahuatl vocabulary in the seventeenth and eighteenth centuries either.[99] As the point of reference and overwhelming majority, especially within the confines of the Nahua world, indigenous people generally needed and received no specific ethnic label as individuals (in Spanish documents, it is the opposite: Spaniards are usually left unlabeled, while people of other ethnicities and especially "Indians" rarely escape an epithet). When it came to collectivities, the writers of Nahuatl documents from the sixteenth century forward, when speaking of themselves or rivals, emphasized the narrow ethnicity of the local altepetl and calpolli-tlaxilacalli rather than broader ethnic categories. They tended to do so even when the contrast between indigenous and Spanish was specifically at issue, as in sixteenth-century Tlaxcalan statements trying to limit Spanish residence in the area, or the order of a noblewoman of Culhuacan in 1577 that some chinampas be sold not to Spaniards but to "inhabitants of the altepetl here" (*nican altepehuaque*).[100]

At times, however, there was no avoiding speaking of indigenous people more broadly. The main expression used from the 1550's until the end of the sixteenth century was *nican titlaca*, "we people here," sometimes expanded to phrases such as *nican titlaca ipan Nueva España*, "we people here in New Spain."[101] By the early decades of the seventeenth century, the Nahuas were beginning to abandon "nican titlaca" in favor of *timacehualtin*, "we macehualtin" (also sometimes in the third person) when speaking of groups whom Spaniards would call "Indians." Usage is best demonstrated in the work of Chimalpahin, apparently mainly written down around 1600 to 1625.[102] In speaking of the preconquest period and most of the sixteenth century, Chimalpahin consistently uses "macehualli" to mean commoner as opposed to noble, and "nican titlaca" for indigenous people as opposed to Spaniards, in both cases apparently mainly following what he found written in earlier texts. With the year 1595 (though the passage may have been composed somewhat later), "timacehualtin" appears in contrast to Spaniards, and this usage becomes standard in discussions of later years up to the point where the annals break off, though a transitional "nican titlaca timacehualtin," pairing the new phrase and the old, continues to be seen on occasion.[103] The new term includes high-ranking people, as can be seen from its use for groups going in religious processions, and it could also refer to non-Nahuas (Mixteca migrants in Mexico City).[104] If there is any doubt about the referential meaning, Chimalpahin resolves it with the passage (unparalleled in his writing) "macuiltin timacehualtin indios," "five of us macehualtin, Indians."[105]

In general, it is fair to say that "macehualtin" came to dominance as a successor of "nican tlaca," but the meaning may have been there almost from the beginning, and certainly it had been in gestation for a considerable time. In a set of annals of Tenochtitlan in the 1560's, apparently written contemporaneously with events and surely not later than about 1570, two entries for 1566 have "timacehualtin" unmistakably in the ethnic sense, exactly as it was to be used later.[106]

Although the two words macehualtin (in the broader sense) and indios designated the same set of people, their connotations and manner of use were quite different. The collective macehualtin was more neutral, and even after it had become established, it was much less frequent in Nahuatl than its counterpart in Spanish. It also continued to have its older meanings. Even in dealing with his own time, Chimalpahin contrasts teteuctin (here meaning noblemen in town government) with macehualtin, and when he speaks of macehualtin doing tribute labor, he unambiguously means commoners; he also uses the traditional "macehualtzitzintin," "poor commoners."[107] The two senses remained close to each other, and at times it is not entirely clear whether indigenous people or commoners (who would also be indigenous) is Chimalpahin's intention.[108]

The new meaning was not restricted to a single Nahuatl speaker located in Mexico City. Since the term, as I say, was not constantly on people's lips, and the types of sources handed down to us have little occasion to use it, evidence is not extensive. But in a text of 1611 from as far away as the Guadalajara region, outside central Mexico as construed here, "macehualli" borders on the sense "indigenous person," and a contemporary Spanish translation renders it as *natural*, "native," and as *indio*.[109] A set of Nahuatl annals from Puebla, composed for the most part in the late seventeenth century, repeatedly shows the broader meaning of macehualli, in explicit contrast to Spaniards and specifically including indigenous nobles and municipal officers. The word is now always in the third person, the "we" having been dropped, and "macehualtzitzintin," earlier used to indicate condescension or compassion, had apparently been repeated so much as to lose its force, becoming the standard form, for this writer at least.[110] As more late annals (the form by its nature most likely to produce attestations) become available and receive close study, it should grow increasingly clear that "macehualli" was the general Nahuatl approximation of "Indian" in the seventeenth and eighteenth centuries.[111]

Like the terms for commoners, those for nobles were undergoing change and loss. As seen in Chapter 2, in the course of the sixteenth century, "tlatoani" came to be used for a governor as well as a dynastic ruler, and the plural "tlatoque" was applied to municipal officers en masse. By about the mid-seventeenth century, the whole traditional terminology of nobility could be said to have fallen into relative disuse. The specific titles of rulerships and lordships are virtually not seen. When "pilli" or "teuctli" appears referring to groups, which is no longer frequent in most areas, they designate office-holders only. "Teuctli" in particular hardly seems to have been retained in the vocabulary of many. The terms for noble status (and macehualli in the stricter sense as well) are found applied to individuals only on the occasion of election disputes in which each faction was anxious to claim high rank for its candidate and brand the opposing candidate a commoner.[112] This state of things represents a marked change from the late sixteenth century and the first decade or two of the seventeenth. As late as the 1580's and 1590's, Tetzcocan documents routinely identified each noble as a pilli or a cihuapilli.[113] Chimalpahin and Tezozomoc, writing from the late sixteenth into the early seventeenth century, were still concerned to label each person, even among their contemporaries, as pilli or macehualli, and had the entire noble terminology at their fingertips.

As with political organization and kinship, so with social rank the middle part of the seventeenth century proves to be a watershed in the evolution of vocabulary and concepts. Are we to conclude, then, as not a few have in the past, that indigenous society by the later colonial period was compressed and homogenized into a single quite undifferentiated rank?[114] The loss of certain overt distinctions is undeniable, and the social range appears to have become progressively less wide, yet the overall conclusion does not follow, especially in its more extreme form, with the implication that a real difference between the mass of Indians and an upper group approximating the nobility of earlier times no longer existed. The self-serving complaints of nobles that they were no longer any different from the commoners, and above all the constant unfounded charges of election factions that their opponents were macehualtin, have at times been too readily believed.[115] At the same time that some distinctions faded, others made their appearance, and some important differences continued even in the absence of clear labeling.

The Evolution of Naming Patterns

Names not only point out specific people, they are capable of making numerous distinctions, potentially covering gender, age, descent, rank, ethnic-regional affiliation, and other matters. The naming system that gradually grew up over several generations after the conquest went far toward replacing traditional social categories.

Not nearly enough is understood about the use of personal names in pre-conquest times. A complex system of hidden, successive, or alternate names for the same person may have existed, at least at certain times and places and for people of high rank.[116] According to the best present understanding, however, at the time of the Spanish conquest the great majority of Nahuas bore only a single personal name throughout their adult lives, except that with lords and rulers the title of office acted almost like a second appellation.[117] In keeping with Nahua kinship principles, nothing about the naming indicated "family," although in certain royal dynasties the same names were used in succeeding generations, at intervals, thus associating a set of names with a specific dynasty and rulership.[118] Apart from that, so far as we know now, naming (among males at least) did not vary greatly with social rank.

In the Cuernavaca-region censuses, the largest available repository of personal names in the preconquest period, the same name types seem to prevail among wealthy and poor, more and less noble. Nearly all are immediately intelligible as normal Nahuatl words (though sometimes apocopated and/or with a reverential added). Some are calendrical, such as Ome Acatl, Two Reed, referring to the time when the person was born; many of the signs being animals, this practice frequently gave rise to animal names. Some refer to prowess in war, some to physical or emotional characteristics, and some are rather lyrical metaphors; others indicate the origin of the person or his parents outside the local community. Very common are mock-derisive nicknames (used as the principal name), pointing out the uselessness, insignificance, or annoying habits of the bearer, an example of the fine sense of humor displayed also in Nahuatl aphorisms.[119]

Irreverence knew no bounds. The tlatoani of Ocotelolco, greatest of Tlaxcala's kings when the Spaniards arrived, bore the (later dynastic) name Maxixcatzin, One Who Urinates, which must, as often with the Nahuas, have originated from noticeable behavior in early childhood. A little later, the Mexica dubbed don Luis de Santa María, governor of Tenochtitlan in the 1560's, Nanacacipactli, Mushroom Alligator, because of his alleged meekness in accepting new tribute obligations.* Possibly everyone originally had a calendrical name, which was ordinarily, or at least often, displaced by another

---

*I am not sure whether the nickname alludes to the hallucinogenic qualities of mushrooms or to their insubstantiality (as if to say "paper tiger"). Chimalpahin thinks the Mexica gave don Luis the whole name and uses it seriously, but the governor seems to have borne Cipactli (Alligator, a calendrical name) from birth (CA, p. 75; CH, 2: 19). The son of one of the great tlatoque of Amaquemecan in 1540 was named Pablo Moquatlahuitec (He Hit His Head Against Something; CH, 2: 12). The tlatoani of the Amaquemecan tlayacatl Tequanipan in 1575 was don Pablo de Santa María Cuitlaquimichtzin (Dung Mouse; CH, 2: 26).

more descriptive term at some point later in life.[120] Whatever the nature of the name, it does not appear that people remained aware of the literal meaning for very long; the retention of the originally scurrilous Maxixcatzin alone shows that. Tables 4.2 and 4.3 give some examples of each of the types mentioned; similar and even identical names are found all over central Mexico.

If there seems to have been relatively little distinction by rank, there was a good deal by gender. All of the above kinds of names in early Nahuatl mundane texts are applied overwhelmingly to males. Of the colorful words and phrases in Table 4.3, only two designate females, and whereas examples for males could be multiplied readily from the same source, ones for females could not. In the most copious early Nahuatl sources, the great majority of women and girls are called by the order of their birth, carrying the names Teyacapan (or Tiacapan), Eldest; Tlaco, Middle; Teiuc, Younger; Xoco, Youngest; or Mocel, Only.[121] This manner of naming is gender-specific; it was not normally used for males. It also involves more rank differentiation than is seen in masculine naming. Although the ordinal names occur also with high-ranking women in the records of both the early Cuernavaca region and Culhuacan later in the sixteenth century, there are exceptions, quite numerous in the Cuernavaca documents, in which females have more descriptive names, and these are likely to involve women of demonstrably high rank (as with doña Ana Cihuanenequi in Table 4.3).[122] In annals of preconquest times, the women mentioned are mainly wives and relatives of rulers and often possess names that are poetic, calendrical, or otherwise nonordinal.[123] The same tendency can be seen in some mundane sources too; thus the wife of the often-mentioned Tlaxcalan teuctli don Julián de la Rosa was named María Cozcapetlatzin, Jeweled Mat.[124]

It was baptism that started the process of change in the indigenous naming system. Each newly baptized person received a Christian and hence Spanish name, which in the beginning must have been chosen by the friar or priest carrying out the ceremony. From the 1520's into the 1540's, essentially the entire indigenous population of central Mexico received baptism, so that well before 1550 everyone had a Spanish name, and the new-style appellations, as well as can be judged from the sources at our disposal, were soon in use in everyday speech (though adjusted to Nahuatl pronunciation).[125] Mainly the names chosen were common among the Spaniards of the time, such as Juan, Pedro, Antonio, and Miguel, or Ana, María, Juana, and Magdalena. But others, like Tomás, Pablo, and Ambrosio, though well known as saints' names, were rare or unheard of among Spaniards of the sixteenth century. Acquisition of the new did not, however, mean immediate displacement of the old. Perhaps because the new repertory was less varied, at least for males, perhaps because of a felt need for continuity, an indigenous name was retained in

TABLE 4.2
Personal Names, Cuernavaca Region, ca. 1535–45

Poetic Metaphors		Sardonic Nicknames	
Quetzalcoatl	Feathered Serpent (preconquest god)	Andrés Chilcanauh	Narrow Chile
		Gabriel Tomiquia	The Death of Us
Pedro Xochitzetzeloa	He Sprinkles Flowers	Antón Acnel	Who in the World's He?
Diego Xochtonal	Flower-fate	Maxtlacozhuehue	Old Yellow Breechclout
Domingo Quetzalhua	Owner of Plumes	Don Pablo Campa huitz	Where Does He Come
Francisco Ecapapalotl	Wind Butterfly		From?
Quauhtemoc	He Descends Like an Eagle (name of tlatoani of Tenochtitlan)	Tochnenemi	He Hops like a Rabbit
		Domingo Ayac icniuh	He Has No Friends
		Cihuacuitlapil	Woman's Tail (a 2-yr-old)
Quauhtliztac	White Eagle	Domingo Tecuetlaça	He Hurls People's Skirts Down
Citlalin	Star		
		Ac mach quichiuh	Who in Heaven's Name Did It (engendered him)?
Martial and Religious			
Teuctlamacazqui	Lordly Priest		
Mihua	Possessor of Arrows	Amo mimich	He's Not a Fish (2-yr-old)
Juan Quachiqui	Scraped-head (warrior)		
Quauhchimal	Eagle Shield	Quenhueltehuantin	How Lucky We Are
Yaotlachinol	The Scorching of War	Quicemitoa	He Says It All
		Canmach	Where in the World?
		Quen opeuh	How Did It Begin? (6th child)
Animals, Things, Calendrical Signs			
Chiucnauh Acatl	Nine Reed	**Nonordinal Female Names**[a]	
Ecacoatl	Whirlwind	Magdalena Teuccihuatl	Lordly Woman
Techalotl	Squirrel	María Tecpane	Palace Inhabitant
Domingo Coyolton	Little Bell	Anican	Not Here
Quauhquimichin	Wood Mouse	Catalina Maçaxochi	Deer Flower
Chichiton	Little Dog	Magdalena Ilamaton	Little Old Woman (5-yr-old)
Xopil	Toe		
Tecolotl	Owl	Magdalena Necahual	Abandoned One
Maçatoch	Deer-rabbit (the symbols of bestiality)	Doña María Tonallaxochiatl	Flowery Water of Summer

SOURCES: AZ; MNAH AH, CAN 549–51.
[a] Most females in preconquest and early postconquest times were named by order of birth, "Oldest," "Middle," etc.

addition to the Christian one. In the Cuernavaca region this was often called the *macehualtocaitl,* "macehualli name," another indication of how near "macehualli" was to being a general designation for all Nahuas from the very beginning.[126] A baptized adult would retain the name he or she already had; infants received a second name in the normal indigenous fashion. In the case of calendrical names, which consisted of a number and a sign, the number was usually deleted, so that Martín Nahui Tochtli (Four Rabbit) would become just Martín Tochtli. To Spaniards, the second element would appear to be a surname, and though the Nahuas doubtless did not feel it as such, and

TABLE 4.3
Personal Names, Culhuacan, ca. 1580

Poetic Metaphors		Sardonic Nicknames	
Diego Maçaihuitl	Deer Down	Juan Quenitoloctzin	What's-His-Name
Pedro Coçamalocatl	Rainbow Inhabitant	Juan Ilcahualoc	He Was Forgotten
Juana Xoxopanxoco	Fruit of Spring		(when they gave out intelligence, etc.?)
Animals and Calendrical Signs		Antón Tepotzitoloc	One Who Is Talked
Miguel Quechol	Quechol (species of tropical bird)	Pedro Huelyehuatl	About Behind His Back That's the Very One
Melchor Quauhtli	Eagle	Juan Çaoya	He Just Left (i.e., without
Pedro Chapol	Grasshopper		saying goodbye, etc.)
Francisco Ayotoch	Armadillo	Juan Otlicahuetztoc	He Lies Fallen on the
Antón Mimich	Fish		Road (probably drunk)
Pedro Olin	Movement	Doña Ana Cihuanenequi	She Imagines Herself a Woman
Martial		Miguel Nacazitztoc	He Lies Looking Sideways
Juan Yaomitl	War Arrow		(is in love, distracted?)
Francisco Chimalquauh	Shield Eagle	Melchor Tleçannen	What's the Use?
Mateo Yaoquizqui	Warrior	Gerónimo Tlaxcalcecec	Cold Tortilla
Miguel Yaochoca	He Makes War Cries	Juan Atonemac	Not Our Inheritance (he's not ours)
		Antonio Tlemachica	What in the World For?
Titles		**Other Descriptive Names**	
Domingo Tlacateuctli	People-lord	Mateo Opan	On the Road (name of a
Pedro Tlacochteuctli	Dart-lord		trader and horse-
Juan Colhuateuctli	Colhua Lord (lord of people of Culhuacan)		owner)
		Juan Tzapa	Dwarf
		Pedro Achane	Homeless One
Altepetl and Calpolli		Pedro Nentlamati	He's Pining Away
Francisco Huitziltecatl	Inhabitant of Huitzillan	Francisco Tlamaceuhqui	Penitent
Antón Atzaqualcatl	Inhabitant of Atzaqualco		
Juan Tocuiltecatl	Inhabitant of Tocuillan		

SOURCE: TC.

did not normally hand it on to members of the succeeding generation, it increasingly came to function as a kind of surname in a system in which a two-element appellation was becoming, although not universal, at least a norm (see Tables 4.2 and 4.3 for some typical examples of this type).

Such names did not occupy the field alone for very long. By 1550 and in individual cases much earlier, Nahuas were acquiring second names which, if not always standard Spanish surnames, were not indigenous either. The main model was apparently a type of name borne by some of the mendicant friars who did most of the baptizing. While many mendicants retained the surnames they were born with, some assumed religious surnames, commonly a saint's name; Cristóbal de Benavides would become fray Cristóbal de San Pedro. In Spain in the late fifteenth century, many newly converted Jews had been named in the same fashion, allowing one to identify them even some generations later by their surnames (though possibly a small minority of Old Christian Spaniards also bore such surnames). As the ecclesiastics embarked upon mass production of surnames, the "de San . . ." formula quickly became the predominant one, so much so that "de San" became an annoying redundancy and was dropped, whether first by the Spaniards or by the Nahuas I am not sure. Thus a person named Juan de San Martín at birth would ordinarily be called just Juan Martín, though he might retain the fuller version on occasions demanding greater formality.[127] By the end of the sixteenth century, this type of appellation, consisting to all appearances of two Spanish first names, was becoming the norm for ordinary Nahuas (and Indians all over Mexico), and it was to retain that flavor until independence, despite many further complications of the system.

With females the end result was the same; Bárbara Agustina, Leonor Magdalena, and the like were archetypal for Nahua women across the entire colonial period. It is not certain, however, that the result was achieved by the same means. A few noblewomen had names incorporating "de Santa" before the second element, but I have yet to find an example of alternation between the two forms as occurs with males, and in some instances the second element does not refer to a saint, as with the popular "María Salomé." In any case, the second element is always a feminine name, just as with males it is masculine.[128]

The tradition of one-element appellations did not die out entirely. As the new names became more familiar, some people used only the single Christian name. In the Tetzcocan region in the 1580's, the heroine of the story told in Chapter 3 (who gave a feast and negotiated the grant of a house site for her family) was called simply Ana, and her husband and son were both just Juan. A propertied woman living in Azcapotzalco in 1695 was given only the name Angelina in her testament.[129] People who in everyday life went without a surname seem sometimes to have drawn on the patron saint of their altepetl subdivision in case of need; Simón de Santiago, who made a complaint to the municipal authorities of Tulancingo in 1584, was from the subdivision of Santiago and was probably ordinarily known simply as Simón, just as he calls the person whom he accuses only Cristóbal.[130] The second element of names sat lightly on ordinary Nahuas, even those who possessed one, and made even less impression on Spaniards, who not infrequently referred to any mace-hualli by his first name plus "Indian": "Juan indio" or "Juana india."

Simultaneously with the double first name, other types were coming into existence, creating social distinctions whether that was the original intention or not. Once "de San" had been mainly dropped, retaining it created a name of greater resonance, likely to be used for people of higher rank. Consider the municipal officers of Tenayuca in 1708 (listed in Table 2.4), with the governor called don Antonio de San Juan in contrast to all the others, who have unadorned double Christian names. The surname Santiago, which did not lend itself to contraction, also stood out from the rest and continued for the whole colonial period to have implications of relatively high position, though as just seen it might be appropriated at times by almost anyone. Surnames based on items of Christian lore and doctrine (also used by the mendicants themselves) were rarer than those of saints and generally indicated higher rank. The great standby was "de la Cruz," sometimes seen as "de (la) Santa Cruz" or "de la Vera Cruz"; others, such as "de la Asunción" or "de la Encarnación," were much less frequent. Another surname type at about the same level was created by taking the entire name of an actual saint, as with doña Catalina de Sena (Coyoacan, 1588), don Nicolás de Tolentino (Mexico City, 1733), and don Gregorio Nacianceno, the governor of Tlaxcala for many years in the early seventeenth century.[131] The names of the Magi were similar, but Baltasar de los Reyes, Melchor de los Reyes, and Gaspar de los Reyes were so popular all across the colonial centuries as to become a bit devalued. (Somewhat along these lines, but more in the nature of an ecclesiastical joke, was the common Domingo Ramos, a play on "domingo de Ramos," Palm Sunday; understandably, this name carried no special implications of rank.)

Highest on the ladder were actual Spanish surnames differing in no way from those used by Spaniards, and in many cases actually taken from some Spaniard who served as baptismal sponsor or in some other way adopted his namesake as a protegé. Surnames of famous conquerors, viceroys, encomenderos, corregidores, and prominent friars headed the list, being assumed by rulers and great lords. The practice began with Hernando Cortés, under whose sponsorship so many tlatoque and sons of tlatoque were baptized don Hernando Cortés that Cortés became one of the most common noble surnames all over central Mexico in the conquest generation and for generations afterward;[132] indeed, in colonial New Spain, a Cortés was much more likely to be an Indian than not, and if he bore the "don" it was almost a certainty. Alvarado, from Pedro de Alvarado and his brothers, was also popular at the highest level, as was Mendoza, from don Antonio de Mendoza, the first viceroy.[133] The local encomendero and the prior of the local monastery were perhaps the most natural and frequent sources of distinguished surnames. The tlatoani family of Zinacantepec in the Toluca Valley took the surname Sámano after the encomenderos of that altepetl, and also adopted the same Christian names,[134] as was usually done when baptismal sponsorship was in-

volved. Páez de Mendoza, a prominent surname among the tlatoque of Amaquemecan, harked back to the days when the Dominican fray Juan Páez was
in service there (and actively intervening in politics).[135] The names of lesser
local Spaniards—notaries, lieutenants, interpreters, nonencomendero estate
owners—would serve as well, especially if they had a good ring to them in
the Spanish context.[136]

In all these cases, the Spaniard probably actually knew or at least met the
Nahua and gave his permission and sponsorship. Some names became so
famous, however, that they seem to have been adopted in the Spaniard's absence, or after his death, though still with some kind of indigenous or Spanish
monitoring, for only the most prominent were eligible recipients. Fray Martín
de Valencia, legendary leader of the first twelve Franciscans, was a notable
example. In Tlaxcala, don Martín Coyolchiuhqui became don Martín
de Valencia long after fray Martín had died, and in Tulancingo there was
another don Martín de Valencia living late into the sixteenth century.[137] The
Cortés surname also seems to have spread posthumously.[138]

Spanish patronymics like Hernández, Sánchez, López, and Pérez were a
somewhat different matter, at least in the long run. Extremely common
among Spaniards of the time, they had a strongly plebeian ring unless accompanied by a higher-sounding second surname. Many of the humble Spaniards
going among Indians as employees of encomenderos, small farmers, petty
traders, or muleteers bore these surnames or others of a similar flavor. It is
probably from them that the Nahuas began to take such names, though it is
also possible that as obvious choices, patronymics were arbitrarily awarded
to many people by friars or priests at baptism. That possibility may be suspected especially with the surname Juárez, which became in time almost as
characteristically "Indian" as Santiago or a double first name.[139]

At any rate, in the first generations even surnames of this type were associated with high rank in the indigenous world. From the late 1540's into the
1570's, a majority of the prominent nobles constituting Tlaxcala's prestigious
220-man electorate had indigenous or religious surnames, and any true Hispanic surname put a person in a small upper category. Lucas García and
Alonso Gómez were governors of Tlaxcala, and Juan Jiménez was a high
nobleman of great influence in the cabildo, repeatedly alcalde.[140] In Culhuacan around 1580, people with names like Juárez and García held noble titles
and municipal-churchly office.[141] In some cases, an unimpressive surname became associated with a tlatoani family and remained prominent and prestigious on into the eighteenth century, as with the Díazes of Cuernavaca.[142] But
from the beginning, the more distinguished Spanish surnames usually went
to the very highest members of indigenous society; even in early Tlaxcala and
Culhuacan, the dynastic tlatoque did not bear patronymics. As time went on,

patronymics and other surnames ranking lower on the Spanish scale became neutral among the Nahuas; they stood out somewhat against the sea of double first names, in the same manner as the religious terms, but either humble commoners or people of high status might use them.

A special characteristic of Spanish surnames in the Nahua world is that, as among Spaniards and in contrast to most second names of Indians, they were frequently passed on to children and grandchildren. Let us first consider the great majority of cases, where second names bore no relation to lineage. A family of the late colonial Toluca Valley (Metepec, 1795) can stand for the usual situation from the conquest generation forward, for the earlier indigenous surnames were treated in the same fashion; Miguel Gerónimo and Pascuala Josefa had a daughter Petrona Martina, who married Cayetano Salvador, and their children in turn were named Gil Antonio and Rafael Valentín.[143] In Azcapotzalco in 1695, the grandchildren of the Angelina mentioned above were Tomás de los Santos, Teresa de Jesús, Jacinto Ventura, Josefa de la Encarnación, and Nicolasa Jacinta.[144] Occasionally, but as well as one can tell from wills and the like not often, children were named after parents, though not in such a way as to imply a lineage surname. In Xochimilco in 1572, Constantino de San Felipe (also called just Constantino Felipe) had named his son Felipe Constantino, a neat reversal that is quite rare in the documentation generally.[145] Somewhat more common was for the child to take the entire name of the parent, as with Juan Fabián, father and son, in the Coyoacan region in 1617.[146] Religious second names, particularly de Santiago and de la Cruz, were sometimes treated as continuing surnames, but overall the bulk of names carried in the same family were Spanish surnames, borne by lines of propertied nobles who held municipal office and had not infrequently originated in a tlatoani or great teuctli. Tlaxcala provides a good example; the same surnames adopted by the lords of that complex altepetl in the mid-sixteenth century are still seen in the cabildo membership in the 1620's and beyond.[147] Many surnames of tlatoani or governor lines were maintained from the sixteenth into or through the eighteenth century: Guzmán in Coyoacan, Páez de Mendoza in Amaquemecan, Maldonado in Tulancingo, Hinojosa in Cuernavaca, Rojas in Cuauhtinchan and Tepoztlan, and so forth.[148]

An element of prime importance in the Spanish naming system was the honorific "don," with its feminine equivalent "doña," in tandem with a person's first name. Since usage was invariant, so that a given person either always had the title or always lacked it, at any time period there was an upper group with "don" and a lower group without it. At the time of the conquest, only the very highest Spanish nobility had the don, and ordinary hidalgos lacked it, though the doña was more widely spread and was used by most women of hidalgo families.[149] Drawing the parallel, the Spaniards awarded the don to most, though not all, of the recognized tlatoque of New Spain at baptism. Within a few years, the Nahuas themselves had taken over management of the title, using it in a similar but not identical way. For Spaniards, the don was primarily a matter of family and birthright; all the sons of a don were also don, from the hour of their birth to the hour of their death. The Nahuas seemed to equate the title more with attained position. Lords and rulers with the don had brothers and cousins without it, as though it were the equivalent of "teuctli."[150] On the other hand, as one attained reputation and position, especially high municipal office, one could acquire the don along with it (see Chapter 2); for early Tlaxcala and Tulancingo, this process is well documented, and variants of the same phenomenon are found in the seventeenth and eighteenth centuries as well. In some places, the title went with certain offices so strictly that a person might lose it after the end of his term.[151] And doña, so widely used among Spanish ladies, was actually less frequent among the Nahuas than don, presumably because the noblewomen did not ordinarily hold an office or head a teccalli.[152] In time, things seem to have evened out to the extent that women in notable families usually bore the doña, but where the husband had risen from low or intermediate status, his wife would often remain without title.

With the don as something that could be acquired within one's own lifetime, inconsistency of use was much more frequent among Nahuas than among Spaniards, although true arbitrariness was rare. Most cases of vacillation involve people on the verge of achieving prominence; ordinary commoners would never receive the title, and the highest-ranking would never be left without it.[153] In the Spanish world, usage evolved quite rapidly; by the seventeenth century, most Spaniards of any prominence at all bore the title, and in the eighteenth century, it spread so far as to be used by almost any respectable and solvent man. The same tendency asserted itself among the Nahuas but never went, relatively speaking, so far. From being at first the prerogative of major tlatoque, the don spread rapidly to other lords and their relatives. On the cabildo of Tlaxcala, the don had hardly gone beyond the altepetl tlatoque in the late 1540's; by the late 1560's, most cabildo members had it; by 1620, all did (except the notary), and a good many of the 220 electors as well.[154] Much the same thing was happening in Tulancingo, although perhaps as much as two decades behind Tlaxcala at any given moment.[155]

Since Tlaxcala was such a large entity, it included more truly eminent families than a normal altepetl. Generally speaking, the don never diffused appreciably beyond the group of families that rotated in the municipal offices of governor, alcalde, fiscal, regidor mayor, and notary, and in some towns, even the last two were not usually included in the circle. In the eighteenth century, especially in the second half, usage seems to have become rather more arbitrary and less consistent, perhaps as a result of the extreme devaluation of the term among Spaniards, who at that point still insisted on its use in addressing others but no longer added it to their own signatures. The effect is partly caused by documents in Spanish; perhaps because of a desire to maintain a distinction between Spanish and Indian names even now when the don was so general in the Spanish world, Spanish writers increasingly declined to apply the title to any Indian, however high ranking.[156]

Overall, then, the naming system of the postconquest centuries was subtle and highly differentiated, as well as changing over time. For much of the sixteenth century, the majority of the population bore indigenous surnames, and the greatest dividing line was between them and those possessing names of all the other types. A party of officials of Mexico Tenochtitlan in 1585 divides sharply into two groups: the high-ranking cabildo members, who all have some sort of nonindigenous name—Juan Martín, don Martín Hernández, Pedro Gerónimo, and Pablo Juárez—and the lower-ranking constables, named Pedro Aca (Reed), Martín Quauhtli (Eagle), and Pedro Ahuexotl (Willow).[157] By the second quarter of the seventeenth century, indigenous surnames had in effect disappeared in most subregions except for a few illustrious dynastic names recognized even by Spaniards, including Maxixcatzin and Moteucçoma. The primary dividing line was now between those with double first names and all the rest. The religious surnames occupied an intermediate position, along with the commonest patronymics. The mark of high distinction in the indigenous world was possession of the don plus a nonplebeian Spanish surname. In both the earlier and the later period, the generality of the indigenous population stood (as it had before the conquest) in a relative anonymity, bearing appellations that had no generational depth and by themselves did not suffice to distinguish one person from another, at least in a larger community. The middle-rank surnames, de la Cruz, Santiago, de los Reyes, and the rest, were only a slight improvement in this respect. The bulk of Indian names were so similar and indeed in a sense so nondescript that to outsiders they all seemed the same. Spanish lawyers frequently got the names of their own Indian clients wrong, mixing up Luisa Clara and Juana Luisa, for example, and the same could happen even with Nahua notaries in larger settlements. In Mexico City in 1596, a notary after writing a long testament had forgotten the testator's all too common appellation, Juana Mocel, and referred to her as *yehuatl fulano*, "that what's-her-name."[158] From the inside, things were very different. In any given situation, certain surnames took on a local coloration, and the nomenclature served to articulate the population, leaving little doubt about lower, intermediate, and higher.

TABLE 4.4

Typical Names of the Mature Colonial Period: Householders
of Teopancaltitlan Tlatocapan (Tepemaxalco, Toluca Valley), 1659

Bernabé de Santiago	Andrés de Santiago	Gabriel de Tapia
Don Gabriel de San Pedro	Juan de San Miguel	Mónica Elena
Francisco Nicolás[a]	Francisca Juana	Ursula María
Baltasar Gregorio	Don Diego de la Cruz	Francisco Hernández
Lucía Florenciana	Agustín Salvador	Diego Francisco
Juan Nicolás[a]	Juan Bautista	Juan Nicolás[a]
Francisco Nicolás[a]	Lorenzo López	Antón Josef

SOURCE: MNAH AH, GO 185, p. 15.

[a]There were two men named Francisco Nicolás and two named Juan Nicolás. The like-named pairs were possibly but not necessarily related.

Let us look at a list of names from a section of Tepemaxalco in 1659 (Table 4.4).[159] Of the twenty-one compound appellations, no fewer than thirteen are double first names. Another, Juan de San Miguel, is the same thing in altered form, for the previous year the person referred to had been just Juan Miguel. Likely he had made a good marriage or prospered in business. In 1653, he held a minor position as church *topile* (constable, general henchman). There are two Santiagos; this surname, which could mean almost anything, had no strong profile in Tepemaxalco and probably does not indicate especially high status in these cases. Two persons possess patronymics. Of these, Lorenzo López was to be master of the church choir in 1666, and alcalde (by then entitled don) in 1682. Francisco Hernández had been church topile in 1653, was master of the choir in this very year of 1659, and was to become alcalde and don in 1672. One person is named Tapia, which had originally been a grand Spanish surname but had spread so widely among Indians as to fall, in general, approximately to the level of a patronymic. Gabriel de Tapia was to become regidor mayor in 1667, then don and alcalde in 1671. López, Hernández, Tapia, and the Santiagos probably all represent persons conscious of carrying on a family line.

Only two of the men bear the don. The surname of don Diego de la Cruz ranks, in general, no higher than de Santiago, but in Tepemaxalco, the governor (as we will see) was a de la Cruz more often than not over a century and a half, so that don Diego was definitely a member of Tepemaxalco's upper crust. In fact, he had himself been governor in 1655. About don Gabriel de San Pedro's background we can say on the basis of his title that he had somehow attained high status. Names cannot, after all, do absolutely everything. In small groups where everyone knew everyone else, even a prestigious family would for whatever reason sometimes revert to a nondescript name, which in the context would soon convey something quite different than usual.[160] Don

Gabriel thus may have been of high rank from birth despite the unremarkable "San Pedro." Another possibility is that he was originally just Gabriel Pedro and through some combination of marriage, merit, wealth, and longevity reached prominence. In 1647, he was already Gabriel de San Pedro (though without don) and made a substantial donation of twenty pesos to the church, indicating solvency. By 1655, he had the don and was serving as alcalde. In preconquest terms, the twenty-one household heads would seem to represent, as of 1659, the approximate equivalent of thirteen clear macehualtin, six people of intermediate or rising status, and two pipiltin. (The proportion of persons eventually attaining the don and high municipal office is higher here than it would be in other parts of Tepemaxalco, for Teopancaltitlan was the ranking subdivision.)

Essentially, the Nahuas were nearly as able and inclined to designate rank distinctions as they had ever been. Although the newer system was nowhere identical to the older one, it resulted in somewhat equivalent distinctions and groupings. "Don" in the later period was overall rather more exclusive than "pilli" had been, rather less exclusive than "teuctli," and more like "teuctli" than "pilli" in representing attained status plus birth rather than birth alone, but it had a function similar to that of the earlier terms. For all the differences, the set of people holding the same prestigious surname in a Nahua altepetl in the seventeenth or eighteenth century constituted a designated lineage hard to distinguish from the pipiltin of a teccalli in earlier times. Although Spanish priests and friars continued to officiate at baptisms to independence and beyond, at some fairly early point, the Nahuas must have begun choosing names for themselves, for by the middle colonial period the system of naming was a perfect fit for their still quite intricate society.

Naming patterns betray many distinctions larger than those of individual rank. During the years when the system was still taking shape, that is, until the third or fourth decade of the seventeenth century, one finds a far higher proportion of nonindigenous surnames in major centers, with a greater Spanish presence, than in smaller and more remote ones, graphically illustrating the earlier impact of change in the "cabeceras."[161] Later, in the time of the mature system, the relative prevalence of names associated with high rank in major centers, together with the plebeian naming of even governors and alcaldes in minor towns, tells one a great deal about the distribution of the prominent and the humble in the Indian world of the late period.

The system as it evolved also set up distinctions between Indians and Spaniards. Even after indigenous surnames faded, it was generally easy to tell an Indian from a Spaniard by his name alone. Not only were the double first names and religious surnames idiosyncratic; until the eighteenth-century explosion of the don among the Spanish population, the very presence of the

don in conjunction with a Spanish surname (and especially with one of plebeian flavor) hinted that the possessor was Indian.* Mestizos of the late sixteenth and early seventeenth centuries such as Juan Bautista de Pomar and
Diego Muñoz Camargo, who went among Nahua relatives but did not use
the don, were thereby signaling that they belonged to the Spanish world, and
there were some mestizo governors of the time who did the same.¹⁶² Later the
don evened out, but at the same time high-ranking Spanish surnames evolved
in the direction of greater complexity, so that a difference remained. Closest
to identity between the two spheres were the simple two-element appellations
of Christian name plus patronymic borne by humbler Spaniards, the ethni-
cally mixed, and some Indians alike; the patronymics seem to have increased
in popularity with the bulk of the Indian population as time went on, and the
trend may be indicative of a more basic rapprochement.†

In the final years before independence, a certain number of Nahuas,
mainly people of some prominence, were adding a second, indigenous sur-
name.¹⁶³ The meaning of this late and secondary phenomenon is not yet clear;
possibly it was an attempt to escape from the relative anonymity of the usual
"Indian" surnames, or possibly it is a back-manifestation of the pride in the
indigenous heritage that Mexican Spanish patriots had been preaching
through the whole later colonial period.

The Persistence of an Upper Group

By 1650 and before, the older Nahuatl terminology of nobility and high
rank was primarily restricted in usage to courtesy titles for municipal officers
and posturing in municipal election disputes. Of the special titles of rulerships
and lordships, so important a feature of the earlier system, only minimal
traces were left, or so it seems in the record. For some reason, the lordly titles
had been almost surreptitious from an early time. The sixteenth-century wills
of lords and rulers leave their titles entirely unmentioned even when the documents designate successors to the positions, and it is mainly from historical

---

*Until a late time, such a name as don Pedro Jiménez did not occur among Spaniards and
would have been extremely ludicrous. Anyone so named could only be an Indian nobleman.

†I have seen a few examples from the Tulancingo region of a phenomenon that may have
been more widespread, an apparent tendency to have one name, more typically "Indian," for the
inside, and another, more meaningful to Spaniards, for dealing with the outside. In Tulancingo
in 1642, a Gaspar de Santiago sold a house, according to a Nahuatl document, but the Spaniard
who bought it identified the seller as "Gaspar Jiménez indio" (UCLA TC, folder 12). In Acaxochitlan in the Tulancingo area in 1768, a person who is Domingo de la Cruz in a Nahuatl will is
called Domingo Rosales by a Spaniard, and his uncle (don) Marcelo Simón is called don Marcelo
Simón Rosales. Something of the same tendency can be seen, potentially, in the names of the
town's governor and alcalde, don Pedro de Santiago López and don Juan de la Trinidad López
(ibid., folder 25).

accounts that we learn of their existence.[164] When dealing with Spanish authorities, from whom little comprehension could be expected, it is understandable that tlatoque and teteuctin should pass over the lordly titles, often representing themselves as the single cacique or natural lord of the altepetl even when there was a complex set of rulers.[165] But it is hard to account for the conspiracy of silence in Nahuatl wills and municipal documents, since all manner of other traditional indigenous social and political concepts crop up there. Possibly the lordly titles were felt to be associated with preconquest religion (though Chimalpahin, for one, had no such feeling, proudly displaying the titles of the tlatoque of Amaquemecan right up to his own time). At any rate, by the middle of the colonial period, the preconquest terminological system for distinguishing the prominent from the lowly was moribund; it had been replaced by a several-tier naming system that was capable of making as many distinctions, though without drawing as sharp a linguistic line between upper and lower.

It was not name alone that distinguished an upper group from the rest. In the example of the names from Tepemaxalco, we have just seen that even in the later colonial period not everyone held office. In most Indian towns of central Mexico, a body of *vocales,* "voters" or "electors," continued to be designated up to the time of independence. A study of the Cuernavaca jurisdiction in the seventeenth and eighteenth centuries finds that from 5 percent to as many as 20 percent of the tribute payers were vocales, with 10 percent perhaps something of a norm; and more fragmentary data for other regions confirm this picture.[166] According to estimates on the basis of early Nahuatl censuses, the proportion of pipiltin in the mid-sixteenth century fell within the same range.[167] Like the earlier pipiltin, the vocales monopolized governmental and churchly office. (But they were not all equal; in a given altepetl, usually only one, two, or a very few families aspired to the governorship, a point to which I will return.)

Economic differences persisted as well. In seventeenth-century Tepemaxalco, when the special field of a church or *cofradía* (lay religious sodality) was to be cultivated, the present and past officers (the same sector as the vocales) brought yokes of oxen, whereas the ordinary people brought only *huitzoctli* (a type of digging stick). Though the upper group is given no name, the lower group is referred to in contrast as macehualtin and *tlapaliuhque,* "farmers, hands, the able-bodied." The de la Cruz family, source of so many governors, contributed at times more money to pious causes than the rest of the officers put together.[168] The persistence of substantial estates among the indigenous ruling group in the Cuernavaca region has been demonstrated, and sharp differences in landholding, much like those obtaining at conquest, have been documented for other places as well in the late period, ranging from the landless or nearly so all the way up to gubernatorial families with quite extensive holdings.[169] It is true that by 1750 few Indian estates could compare with those of even middle-level Spanish families, and it is also true that to some Spaniards, and especially to observers fresh from Europe, Indians seemed all the same, reduced to a single level. Yet meaningful, systematic differences continued to exist, closely comparable in type to those obtaining when the Spaniards first arrived. Even the flexibility and in some cases indeterminacy of status had good preconquest precedent.

One might say that the prominent of the late colonial indigenous world had been reduced to the level of macehualtin in the sense that, when not holding office, they had the same tribute obligations as any ordinary Indian. In fact, however, as we have seen, Nahua lords and noblemen had always paid tribute in kind to the altepetl, if not exactly for themselves then at least by virtue of the lands they held and for their dependents, and it was only their great and for a time successful scam of extolling their privileges and sweeping their duties under the rug that hoodwinked Spanish authorities into thinking they had been exempt. To be sure, earlier Nahuatl nobles had been truly exempt from the coatequitl or draft public labor, whereas in late colonial times, they had the same formal obligation to the Hispanized form of the institution, the repartimiento, as the rest of the population. But the repartimiento was no longer meaningfully operative in many parts of central Mexico after the early seventeenth century, and even where it was, as in the Cuernavaca jurisdiction and the Toluca Valley for the neighboring silver mines, further research will probably establish that members of the "vocal" group bought their way out or otherwise managed to avoid the duty.

The late colonial "gubernatorial" lineages appear to have a good deal in common with the tlatoani lineages of the sixteenth century. To what extent is this appearance only? For the Valley of Mexico, it has already been demonstrated that although the formal tlatocayotl was often legally buttressed by Spanish governmental decrees granting the right of succession, confirming rights to the labor of dependents, and giving the ruler's holdings the status of an entail, the institution was in rapid decline by the early seventeenth century. Some lines died out, others persisted but on the edges of the ruling group rather than at its center, and some flourished indefinitely, a few in a very large way, though they did so because of the reputation of the line, the astuteness of its members, advantageous alliances, or luck rather than because of the power and wealth of the rulership as such.[170] In the late colonial period, the concept of the tlatoani as the dynastic head of state of an altepetl or tlayacatl, if it did not absolutely disappear, then at least went underground. The latest use of tlatoani to mean dynastic ruler that I have seen in a Nahuatl text is from Amaquemecan in 1661; a don Francisco Cosme is called in passing the "Tequanipan tlatoani," Tequanipan being one of Amaquemecan's sub-altepetl.[171] By this time and even earlier, "tlatoani" was coming to mean no more than prominent person (in almost any capacity). Already in the six-teenth century, the plural tlatoque had often referred to groups of municipal officers none of whom was a dynastic ruler, and by the middle colonial period, even the singular, which until then had designated at the least a cur-rently officiating governor, was being used in the same way. A Nahuatl text from the Toluca Valley in 1645 speaks of the "tlatoani don Simón de Santiago, fiscal mayor."[172] In Acatlan in the Tulancingo area in 1659, a notary refers to don Francisco de Larios, a wealthy landholder and former governor, as "the tlatoani," though there is no hint of a formal tlatocayotl.[173]

Just as in studying the evolution of the concept altepetl the Spanish "pueblo" becomes relevant at a certain point, so to understand late colonial concepts of nobility and rulership one must discuss the Spanish terms *cacique* and *principal*. "Cacique," though not invariably used in grants of rights to indigenous rulers ("señor" was an alternate term), was the operating concept among Spaniards in the sixteenth century, and the ensemble of rights and holdings surrounding the rulership was called a *cacicazgo* by analogy with Spanish *mayorazgo*, "entail." At this time, "cacique" was fully equivalent to traditional Nahuatl "tlatoani," and "cacicazgo" to "tlatocayotl." Declining to call Indian noblemen hidalgos or caballeros (those being the most common Spanish terms), the Spaniards soon settled on "principal," "important per-son." Applied to Indians, the word may not have conveyed nobleman in the strictest sense, for it was sometimes used in the Spanish world to speak of persons of great influence but undistinguished birth, and it can be found re-ferring to leaders at the macehualli level.[174] Yet all in all, "principal" in the sixteenth century is simply a translation of Nahuatl "pilli."[175]

Such clarity was not long maintained. The Spaniards were mainly con-cerned with rulers and lords as figures of authority, not with nobles or no-bility as such. In effect, most of the "principales" with whom they dealt were "caciques," and even by 1600, one begins to see the two terms used in tandem more than separately.[176] The two increasingly became equivalent. If this served to raise the connotation of "principal" somewhat, its main effect was to broaden "cacique." By 1700, cacique in Spanish no longer usually had the meaning "holder of a tlatocayotl or cacicazgo." In much usage, it tended to displace "principal" almost entirely, referring to any prominent, propertied person of an officeholding family; the women of these circles were called *ca-cica*.[177] A single minor town could have several caciques. In the San Sebastián district of Mexico City in 1733, don Nicolás de Tolentino, don Miguel Juá-rez, and don Vicente Ramos, all three called "cacique y principal," lived side by side. Two had been alcalde; they were, respectively, a carpenter, a candle-maker-choirmaster, and a mason.[178] Since the crafts had always been practiced by some Nahua pipiltin, and in any case in postconquest society, many indigenous noblemen carried on profitable activities that were middling to low on the Spanish scale, the trades of these gentlemen by no means demote them to low status in the indigenous context. Nevertheless, the thrust of "cacique" had clearly changed.

Late colonial "cacique," then, was not far from meaning what Nahuatl "pilli" had meant earlier, though it was used more pragmatically than genealogically and had little or no legal standing. But "cacique" continued to mean "holder of a cacicazgo" as well, for those cacicazgos that still existed. As "tlatoani" continued its long evolution toward meaning simply "Mr.," "cacique" in its broader sense began to be used by the Nahuas, though more in dealing with Spaniards than when speaking Nahuatl.[179] It was, however, by now the only term left in either Spanish or Nahuatl that referred to formal dynastic rulership, and in a testament from Tepetlixpan (Chalco region), dated 1733, it is actually used in the Nahuatl text in that meaning instead of "tlatoani."[180] The two meanings could be played off against each other. In the 1760's, a former governor of Coatlichan (Tetzcoco region), don Sebastián Ignacio (de Buendía), claimed in a Spanish court to be a cacique, meaning without a doubt in the broader, devalued sense, which to every appearance was true. But the opposing party denied the claim, saying that a cacique did not pay tribute as don Sebastián did, for the possessor of a formal cacicazgo was in fact usually relieved of tribute obligations.[181]

Some cacicazgos did continue to function on into the eighteenth century much as they had before, although the phenomenon may be confined to the eastern region, where, as seen earlier, the teccalli had always proclaimed itself especially strong. The only full-fledged example I know of comes from Cuauhtinchan.[182] In preconquest times, the Tecpanecatl teuctli had been one of Cuauhtinchan's seven tlatoque, perhaps the ranking one. As of 1576, this tlatocayotl was held by don Diego de Rojas, a grandson of the incumbent at the time of the conquest, who bequeathed it in that year, along with extensive buildings, landholdings, and dependents to his son don Tomás. Some 130 years later, in 1707, don Antonio Tomás de Rojas, "cacique y principal," a direct descendant although through his mother, was in possession of a cacicazgo specifically so called (his will is in Spanish) and left the rulership and most of his property to a daughter and son-in-law, since the whereabouts of his son was unknown. Not only the surname Rojas, but the first names Tomás, Antonio, Diego, Antonia, and María had now been kept in the family for many generations. Don Antonio Tomás had a large house compound in town, not said in so many words to belong to his cacicazgo, but a rancho and six *caballerías* of land were specifically cacicazgo property. The rancho was leased to a

Spaniard; of the six caballerías, don Antonio Tomás rented thirty lots to his "vassals and tenants" for two pesos annually each and let them use the rest in return for the customary service to him, "since they are subject to my cacicazgo." Proceeds from other cacicazgo land leased out to Spaniards went for an annual festivity of Santo Tomás, which seems to have been held at the place where the six caballerías were, constituting a "barrio that they call Tecpanecatl," so that in a slightly disguised form even the title of the tlatocayotl had survived. The first tlatoani baptized had borne the name Tomás, doubtless coinciding with the "barrio's" patron saint and Spanish name.

Although the heirs of don Antonio Tomás de Rojas were expected to carry on in the same fashion, the 1707 document seems to be the last known of the cacicazgo. Possibly the family and its holdings evolved in the same direction as in the case of another Tecpanecatl teuctli, this one the tlatoani of Tepetlix-pan (originally a tlayacatl of Chimalhuacan) in the southern part of the Chalco region. Although the documents are sketchy, something of the story can be pieced together. In 1629, a don Juan Pacheco headed a party of officials and other citizens of Tepetlixpan, all with names far less distinguished than his, who bought four caballerías of land called Tetepetlac, in their own district, from a nobleman of Tlalmanalco, to be community property. Other Pachecos, in the late seventeenth and the eighteenth century, were alcaldes of Tepetlixpan and connected with the tlatoani family, which by 1690, in the person of (don) Josef de Aguilar, claimed ownership of Tetepetlac among other lands. I deduce that don Juan Pacheco was the Tecpanecatl teuctli and as such took the "community property" for himself and his heirs. In 1690, though nothing was said about any cacicazgo, the family was still flourishing. In 1704, strains were beginning to show. Doña Francisca Ceverina, who had held the inheritance until then, lived in a compound sporting an oratory with many saints, and she still treated the Tetepetlac land as her own, but she considered her son Gaspar (de los) Reyes a drifter and loafer and tried to leave everything to her daughter-in-law Magdalena Ursula instead. (Note the deterioration in the family's surnames, from a high-sounding Spanish surname to religious names and double first names, with loss of the "don.")

By 1737, the last known of the Pachecos said in his will that Tetepetlac had been wrongly lost to an hacienda—probably through a mismanaged lease—but was really the property of the Tecpaneca caciques (using the Spanish word in Nahuatl, as mentioned above). Doña Francisca is actually referred to, posthumously, as "the Tecpanecatl," the latest instance known to me in which a preconquest lordly title is attributed to an individual. The family did not regain the land. In 1791, a current and a past governor of Tepetlixpan brought the grandson of Gaspar Reyes, Miguel Castillo, to Mex-

ico City to press further claims. It is apparent that the town officials were
propping up Miguel, whose greatest eminence was that he had once held the
lowly post of merino, in order to win back some of the land for the whole
community, and that the descendants of the tlatoani family no longer played
an appreciable role in town affairs.[183] In fact, it is not certain that any of the
participants in the 1791 appeal were fully cognizant of the genealogy of
the tlatoani line, for no open reference is made to cacicazgo. Nevertheless, the
title had been carefully handed on, sub rosa, into the eighteenth century, and
the same may have been true in other altepetl where not even as slight a
documentary trace is preserved as in Tepetlixpan.

But in many places there is little reason to think that those prominent in
the seventeenth and eighteenth centuries had any genealogical affiliation with
a preconquest tlatocayotl. Because of some quasi-personal Nahuatl records,
the best available example is that of the de la Cruz family in the Toluca Valley
municipality of Tepemaxalco (the lower ranking of dual governments in the
Calimaya region) in the late seventeenth and eighteenth centuries. A certain
Pedro de la Cruz, organist of the church, began keeping a book of income
and expenses related to the local churches and cofradía, starting with a campaign of 1647 to raise money for a new organ. In time, others added entries,
often having to do with municipal business; someone put in a page or two of
historical annals, and notable events like earthquakes were reported as they
happened. As a result, a rather intimate if highly sporadic and partisan account of municipal affairs emerges. Pedro de la Cruz the organist became
governor don Pedro de la Cruz in 1657 and held the office for virtually the
rest of his life, until 1674, with minimal interruptions. The last part of the
century was dominated by don Juan de la Cruz, a son-in-law rather than a
son but nevertheless principal heir to all don Pedro's interests, his own male
children having died early. Don Nicolás de la Cruz was governor in the
middle eighteenth century, and at the end of that century, don Bernardino
de la Cruz y Serrano held the office (see Table 4.5). Although the records do
not provide an exhaustive series of incumbents in the governorship, there is
every reason to think that the de la Cruzes held the post essentially as often
as they wanted to when they had a mature and capable candidate. In the time
of don Pedro, the best-documented family member, don Juan Pablo was a
stand-in governor in the second half of 1662 when don Pedro must have been
sick; otherwise he was Juan Pablo the notary. The term of don Matías de San
Francisco in 1671 was probably in the nature of a crumb to an old friend, for
he had been master of the church choir when don Pedro was organist, and
don Pedro doubtless held the reins even that year.

During don Pedro's tenure, he personally made large donations, sometimes
hundreds of pesos, to build and repair altars and chapels and to enlarge the

TABLE 4.5

Known Governors of Tepemaxalco (Toluca Valley), 1605–1813

Tenure	Name	Tenure	Name
1605	Don Diego Felipe	1671	Don Matías de San Francisco
1610	Don Francisco Martín	1672–74	Don Pedro de la Cruz
1616	Don Daniel (Velásquez?)	1678	Don Juan Martín
1624, 1647	Don Baltasar de los Reyes	1682–83	Don Juan de la Cruz
1655	Don Diego de la Cruz	1684	Don Francisco de la Cruz
1656	Don Matías de San Francisco	1733–34, 1745–46	Don Nicolás de la Cruz
1657–70	Don Pedro de la Cruz	1772	Don Josef de la Cruz
	(don Juan Pablo for 6	1791–92, 1795,	Don Bernardino de la Cruz
	months in 1662)	1809, 1813	y Serrano

SOURCES: CFP; AGN, Tierras 1501, exp. 3, ff. 2 (don Josef), 19 (don Diego Felipe), 20 (don Francisco); Tierras 2533, exp. 2, ff. 36v–37 (don Bernardino).

organ; his contributions were always substantial, and in many cases, he was the sole significant source of funds. Clearly he was a wealthy man. The next de la Cruz to take over, don Juan de la Cruz, had large landholdings scattered across the district and was able to leave lands and oxen to each of an impressive number of children. Both don Pedro and don Juan had permanent employees (gañanes). In the mid-eighteenth century, governor don Nicolás and two nephews surnamed de la Cruz by themselves paid for a new bell for the church. The de la Cruz family thus gives every indication of having formed a dynasty, ranking at the very top of Tepemaxalco society socially, economically, and politically for generation after generation, thereby behaving for all the world like a tlatoani lineage.

One looks in vain, however, for any assertions of noble descent on the part of the de la Cruzes. Not only do they never speak of any forebears or cacicazgo; they virtually never even call themselves tlatoani, teuctli, or pilli, terms that hardly appear to have been in their vocabulary. The appellation de la Cruz, as indicated earlier, was only of medium status generally speaking and was not always treated as a continuing surname. By 1650, the family was becoming well established, for Pedro de la Cruz the organist was already son of a (don) Juan de la Cruz who had been alcalde, and in 1655, don Diego de la Cruz assumed the governorship. Yet the family's historical researches seem not to have turned up a de la Cruz governor before that. Possibly (though by no means necessarily, given the commonness of the name) the line went back to an apparent muleteer of the late sixteenth century named Pablo de la Cruz, who was said in some Spanish records of Toluca to have been from Calimaya (Spaniards often failed to make any distinction between Tepemaxalco and Calimaya, ignoring the former). When don Bernardino de la Cruz, who had gone over to writing in Spanish, was given custody of the records in 1791, he called them "the book of my antecessor don Pedro de la Cruz Serrano, who was conqueror and founder." Leaving aside for the moment the seeming utter inappropriateness of these terms, literally applicable only to sixteenth-century Spaniards, it can be seen that don Bernardino considered his family's fame and high position to have begun with the great don Pedro. The seventeenth century does seem to have been, if not the time of origin of the de la Cruzes as a self-conscious line, then at least the time of their rise to prominence.[184]

Dominance as pure and lasting as that of the de la Cruz family may have been quite rare. Larger towns of the late colonial period were more likely to have two or three dynasties vying for the governorship and general preeminence, as in Cuernavaca and Tepoztlan, although the disputants might be so intertwined as to seem rival branches of a single dynasty, a common situation in the preconquest period.[185] A few such families derived straightforwardly from sixteenth-century tlatoque, others had some slight affiliation with them, and yet others arose in the later period, at times helped by a matrimonial alliance with someone from the Hispanic world. Once a position was established in one way or another, the origin seems to have mattered relatively little. Dynasties behaved the same and were viewed the same whether they went back for centuries or for only two or three generations; in central Mexico by the middle colonial period, although traditions of current practice were handed faithfully and tenaciously from one generation to the next, perspectives over longer time spans were often blurred. In late colonial times, preconquest tlatocayotl was no longer a necessary ingredient of the biological heritage of gubernatorial families, nor was it a major part of their conscious rationale, but as a precedent and a pattern it was historically important in shaping the nature of their activities and their general position. Despite all the loss, transformation, and renaming, late colonial Indian towns still had a mainly hereditary minority group, of greater wealth, prestige, and education than most, who held the bulk of corporate offices, and among that minority, a few continuing families were the wealthiest of all and dominated though not always monopolized the governorship.

Other important aspects of the articulation of society have left too little evidence of themselves, or so it presently seems, to allow for systematic discussion. Although age differential must have continued to play a significant role, little was written down on the topic other than occasional complaints that a governor was too young for his post. The word *huehuetque*, "elders," continued to be used at times for the authorities of subdivisions and even for the municipal officers as a group, but the term seems to represent more a political formula than a description of chronological age or a high evaluation of older people. Persons in authority were frequently called on as witnesses, causing them to declare their ages, from which one can form an impression that officeholders were all mature adults and often of middle age or over, but people in their thirties also appear.[186] As we would expect from what was seen above about the importance of family connections in the upper reaches of society, rank was far from being a mere function of age.

Gender too is little spoken of in the records. The complaint of a Tetzcocan noblewoman in 1589 that she could not manage her late husband's properties adequately "because I am a woman" is quite without parallel.[187] The general picture arising from the study of inheritance and naming patterns is that both women and men held property, influenced family decisions, and shared in the family's social rank whatever that might be, all of which, aside from being hardly any different from Spanish patterns, had also been true before the conquest. Spanish influence can sometimes be detected, as in calling the governor's wife the "gobernadora,"[188] but in the main the two models must have reinforced each other. A pattern of segregation of the sexes, possibly implied by the separate education of boys and girls in preconquest times, is hardly confirmed in postconquest records. In house compounds, the structure called *cihuacalli* ("woman-house," as seen before) is not very clearly a place for women only, and its counterpart *oquichpan* ("where the men are") is attested only once. Both terms fade out as the colonial period progresses. The mysterious minor office of *cihuatepixqui*, "female person in charge of people," presumably designates an official in charge of the women as a group in churchly and other organizations; it too is seen primarily in records of the sixteenth century, with one seventeenth-century example.[189] The long lists of witnesses to wills and the like, first all the men and then all the women, which are frequently seen in Nahuatl texts of the sixteenth century, diminish and are less formally organized by male and female in later centuries; also, witnesses in the later time are much more likely to be all men, probably because of Spanish influence. Women did not hold public office, though they might succeed to a cacicazgo in the absence of male heirs; certain women who were said to be movers in political affairs often are found to have been widows of well-known figures or the only representative of that generation of an outstanding family, though some feminine political leadership seems to have originated primarily in the unusual personal gifts of the women themselves.[190] A rare set of cofradía records from Tula shows an important role for women as supporting officers, part of a possibly very influential position in the organization as a whole. (We will return to the point in Chapter 6.) Hints of special functions of women in making petitions and public protests remain, for now, tantalizing suggestions.[191]

It is also evident that the role of occupation in grouping the indigenous population was as great as ever, if indeed it did not gain in importance. In Spanish society, the terminology of nobility was also being deemphasized across the colonial period, and the hierarchy of professions and trades, together with the modulation of names and the use of ethnic epithets, represented perhaps the most basic means of ranking the population. The same may well have been the case among indigenous people, and we know in general that many Hispanic as well as indigenous trades were practiced, but the records are such that they rarely connect a specific person with a specific trade. It can be seen, however, that economic activities low on the Spanish scale, including petty regional commerce, regional and interregional transportation, and the most common Hispanic crafts, could be associated with relatively high rank among Indians.

Nor do the three large areas of age, sex, and trade exhaust the Nahua social distinctions that must remain relatively unexplored. The upper group did not speak Nahuatl in exactly the same way as the ordinary folk, and at any given time they tended to know more Spanish; speech patterns also served to differentiate people by age, gender, and region. As little as is currently known about all these matters, they bear mention in the present context because they serve to remind us how richly differentiated the Nahua world remained, up to and including the last decades before independence.

5

Land and Living

IN THE MAINLY Nahuatl sources of this book, documents in annual series with precise specifications of prices and other quantities are rarely found, nor is there much detail on techniques of production and distribution, so that without using altogether different materials it would be difficult to undertake economic history in the usual sense, and such is not my intention. Yet some aspects of economic life, often related to the kinds of social and political organization discussed in the previous chapters, emerge clearly enough and will be treated here at some length. Since the documents are much more expansive on land tenure than on all other aspects of the indigenous economy, the pages that follow are necessarily heavily weighted toward that subject.

Land Tenure at Contact

It was ultimately a rich, intensive, permanent-site agriculture that gave central Mexico at the time of the conquest preeminence in population size and many other respects over areas of southern Mesoamerica better provided with prestige goods, from jaguar skins and the plumes of tropical birds to the crucial quasi-staples cotton and cacao. Although the plant varieties and growing techniques that had developed over centuries, not to speak of the climate, were at least as important as the land itself in the flourishing of central Mexican agriculture, they were constants, equally available to all, so that land became the principal determinant and attribute of wealth as well as the primary basis of taxation. Elaborate vocabulary and procedures evolved (presumably all or nearly all with long-standing Mesoamerican precedents) to classify, measure, and allocate land and to record tenancy. Preconquest practices related to land were as relevant to postconquest land tenure as the altepetl was to postconquest political life, so it will be necessary to give the preconquest situation ample discussion.

Corporate Land Management

It is important to note at the outset that in preconquest times, the keeping of land records was in the hands of altepetl and calpolli authorities, and so to a large extent was allocation. This strong corporate role, together with a predisposition on the part of early scholars to identify the Mesoamericans with Indians of northeastern North America, led to the persistent notion that central Mexican landholding was communal. Recent scholars have now repeatedly shown that as far as arable land is concerned, in actual practice individuals and households worked it, held it on a long-term basis, and inherited it.[1] This side of land tenure deserves and will receive emphasis here, for it brings indigenous patterns far closer to those of Europe than once thought. Yet there is no doubt that the corporate entities retained residual rights to all lands (as in Europe) and, with fertile land at least, took a more active role in allocation and reallocation than their contemporary European counterparts.

Two of the most basic Nahua land categories were *altepetlalli*, "altepetl land," and *calpollalli*, "calpolli land" (*tlaxilacallalli*, "tlaxilacalli land," does occur with approximately the same meaning as calpollalli, but much less frequently).[2] The two were in fact different ways of referring to the same thing; presumably there was no altepetl land that was not at the same time calpolli land. In some sense, the entire jurisdiction of an altepetl must have fallen into these categories, but in practice they were used as the opposite of land held by nobles, and indeed a frequent implication was that the land was not held at all and hence was open to reallocation. All these points are illustrated by a case of 1575 in Coyoacan, in which an individual petitioned to be given an empty piece of altepetlalli described also as "calpollalli that no longer belongs to anyone and lies idle."[3] Of the two terms, calpollalli was much more common, reflecting the importance of the calpolli/tlaxilacalli as the primary land-distributing unit for the general population.

Nahuatl documents of the early to middle colonial period deliver considerable evidence pointing toward an earlier corporate division of at least the most fertile lands into relatively uniform plots, allocated to the population at a single time in the past. Plots held by individuals are described as measuring twenty units, or some multiple thereof, far too frequently for such a result to have arisen from chance. In places at least, whole tracts must have been divided into plots of twenty units of measure (sometimes square, sometimes with a lesser width), arranged in long strips side by side; some people got only one plot, some several, and calpolli leaders or important nobles might receive many times an ordinary commoner's allotment. The best extant example is provided by the early census and tax records of the Cuernavaca region,[4] where, in some districts at least, a plot twenty units long was the normal allotment for a nuclear or small extended family, wealthier families might have forty, sixty, or even eighty, and leaders often had a hundred, two hundred, or more. In different parts of the region, the width of the twenty-unit plots varied from five to twenty (making them square), but in a single calpolli or large tract, plot width was often uniform, so much so that in the majority of cases the officials making the survey took it as a constant and left it unrecorded.

On the other hand, many plots described in Nahuatl testaments of the sixteenth century, probably the absolute majority, do not have even dimensions. Records made in Tepetlaoztoc (Tetzcoco region) around the 1540's, the only known painstaking and comprehensive land surveys of portions of a given region in preconquest style, also show predominantly plots of irregular shape and uneven dimensions.[5] The registers, however, contain two separate sets of measurements for each plot, one giving the shape and lineal dimensions, the other the area in square units. A special sign is attached to any field of less than 400 square units, or in other words, less than the equivalent of twenty by twenty. A possible implication is that twenty by twenty was the normal plot size, and the irregularities arose in the process of adapting a uniform scheme to the features of a sloping and varied terrain.[6]

The corporate management of fields extended beyond the original subdivision and allocation to ongoing reallocation and the maintenance of up-to-date records. The Cuernavaca-region censuses contain numerous instances of outsiders who are given fields at some point after their arrival on the local scene, or of young newlyweds given their first allotment, or just as significantly, of people in these two categories who are still awaiting their allotments and meanwhile are performing less than full duties for the group. The lands are assigned by the calpolli officials (calpoleque) or by "the nobles" (pipiltin), presumably meaning higher authorities of the altepetl.[7] A crucial feature of the preconquest system was the keeping of glyphic-pictorial registers of all arable, taxable lands in each district, together with the names of the current holders. The posterior Spanish chronicles assert that such was the preconquest practice,[8] and the Tepetlaoztoc records represent a concrete example, exhaustive land registration still being carried out about a generation after the conquest. The Cuernavaca records, apparently for the most part done a little earlier, do not contain such a register, but they imply its existence and currency. To judge by the Tepetlaoztoc example, the notational conventions used by central Mexicans in registering land continued to be indigenous after the conquest, with the gradual addition of some (essentially superfluous) alphabetic glosses in Nahuatl. Further full examples are not available, but fragmentary records from Xochimilco in the late 1560's show that the details of the traditional manner of registration were still known: altepetl officials

TABLE 5.1

Terms for Fractions of the Primary Unit in the Indigenous Measuring System

Term	Literal translation	Equivalent
matl	arm, hand	four-fifths of a unit? (distance between outstretched hands?)[a]
mitl	arrow	half or three-fifths of a unit? (distance from one outstretched elbow to the far hand)
yollotli	heart	two-fifths of a unit? ca. 2.5–3 ft.? (distance between heart and outstretched hand)
acolli	shoulder	arm's length, from the shoulder to the fingertips
ciyacatl	armpit	arm's length
matzotzopaztli	flat part of the arm from elbow to wrist	cubit, from elbow to fingertips
molicpitl	elbow	cubit
omitl	bone	cubit
tlacxitl	foot	10–12 inches?
iztetl, iztitl	nail (of fingers or toes)	ca. 6 inches (a Spanish *jeme*, distance from tip of thumb to outstretched forefinger)

EXAMPLES: *matl*, BC, p. 154; Williams 1984; *mitl*, AGN, HJ 298: 4 (translated as half a braza); *yollotli*, BC, p. 90 (construed by translator as a Spanish yard), TC, p. 20; *acolli*, AGN, Tierras 30, exp. 1, f. 37 (Mexico City, 1570); *ciyacatl*, NAC, ms. 1481 (Tlatelolco, 1581); *matzotzopaztli*, AGN, HJ 298: 4 (translated as almost half a braza); *molicpitl*, AGN, Tierras 56, exp. 8, f. 3 (Tlatelolco, 1579); *omitl*, AGN, HJ 298: 4 (translated as cubit); *tlacxitl*, BC, pp. 88, 165; *iztetl, iztitl*, NAC, ms. 1481 (Tlatelolco, 1589; uses *omiztitl*).

[a] More often, in most places, a full unit.

called *tlalhuehuetque* ("land-elders") existed, and the fragments appear to be extracts from complete registers still kept current.[9]

Registration involved exact measurement, something that indigenous central Mexicans were fully capable of. We know little of the techniques used, how angles and areas were calculated, but the results show that the means were adequate. And although it may not be possible to establish absolutely precise equivalents for the units of measure, it is clear that each subregion or altepetl had its own version of a refined system of standard units capable of handling both large and small dimensions. The primary unit was a largish one, most often of perhaps eight to ten feet. In some places it was called the *quahuitl*, "stick," after the measuring stick used. (In the Tetzcoco and Tepaneca regions, and perhaps elsewhere, the term was often expanded to *tlalquahuitl*, "land-stick".)[10] In other places, it was the *matl* or *maitl*, literally "arm, hand," referring to any of various ways one can indicate distance by arm extension. "Quahuitl" and "matl" often seem synonymous, but in Tetzcoco and Coyoacan at least, the matl could be a fraction of the quahuitl.[11] A considerable vocabulary, based on the length of body parts, was available to designate various fractional units (see Table 5.1).

As to the size of the primary unit, Spaniards often translated "quahuitl" and "matl" as *braza*, "fathom" (about six feet), but it appears that the principal indigenous measure, though varying from place to place or occasion to occasion, was generally larger than that, and Spanish translators sometimes recognized as much by writing *braza de indios*, "the braza of the Indians."[12] The relative uniformity of the measure at any one time and place led many writers in Nahuatl to omit the name of the unit, but some Nahuas and Spaniards, aware of the overall variation, were at pains to describe the measure used. A Nahuatl document of 1554 from Coyoacan mentions the use of a quahuitl containing ten (Spanish?) feet as the customary one there, though a contemporaneous document from that region specifies a twelve-foot quahuitl.[13] The quahuitl used in Xochimilco in 1568 had the special name *nehuitzan* (for which I have found no analysis); the Spanish translator called it an "old-style measure" ("vara de las antiguas") and more usefully, a braza "measured from the foot to the hand," that is, apparently the distance from the ground to the hand of a standing man held as far as it would reach over his head, perhaps seven to eight feet or more depending on the person's height.[14] A Nahuatl document from Amaquemecan in 1661 specifies that the quahuitl used in the case at issue contained three Spanish yards (varas).[15] Another from Azcapotzalco in 1738 mentions that the tlalquahuitl employed on that occasion was called *cennequetzalpan*, derived from a word for standing erect; said to contain two and a half varas, seven and a half Spanish feet, it too was probably based on a standing person raising his hand over his head.[16] Scholars working on the Tepetlaoztoc land records have arrived at an equivalence of 2.5 meters for the tlalquahuitl there; to aim at such exactitude may be somewhat illusory, but the estimate falls well within the general range of variation.[17]

A measuring stick of a locally customary size, then, was used for determining relatively small linear dimensions. For larger dimensions, ropes came into play, or so one can conclude from the fact that *mecatl*, "rope, cord," had the extended meaning of a plot of land of a certain size. In Culhuacan, the term is found once possibly referring to a piece 200 by 20 units, or 4,000 square units, and in the Cuernavaca region another equivalence occurs.[18] In general, however, the mecatl seems to have been the basic standard plot twenty units square, called by Molina "an allotment of land" ("una suerte de tierra"). The most usual measuring rope must have been twenty units long. In fact, it does not seem to strain speculation too far to imagine that at some distant time, possibly before the Nahuas had arrived on the Mesoamerican scene and adopted intensive agriculture, the twenty-unit measure was the primary one, delineating one side of a square plot thought to be sufficient to maintain a small family, and the quahuitl or matl was derived by dividing the larger unit by the even number (in the vigesimal system) of twenty. If the quahuitl was eight feet, the basic plot was 160 feet square; if it was ten feet, the plot was 200 feet square. Under optimal conditions of water and fertility, such an area (25,000 to 40,000 square feet) might have been enough to provide the primary support for a group of four to six people.

The systems of land measurement, allocation, and registration, then, show that the altepetl and calpolli were deeply involved with landholding. But to what extent is use of the word "communal" justified? Modern governments dedicated to the notion of private property also maintain exhaustive cadastral records and peg taxes to land held; in new areas especially (as on the North American frontier), they may lay out plots of uniform size and shape and distribute them to the populace. They may even from time to time redistribute some land. They do not, however, make allocation a primary means of land redistribution, and to the extent that indigenous altepetl did so, their system of land tenure could reasonably be called communal even though the bulk of the arable land was held and worked by individuals and households.

Yet it does not follow that the indigenous governmental units could reallocate at will or that corporate reallocation was the predominant means by which land changed hands. Consistent ongoing reallotment according to need would seem to be incompatible with what has been discovered for the best-documented areas for the early postconquest years, the Tetzcoco and Cuernavaca regions, where we find not only great variance in the amount of land households held, but no particular correspondence between household size and holding.[19] The situation in Tepetlaoztoc, where some households held six or seven plots, others one, giving some far more arable land per person than others, appears to be primarily the result of the vagaries of inheritance over the generations. The implication is that the authorities could not or did not interfere with inheritance as long as there were living heirs and the land continued to be worked, and indeed, statements to this effect can be found in the postconquest chronicles.[20] As to more direct evidence, the tlatoani of Coyoacan is seen at mid-sixteenth century confirming the rights of individual spouses and offspring of commoners to inherit the latter's lands, or dividing the inheritance between disputing relatives.[21] From the late 1540's onward, Nahuatl testaments show nobles freely leaving their lands to their heirs, and as the testaments of commoners mount in numbers later in the century, the same pattern obtains.

The editors of the Cuernavaca censuses, however, take the position that (there at least) inheritance could not be used to accumulate land, since for the great majority a single amount is given, for irrigated land, with at most, in a certain number of cases, a separate amount for additional unirrigated land.[22] The question of how the land was acquired is usually not broached; in only a small minority of the instances is the allotment said to have come from the altepetl or calpolli officials. What is most frequently seen is that the head of the household allots a portion of his (i.e., the household's) land to some other member without breaking up the household's unity. In my opinion, the Cuernavaca records are not inconsistent with widespread inheritance and accumulation. The editors attribute the differential to the varying size of the plots originally allotted,[23] and I by no means discount this possibility, especially in the case of nobles and leaders. But I take it that most of the heads of household must have acquired their land through inheritance. The suballocations seen within households look very much like the inheritance division described in the chronicles and often may well have been preliminary to definitive inheritance on the death of the household head. The fact that the Cuernavaca records, which are primarily tax documents, list sixty or eighty units of land together in a single sum does not mean that they necessarily made up a single plot. I imagine that as in all other known situations, many if not most holdings above twenty units (other than those of nobles, whose plots often took the form of large tracts) were in separate and probably noncontiguous fields, and there is no reason why they could not have been accumulated through inheritance.

Overall, the picture suggesting itself is that on relatively rare occasions such as altepetl foundation, large-scale migration, and major defeat or victory in war, corporate authorities laid out the best lands in plots and divided them among the members of the group according to their rank and need, but that subsequently inheritance and spontaneous sharing or division among the people holding and using the land was the principal mechanism of continuity and redistribution, much as in Europe. Corporate reallocation, although a constant factor and an important part of the rationale of land tenure, would have played a supplemental or secondary role, taking over essentially only when a household died out or land was left abandoned for some other reason.

A further large question is what part individuals and corporate authorities respectively played when new allocations did occur. Who took the initiative? The larger land and census records have virtually nothing to say on this issue. When the authorities gave plots to newlyweds or new arrivals from other districts, surely the recipients first requested an allotment, and in a few passages in the Cuernavaca records such requests are explicit.[24] But could it happen that individual initiative went even further? Our only glimpse into this question is a unique document from the Coyoacan region, dated 1554, describing an inquiry into landholding and a partial redistribution that took place at Atenantitlan in the southeastern part of the region after it was reassigned from the district of Palpan (San Agustín) to the district of Hueipolco.[25] Although thirty years had passed since the conquest, the document belongs to the earliest land records preserved and is the only one known in which the fate of several plots over a period of years is detailed.

Most suggestive of all of the stories is that of a certain plot measuring thirteen by eleven units, newly assigned in about 1544 to one Martín Quauhtli, who after working it for three years left the Coyoacan area for Xochimilco. Later, an altepetl constable came to assign it to a new holder, Francisco Cihuaihuinti, who though he must have requested it, left it lying idle for years, despite continuing to live in Atenantitlan. Finally, not long before February 1554, a Francisco Xico took it upon himself to cultivate the plot. As he testified, "Just recently I broke the ground for myself; no one gave it to me." His rights were apparently confirmed. Other plots as well were assigned upon the previous holder's death or departure to new recipients who either went elsewhere after a time or never used the holdings at all. The chain of action seems to begin with a particular individual seeing land left vacant for whatever reason and moving to occupy it, probably with the informal assent of neighboring landholders aware of the overall local situation. The calpolli authorities are then prevailed upon to give the applicant the land he wants and may have already started working, and finally an official from the altepetl, a constable, alcalde, or regidor, comes to give final approval and see to measurement and proper recording. The dynamism in the system comes from spontaneous developments at the level of individual and family— migration, death, the filling of vacuums, the capacity or lack of capacity to work certain lands—leaving the corporate authorities primarily the function of legitimizing the existing situation. The entire Atenantitlan investigation was carried out at the request of the local people to liquidate Palpan interests in the area and legitimate the subdivision among several local residents of a large plot left vacant by a nobleman presumably now deceased. Pedro de Paz, the Coyoacan regidor who represented the altepetl (though possibly affiliated with the locality too),[26] reported: "I distributed their land to those Atenantitlan householders just as they wished it. . . . I merely followed their statements about how they had distributed it among themselves." The regidor may in fact have exercised some discretion, but the very nature of the proceedings suggests that he used local information and preliminary allocations as the basis of what he did.

In its day-to-day, year-to-year functioning, then, the system seems to have shared a great many common traits with European modes of land tenure, although surely there was less tolerance of individual land rights in the absence of active cultivation, and community consensus on landholding matters counted for more. In a land transfer of almost any kind, consulting local community opinion was an essential part of the procedure. Even with new allocations of empty land, inquiries were made to be certain no one had prior rights to it.* Those asked are usually called "tlaxilacaleque," which can mean either the calpolli elders or calpolli citizens in general, so that it is hard to be sure which is intended, but in any case, opinion is practically always unanimous, representing a local consensus on the status of the land and the legitimacy of the transfer. If at times the three or four persons interrogated are clearly district officials, at times there are ten or more people with humble names who appear to be simply neighboring houseowners.[27] Sometimes the group is referred to specifically as householders or even "all the householders," their individual names not being mentioned.[28] A report of the kind of thing actually said on such occasions comes from Tlatelolco in 1596. The governor and alcaldes, about to give possession of a house and lot after a sale, went to the site:

When they arrived, the householders there, the tlaxilacaleque, were summoned, and these people next to the house were told: "Come, what do you think about this house? Whose property is it?" They answered and said: "Oh rulers, María Salomé was truly the owner [*axcahua*]; now her grandmother María Juárez and Miguel Juárez, whose wife it was that died, are the true owners, and no one is claiming it from them."

Thereupon the governor gave formal possession to the new purchaser.[29] Anonymous groups of district citizens continued to participate in legitimizing indigenous land grants and sales into the eighteenth century.[30]

General public assent was not the only rite associated with taking possession of land. The new possessor sponsored a feast, or at least gave something to eat and above all something to drink to the officiating authorities. The feast is best documented for confirmations and transfers affecting one or more entire altepetl, but sufficient hints exist to indicate that it was standard practice among individuals as well.[31]

The Structure of Individual Holdings

At the individual level we encounter perhaps the most characteristic aspects of Nahua landholding. Although specific individuals held specific plots, they did so, from the point of view of the corporation at least, in the capacity of *cale*, "householder, head of a household." Thus in some sense it was the household that held land, rather than its constituents, even though the person designated household head was in charge of all the lands, and other members might be assigned specific rights to specific plots.

---

*To be sure, before granting land or giving final possession, Spanish investigators often canvassed all the neighbors brought together as a group to ensure that the action was without prejudice to third parties, approximating the same procedure. But there was an important difference. Spanish officials were trying to determine if any individual or individuals felt the action violated their particular rights; Nahua officials were trying to determine whether the consensus was for or against the action.

Lands held by the household fell into two great categories, one well defined, the other defined mainly as not being the first. As seen in preliminary fashion in Chapter 3, the core of the holdings was the *callalli*, "house-land," apparently meant to provide the family's primary sustenance and constituting the most permanent element, more closely associated with the household as a cross-generational entity than other lands. I say "apparently" because everything must be deduced from the practical use of the relevant terms in texts produced by the Nahuas; no straightforward discussion of these matters is found in either Nahuatl documents or Spanish chronicles. In the most systematic of the early cadastral records, still mainly glyphic in nature, the first listed of a household's plots bears the glyph for *calli*, "house," signifying "callalli." [32] Some of the signs are accompanied by the Nahuatl word written with alphabetic characters, leaving no doubt at all of the intention. [33] The callalli went far beyond being merely a site for a house; intended for agricultural use, it was if not the largest of the family holdings then at least a plot approximating standard size, [34] and it was possibly the best situated, best watered, and most fertile. In Culhuacan, the callalli most often consisted of a set of chinampas. [35] Ordinarily the house complex would be found physically located on the callalli, but this was not an absolute requirement; land at some distance could be understood to be attached as house-land to a certain household. [36]

For lands other than house-land, no single term emerges. Such plots are most often described simply as separate or in another place. In the 1554 Atenantitlan investigation, land not awarded as callalli is called *inic occan itlal*, "his land in another (or a second) place." [37] In Tulancingo some fifteen years later, we find the term -*huecamil*, "one's distant field," juxtaposed with the primary plot. [38] It is natural to speculate that the secondary fields were often relatively marginal land, or at least less fertile than the callalli, but specific statements about relative value have no occasion to appear in testaments, the main potential source of such information. Although in the Cuernavaca census records irrigated land is listed before unirrigated, this is not entirely conclusive, since the figures appear to be totals rather than the dimensions of individual plots.

Holdings organized by the distinction between the central callalli and scattered non-callalli can be said to have been universal in Nahua society. In Nahuatl wills, people who have more than an absolute minimum of land practically always have multiple holdings located away from the central plot. This is as true for lords and even for tlatoque as for commoners. Around 1550, don Juan de Guzmán, tlatoani of Coyoacan, had scores of fields scattered all across his kingdom, but at the center was some callalli, attached to his palace. [39] Indeed, if one equates the teuctli or lord with the householder,

TABLE 5.2

Land Scattering: The Estate of Félix de Santiago, Calimaya (Toluca Valley), 1738

Description	Size	
	Almudes	Acres[a]
—a house on a lot (solar) in town, near the jail	—	—
—a field at the border of the San Marcos jurisdiction	—	—
—a little field on the Metepec road, near a small hill	1	0.7
—a field on the Metepec road where there is a crossing to San Lorenzo	4	2.8
—a field on the Metepec road, lower down	3	2.1
—a field on the Analco road	4	2.8

SOURCE: NAC, ms. 1477 B [1].
[a]The acre equivalents are uncertain.

the teccalli or lordly house with the household, and the tecpancalli or palace with the house, organization is fully parallel for nobles and commoners. The manner of describing plots rarely allows us to tell just how far apart holdings were unless, like those of the tlatoani just cited, they were located in different calpolli districts. With lesser figures this was not often the case, and secondary plots are identified only as being either in a separate place (*cecni*) or at some named place that does not appear among the known calpolli.[40] Most often such names seem to refer to the kind of sizable tract of land (probably defined by natural features) that the Spaniards called a *pago* or a *paraje*.[41] Holding lands in different parajes would constitute significant scattering, and it was very common, to judge by the frequency in Nahuatl testaments of plots in differently named locations. On the other hand, a household's plots could be located in a single paraje and even at times be mainly contiguous, as shown in a recent reconstruction of a tract in Tepetlaoztoc.[42] Furthermore, there is no doubt that many households, in some places the majority, held but a single plot. Yet just as the existence of many single-structure dwellings did not negate the general structure of the household complex, so single-plot households, perhaps often inhabited by young couples or new arrivals, fit the landholding pattern in that any expansion with time would bring them into line with it, and their single holdings had the status of callalli. The pattern was as pervasive across time as across region and rank. As late as 1763, the holdings of a Josef de la Cruz in Tlapitzahuayan, near Chalco Atenco, consisted of the callalli plus four other apparently noncontiguous pieces of land.[43] Table 5.2 gives another eighteenth-century example.

What are the implications and rationale of the system of callalli plus scattered additional holdings? It can be seen as another form of cellular organization, treating a whole estate as a set of discrete independent parts related to each other not directly but in their common connection with the holder, who would attend to them sequentially and separately (as, for example, in the relationship of tlatoani and calpolli). On a larger scale, the same mentality manifests itself in the general notion of dividing up the fertile land of the altepetl into many distinct, relatively small and uniform plots that retained their identity no matter who held them. Estate structure apparently had no room for numerical symmetries (other than the even dimensions of some plots), and it violated the principles of cellular organization by putting one plot, the callalli, on an entirely different plane from the rest. Yet it was surely comparable to the organization of the house complex into separate parallel buildings and even directly congruent with it, in the sense that just as each adult relative was likely to have a separate residential unit within the compound, he or she might have separate rights to one of the household's plots, or in the case of a male, actually work a plot separately.[44] Among the more concrete motivations of the system, a primary concern, at least at times of large-scale distribution, must have been to avoid giving an undue proportion of the best land to a few; the system of scattered multiple plots allowed a larger number to have at least some part of the most fertile areas, supplemented by less desirable land elsewhere. Multiple separate plots also facilitated the usual division of the inheritance among all heirs. For landholders who were lords or tlatoque, their lands could be close to dependents located in different entities and subentities.[45] Diversification would also have been possible, each larger household growing the various types of crops best suited to various soil types and other conditions. However, although the Nahuas classified lands by soil type, availability of water, and slope, and integrated these categories into their landholding records,[46] no overt evidence has been found for a conscious effort to obtain complementary kinds of lands.

Certainly there is nothing to make one think of the large-scale, systematic attempts seen in the Andes for each household or small unit to use all ecological niches, often leading to holdings many miles removed from each other and a quasi-migratory way of life.[47] The central Mexican system was compatible with either a diffuse residence pattern of households scattered here and there across the land or a quite high degree of urban nucleation (especially when the house-land was physically separated from the house complex), but its natural affinity, probably associated with the original rise of the system, was for an intermediary settlement type in which people would live quite close to each other on the most fertile parajes, working their primary plots there, and go out frequently to work supplemental plots in surrounding parajes, perhaps less favored by nature. The addition or loss of supplementary plots would hardly affect the location of settlements and households. Life would be fully sedentary, but there would be a great deal of short-term motion back and forth across the locality.

Land Sale

Among the considerations speaking against a thoroughly communal interpretation of indigenous central Mexican landholding is evidence that individual holders sold land to each other in preconquest times. The chronicler Ixtlilxochitl claims that one of twenty ordinances issued by Neçahualcoyotl, king of Tetzcoco in the fifteenth century, specified that if a person sold the same piece of land twice, the first buyer should keep it and the seller should be punished (for the duplicity, apparently, rather than for the sale proper, which here appears to be recognized by the highest authority as a legitimate possibility). The term *tlalcohualli,* defined as land that is sold and bought, is included in the encyclopedic volumes compiled under the direction of Sahagún.[48] Although these are not conclusive proofs, since Ixtlilxochitl is far from reliable on preconquest matters, and Sahagún's work sometimes includes phenomena of the postconquest period, mundane Nahuatl texts point in the same direction.

In the Cuernavaca-region census records, done surely no later than 1544, with local society showing minimal change, a calpolli head of Tepoztlan is listed as possessing purchased fields amounting to forty units, in addition to eighty units of other land, and this is not the only such listing.[49] Above all, an entire calpolli of Tepoztlan was named Tlalcouhcan, "where land is purchased," strongly implying the antiquity and generality of the practice.[50] The lands of don Juan de Guzmán in Coyoacan (ca. 1550) included many scattered pieces of tlalcohualli, distinct from and often smaller than his numerous patrimonial or lordly holdings.[51] In Tlaxcala as early as 1547, indigenous people were coming from outside the area and buying land locally; the cabildo was concerned, but primarily, it appears, because it wanted the new purchasers to perform tribute duties, not because it saw anything untoward about the buying itself.[52]

From the earliest postconquest documents one finds land referred to as someone's property (-*axca*) or the landholder called a property owner (*axcahua*).[53] That "-axca" labels an item as special to a given person or persons rather than others is clear, but that the concept had all the connotations of "property" in European languages is hard to demonstrate; indeed, it is unlikely. Likewise, -*patiuh*, often translated as "price" or "payment," equally meant "value," and it is probably derived from a root implying replacement and exchange in a very general sense.[54] Though words taken by early lexicographers to be equivalent to European "buy" and "sell" existed in Nahuatl, the same question arises. *Namaca*, "to sell," by origin meant "to give in return," and although *cohua*, "to buy," is more obscure etymologically, it too seems to have to do with reciprocity.[55] These words were used in the earliest recorded postconquest money transactions, but what was their content in preconquest times?

A sixteenth-century Tlatelolco land case gives an answer to this question and throws additional light on the context and meaning of preconquest land sales, for not only does it tell far more than usual about the circumstances, but the reported sale is the earliest one documented.[56] In November 1558, relatives and witnesses affirmed that thirty-seven years before, by one reckoning, or three years after the arrival of Cortés by another, Magdalena Teyacapan, then doubtless still unbaptized, bought a piece of land at Tolpetlac (a northern dependency of Tlatelolco) from a man named Acxotecatl for twenty lengths of tribute cloth, or *quachtli*.[57] Since quachtli cloth was an important form of currency in preconquest Mesoamerica,[58] the transfer from Acxotecatl to Magdalena approximated a sale in the European sense, not merely some sort of trade. Immediately after the transaction, Magdalena went to the elders (huehuetque), also called *tetahuan*, "the fathers," who were altepetl officials in Tlatelolco proper rather than calpolli officials in Tolpetlac, and said to them: "Here is a bit of pulque that came from Tolpetlac, where I bought some land; it is so you will be informed that I am keeping the land for you, lest the person I bought it from, Acxotecatl, resident of Tolpetlac, should ever change his mind."

A land sale, then, was openly brought before the authorities, and a feast-like ritual accompanied the transfer like any other. Indeed, one way of looking at a transaction of this type is that the seller for a consideration relinquished his allocation from the altepetl/calpolli and permitted the authorities to reallocate it in the usual way to the buyer.[59] Sale in those circumstances would not contravene residual altepetl rights; nor would it by itself constitute sufficient legitimation of the transfer, or create an entirely separate category of land. Yet since individuals played the primary role, and going to the authorities was a second step that many may have omitted when the buyer felt sufficient confidence,[60] sale rather than reallocation was the effect, and throughout the colonial period indigenous people were to emphasize the distinction between tlalcohualli and other altepetl land.

The existence of land sale in return for currency did not preclude the exchange of one piece of land for another, and though we have little or no evidence for the preconquest period, trading is documented in Coyoacan in the time before 1575. One Juan Alvaro had accumulated six separate pieces of land, three by money purchase and three in exchange for land he already held. Although the term tlalcohualli does not appear as such, all six pieces are treated the same and apparently had the same status.[61]

In terms of the overall preconquest land tenure system, sale would seem to have ranked third behind inheritance and corporate allocation as a mechanism for redistribution, but it was a normal, recognized feature. Data are not sufficient to say more with certainty. It would have been natural if sellers were primarily those who had inherited more land than they could work and if the land affected was usually other than callalli. The role of the corporation would thus have been stronger with the most fertile and densely settled lands, weaker with those that were more remote and less productive, at least in terms of maize. In postconquest times, however, as we will see, all sorts of holdings were sold, and there is little to tell us whether the pattern was new or old. Some scholars have proposed that selling was more common among the high-ranking; many early examples tend to confirm this proposition, but the mere absence of specific instances involving the humble, especially in the first decades, when they had only begun to appear in documents, is not entirely conclusive.[62] At any rate, we can say that the Nahuas had traditions close enough to European practices of buying and selling land that they could immediately begin to act within the framework of the Spanish conventions.

Further Aspects of Land Categorization

The above discussion of some of the most basic features of the indigenous land regime has already defined several key concepts, but it has hardly touched the welter of categories, found in a variety of sources, that either show every sign of belonging to the preconquest system or openly purport to do so. A thorough treatment of the matter would assume frightening proportions without perhaps leading to a corresponding number of definitive conclusions. My intention here is merely to make one or two general points about land categories and then proceed to discuss a few of the ones with the most implications for postconquest times, trying above all to relate them to each other.

One of the largest, most intractable problems is the gap between, on the one hand, those sources—mainly synthesizing, mainly in Spanish—that devote space to a self-conscious description of preconquest land categories, and, on the other hand, sources—mundane, concerning individual postconquest cases, often in Nahuatl—that show comparable categories in actual use. A scholarly tradition has formed that approaches these two sets of materials by rationalizing the categories in the chronicles, comparing them with the mundane sources, and concluding from the difference a quick, sharp, and general loss of categories.[63] The list of classes considered basic does not always agree in detail from one version to another, but the impression arises that the categories are fixed and mutually exclusive, even though some of the objections to such an interpretation have been recognized and well stated: that the chronicles are vague, arbitrary, and self-contradictory; that practice and the use of terms varied strongly from region to region; and that the descriptions given are normative and partisan.

Let us assemble the terms included in three such listings, disregarding which of them different scholars subsume under the same grouping. They are *teopantlalli* or *teotlalli*, land of the temples and gods; *tlatocatlalli*, ruler's land; *tecpantlalli*, palace land; *pillalli*, noble's land; *teuctlalli*, lord's land; *milchimalli*, "army" land; and calpollalli. I propose that these categories were not mutually exclusive, that they were controversial, that terminology varied with time, region, and even speaker, and that hence without contemporary case material from the preconquest period, which it appears we will never have, we cannot take the chronicles at face value on preconquest land categories. Certainly we cannot simply compare the chronicles with the postconquest mundane records and interpret the difference as change. It is at least as likely that those records give us a truer view of the situation in preconquest times than the chronicles do.

In my view, tlatocatlalli, tecpantlalli, pillalli, and teuctlalli all refer to some particular way of looking at the lands of the teccalli or tecpan, the lordly establishment discussed in Chapter 4. We have already seen that tlatocayotl or rulership was teucyotl or lordship writ large. "Tecpantlalli" emphasizes the corporate institution of the lordly house, and "pillalli" the individual holder of land, while "tlatocatlalli" and "teuctlalli" can be taken as emphasizing either the individual or the office. The status of "tecpantlalli" must have been as variable and controversial as the status of the lordly house itself, some maintaining that such land was separate from the altepetl/calpolli and at the discretion of the lord, others that it was held as a function of altepetl/calpolli office. No doubt the concept of a distinction between lands given by the corporation for a corporate purpose and lands inherited or acquired as an individual existed,[64] but there is no reason to assume that the distinction resulted in well-defined sets of entirely discrete holdings. Much land must have come under several categories simultaneously and uncontroversially; just as a tlatoani was at the same time a teuctli and a pilli, so presumably tlatocatlalli could at the same time be teuctlalli and pillalli. For an early postconquest example (ca. 1550), some of the same lands on a list of the *tecpillalli*, "lordly noble's land," of don Juan de Guzmán, tlatoani and governor of Coyoacan, appear in another list giving palace and patrimonial lands clearly pertaining to the rulership.[65]

As for teopantlalli and milchimalli, the most probable interpretation is that these words name portions of the calpollalli set aside, possibly on an ad hoc, shifting basis, to help meet the needs of worship and warfare. With teopantlalli (far the more frequently mentioned of the two categories) there is no lack of indication that this may have been the case. One scholar has found calpollalli actually meaning land dedicated to purposes of worship.[66] With relatively few examples of usage, it may be impossible to distinguish between passages, if any, in which calpollalli truly carries the meaning "religious land," and those in which calpolli land is simply being used for such purposes. Nevertheless, the more specifically religious meaning would not be at all far-fetched. Every calpolli possessed some sort of divinity associated with its origin legend, and there are indications that in postconquest times, the Nahuas viewed the saints, the successors to the gods, as the residual owners of the land (see Chapter 6). Calpollalli could hence have been primarily and originally the land of the gods, and only by extension the land of the corporation. Another possibility is that lands held by temple functionaries on much the same basis as tlatocatlalli or teuctlalli could have been called teopantlalli (again, partial postconquest analogues exist). In any case, a student of preconquest religious festivities has emphasized the intertwining of priests with other nobles and of temple life with government, opining that most support for religious display came from altepetl officials.[67] It is unlikely that large surfaces were ever temple land to the exclusion of belonging to individuals or other entities, and even less probable that the constant wars of preconquest times were supported by the product of large plots permanently dedicated to that purpose alone. Of the categories commonly considered basic, then, only two emerge as sharply distinct from each other, namely, calpollalli and the land held under any of several appellations by rulers, lords, and nobles. Even between these two the line is sometimes hard to draw.

A category running parallel to calpollalli, used apparently for the same lands and contrasted in the same way with classes such as tlalcohualli and pillalli, is that of tribute land. The exact shape of the term varies considerably. *Tequitlalli* and *tequimilli* ("tribute land, tribute field") incorporate the noun *tequitl*, "tribute, duty," whereas *tequitcatlalli* and *tequitcamilli* are derived ultimately from the verb *tequiti*, "to perform tribute duty, pay tribute."[68] The two sets apparently mean the same thing. Another formulation is created by adding the modifier *tequio*, "that which owes tribute," to the main word denoting the piece of land, whatever that should be.[69] Most common of all is a statement made about a given holding that *ipan tequiti*, "he pays tribute on it," or *ipan tequitihua*, "tribute is paid on it."[70] Since such expressions occur in Nahuatl documents from the earliest known to the eighteenth century, the category may be presumed to have existed in preconquest times. Not only do references to tribute land occur in the same situations where one might expect mention of calpollalli, but in a document of 1596 from Tetzcoco, a plot is actually called by both terms at once ("tequitcamilli calpollalli");[71] such a pair is frequently used in Nahuatl to form a complex appellation by specify-

ing two slightly different aspects of the same thing. In Culhuacan in the
1580's, some people at death returned certain lands to the tlaxilacalli authorities for redistribution because the holdings were subject to tribute.[72] The
phrase thus conveyed that the land was under the direct administration of the
tlaxilacalli, to be allocated to other members at need, which was precisely
the thrust of the term calpollalli. An eighteenth-century Spanish translator
rendered "tequitlalli" as "land of the barrio," and in another document of
that period, some land called tequitlalli in Nahuatl is called *tierras de repartimiento* ("lands to be distributed") in Spanish.[73] The Spaniards used one or
the other of these terms to denote the bulk of the calpollalli.

Matters would be considerably simplified if we could ascertain that there
were two separate sets of categories, one referring to the status of land relative
to the altepetl/calpolli, the other to status within the household. To an extent,
such groupings exist. Callalli or house-land, non-callalli or additional land,
and tlalcohualli or bought land refer in the first instance to household-internal
status, pillalli and calpollalli to altepetl status. All three types in the first set
could occur in a single nobleman's holdings and thus in some sense be pillalli.
To be fully accounted for, any plot would need to be placed in two categories.
In fact, however, whatever the primary thrust, most categories seem to have
implications for both spheres.

Let us take the example of the common category *huehuetlalli*, literally
"old land." The element *huehue-*, "old," can be attached to such words as
"field," "house," and "property" with the same effect, which according to
Molina amounts to "patrimonial." As one scholar has observed, huehuetlalli
in practice comes close to meaning inherited land pure and simple.[74] But the
corporation could give someone land so designated from the first moment, as
when in 1567 the altepetl of Xochimilco awarded Martín Iuctli some chinampas "that become his huehuetlalli that he will leave to his relatives so that
they will always eat and drink from it."[75] Huehuetlalli thus tends to fall together with callalli as the more central and permanent part of a family's holdings. For commoners, callalli was definitely simultaneously calpollalli at its
origin and had the characteristic associated with calpollalli of not being
lightly alienated.[76] Nevertheless, the longer callalli stayed in a household, the
more distinct it must have seemed from the empty or quickly reallocated
portions of the calpollalli. The term huehuetlalli appears to have been used
above all to denote holdings of the callalli type, with emphasis on the holders'
discretion to dispose of them and the difference between such lands and ordinary calpollalli. Thus when a Pablo Huitznahuatl began to work some temporarily unused land in the Tlatelolco jurisdiction around 1550, "he did not
say it was his huehuetlalli, but only made it his tequimilli."[77] Landholders
used huehuetlalli status as justification for any action they saw fit to take,

either bequeathing the land to relatives or selling it.[78] With such connotations, "huehuetlalli," although more than anything else a household-internal category, came to imply a restriction of altepetl/calpolli claims on the land, while "tequimilli," primarily an altepetl-related category, came to imply secondary holdings in the household (i.e., non-callalli).

Further complications arise with huehuetlalli, however, for the term was used not only by individuals and households but by larger groups and corporations. According to Chimalpahin, in the early seventeenth century the citizens of the tlaxilacalli of Xolloco (Mexico City) claimed that the land on which a cross had long stood was their *huehuetlatquitl*, "patrimonial property."[79] Here what is meant is a holding of the corporation as such, and no contrast with calpollalli obtains. Indeed, in such cases calpollalli was precisely what was being referred to, as a passage from Tulancingo (ca. 1570) makes clear. A party from one of the constituent parts of the altepetl complained to the Spanish alcalde mayor that a certain nobleman had sold off "the fields that are our calpollalli . . . truly the fields of our fathers and grandfathers, our *huehuemilli* [patrimonial fields]."[80] The sense remains the same—long-term possession with an aura of full discretion and close association between holder and holding—but the type of possession varies, and the holder can be an individual, a small group (household, family), or an entire corporation. So huehuetlalli is no more a fixed land category, susceptible to the same interpretation in every use, than any of the other Nahua land categories, meaningful though they are.

Even less fixed, probably not deserving the name of a land category at all, is -*tlalnemac*, literally, "land that is given to one, land-portion," hence usually "one's inherited land," but also a plot awarded to one in judicial proceedings.[81] The term apparently always refers to an individual or individuals, never to a whole household or corporation, and means essentially no more than one's share within any of various frameworks. For this reason it is always, in my experience, in the possessed form, whereas huehuetlalli, though also possessed more often than not, does occur in the absolutive. It places emphasis on the possessor's particular rights, not the source of the rights or category of land per se. Thus we find in a text the phrase "huehuetlalli nonemac," "the huehuetlalli that is my share (inheritance, portion)."[82] Other types of land could also be one's -tlalnemac.[83]

Seen occasionally in sixteenth-century Nahuatl texts, once with specific reference to the preconquest period, is the word *cihuatlalli*, "woman-land, woman's land." Although such land is most often possessed by a woman, the term seems to be a true land category meaning more than simply land that happens to be held by a woman at the moment. A preconquest king of Tetzcoco apparently presented his daughter with land called cihuatlalli on the

occasion of her marriage, giving the appearance that the term refers in effect
to dowry land.[84] Other instances are compatible with such an interpretation
but could as well refer to land a woman had inherited in her own right,
regardless of marriage, or even acquired in other ways.[85] The thrust of the
term seems to be that the land came into a household through a woman, and
that she or her successors retained special claims on it in that context, not to
place any restriction on what could be done with the property. Status as cihuatlalli was somewhat independent of the woman who first brought the land
into the family; the word could be used in the unpossessed form, and the
category could remain viable even when the land passed into the hands of a
man, as when a male citizen of Coyoacan referred to "his" cihuatlalli.[86] Comparing the category with the last two treated, cihuatlalli could and usually
would be someone's -tlalnemac, but differed in principle from huehuetlalli in
being less closely identified with the household as a whole, carrying instead
the presumption of recent acquisition from the outside. It remains entirely
possible, however, that huehuetlalli in one household could go to a woman
as her inheritance and become cihuatlalli in another.

There are other, less well-understood and -attested land categories that I
have ignored, but those discussed above (and summarized in Table 5.3) are
central to the system as I understand it.[87] In general, though the evidence on
indigenous land categorization is relatively copious, it does not suffice to allow a complete reconstruction of the principles of the system and far less to
understand the details of a subtle and varying practice. The existence of an
extremely well-developed set of concepts and principles governing land tenure—in effect, a large body of land law, understood and enforced by both
governmental officials and the community at large—cannot be doubted. Inheritance, individual and family rights to land, and sale gave Nahua land
tenure many points of contact with the European tradition, as did the role of
government in recording and legitimating. But for all the similarities, differences were profound. Not only did any single Nahua category fail to overlap
entirely with any European category, differing substantially in the ensemble
of its implications, but the relationship between public and private was not at
all the same. One scholar has ventured the opinion that the most general
division in the indigenous system was between public and private domains.[88]
In fact, perhaps one of the most persistent sources of friction over land in
preconquest times, and certainly in postconquest times, was the question of
the rights of individuals or families relative to larger entities. Yet no terms
that could be comfortably called "public" and "private" have yet appeared
in Nahuatl land documentation (or in older Nahuatl in general, for that matter). We can identify entities of a clearly public nature that had land rights
(the altepetl, the calpolli, the local community or subsection) and entities of

TABLE 5.3

Overview of Indigenous Land Tenure Categories

Category	Translation	Remarks
1. altepetlalli	land of the altepetl	Can encompass any land over which the altepetl had residual control, but usually in effect means empty or loosely claimed land; generally falls together with the much more frequent calpollalli (2)
2. calpollalli	land of the calpolli	Primary term for land on which the corporate claim was strong, subject to reallocation; often contrasted with pillalli (4), huehuetlalli (7), tlalcohualli (8), and other categories emphasizing the holder's discretion over the land
3. tequitcatlalli, tequitlalli	land with tribute obligations	Essentially the same land as calpollalli (2), with emphasis on the direct obligations of the holder to the corporation
4. pillalli	land of nobles	Most frequent of several often overlapping terms referring to the holdings of high corporate officials, lordly and rulerly establishments, and nobles as individuals; often contrasted with calpollalli (2)
5. callalli	house-land	The plot or plots most closely and permanently associated with a given household; existed among both nobles and commoners; with commoners often assigned as calpollalli (2), but with time could be contrasted with it, falling together with huehuetlalli (7)
6. hueca tlalli, inic occan tlalli	distant land, land in another place	Plots held by a household over and above the callalli (5); usually but not necessarily noncontiguous with the callalli and each other; with commoners often falls together with calpollalli (2) and tequitcatlalli (3)
7. huehuetlalli	old land, patrimonial land	Land that has been or is expected to be inherited within a household indefinitely and hence is at the holder's discretion; existed among both nobles and commoners; often falls together with callalli (5) and is contrasted with calpollalli (2) and tequitcatlalli (3)
8. tlalcohualli	purchased land	Often contrasted with calpollalli (2) and tequitcatlalli (3); existed among nobles; existence among commoners in preconquest times not yet definitely established but probable

NOTE: Categories connected by lines and arrows have a tendency to refer to the same land.

what we would consider a private nature (the individual, the household), with some seeming to partake of both characteristics or to lie on the borderline (lordly houses and palatial establishments of various kinds). We cannot, however, point to lands that belong entirely in one domain or the other. Everything seems to belong to the two at once; even empty calpollalli was merely awaiting assignment to some individual, and a single individual holding land did so as a calpolli member and potential household head.

It is true that one could say much the same, in principle, of European land tenure, where all private holdings entail public responsibilities and under certain conditions can be repossessed by public agencies. Nevertheless, the dominant relationship between public and private in the European tradition is that land is either one or the other, while the dominant relationship in the Nahua tradition was that it was both at the same time. Words like "-axca" (property) and "huehuetlalli" (patrimonial land) could be used in relation to larger as well as smaller entities. The system followed the usual principles of cellular organization, with large units consisting of compartmentalized constituent units that were themselves compartmentalized: altepetl land was thus divided into calpolli land, calpolli land into household land, and household land into plots that individual family members worked and expected to inherit, with no one place for division into "public" and "private." The relationship of calpolli to household land was precisely that of household land to individual holdings. As in Nahua politics, constituent entities were forever working toward greater independence, trying to establish their own autonomous land rights, but within any successfully established domain, the process of subdivision and new thrusts toward autonomy repeated itself. The controversial status of teccalli land and the special rights families claimed to both callalli/huehuetlalli and tlalcohualli were entirely expectable under such circumstances. Statements that the lines between institutional and private ownership were blurred in specific cases or in general are true in their way but hardly do the situation justice.[89] Closer to the mark is one scholar's recognition that lands that had stayed in the same hands for generations were viewed differently from those more recently assigned by larger entities.[90] I would raise this to a general principle of Nahua landholding: that the longer any entity held land and the more removed the land was from the original allocation, the more unrestricted power that entity had over it, and the less power resided with the original allocating agency.

After all, collective entities, including both the household (with its noble variant) and the calpolli, were a more integral and active part of landholding in indigenous central Mexico than their counterparts in Europe, yet their role was not incompatible with intensely individual land rights, personal initiative, or inheritance and voluntary transfer between individuals. The multiplicity of potentially overlapping categories and the sliding scale of more rights with greater distance from allocation, without creating a strictly intellectual confusion, allowed for an infinitely varying interpretation of cases, giving us every reason to believe that the struggles over the status of land seen from the early postconquest period went back into the precontact period as an endemic feature of the system. They would have been held in check, however, by the pressure of a well-informed community consensus and extraordinarily detailed recordkeeping by local officials.

Land in Postconquest Times

Many aspects of the indigenous land system survived past the conquest into the following centuries. In fact, as we have seen, the middle and later sixteenth century has left us an essential part of the evidence with which the preconquest period can be studied. Indigenous municipalities remained in charge of their own land tenure management until independence and beyond. The pattern of estates consisting of many separate relatively small pieces, usually scattered in location, also continued to be dominant in all areas for the whole time. Several of the important categories dealt with above continued in use in their traditional meanings well into the second half of the colonial period. "Calpollalli" is attested as late as 1722 (Cuernavaca region), "tlaxilacallalli" 1738 (Azcapotzalco), "tequitlalli" 1723 (Chalco region), "callalli" 1763 (Chalco region), "huehuetlalli" 1659 (Tulancingo region), "tlalcohualli" 1738 (Azcapotzalco).[91] Given the spottiness of the record and the fact that fewer Nahuatl documents are preserved from the time after about 1770, partly because they were becoming less acceptable to Spanish authorities, it is likely that these terms and the concepts they bore remained viable among many Nahua groups through the entire eighteenth century. Not everything, of course, remained the same. Vast substantive changes aside, some categories seem to have faded quite early. "Cihuatlalli" is not attested after the late sixteenth century. "Pillalli" and other terms referring to the lands of lords, rulers, and lordly establishments carry on into the early seventeenth century, but in the second half of the colonial period, they appear only, so far as is now known, in the Cuernavaca region.[92]

With presently available sources, it does not seem possible to trace and date continuity or change in postconquest indigenous landholding practices with great precision. One large reason for the difficulty is the deterioration in the quality of the indigenous community's land records as the postconquest period proceeded. But this trend in itself, if interpreted, can tell us much. If we look at the overall situation in the sixteenth century after the Spaniards had established themselves, the fact that the newcomers began to appropriate some land seems to have affected Nahua landholding less than the drastic long-term indigenous population loss. Land values were low for both Spaniards and Indians; as late as the early seventeenth century, there was little indigenous reluctance to alienate lands and equally little interest in consolidating corporate rights to them when the opportunity presented itself.[93] To all appearances, there was plenty of land available for the survivors, the more so as the effects of the series of epidemics of the sixteenth century mounted. Measuring lands practically to the inch (far more exactly than Spaniards in the Indies customarily did) and keeping meticulous, complete, unified, up-to-date records of all holders and holdings (something else the Spaniards did not do) were now far less necessary than when the population pressed heavily on resources. For some time, until perhaps 1550 or 1560 generally and until 1600 in some places (perhaps especially in the intensely cultivated chinampa areas), the full system was maintained. But by the seventeenth century, and surely by the third or fourth decade of that century, it was gone. Often the measurements for a given plot were specified inexactly or not at all, and above all, unified registers ceased to be kept. This change can be correlated partly with the general decay of preconquest pictorial/glyphic writing, the medium of indigenous land records; with Spanish influence (since the Spanish tradition emphasized titles kept in individual hands rather than unified ca-dasters); and even perhaps with the long-term process of the weakening of the indigenous corporation and its loss of various functions. Yet the strongest factor seems to have been simple lack of need, much as in the case of the fading of indigenous military lore after the conquest.

Under the circumstances, with empty land available for people to take when needed, things probably worked well enough. Litigation over individual plots is hardly preserved from the early colonial period except for chinampas and urban properties. Appeal to the knowledgeable consensus of the local community was presumably as effective as ever, and it continued as late as the eighteenth century.[94] By the middle of the seventeenth century, however, things were changing: the Hispanic population and economy had expanded greatly and taken vast amounts of land, indigenous population loss had nearly halted, and land values were on the rise. Suits involving pieces of land of all sizes were now commonplace, between Spaniards and Indians as well as inside the community. It would have been well, for many, if the old regis-ters had still existed, but it was too late to revive them (it apparently did not even occur to anyone to try). For some, the new situation had its advantages. Claims to special rights to land could be pressed more successfully when there was no exact record to contradict them. Factionalism always played a large part in indigenous life. If the community climate was unfavorable to the claims of a person, family, or group, it was possible to appeal to Spanish authorities, who would view the matter with little contextual knowledge, not much respect for informal consensus, and great reliance on written documents.

For most indigenous people, however, especially commoners, land rights rested on informal consensus or equally informal action (at least in the sense of leaving no written record) by altepetl/calpolli authorities. Very few reallocations of land were ever written down as land grants in the Spanish manner. More frequent were bills of sale, but even sales apparently most often went undocumented unless the purchaser was a Spaniard.[95] If there was any document at all, it was likely to be the testament of a family member mentioning the piece of land in contention. From the Spanish point of view, the use of a will to establish title begged the question of whether the land belonged to the testator in the first place, but this aspect of the matter did not cause many problems because from the Nahua point of view, a testament issued before the proper local authorities and some witnesses representing the community guaranteed that the testator had authentic rights to what he bequeathed. A greater difficulty was that the document often lay more than a generation back in time and did not mention the person currently raising the claim.[96] Another hazard was the repetitiousness of naming patterns, leading to any number of people named Juan de Santiago or Ana Francisca in a single district over a stretch of years.

But by far the thorniest problem was the identification of land. Nahuatl documents of the second half of the colonial period, whether wills, sales, or records of municipal action, usually fail to provide adequate information to differentiate the plot involved from others in the same district (this is true of many documents of the first half of the period as well). Even when some sort of measurement is given, it is often a standard one, and though a paraje name or other geographical indication ("on the road to Toluca") is sometimes present, the same wording would cover many other plots; the intention of such descriptions as there are is primarily to distinguish among a testator's various properties. The names of parajes and subdistricts in any case merge with ad hoc descriptions ("at the road crossing," "at the edge of the ravine") and repeat as constantly as personal names. In Coatlichan (Tetzcoco region) in the years 1762–64, a suit revolved about the question, never firmly settled, of whether the piece of land concerned was the whole paraje of Cihuateopancaltitlan, or the whole paraje of Yancuiccalco, or just one part of Cihuateopancaltitlan.[97] In a long suit in Tenayuca (north of Mexico City) from 1697 to 1709, a major recurring problem was to try to identify a rancho one Miguel Francisco was administering for the municipality; Spanish and indigenous authorities seemed unable to establish whether certain land he had leased or sold was the rancho or not.[98] The same thing could happen even in the indigenous community of Mexico City, where in 1697 a Juan Pascual presented papers dated 1600 giving title to a house and chinampas; these documents were recognized by all as valid, but the opposing party affirmed that they related to Juan Pascual's residence, not the property in litigation.[99] Nahuatl documents, then, from the beginning to some extent, and increasingly as time went on, gave specific people clear rights to specific lands but were not in themselves sufficient basis for successful claims because in the matter of identification of the property they simply referred to common knowledge and community consensus. If a document happened to have been prepared a generation or more before coming into dispute, it might prove impossible to relate to community consensus at all.

Adoption of Spanish Procedures

In the above it has already been seen that indigenous landholding remained a matter primarily regulated inside the community, following norms largely derived from, if not literally identical with, those of the preconquest period, and that specifically Spanish procedures were not uniformly introduced. But here as in other spheres, Spanish terminology and ideas, originally often little more than a cover for some partial indigenous equivalent, in the long run had a considerable effect.

The old ways of measuring persisted to some extent through the entire colonial period. A document from the Toluca Valley at the very end of the eighteenth century, for all its late colonial idiom, still relies entirely on the classic style of measurement. The term quahuitl is employed to describe the unit, only the length is specified (on the presumption that the width is uniform and understood), and the quantities are round in vigesimal terms (80, 20, 10).[100] Even when Spanish terms occur, the content can still be indigenous. Measurements of a piece of land in Azcapotzalco in 1738 are given in the Spanish *brazada*, yet not only are the dimensions an utterly traditional 40 by 20 units, but the measuring stick used ("tlalquahuitl") contained two and a half varas, within the range of the indigenous quahuitl/matl.[101] Nevertheless, the vara or Spanish yard did make headway. It is found in 1630 as a fraction of a matl, and repeatedly from 1620 through the eighteenth century as the principal measurement.[102] But increasingly in the late period, both the quahuitl and the vara were used only to measure small strips, urban house lots, and the like. For larger holdings, the Nahuas began to adopt the highly imprecise Spanish system of stating the extension of land by the amount of seed that could be planted on it (in the indigenous context, the seed was generally understood to be maize, as was sometimes in fact made explicit, although the concept was occasionally applied to wheat as well). A *fanega de sembradura* is thought by some to have equaled about 8.8 acres, a *media fanega* (half) consequently 4.4, a *cuartilla* (fourth) 2.2, and an *almud* (twelfth) 0.73, but the values undoubtedly varied with time, place, and purpose, often being mere estimates.[103] Nahuatl documents show that "fanega" and "almud" were borrowed directly from Spanish in this meaning, whereas an indigenous equivalent, *tlacoton* (literally "little half"), took the place of "cuartilla."[104]

An even vaguer Spanish way of describing extension also found its way into Nahuatl vocabulary: talking in terms of yokes (of oxen), that is, giving the number of yokes it would take to work the land.[105] By now, the reader of these pages will not be surprised to learn that the middle of the seventeenth century was a watershed in the manner of expressing the dimensions of landholdings, with the new modes making their appearance in the 1640's and 1650's.

Spanish legal procedures involving land tenure began to be introduced much earlier, in the mid-sixteenth century, as part of the Hispanic reorganization of altepetl mechanisms more generally. Documents of that time from Coyoacan already include all the most important items: grant, possession, and bill of sale.[106] To what extent, however, did these genres match the Spanish originals? For one thing, European-style written records about land dealings were most likely to be drawn up, and to approach Spanish models most closely, when a Spaniard was involved in the transaction.[107] Even so, a punctilious observation of written and other formalities sometimes characterized purely indigenous land dealings as well.[108] In general, over time the documents tend to come ever closer to Spanish counterparts.

Some were quite close from the beginning. In Coyoacan in 1575, one Joaquín Flores, of the district of Atepotzco, came before the governor and alcaldes and presented a petition asking that he be granted some empty town land in his home territory. District authorities appeared on his behalf, verifying the facts and supporting Flores's request, whereupon the governor and alcaldes granted him the land for himself and his children after him, and sent the chief constable out to give him full possession. The notions of petition and possession are both conveyed through Spanish loanwords.[109] Almost two centuries later, in the Toluca Valley town of Calimaya in 1750, a Marcelino Antonio and his wife came before the governor, alcaldes, and other officials with a petition requesting a specific piece of land, and the story repeated itself, this time the governor himself proceeding to the spot to give possession (which is reported in some detail).[110] The second document especially has many local peculiarities, but both reproduce the main elements of a Spanish land grant.

Looking beneath the surface, we can say, first of all, that the Spanish mode differed little from already established indigenous practice. We have already seen that as well as can be reconstructed, in preconquest times a person would ask the authorities for land, often a specific piece he had already identified and perhaps begun to work, and after verification they would give it to him, carrying out formalities of measurement and making a record. There was surely no written petition, and no sources tell us just what the applicant said on this occasion, but the Nahuas were such masters of formulaic speeches that it would have been most uncharacteristic if there were no set speech for the purpose, and likewise for the finalization of rights. Procedures diverged, then, primarily in the type of written record kept and in the detail of formula and rite. It was perhaps because of the variance of the Spanish forms that the Nahuas frequently used Spanish terminology for the acts of petitioning and taking possession, but just as likely it was because of the emphasis Spaniards placed on them as necessary steps in the process of establishing title.

Yet the gestures in the direction of Spanish ritual did not mean that indigenous ritual was abandoned, even if it was not ordinarily reflected in the written record. A certain amount of subtle, even profoundly significant evidence of continuing indigenous thought and practice can be found buried in records ostensibly following a Spanish model, but writers definitely tended to emphasize what would have legal value within the Spanish framework and to omit what would not, so that the more purely indigenous side of practice is hard to detect. It is seen in Spanish complaints that indigenous officials were always eating and drinking and receiving gifts for their cooperation, and sometimes in statements made by parties to litigation about how things really worked.[111] Rarely was a Nahuatl notary naïve enough to put everything that happened on paper, but in San Miguel Tocuillan (Tetzcoco region) in 1583 one writer did just that. A precious source for various purposes, the document (no. 1, Appendix A) has already been used in previous chapters.

Since Tocuillan, despite its location in the central part of the Valley of Mexico, was no major settlement, and indeed possibly merely a subconstituent of Tetzcoco, the writer may not have mastered the Hispanic formulas, causing him to resort instead to a full dialogued account. Even so, his version is artful and condensed, representing formula of a different kind. Perhaps it is a descendant of the memorized oral recitals that must have accompanied reference to written cadastral records in preconquest times. At any rate, to set the scene again, a woman known only as Ana, having fallen on bad times, moves in, together with her husband and young son, to live with her older brother Juan Miguel, a regidor, until, the arrangement becoming burdensome, she suggests that they request some land for a site where she can build a house. Juan Miguel then sets out to collect a set of four notables from as many subdistricts, first telling Ana to prepare some tortillas and get out the pulque, of which there is a plentiful supply. Whether these men are heads of calpolli or sub-calpolli, with Juan Miguel a regidor in a larger municipal entity, or whether they all together constitute a cabildo or full set of officers for Tocuillan is not clear. In any event, when they arrive at Juan Miguel's house, they partake of the tortillas and pulque, and after polite small talk, Ana requests "a bit of the land of San Miguel" (the town saint) on which to build a house. They assent, go out with Ana to the general area, ask her to designate a site, and after one of their number (the one who usually performs the task) has measured out the land, award it to her, saying "that's how much land we're giving you." Ana and her husband weep on receiving the plot, and she promises to keep candles and incense burning at the altar of San Miguel in gratitude. She makes the gesture of asking everyone back to the house for some more pulque, which is politely declined. All five officials speak, everyone embraces, and the occasion is over.

Since the account, although longer than a terse Spanish grant document, is still highly compressed and selective, it appears to be not merely a story told in colloquial idiom about the events of a day, but a reporting of the proper performance of legitimating ritual. Before Juan Miguel even left the house, it had probably been decided that the site would be awarded, and where. The document tells of the carrying out of a feast and other requisite niceties in the same spirit as Spanish title papers specifying the proper sequence of legal acts and bearing the necessary signatures. Although close parallels to the Tocuillan document have not been found (and with most writers having been better trained in Spanish documentary genres, few must ever have been written), I believe that grants and other transfers within Indian communities across the entire period under consideration were accompanied by food, drink, and various ritualistic negotiations and transactions (including outright payments to those officiating), all phenomena with roots in the preconquest period.

At the same time, Spanish land ritual, especially the concept of "taking possession" and the acts accompanying it, became meaningful to the Nahuas. The Spanish manner of having the principal officer present take the new possessor by the hand and lead him over the property, while the latter carried out symbolic destructive acts showing his full rights (pulling off twigs and throwing stones), seems to have become deeply embedded in Nahua practice, though the Spanish rite may have been affected by indigenous elements (entirely aside from a separate substratum of indigenous rites). Thus some extant examples contain hints of the traditional Mesoamerican emphasis on the cardinal directions and four-part gestures. In acts of possession in Tlatelolco and Mexico City in 1620 and 1630, the new possessors indeed threw stones, but specifically in the four directions (*nauhcampa*).[112] The governor of Calimaya, in giving possession to Marcelino Antonio in 1750 (see above, at n. 110), was careful to stroll him about all four corners of the property.[113] Even so, the "possession" functioned very much as in Spanish land law, as something to which the new holder could appeal in the first instance to ward off any other claim, and something without which (in theory) any claim, however valid, that he himself might have to the land could not be made operative. At times, the possession even carried the Spanish implication that the holder was now the primary repository of the materials for the future defense of his rights, as when in Mexico City in 1630 the buyer of a house, as part of an act of possession, was given the original testaments of previous owners, as well as the bill of sale and record of the current proceedings, to keep always.[114] In the majority of unwritten transfers involving humble people, eating, drinking, and other indigenous ritual may have outweighed the Spanish trappings, but a mixture of both sorts of legitimation was probably the norm, and surely both became part of standard Nahua procedural lore.

Postconquest Forms of Non-calpolli Land

As we have seen, in preconquest times a tension existed between calpollalli, quite directly under the control of the general corporation, and lands that under various headings were under more autonomous control by subgroups of individual members of the corporation. Although several of the non-calpollalli categories fell into disuse, others did not, and the often disputed distinction continued to be a marked characteristic of indigenous landholding in the postconquest centuries. The nature of the sources for both periods precludes any definite statement that the tension increased in absolute terms, nor can it readily be shown, though it may be suspected, that the noncalpollalli sector grew in relative size. Spanish cultural influence and actual pressure from Spaniards in and out of government certainly played a role in the process, but often Spanish factors prove to coincide with indigenous counterparts. The subject is thus full of ambiguities and for now must remain so. Still, something can be said about the forms and rationale of attempts to remove land from the calpolli domain.

As noted above, the indigenous category tlalcohualli (purchased land) remained current in central Mexico through the whole colonial period, and it was common for one person or married couple to sell land to another. In many such sales, probably the majority of those of which record is preserved (since records were needed for subsequent title validation proceedings in Spanish courts), the buyer was Spanish, and the piece of land was lost to the Indian community forever. But in some documents only Nahuas are involved, and many others (above all testaments) report such sales indirectly, leading to the conclusion that between indigenous people land sales without written record were, if not the rule, at least a frequent phenomenon. Nevertheless, the Spanish bill of sale (*carta de venta*) became part of the repertory of Nahua notaries from an early time.[115] As with the petition and the possession, apparently the primary motivation was to cement certain rights within the Spanish framework, so that the simple use of the term as a catchword seems for some to have been the crucial factor, the actual content of the procedure being relatively unimportant. Yet the wording does often approximate the Spanish

model, implying that the transaction occurs between two absolutely free economic agents acting as individuals and in no other capacity, and transferring
the property sold to the absolute control of the buyer for all time to come. If
taken literally (whether it was or not is virtually impossible to judge), the
language would mean the introduction of a quite pure form of the European
conception of private property into Nahua thinking. In my opinion, although
the Nahuas translated and understood the Spanish formulas, the two traditions had so many points of contact that there was nothing to keep indigenous people from interpreting the statements within their own framework.

Spanish authorities were aware of land sale by and among Indians, and
perhaps moved in part by the apprehensions of indigenous authorities about
the possible results of unrestricted sale under postconquest conditions,[116] were
always passing ordinances demanding full justification of any sale, especially
evidence that the seller was not being coerced and was fully aware of what he
was doing, that he was not being impoverished by the sale, and that he had
good reason for it. The response was the appearance of additional formula in
Nahuatl bills of sale. An affirmation of voluntary action was within the Spanish tradition, but the rest was neither purely Spanish nor purely indigenous,
reflecting rather specifically postconquest circumstances. The seller would
likely affirm that he had other land to support himself, that the land being
sold was in disuse or useless (flooded, next to a highway and exposed to
damage by livestock, etc.), and that he needed the money to pay his tribute,
cover other debts, or have masses said for relatives. He might add that for a
specified reason the land sold was not calpollalli or tequitcatlalli.[117] Although
in an individual case these assertions were not necessarily untrue, they were
not necessarily true either. They were above all legal language designed to
ensure the validity of the transaction in Spanish and indigenous courts, and
they owe their plausibility primarily to the fact that Spanish ordinances in
these matters spoke to widespread conditions.

Sale documents are thus only the façade for processes that become visible
all too rarely—usually only when a disagreement caused someone to dispute
the legality of a sale. Consider the case of José Lázaro in Amecameca in the
late eighteenth century. In May 1767, a document was drawn up confirming
the sale of a piece of land by José de Santiago and his wife Catarina María to
José Lázaro and his wife Luisa Juana, for fifteen pesos. The land was in the
tlaxilacalli of Huehuecalco, next to another piece José already held, and Catarina and her first husband had themselves bought it many years previously.
The listed witnesses, three people entitled "don," of whom one was fiscal of
the church, are referred to by José as "notlaxilacaltlahuan," "my tlaxilacalli
uncles," so that they seem to have been figures of authority in the district.
Nevertheless, irregularities abounded. When the document was drawn up,

only nine of the fifteen pesos had been paid; the rest was to follow at an unspecified rate, and in fact José Lázaro gave Catarina María only small bits whenever he could, taking over ten years to pay the full amount (which he claimed was sixteen pesos, not fifteen). Because of the drawn-out nature of the transaction, some neighbors took the position that the land was in hock rather than being sold. The notary who drew up the document, though he had frequently been Amecameca's municipal clerk, was not in office at the moment, and above all, the governor and alcaldes were not called upon as was the custom. José Lázaro claimed that if he had brought in the full set of municipal officials, all the money he had paid to Catarina María over the years would have had to go instead for snacks and pulque for them, and he would have been liable besides for a money payment of three pesos, called the *tlatlaqualoni* (literally "something to eat with"), which they were customarily given on the occasion of a sale. The out-of-office notary said he had agreed to take care of the sale by himself because the amount involved was small. In June 1781, after appeal to Mexico City, although no one denied that the money had changed hands, the Audiencia declared the sale false and ordered the land returned to Catarina María (not quite the same as her actually receiving possession, of which there is no record).[118]

Halfway between formal and informal procedures, José Lázaro's story contains many elements in common with cases less well recorded. Payments made bit by bit on an undetermined schedule (or not made at all), each side having a divergent interpretation of the total amount and of who now really owned the land, are mentioned in other sources as well.[119] The lack of ready cash among humble people amply explains the practice. When, as often, the value of the land was even less than in José Lázaro's case, the motivation to avoid written and other formalities was even greater. Transactions often reached the level where sale was only one aspect of the transfer, and one could legitimately doubt whether "sale" is a proper description. Purchase terminology is sometimes used in the sources for dealings of this type, sometimes not.

A purchase such as José Lázaro's is straightforwardly economic, since it took place between nonrelatives and had the purpose of increasing José's productivity by adding land located nearby and easy to work. We have no reason to doubt that many other transactions were of that nature, and at times evidence appears of systematic speculative activity.[120] A great many sales, however, were motivated by the need to pay funeral and other emergency expenses. A glance through collections of Nahuatl testaments will show how frequent it was to order property sold for masses for the testator's soul. Most often such sales were carried out by relatives, officials, or others assigned the role of estate executor. But there could also be mixed, anticipatory arrange-

ments. During his lifetime, Constantino Esteban of Tlatelolco made an agreement with Miguel Hernández of the neighboring district of Santa María in
Mexico City to sell him his house and lot for seventy pesos. Constantino
received only thirty pesos at the time; then when he fell ill in 1620, he had a
testament drawn up ordering Miguel to give thirty pesos to his wife and children and pay ten pesos for requiem masses for his father and himself. Miguel
did so, and then received the property with all formalities.[121]

Many sales were the result of family contingencies only on the seller's side,
with the buyer acting impersonally, on market principles. But often family
was involved on both sides, so that sale and inheritance came close to merging. In Tezontla (Tetzcoco region) in 1689, a Juan Miguel, struck with an
illness, made a will stating that he had already transferred a small piece of
land at Calinatoxtitlan (Granadostitlan, "next to the pomegranates") to his
nephew Diego Gabriel, who had given him half a peso for it. Juan Miguel
then survived his illness to make a second will over twenty years later, in
1710; this time he merely stated that he was leaving the land to his nephew
(who had doubtless possessed and worked it the whole of the time). In 1713,
Juan Miguel's widow in her will, presumably to avoid all possibility of coun-
terclaims, once again left the same piece of land to Diego Gabriel, saying
nothing of the background.[122] It is entirely possible that Diego Gabriel would
have inherited the land anyway, and the transaction could be seen less as a
sale than as payment for the right to enjoy one's inheritance early. It is also
likely, though as usual in these cases not demonstrable, that Diego Gabriel
paid less than the going rate.

Other cases have even less of an aura of sale. A testator might make what
looks like a normal bequest to a relative, then follow it with a request or
order that the relative make a payment, at times specifically destined for
masses or other funeral expenses (and probably so intended even when no
specific purpose is given). The money might or might not be overtly labeled
as a quid pro quo. Money might not be mentioned at all. María Teyacapan,
who left two buildings and fifteen chinampas to her nephew in Culhuacan in
1580, simply added "and he is to favor me with a mass"; no amount was
named, but the effect was the same.[123] Aside from functioning as the vehicle
for a kind of inheritance fee, intrafamilial sale could facilitate redistribution
within the family beyond the scope of normal inheritance. In a family of the
Tetzcoco region in the seventeenth century, the holdings were divided among
the children in the normal way, but in the event, one brother flourished and
the others did not. As his siblings one after another fell into straits or suffered
illness, he would give them money, take care of their children, and see to their
burials in return for their land, thus reintegrating family properties that might
otherwise have gone their separate ways.[124] On the other hand, just such fa-

milial cooperation might have taken place equally well in preconquest times under the rubric of the special responsibility of uncles, with no connotation of sale.

One effect, with possibly major implications, was that those who acquired land from relatives for a consideration, even though it had been calpollalli and they might have inherited it in any case, did not hesitate to call it tlalcohualli (purchased land). How well they succeeded in obtaining more general acceptance of such a view seems impossible to establish from the available sources, but if a significant percentage of the lands changing hands in this manner escaped the duties imposed on calpollalli/tequitcatlalli, the domain of taxable, reassignable land must have been constantly diminishing. In view of the general situation with postconquest land tenure, the status of such land was probably precarious and controversial. The potentially mushrooming amount of tlalcohualli among indigenous holdings may not have gone unchallenged, but it did provide a much-used pretext for reselling land alleged to have been sold before.

Presumably the popularity of the appeal to the special standing of tlalcohualli, though growing out of the indigenous heritage, was reinforced by the introduction of the bill of sale genre, by Spanish notions of unlimited rights to sell private property, and by common practice in the local Spanish economy (though there is no evidence of any overt Spanish campaign to Europeanize the indigenous land regime). Another and even more basic land category, huehuetlalli (old land), also coincided with Spanish concepts closely enough to merge with and perhaps be influenced by them. As inherited or inheritable land tied to a family's fortunes, huehuetlalli was generally translated into Spanish as "patrimony, patrimonial land." Spanish *patrimonio*, while referring to an inherited family estate in toto, also had, when applied to a single individual, the connotation that his patrimony was his special share, all other claims having been previously resolved, so that while the holder of the patrimony had a serious responsibility for its preservation, he was completely free to do whatever he wanted with it. By the late sixteenth century, the Spanish term had been introduced into Nahuatl, and by the seventeenth, it was being used standardly along with or even instead of huehuetlalli to justify the right to sell land and differentiate it from tribute-paying calpollalli.[125]

Pillalli (nobles' land), together with its related categories referring to office or lordly establishments, had been the main opposite pole of calpollalli in preconquest times. After the conquest, however, these terms gradually fell into disuse, unlike others that were often distinguished from calpollalli (tlalcohualli, huehuetlalli, callalli). First to go were all those relating to office and palace lands (tlatocatlalli, tecpantlalli, and equivalents), which do not appear in known documents after the early seventeenth century. Such lands are seen spoken of in the later colonial period mainly in Spanish, as cacicazgo lands. "Pillalli" (also in the variant "tecpillalli") held on more strongly, perhaps because it emphasized the rights of the individual holder rather than those of a larger entity, but it too faded in the second half of the seventeenth century and was generally speaking a rarity in the eighteenth.[126] Does this mean that nobles' lands became indistinguishable from calpollalli, or at least from the various gradations of the holdings of ordinary commoners? Although it seems to be true that the lines became more blurred, I believe the answer to this question should ultimately be in the negative. The evolution is closely parallel to developments with the indigenous nobility in general, as dealt with in Chapter 4. There it was seen that indigenous terminology for noble rank decayed after the early seventeenth century, but new types of distinctions were made, and a recognizable, self-perpetuating upper group continued to exist. Just so, that same upper group (despite the sale of much of its land to Spaniards before 1650) continued to maintain landholdings larger than and in some ways distinct from the rest, in spite of the loss of the old terminological distinctions. For one thing, it was mainly nobles who sometimes went beyond Hispanic-style procedures and records within the indigenous community to confirm their rights in the Spanish context, having sales, grants, and acts of possession carried out directly under the auspices of Spanish officials, much as any Spaniard would do, with consequently firmer title anchored outside the local altepetl.[127] In the late colonial period, the holdings of the class of people who functioned as governor, alcalde, and fiscal, at least in some of the larger towns, sometimes approximated Spanish haciendas or ranchos, or more often took the traditional shape of numerous scattered plots, but in either case were differentiated by their scale, staff, and equipment from most estates of ordinary plebeians even when described in the same terms. As in times past, altepetl officials often used their position to assure the allocation of lands to themselves.[128]

All the forms of non-calpollalli landholding in the later colonial period, both those overtly resting on indigenous categorization and those involving its replacement, showed signs of Spanish influence, and it is a fair statement of the general trend to assert that there was movement in the direction of a more individualized conception of landholding in the European style, in which the landholder stood in contrast to larger entities rather than forming part of them. On the other hand, the new concepts were reinterpreted, receiving indigenous content, and all of them represented variants on a traditional distinction between calpollalli (as land held by individuals but under the close supervision of the community) and other lands, a distinction that had no near counterpart in the European tradition. Ultimately it was still the indigenous concept of calpollalli/tequitcatlalli that defined, albeit negatively, all other civil categories of landholding.

In a flux between two traditions, indigenous landholding was in a potentially precarious state by the eighteenth century. Despite great losses into
Spanish hands, in most areas indigenous towns still had considerable
amounts of land and administered it for the most part autonomously, following a regime in which indigenous elements still predominated. Yet with the
double tradition, two sets of authorities to whom to appeal, the loss of exhaustive indigenous record keeping and surveying, and the fragmentation of
the altepetl into entities often unable to exert any wider influence, a fragile
neighborhood consensus was left as the only stabilizing force. People must
often have done as they pleased, interpreting evolving community norms to
suit themselves, and there was no easy or fully satisfactory way to settle serious disputes.

Economic Life and Material Culture

Having understood something of how the Nahuas held land, we may now
turn to the question of what they did with it, or more broadly, of how they
lived and made a living. On these important matters, the internal sources of
the indigenous world prove far less generous than on political and social
organization, inheritance, or land tenure. Since the routine of daily life consists of an almost infinite number of discrete small actions and strategies, its
elements must have seemed individually too insignificant (as well as too obvious or presupposed) to deserve space on the written page. Though Nahuatl
documents are rich, enlightening, and not infrequently graphic, they fall into
well-defined, highly selective types that by no means blanket the field of potentially interesting information. Nahuatl writing is never merely discursive
but always for a specific purpose; in mundane Nahuatl documentation, that
purpose is generally to claim or protect rights or possessions that might be
legally challenged. In the sphere of marketplace activity, the crafts, and the
production, sale, and consumption of agricultural commodities, challenges
apparently did not reach the level of legal action within the altepetl
framework.

Indeed, this whole domain seems to have gone substantially without altepetl regulation of any consistent kind, at least after the third quarter of the
sixteenth century. One reason may have been the small money value of dealings in such areas. It is also possible that a great deal of Nahua economic
activity spilled over into the general Spanish economy, escaping the purview
of the altepetl and falling directly under the jurisdiction of Spanish authorities. Whatever the reason, Nahuatl litigation and sale documents tend to deal
with land, not products, and the Nahuatl wills that specify all the testator's
lands and their destination say little about what was grown on them or how,
much less about any other routine activity. To attempt to treat somewhat

systematically the productive and nonproductive aspects of daily life among indigenous people, it would be necessary to resort to Spanish sources, many of a synthetic nature, and as in other parts of this book, that I am reluctant to do without adequate indigenous sources as a check. Moreover, such a treatment is already available.[129] Here I intend only to devote some pages to those aspects of economic endeavor and material culture that find expression in Nahuatl sources, as a supplement to what may be seen from other perspectives. (See Chapter 3 for some relevant discussions of household life and appurtenances.)

Money and Money Dealings

Although preconquest Mesoamerica lacked coinage or an exclusive reliance on precious metals as a medium of exchange, currencies existed. One reads in chronicles of copper artifacts, beads, and quills filled with gold dust serving in this capacity, as no doubt they did,[130] but the items most commonly mentioned, and the only ones still found operating in early postconquest mundane records, are lengths of cotton cloth called *quachtli* (often used for tribute) and cacao beans. Both were commodities of ordinary consumption, especially for people of means, but in temperate central Mexico they had the aura of luxury goods because cotton and cacao grew only in warmer lands, mainly located to the south. Quachtli, arranged in standard bundles of twenty, were used to buy the indigenous slaves who were still owned in the Cuernavaca region around 1540.* (They also, as indicated at nn. 56–57 above, appear as payment in the earliest recorded postconquest land sale, in the Tlatelolco jurisdiction.) Cacao as a medium of exchange appears again and again, in both Spanish and Nahuatl documents, throughout the sixteenth century and on through the colonial period. Cacao could be amassed to represent substantial values, but ordinarily it came into play for small transactions worth less than a quachtli; at any particular time, with adjustments in a given case for the relative quality of the two products, a standard rate of cacao beans per quachtli prevailed.[131]

Spanish money entered the Nahua world very quickly; it figures prominently in one of the earliest extant Nahuatl documents, a Tlaxcalan market price list of 1545,[132] and it continues to appear as a standard item in documents of all kinds through the postconquest centuries. The Tlaxcalan cabildo records of the 1550's and 1560's repeatedly show a conceptual mastery of the Spanish monetary system; furthermore, by the nature of the taxes imposed and by general descriptions of the local economy, they imply that most indigenous people including commoners actually had some money in their pos-

---

*AZ, 2: 1, 3. *Quauhnahuacayotl*, cloaks of a specific type ("Cuernavaca-style"), were given in tribute like quachtli and on occasion were used to pay for slaves as well. The same presumably applies to other types of cloth and cloaks in different regions.

session in the course of a year.[133] Documents from Coyoacan show money circulating in the altepetl market by the middle of the sixteenth century, with the various specialties all able to pay money assessments.[134] Similarly, the Culhuacan testaments (ca. 1580) show money in the hands of almost everyone, including women and very humble people; not only land, houses, and transport animals, but things such as household gear and ordinary foods bore a money value and were exchanged locally on that basis.[135] The word *tomín*, signifying a coin, gold weight, and standard of value equal to the *real* or eighth of a peso, is one of the first attested Spanish loanwords in Nahuatl, and "peso" itself was not far behind (1548).[136] Both, as well as *medio*, half a tomín or *real*, were an indispensable part of the Nahuatl vocabulary from the mid-sixteenth century forward.

How much change did the introduction of the Spanish monetary system represent, and was the adjustment a difficult one? The transition to money occurred with great speed in all known parts of the area, and there is no evidence that the Nahuas had any difficulty in comprehending money's significance; prices seem rational, and money was prized and sought after by all. No strong indigenous reinterpretation, such as that affecting borrowed land categories or introduced governmental offices, seems to obtain. On one occasion, the Tlaxcalan cabildo took an apparently antimonetary position, condemning the commoners who neglected their duties and sustenance crops in growing cochineal for money, which they pointedly noted could not be eaten in time of famine. This is a statement, however, with few parallels in indigenous records (though some can be found in the annals of various other civilizations), and it covers up the fact that the nobles on the cabildo were themselves growing and selling cochineal for the money it brought them.

The transition from one system to the other was only partial in any case, for the two became integrated. The tomín/*real* and its multiple the peso quickly replaced the quachtli for larger transactions, but for items worth under a tomín or half a tomín, cacao beans continued in use. It was not a question of competing currencies, but of cacao beans functioning as change for the Spanish coins. This ability to build one system into the other implies that the conceptual distance between the two was not insurmountable. Mesoamerican trade is often considered to have contained a very large element of barter because by many descriptions currency appears to have been at most supplemental to the direct exchange of goods. In the early Tlaxcalan market price list just referred to, however, each item has a price in cacao beans. What looked superficially like barter was actually an exchange of something worth a given amount by an abstract standard for something of equal value by the same standard. Such an interpretation is reinforced by hints of the use of cacao beans as change to even out market transactions.[137] This business strategy had the advantage of making sparing use of the rare currency. The use of a mainly fictional currency had much in common with Spanish practice in the Indies, in which pesos often represented an instrument of evaluation, a means of reckoning shares of investment, or an almost totally abstract credit amount likely to be traded from one person to another for months and years, all in the name of getting along without rare cash. In both systems, standards of value existed and were normally applied in all kinds of business transactions even though the amount of currency in circulation was far from sufficient to proceed on a cash basis.

Despite their currencies, it is not clear that the preconquest Nahuas had any well-defined term in the semantic range "money, currency, cash." Molina's dictionary entry *tlacocohualoni*, "that with which various things are bought," might be suspected of being no more than an attempt to account for Spanish *dinero* were it not for the fact that the term appears quite regularly in the early Cuernavaca census records, in specific application to quachtli given as tribute.[138] Nevertheless, it did not become part of the standard postconquest vocabulary; I have yet to find it in any other text. Even if "tlacocohualoni" really was a general term meaning "medium of exchange," indigenous people still felt that Spanish-style money was sufficiently different to require a new word. They did not, however, borrow Spanish "dinero," possibly because the Spaniards themselves used it relatively little. Instead they extended the meaning of the tomín, the coin most used in all sorts of transactions, employing it first, especially in the plural, in the sense "coins," and then in the more general meaning "cash, money." The entire evolution took place very early, as can be seen in the phrases *cempohualli ommatlactli pesos tomines*, "thirty pesos in money (cash, coin)," and *itomin atl tepetl*, "the money of the altepetl," both written in 1548. "Tomín" must have come into Nahuatl by about 1540, and since the extended meaning surfaces in the first dated Nahuatl documents of the late 1540's, it too must go back to earlier in that decade. "Medio" (half a tomín; in Nahuatl usually "melio") also took on the broader meaning, at least for some speakers. Both words have retained that sense to this day, so that even in the twentieth century, "dinero" is not among Nahuatl's by now vast repertory of Spanish loanwords.[139] The early freezing of usage can also be seen in the fact that though Spaniards soon nearly dropped the tomín, speaking instead of reales, Nahuatl did not follow suit. "Tomín" continued to be the ordinary Nahuatl term for one-eighth of a peso as well as meaning money or cash, and though used abstractly, it was apparently limited to money in the specifically Spanish style; there is no indication that cacao beans could be included under that rubric.

Using the name of a coin for the general concept of money does not necessarily imply either naïveté or the predominance of tiny transactions in the indigenous world. Among the Spaniards themselves, the main way of saying "in cash" was *en reales*, and when money changed hands even in very large amounts, it was usually in silver reales rather than larger denominations. Transactions among the Nahuas were indeed rarely very large by Spanish standards, but dealings in the range of five to fifty pesos abounded in all time periods and were spoken of in terms of peso amounts just as would have been done in Spanish documents. Technical Spanish terminology for different kinds of pesos (*pesos de minas, pesos de buen oro,* etc.) was also employed as appropriate.[140]

The alacrity with which the Nahuas took to money casts doubt on the often-expressed opinion that tribute obligations to the Spanish government gave the principal impetus to indigenous acceptance of the new system.[141] The relevant vocabulary took shape at a time when money tribute was not yet fully incorporated into the postconquest framework and surely did not impinge on the ordinary person. I am convinced, in fact, that the causal flow is in the other direction, that is, that to the extent that indigenous people acquired money and it circulated among them, money tribute became possible. No doubt a dialectic was eventually set up in which each factor promoted the other, but consider that the money tribute remained differential by region, being higher in areas more economically active and connected to the Spanish economy.[142] As a people already commercially oriented and in possession of currencies, the Nahuas needed no special pressures to understand and adopt a monetary system, but would do so as a simple function of their degree of access to Spaniards and the Spanish economy.

Financial transactions in the indigenous world were not limited to the sales of real estate dealt with above (and of other items—livestock, household goods, foods, and the like—of which no written record was made). By the middle of the colonial period, Nahuas were entering into dealings as complex as mortgages (*censos*), but in these cases one of the parties was always Spanish, the indigenous party being a wealthy noble, and the transaction took place in Spanish before a Spanish notary, essentially outside the indigenous context.[143] The same tended to be true of leases (*arrendamientos*); in the most common type, the indigenous corporation or a community member acting in its name leased a large piece of corporate land, sometimes a rancho or estancia, to a Spaniard. The revenue was usually intended to pay for religious observances. Such dealings were often less well documented than mortgages and led to controversies over the true ownership of the land.

Leasing did occur on occasion within the indigenous community, however. In 1726, don Antonio and don Manuel de Galicia y Castilla, of Ayapango in the Chalco region, leased four and a quarter fanegas de sembradura of land to doña Antonia de la Concepción of nearby Amecameca for nine years at a total rent of 459 pesos, which the lessors received then and there. The document was drawn up in Nahuatl, and notaries from both towns were present. Maize and wheat crops were grown alternately on the property, possibly under the direction of the Hispanic person who noted down in Spanish on the back of the document what was done with the land each year. The product was probably intended for markets in Mexico City, or at least for the growing urban concentration in the town of Amecameca, and the lease rate was close to that current among Spaniards in Chalco, so that the entire operation was barely within the indigenous sphere. Controversy arose because the document mentions that the land would be left fallow periodically without making clear whether or not fallow years would count as part of the term of the lease.[144] The parties would no doubt have done better to use a Spanish notary more accustomed to the technical language of leases, and other indigenous lessors and lessees may have done just that.

The names of the participants and the amount of money involved betray that the Ayapango lease took place in the upper circles of indigenous society. At lower levels, informal renting between individuals may have gone on, but if so it has left very little trace. A Miguel Huantli (Culhuacan, ca. 1580) grew some crops for himself on a few chinampas not belonging to him (as well as working his own chinampas), but fails to tell us just whose land it was, or whether or not he paid any rent.[145] Presumably such arrangements followed preconquest precedent, but treatment of the topic in Spanish chronicles tends to confuse renting with dependent status,[146] so that these writings do not contain much good evidence for the existence of simple payment in compensation for the temporary use of land, as opposed to rendering services and helping with the tribute in return for being allowed to live on someone's property as a dependent.

Another Spanish economic concept adopted by the Nahuas was that of putting goods in pawn or hock (*prenda*) in return for cash. The term appears as a loanword in Nahuatl texts starting in the late sixteenth century,[147] and the goods affected could be either valuables or real estate. Rarely were such dealings committed to paper (we find out about them mainly from after-the-fact assertions in wills), but an example is extant from Coyoacan in the mid-seventeenth century. In 1654, one Juan Francisco and his wife Juana Ursula placed an orchard, which they had bought in 1642 for twenty pesos, in hock with a Simón Gabriel and his wife Juana María for ten pesos, to be repaid in two years. In the event of nonpayment within the term, the products of the orchard were to be used to pay off the debt. Apparently it was already realized that the repayment process might be a long one, since the document carefully specifies that the land would eventually be passed on to the owners' son.[148]

Such a provision must be deemed prudent, for in fact leases and pledges sometimes eventuated in a permanent transfer of possession. It is possible that in the minds of indigenous people of the postconquest period the line between selling, leasing, and pawning was less firm than among Spaniards. On the one hand, the Nahuatl verb *cohua*, "to buy," could be used when one was acquiring services only temporarily,[149] and on the other, whenever a person paid out money or was in possession of something for a certain time, he seems to have been well on the way to establishing a claim to permanent ownership. Yet the Nahua principle that use makes for ownership was not the only factor at play. I believe that many Nahuas fully understood the distinctions between the types of transactions, but since most agreements were oral and there was a double framework for interpretation, each party was relatively free to interpret a transaction as best suited him, which tended to give an advantage to the possessor of the moment.

The Nahuas were not, it is true, alone in thinking that use makes for firmer rights, since the Spaniards too gave great weight to uncontested possession over a period of time in deciding questions of ownership, and this fact helped some long-term Spanish lessees of indigenous lands to become permanent owners. In the Spanish system, however, possession took second place to documentation, and a family could rent a piece of land for a hundred years without coming a whit closer to ownership if someone else held a valid title. By the middle colonial period, very few Nahua landowners had demonstrably valid title (by Spanish criteria) with which to quash other claims. Another factor blurring the line between temporary and permanent transfers was the perennial lack of cash. Since many indigenous people were unable to pay in cash even the relatively modest prices they usually charged each other for land, houses, or animals, there was no alternative to paying in installments. Until payment was complete, possession was not fully clear, and if the complete price was never paid, of course the seller would want his goods back.[150]

What of European practices of owing, lending, and borrowing money? Nahuatl seems to have had little if any special vocabulary in this range. The common verb *tlanehua* and related forms could mean "borrow," and the causative derivative *tlaneuhtia* meant "to lend," but the object borrowed or lent could be anything whatever (including people); the emphasis in this set of terms, as usually seen, was in any case on the transitoriness of the holder's possession, rather than on the necessity and means of returning the object.[151] Another Nahuatl verb, however, proved more immediately applicable to the new situation. Molina (whose work, let it be remembered, took place in the time from the 1540's to about 1570) makes distinctions between forms related to "tlanehua" and others related to *tlacuia*, also meaning "to borrow," but with broader options on the form in which the item was to be returned.*

---

*Molina is contradictory and for once apparently confused on the difference between *tlanehua* and *tlacuia*. In the Spanish section, f. 98, his glosses imply that *tlanehua* forms were used when the very thing borrowed was to be returned (consonant with their occasional use for renting, as seen in glosses on f. 128v of the Nahuatl section and in n. 151, above), whereas *tlacuia* forms were used when the thing borrowed was to be returned in kind, as, presumably, when one lent someone supplies to be consumed (firewood, food, and the like), expecting to get back the

By the late sixteenth century (perhaps earlier), "tlacuia" had become the standard word used for borrowing money, so much so that it and derived forms were understood to refer to money even when no more specific mention of it was made; the nominal *netlacuilli*, "that which one has borrowed," meant "(money) debt."[152] Yet as a word for the complementary notion of lending money, by the late colonial period "tlaneuhtia" became more common than the causative of "tlacuia."[153]

With the terms related to monetary borrowing, it is quite clear that a semantic evolution occurred in the course of the sixteenth century, leading to the formation of concepts without exact parallels in preconquest times (though not without precedent in a general fashion). With the concept of owing money, the lack of parallels and the subsequent conceptual reorganization become even clearer. Under "to owe," Molina gives some phrases that may or may not be applicable to money, but that in any event are not found in mundane Nahuatl texts.[154] A related form, -*tech ca*, "to be attached to one," is used at times in postconquest texts where "owe" would fit,[155] but the meaning is actually broader, "to be counted against someone," and the phrase could be used with anything for which a person was accountable. The word that first gained currency as an equivalent for "owe" was *pialia*, derived from the verb *pia*, "to keep, guard, have custody of," so that the literal meaning of the applicative "pialia" was "to keep something for someone." Only the latter sense figures in Molina; the meaning "to owe" first appears, to my knowledge, around 1580, in one of the testaments of Culhuacan: "atle ma itla nicnotlacui anoço itla aca nicpialia," "I have borrowed nothing at all, nor do I owe anything to anyone."[156] In the late sixteenth and early seventeenth centuries, "pialia" apparently became the dominant term, although "pia" itself, since notions of guarding and custody inherently involve obligation to another person, at times bordered on "owe."[157] The related form *pialtia*, the causative of "pia," meaning "to make someone custodian of something," in this time was sometimes used to mean "lend (money)."[158] After about the second decade of the seventeenth century, however, "pialia" and related words are found no more in connection with debts. The probable reason is that "pia" was evolving, becoming an equivalent of the Spanish verb *tener*, "to have," and thus often connoted permanent possession (a point we will return to in Chapter 7).

Replacing "pialia" definitively was *huiquilia*, the applicative form of *huica*, a verb with traditional meanings including "to carry, take, accompany,

---

equivalent but not literally the same supplies. Such a distinction would readily explain the easy applicability of *tlacuia*; no change whatever would be required for money borrowing to fit the definition, and with use the association with money would become ever stronger. But in other places (Spanish, f. 51, Nahuatl, ff. 120, 128v), Molina says that *tlanehua* forms imply return in the same kind ("en la misma especie"), and *tlacuia* forms imply return in a different kind of thing ("no en la misma especie").

be responsible for." The earliest presently known attestation in the sense of monetary obligation is in a text of 1611 from the Jalisco region, well outside central Mexico,[159] but I take the provenience of the expression to be central Mexican. By mid-seventeenth century, the grammarian Carochi considered "huiquilia" the normal word for "owe"; it continued to appear in this meaning throughout the colonial period to the exclusion of other words, and it is still in the language today.[160] Surely it is no coincidence that as an equivalent to the European concept of having a monetary obligation, Nahuatl fastened successively on two words emphasizing custodianship. The European way of thinking of owing money was clearly unfamiliar to the Nahuas, and though in fact they seem by the second half of the sixteenth century to have been incurring and collecting debts in the same manner as Spaniards, they may have conceptualized the activity differently, at least during a long transitional period. For one thing, until late in the game, the "owe" equivalents appear to have been used primarily when an actual cash amount had changed hands and was in a sense being kept for someone. When it is a question of money owing for a purchase, money not yet really in existence, the sources usually say merely "not yet paid."[161]

As to the actual process of making loans, the vast majority of transactions were carried out informally and involved small amounts, almost always under ten pesos, usually under five, and frequently under a peso. A loan at the corporate level, 400 pesos lent by the altepetl of Calpan to the altepetl of Tlaxcala in 1562 with a formal acknowledgment of debt (*conocimiento*) and a fixed term (*plazo*) of ten months, is unique in all respects.[162] Not only were loans left unrecorded unless they had not been collected at the time of the creditor's death, but nowhere does one find any indication of a fixed term or schedule of payment. Generally no purpose is specified, though in a few cases it emerges that people borrowed money in emergencies—to treat injuries or get out of jail.[163] Most loans were isolated transactions by people who show no sign of having lent money to anyone else. Indigenous merchants (*pochteca*) and petty traders, however, might make the lending of money a part of their business. In 1608, when she made her will, one Bárbara Agustina of Chiucnauhpan in the Coyoacan district, who sold pigs, turkeys, and doubtless other things (since she owned a mule to transport them), was owed no fewer than eight money debts, ranging from half a tomín to one peso. She had lent out 200 cacao beans as well.[164] The smallness of the amounts and the humble names of the debtors, most without a second appellation, are testimony to the depth of the penetration of monetary dealings into the indigenous world by the end of the sixteenth century. A Juan Fabián, also of the Coyoacan region, who in the time around 1615 owned an orchard and pack train and sold fruit, does not seem to have been an actual moneylender, but he did frequently both lend and borrow up to five pesos, dealing with both Nahuas and Spaniards.[165]

How moneylenders received profit from their loans is nowhere hinted at in any mundane Nahuatl documents that I have seen. I do presume, however, that except among relatives and close friends, the lender received some monetary consideration or other significant economic advantage. (Among Spaniards, the traditional procedure was to lend less than the nominal amount, then receive the full amount on repayment.) I hesitate to resort to literary evidence, but faute de mieux I will do so, presenting for whatever it is worth some material from a moralistic play in Nahuatl, possibly dating from around 1627, which has a pochtecatl or merchant as its protagonist and concentrates on the theme of usury.[166]

Moneylending is the only activity of the pochtecatl that we are shown; the only hint of other dimensions is the fact that his house is at the edge of the marketplace. He takes high rates of interest for short time periods, varying with the situation. The conditions are described precisely, though no word for interest as such is evident. With a small, short-term loan, the pochtecatl demands four tomines per peso, amounting to 50 percent in two weeks. With 4,000 pesos over a somewhat longer time period, he demands 400 pesos, or 10 percent, a month. People also give him large amounts of money in safekeeping, which he later denies ever having received. One of the means he uses in his manipulations is to have a notary write out a false bill of sale for land. Needless to say, the bad deeds of this particular pochtecatl have been exaggerated for effect (he curses beggars and tries to get sexual favors from a poor girl needing money), but I offer these tidbits in the hope that they have some of the same social accuracy found in the parallel playlet about the sharp practices of the executors of wills (see Chapter 6), where we have enough other evidence to be on firmer ground.

Markets, Traders, and Nonagricultural Occupations

Along with its tlatoani and its specific divinity, one of the principal integrating elements of a preconquest altepetl was its central market. All three phenomena had significant successors in postconquest times, and indeed, by external accounts, the market was of the three the one that underwent the least change, but it is by far the least well represented in surviving internal Nahua records. Nothing indicates that market operations had ever been as carefully recorded as land tenure; the very nature of such dealings would resist it. Yet the preconquest tlatoani and other altepetl officials had carried on market supervision as one of their primary duties, and the tlatoani in particular derived revenue and services from the market, which was thought in some sense to belong to him.[167] The first flush of Nahuatl documentation

in the mid-sixteenth century delivers a reasonable amount of information on
market organization, after which the topic disappears from indigenous records except for some chance oblique reference.

Information comes from the three important centers of Coyoacan, Mexico City, and Tlaxcala, each having left some sort of internally generated
listing of products sold or groups of vendors.[168] Since the lists were made for
somewhat different purposes, they manifest different criteria and vary from
each other to an extent, as can be seen in Table 5.4. Nevertheless, they agree
on the general kind of thing available and on many specific staples. Given the
restricted nature of the documents, it is my belief that all the things mentioned
in all three listings, and many other items as well, were for sale at the market
of any major central Mexican altepetl.* For Coyoacan and Mexico City, each
entry represents not merely a single item sold, but an entire organized group
making and selling it, which implies that each group would deal in additional
related products, as they do in the descriptions in book 10 of the Florentine
Codex. The variety of goods is impressive, the importance of the market to
the everyday life of the people obvious. Luxuries are not emphasized, a possible change since preconquest times, although some ingredients for fancy
garments (feathers, dyed rabbit hair, fringes for cloaks and skirts) are in evidence, as well as some jewelry and bells. In any event, most of the things sold
could have been converted into luxuries if of sufficiently high quality or
brought from afar, which may have been precisely the function, for example,
of the organized groups of merchants (*oztomeca*) attested in the Coyoacan
market. The market supplied firewood and kindling, much in the way of
household paraphernalia and other items of daily use, and a considerable part
of the daily diet. Yet of the greatest staples—maize, beans, and pulque—
pulque does not appear at all, and maize and beans only on the Mexico City
list (despite the fact that the Tlaxcalan list is primarily devoted to foods). It
is my impression that the maize and beans in the Mexico City market reflect
the urban nature of the population, and in any case were likely choice varieties from a selection of regions rather than the ordinary product in bulk.
Although society as a whole could hardly have existed for long without the
market (consider the standard items firewood and salt), nearly everything in
it was in some sense a specialty, extra, or supplement. Finished clothing was
for sale, but just as important were supplies of all kinds for textile manufac-

---

*The items of Table 5.4 agree well with Spanish lists of what could legally be sold in the
markets of Ecatepec, Xochimilco, and Acolman in 1551 (Gibson 1964, p. 356). Generally speaking those lists are less varied, but they do contain some things not in the table (digging sticks,
melon seeds, boats, needles, grinding stones). I am sure that these goods would have been found
somewhere in the Coyoacan, Mexico City, and Tlaxcala markets as well (except possibly for
boats in Tlaxcala). I do not believe that sporadic Spanish orders restricting what could be sold
in Indian markets (see Gibson 1964, p. 355) had any appreciable effect whenever given items
could be produced and there were customers to buy them.

TABLE 5.4

Items Sold in Some Central Mexican Markets, Mid-16th Century

Coyoacan, ca. 1550	Mexico City, 1540's–50's?	Tlaxcala, 1545–63
FOOD AND TOBACCO[a]		
cacao	cacao	cacao
chiles	chiles .	chiles
chia	chia	tamales
tamales	shelled maize	fish
atole (maize gruel)	beans	venison
fish	pinolli (flour of maize and chia)	rabbit
meat	atole	axolotl (salamander)
lake scum (tecuitlatl)	chocolate drink	quail
salt	tortillas	turkeys, eggs
lime (for tortillas)	fish	avocadoes
tobacco	meat	tomatoes
smoking tubes	duck	guavas
cigars	greens	sapote fruit
	fruit	cactus fruit
	honey? (neuctli)[b]	smoking tubes
	salt	
	lime	
	tobacco	
	smoking tubes	
CLOTHING-RELATED ITEMS[c]		
clay dye	colors	cochineal
bark-clay concoction (a dye)	rabbit hair	feather ornaments
colors	feathers	dyed leather
warping frames	borders of cloaks	sandals
spindles	borders of shirts	
canes (for hand looms)	hides	
rabbit hair	yarn	
feathers	cotton	
cloth borders	wool? down? (tomitl)	
hides	women's shirts (huipiles)	
sandals	skirts	
	cloaks (of wool? tomitilmatli)	
	sandals	
HOUSEHOLD AND WORK ITEMS		
pots	pots	pots
clay vessels	cups (xicalli)	bowls
sauce bowls	baskets	mats
griddles	mats	(fire)wood
baskets	pine torches	pine bark
brooms	metal items[d]	copper items
mats	clay bells	
(fire)wood	paper	
tumplines		
medicine		
obsidian blades		
metal items[d]		
worked wooden items		
clay bells		

(continued)

TABLE 5.4 *(continued)*

Coyoacan, ca. 1550	Mexico City, 1540's–50's?	Tlaxcala, 1545–63
	SPANISH-STYLE ITEMS[e]	
collars (cabezones)	Spanish bread ("Castilla tlascalli")	chickens, eggs
upper garments (chamarros)	collars	
shirts (camisas)	hats	
candles	leather belts (talabartes)	
	blankets (frezadas)	
	capes (capas)	
	coarse cloth (sayal)	
	silk	
	soap (jabón)	
	guitars (mecahuehuetl)	

SOURCES: BC, docs. 25, 34, pp. 138–49, 208–13; TA, passim; Durand Forest 1971, pp. 121–24.

[a]The "boat people" mentioned in the Coyoacan lists probably were traders in various aquatic foods, but they may have sold other goods, and it is conceivable that they actually sold boats.

[b]Possibly maguey juice, not honey.

[c]On the Mexico City list, "chiquipon" must be *chiqui(uh)pan*, associated with colors.

[d]These may well have included objects of iron in the Spanish style.

[e]The item *cordón*, "rope, twine," on the Mexico City list has a Spanish name, but it is not clear what was Spanish about the product.

ture at home. In all the main departments, including food, clothing, and hardware, goods were overwhelmingly indigenous in type, as one would expect, but Spanish-style items had already made a significant impact in at least the two Valley of Mexico markets. Coyoacan had whole trade groups devoted to European collars and shirts, and another to candles. Chickens and their eggs were standard fare in the Tlaxcalan market. In Mexico City, a whole range of European clothing and cloth was available, as well as soap, guitars, and Spanish (wheat) bread. In the home of the largest and wealthiest Spanish population of all New Spain, some of these things, especially the wheat bread, may have been primarily for a Hispanic clientele, but they were being sold and surely in most cases produced by indigenous people.

In its manner of organization, too, the market retained predominantly preconquest characteristics. A separate spot reserved for each specialty, as shown in the Mexico City diagram, and the separate organization of each trade, as seen in the Coyoacan records, were both preconquest modes. So too was the correspondence seen there with altepetl organization. One of the lists is divided in two, one part for each of Coyoacan's great halves, and this may reflect an actual physical and organizational division in the marketplace. At any rate, the taxes of the two were at times collected and totaled separately. Several trade groups are described by the name of a constituent unit of the altepetl, and the most geographically explicit listing raises the likelihood that all the groups in the market were based in some specific subunit, consisting of people only from that unit. The subunit was not coterminous with the trade group, however, since some altepetl units fielded as many as four or five groups; from Apçolco came chile sellers, pine-torch splitters, fish dealers, shirtmakers, and candlemakers. Nor did any one unit necessarily have a monopoly on any one line. Groups of dealers in wood and chia, chile sellers, and merchants came from different units. Commonly enough, however, one subunit apparently had only one specialty and was the only group in the market purveying it. Except for a few from nearby places, including Mexico City and Iztapalapa, the groups were overwhelmingly from within the Coyoacan region itself, even the merchants. With the wood dealers coming from wooded regions and the fish dealers and reed makers from the lake shore, the market was a vehicle for the exchange of complementary goods from the entire district and thus an important force for altepetl integration. It must be remembered, though, that Coyoacan was a major complex altepetl with a large population and a diverse territory. The market of nearby Huitzilopochco, a much smaller and more uniform entity, could not have been so integrated and self-contained, nor could the markets of most towns.

About the nature of the trade groups very little emerges. The group names occurring in the Coyoacan market fall into four main categories: makers (-*chiuhque*), sellers (-*namacaque*), and dealers (-*neculioque*) in respect to various wares, plus some oztomeca or merchants. The first two types constitute a large majority of the groups; see Table 5.5. (It remains entirely possible, however, that some trades or types of trades were more heavily populated

TABLE 5.5

Classes of Trade Groups in the Coyoacan Market, ca. 1550

| Category | List | | | | Total | Percent of Total |
	1	2	3	4[a]		
Makers (-chiuhque)[b]	16	15	14	21	66	40.5%
Sellers (-namacaque)	15	12	18	10	55	33.7
Dealers (-neculioque)	5	4	3	5	17	10.4
Merchants (oztomeca)	5	4	2	3	14	8.6
Other[c]	3	3	3	2	11	6.7
TOTAL	44	38	40	41	163	99.9%[d]

SOURCE: BC, doc. 25, pp. 138–49.
NOTE: Each separately named group is counted, even when the same trade figures twice on a list. In each case, the criteria of the original list makers were somewhat different; omission and grouping together appears to have occurred each time. Using all four extant lists, it is hoped, counteracts this factor to some extent, but one must be aware that most of the groups appear on all four, and that the absolute totals are consequently much larger than the number of groups actually active at any one time.
[a]A category not yet well understood (*tlayehualli*) is omitted from the count.
[b]Includes certain more specific terms for productive activity, such as pine-torch splitters, metal forgers (smiths), and wood shavers (carpenters). "-Chiuhque" is, however, by far the predominant form.
[c]Includes "boat people" and a group named only by its unit of origin.
[d]Column does not total 100 percent because of rounding.

than others and dominated the market far more than would appear in such a category count.) The sellers as well as the makers probably produced their own goods in many cases. The dealers were possibly involved in production too, though they must have collected goods in some fashion from colleagues to sell (as with the dealers in wood, fish, or chia).* Dealers as well as makers and sellers specialized in a single commodity, unlike the merchants, for whom no one commodity is listed.[169]

In Coyoacan, each trade paid its taxes as an entity; though members must have contributed individually, the round numbers show that a single assessment was first made for the whole group.[170] Figures called *tianquizhuaque*, "holders or possessors of the market," paid the tax to the tlatoani's representatives, first having collected it through unknown mechanisms inside the trade groups. Doubtless there was one such officer for each group, possibly the same as the *topileque* (minor officials, constables) seen for some trades in the late-sixteenth-century Culhuacan testaments.[171]

In mid-sixteenth-century Tlaxcala, market constables were appointed annually, one for each of the sub-altepetl, and in addition members of the cabildo took turns functioning as *diputados* (delegates, deputies), judging market cases and supervising activity. The prices of cacao imported into the market, for example, were to be announced to the officials and then to the public. An effort, not too successful by all indications, was made to restrict the exchange of goods handled by the trade groups to the marketplace proper.[172]

By the later part of the sixteenth century, systematic internal sources on indigenous markets dry up. We know that the mainly preconquest features we have just been discussing persisted to some extent, for the simple reason that some have been preserved to this day. Taxation and supervision by the altepetl also continued, if perhaps more sporadically.[173] But a Hispanic presence in the market was not long in making itself felt. Even the Tlaxcalan

---

*Molina defines *necuiloa* as "to deal, retail (petty items), or twist something" ("contratar, regatonear, o entortar alguna cosa"). The root seems to have to do originally with twisting and turning (although it appears superficially to contain within itself *ne*, reciprocal or reflexive prefix, and *cui*, "to take"). There are several interesting related items in Molina's dictionary. *Tlanecuilo* is defined either as "petty retailer, dealer," or "swindler, sharp dealer" (the latter connected with the sense of twisting). *Necuiloloni* (lit., "that which is dealable") is glossed as "something bought to be resold." -*Tech necuiloa* (lit., "to deal with someone") is glossed as "logrear," that is, to give something to someone else to sell on a speculative basis. *Necuilhuia*, the applicative of *necuiloa*, has the gloss "to deal with another's property." The conclusion arising from the linguistic evidence is that a dealer or "necuilo" had usually acquired the bulk of his goods from others, and that he might either have bought them outright or be selling them on commission. The "sellers" (-*namacaque*) in the Coyoacan market may overlap with both dealers and makers. The chile sellers were most likely dealers, whereas the tamale sellers most likely produced their own wares. One group is called "candlemakers" part of the time, "candle sellers" at other times, and the same occurs with "fish sellers" and "fish dealers."

market price list of 1545 owed its existence to the related facts that Spaniards were making large-scale use of the Indian markets and Spanish officials wanted to regulate them. *Tiánguiz* or *tiánguez,* from Nahuatl *tianquiztli,* "market, place of commerce," entered Mexican Spanish almost immediately after the conquest. As time went on, the Spanish population relied on the market more and more for its daily needs.[174] Pedro de Arenas, in his early-seventeenth-century manual of Nahuatl for Spanish speakers, takes it for granted that Spaniards will acquire most of their food in the market, either buying it themselves or sending an Indian employee. In Puebla, by the late seventeenth century Spaniards appear to have been relying primarily on Indian bakers and vendors in the marketplace for the great Spanish staple of wheat bread.[175] Already in the course of the sixteenth century, we hear Spanish reports that markets were becoming less orderly, meaning for the most part, apparently, the weakening of organization in terms of strong exclusive trade groups, each with its strictly defined site within the marketplace. One major element in such weakening was the entry of nonindigenous people as active participants in marketplace business, in direct response to the growth of a Hispanic clientele and greater potential profit. These intruders—most often blacks, mulattoes, or mestizos, but including low-ranking Spaniards as well—had no relation to altepetl-based organization; rather they became important in interregional and intersector market articulation, and they tended to draw Spanish supervision attempts in their wake.[176] It was where the most Spaniards congregated (in Spanish cities, corregimiento capitals, and towns on highways) that the changes and pressures were greatest, but in central Mexico they were ubiquitous. Thus despite escaping a sustained campaign of direct reorganization such as affected altepetl government and the religious cult, the market was a greater arena of cultural, social, and economic interaction between indigenous and nonindigenous people, and in due course documentary avenues must be discovered that will provide an adequate vision of things in this sphere.

Merchants, long-distance traders in goods of relatively high value, were prominent in the preconquest economy; they participated in marketplace activity, but transcended any single altepetl market and may have dealt outside the framework of organized markets for some purposes. The principal term applied to them was "pochtecatl," with "oztomecatl" an apparently exact equivalent sometimes paired with the other word, sometimes used in its stead (as in the Coyoacan market lists). Although we might reasonably assume that the two terms correspond to two types or aspects, one perhaps associated with longer distances or more luxurious goods than the other, documents seen to date fail to bear out such a distinction.[177] The main source on preconquest pochteca, book 9 of the Florentine Codex, tends to be more informative

on the group's ceremonial aspects and political connections than on its economic activity and internal organization. Produced apparently by descendants of Tlatelolco merchants, it portrays the pochteca idealistically and nos-
talgically as a tightly cohesive and highly prestigious hereditary group,
indirectly emphasizing their uniqueness.

All the same, parallels can be observed between the pochteca/oztomeca
and other trade groups. Both names by origin referred to ethnic-political
units; pochtecatl means "inhabitant of Pochtlan," oztomecatl "inhabitant of
Oztoman," and the names probably go back to groups then famous for trading activities. The ethnic connotations may have faded in certain contexts,
allowing the terms to become pure trade designations, as had happened also
with *amantecatl* (originally "inhabitant of Amantlan," which came to mean
"featherworker, skilled craftsman in general") and *toltecatl* (originally "inhabitant of Tula," acquiring the additional meaning "craftsman, artisan").
Yet the words are symptomatic of the closeness of pochteca organization to
the altepetl/calpolli, just as with the producer-vendors and local retailers of
the marketplace. In late preconquest times, Pochtlan was a name still in use
for an actual entity among the Tlatelolcan merchants, and they were grouped
into six calpolli subdivisions, each with a leader.[178] Nor does the hereditary
aspect distinguish merchants sharply from other tradesmen, for the crafts too
are said to have stayed within the same family and locality.[179]

After the conquest, pochteca/oztomeca were still functioning as groups
concentrated in certain altepetl units in the 1550's and 1560's, as seen in the
Coyoacan market lists and the Huexotzinco census materials.[180] A group of
pochteca, not named as individuals, also appears in the Tlaxcalan cabildo
minutes of 1551, where they are given forty pesos to invest on behalf of the
altepetl government, an apparent continuation of their dealings as representatives of preconquest tlatoque.[181] An anonymous annalist of Tenochtitlan in
the 1560's tells of continuing corporate activity by the pochteca, noting that
they decorated a Christian cult object with feathers and displayed a new
saint's image in a procession.[182] Spanish sources report that well into the second half of the sixteenth century, Indian merchants of the Valley of Mexico,
Tlaxcala, and Cholula went on long expeditions, particularly to the south, to
bring back tropical fruit, cacao, feathers, and other regional specialties, much
in the manner of their predecessors.[183] In the bulk of Nahuatl documentation,
however, pochteca are seen, when seen at all, as individuals, and rarely are
they specifically called by the professional name. The nature of the documents
may well magnify the extent of the change across periods. The fact that there
were well-organized groups does not mean that within a given framework
individual action, including competition, could not have been the norm, as it
was in other aspects of Nahua life. At one time, when guild regulations were

the main thing studied about Spanish merchants, they were imagined to be a highly unified, monopolistic, even anticommercial group, but when trial and notarial records opened up, the most individualistic, cutthroat traders conceivable were revealed, united only when it came to combating other sectors of the economy. So it may well have been with the pochteca of preconquest times.

Actually, the postconquest pochteca have left very little documentary trace. The only persons who can be identified as such with certainty are an Antonio de Santa María and his son and successor, Luis Tlauhpotonqui, who lived in Culhuacan in the late sixteenth century.[184] The son followed his father's path according to the preconquest pattern, and the women of the family also married traders. Among the goods they stocked were the traditional *tecomates* (deep cups for beverages, made either of clay or of gourds brought from tropical areas), including elaborate painted ones and one in the form of a bird. As one would expect, they had dealings outside Culhuacan, though as far as emerges not outside the immediate Mexico City orbit. The father had given a colleague twelve pesos' worth of merchandise on credit, the amount to be paid back out of his profits on resale; this sort of cooperative speculation may well have had preconquest roots. Other activities of Antonio and Luis, however, were Spanish-influenced at least in the form they took. The father owned horses, which he not only used to transport goods but sold on credit to other indigenous people. He made substantial money loans, in amounts of up to twenty pesos; indeed, in the son's will these appear to have been a very large part of the business, probably because several debts proved hard to collect and were still outstanding when father and then son made their wills. In addition to its mercantile dealings, the family owned a quite impressive collection of scattered chinampa land.

Other likely pochteca include a Pablo Quechol, living in Culhuacan at the same time, who had in his possession smaller or larger amounts of tecomates, baskets, bowls (some stored in large pots), metal-tipped digging sticks, men and women's clothing, and 2,000 cacao beans to help toward his marriage (which he died before arranging), as well as some chinampas.[185] He lacked horses and mentioned no debts owed him, which seems to place him at a lower rank than our first example. Another probable merchant was Constantino de San Felipe of Xochimilco, who made his will in 1572.[186] In addition to several chinampas and a house, he had some wares on hand: twenty tecomates with some stirring sticks kept in a (Spanish-style) chest, and sixty cloaks or lengths of cloth (*tilmatli*), which is to say, three of the standard bundles of twenty each. No debts were owed him, but he did have a horse. Both these traders had received some or all of their goods from their parents and so were presumably pochteca of at least the second generation.

Among the testators of Culhuacan are several people who do not mention debts or salable goods in commercial quantities and whom we might not suspect of being traders, much less full-scale merchants, but for the fact that they share two characteristics of the known pochteca: owning one or more horses or mules and having out-of-town connections or actually being from out of town.[187] Some of these people then prove to have been in direct contact with those just mentioned, giving us some sense of the profile of the specifically commercial sector in the indigenous world by the late sixteenth century. Cross-altepetl connections or mobility; ownership of European transport animals; and the use of specifically Spanish economic arrangements—including moneylending, pawnbroking, and even sometimes entering into *conciertos* (stipulated agreements) and *compañías* (formal partnerships)—are key characteristics. None of the traders were literate enough to sign their own names, and as a group the names were not particularly prestigious. None of these people are known to have held altepetl office. A few were landless, though most had moderate amounts of productive land. No direct connections emerge between this group and the nobles who dominated altepetl government and churchly organizations.

After the late sixteenth century, the term pochtecatl appears in known mundane texts no more, nor do people in possession of the typical wares, neither the exotic luxuries nor the tecomates and bundles of cloth.[188] On the other hand, a few people owning horses or mules and engaged in some sort of local trade do continue to show up here and there. Examples from the early seventeenth century still display much the same social profile; the two fullest ones were already mentioned above in connection with borrowing and lending money. One was the previously mentioned Juan Fabián of the Coyoacan region, who owned several pieces of land including an orchard, the apparently indigenous fruit of which he sold not only in Coyoacan but in neighboring Indian towns. At times, he hired local workmen (carpenters) in relation to his orchard and lands. Thus he was a producer and entrepreneur as much as a trader. But he did have a packtrain of horses and mules (some of them hired from Spaniards) to carry his fruit, along with other things perhaps, to be sold outside the immediate area, and he had outside connections. His son-in-law Diego Francisco, from neighboring Huitzilopochco, often took a horseload of fruit to sell on behalf of the family enterprise, probably in Diego's hometown. In all probability, Juan's financial activity (seven transactions outstanding, several of them with Spaniards, when Juan made his will), was merely a by-product of his central business. He hoped to initiate his namesake son into the trade, putting him in charge of the packtrain and relations with subordinates; in the event, both son and son-in-law failed him, losing animals and withholding money. Juan Fabián's humble name speaks for itself; he was illiterate, held no office, and gives no sign of having had connections with anyone who did. Thus he manifests nearly all the diagnostic characteristics of a pochtecatl of the late sixteenth century. At the same time, he is close in type to the Hispanic muleteers, petty dealers, and small growers (activities often combined) who were to be found at the lowest rungs of Spanish regional trade, and indeed the Spaniards from whom he hired animals and with whom he maintained debts and credits seem to have been of just that type.[189]

The other example, at a lower level, is Bárbara Agustina, who lived in the Coyoacan district at near the same time; her petty lending of money and cacao to humble local Nahuas was detailed above. A series of very small outstanding debts dominate her will, but she also had pigs and turkeys on hand and had sold the same items to others, so that raising and selling small livestock must have been an important part of her activity. A widow, she had no real estate beyond the house she left to her daughter. The place may have belonged originally to her husband's family, for on several occasions she mentions her late mother-in-law, to whom she still owed money, and whose successor in trade she may well have been. Bárbara Agustina can be taken as an illustration of a type present in the local market, but she also owned a mule worth the very considerable amount of thirty-five pesos, which she must have used to transport goods to other markets.[190]

The general question of the role of women in trade both before and after the conquest is as elusive as many other important matters pertaining to the indigenous economy. Because of Nahuatl's reluctance to specify gender, indigenous lists of tradespeople and descriptions of market and merchant activity tell us hardly anything about the relative functions of men and women. Pictures accompanying the Florentine Codex show many women vendors in the market, especially in everything related to food and clothing.[191]

The annalist Chimalpahin, in the course of telling about other things, reveals some tidbits about the market women of his day. In 1612, María López, a chocolate drink seller, was living in the San Juan section of Mexico City. She had originally come from Tetzcoco but had made San Juan her home, become a district citizen, and married a local man, Juan Pérez. Chimalpahin mentions her because she complained all the way to the Royal Audiencia about the way a Franciscan friar had her husband stripped and given lashes even though he was already very ill. We also hear from Chimalpahin of a female vendor of bitter atole, named only María, who in 1613 was living in a house she apparently owned behind the church of San Antonio Abad in the southern part of Mexico City. A widow (her husband had been the tailor Francisco), she seems to have headed a household that included her son-in-law. She comes into Chimalpahin's story by virtue of claiming that the road in front of her house was her property and demanding payment if district boosters erected a cross there as they planned. María was publicly vociferous in her cause, so much so that Chimalpahin says he could not repeat her filthy language. The cross, however, was erected, and María died of illness shortly after, which both Chimalpahin and the neighborhood took to be a judgment of God (we will hear more of her in Chapter 6). Both of Chimalpahin's vendors are seen to be specialized in one kind of product, permanently rooted in the community, and assertive members of it. But perhaps the most suggestive of Chimalpahin's tidbits is in his report that when Spanish officials were trying to move and reform Mexico City's markets in 1592, it was the women ("Mexica cihua") who brought suit, as though he were taking for granted that the market was primarily a woman's affair.[192]

But what of women as pochteca? Nothing in the sources for the preconquest period hints that they ever assumed that role directly, and they do not appear among the identifiable pochteca of the late sixteenth century. A woman named María Tiacapan, wife of one Culhuacan pochtecatl and cousin of another (the aforementioned Luis Tlauhpotonqui), does assert that of the two horses she and her husband had, she was jointly responsible for the acquisition of one of them and hence joint owner, but she mentions no other mercantile dealings or assets.[193] At the same time and place, Ana Tlaco, whose home was in Yecapixtla (just south of the Chalco region) but who died in Culhuacan, owned a horse or mule and gives some indication of having been a petty producer and trader of clothing.[194] By present indications, it seems unlikely that women in trade went much beyond figures like Bárbara Agustina, essentially market women owning a transport animal that permitted them to engage in regional trade in a very small way. In both Spanish and Nahuatl sources, the owners and conductors of packtrains always turn out to be men.

By the eighteenth century or before, even the rough equivalents of pochteca (people of middle rank with pack animals and trade involvement beyond a single local market) have largely disappeared from Nahuatl sources, though Spanish sources point in the direction of a continuing or even increasing role of Indians in the lower levels of interregional trade. In the later period, most of the known larger entrepreneurs and owners of transport animals are noble members of the officeholding group.[195] The entire subject is drastically underdocumented. I do not believe that traders at the middle and lower ranks of indigenous society actually ceased to exist; I think rather that mules and especially horses—the two primary diagnostic signs—so decreased in value over the decades and centuries that they received less mention in testaments.

Surmising developments from what is known of the overall structure of the situation, it can be said that indigenous society's pochteca sector was under severe challenge in the postconquest period. The pochteca's role as primary purveyors of high-value goods acquired through long-distance trade soon faded as Spanish merchants, traders, and entrepreneurs invaded and with time practically preempted any aspect of interregional trade that showed a strong profit potential. For a time, the pochteca had a special niche in the supply of goods from warmer climates that were desired only by Indians. But the staples of this trade, cacao and cotton, were so in demand in the indigenous sector that before long, with indigenous people increasingly able to pay in money, Spaniards entered and eventually dominated the field, stimulated further by the development of direct Spanish demand for the products. Spaniards had no interest, either as traders or as consumers, in feathers, jade, and other Mesoamerican exotica, which were hence left to the pochteca, but cultural change was rendering these items, once so important to war, religion, and social differentiation, obsolete in indigenous society itself.

With the scope of indigenous trade thus restricted and its content altered, there was little left to distinguish a pochtecatl from a producer-vendor who could afford some pack animals. The overall commercial structure was transformed, the Spanish economy taking over most of the function of large-scale interregional articulation. At the same time, transport and the handling of certain marginal goods were relegated to members of the lowest ranks of Hispanic society. These traders and muleteers were in constant contact with indigenous people, buying from them, employing them, and sometimes dealing with them as equals. Once the Nahuas had learned some basic skills and acquired some capital goods, they could compete successfully at this level. By the late colonial period, in fact, transport and petty commerce in regional specialties, though low on the Spanish scale, were among the prime economic opportunities available to indigenous people, and it is not surprising that the upper group, the heirs of the preconquest nobility, moved into this kind of enterprise. By the second half of the period, no one indigenous group seems to have dominated activity in interregional trade; rather people across the whole spectrum took part in it to the extent of their ability. Aspects of the pochteca heritage must have remained alive in the indigenous world and affected behavior, but the new situation no longer called for just that kind of specialist.

As to the other kinds of nonagricultural occupations the Nahuas practiced across the entire period, known Nahuatl sources add little to what the Spanish record tells us,[196] other than the glimpses of marketplace trades already presented. Organized craft groups are seen a few times in sixteenth-century texts attempting to avoid their apparently traditional duties of performing certain work for the tlatoani or the altepetl.[197] In Tlaxcala in 1550, a group from the district of Acxotlan wanted the work they were doing on an altarpiece in the monastery church considered a fulfillment of their own vows, not tribute duty, to which notion the cabildo and the Franciscan friars objected.[198] In Tulancingo in 1570, a group of eleven painters complained to the Spanish alcalde mayor that they had worked for three months painting buildings and cloths at the church, and that their pay had been withheld by altepetl officials, not for the first time.[199] The officials would no doubt have responded that the painters did not deserve pay for doing their normal duty to the corporation. In time, the issue seems to have been resolved mainly in favor of pay for craftsmen working for public purposes, though examples can be found of individuals donating their services to a church as late as the eighteenth century, a continuation of the tradition even if now viewed as voluntary behavior.[200]

One occupational specialty about which Nahuatl sources have a certain amount to say is weaving. The early Cuernavaca-region censuses show weaving as a virtually universal activity of women, both noble and commoner.[201] The wives and other women associated with household heads produced the cloth that dominated tribute in kind. By the late sixteenth century, cloth tribute was a thing of the past in central Mexico, but the Culhuacan testaments make clear that essentially all women did spinning and weaving, using indigenous hand equipment, which, together with yarn and half-finished clothing items, appears frequently in their wills. Often they were making things for themselves or for the family, but in some cases they intended the product for the market from the beginning.[202] Mention of this kind of home weaving by women continues into the seventeenth century,[203] and then, like so many other things, fades out. Surely Nahua women continued to weave; perhaps what they produced was of less value relatively, or perhaps the phenomenon is to be attributed exclusively to the less generous nature of the later documentation. It is possible, however, that Spanish textile works (*obrajes*) had a considerable impact, and also that Spanish-style looms partially displaced indigenous techniques in the home; a couple of examples of mechanical looms and associated equipment appear in Nahuatl wills, apparently both owned and operated by men.[204] In these cases, weaving can be presumed to have been the man's primary occupation, along with work on the family fields.

Indigenous Dress After the Conquest

The production and exchange of clothing constituted a large part of the indigenous economy even after the conquest, so it behooves us to attend carefully to documentary hints about the kinds of garments Nahuas wore. The last well-attested example of full preconquest garb is that of don Julián de la Rosa of Tlaxcala, who in 1566 owned not only several elaborate and valuable cloaks of traditional design, including one covered with feathers (though the feathers were those of the European domestic duck), but also—doubtless as heirlooms and for special occasions—full war regalia, including a monkey uniform of feathers with a pheasant head device, a coyote headdress, and a shield with 200 quetzal feathers.[205]

But change came quickly. We have seen that already by 1550 the European fitted and buttoned shirt had become so popular that whole trade groups were devoted to making shirts and collars. *Camisa* was one of the earliest and most widespread Spanish loanwords entering Nahuatl; coming when it did, it was one of only a handful of borrowed nouns incorporating the indigenous absolutive ending *-tli*, which it retains in Nahuatl speech to this day.[206] Given the frequency of reference to shirts, it is hard to agree with the remark of the late-sixteenth-century official and writer Gonzalo Gómez de Cervantes that Indian men except for noblemen went naked save for "a bandage to cover their private parts" and a cloak so light it appeared made of netting.[207] In 1584, even Cristóbal, the unemployed turkey thief and lowlife of Tulancingo we met in previous chapters, wore a *camixatli* in addition to his indigenous loincloth and cloak, though all three were old and easily tore off in a fight with the turkey's owner, leaving Cristóbal naked.[208]

As Cristóbal's example shows, trousers were slower than shirts in becoming normal wear for males; conceivably, Gómez de Cervantes was right that in his time only people of substance wore them. Nevertheless, they were coming into use in the second half of the sixteenth century. The type first mentioned were *zaragüelles*, usually thought to have been very wide, loosely fitting long trousers.[209] The zaragüelles that Juan Velásquez of Culhuacan had in 1581 were green, and they were bought (not long before) rather than made at home.[210] As time proceeded, *calzones*, the word for the usual Spanish trousers, began to displace "zaragüelles," presumably corresponding to a change in the items themselves. In 1639, Baltasar Bautista, a baker of Mexico City, had two pairs of calzones, one of Rouen (a printed cotton cloth) and the other of *lampote* (a cloth made in the Philippines).[211] Jackets (*jaquetas*), doublets (*jubones*), hats (*sombreros*), and shoes (*zapatos*) are also attested after the middle of the sixteenth century.[212] But apparently even the most Hispanized in dress did not soon abandon the indigenous man's cloak, or tilmatli. Both Juan Velásquez and Baltasar Bautista had tilmatli with embroidery on them (*tlamachyo*) to go with their European pants. European influence is not lacking, however, even with the tilmatli. In addition to Baltasar's three red cloaks (apparently his normal wear) and his embroidered one, he had one of Rouen. Some men speak of a *frezada* (in Spanish usually a blanket used to cover a bed or a horse) where one would expect "tilmatli," and the two words are even found equated.[213] The clothing that the well-off Lucía María of Atocpan (near Milpa Alta in the southern part of the Xochimilco district) was keeping for her sons around the year 1635 represents the most complete known listing of a Spanish-style outfit. There was a shirt, a doublet, pants (calzones, one pair of them woolen), shoes, and a hat, as well as several tilmatli, one of Rouen with Spanish-style lacework (*randas*).[214] The mother had made some of the trousers and cloaks herself, the others then apparently having been bought.

Women's clothing, as often in such situations in world history, was more conservative than men's, but then, it had resembled the European manner more from the beginning, consisting primarily of a long full skirt and an upper garment. Since the skirts are never found described in any detail, we learn nothing about whether or not indigenous skirts were influenced by Spanish counterparts. But it is clear that women retained the indigenous upper garment, a kind of shift called a *huipil* (Nahuatl *huipilli*), sleeveless, unfitted, and reaching well below the waist. Even Lucía María, whose sons were so up-to-date, wore a huipil, albeit a new and probably fancy one. Among her accessories, a bracelet of feathers (*machoncotl*), including quetzal plumes, was definitely of indigenous type, and so apparently was her carrying apparatus (*mamalhuaztli*). Her headgear may have been Spanish influenced; her -*tlapachiuhca*, literally "covering," had a Nahuatl name, but it probably was a type of shawl introduced from Spain.[215] A hundred years later (1734), doña Felipa de Jesús, wealthy widow of a member of the officeholding group of Soyatzingo (Chalco region), had shawls called in Spanish *rebozos*, but she too still wore huipiles, some of them from Pachuca and Oaxaca.[216]

Aspects of Land Use

What Nahuatl documents (and other sources too, apparently) have to say about plant and animal varieties and techniques of propagating them falls so far short of the copious material on land tenure that I mention a stray fact or two here only to make clear how unbalanced our knowledge is. As to tools, which at times are mentioned in wills, by the later sixteenth century the Nahuas were using a combination of indigenous and Spanish implements. The evidence is rather skewed, since only a tool of metal, hence probably European or European influenced, would be likely to be worth bequeathing. Most frequently mentioned is the *tlaltepoztli*, literally "land iron," which can be safely considered to be a Spanish hoe or mattock (*azadón*).[217] Also found, however, is the *huictli*, or indigenous digging stick with a flat blade, usually in the form *tepozhuictli*, with the addition of the word for "metal, iron," apparently signifying that the blade was now made of that material. Several of these are found among the stock of a Culhuacan pochtecatl in 1581, and at the same time and place another possessor of a tepozhuictli had paid six tomines (three-fourths of a peso) for it, so the item was of more than negligible value and must have ordinarily been purchased rather than manufactured by the user.[218] The latest presently known attestation of the word tepozhuictli is from 1689,[219] but since the tool has survived in some places to the present century, it must still have been in use in the eighteenth. The *huitzoctli*, a pointed oaken pole for levering sod loose or planting seed, is not mentioned in known testaments, but a document of the mid-seventeenth century asserts that in breaking the ground of a field dedicated to religious ends, the ordinary people brought "only" huitzoctli, whereas the more illustrious brought a yoke of oxen, if not several.[220] By the seventeenth century, some of the wealthier Nahuas had surprising numbers of oxen,[221] and the general impression arising from both Nahuatl and Spanish sources is that oxen were ever more prevalent among the general population as well, but at present there is no way to gauge the exact rate and extent of the development. The hand tools of agriculture were in the male domain, and they can be found given to a son on the explicit ground that the recipient is male.[222]

As for crops, one surprise in the documentation is that the chinampas of sixteenth-century Culhuacan seem to have been used more for the staple maize and beans than for the multitudinous specialties with which the chinampas of the southern lake region are often associated.[223] In general, however, the staples are little mentioned, ceding in interest to the land that produced them. More often felt worth bequeathing were the magueys that bordered many fields and to which some lands were entirely devoted.[224] Quite often seen, because of their revenue-producing potential, are orchards in the Spanish manner or individual European fruit trees. The word *huerta* was borrowed into Nahuatl before 1550, and orchard owners, most often but not always nobles, are no rarity from that time forward. Peach and pear trees are perhaps most frequently mentioned, but apple, pomegranate, walnut, fig, apricot, and quince also occur. Such orchards could also include native trees like the avocado and sapota.[225]

Horses and mules appear in Nahuatl sources, as seen above, mainly in packtrains or as individual animals for transport or riding, and mainly in the hands of nobles or entrepreneurs; only occasionally is it specified that a noble owned a whole herd of larger livestock.[226] The European chicken receives frequent mention under various names, especially in the sixteenth century when it was still something of a novelty.[227]

At one time it was thought that the Spaniards destroyed and revolutionized Nahua political and religious life while leaving the fabric of ordinary economic life at the local level nearly untouched. Though only scattered morsels related to economic activity as such are to be found in Nahuatl documents, they imply that no such differential obtained. In the economic realm as in the others, a strong indigenous base continued to provide the framework while Spanish items and modes quickly entered everywhere, not so much displacing as infiltrating, interpenetrating, and being assigned to niches already existing in the indigenous cultural scheme. Indeed, it may be that the economic sphere, as the least formal of all the major sectors and the one of greatest concern to the bulk of the Hispanic population, was the arena of the most direct and pervasive interpenetration. Several economic phenomena of the indigenous world appear to have persisted unchanged in the essentials, but we can be sure that nothing was left literally untouched.

6

Religious Life

THE RELIGIOUS HISTORY of postconquest Mexico has often been seen in terms of successful or unsuccessful resistance to a Christian conversion campaign. In fact, conscious, overt indigenous resistance was not utterly lacking from the picture, and it is not entirely inappropriate to speak of some effort on the part of the Spaniards to convince or "convert" the Indians in the manner of evangelists of our own times. But neither category, conversion or resistance, truly hits the mark. As in politics, existing Nahua patterns were what made the quick apparent success of Spanish modes possible; the altepetl was as important in religious as in political organization. One can hardly speak of an indigenous inclination to disbelief in Christianity. For the people of preconquest Mesoamerica, victory was prima facie evidence of the strength of the victor's god. One expected a conqueror to impose his god in some fashion, without fully displacing one's own; the new god in any case always proved to be an agglomeration of attributes familiar from the local pantheon and hence easy to assimilate. Thus the Nahuas after the Spanish conquest needed less to be converted than to be instructed. Spanish ecclesiastics seem to have taken much the same view of the matter, since they spoke mainly in terms of instruction or indoctrination rather than conversion, and never referred to themselves as missionaries, the word so many modern scholars have anachronistically preferred.

Mesoamerican religion, including that of the Nahuas, was highly developed. A complex pantheon of deities possessed specific iconographic and other attributes and was embodied in images inhabiting sumptuous temples; there a hierarchy of religious specialists held forth, overseeing the observance of a full calendar of festivities, replete with processions and rich costumes, throughout the year. Sacrificial and penitential practices affected all levels of the population, while divination and shamanistic rites played some part in every aspect of daily life. Religion was an integral part of sociopolitical organization. A special ethnic god (like the Mexica's Huitzilopochtli, often at once a deified ancestor and a variant of one of the general Mesoamerican deities), was one of the main unifying forces of the altepetl, and his temple was the primary symbol of its sovereignty and power. A lesser god with a lesser temple fulfilled the same function for each calpolli; and it appears that the pervasive if little understood gods or spirits of the household may have done the same at that level. In theory, the god gave his people their land and clothed their rulers with title and authority. The upper level of the priestly hierarchy was recruited from the same noble lineages as the political officers of the altepetl; the same person might hold religious and political posts in succession, and altepetl officials as such had important religious duties. By present understanding, religious and political functions were even more intertwined and undistinguished from each other than was the case among the Spaniards, who had themselves gone a considerable distance in that direction.

A veil covers the first years of postconquest reorganization in religion, just as it does in the sociopolitical realm, and for the same reason: the lack of knowledgeable contemporaneous reports or other types of direct evidence from the inside in the time before the Nahuas had learned to make use of the European alphabetic script. The darkness is in fact greater in the case of religion, for whereas we have every reason to believe that the tlatoani and lesser officials of the altepetl continued to act virtually as before the conquest, and in the earliest Nahuatl documents we actually see them still doing so, the Spaniards could not allow indigenous priests and temples to continue to function in the preconquest manner for any extended period. Spanish ecclesiastical accounts emphasize the speed, thoroughness, and voluntary nature of the changeover, but they are suspect on the grounds of being partisan and relatively uninformed, and the same can be said of indigenous claims of quick total conversion made in the second half of the sixteenth century with the transparent purpose of gaining the favor of Spanish officials. Indeed, one of the most prominent testimonies of the latter type, a 1560 letter from the cabildo of Huexotzinco, while asserting the Huexotzincans' immediate enthusiastic adoption of Christianity, gleefully tells of widespread reluctance and even outright resistance in the rival altepetl of Tlaxcala.[1] Charles Gibson's careful reconstruction of the early Tlaxcalan situation from sources of this type (the best such survey yet made) comes to the conclusion that the Spaniards did continue to tolerate certain overt preconquest practices for some time, and that some indigenous factions were less hospitable to Christianity than others.[2] In all likelihood, such differences were by no means purely doctrinal. Religion being tied as closely to politics as it was, a group or faction that favored continued military resistance likely took a similar position on Christianity as a matter of course; nor, probably, was the inclination to resist in either sphere the product of any special attitude toward the intruders, but rather the outcome of internal tensions. We can imagine a process like that known to have occurred in Valley of Mexico altepetl such as Tetzcoco, that is, if the ruling tlatoani decided for the Spaniards and against the Mexica, his principal dynastic rival (and following) would automatically do the opposite.

The earliest known substantial Nahuatl records, the census volumes from the Cuernavaca region (apparently dating from ca. 1535–40 or a little later for the most part), do not speak directly of religion, but do show a large portion of the populace still unbaptized, going about their business on the same basis as those who had already undergone baptism and received a Christian name. The proportions varied from altepetl to altepetl, calpolli to calpolli. The higher-ranking were more likely to be baptized, but not always. Sometimes baptism or the lack of it went by whole families, sometimes by individuals within families; the elderly were not infrequently left unbaptized, as though it were too late or no longer mattered. The general impression is of an unhurried process tending ultimately toward universal baptism but not bringing about large attitudinal change at any one time. The records report, without comment, quite a few cases of polygamy, some involving people who were baptized.³

One spectacular Nahuatl document does speak directly of the first moments of confrontation between indigenous and European religious beliefs. A set of *Coloquios* composed in Nahuatl under the direction of fray Bernardino de Sahagún purports to reproduce in dialogue form what passed at meetings between the founding party of twelve Franciscans and the high priests of Tenochtitlan when the friars first arrived in the capital city in 1524.⁴ It turns out, however, that the *Coloquios* were written in the 1560's without, as far as we know, the benefit of the testimony of any eyewitness to the original proceedings. We have no way to determine the respective parts played by authentic oral transmission, posterior legendary heightening, and conscious shaping of the material for exemplary purposes. The last aspect is at least present; indeed, the *Coloquios* put one in mind of the Nahuatl religious plays intended for performance before an audience. To summarize the contents, the Franciscans, having assembled the native religious authorities, proclaim the existence of their God and the falsity and perversity of the native deities, actually demons. The reply of the indigenous priests, often anthologized, is the most striking thing in the whole composition. They do not challenge the strangers' god directly but instead argue for preserving their own divinities, who from time immemorial have provided the spiritual and material means through which they and their forebears have sustained life. Thereupon the friars, rather than debating, launch into telling the central events of the Old and New Testaments (the document in its extant form breaks off before the finish). Whatever their degree of factual authenticity, the speeches presented correspond to our general understanding of religious interaction between the two peoples in that the indigenous priests, instead of casting doubt on the new doctrine, insist on the necessity of retaining the core of their own traditions, while the friars, rather than employing persuasive arts, immediately undertake detailed instruction on the basic tenets of Christianity.

Religion and the Politics of the Altepetl

The process of creating parishes in Nahua territory began as early as the 1520's and was virtually complete by the 1540's. Despite a multitude of variations, a parish was generally a function of an already existing encomienda and hence was based, as a norm at least, on a single altepetl. The original Nahua parishes were almost all manned by one or another of the three orders, Franciscan, Dominican, and Augustinian, with the first as earliest arrivals getting the lion's share. Details of parish creation are little understood. The friars tended to present the parishes as the product of their own free and arbitrary decisions, ignoring both the encomienda and the altepetl. Nevertheless, the encomienda supplied the parish much of its revenue, and the altepetl provided its whole internal organization and working mechanisms. The monastery churches, which though often not completed until far into the sixteenth century, were usually planned or begun quite early, were normally built near the old main altepetl temple, sometimes on literally the same site. Whether it was in the same place or not, the Nahuas took the Christian church as the analogue of the preconquest temple. They enthusiastically participated in its construction and decoration in the same spirit as with its predecessor, looking to magnify the central tangible symbol of the altepetl's sovereignty and identity. The nobles of the altepetl expected to and did serve as officials involved in seeing to church operation, as they had supervised the functioning of the temple before the conquest. Following established preconquest precedent, altepetl officials used labor and tribute mechanisms to supply the church's needs and make sure its public rites were well attended. Since one church, however large, was not enough to serve an entire altepetl district in the long run, secondary churches or chapels without resident priests, to be visited periodically from the main church and hence called in Spanish *visitas*, soon began to be created, one for each calpolli, like the secondary temples of preconquest times.[5]

Exactly how given orders acquired given parishes has never been ascertained with any clarity. As we saw, the Franciscans originally got most of them, simply by virtue of arriving before the others. Later, the Dominicans and Augustinians took over some of the Franciscan parishes, plus whole unoccupied peripheral areas, where they became respectively dominant. Robert Ricard presumed that these assignments came about entirely through sovereign choices on the part of the ecclesiastics, including disputes and gentle-men's agreements among them.⁶ Indeed, the results plotted on a map, with a mainly Franciscan center broken by just enough Dominican and Augustinian foundations to give the other orders some kind of presence in the area and form communication chains leading to their outlying bailiwicks, tend to con-firm such an interpretation. That encomenderos might have made the original choices, as they often did in Peru, is not confirmed by remaining evidence. But hints and claims do exist in Nahuatl records that the local people them-selves took an active part in the decision, for political reasons reminiscent of those I have surmised to have motivated some of their actions in the conquest period proper. Though the accounts are posterior and partisan, they will bear repeating.

In 1556, in the four-part complex altepetl of Tlaxcala, a political crisis followed upon the viceroy's deposition of governor don Martín de Valencia after only one year in office instead of the normal two. Since the governorship rotated among the four subkingdoms and don Martín was from Quiahuiz-tlan, that entity was hard hit, and in the cabildo session called to discuss the matter, it was the members from Quiahuiztlan who made the strongest and bitterest statements. One of them, looking back to the time of strife among the four altepetl before a definitive system of office rotation was established in 1545, recalled that Quiahuiztlan in that period had seceded from Tlaxcala and brought in the Dominicans (to replace the Franciscans who already held the province). Now, he threatened, Quiahuiztlan might do the same again.⁷ The Quiahuiztlan people in fact did not do the same again, nor is there any other known record of exactly what they did the first time, or when. If we take them at their word, at some point in the 1530's or 1540's Quiahuiztlan on its own initiative expelled the Franciscans and put the Dominicans in their place as a gesture accompanying its departure from the Tlaxcalan confedera-tion. If so, it must have disinvited the Dominicans and taken the Franciscans back when it returned to the fold.

A somewhat similar account comes from the much later hand of the Ama-quemecan annalist Chimalpahin; the time is not fully clear but again appears to fall into the general period of the late 1530's or the 1540's. Amaquemecan was a complex altepetl of five parts; apparently at the time in question no decision had yet been made on whether the whole entity would be a single parish or not. The Franciscans were present, staying at the palace of don Tomás de San Martín Quetzalmaçatzin, tlatoani of the ranking sub-altepetl, but they had not yet built a church. The tlatoani of the second-ranking entity, don Juan de Sandoval Tequanxayactzin, was the rival of don Tomás, anxious to outshine him and dominate all Amaquemecan. Don Juan therefore had a church built and summoned the Dominicans from a nearby monastery to say mass there, making much of them. Nor did he fail to use them to take a jab at don Tomás, wondering aloud what kind of people his rival's friars were, going about in filthy rags and unshod, when his own Dominicans were splendidly gotten up in clean habits and shoes. In this atmosphere, the Franciscans may have felt, says Chimalpahin, that no one was very concerned about them, and so they soon departed, leaving the field to the Dominicans.[8] We must suspend full belief in this tale, written down perhaps eighty or ninety years after the events by a reporter ill disposed toward don Juan and his faction, but it is true that Amaquemecan ended up as a Dominican parish. The story in any case gives us an indigenous perspective on the manner and rationale of parish assignments.

It would appear, then, that for the Nahuas the question of which order held a parish was inextricably wrapped up with the definition of indigenous sociopolitical entities, their autonomy, and their solidarity or fragmentation. When an altepetl came to terms after the conquest on a (partly) new religious orientation and self-definition, the arrangement was not merely with the Christian church in general but with a specific order, which became an integral part of altepetl identity. What preconquest precedent there may have been for the Nahuas' sharp distinction among the different orders is not clear. Possibly they simply perceived the importance that the Spaniards themselves gave to the distinction, calling the orders "religions" and making them the focus of vast political and doctrinal battles. The Nahuas may also have detected the Franciscan strength within the Spanish establishment from the conquest forward, and that perception may have made them especially resistant when Spanish policy called (as it sometimes did to correct the early imbalance) for the removal of the Franciscans from a given altepetl in favor of another order or, later, secular priests. We would be naïve to believe, as the friars maintained and as Ricard tended to accept, that indigenous actions and reactions in the matter of order affiliation had primarily to do with the order's popularity or an indigenous group's devotion to it or to certain of its members.[9]

Consider the story Chimalpahin tells of how the indigenous people of San Sebastián Atzaqualco in Mexico City did all they could in 1608 to retain the Carmelites at their church and not accept the Augustinians. The reason Chimalpahin gives for their action is not any attachment to the Carmelites (a factor that goes unmentioned) but the fact that in the eyes of the Atzaqualca the church was theirs, built on their land by their fathers and grandfathers, and they were afraid they would lose it. They seemed to fear it would become a mere visita of the Augustinian monastery, with no resident cleric.[10] These things happened before Chimalpahin's eyes; for the Mexico City of his time, he must be considered a good witness.

Central Mexican parish creation was said above to have neared completion in the 1540's only in the sense that the entire territory was now assigned to some ecclesiastical jurisdiction. Many early parishes served complex altepetl or dual kingdoms with vast populations, large territories, and highly distinct constituent parts that might not even be on good terms with each other. As the number of Spanish clerics grew, a second wave of parish creation got under way, leaving the cores of the original jurisdictions intact but carving out new parishes on the edges. The second-generation parishes, like those formed earlier, followed the lines of indigenous sociopolitical organization, fastening on some well-defined altepetl-like unit. The Mexican-born Spaniards who began entering the church in the second half of the sixteenth century often became secular priests rather than friars, in part because in that capacity they could better serve the economic interests of their families, and thus strong pressures were brought to bear to assign the new parishes to the secular hierarchy rather than to the orders. Now that the interorder battles over dominance had faded, new combats raged between the secular clergy and the orders in general, with the seculars often victorious in creating parishes for themselves inside previously mendicant jurisdictions.[11]

Jurisdictional rearrangements, like the original parish creations, were strongly affected by developments on the indigenous side. As the grand monastery churches belonging to the whole altepetl reached completion in the second half (and mainly the last quarter) of the sixteenth century, indigenous attention naturally turned increasingly to the network of lesser churches, each subunit being of course concerned primarily with the construction and maintenance of its own. The effects of this normal and predictable shift of emphasis go far toward explaining the impression of some observers that by the seventeenth century the Nahuas had become alienated from the clergy and more specifically from the friars.[12] Secondary church construction and parish proliferation coincided and interacted with the gathering forces of altepetl fragmentation, which met the ambitions of the secular clergy halfway. An impressive calpolli church could be an argument for a new parish but also for political independence from the altepetl, and much religious construction was undertaken precisely with that object in mind.[13] The late seventeenth and the eighteenth century saw a crescendo of such movements, but they had begun long before. In 1570–71 (whether on his own initiative or at local urging is not known), the friar stationed at San Luis Huamantla on the edges of the Tlaxcala district founded a new church, which the local people used as a pretext to establish an independent altepetl; thereupon authorities from greater Tlaxcala came and brusquely put a stop to both developments, forcing some of the plotters into temporary exile, though they continued to litigate for permission to found a new church.[14]

The intermingling of religious life and altepetl politics went far beyond parish assignment and church construction to affect religious phenomena of nearly every description. To illustrate, let us again call on Chimalpahin and his reports on events in Mexico City. In 1593, the people of the Tenochtitlan sub-calpolli Nativitas Tepetlatzinco proudly had a new monstrance consecrated, but no sooner had they done so than the apparently neighboring people of Huehuetitlan also got themselves a fine one. This tit for tat gives every sign of relating as much to community pride and jockeying for position as to pure religious devotion. Chimalpahin is explicit on this point when he says that having the Holy Sacrament placed in the church of San Juan Bautista de la Penitencia lent honor and renown to the whole district of San Juan Moyotlan (the Molotecayotl).[15] The right to go in religious procession separately from other groups was another symbol of independence and source of community prestige. In 1613, the people of Santa Cruz Contzinco wanted to have a procession all by themselves, but a representative of San Pablo Tlachcuititlan, of which they were a part, brought suit before Spanish authorities to prevent it. The Santa Cruz people therefore went out secretly at night on their procession, getting home before dawn and avoiding any confrontation or penalty. With the precedent set, they later got permission to do as they wanted.[16] As so often, the goal was heightened community identity and greater autonomy in all respects, and as usual, the umbrella community resisted.

The Church People

Throughout the entire colonial period, the ordained priest or priests assigned to a parish were almost always Spanish, and as a result, the indigenous staff of the church took on special importance. The priest as an outsider neither fully identified himself with the parish community (that is, the altepetl or altepetl subdivision) nor fully understood its language and ways. It was up to the church staff to represent the community and to mediate between the priest and the congregation. In visita churches, the staff was in complete charge of day-to-day operations, and even in the monastery or parish churches, though the priests tended to develop a close relationship with their aides, they usually rotated at fairly short intervals and were often absent in the city, whereas the staff was always present and in addition remained markedly stable over the years. No wonder that the local people considered themselves sole owners of their churches.

The leader of the church staff was the *fiscal (de la iglesia)*, the general steward and manager of the church and all its assets and activities, the right-hand man and principal intermediary of the Spanish priest. The Spaniards introduced the office and the term into many of their American territories from a very early time, apparently seeking to establish an equivalent of the cacique in ecclesiastical matters. Among the Nahuas, the fiscal of the mature colonial period was a person of great social prestige, usually of noble lineage, and structurally the second-ranking community representative after the gobernador/tlatoani. Whether or not the position was, on the indigenous side, a carryover from the high priesthood of the altepetl deity in preconquest times is a moot point, but its aura and characteristics surely were part of a continuing tradition.[17] As in the preconquest period, religious and political office intermeshed, and the fiscal often acted for all the world as though he were an important member of the secular altepetl cabildo.[18]

It is not at all clear, however, that this eminence attached to the post of fiscal from the beginning, in the manner of the altepetl governorship. Since the notion of the indigenous fiscal as aide was part of the general Spanish cultural baggage in the Indies, friars must have started filling the post as soon as they started consecrating churches. But in Nahuatl documents I have yet to see a fiscal mentioned before 1570. In later times, the fiscal was a perennial witness to testaments; not so in the earliest Nahuatl wills. The word never appears in the copious municipal records of Tlaxcala stretching from the late 1540's into the 1560's.[19] The absence does not mean that the Tlaxcalan monastery had no fiscal, but if it did, he surely was not yet playing any appreciable role in cabildo activity. The first attestation of the word presently known to me occurs in a Tula cofradía membership list written in 1570. But "Juan García, fiscal" lacks the "don" adorning the name of the governor; in fact, he appears far down the list and at a distance from the governor and alcalde, whose names come first of all.[20] Other sixteenth-century examples are less suggestive, but there too the fiscal does not appear to cut much of a figure.

In 1575, however, we find don Toribio Silvestre, of impressive name and title, officiating in Coyoacan, surrounded by lesser members of the church staff, and being called on to witness various kinds of transactions.[21] The fiscal don Juan Téllez, of Culhuacan, who died around 1580, also already fits the classic mold: noble, wealthy, married to a noblewoman, taking a free hand in the general management of economic transactions between the church and the community.[22] In Amaquemecan in 1588, the tlatoani of one of the five sub-altepetl was acting as fiscal.[23] Here, then, we have an instance of a major organizational feature in which, contrary to the general pattern, the preconquest mode did not serve as a transitional device, and direct continuity between pre- and postconquest periods seems to be lacking. The reason appears to be the brusque sweeping aside of the indigenous high priesthood and its more overt manifestations, so that it took some time for an approximate equivalent, adjusted to the changed situation, to grow up.

Originally, a whole altepetl would have had a single fiscal, attached to the district's main church, but as jurisdictions and churches multiplied, so did fiscales. Though the process is hard to follow systematically, it appears that in due course an appointment was made for every consecrated church, including very secondary ones. In a small calpolli church, one would not necessarily expect the holder of the office to be of illustrious lineage; Juan Vicente, fiscal in the San Bartolomé Atenco tlaxilacalli of Coyoacan in 1617, would seem to have been the same sort of substantial commoner as the Juan Fabián for whose estate he served as executor,[24] and there were many like him. Main churches sometimes came to boast a hierarchy of fiscales, perhaps especially when the altepetl contained major ethnic-political divisions, as in the case of Metepec, where in 1795 three such officials are mentioned: a *fiscal mayor*, a *fiscal mexicano*, and a fiscal for Ecatepec.[25]

Nahuatl documents tell little about the fiscal's more properly religious duties, in which department it is hard to improve substantially on Ricard.[26] Spanish monastery records emphasize the extent of the friars' reliance on the indigenous official, who in at least some cases kept his own accounts, had custody of all church funds including those to be spent for members of the order, converted revenue in kind into cash, made purchases and loans, and paid salaries.[27] Indigenous complaints about abuses by the fiscal, which abound if one seeks them out, drive home the extent to which custom allowed him to exact revenue (whether for the church or for himself is never certain) from a wide range of religious activities.

One target of complaints was a Josef de la Cruz, who had been fiscal in San Pedro Atocpan, in the district of Milpa Alta, itself within Xochimilco's jurisdiction, for fifteen years or so before 1638. Witnesses said among other things that at sowing time he required every boy and girl who came to catechism to bring him a small gourd full of maize. The Nahuas loved to bring their personal images of saints to the church to be blessed and viewed publicly, with as much pomp as possible. To get permission to do so in Atocpan, the owner of a saint had to pay Josef de la Cruz three or four reales. If the person wanted the accompaniment of trumpets, as of course those who could afford it did, he had to pay as much again, even if he had already paid the trumpeters their own fees.[28] Both practices may contain preconquest elements.

What does leap to the eye in extant Nahuatl documentation is that the fiscal was the most called upon of all the altepetl dignitaries, even more than the past and present governors, as a witness to and especially as an executor of wills. Not only was the fiscal a figure of high standing in the community and expected to be an expert in the management of money and affairs, but every person of property needed to request a mass or masses in his testament, for which purpose some property usually had to be sold, and the fiscal would in any case be the recipient of the money, as well as ultimately directing the whole corporate aspect of the funeral ceremonies. But though this natural arrangement must have worked well in many cases (else the Nahuas surely would have ceased to rely so heavily on the fiscal in these matters), it also led naturally to trouble because of the persistent tendency, doubtless in part left over from the preconquest period, not to differentiate between private and churchly affairs.[29] Another witness against Josef de la Cruz accused him of taking all the goods of the dead for himself except the houses, and he would have taken them too, according to the accuser, had he been able to find buyers.[30]

At this point, we need to stop to consider the role funeral rites played in the Nahua economy in general and in the life of those directly affected in particular. The customary funeral feasting, with precedents in both the indigenous and the European tradition, was by itself a considerable expense.[31] Further and larger expenditures were required to pay for the priest, attendants, musicians, and use of equipment during the actual burial. And then there was the cost of having, when possible, one or more masses said for the soul of the decedent. Whether because in preconquest times the relative pomp of personal rites of passage signaled the status of the individual and his line, or because of the Spanish practice of counting a family's status by the number of masses it could afford, the Nahuas were soon acting just like the Spaniards: the wealthier, the more masses. In their especially cash-poor sector of the economy, the money for all the expenses was usually acquired by the sale of real estate. People who had argued with relatives or had none were likely to order virtually everything to go for masses.[32] Moreover, as was seen in Chapter 5, major purchases in the Nahua world tended to be paid for by sporadic installments dragging out over the years, and the same was true of loans and pawning arrangements. All the obligations came due once and for all at death, occasioning yet more selling to acquire cash. The upshot was (as Chapter 5 anticipated) that death and funeral rites had a large impact on the cash economy by causing property transfer not only through inheritance but through sale, with the two transfer types closely intertwined. The preferred recourse was a quasi-sale in which relatives assumed the various expenses in return for inheriting assets (most often land), thus keeping the property in the family. The principle becomes explicit in the 1581 will of Joaquín de Luna of Culhuacan, who gave his horse to his younger sister with the stipulation that she have six masses said for him, "as though she were paying for it."[33]

In fact, the relatives so called upon did not invariably comply. They might lack either the money or the inclination. In the Culhuacan testaments, far fewer masses were paid for and performed than were requested. Several explanations are possible, as we will see, but one gets the impression that in many instances relatives and officials unanimously felt the dying man or woman had overdone it in the moment of extremity and through a silent conspiracy simply retrenched. To have at least one requested mass said was a solemn obligation that few would dismiss outright, but relatives or friends named as executors were much tempted to put the obligation off indefinitely, and death caught many of them in turn with that mass still not paid for.[34] The executor could even turn the matter into a business venture, selling the land as instructed but investing the money in his own dealings and letting the profit mount, he hoped, far beyond the amount required for the mass before finally having it said, if he ever did.[35]

The practice was so common that, probably in the sixteenth or early seventeenth century, someone wrote a moralistic playlet on the topic.[36] After a first scene in which an elderly couple expatiate on the virtue of leaving property to be sold for masses for the souls of the dead, two executors, apparently of this very couple, appear. They immediately start musing that since the dead do not return, there is no reason not to split the money two ways, profit from it, and worry about the mass later. Demons in the wings rub their hands as they listen to the conversation, and the executors eventually go to perdition.

When a testator ordered property sold for a mass, and the money for the mass then failed to appear, it could be considered incumbent on the fiscal, who was so often a witness to the testament if not actually its executor, and who was also generally designated to receive the mass payment at some point, to take action. With such justification and sometimes on flimsier grounds, fiscales were often all too ready to intervene. Some of the possible implications of this intervention can be seen in the case of don Juan Miguel (Velásquez), who served as fiscal in Tezontla, in the Tetzcoco jurisdiction, at least from 1689 to 1721, apparently without interruption.[37] In 1720, various broad accusations were made about his behavior, but the most specific complaint, which may have brought matters to a head, went as follows: a testament had called for eight pesos' worth of masses, which were actually said in expectation of the payment; then, although the will spoke of leaving lands to relatives and making them responsible for the masses, don Juan Miguel sold the land to get the money. One can conclude that he probably did so because payment was not forthcoming from the relatives. No one claimed, in this case, that he had pocketed the money instead of paying the priest. The benefit he was said to seek was the opportunity to sell land, doubtless too cheap, to his own relatives and followers.

In his over thirty years in the position, don Juan Miguel had perfected ways of dominating the local situation. In 1710, he was alcalde (apparently Tezontla's highest secular officer during this period) and fiscal at the same time, probably not the only year he filled both posts. In 1720, both the current alcalde and a past alcalde who testified in the litigation were his nephews. He kept all the testaments issued in the jurisdiction in his own possession and did not, it was implied, give others access to them in case of suspected irregularities.* In general, as here, when indigenous people felt the land-for-masses nexus was being abused, they were much more inclined to blame the fiscal, the more visible figure to them, than the Spanish priest, who in the Hispanic sector was the favorite target of this kind of criticism.[38]

Don Juan Miguel's simultaneous double officeholding was a little unusual, but as shown in Chapter 2, the interpenetration of secular and ecclesiastical officers and functions, with the fiscal as the primary liaison, was normal. In 1585, the governor and alcaldes of Tula sent the fiscal to investigate whether there were any heirs for a certain piece of vacant land. The fiscal thereupon negotiated and signed a land sale agreement, and brought the money received to the cabildo, which immediately gave it back to him to buy what was needed at the church.[39] That is, the fiscal here was meeting with and acting on the authority of the secular cabildo, but at the same time the entire proceedings were carried out in the interest of the church. Funds flowed in the other direction too on occasion. The early-seventeenth-century fiscal of the monastery of Tula lent church money to the governor to pay taxes to the royal government.[40] And we sometimes find secular officials operating within the church hierarchy. In 1620, the father guardian of the Franciscan monastery of Tlatelolco sent out not only the fiscal but the alcalde to inspect a piece of land and give the buyer possession.[41]

Not surprisingly, the exact powers of the different officers were the object of contention at times. In Tocuillan (Tetzcoco region) in 1757, an aggrieved party claimed that the alcalde and other secular officials, not the fiscal, should litigate over land.[42] But the final agreement was issued by the fiscal and alcalde jointly. A fiscal would often be seen taking a turn in the town's highest secular office, alcalde or governor as the case might be.[43] Perhaps the greatest single responsibility of both sets of officials, from the indigenous point of view, was to maintain the splendor of the church, the saint's cult, and the festivities as a unified expression of altepetl well-being and religious devotion.[44]

The fiscal was only the ranking, most visible figure of a staff usually referred to as the *teopantlaca*, the "church people." Nowhere is the term found rigorously defined; when one sees it in texts, the context is usually that a testator near death is asking the teopantlaca to come get his body and perform the honors, promising them alms for the service.[45] From such instances,

---

*The fiscal did not always keep the testaments. Often the notary did, and in a great many cases, which provide the backbone of extant Nahuatl documentation, the heirs retained the original.

one gradually forms the opinion that the word refers primarily to the church cantors. Indeed, the first known certain attestation, from Tulancingo in 1569, speaks of the "teopantlacan cuihcanime," or "church people, singers"; the potentially ambiguous wording is clarified somewhat by the fact that parallel entries for the two previous years speak of the singers only.[46] In some texts, the Spanish loan *cantores* is found at the juncture where the Nahuatl word is expected, hinting further at the equivalence of the two terms.[47]

Preconquest Nahua notions of the role and aura of temple personnel seem to have affected the postconquest church staff profoundly, and it begins to appear that the actual word teopantlaca is a carryover, as well as *teopan*, "church," on which it is based. Yet as just noted, I have at present not found an example of the full-fledged term before the 1560's.[48] In a reference to church singers in Coyoacan around 1545–50, the indigenous word for singers is used, modified by the Spanish loan *capilla*, "chapel" or "choir."[49]

We have good reason to believe, however, that the concept "teopantlaca" was not strictly confined to the singers. Chimalpahin has the group contending with the governor of Amaquemecan and actually getting him thrown in jail, a type of action better suited to the whole churchly establishment from fiscal on down than to the musicians alone.[50] In a Culhuacan will of 1583, five people are specifically designated teopantlaca, and these include a church constable and a *diputado* ("deputy," a post varying greatly in its duties from one place to another).[51] As a matter of fact, Spanish "cantores" was often used the same way, designating the entire church staff by its largest component. The Nahuatl term in practice meant exactly the same as the Spanish one, naming the whole group but associated most closely with the musicians as predominant, although in this case employing a word that literally refers to the larger grouping.

In preconquest times, temple personnel seem to have received lands by way of remuneration. We see the same system operating in the Coyoacan document of 1545–50 referred to just above. Don Juan de Guzmán, the tlatoani/governor, surrounded by high noblemen of the realm (some of whom were cabildo members, though the group does not proclaim itself to be or represent the cabildo), gives sizable plots of land, apparently as personal property without restriction, to a group of nineteen singers, the largest piece going to a Gonzalo López who heads the list and must be the leader, although he bears no special title. The declared rationale of the grants is to ensure that the singers will always continue to perform in church and teach singing to others.[52] No comparable document is known from any later period, and I presume that the custom did not long survive in its pure form, going the way of special land allotments for altepetl officials generally. In the 1560's, the church singers of Tulancingo were annually receiving sums of money, specifically called their pay ("yntlaxtlahuil"), from the municipal government, but the three or four pesos given out to the whole group each December could hardly have made anyone rich.[53] Nor is the practice known to have been common.

The staple benefit of the church people, presuming the fiscal did not intercept it, was the half peso or so that all across the colonial period the dying usually dedicated to them as a group for their part in the funeral rites,[54] plus their fees for participating in corporate festivities. The master or teacher of the musicians (usually called by the Spanish loan phrase *maestro de capilla*), who might later become fiscal or a high cabildo member, may have had certain prerogatives. The choir normally consisted partly of boys, and in 1763, a former alcalde of Quauhtlalpan (central Valley of Mexico, near Coatlichan) remembered that when he was a choirboy, the master used to send his young charges to harvest his wife's magueys.[55] Another former alcalde testifying had also been a choirboy; lesser church positions must have sometimes served as a training ground for future high officers of the municipality.*

One reason why the term teopantlaca enjoyed such currency may have been the lack of specialization among the church staff. Sacristans, constables, deputies, and custodians appear to have carried out one another's functions at need and sometimes turn out to be the same people wearing different hats; many of them were probably also in the choir.[56] The two types of official with the most distinct profile were the church constable (*alguacil de la iglesia*) and the church notary (*escribano de la iglesia*); these are the most frequently observed in the company of the fiscal, whether seeing to testaments or dispatching other business.[57] The constable was the primary executive arm of the fiscal; he must be distinguished from the other church people sometimes called *topile*, even though the Nahuatl word can be translated "constable" and on occasion was applied precisely to the official we are discussing.[58] *Topilli* means "staff," and its derivative "topile" (literally "staff holder") can refer to anyone in an official position exercising specific responsibilities at an intermediate level, both supervising and supervised. In several examples in the Culhuacan testaments, a topile is seen to be anything but a constable; these include Juan Jaso the "teopan topille tlachpanqui," "church topile who sweeps," probably in charge of the custodians and cleaning crew, though the title and position may have been quite prestigious in view of the preconquest

---

*Which is not to say that the modern *cargo* system was already in existence. Whereas in that system's ideal form (which may or may not actually exist), every officeholder if he lives long enough and performs up to minimum standards goes through the entire office sequence in an egalitarian fashion, in the older period only a certain proportion, standing out by reason of wealth and high lineage, advanced to the top, and some were so illustrious that they never had to serve in lesser posts at all. Some recent ethnographers are finding, in the Mayan region at least, that on closer examination many vestiges of the older system can still be detected (Kathleen Truman, personal communication). See also Chance and Taylor 1985.

tradition of sweeping the temple as a high ritual duty and prerogative, and Juan Bautista the "coro topille teopan," "choir topile at church."[59]

The church notary is not so easily confused with other church personnel; the problem is to distinguish him from the notary of the municipality. Since we rarely have exhaustive information on both the secular government and the church hierarchy in a given altepetl at a given time, categorical statements cannot be made, but it appears that very often the notary of both organizations was one and the same. Certainly Martín Jacobo de Maldonado, when he was writing testaments in Culhuacan in 1579–80 in company with the fiscal and other church people, was an altepetl functionary, subject to dismissal by the cabildo.[60] In the sixteenth century, wills were most often penned by a person styling himself notary of the cabildo; later, the writer was more often called the notary of the church.[61] I am not sure whether or not this trend reflects any change deeper than that of title, but it may be that after 1650 the secular cabildo, having at first taken an active role with masses, property sale, and inheritance, increasingly relinquished direct control to the fiscal and his men. As a person who acquired a good understanding of religious formulas and of the workings and implications of the whole funeral business, the notary was especially apt to advance to fiscal himself (as well as to cabildo office).

It is likely that the constables and notaries were involved in the manipulation of testaments and property along with the fiscal and thereby received part of their normal, if unofficial, remuneration. Again the Culhuacan testaments provide the best examples. The main notary, who wrote most of the extant wills and kept them together in his possession, was removed from his post for taking many of them out of the book, presumably so that he or confederates could with impunity sell property and keep the money rather than having the masses said. A second notary, Miguel García, in his own will admits having "borrowed" the money of several testators. And the general executors (for *albacea* was at this time in Culhuacan an official post much like constable) seem to have done the same.[62]

Cofradías

Almost a part of the church staff were the officers of the cofradías, lay brotherhoods founded at first at the instigation of Spanish clerics, and later increasingly on the initiative of local people. A few of these sodalities are known to have originated during the first postconquest generation, but the campaign to organize them began in earnest in the latter part of the sixteenth century, and during the seventeenth and eighteenth they were a standard feature of the scene, tending to expand in number until there was a cofradía-like body for every self-conscious indigenous community and subcommunity (as occurred also in the Hispanic world). In the present state of knowledge little can be said about the timing of this process or how far it went toward actually reaching its logical conclusion.[63] The Nahuatl records of central Mexico leave their readers with some sense of the ubiquity of cofradías by the seventeenth century, but not with much reason to think that they were dominant, aggressive, or even particularly elaborate and well-defined entities in the general scheme of religious and sociopolitical organization. One pair of scholars has already observed that the cofradía seems to have been better developed on the periphery, where the strong mechanisms of the altepetl or its equivalent were lacking, than in central Mexico and Oaxaca.[64] Nahuatl documentation coming to light to date bears out this interpretation, not only in the little emphasis on the organization seen in central Mexican records, but in the high profile the cofradía assumes in the few Nahuatl records we have from the western part of the country.[65]

Proliferation along the lines of sociopolitical units may have been retarded by the fact that the principal cofradías were rarely dedicated to the patron saints of specific entities. Rather the same advocations as among Spaniards appear again and again, doubtless because Spanish ecclesiastics originally insisted on them, after which they became the expected thing and would be the indigenous people's spontaneous choice in any case. The Most Holy Sacrament, Souls (of Purgatory), the Rosary, the Holy Cross, and the Holy Communion, all named by Spanish loanwords, were the most common, and if several sodalities were established at one church, it would often be in that order. Some other common advocations did have a greater potential for personification, such as the Burial of Christ, the Child Jesus, Saint Mary of the Rosary, the Solitude of Saint Mary, and Saint Francis, yet all these were generalized concepts or personages not tied exclusively to any one entity. I am not sure that officially recognized cofradías were *ever* devoted to the saint of the local altepetl or calpolli; at present I know of no example.[66] Identification with the unit was also undercut by the not infrequent practice of one person belonging to more than one cofradía.[67]

An official cofradía was licensed by a bishop, based in a consecrated church, and inspected periodically by a priest, who might also oversee the organization's elections. Yet there was room within this framework for indigenous people to assert themselves, using the sodalities for a combination of personal piety, unit patriotism, and factional strife that for the most part we can only imagine. Chimalpahin, however, gives us some rare anecdotes garnered at his observation post on the Nahua world in late-sixteenth- and early-seventeenth-century Mexico City. His stories frequently involve the politics of altepetl and ethnicity.

In 1591, a cofradía of the Solitude was established, at the special request of "the governor, nobles, and commoners of Mexico City," at the indigenous chapel of San José (attached to the Franciscan monastery). It was to be specifically for the Mexica, and not for the Spaniards. In 1596, the flock of the same chapel was proud to acquire the first cofradía of San Diego to be founded in any monastery in all the city; "they had an ash-colored banner, and they wore an ashen scapulary on their chests." In 1603, the San José cofradías joined their Spanish counterparts in a procession to appeal against the year's excessive rain and flooding; Chimalpahin is careful to say that the Tlatelolco sodalities came last in line, after the Mexica.[68] In 1612, Tlatelolco got permission to establish a cofradía of Saint Mary of the Rosary. Chimalpahin says that this was done at the petition of Diego López, a woodcarver, whom he considers the founder; then in another passage he calls the then-governor of Tlatelolco the founder along with Diego López. In 1613, the new organization got permission to parade on the prestigious long route all around the city, but at the same time it was somewhat mortifying that the Spaniards of the cofradía of the Rosary based in the Dominican monastery refused to cooperate. In the procession of the cofradía based in the nunnery of San Juan de la Penitencia, however, Spanish and indigenous members paraded together, and the Mexica, specifically the people of the Tequicaltitlan tlaxilacalli of the San Juan Moyotlan quarter of Tenochtitlan, went first of all. All participants in these affairs, of course, paid close attention to the relative size and splendor of the images carried. On this same occasion, the Mexica were especially offended because the unpopular father Zárate denied them permission to take out two new saints' images they had just made. Chimalpahin reports that the Mixteca foreigners in Mexico City also established a cofradía and paraded, but he is at pains to note that their image of the virgin of the Rosary was "rather small."[69]

The principal officer of a cofradía, following Spanish precedent, was the majordomo, often accompanied by assistant stewards with the title *diputado* or *prioste*, and a notary-clerk. At intervals the full membership, in the presence of a priest, elected the officers. Such a mechanism would seem to hold the possibility either of simple priestly domination or of a more democratic way of doing things than is seen elsewhere in the Nahua sphere, but it is unlikely that either alternative fully materialized. What one seems to glimpse is a consensus allowing the same notables who appear everywhere else to operate the cofradía as well. Still, as we will see, direct community participation may have been greater, since here women could take an active part in the organization, a phenomenon otherwise hardly detectable in formal institutional structures in the postconquest Nahua world. In general, we lack sufficiently detailed internal testimony on these matters to assess them properly.

For that very reason, I will dwell a bit on the unique book of records of the cofradía of the Most Holy Sacrament in Tula, containing (with many gaps) entries from its foundation in 1570 up to 1730, most of them in Nahuatl and the great bulk composed by indigenous cofradía members.[70]

Introducing the book is an item of considerable potential interest, the complete ordinances of the cofradía written in an elegant Nahuatl. The interest is reduced, however, when one begins to sense that the document is a close translation of a Spanish original; indeed, the last few pages of that original are still in the volume. Judging from the contents of the regulations, a Spanish cleric made them up nearly whole cloth, hardly consulting the local indigenous people. Except for provisions that Indians would pay lower entrance fees than any Spaniards joining (also receiving correspondingly fewer honors gratis at death), and that offices would be shared between the two ethnicities, the entire statement could describe any Spanish sodality, from the processions, masses, and forests of candles to the funeral benefits, bier, and bell ringing.[71] The Nahua citizen of Tula who seems to have made the translation in 1570, perhaps a bit provincial and behind the times compared with his fellows in the Valley of Mexico, was not entirely familiar with some of the Spanish theological terms used and would thus give both the Spanish word and a Nahuatl equivalent to make himself clear, as with "the loving of people called Charity."[72] Though the writer knows and employs the Spanish word *campana*, "bell," he reverts in one place to the first-generation circumlocution "miccatepuztli," "dead-person metal," that is, the metal object sounded to announce someone's death.[73]

Entering the sodality of the Most Holy Sacrament cost half a peso for an indigenous adult and a quarter peso for a child. A membership campaign got under way immediately upon the organization's establishment, and the clerk recorded in the book the name and monetary contribution of each new member. Great care was taken and with some lapses continued to be taken over the following years and decades. If a person made only partial payment, that was noted, as was the subsequent final installment. Two people entered as children, for a fee of two reales each; then some fifteen years later, having become adults, they paid two more each, and the clerk went back to the original entry to make an annotation to that effect.[74] Such lists inspire an ambition to determine the size and attributes of the cofradía membership. What can be accomplished, however, is severely limited.

As to attributes of the members, only a few trades are given: cook, baker, butcher, feather worker (*amantecatl*, possibly meaning only "artisan"). High positions in the local cabildo and church staff are mentioned frequently enough to make it clear that the governor, alcaldes, and fiscal were expected to join. Inspecting the names of the members as a further source of enlightenment, a top echelon of the membership bore the "don" or "doña" or had prestigious Spanish surnames. Most, however, lacked such ornaments. Although names of all the standard postconquest types were present, the majority of the members bore indigenous surnames. Some hinted at relatively high position (such as Pochtlantiachcauh, "leader in Pochtlan"), but most were standard preconquest Nahuatl names, with few implications for rank. For the time (the second half of the sixteenth century), the names as a group are unexceptional; they look like a cross-section of the community, but not necessarily so, since at this date people of fairly high rank might still have Nahuatl surnames. In a new list started in 1604,[75] the proportion of nonindigenous names is sharply higher, especially for males, but adjusting for changing styles, the ambiguities remain the same. Family participation was strong. A married couple was the normal or ideal entry, man and wife both being named, quite often with children of both sexes as well, but such entries did not constitute a clear majority because of the many widows (as well as a few widowers) and unmarried young people. Some children also joined without their parents.

Though it is impossible to determine the cofradía's exact size and geopolitical distribution, the records allow one to make some rough guesses. For the periods during which care was exercised, we appear to have the names of virtually all the members, but nowhere is the total number at any one time stated, and though deaths were erratically recorded, no dates were supplied. After the foundation of the cofradía in October 1570, the clerk kept adding new names with no break in the listing until May 1573; during this period, about 430 people of different genders and ages became members.[76] Presumably most were still alive after two years and eight months, but the 1570's, and particularly the latter part of that decade, were a time of virulent epidemics, taking place against a background of long-term population decline over the whole sixteenth and early seventeenth centuries.[77] Some of the members in any case only entered at the point of death, in order to enjoy the indulgences. With new enrollments at the rate of fifty or sixty in good years, less than half that in bad years, it seems unlikely that late-sixteenth-century membership ever exceeded 500, which would have represented surely no more than 300 households. A new registration campaign starting in 1604, with all the same ambiguities, leads to similar conclusions. From about 1615 until 1730, the last date in the book, the records are so erratic, with new members going entirely unrecorded in many years, that no basis exists for an estimate of absolute numbers.

Out of what pool were our perhaps 500 people in 200 or 300 households drawn? Scanning the inconsistently recorded affiliations of the members, one first notices that they came from all over the greater Tula region. The Tula parish included not only the altepetl of Tula proper, but on a visita basis several other altepetl that became separate encomiendas and had their own governors and cabildos. Essentially all of them are represented. The name Tula (Tollan) is very rare in the entries, not occurring at all in the lists of the early years, but the twenty-odd affiliations given that cannot be identified as separate towns prove to be constituent parts of Tula. Tula proper, then, contributed the bulk and core of the membership; in the first undivided stretch of names, tlaxilacalli of Tula occur eighty-eight times, surrounding towns twenty-five times.[78] Even though the tlaxilacalli names fail to give us a good idea of the internal organization of the altepetl, their distribution suffices to show that the membership was broadly based, recruited from many (apparently all) of the town's districts and not concentrated in any one, two, or several dominant parts. The members from places other than Tula included many town governors, sometimes with their wives, and other dignitaries, from which it can be inferred that the non-Tula minority consisted mainly of people prominent in their own communities. As the lists advance chronologically they become less suited for even rough statistical analysis, but the structure of a varied Tula majority with a minority of prominent outsiders never changed during the time covered by the book; as late as 1700, we see the governor of San Lorenzo Xipacoyan entering the cofradía.[79] That the Most Holy Sacrament, the premier sodality wherever it was to be found, retained the function of helping to integrate the whole altepetl of Tula and to some extent the larger region does not mean that all cofradías of this and other regions were similar; organizations founded later could be expected to serve more specialized constituencies.* Within Tula proper, the membership, at least up until the 1630's (after which the records no longer give an adequate notion), represented a significant fraction of the total local population, but still only a minority. Since the members' names are ambiguous and the membership fee was not prohibitive even for the poor, we cannot be sure whether or not the cofradía drew exclusively from the upper stratum of local indigenous society, though it definitely contained the very highest-ranking figures in that society.

Officership in the Most Holy Sacrament was closely linked to high position in the general governmental/ecclesiastical establishment. Majordomos and diputados might already hold or have held other high office, or they might come to hold it later. In the absence of complete listings of any of these

---

*Because the Tula region was so thinly settled and thinly manned by friars, with only one monastery for several altepetl, the cross-altepetl integrative function of the Most Holy Sacrament in Tula may well have been more pronounced than in the Valley of Mexico or surrounding valleys, where most altepetl had their own monastery or other parish church, but that remains to be seen, and something very similar could easily have existed in great complex altepetl like Xochimilco and Coyoacan.

TABLE 6.1

Officers of the Cofradía of the Most Holy Sacrament of Tula, 1632 and 1640

Position	1632	1640
Majordomo	Don Diego Juan del Castillo[a]	Don Diego Larios
Diputado mayor	Don Francisco de San Pablo	Alonso Mateo[b]
Diputados	Alonso Mateo	Josef de Santiago
	Josef de Santiago	Tomás Diego
Notary-clerk	Francisco de Rosas	—[c]
Diputadas	Doña María de los Angeles	Doña María de los Angeles
	Doña María Jiménez	Doña María Salomé
	Doña María Salomé	Constanza de Santa Ana
	María Salomé	María Salomé
		María Jacoba
		Ana Xochitl

SOURCE: TCB, pp. 70, 76. The original order of the names is retained.
[a]The list mistakenly says "don Diego Luis"; the error is made apparent by several other mentions of the same person as "don Diego Juan."
[b]Alonso Mateo by his position seems to be the diputado mayor, although he is not specifically so called.
[c]Position not mentioned.

TABLE 6.2

Officers of the Cofradía of the Most Holy Sacrament of Tula, 1667, 1668, and 1674

Position	1667[a]	1668	1674
Majordomo	Don Diego de Acevedo Acamapichtzin	Don Hernando de Mendoza	Don Sebastián de San Antonio
Diputados	Don Sebastián de San Antonio	Don Nicolás Feliciano, alcalde	Don Gaspar de los Reyes y San Francisco
	Don Lorenzo García (and others, unnamed)	Juan de Mendoza, alcalde	Don Lorenzo García
		Diego de Mendoza	Don Hernando de Mendoza
			Diego García

SOURCE: TCB, p. 77. The original order of the names is retained.
[a]Incumbents when the election of January 15, 1668 was held; they may have been in office for more than one year at that time.

types of position, one cannot call the trend universal (and indeed some of the humbler officers probably never held any other post), but it was certainly pervasive. Among the cofradía's officers at its foundation in 1570 was Juan Damián, currently alcalde.[80] In 1621, don Andrés Luis de Tapia, current fiscal and sometime governor, was majordomo, and in 1631, Francisco de Rosas was simultaneously fiscal and diputado (then notary, the next year; see Table 6.1).[81] In 1668, two current alcaldes were diputados (see Table 6.2). On the other hand, Rafael de los Angeles, diputado in 1590, was to be alcalde in 1604, and Juan de Contreras, notary of the cofradía in 1604, was soon to be fiscal.[82] Other officers for whom data are not available bore names proclaiming that they were gubernatorial timber: don Diego Juan del Castillo, don Diego de Acevedo Acamapichtzin, don Hernando de Mendoza.* By 1600, it had apparently become important that the cofradía at all costs should have such a person as a figurehead in the majordomo post, and when necessary one may have been recruited from outside the current membership. The don Andrés Luis de Tapia mentioned just above entered the cofradía and paid his fee at the same time as he became majordomo.[83] Other officers, just as in the cabildo and church staff hierarchies, were of less illustrious origin and had less soaring careers. Alonso Mateo, humbly named for that epoch, was frequently diputado in the 1630's and 1640's (Table 6.1), but probably never rose higher than diputado mayor.[84]

Although the ordinances foresaw annual elections, the replacement of officers was irregular. The very first set named served an uninterrupted two years and eight months before an election was held.[85] No uniform election date was ever developed. At times, a new election seems to have come as part of a clean sweep brought on when an ecclesiastic carried out an inspection and found an unsatisfactory state of affairs. In early December 1604, the father guardian fray Juan de la Torre was inspecting the monastery preparatory to leaving office. Summoning the cofradía officers to give account of the candles and money in their possession, he was shocked to be told that there were only eight large tapers, some sixty very small candles, and less than three pesos in cash. The father guardian reprimanded the officers, asking if they had forgotten their duty, and as a fund-raising device, ordered a membership campaign in which even old members would have to pay their fees anew. At the same time, new cofradía officers were selected, in the presence of the entire cabildo of the municipality.[86]

Much the same sort of thing happened again in 1631, this time with the blame laid specifically on the length of the current officeholders' terms. The friars, cabildo, fiscal, and cofradía members assembled to see to the election of new officers, lamenting that the organization was going entirely to ruin. There were no candles, and nothing was being done about it; "the majordomo and diputados have never been changed; it is because of this that they have just neglected things."[87]

Even when elections took place frequently, officers might repeat. Alonso Mateo was elected diputado in 1631, 1632, and 1640, and possibly in intervening years whose elections went unrecorded. As one can see in Table 6.2, the same circle tended to rotate in office. Don Sebastián de San Antonio,

*Note the presence of the "don" and the high tone of the Spanish surnames. The addition of an assertively dynastic indigenous second surname after a good Spanish name, as in Acevedo Acamapichtzin, is the superlative grade of ostentatious naming. Don Hernando de Mendoza, majordomo in 1668, is specifically referred to in a Spanish text as "principal y cacique" (TCB, p. 77).

diputado in 1667, was majordomo in 1674 and again in 1683.[88] Don Hernando de Mendoza, majordomo in 1668, was diputado in 1674. Don Lorenzo García was diputado in 1667 and 1674. In a word, officer recruitment in the cofradía of the Most Holy Sacrament operated on the principles governing officeholding in the whole cabildo-church establishment, of which the cofradía was but one relatively subordinate part.

Some idiosyncrasies did emerge over time. When don Hernando de Mendoza was elected majordomo in 1668, he proceeded to name his own diputados, including two people named Mendoza (Table 6.2). The precedent did not stand, however, since in 1674 the diputados were directly elected as they had been previously. One innovation that did take hold was the addition of more diputados. Two in number through 1631, in 1632 they became three, a diputado mayor being added, and by 1674, there were four.[89] In a list of 1683, we find a diputado mayor followed by a "second diputado" and no fewer than forty-four other diputados (each time spelled "tiputado," by a clerk who was writing Spanish but retained a pronunciation much affected by Nahuatl).[90]

The proliferation of office up to the number of major subunits in the relevant sociopolitical entity is normal in any Nahua institution, and the increase up to four looks classic. It is not to be imagined, however, that forty-four or forty-five distinct units were in need of representation. One's first thought is that all the members had become diputados, but the list contains some ordinary members at the end and is followed by new enrollments of others. The system seems to amount to a distinction between first-class (probably senior) and second-class (probably newer or less active) members.

The greatest constitutional irregularity and indeed by far the most interesting thing about the cofradía of the Most Holy Sacrament is the role played in it by female officers, and possibly by the female rank and file as well. It is not, in all probability, that the phenomenon of active female participation in Nahua organizations was truly rare, as shown by the shadowy *cihuatepixque* in the realm of secular governance (see Chapter 2), but documentary evidence is extraordinarily uncommon. The ordinances of 1570 make no mention of women in an official capacity, and men in fact were always to occupy the offices of majordomo and diputado mayor, though from the first females became cofradía members in large numbers, as married women, widows, unmarried young women, and children. Everything indicates, indeed, that the membership was well over half female. The 1570–73 membership list includes by my count 264 females to only 166 males.[91] Women who were single for one reason or another were numerous in the organization, whereas practically all adult males were accompanied by their wives. It seems not unlikely that female pressure often brought the married men into the cofradía in the first place. With rare exceptions, the only adult men entering alone did so at the moment of death. Even among the young children enrolled, girls appear noticeably more frequently than boys.

Not until 1604, however, do we see proof that women were going beyond informal influence to an open exertion of authority in the organization. In that year, the cofradía had reached a low ebb, and, as we have seen, a sense of crisis and need for reform inspired a new election and a re-registration of members. After recording the names of the new regular officers, the minutes go on to say that in addition "four old women" were chosen, who "will keep people in order, so that the holy things (sacraments) will be respected and the offerings will not be [wasted]; they too will approve what is used (spent), and they will admonish people and instruct them to be prudent."[92] Who chose the women, or whose idea it was to choose them, is not said, nor are their names given. The fact that there were four smacks of typical Nahua organizational procedures. I surmise that they had been almost spontaneously if somewhat informally present from the foundation of the cofradía forward, carrying out a function normal in any Nahua mass organization. Now, at a moment of corporate self-assessment, they received formal recognition. In 1631, they are mentioned again, as "four mothers of people in holy matters, to take good care of the holy cofradía so it will be much respected, and they are to urge those who have not yet joined the cofradía to enter, and they are to take care of the brothers [and sisters] who are sick, and the orphans; they are to see to what is needed for their souls and what pertains to their earthly bodies."[93]

In 1632, the four "old women" or "mothers" entered fully into the fold of the cofradía officers, for they became *diputadas* and were listed along with, though after, their male counterparts, much as women had appeared in early lists of witnesses to Nahuatl testaments. In 1640, the diputadas resurface, now having increased their number to six (see Table 6.1). Like the male officers, they prove to include persons of varying social status, the higher ranking generally listed first. Three of the diputadas of 1632 were in office again in 1640; one suspects that they had served the entire time, and that the fourth had meanwhile died. Seniority must have been very important, but social standing could supersede it. Note that Constanza de Santa Ana, whose name outranks that of María Salomé, precedes her on the list even though she is junior.* The next elections recorded fail to mention the diputadas (see

---

*The 1640 diputada list is a textbook illustration of the ranking of names. The two women with a "doña" precede the four without it. Among the doñas, the one with a religious surname precedes the one with two first names. Among the non-doñas, the one with a religious surname again leads two women with two first names, while the woman with a Nahuatl surname comes last. Nevertheless, wherever possible seniority is respected. Of the non-doña women with two first names, the woman senior in office precedes the junior.

Table 6.2), but probably only because they were growing in number and those already in office always repeated.

The 1683 list mentions a grand total of fourteen diputadas. Most are at the tail end of the compilation, with its stunning total of forty-five male diputados, but two are quite near the top, together with their diputado husbands, and doña Agustina de la Corona comes tenth all by herself.[94] The original four elder women may have represented as many subdivisions of Tula, but, as with the men, the position of diputada in its proliferation probably went beyond any allocation according to units. Indeed, after a high point around the 1630's and 1640's, women hardly transcended the formal position of auxiliaries in the cofradía, even though in de facto terms theirs may have been the predominant voice, and their role here gives us a sense of patterns that probably obtained in any organizational setting involving both sexes and a major segment of the community.

As 1700 approaches the Tula cofradía book peters out, with desultory enrollments of single individuals, male or female, never pairs, and the amount paid is often two reales rather than four, even when the new member seems to be an adult. If the members listed are all there were, the sodality had fallen on hard times, but I believe rather that as things became more routine, less was written down, and while we do not know much about what was going on in the later years, there is no reason to doubt that the organization continued along much the same lines, adapting of course to the changing times. The last entry in the book is a proud assertion of the acquisition of a new silver ornament with the insignia of the Most Holy Sacrament. The majordomo responsible was don Matías de Tapia, doubtless a descendant of the Tapia who was majordomo and fiscal in 1621.[95]

It is clear that the principal cofradía of Tula owned no real estate or livestock and ran no business enterprises. The episode of 1604 implies that it relied heavily on membership fees for income. Yet those alone cannot have financed the requisite masses, candles, and processions. The original ordinances mention voluntary contributions without setting any schedule or procedure, and we can imagine that the cofradía did rely on collections. Perhaps things operated somewhat as shown in early-seventeenth-century Nahuatl records of the cofradía of the True Cross in Xochimilco. Contributions were of two kinds and were given on two different occasions: cacao beans on Saturdays, cash on Sundays. The cofradía must have had a regular meeting by itself each Saturday; then on Sunday a collection was taken in church, perhaps soliciting the congregation in general, before or after mass. Income also accrued from helping to bury people (the cofradía apparently charged for bringing the bier to carry the body). At fifty cacao beans per real, the Saturday contributions were generally worth more than the Sunday money. In October 1610, with four Saturdays and Sundays, the cofradía realized a little over one peso, five reales in cacao proceeds, four and a half reales in Sunday contributions, and four reales in burial fees. Each month receipts were compared with expenses, which apparently were mainly for masses.[96] Again we see the cofradía merging with the church in general, joining with the "church people" in providing burial services (and on the same basis), as well as taking up collections in conjunction with the meeting of the larger congregation.

The Church as Personal Property

Despite the strongly corporate nature of Nahua Christianity, individuals, kin groups, and cliques were forever trying to make its central monuments and ritual objects their own in a special or even exclusive way. The dialectic we have seen at work in land tenure, where everything belonged simultaneously to an individual and to the commonwealth, with the exact status of any one holding never fully stable, obtained in religious matters as well. Those most likely to do the appropriating, it is true, were people of relatively exalted rank who thought of themselves as the true embodiment of the larger unit.

In a set of Nahuatl documents from Quatepec (Coatepec?), in the Sultepec district well off to the southwest of the Valley of Mexico, don Pedro de Santiago Maxixcatzin makes a testament-like statement to his children and grandchildren, the first part of which deals with the church. The documents have the flavor of "primordial titles," so the date (apparently 1660 or 1680) and even the historicity of the main figure must be viewed as uncertain, aside from the ambiguities and inconsistencies typical of the genre; yet the thrust of what is said bears repeating. After being baptized by the Franciscans, don Pedro and/or his brother don Juan—and not the Spaniards—built the local church dedicated to Saint Michael. Don Pedro (or a descendant?) went to Mexico City to get the license for the church and served in turn as maestro de capilla, alcalde, fiscal, and governor. Now don Pedro tells his heirs to take good care of their property ("amoaxca"), which includes not only the church but all the hangings, vestments, and ornaments therein. He specifically bequeathes them a velvet cape to adorn Saint Michael, and goes on to speak of fruit trees he planted, presumably in the church patio. As so often, however, the message is not entirely one of personal property and privilege. Although don Pedro makes much of the accomplishments of himself and his close relatives, giving no one else any part in the creation and decoration of the church, his phrase "my children and grandchildren" ("nopilhua noxhuihua") can be interpreted as referring more broadly to all altepetl citizens, now and in the future. A continuation of the document defines the borders of the altepetl and asserts its territorial rights in a fully corporate fashion.[97]

The strongest expression of exclusivity yet to come to my attention is a rare but not uncharacteristic quasi-ledger kept by the de la Cruz family of Tepemaxalco, the apparently lower ranking of the Calimaya/Tepemaxalco pair of altepetl in the Toluca Valley.[98] The first entries were made in 1647 by the effective founder of the dynasty, Pedro de la Cruz the church organist, soon to be don Pedro de la Cruz and governor of Tepemaxalco (though Pedro's father [don] Juan de la Cruz, who was alcalde at times and amassed considerable wealth, got him off to a very good start). Succeeding generations continued to write in the book sporadically through the eighteenth century on into the nineteenth, the latest date being 1842. Although the document contains some cabildo business, a rudimentary set of town annals, some personal memorabilia such as the marriage of a family dependent,[99] and other tidbits, it is above all an unsystematic account book of church-related receipts and expenditures, with emphasis on those in which the de la Cruzes had a part. From the beginning, the writers adopted the position that virtually all religious construction, adornment, and maintenance were the work of a select circle; they fiercely and rather gratuitously denied the existence or belittled the importance of the contributions of others.

No better example could be found than the book's very first entry, a fund-raising list for Pedro de la Cruz's pet project, a new organ (see Table 6.3). Indeed, the acquisition and maintenance of organs become a leitmotif carrying on to the final entries, generations after the founder was dead. In 1647, nine individuals, foremost the de la Cruzes themselves, donated the bulk of the 410 pesos raised; six of the seven male contributors either at that time or later occupied some place in the cabildo or churchly hierarchies.[100] The cantors put up an additional seventy pesos, the proceeds from a field dedicated to religious expenses, and parishioners in general contributed a total of only twenty pesos.[101] At the end of the list, the names of the nine individual contributors appear again, as though they had signed (all being, however, in the same hand), accompanied by the statement, "We all place here our signatures; they are not to say sometime that perhaps everyone bought the organ, for only a few people bought it."[102] The tendency to exclude at times knows no bounds. From 1652 through 1654, Juan and Pedro de la Cruz, with three associates, cultivated the special field to buy an image of San Juan and accessories, but Pedro makes a point of saying that one of the others helped for only a few days, and that in 1654, he and his father worked the field all by themselves (with oxen, that is, and probably employees as well). The ordinary people come in for no end of snide comments on their efforts: "they just helped thatch the granary; only a few people dragged wood," or, "None of them has a yoke of oxen. They just worked one day each; they only brought digging sticks. Only a few people worked."[103] Yet another target of belittle-

TABLE 6.3

Contributions for the Church Organ, San Pablo
Tepemaxalco (Toluca Valley), 1647

Contributor	Pesos
(Don) Juan de la Cruz (alcalde, father of Pedro de la Cruz)[a]	110
Pedro de la Cruz, organist	40
Matías de San Francisco, maestro (de capilla)	10
Don Baltasar de los Reyes, governor	50
The ordinary people (tlapaliuhque)	10
Gabriel de San Pedro	20
Juana Salomé, widow	20
Angelina Francisca	10
Baltasar de Santiago	5
Pedro Joaquín	5
The cantors, from their special field (tequimilli)	70
The San Lucas people	10
Pedro de la Cruz again, paid to a Spaniard[b]	30
TOTAL	410[c]

SOURCE: CFP, ff. I–IV.
NOTE: What church the organ was for is never said, but it was probably the monastery church of San Pedro y San Pablo of Calimaya/Tepemaxalco.
[a] Juan de la Cruz was just reaching the point of being called "don," and usage wavers.
[b] The name is not given, but the entry is in the first person, and on subsequent pages it is specified that "I" is Pedro de la Cruz.
[c] The column actually totals 390; one contribution was probably omitted or understated.

ment was Tepemaxalco's senior partner Calimaya, which shared the monastery church of San Pedro y San Pablo, claiming San Pedro for its patron, as Tepemaxalco did San Pablo. Mainly the writers of the de la Cruz book preferred to ignore the existence of Calimaya entirely, but in 1667, when now-governor don Pedro de la Cruz paid eighty pesos plus other expenses out of his own pocket for a new door and stone arch on the main church, the person recording the events remarked, "and the Calimaya people gave no money, they only fed people," adding that don Pedro fed the principal craftsman himself.[104]

In their insistence on their own role, the de la Cruzes and their circle even made statements that sound hostile to the altepetl itself: "No one is to say that perhaps the altepetl bought it," or, "They are not to say sometime that perhaps the altepetl made the granary; we cantors made it."[105] A different and probably truer perspective emerges from a 1683 entry in which, after admonishing the commoners as usual not to make claims, the governor don Juan de la Cruz refers to himself, the alcaldes, and the fiscal as "we who are in charge of the altepetl for our lord God."[106] It is much to be doubted that any other long-term record of Tepemaxalco altepetl and church activity ever existed than the book of the de la Cruzes. All in all, what they seem to have desired is not so much to monopolize buildings or rites as to avoid sharing credit for their sponsorship. They were also apparently concerned about legal claims that might be made against them later, presumably because some had been made in the past. When, in 1658, don Pedro as governor recorded that he planted magueys on one of the special fields with the help of a group of ordinary folk, he stated that "they are never to say that it all belongs to the altepetl," and proceeded to have those present take oath to that effect, listing as witnesses a series of prominent people by name, along with the ordinary citizens as a group.[107]

It was doubtless not unheard of to accuse a generous donor in an official position of having taken the altepetl's money to make the gift possible. In the time of the governorship of don Pedro, his private donations went from large to immense (by indigenous standards), and one might well wonder where the money was coming from. The small churches of don Pedro's immediate neighborhood were the first objects of his concern, though ultimately not the targets of his grandest charities. In the central Tepemaxalco settlement cluster were at least two local churches or chapels aside from the great monastery church and a chapel of Guadalupe (which was in existence by 1683).[108] The church of San Francisco was in the district of Pochtlan.[109] The church of San Juan, to judge from don Pedro's close association with it before he was governor, may have been in Paxiontitlan, don Pedro's home district.[110] Each had a piece of land where maize and maguey were raised, under the direction of a majordomo, to help maintain the cult and the church building.[111] Governor don Pedro usually limited himself to supplementing the normal sources of income for these local chapels, though when the San Francisco church was in need of repair in 1674, he took care of everything, donating forty pesos, having his mules transport the sand and earth, and paying the needed workers ("cayanixti," i.e., "gañanes" or permanent employees, probably his own).[112]

One of don Pedro's greatest splurges was the upgrading of Santa María de la Asunción, the second-ranking of the outlying districts of Tepemaxalco. He may have been simply filling a felt need, or perhaps he had close family connections there. At any rate, in two steps don Pedro poured a great amount of money into the project. In 1654, he spent 120 pesos on church construction and a new altarpiece, so much that he had a special promise put into the book that neither he nor his heirs would change their minds (that is, presumably, not claim the money had been a loan). This led to consecration ceremonies in October 1665 involving two days of bullfighting and banqueting at the expense of the public officials. Then in 1668–69 don Pedro donated garments for the saint and had a vault built for her, to the tune of 200 pesos, topped off by having the image taken to the monastery church for reconsecration in a celebration with candles and fireworks so lavish that the total bill, completely footed by don Pedro, was 300 pesos. But perhaps even the Santa María enterprise was outdone when, in 1673, don Pedro, remembering his beginnings or indulging a lifelong passion, gave the monastery church an organ costing 650 pesos.[113]

After don Pedro de la Cruz, the sequel could only be anticlimactic, but the lineage long continued to act in the same vein if on a smaller scale. In 1679, when income from the land was not sufficient to buy a canopy for San Francisco, don Juan de la Cruz, soon to be governor, donated fifty pesos, and as governor he continued to pay for the provisions of artisans working on church projects.[114] In 1746, don Nicolás de la Cruz, simultaneously governor and majordomo for the Virgin of Guadalupe, joined with two nephews in paying nearly all of the seventy-odd pesos needed to acquire bells for the chapel. As late as 1829, when one of the bells had to be recast, it was another de la Cruz who funded the job.[115] In our present state of knowledge, one cannot deny the possibility that the de la Cruz governors were milking the altepetl to obtain some of the means for their religious philanthropy, but it seems nearer the mark to say that their wealth and philanthropy were important factors in keeping them in their position. Don Pedro's mules and hired hands point to a strong private economic base, and the sums he spent must have far exceeded total altepetl income in many years. The governor was still expected to subsidize religion, even if he no longer possessed the formal office lands of the preconquest tlatoani. Devotion to the saints, local patriotism, political and economic advantage, and family pride all merged to motivate the de la Cruz tradition.

One group that rarely if ever finds its efforts and contributions minimized in the de la Cruz ledgers is the corps of church cantors, among whom don Pedro first came to prominence and with whom he (and doubtless his successors as well) felt solidarity. In the Tepemaxalco of the seventeenth and eighteenth centuries, the Spanish loanword *cantores* was used in preference to the Nahuatl term *teopantlaca*, or "church people," though the latter does appear once or twice.[116] This does not mean, however, that the group was any more restricted to the performance of music than in other areas of the Nahua world. The Tepemaxalco cantors mainly appear in the records making monetary contributions for various religious expenses, usually obtained from "their" maize and maguey, harvested apparently primarily by themselves, but at times assembled by each of them putting a couple of reales in the pot (that they had a cantors' field distinct from the saints' fields remains unestablished, despite one instance where such a field is called theirs).[117] Their fund could mount up considerably, as in 1666, when don Pedro looked into their accounts and found they had 170 pesos, whereupon they contributed 100 toward an organ. At other times their coffers were empty.[118] They also became involved in such joint tasks as building a granary on a saint's field.[119] Although the common people were expected to help with the saints' lands, their time and funds were limited and their efforts sporadic, so that the better equipped cantors, aided further by their corporate strength and continuity, in the end usually did most of the cultivation and not infrequently carried it out entirely on their own.[120]

As to the cantors' organization, the leader and chief representative of the group was the maestro de capilla, aided by a topile or second in command, at the head of a corps of unknown size; one group labeled "cantors" that assembled as witnesses to a transaction consisted of five ordinary cantors plus the topile, but we have no reason to think there were not more of them (the maestro was absent in any case).[121] After every few years the maestro would change; for the topile we have too few examples to say, but one Mateo Nicolás held the post at least from 1657 into 1660.[122] Past members, however, might still take an active part, as Francisco Hernández, maestro pasado, did in 1660, when he contributed to a donation the cantors made.[123] Most higher political officers seem to have been former cantors. The position of maestro was particularly strategic: a large number of alcaldes had previously served as maestro, and so had the two notables (don) Matías de San Francisco and (don) Juan Pablo, the only persons who were permitted to hold the governorship for short periods during the long reign of don Pedro de la Cruz.[124] The cantors were clearly an upper-level club, an integral part of political advancement, and an important economic support group for religious activity. Yet they were also, at least in the time of don Pedro, very serious musicians. In the 1650's and 1660's, sometimes with their own money, sometimes with don Pedro's, they bought at least two trumpets, three sackbuts (trombones), two bassoons, a guitar, and a rebec. On this impressive set of instruments they played up-to-date Spanish sacred music; in 1660, the governor gave them two pesos to buy a mass (that is, the contrapuntal score for one) and the music for a song (*villancico*) devoted to San Pedro, don Pedro's name-saint.[125]

Each town in central Mexico had its own particular mix of the standard organizational elements, and in Tepemaxalco the strength of the cantors and the active role of the governor left little place for the fiscal. The office existed, since in the records three persons are so titled, one for the church of Santa María de la Asunción, and the other two presumably for the Tepemaxalco half of the monastery church (especially the officer called fiscal mayor).[126] But their names come low on lists, and no contributions or responsibilities are attributed to them. More obviously active in the Tepemaxalco scheme of things were the majordomos of the small district churches, who were likely to serve simultaneously as majordomos of unofficial cofradías of that church's saint (I doubt, indeed, that local people made any distinction between these two offices and functions). Don Pedro de la Cruz was majordomo of San Juan in 1655, only two years before he became governor.[127] As mentioned above, don Nicolás de la Cruz was both governor and majordomo of the Virgin of Guadalupe in 1746. Rank within the Tepemaxalco civil/religious hierarchy seems to have descended from governor to alcalde to maestro to majordomo, with the fiscal to one side of the mainstream but comparable to the majordomo.[128]

The uncomfortable relationship of two altepetl competing in a single monastery church may have affected Tepemaxalco's structure considerably. In 1677, the Tepemaxalco cantors were on the verge of being ejected from the monastery choir loft in a controversy over their right to use it during a certain week for a fiesta, until don Juan de la Cruz intervened with the father guardian.[129] San Pablo, titular saint of the altepetl, plays little role in the de la Cruz book; most of the interest is in the saints of the constituent parts and, as time passes, in Guadalupe. It may be that the lack of an uncontested base pushed the cantors out into more extensive district activity than normal. But everywhere the church people were an altepetl-wide organization, not tied exclusively to one ecclesiastical foundation within the jurisdiction. In relatively few situations, perhaps, was the group led generation after generation by the same lineage acting in a proprietary spirit as in Tepemaxalco, but that spirit can be frequently detected on the larger central Mexican scene.

Saints

Asked to specify the nature of postconquest indigenous religion in central Mexico, someone whose experience of the matter consisted primarily of reading mundane Nahuatl documentation would inevitably answer that religion was about saints. Saints leap out of wills, municipal decrees, sales, leases, annals, primordial titles, indeed almost everything the Nahuas wrote without supervision and primarily for their own eyes. No other aspect of Christian religious belief and ritual had a remotely comparable impact on the broad range of their activity (especially if we consider that Jesus Christ and often the cross were in effect treated as so many more saints), with the possible exception of the rites associated with death. The saints have therefore already been frequently mentioned in preceding sections of this chapter as well as in the chapters on the household and economic life.

In part recapitulating, I will try to state here somewhat succinctly the role of saints in the corporate and individual life of the Nahuas by the time the postconquest period had crystallized. At the corporate level, a saint was the primary symbol identifying and unifying each sociopolitical entity, not only the altepetl but its constitutent parts. Note that in the earliest known postconquest Tlaxcalan usage, the general term for a named subentity of the altepetl was *santopan*, "where a saint is."[130] Although by no means all Nahua ethnic-political assertiveness expressed itself under a saint's banner, the saint became identified both consciously and subconsciously with preconquest group symbols. In the legend of Sula (Tlalmanalco area, on the northwestern edge of Chalco), as it was written down sometime in the late seventeenth century, the choice of Santiago as a patron took place in the following manner. When the Spaniards not long after the conquest said it was time for Sula to decide on a saint, the people delegated the task to the two oldest and wisest among them. Sleeping on the matter, each had a dream in which Santiago appeared in great splendor, declared himself to be from Persia (i.e., far away), and announced that he would be Sula's saint. Still in doubt the next morning, the two elders questioned each other, and on discovering that their dreams had been identical, proclaimed the choice of Santiago to the populace. These two eldest citizens are (though named differently) an embodiment of the autochthonous pair, representing Sula's dual organization, which dominates much of the narrative; one of them as "Quail-lord" and "Quail-serpent" also represents the preconquest totemic deity. Thus the indigenous bearers of ethnic identity are made to endorse and become associated with the saint, who can be viewed as having been thereby consecrated in the role of sacred symbol of the community.[131]

A far more deliberate, theatrical gesture, carrying a similar message, was made in Mexico City in 1593, on the day of Saint Francis. As part of the celebration, local artisans made a representation of the Mexica eagle sitting on a cactus, with Saint Francis riding the eagle like a horse, and they set it up under the cross in the patio of the indigenous chapel of San José, to general admiration. Then on the day of San José in 1594 came a further innovation: a banner of crimson damask, decorated along the edges with preconquest war scenes and the kings who had ruled in Tenochtitlan, each holding a cactus in his hand; in the middle, apparently, was an eagle representing the rulership, and again Saint Francis rode him like a horse, holding a cross and displaying a written message. The Mexica hung the banner above the portal of the San José chapel, where all who saw it, including the viceroy and members of the Royal Audiencia, are again said to have admired it.[132]

In preconquest times, the main temples, which were themselves important expressions of the glory and identity of sociopolitical units, were seen as the houses of the particular gods who were honored there (as seen in the word itself, *teocalli*, "god-house"). It is true that in Nahuatl writings Christian churches are sometimes called "the churchly home of God" or the like, but at least as often they appear as the home of the particular saint to which they are dedicated.[133] Saints were imagined as the parents of their people and as the true owners of the unit's land.[134] It follows that local institutions should lavish attention on the saint and the saint's residence. We have already seen examples of the extent to which high governmental and ecclesiastical officers devoted themselves to the cults of patron saints, and all accounts, both Spanish and Nahuatl, lead us to believe that the feastday of a unit's patron saint was the greatest occasion of the year for the whole population, involving general participation and the display of the unit's strength and internal organization.

At the personal level, by the seventeenth century, and probably well before that, it was the goal of every household to possess one or more images of saints. As early as Monday, May 29, 1564, the anonymous author of a set of Nahuatl annals broke ground at his Mexico City home for "my little building where an image is."[135] The pattern of a separate "saint-house," with the saint occupying his or her own building, just as the other component parts of the household did, can be detected in occasional documents all across the colonial period,[136] but since the specific location of the saints is quite rarely mentioned, it may well be that the present-day practice of placing them at an altar in one of the residential buildings also appeared during this time. Though large-scale quantification remains unfeasible, we have no reason to presume that only the wealthy had saints. In Mexico City marketplaces of the late sixteenth century, indigenous artisans sold glazed incense burners in the form of male or female saints. In 1598, the Holy Office forbade their production because people had been putting preconquest magical substances like tobacco in them,[137] but if things followed their usual course, the objects did not actually disappear. Some people's household saint collections were impressive; in 1621, an unnamed benefactor of the church in Coyoacan had images of the Trinity, San Francisco, San Nicolás, and Santa María de la Asunción, plus an Ecce Homo and another crucifix.[138] Note that none of these were the patron of the altepetl, San Juan Bautista, and not more than one of them can have been the patron of the tlaxilacalli (although people did sometimes have home images of the unit's patron). It is my impression that saints are mentioned more frequently and in more detail by women than by men, but it is only a difference of degree. Both men and women bequeathed, inherited, and maintained saints, who may be imagined as pertaining above all to a household.

We should be aware of the implications and limitations of the term image in postconquest Nahuatl documents. In sixteenth-century texts, one sees *ixiptlatl*, "image, replacement, representative," thus a very good translation of Spanish *imagen*, which as a loanword appears as well. Either term could be used alone, but in the sixteenth century the two are often seen together, as if it were still necessary to explain what the Spanish word meant.[139] By the early seventeenth century, however, "imagen" had won out in usage, usually appearing alone.[140] As in the Spanish of that time, the word could refer to either a painting or a figure in the round.[141] Both types were common, and the external form seems to have made no difference. Most frequently no such word as "image" was used at all in speaking of the saints, and after about mid-seventeenth century, such terms seem to have gone almost completely out of fashion. It is as though, after experimenting with the Spanish ecclesiastical notion of emphasizing the distinction between representation and thing represented, the Nahuas had reverted to their habit (and perhaps the popular Spanish habit as well) of looking at the spiritual being and the tangible form as fully integrated. What the Nahuas had in their houses *were* the saints, in a particular manifestation, and they constantly spoke of them correspondingly.[142]

What was the position and function of the saints in the household? Although the house complex was thought of as belonging to God,[143] the saints seem to have symbolized household identity and continuity. Even when ostensibly bequeathing saints to heirs, testators often expressed concern that the images stay in place, and they might make concrete provisions toward that end, such as specifying that a certain structure belonged to them and should be reserved for their residence.[144] The saints presided over the household, in effect deities whom the household members served as priests or acolytes, though this is never said in so many words.

The universal imperative to heirs was to "serve" the saints (using the word *tequipanoa*, or sometimes *tlayecoltia*);[145] indeed, saying "to serve the saints" in a certain house was tantamount to saying "to maintain residence" there. This service, whenever it is described more closely, turns out to have to do with maintaining the cult. Sweeping for the saints is frequently mentioned and could even be used as the general term for service and residence.[146] An important ritual activity in preconquest times, sweeping as a religious act was not unknown to the Spaniards either.[147] One was to keep the saints supplied with "candles, flowers, and incense,"[148] again a coincidence of indigenous and Spanish practice, though the emphasis on flowers is especially characteristic of indigenous ways. One was also to make sure the saints were always "clean," that is, in a reputable state of repair.[149]

A plurality of saints was the norm; where there is any mention of them at all, quite rarely does a household prove to have only one saint. Often they were a mixed group, both male and female. At this remove, it is hard to know whether the mention of both genders stems from a conscious attempt to have both represented or results simply from the fact that the Nahuas borrowed *santo* and *santa* as separate words, not using the male gender as a generic form, as the Spaniards did.[150] I have been unable to detect any tendency for male saints to be bequeathed to males, female saints to females; both seem to go to both. My impression needs systematic confirmation, but it appears to me that whereas male saints predominate as altepetl patrons, female saints had a numerical predominance in the household.

One possible motivation for acquiring several images was that, in the minds of some at least, the saints were apparently cast in the role of formal or ceremonial owners of a household's land; since most Nahuas owned land in scattered plots, and the plots were inherited by different household members, it would be well to have a saint for each plot (possibly there was a household god for each field in preconquest times). Nowhere is such a principle explicitly stated, nor are very many situations spelled out in enough detail to allow firm deductions, but some documents are very suggestive. Take the case of Angelina of Pochtlan (Azcapotzalco jurisdiction). In her will of 1695, she gives a piece of land to Our Lady of Candlemas for her grandson Tomás de los Santos to use in the saint's service, at the same time giving the saint to Tomás. Likewise, she gives a plot to Santa Catarina, for her granddaughter Teresa de Jesús to use in her service, at the same time giving the saint to Teresa. Another granddaughter, Nicolasa Jacinta, receives a third piece of land directly, without any statement that it is given to a saint, but with the stipulation that with it she is to serve Our Lady of the Rosary. In all likelihood, Angelina was devoted to the Virgin of the Rosary but had not yet acquired an image of her, or knew that her granddaughter already possessed one.[151] Cases this pat are rare indeed, but we have another telling example in Félix de Santiago of Calimaya (1738), who although he left everything to his son for once detailed both the lands and the saints meticulously. He proved to have five separate pieces of land and exactly the same number of saints: a Virgin of Guadalupe, "two little Christs," Santa Lucía, and San Francisco.[152]

In any event, stating that one was giving the land to a saint to be in the custody of a relative was a set formula, the true intention being to give the land to the relative with the saint attached to it.* Sometimes the formula could apply to income-producing possessions other than land, as when in 1608 in the Coyoacan region Bárbara Agustina gave her mule to her image of the Virgin for the saint's service, with the provision that the mule would be in the custody of Bárbara's nephew Juan Pedro.[153]

We saw earlier that when people could manage it they sought to bring

* An exasperated heir whose family had lost some land to the altepetl because of a too-literal interpretation of the talk about the saint owning the land came as close as anyone in my experience to enunciating the principle and describing the practice explicitly. He argued that by custom indigenous people in their testaments left such and such a piece of land to a child to serve a favorite saint but had no intention of taking the land away from the heir (AGN, Tierras 2533, exp. 3, f. 5; Santa María de la Asunción, Tepemaxalco/Calimaya, Toluca Valley, 1803).

their household saints to the altepetl church for a ceremonial visit. Saints or their lands in fact easily crossed the line between the spheres of household and altepetl, in either direction, though often at the expense of some controversy. First let us look at an example showing movement from the smaller into the larger arena. The story of Our Lady of the Immaculate Conception and another de la Cruz family, this one of Tlapitzahuayan (in the jurisdiction of Chalco Atenco), deserves telling in some detail because it reveals so many of the common elements and ambiguities of the saints' lands situation.[154]

Around 1700 or before, a man named Josef de la Cruz, who had been born in Chalco Atenco proper, came to Tlapitzahuayan to marry and settle down. He and his descendants were not usually called "don," even in Nahuatl,[155] but since they kept their surname on a cross-generational basis, were sometimes referred to in Spanish as principales, and held five separate pieces of land over a period of many decades, the family can be said to have enjoyed a certain position. In his house, Josef had an image of the Virgin of the Immaculate Conception. The townspeople were devoted to the saint and held an annual celebration in her honor. However, they lacked an image of her, so the town fathers, or in one account the town's young unmarried women,[156] asked Josef for permission to use his saint in their celebration until such time as they could have one made and put in the church. Josef gladly lent them his saint. This much was agreed on when the divergent interpretations that the parties had held over a large portion of the century led to direct conflict in the 1760's.

According to the town officials, they had donated a piece of land (a fourth of a fanega, possibly about two and a half acres) at a place called Atocpan to the de la Cruzes in return for the use of their household saint. When a new image was installed in the church, the original agreement lost its validity, but the de la Cruz family was allowed to retain the land under obligation to help with the yearly festivities. According to the de la Cruzes, the piece of land had been theirs all along. A Nahuatl document of 1716 in which Josef de la Cruz and his two sons enter into an agreement with the town's alcalde fails to clear up the doubts. Although the Atocpan plot is called the property of Our Lady of the Conception and related to duty to the altepetl,[157] the signatories also affirm that Josef de la Cruz has received twelve pesos from the town officials, which he is to pay back at two pesos a year, making it appear very much as though the land already belonged to Josef and he was hocking it to the city fathers.

Josef de la Cruz was succeeded in due course by his namesake son, in whose time things continued as before; indeed, with the passing of the years, the town officials tended to fuse father and son into one person. The townspeople apparently saw Josef the younger as something of a majordomo for the saint, who was expected not only to look after her cloak, crown, cande-labras, and other ornaments, but also to pay for a yearly mass in her honor. Josef continued to see his contribution as voluntary. He was willing to pay two reales a year toward the saint's mass (a general obligation of all house-holders who held town land) and an extra two reales toward paying the can-tors who carried the image in procession, but for the rest he considered him-self the owner of the Atocpan land who happened to have a private image of the Virgin of the Conception in his household and was free to do as he pleased in respect to her public cult.

As the position of both sides hardened, the town forced Josef into an agreement (probably in 1753).[158] The first part of the Nahuatl document looks like Josef's premature will, leaving his house and all of his lands, in-cluding the plot at Atocpan, to his minor sons under the supervision of his son-in-law. A second, contradictory part calls the Atocpan land the property of the saint and commits Josef and his wife to paying a peso each year on the saint's day. The apparent contradiction arises from divergent interpretations of the same wording, a crucial ingredient of many of these cases. Josef would have agreed that the land belonged to the saint, but he meant the household saint, whereas the town officials meant the saint of the altepetl (for a new image had long since been made and placed in the church). The two manifes-tations were closely related indeed but had very different implications in the realms of duty and ownership.

At any rate, Josef paid the yearly peso for ten years before refusing to continue, denying that there was any custom that obliged him to do so. The altepetl thereupon seized the land for the cult and festivity of the Virgin, claiming that it had belonged to the saint from time immemorial, and that she was in need because there had been no procession the preceding year and she had no cloak. The plot was reassigned to a citizen willing to assume the obligations. Josef de la Cruz protested, saying that the reason for the lack of a procession was that the townspeople failed to pay their yearly two reales each; as a result of his representations, in March 1764 the Spanish alcalde mayor returned possession of the land to Josef. This was followed, in June, by a new decree from Mexico City, which confirmed Josef in possession of the land but insisted that he keep paying the yearly peso, bringing things back to the point where they had broken down. The troubles probably continued to simmer.[159]

The direction of the process was often reversed, that is, lands originally intended to subsidize the cult of the altepetl saint gravitated into private hands permanently (I have never seen a case in which an individual laid per-sonal claim to an image clearly belonging to the town or district). Tenayuca (a little north of Mexico City) had two caballerías of municipal land held under viceregal grant, located in the district of Iztaccallan; since there were some buildings and a threshing floor on it, it was often called a rancho. For years, the elder nobles of Iztacallan as a group had leased it out to get income for the feastdays of the titular saints San Bartolomé and San Juan. But at some point in the second half of the seventeenth century, apparently because of difficulties in handling things on a corporate basis, the Tenayuca authorities turned the matter over to a single person, and in fact to a prominent woman, Lorenciana Angelina (probably "doña" in Nahuatl). She then leased the rancho to various local Spanish haciendas and small farmers, taking responsibility herself for supplying everything necessary for the festivities and other expenses, and giving account to the community. After her death, her son (don) Miguel Francisco, a sometime alcalde, took over, aided apparently by the fact that he was serving at that time as the church fiscal's constable. Though the rancho now produced an income of sixty pesos a year, the new manager ceased to give any account of the earnings, sold some strips to Spaniards, and in general acted as though he had inherited the land. The town brought suit in 1697, inaugurating a prolonged indecisive legal battle that continued at least until 1709.[160]

Thus the obligations owed to household saints were forever being appropriated by the altepetl, and assets assigned to altepetl saints were appropriated by individuals. Individuals' desire to show off their saints and have official sanction for their household arrangements opened the way for absorption by the altepetl. Local government and the populace were attached to the saints and wanted their cult honored, but the corporation was unwieldy, and the generality as individuals were not always eager to pay out of their own pockets, so the duties tended to devolve upon capable and interested people whose heirs and successors thought of the assets used as their own by birthright.* With saints as with lands, rather than pertaining to a well-defined private or public domain, everything was always simultaneously individual and corporate. It is small wonder that the Nahuas sometimes called their domestic saint-houses churches.[161]

To this point I have been treating, in a relatively atemporal manner, aspects of the mature saints complex that are characteristic of the entire longer haul of the colonial period. Although much remains to be fully substantiated, and subtleties of variation over time and region must still be investigated, I am convinced that the core practices described were customary in much of central Mexico at least by 1600. Let us now reexamine the evidence for the origins of the cult of the saints as something affecting the life of the individual.

Above we have seen something like a "saint-house" as early as 1564, and

---

*Leasing altepetl land to help the saints led even more frequently to possession by Spaniards, but that is another story.

in 1583 a woman speaks of providing the patron saint with candles and incense in return for giving her land for a house.[162] In no Nahuatl testament written before the 1580's, however, have I seen an unambiguous reference to the cult of saints.[163] If we look closely at the largest known sixteenth-century collection, the Culhuacan testaments of around 1579–80, few of the phenomena of the full-fledged saints cult appear. Individual saints are not much mentioned, not even the patrons of the altepetl and the various tlaxilacalli, though one woman did name two of her daughters Magdalena after the tlaxilacalli saint.[164] Heirs are never exhorted to serve the saints or to maintain their altars. Of two cases involving images, one is specifically called a crucifix, and the other, an "image of our lord" for which a house is to be built, seems to have belonged to the same type. Although the identification with the household is already strong here ("the crucifix standing here is my own property, and I declare that it is not to be taken somewhere else but to stand here at my home"), the burgeoning variety of saints seen in later documents is lacking.[165] Crosses, especially Christs on the cross, may have been a transitional step in the late sixteenth and early seventeenth centuries on the way to the fully developed cult of the saints.[166] Indeed, one of the earliest saints mentioned by Chimalpahin came to prominence precisely through association with the cross; in 1583, the crucifix on which San Guillermo was said to have appeared at Totolapan was brought to Mexico City to be honored.[167]

As to exactly how the saints gained their popularity—whose idea the cult was, what the intentions of the originators were—we are left with as good as no firm evidence. There is no doubt that a close parallel existed between the Spanish and preconquest Nahua religious systems. In Spain, the corporate aspects of local religion were expressed through images of saints with specialized supernatural powers, each image having its own attributes and being associated with a particular region, town, social group, or subdistrict.[168] Among the Nahuas, a pantheon of specialized gods behaved in precisely the same manner. A general principle of Spanish-Nahua interaction is that wherever the two cultures ran parallel, the Nahuas would soon adopt the relevant Spanish form without abandoning the essence of their own form. With the saints, the expected in due course happened. It is clear that as soon as the Nahuas grasped the nature of the saints in Spanish regional religion they would have made the identification and taken advantage of the opportunity in just the way they did. The question is how or indeed whether they ever learned much about the saints of Spain.

If we resort to simple speculation, as under the circumstances we must, the potential actors in the matter are the Spanish clergy, their indigenous linguist-aides, the Spanish laity, and the indigenous altepetl authorities. Everything indicates that in the first couple of generations, the Spanish ecclesiastics did not emphasize saints. The secular clergy may have been more prone to do so; from the polemical reports that have reached us it is hard to say.[169] One scholar has put forth the theory that the friars, in a spirit of "guided syncretism," deliberately fostered those saints sharing the attributes of local gods.[170] The idea is perfectly reasonable but not very compatible with what is known of the attitude of the friars in the first generations, and hard evidence is lacking. More likely is that the meaning attached to the saints in Spanish religion gradually seeped through to the Nahuas as they came into contact with ordinary Spaniards and with ecclesiastics in their capacity as ordinary Spaniards, just as happened with material objects, crafts, and economic dealings.[171]

I suspect that the ecclesiastics' linguist-aides—who with rare exceptions like the erudite friars Molina and Sahagún were the only people well apprised of iconography, symbolic meanings, and ritual practice on both sides of the fence—played a crucial role in the original assignment of saints and in the cult arising around them. The altepetl authorities, who at least in retrospect were sometimes imagined to have chosen patrons from among the saints, must have known little indeed about these new Spanish supernaturals, but if they really did have anything to say in the matter, they would probably have chosen a saint whose feastday fell near to that of their ethnic god, or if shown pictures, one with similar iconographic attributes. For the friars, despite their early emphasis on the Trinity, did insist, the moment they began founding churches, on each unit's having a patron saint; and given the Nahuas' propensities, many of the other phenomena would have followed from that alone, even without the reinforcing Spanish example.

At what point did the Nahuas begin to associate saints' images with miracles? Of those that are said to have occurred the earliest, most reports are posterior by decades and come from the mouths of Spaniards. The only accounts by a Nahua that I know of are in the diaries of the often-mentioned Chimalpahin, produced as the reader will recall in Mexico City in the last years of the sixteenth century and first two decades of the seventeenth. Perhaps Chimalpahin's uniqueness is more than chance; a new series of sweating crosses and the like appeared in Spain itself from 1590 forward.[172] It will be worthwhile to repeat Chimalpahin's stories and reflect on them briefly. We have already seen that the crucifix on which San Guillermo appeared was brought to Mexico City in 1583. In 1597, the miracle-working image of Santa María de los Remedios of Totoltepec visited Mexico City. Everyone went out to greet her, carrying candles, "the (indigenous) men and women, the Spaniards and Spanish women," some going all the way to Totoltepec and others just meeting her along the way.[173]

In 1600, San Diego brought a presumably indigenous child back to life at the prayer of his mother, who had laid the body before the saint's image; all the friars and Spaniards saw it too, and Chimalpahin specifically calls it a great miracle ("huey tlamahuiçolli"). A few days later, San Diego revived another child.[174] In 1611, San Nicolás de Tolentino miraculously saved a Spanish woman who had been buried under ruins in an earthquake, as a result becoming the patron of both Spaniards and indigenous people.[175] In 1615, San Nicolás entered the child-resuscitation field as well, reviving a one-and-a-half-year-old plebeian Mexica child who had fallen in a well and lain dead for two and a half hours. Bells were rung in all the churches (as they had been with the previous children), and when the Spaniards burned wood on their roofs and set off rockets, many indigenous people followed suit. From then on, a big celebration was held in Mexico City every year on the day of San Nicolás de Tolentino.[176]

The year 1613 saw two miracles, or so Chimalpahin calls them. First, two indigenous skirt-makers ("cuechiuhque") and some other local residents of the district of Xolloco wanted to set up a cross at an intersection not far from the church of San Antonio Abad where Chimalpahin worked, but a widow María, a seller of bitter atole ("xocoatolnamacac"), violently opposed the project, saying the site was on her property, and she even had the cross builders arrested. Nevertheless, the viceroy gave them permission, and almost immediately María died, miraculously punished for her opposition to the cross. In the second episode, a Spanish couple wanted to get rid of a cross the Xolloco people had set up many years before at a place called Acatla because it was too close to their house. The wife was the worst offender, using bad language in public, and it was she who soon became ill and died. The local people called it God's justice and proceeded to win their suit to retain the cross.[177]

When we look at these items, certain things stand out. Chimalpahin, far from showing skepticism about such marvels, hardly even betrays surprise. Miracles associated with images clearly fit within the normal operation of his world (unlike the party of Japanese who marched into Mexico City one day and truly did surprise him).[178] As we have noted before, crosses come into these matters frequently. Above all, though Chimalpahin makes a distinction between Spaniards and local people as groups, he makes no distinction in their relation to saints, images, and miracles. The Virgin of Los Remedios is not merely something Spanish as she has sometimes been seen;[179] local people go to greet her, too, and even get mentioned first. That a miracle affected a Spanish woman does not prevent the Nahuas from adopting the saint who performed it. When an indigenous child is the one affected, Spanish participation and confirming testimony are meaningful to Chimalpahin. The opponents of crosses, struck down for their attitude, are both Spanish and indigenous. What we see here is the two populations in parallel relation to the same holy objects, sometimes directly interacting and reinforcing each other's beliefs. The situation (most pronounced surely in the capital but not impossible to duplicate to some extent in many other settings) provided ample opportunity for Nahuas to acquaint themselves with Spanish lay beliefs and practices. In Chimalpahin's reports, despite the full assimilation of the world of saintly miracles, we still find occasional hints that in some things the Spaniards continued to be the style leaders, as appears to have been the case with setting fires on rooftops in response to a miracle.[180]

As I have already made clear, the mature saints complex extends forward in time indefinitely (many of the cases cited above were from the eighteenth century). The one great modification after 1600 was the growth, from the mid-seventeenth century on, of a supra-altepetl saint of national dimensions, the Virgin of Guadalupe. In the classic form of the legend, the Virgin appeared at Tepeyacac a little north of Mexico City in 1531, and by around mid-century there was in fact a well-known, even controversial shrine there.[181] The Virgin of Guadalupe was never an altepetl patron, but instead appealed to the populace of the general Mexico City area regardless of their unit affiliation. In this, she was very much like Marian saints in the Spain of that time, and specifically like the Spanish Guadalupe after whom she was named. As in Tepeyacac, the Spanish images and their shrines were generally located at the edge of town or outside it on a site defined by some striking natural feature.[182] Assuming that an important preconquest temple to a mother goddess really was located on the same site, as was said by a good authority at an early time,[183] the Guadalupe cult was well grounded on both Spanish and indigenous sides. It did not, however, spread like wildfire through central Mexico in the sixteenth century, or even in the early seventeenth. Guadalupe is not mentioned in presently known Nahuatl materials originating beyond the general environs of Mexico City in the entire time before Lasso de la Vega's publication of her legend in 1649.

Even in the neighborhood of Mexico City, references build up slowly, by no means overshadowing devotion to altepetl and tlaxilacalli saints.[184] In a brief historical section, the anonymous annalist of Tenochtitlan through the 1560's (referred to earlier) mentions the appearance of the Virgin at Tepeyacac, dating it in 1555, a generation later than the now traditional version.[185] These annals contain one other reference: in 1566, a Spaniard named Villaseca donated a golden image of the saint and a house where the sick could sleep, leading to a major consecration ceremony attended by the Audiencia judges and the archbishop, for whom Villaseca provided a feast. The emphasis is on the Spanish donor and the dignitaries, though it is said that the indigenous people (of Mexico City) also went out to watch.[186] In 1588, a noblewoman of Coyoacan donated half a peso to "our precious mother Santa María" at Tepeyacac above and beyond the usual local contributions.[187] From that time forward, people in Mexico City and the settlements closely associated with it (although not as far as Xochimilco or Chalco, to my knowledge) routinely mention Guadalupe or possess one or more of her images.

Chimalpahin's entries can add to our grasp of the position of Guadalupe around Mexico City in his day (ca. 1590–1620). Her special importance in his eyes is implied by the fact that, like the anonymous annalist before him, he gives the date of her apparition, something he does for no other saint (agreeing closely with his predecessor, he dates the event in 1556).[188] Still, among all the saints carried in the numerous processions in which Chimalpahin so revels, Guadalupe does not appear even once.* Chimalpahin refers to her (as far as I am aware) only three other times, all of which (much as with the earlier annalist) have to do with high Spanish officials: once the officiating viceroy made a pilgrimage to her shrine on Ash Wednesday, himself in ashes (1568); once a viceroy was feted there on first arrival (1595); and once an arriving archbishop spent the night there (1613).[189] Nothing Chimalpahin says has any implication that the Guadalupe cult was exclusively or even mainly directed at or carried on by indigenous people.

The shrine the just-mentioned dignitaries visited seems to have been but one of several shrines in central Mexico, most of them Marian, which in the course of the sixteenth century gained a certain regional following beyond their respective altepetl. The first publication on Guadalupe itself gives the location of some other prominent Marian shrines: Totoltepec, Cozamaloapan on the Veracruz coast, Temazcaltzinco, and "other towns."[190] Perhaps the Tlaxcalan Virgin of Ocotlan, the Lord of Chalma, or the Sacromonte of Amaquemecan should be added, but it is very hard to find contemporaneous documentation of the early stages of regional image devotion and associated pilgrimages, and there seems to be virtually none in the characteristic sources of the present work.[191]

Bachiller Luis Lasso de la Vega's Nahuatl book *Huey tlamahuiçoltica . . .* (Through a great miracle . . .), published in Mexico City in 1649, is a turning point in Guadalupan history in more than one sense. Besides giving us the first Nahuatl account of the legend in its now-classic form, it coincides with the beginning of a quick expansion of the devotion to Guadalupe over large parts of central Mexico, if not farther. I do not say that the book necessarily brought on or was even highly instrumental in the expansion, though it certainly could have been. It is entirely possible that the publication responded

---

*It is true that a majority of these saints were patrons of sociopolitical units, which would eliminate Guadalupe, but some units were beginning to display more than one image, and cofradías were also adding greatly to the variety.

to an already beginning ground swell. At any rate, during the second half of the seventeenth century and through the eighteenth, images of Guadalupe, chapels devoted to her, and a preoccupation with her apparition as a historical event of major significance appear in Nahuatl documents from Toluca in the west through the greater Valley of Mexico, including Chalco, to the Tlaxcala-Puebla region.[192] The same can be said of no other saint.

In many ways, the time was ripe for the development of a proto-national or macroethnic saint who would symbolize the larger unit now becoming more meaningful. As we saw in Chapter 2, the fragmentation of the altepetl was well under way. At this point, the Nahuas were far more open to the supra-altepetl, countrywide society and economy, primarily Hispanic in character (or at least in tone), through direct contact with Hispanics in residential, commercial, and work settings. And because of widespread bilingualism and the amount of Spanish vocabulary now incorporated in Nahuatl, such contact represented a far more efficient vehicle of communication than in earlier times. Migrants had been moving across the face of central Mexico and beyond, often motivated by work opportunities, for over a hundred years now. The world beyond the altepetl and tlaxilacalli had greater immediacy and constituted a larger proportion of life's concerns than before. The Nahuas had always acted as individuals, but mainly inside the local corporate framework. Now they were increasingly dealing with Spaniards and with each other outside that framework, and a devotion that was less tightly tied to the local unit (thus more individual even though in some sense representing a still larger unity) had its special appropriateness.

Yet even in the late colonial period, the Nahuas, and most surely those not living in cities or on haciendas, were still oriented above all to their own local units, to which, however fragmented some might be, they continued to give primary political and religious allegiance. It is hard to imagine that they by themselves would have generated this new symbol. Although the postconquest Nahua world did act as a unit, with similar things happening and the same terms, concepts, and practices appearing everywhere without much time differential, so that the Nahuas were clearly in some sense all in touch with each other, conscious concerted action was largely absent above the level of the altepetl. As early as the mid-sixteenth century, with the development of the northern silver mining industry, the nascent macroregional entity we can call Mexico or New Spain was integrated primarily by Hispanics and Hispanic structures, even in areas like central Mexico where a preconquest tradition of large-scale integration existed. It was the Hispanics who had a common consciousness, and it is from them that one would expect the first demand for a national saint. Indeed, we have already seen that native Mexican Spaniards were deeply interested in the Guadalupe cult in the middle and later seventeenth century, and it is they who probably created, at some point, the apparition story in the form in which we know it.[193]

Thus not only were Spaniards involved in the development of the Guadalupe cult; it flourished among them, and not exclusively among Indians. A study based on naming patterns shows that all over New Spain Marian devotion was strongest in the most Hispanized areas.[194] Returning to Lasso de la Vega, the fact of his publishing the Guadalupe story and supporting materials in Nahuatl, and Nahuatl only, surely demonstrates that he was directing himself to an indigenous audience. Moreover, some of the descriptions and exhortations accompanying the story specifically emphasize that the Virgin purposefully appeared to indigenous people and wanted to help them. His phrases, though, at times have the implication that these very people do not yet know the story and need acquainting with it ("let them see, let them hear in their language, all the things you have done to befriend them, which in the course of time had been very much forgotten").[195] From the point of view of Lasso de la Vega, the story itself seems in a sense only a preliminary to the following section, where one reads of Guadalupe's miracles, mainly of a curative nature, which turn out to have benefited Spaniards as much as Indians, or more so, if one goes by numbers alone. Of the fourteen miracles listed, seven affect Spaniards, five affect indigenous people, and two can be considered neutral.[196] Furthermore, the Spaniards were acting out models of conduct brought from the Peninsula; some of them made contingent promises before the cure and then afterward presented the shrine with silver effigies of their maladies.[197]

It is now known that the Mexican Guadalupe story closely imitates that of the Spanish Guadalupe, down to the tale's humble protagonist having a sick relative who is cured after the apparition as a by-product.[198] The finger of suspicion naturally points first to Lasso de la Vega himself, since as curate of the Guadalupe parish he had much to gain from increased traffic through his shrine. But Lasso de la Vega had a Spanish-language predecessor, whose closely parallel version of the story appeared only one year before Lasso de la Vega's.[199] It is also possible that Lasso de la Vega recapitulated a tale many a Spaniard before him had told, for the Guadalupe shrine in Spain was that country's most important, and such a story would have been on the tip of the tongue of any Spaniard apprised of a new Virgin of Guadalupe. Indeed, the Spanish background was even broader than the specific precedent of Guadalupe; there were several Marian shrines in Spain with stories of the Virgin appearing to a humble person in a rural setting, who then had to convince the authorities of what he or she had seen.[200]

All in all, it seems to me that the most likely scenario is that the repeated telling of tales of this type by Spaniards who knew the original built up a local tradition that was then taken over by the Indians of the area as well. The censor of the 1649 publication considered it faithful to the local tradition.[201] The story proper is in such fluent and idiomatic Nahuatl that Lasso de la Vega would have had to possess very unusual language gifts to have written it himself unless he was guided by an already existing model; indeed, the tale itself is so smooth that it gives the impression of having been through the polishing process of frequent telling by various narrators. The entire Lasso de la Vega publication is in excellent Nahuatl. Lasso de la Vega specifically says that he wrote it,[202] but since Spanish ecclesiastics had long been wont to ignore the fact that their indigenous aides actually put the texts they published into Nahuatl, there is nothing to prevent us from assuming the existence of a Nahua ghostwriter who could have had much latitude, writing as he pleased, or alternatively could have been narrowly restricted to translating Lasso de la Vega's Spanish or correcting his Nahuatl drafts. On the other hand, we cannot be absolutely sure any such figure was involved. To me, the introduction and appendix have the flavor of translations from Spanish, while the story proper does not. (Deep textual investigation might throw more light on this question.) The story is in a Nahuatl that could have been written at any time from 1550 or 1560 forward, with overwhelmingly indigenous and traditional vocabulary and idiom, no obvious calques, and a few Spanish loan nouns; in other words, the text bears the earmarks of what I call Stage 2 (see Chapter 7).

Ultimately, the rise of a cross-regional, cross-ethnic saint like Guadalupe in Mexico at approximately the time that the development actually took place can be viewed as natural if not inevitable, not unlike the rise of Santiago de Compostela in Spain in a much earlier age and later the Spanish Guadalupe, reflecting a change of the country's center of gravity. The Guadalupe of Tepeyacac gained from being located at the hub of Spanish Mexico, the focal point of a great deal of migration back and forth within the indigenous world as well. If we add to this the mere connotations of the word Guadalupe in Spain, that is, a premier shrine looked to across a whole country and in some sense symbolizing its essence—the very thing that a new Spanish-dominated area attaining some maturity, cultural identity, and autonomy would wish to emulate—then the rest simply follows.

Attaching the name Guadalupe to the shrine and its Virgin (how this happened is not at all clear) was the transcendentally important step. The gesture toward the indigenous population could well have been more an attempt to base a new if parallel identity on the principal peculiarity of the local scene than an attempt to reach the indigenous population (it could simultaneously have been that, too). The originator or originators acted long before conditions were right, and so Guadalupe went through a long period of gestation in which her cult drew little attention in broader central Mexico, but when the time came in the mid-seventeenth century, explosive growth started, leading along the lines already laid out toward a symbol with which all native-born Mexicans could identify.

The Question of Beliefs

In general, the materials the postconquest Nahuas have left us relating to religion lend themselves to the study of certain patterns and trends in behavior (such as the practices surrounding saints), attitudes (such as the way both individuals and corporations identified themselves with those saints), and concepts and structures important in organizing the cult (such as the "saint-house" or the teopantlaca and their connections with altepetl government). It is much harder to get at the doctrinal aspect of the religious complex, the actual substantive beliefs people held, for rarely indeed are such matters discussed in mundane Nahuatl documents, including those of a specifically religious nature like cofradía records or the Tepemaxalco religious account book.

Our first recourse must be the preambles of testaments, the most straightforwardly doctrinal statements in the Nahuatl documentary corpus. The essential contents are usually an invocation of the Trinity and a declaration of belief in the teachings of the holy mother church, with a standard example or two, such as the omnipotence of God, followed in many cases by something on the order of the testator's hopes for the intercession of Mary and other saints, the confiding of the soul to God while the body returned to the earth whence it came, and so forth. In its substance, the preamble varied little with region or over time. The entire set of formulas was taken from Spanish testamentary convention, with only the changes demanded by the use of Nahuatl as a vehicle. We have no reason to suspect that the Nahuas did not subscribe to these statements; but in what way and to what extent either the notaries who wrote them or the testators in whose names they were issued understood them, or what importance they attached to them, are not easy questions to answer.

One clue is the fact that of all the matter produced by Nahua notaries, the preambles of testaments are the most riddled with errors, not only a heavy dose of the usual omission and repetition of syllables, but wrong words, ungrammatical statements, and truncated sentences. It gradually becomes clear to the explorer among these materials that the notaries were often bored and inattentive when writing preambles, taking the attitude many of us take today toward the fine print of contracts. (If we look into the background of this attitude, it involves not skepticism, but fatigue on the part of the expert who knows the points all too well and takes them for granted, and a public that is less well informed but inclined to think the formulas must be all right.)

The introductions to some testaments, it is true, are done with care and elegance, and if one inspects a sample from various regions and times, they will be seen to vary in details. Testaments from one altepetl over a given stretch of time, however, ordinarily show a strong uniformity or are partial realizations of a common set of stock phrases. Thus testaments of Coyoacan in the early seventeenth century often include, as an embellishment of God's omnipotence, his creation of all things visible and invisible.[203] These things are more a matter of local style than of doctrinal content. Likewise, a given notary will have his own formulas, varying slightly from other notaries of the same town but quite consistent across all his documents.[204] At times, to be sure, the introduction is somewhat tailored to the testator and may actually include some of his words, as with the statement, "My body has grown old," but this does not affect the vocabulary or content of the opening section.[205]

It would seem that the preamble was a privileged or frozen zone, where only the most conservative and orthodox material could appear, the most hallowed formulas (which could also be un-understood mouthings and clichés), as opposed to the body of the testament, where expression was freer and a more vernacular vocabulary came into play. In this, the preamble is a good deal like an incantation. The most striking distinction between preamble and body is in the treatment of the Virgin Mary, who, though her presence is not obligatory, is frequently mentioned in both section-types. One of the few expressions of normal Nahua Christianity to bear any prima facie implication of an important doctrinal alteration of Spanish orthodoxy was the description of Mary as "our precious mother" (*totlaçonantzin*). Unlike the European "our lady" and "mother of God," this wording has the flavor of setting up a mother goddess for humanity parallel to the father God (similarly called "our precious father," *totlaçotatzin*, in some Nahuatl texts).[206] Sahagún specifically objected to *tonantzin*, "our mother," put off not only by its inherent implications but by the existence of a preconquest goddess by that name.[207] Possibly because of this convergence, but more likely because *tlaço-*, "precious, dear," was routinely added to the description of almost any benevolent Christian supernatural, the simple form "tonantzin" was avoided; I have yet to see it in any Nahuatl document in reference to the Virgin. But by the late sixteenth century, if not before, "totlaçonantzin" had won a clear victory over any objections and continued to be used without inhibition by everyone speaking and writing in Nahuatl.* It is seen in wills, the orthodox

---

*Nahua yearning for a mother figure or for a creator pair, or Spanish ecclesiastical willingness to bend in meeting such desires, may have been very important in helping bring about the end result, but we should not ignore the exigencies of language either. Nahuatl has nothing as smooth or stylish as "our lady" or "nuestra señora" in that general semantic range. The necessity of adding the cumbersome *cihua-* ("woman, female") to *pilli*, "noble," or *-tecuiyo*, "lord," to achieve approximate equivalents deprives the resulting expressions of pithiness or emotional force, and *-tecuiyo* was already preempted by God and Jesus anyway. Nor does *inantzin Dios*, "mother of God," roll trippingly off the tongue, especially in the vocative, which was precisely

religious professional Chimalpahin uses it, and even the Spanish cleric Lasso de la Vega employs it (or permits it to be employed) again and again, starting with the very title page of his Guadalupe publication.[208]

In the preamble of wills, however, "totlaçonantzin" is generally not to be seen.[209] Preamble language for the Virgin includes "eternal virgin," "heavenly lady," "dear mother of Jesus," and "our intercessor."[210] The distinction can be seen not only in the corpus of testaments in general but sometimes within a single testament. Thus in the will of Bárbara Agustina, written in the Co-yoacan region in 1608, the preamble has "the eternal virgin Saint Mary, our intercessor," whereas in the body, when Bárbara speaks of her image of Mary, she calls her "our precious mother."[211]

A common notion has it that the ecclesiastics of the first generation or two suppressed the Nahuatl term *teotl*, "god, deity, divinity, holy thing," in favor of Spanish Dios to avoid possible doctrinal confusions.[212] On the contrary, they permitted its free use as the generic term for deity, as opposed to Dios, which was more like the proper name of the Christian God. In this way, "teotl" entered into preamble language; there it was frozen and continued to appear until the end of the colonial period, when it for all intents and pur-poses had long since dropped out of the living language.[213] The preamble of a will written in the Azcapotzalco district in 1695 speaks of "my god ['noteo-tzin'] and ruler, God ['Dios']," and another done in the Valley of Toluca a hundred years later, in 1795, has the identical phrase; in one from the Tlal-manalco district in 1736, we find the traditional "only one very true god God ['teutl dios']."[214]

The soul as something that will survive and, the testator hopes, go to God in heaven is a fixture of preamble vocabulary. From the earliest testaments, the Christian concept is conveyed by the Spanish loanword *anima* (always possessed and usually "animan"). The beliefs expressed in this connection are invariably strictly orthodox Christian. The Nahuas' initial unfamiliarity with the notion shows in the fact that in sixteenth- and early-seventeenth-century testaments, the Spanish term is most likely to be accompanied and elucidated by what at first may have been the ad hoc explanation or circumlocution *(no)yolia*, "(my) means of living, what makes me live."[215] "Anima" can occur by itself quite early; gradually "-yolia" fades out (though never entirely, and in some subregions it became frozen into the formula), so that by the slight indications we have, the Christian concept of the soul, however naturalized, had become entirely familiar. In any case, we can say that the Spanish term came to dominate the field, at least within the open public sphere. "Anima"

where a term was most needed. There were no easy alternatives to *totlaçonantzin* for constant everyday use, and I suspect that rather than doctrinal considerations, it was usage's insistence on a concise and affectionate yet respectful term that was ultimately decisive. The potential impli-cations, nevertheless, remain enormous.

must have been a basic part of every Nahua's vocabulary well before the end of the sixteenth century.[216]

Considering the number of Nahuatl testaments extant and in one way or another available, and the haste and carelessness with which preambles were sometimes written, doctrinal error in them is insignificant. The Culhuacan notary who in 1580 or so set down that the Trinity was "çan ce persona," "just one person," probably only absentmindedly mixed up the still somewhat exotic loan words *persona* and *esencia*, or conceivably he thought "persona" meant essence (usually rendered -*yeliztzin*, "being").[217] For the most part, generations of notaries across central Mexico handled the "three persons" passage of the opening statement perfectly, using either the Spanish word or the Nahuatl *teotlacatzitzintin*, "god-persons, divine persons," or both.[218] Perhaps, it is true, an example from Tenayuca (a little north of Mexico City) goes too far: "three gods but just one god God."[219]

At the border between the preamble and the body of the testament comes the section on burial and masses. Every now and again one will find the mass or masses justified by the statement, "so that my soul will not spend long in purgatory."[220] Generally, the word used is Spanish *purgatorio*, but one eighteenth-century example has the graphic "tetlechipahualoya," "place where people are cleansed or purified by fire."[221] Since such passages are quite rare, one might imagine that the testators in these cases were especially convinced of the reality of purgatory and were deeply concerned about their own fate there.* From the identical wording in all instances, however, I tend to think the phrase was a stock element that some notaries learned and used on certain occasions, perhaps when they were giving the client the full treatment. There is no way to be sure.

The preamble tends to belong to God and the body of the testament to the saints, though they do cross into each other's territory somewhat. In a sense, God's domain was the unchanging religious framework of salvation, eternity, and the sacraments set up around the middle of the sixteenth century and not normally the center of attention thereafter; the saints' domain, more at the forefront, was the everyday organizational and economic life of the altepetl and the household, the world of living, evolving experience. It was expectable, as well as orthodox, that the otherworldly soul should go to God (or occasionally Jesus Christ) rather than to the saints.[222] Land, on the other hand, belonged to the saints as we have seen; if God had residual possession, it is hardly ever mentioned. But the household complex itself, despite the residence there of so many saints, and the primary obligation of serving them, belonged to God, as shown by the pervasive formula "the patio and exit of

---

*But is one to think, then, that the multitudes who did not mention purgatory were skeptical and unconcerned?

our lord God."[223] Again God provides a general framework, within which the saints operate.[224]

In everyday working documents produced by the Nahuas, then, directly expressed beliefs, though suggestive, are not sufficient to reveal the outlines of the religious system as a whole. If, in search of at least some provisional hypotheses about what beliefs the people considered important, we simply ask what is spoken of and what is not spoken of in mundane Nahuatl documents (including historical annals), then in the corporate sphere, including the household as a small corporation, the immediate answer is once again that the emphasis is on saints. The primary function that can be detected is that of heightening and giving generational continuity to various levels of corporate identities, lending them emotional depth and reinforcing social, economic, and political organization. The propitiation of the saints may have been important, too, or even the ultimate aim of the activity, but if so, that does not emerge clearly from the Nahuatl documentary legacy.

At the level of the individual (although these matters of course have a corporate side, too), the documents the Nahuas wrote emphasize rites of passage, above all the basic ceremonies associated with death, birth, and marriage. It is my impression that the order just given corresponds to the relative importance the Nahuas gave these rites, although since burial arrangements are seen above all in wills, and baptisms and marriages in parish registers, the judgment is subjective. We have seen that masses for the soul and other burial formalities became a business, and an important one, and that mainly non-religious factors determined who would request many masses and who only one. Nevertheless, I am convinced that at the root lay an unquestioning acceptance of the religious validity and necessity of the rites. Such acceptance is not, of course, quite the same thing as an overriding concern with salvation and the afterlife. Of that one sees little indeed. The entire set of funeral rites at once defined the individual's relation to his surroundings, above all his social surroundings, and by their final seal allowed his relatives and fellow citizens to adopt a different stance toward him. Baptism and marriage likewise gave supernatural approval of the individual's passage from one stage to another. It appears that many couples living together may have remained unmarried, but more for economic reasons than out of disinclination or disbelief.[225] No one remained unbaptized, however, or at least no one admitted to it, so that we seem justified in the conclusion that the Nahuas felt a greater sacramental urgency about baptism than about marriage (Spaniards were the same).

Another potential resource in the investigation of indigenous beliefs is a quite extensive corpus of formal religious writings in Nahuatl, including confessionals, catechisms, psalms, sermons, and religious plays. Most were written in the sixteenth or at latest very early seventeenth century, although some (mainly derivative) new materials continued to be generated throughout the colonial period, and the original works still circulated to some extent. Spanish friars and priests appear as the authors, except for the plays, which were not published and remain anonymous, though it has often been assumed that they, too, were written by clerics. In recent years, however, scholars have begun to realize that although the ecclesiastics did instigate, oversee, and in large part determine the basic content of the works of this genre, their Nahua aides, if not always the actual composers of the Nahuatl texts known to us, at least were responsible for the fine points of the phrasing and syntax.[226] Sahagún openly acknowledged his aides, which few others were gracious enough to do, but his practice was the customary modus operandi.[227] One of the clearest examples of its results is the way that many confessionals and sermons draw heavily on preconquest rhetoric.[228]

Although the contents of works in this vein generally appear doctrinally immaculate at first reading, they characteristically contain some approximations of preconquest religious language that are susceptible of interpretation in the old sense.[229] It has been shown that certain passages speaking of Jesus Christ as a source of light or illumination can be interpreted as making him into a solar deity of a type very familiar to Mesoamericans, even though the Nahuatl hews quite closely to Christian originals.[230] How much of this kind of thing the ecclesiastics grasped, how the Nahua writers intended it, and how the Nahua audience received it is hard, if not impossible, to ascertain. This subfield is still quite embryonic; we lack even up-to-date transcriptions and translations of a sizable sampling of texts.[231]

Here I wish only to make a few comparisons between these Spanish-sponsored religious works and the writings produced more spontaneously by the Nahuas. The vocabulary is much like that of testament preambles, that is, it generally lacks the saints and their service. The central figure is an omniscient, omnipotent, omnipresent God, often described by a series of epithets apparently taken from the god Tezcatlipoca, which show up rarely or never in mundane documents.[232] Above all, this whole literature is highly moralistic and individualistic in tone and content, in stark contrast to the corporatism and ritualism reigning in more specifically Nahua expressions of Christianity. One must wonder to what extent the Nahuas ever really incorporated or even took cognizance of this corpus of teaching, especially the many parts of it whose explication relied on the relatively rare presence of a Spanish ecclesiastic. Yet some echoes of it do appear here and there, as we will see.

Very different from the writings emanating from the upper echelons of the religious establishment are the Nahuatl "titles" produced in the time after 1650, primarily to justify altepetl land rights. The titles stand apart from the main body of older Nahuatl documentation in being written, at least in many cases, by people less skilled in the normal documentary conventions of the time, and also in recapitulating much local oral tradition. On both counts, they give us a window into the more popular side of religion, though since their emphasis falls elsewhere, the view is again only partial. In brief (for I will return to the titles in Chapter 9), we are here again in the domain of corporate religion and the saints.[233]

The main church, which the local people usually take entire credit for building, has a central place as a symbol of the altepetl. The acceptance of Christianity is seen as having raised the altepetl to a new level. Although Spanish clerics are little mentioned, the titles do contain some trace of their teachings. The documents often begin with an invocation on the order of a testament preamble or catechistic lesson, and one finds biblical references here and there, though rarely used as they would have been in a sermon. The individual-ethical element is entirely missing except when elders speak to future generations outside a religious context. Some open syncretism surfaces in the titles, with magical-totemic altepetl leaders; one of them transforms himself into a totemic god-animal to deter outside aggression; others show messianic dimensions. The writers seem quite unaware that Spanish ecclesiastics would frown on such beliefs; they show them openly and do not seem to mean them as anti-Christian or non-Christian at all. In fact, they seem to have considerable difficulty in distinguishing the Christian from the non-Christian (as well as little interest in doing so) or in imagining a time when their forebears were not Christian.[234]

But what appears in the titles is the merest hint of what we know from many contemporary Spanish reports to have been a widespread survival of relatively unchanged and unintegrated indigenous religious beliefs and practices, a phenomenon confirmed by numerous vestiges ethnographers have found in the present century.[235] We will probably never be able to assess the nature and extent of such survivals fully; these disapproved practices are a topic that the Nahuas (who are the ones who knew the most about them) generally avoided in the writings that have reached us, and Spanish reports tend to be both alarmist and uninformed. Fortunately, a rural priest of the early seventeenth century, Hernando Ruiz de Alarcón, who knew Nahuatl well, systematically investigated "idolatry" in the region where he operated, the Taxco-Cuernavaca area and much of what is now Guerrero, collecting incantations that he had Nahuatl speakers write down for him (a few, indeed, had already been surreptitiously put on paper). He then wrote a uniquely valuable treatise (dated 1629, with some parts done at least as early as 1617), consisting of the transcribed and translated incantations, together with descriptions of something of their context. He also at times tells of specific cases he saw himself, involving people whom he precisely names and locates.[236] The work thus approaches the value of an indigenous survey of the matter.

Nowhere does Ruiz de Alarcón suggest that he uncovered any disbelief in Christianity. He found rather that in a great many affairs of everyday life, not directly touched by Christian rites but pervaded by preconquest ritual, that ritual was still practiced, by high and low alike and by laymen as well as specialists. He does not claim the practices were universal, emphasizing that, as one would expect, they were most predominant in settlements located in the hills and thinly populated areas, remote from the main centers of Hispanic population.[237]

There were incantations for good fortune in many sorts of productive economic activity—hunting, fishing, woodcutting, lime production, load carrying, farming—as well as for divination, influencing the emotions of others, and curing diseases (a large variety).* The texts use a restricted but highly metaphorical vocabulary involving preconquest calendrical names, symbolism of number, color, and direction, and above all a pantheon of gods, identified by name and specifically so denominated (*teteo*). Despite the ritualization, the users of the texts clearly grasped the divinity of the gods as well as the meaning of most of the other terms, for they were able to explain a great deal to Ruiz de Alarcón.[238] Some sacrifice by self-bleeding still occurred, as well as some offerings to the sun and spirits in high places.[239] Nearly all incantations were accompanied by some use of or reference to hallucinogenic or narcotic substances, which were themselves conceived to be gods and kept in a special basket or chest, along with offerings. Wherever Christianity left a niche unfilled, it appears, there preconquest beliefs and practices tended to persist in their original form.[240]

The remarkable thing is how unchanged and untouched these practices remained. A reader can survey one incantation after another without finding even a Spanish loanword, much less anything smacking of Christianity. Much as with the two parts of testaments, but more pronouncedly, two separate zones had been created, with a well-defined if invisible line dividing them. As we look closer, we see that a certain amount of interpenetration does occur, and it is useful to make distinctions in this respect. First of all, the incantation users can have a purpose compatible with orthodox Christianity or even serving it. Thus the searchers for beehives said that bees were to be revered because the wax they produce "is to be burned before our lord God."[241] But

---

*Ruiz de Alarcón does not include market activity or any ordinary household chores in the repertory, or any kind of interaction with Spaniards. An interesting aspect of the incantations is that though some seem to fall in the domain of high religion, such as those concerning maize agriculture, and some into the realm of shamanism, all have the same format, use the same metaphors, and call on the same gods. Preconquest Nahua religion appears to have been far more integrated than its European counterpart.

such words do not enter into their incantation in any way. The hallucinogenic substances were often put on the altar in the saint-house or oratory, or in other ways associated with Christian paraphernalia. I take it that these substances were thought of as providing a neutral spiritual energy, which could be used for many different purposes, a sort of fuel that could also act as an offering. Since copal and native flowers were used at Christian altars, why not *ololiuhqui* (morning-glory seeds) and peyote? This principle also worked in the other direction; the wax candles brought by the Christians might now be lit before a stone idol on a hilltop.[242]

Ruiz de Alarcón does not say so, but if Nahua shamans were like some of their fellows elsewhere in the world, they must from time to time have received new powers, techniques, and texts in visions. The visions of this type he reports are Christian in coloration. A woman healer had a dream of being crucified while an angel taught her cures. One Domingo Hernández dreamed that he got his powers and his words from the Virgin Mary, Saint Veronica, and another saint whom he failed to recognize. Yet these healers' incantations were entirely in the traditional vein, and the one recited by Domingo Hernández was already known to Ruiz de Alarcón word for word from other sources. Or nearly all of it was. Domingo's version ended with the Latin words, "In the name of the father, the son, and the Holy Ghost." The addition, however, is in the nature of a coda and not part of the actual incantation. Another healer descended in a trance to hell, where God gave him his medicine; he wore a long rosary and attached a cross to his staff.[243] In such cases we see Christian supernaturals being called on to legitimate preconquest rites, but not to enter into those rites.

Christian elements do come yet deeper into the system at times. The clients or patients of practitioners had various designations in the traditional vocabulary, many of them ad hoc. Perhaps the most basic of them, still occurring standardly in Ruiz de Alarcón, was "child of the gods," "teteo ynpiltzin." But now we sometimes see the client called "imacehualtzin dios," "the subject of God," or "Dios itlachihualtzin," "God's creature."[244] A prime cause of disease in the preconquest system was the anger of supernatural beings, to whom the Christian set could now be added. The traditional interrogatory might now run, "Who is angry? A saint?" If that proved to be the case, the continuation could be "Who are you who is angry? Our Precious Mother? San Gaspar? San Juan?" Moreover, angry Christian deities had to be placated in a Christian manner, with a new image, clothing, veil, or ornament, or a celebration on the proper day.[245] These intrusions, though few in the corpus of incantations, were serious in principle. Yet to Christianize the target and the beneficiary of the incantation was not to Christianize the device itself; the magical words and the beings called on for help remained resolutely

indigenous even in these cases. The Nahuas must have viewed the entire supernatural sphere as a unit at some level, meshing and serving ultimately the
same purpose from the point of view of the individual and the corporation,
yet they held certain realms, distinguished by time and manner of genesis,
carefully apart from each other.[246]

    With time and with the advance of the Spanish Mexican world ever far-
ther into the countryside, the preconquest personae and rhetoric must have
receded correspondingly, though not without leaving many traces. A modern
ethnographer regards the religion of the Tlaxcalan community he studied as
still basically propitiatory though mainly Christian in form, with a small well-
segregated preconquest arm as a vestige; the system is not moral-ethical at
all, that function being performed by personal interaction in society.[247] In my
opinion, this analysis applies fully to Nahua religion in the postconquest centuries, although I have seen little direct evidence of the propitiatory aspect
because of the nature of the documentary base, and I would add the ritual
and corporate-identificational aspects as elements of equal importance. As so
often, indigenous and Spanish patterns reinforced each other, for whatever
the views of certain clerical reformers, early modern Spanish religion as practiced by the bulk of the population was also primarily ritual, propitiatory,
and corporate.[248]

7

Language

BY NOW THE READER will have noticed that a basic rhythm appears again and again in different branches of postconquest Nahua life. First came a short time of relative stasis; then a wave of reorganization swept the Nahua world about a generation after the Spanish conquest, followed by another around the middle of the seventeenth century. Nowhere is this three-stage process so clearly defined, or the reason for it so readily apparent, as in the area of linguistic evolution. It was, indeed, in study aimed specifically at the language contained in Nahuatl documents that I first became aware of the three stages and their timing, and in view of their special distinctness in this sphere I will organize the present chapter around them. To anticipate briefly, Stage 1, from the arrival of the Spaniards in 1519 to a time that can be set at between 1540 and 1550, was characterized by virtually no change in Nahuatl. Stage 2, extending from then until close to the mid-seventeenth century, saw massive borrowing of Spanish nouns, but the language remained little altered in other respects. Stage 3, with some advance signs coming earlier in the seventeenth century, stretches from about 1640–50 until today, wherever Nahuatl is spoken, and involves a deeper and broader Spanish influence betraying widespread bilingualism. When one surveys the whole process, it is evident that the stages correspond to the increasing frequency and intensity of contact between Nahuas and Spaniards, eventually leading to the formation and expansion of a group of bilinguals who served as an open channel between the two speech communities. Linguistic phenomena prove to be the most sensitive indicator the historical record contains of the extent, nature, and trajectory of contact between the two populations.

It is a testimony to the unity of central Mexico and the Nahua culture area in the centuries after the conquest that the evolution of the various subregions appears to come within a decade or two of simultaneity in most ways that are presently susceptible of being determined, so that the entire development can and for the most part must be treated in a unitary fashion. This does not mean, however, that subregional variation lacks potential significance. The theory that the rate of linguistic change in Nahuatl is a function of the amount of contact between the two populations involved automatically predicts that change will come first where the largest number of Spaniards and Nahuas had daily encounters and subsequently spread out to the rest of the Nahuatl-speaking community. The greatest caldrons of contact were the Spanish cities, and I suspect that much of the innovation took place in Mexico City and its environs (including such areas as Coyoacan and Tetzcoco). Some evidence to that effect already exists, and I will point it out in the course of the following presentation. In the not distant future, I expect that the dynamics of subregional linguistic evolution will become much clearer, but even then the relative contemporaneity across central Mexico will remain a fundamental part of the picture.*

The matter of primary interest here is the adaptation that Nahuatl speakers made to Spanish across the colonial period, as something occurring within the indigenous context like the other major topics of the book; the Spanish spoken by Nahuas outside that context belongs more to the history of Hispanization—the absorption of indigenous people into Hispanic society—the study of which would be a project at least as massive as the present one, though very different. In the late colonial period, however, the speaking and writing of Spanish by Nahuas became in some areas and circles a corporate phenomenon, and some Nahuas even used Spanish to communicate with each other. Some extant examples of their language show that it retained a strong Nahuatl substratum, and I will deal with it briefly here as a "Stage 4," intending to indicate by the quotation marks that although this development occurs well after the onset of Stage 3 and partially as a consequence, it does not belong fully in the same series, for it did not replace Stage 3. Rather a kind of bifurcation took place, and Stage 3 Nahuatl survived until our times, whereas Nahuatl-influenced Spanish would later give way for the most part

---

*Enough Nahuatl documentation has been amassed and surveyed that first and last attestations of given phenomena (especially those frequently occurring) are meaningful, and that rough, intuitive judgments of frequencies can be made. In fact, the texts used are extensive enough that they would have allowed for rigorous statistical frequency counts, but the requisite exhaustive data collection would have unduly slowed other aspects of the present project. When documents for regions such as the Toluca Valley and the Cuernavaca area or subregions of the Valley of Mexico, such as Chalco, Xochimilco, Coyoacan, or the Tetzcoco orbit, reach a mass somewhat comparable to the present overall total, and I believe that in some cases this will actually happen before too many years pass, then each restricted body can be tested for frequencies against the overall corpus. I believe that, once an adequate mass is attained, first attestations of innovations will ordinarily not vary from one outlying region to another by more than a decade or two, but new developments may prove to have been much more widespread in some regions than in others at a given time. I have a strong impression, for example, that Stage 3 phenomena appear more sparingly in known 18th-century texts of the Cuernavaca region than in those of the Toluca Valley. To date, however, there is a paucity of testaments (the staple of the documentation) from the late colonial Cuernavaca basin, and if that situation should change, the perspective might change as well.

to ever more standard Spanish speech, even by those who continued to speak Nahuatl as well.[1]

Documents written by Nahuas in Nahuatl are the source of the overwhelming bulk of what we know about their language from the conquest through the eighteenth century. Nahua writing practices are thus intimately related to the topic of the present chapter, but let me perhaps superfluously remind the reader beforehand that the writing has its own separate history, and though it is through that window that we see Nahuatl speech, the fact of writing is not what caused the language developments. Much the same processes of linguistic adaptation have occurred among indigenous peoples without a writing tradition.[2]

Stage 1

During the brief military phase of the Spanish conquest, confrontation predominated over contact between Spaniards and Nahuas (by "contact" I mean normal, peaceful, person-to-person interaction). Then in the fifteen or twenty years following the definitive conquest of 1521, although hostile confrontation receded, several factors conspired to keep contact at a minimum: the simple paucity of Spaniards; their distribution, concentrated in a very small number of widely scattered cities from which only dire necessity could budge them; their instability as they went from one part of the country to another seeking some firm basis in an economy whose potential was unclear until the development of the silver industry in the 1540's; the encomienda system, in which a minority of the Spaniards and the higher authorities of the Nahuas bore the brunt of social interaction; and finally, in a circular fashion, the total lack of relevant communication skills on the part of the bulk of both populations, which forced reliance on a small corps of intermediaries. The only two groups of Nahuas who found themselves in the position of communicating verbally with Spaniards on a daily basis were the servants and other permanent employees of Spanish laymen and the aides and students of Spanish ecclesiastics. In both cases, the Nahuas involved were to some extent removed from their original social context. Thus contact between the two populations as such can hardly be said to have existed, and linguistic adaptation was consequently almost nil, even though the Nahuas were experiencing new things and finding ways to express them. The new came to them in the form of direct experience of objects and actions rather than in words. They were seeing things rather than hearing about them.

Among the difficulties in studying Stage 1, the greatest is not its brevity or its earliness, but the fact that our primary source of knowledge about the language, writing in Nahuatl, had not yet been developed. Regular and widespread production of mundane alphabetic documents in Nahuatl began about 1545, that is, simultaneously with the onset of Stage 2. The only known larger Nahuatl document that could be said to belong fully to Stage 1 is the often-mentioned set of census records of the Cuernavaca region, apparently composed at various times between 1535 and 1545.[3] In addition, some Nahuatl documents of the late 1540's and the 1550's, although already belonging to Stage 2, are transitional and contain vestiges of the earlier mode. The greatest resource for the early period is the Nahuatl dictionary of fray Alonso de Molina. Though the 1571 edition is the fullest, much of the material was already in the first version, published as early as 1555, and the work clearly had been in gestation for many years before that. Molina and his indigenous aides constantly added new items but apparently rarely subtracted old ones, so that the end product, though fully representative of Stage 2, is also a mine of information on Stage 1. Quite a few of Molina's entries contain both a Stage 1 and a Stage 2 rendition of a Spanish term.

During the first twenty years or more after the arrival of the Spaniards, the Nahuas used primarily the resources of their own language to deal with the phenomena the newcomers introduced.[4] From the beginning until the process of adaptation was very far advanced, the occasion for linguistic innovation was generally a Spanish introduction, in particular one that struck the Nahuas as so new and different that no existing Nahuatl word or expression seemed appropriate. By no means all of the Spaniards' modalities and paraphernalia qualified as substantially different in the Nahuas' eyes from their own, so that many indigenous words and meanings were applied to Spanish people and things completely unchanged (nor was there in most of these cases any need for change in later centuries). The language for basic categories like life and death, speed and slowness, truth and falsehood, happiness and sadness, or goodness and badness, varied hardly more between Nahuatl and Spanish than between any two European languages, and there was never any question but that the same terms would be applied in these spheres to the affairs of Spaniards as to those of the Nahuas or their neighbors.

Introduced beings and tangible objects presented a greater problem. In some cases, as with the parts of the human body, the principle of identity could apply with equal uncontroversiality, but generally speaking, the Spaniards themselves and all the things they brought with them differed to some degree in appearance, structure, or manner of operation from the nearest Nahua equivalents. The seemingly so clear-cut process of creating a new expression for each new thing turns out to have been extremely subtle and at least superficially unpredictable, depending on judgments of degree. In some cases, the Nahuas simply ignored the differences, whether as unimportant or as subsumed under their own terms it is impossible to say. In others, they invented new expressions or gave old ones a different meaning. In yet others, it is hard to determine whether the expression should be considered an innovation or not. Where the introduced phenomena were noticeably distinct, and most were, there is no difference in kind between an identification and an extended meaning or metaphor.

The Spanish-style house, with its windows, swinging wooden doors, and intercommunicating rooms differed from the Nahua house complex, but the two were so alike in other respects, closed off from the outside, with an internal patio and often similar building materials, that it is no wonder the Nahuas soon settled on their usual word *calli* to refer to a Spanish house and never thereafter had reason to change that designation. It is entirely possible, however, that although all houses in the Nahua world belonged to a common type, the word "calli" should be construed as meaning "residence" or "structure to contain something" more generally, and would have been applied to Spanish houses even if the differences between the two house types had been far more striking than they were. Similarly, because of the generic similarity, *itzcuintli* was used for European dogs despite sharp differences of size and appearance. And *acalli*, "boat," referring among the Nahuas usually to a dugout vessel, was long employed to describe the vastly different European ship because of the identity of function.[5] After what may or may not have been some hesitation, the Nahuas decided that the Spaniards were, as they seemed to be, human beings like themselves, and called them by their normal term *tlacatl*. And though they clearly recognized the uniqueness of the European fruit trees, which were to be important to them and whose Spanish names they were to borrow in Stage 2, they grouped them under the generic *quahuitl*, just like any of the various kinds of indigenous trees.

When an existing Nahuatl word seemed inadequate, a description of the phenomenon was the first recourse (or so I surmise, for we have no source of sequential information on Stage 1); if one takes the still unborrowed and probably entirely unknown Spanish word as a starting point, this way of dealing with the problem amounts to circumlocution or definition. In the descriptive mode, the Nahuatl rendition of the new phenomenon consists of one or more transparent words relating to the phenomenon's appearance or other sensory impact, manner of action, or function. Some examples are included in Table 7.1, and as can be seen there, function tends to predominate.

The expressions vary greatly, as free descriptions naturally do, but two types stand out. The first is a qualified identification, that is, it consists of an identification plus a second word modifying it, as with *xicocuitlaocotl*, "beeswax torch," for "candle," or *oztomecacalli*, "traveling-merchant house," for "inn." The second type is a verbal substantive (an impersonal agentive), usually recognizable as ending in *-loni* or *-oni*, which names something as an

TABLE 7.1

Early Nahuatl Descriptions of Spanish Introductions and Concepts

English (Spanish)	Nahuatl equivalent
To appeal	*oc ceccan moteilhuiz,* "to sue in another place"
Arch (of stone) or stone bridge	*huitoliuhqui,* "something bent"
Bacon (*tocino*)	*coyamenacahuatzalli,* "dried pig meat"
Bellows	*ehuatlepitzaloni,* "hide instrument to blow on a fire"
Bier	*miccatlapechtli,* "dead-person platform"
Boundary stone (*mojón*)	*tetl quaxochmachiotl,* "stone that is the sign of a boundary"
Carpenter's plane	*tlatemmelahualoni,* "instrument for straightening something's edge"
Cattle prod (*garrocha*)	*quaquammiminaloni,* "instrument for sticking repeatedly into cattle (horned ones)"
Cucumber	*ayotontli xoxouhcaqualoni,* "little squash to be eaten raw"
Door (of wood)	*quauhtlatzacuillotl,* "wooden closing"
Hat	*nequacehualhuiloni,* "thing for shading one's head"
Heavy wax candle (*hacha*)	*malinqui xicocuitlaocotl,* "twisted beeswax torch"
Inn (*venta, mesón*)	*oztomecacalli,* "traveling-merchant house"; *techialcalli,* "house where people are attended to"; *nenenque incochian,* "travelers' sleeping place"
Justice, the law (*justicia*)	*tlamelahuacachihualiztli,* "doing things straight"
Key	*tlatlapoloni,* "instrument for opening something"
Lock	*tlatzaqualoni,* "instrument for closing something"
Pirate	*acalco tenamoyani,* "one who robs people on a boat"
Plow	*quaquauhe ielimiquia,* "means by which an ox cultivates"
Shop, store	*tlanamaquizcalli,* "sale house"
Surgeon	*tetecqui,* "one who cuts people"; *texoxotla ticitl,* "doctor who rips or saws people"
Vault	*tetlapachiuhqui calli,* "structure roofed with stone"

SOURCE: Molina, passim.

instrument (in the broadest sense) for achieving a certain purpose; among the examples in Table 7.1 are *tlatlapoloni,* "instrument for opening something," for "key," and *tlatzaqualoni,* "instrument for closing something," for "lock." These constructions are based respectively on *tlapoa,* "to open," and *tzaqua,* "to close." Both of the most common description types, the two-element compound and the *-loni* instrumental construction, were already part of the normal equipment of Nahuatl before the Spaniards came.

To pass beyond the status of an ad hoc expedient and enter into the vocabulary of Nahuatl for even a brief time, an expression had to have brevity. In the table, *ayotontli xoxouhcaqualoni,* "little squash to be eaten raw," for "cucumber," is admirable for hitting the nail on the head but does not fall trippingly from the tongue. Doubtless it was the momentary inspiration of one of Molina's aides.[6] It is my impression that, counting the nuclear constituents of compounds as separate words, few if any new expressions containing more than two words ever gained real currency in the Nahuatl speech community. Even such a relatively compact and apt phrase as *nequacehualhuiloni*, "thing for shading one's head," for "hat," never got off the ground, it seems.[7]

Now let us look at some successful expressions. Perhaps the most widespread newly coined description during the era of the conquest was the two-element qualified identification *tlequiquiztli*, "fire trumpet," for a European firearm. A *quiquiztli* was a conch-shell trumpet or horn; perhaps "fire horn" would be as good an English version. At any rate, in this case it was the sensory impression, the sight and sound, that gave rise to the term rather than the instrument's lethal aspect.* The word is found not only in Molina but in book 12 of the Florentine Codex and other early Nahuatl writings; though it eventually faded out, Chimalpahin was still using it in the early seventeenth century.[8] The term strikes one as an absolute neologism and in a sense may be so considered, yet it conforms perfectly to one of the most used descriptive conventions.

Once a new expression had taken hold, other major coinages were not to be expected in its semantic proximity. Economy in innovation was achieved by using the new word as the key element in a whole set of expressions describing various dimensions of its orbit. The complex that arose around "tlequiquiztli," shown in Table 7.2, can illustrate the principle. Quite technical aspects of gunnery are adequately handled without recourse to further striking neologisms. The device most used, in this as in other such complexes, is a second-generation qualified identification with the new expression acting as the modifier, as in *tlequiquiztlalli*, "fire-trumpet earth," for gunpowder. (Here we appear to have a successful expression of more than two elements, but having become part of the general vocabulary in a new and unitary meaning, "tlequiquiztli" now counts as but a single word.) Or the new expression might itself be modified, as in *matlequiquiztli*, "hand fire trumpet," for harquebus.

Another neologism that apparently attained currency for a time, though it was to yield to a Spanish loan early in Stage 2, was *quauhtemalacatl* for cart. The word is itself a secondary formation, based on the Nahuatl render-

---

*This does not necessarily mean that the Nahuas ignored purpose in this case. Rather, whether by chance or not, they homed in on the true function of firearms in most encounters between Spaniards and sedentary Indians in the conquest of America. Killing was accomplished primarily by the steel blade, while guns, too few, too slow, and with insurmountable ammunition problems, were mostly relegated to impressive blustering at the beginning of a battle, sharing the function of the trumpets with which the Nahuas so correctly associated them. (Compare Lockhart 1972a, pp. 10, 370.) The exact quality of sound intended by *quiquiztli* remains unclear. Conch-shell instruments generally produce a deep roar; yet as we will see, the Nahuas were to identify the conch *quiquiztli* with the European trumpet, of high, piercing sound. Consider also that the word for "to whistle," *tlanquiquici*, contains the same root (Molina, Spanish, f. 109).

from neologism to loan word.

TABLE 7.2

The Early Complex Around "Tlequiquiztli," "Firearm"

English (Spanish)	Nahuatl equivalent
Firearm in general	*tlequiquiztli*, "fire (conch) trumpet, horn"
Harquebus (early musket, *arcabuz*)	*matlequiquiztli*, "arm or hand fire trumpet"
Cannon	*tomahuac tlequiquiztli*, "thick or fat fire trumpet"; *huey tlequiquiztli*, "big fire trumpet"
To discharge a firearm	*tlequiquizoa*, "to operate (play) a fire trumpet"; *tlequiquizhuia*, "to use a fire trumpet on something"; *tlequiquiztlaça*, "to hurl, let go a fire trumpet"
Match	*icpatlamalintli ic motlequechia tlequiquiztli*, "twisted yarn with which a fire trumpet is set on fire"
Cannonball	*tlequiquiztelolotli*, "fire-trumpet sphere"
Gunpowder, saltpeter	*tlequiquiztlalli*, "fire-trumpet earth"
To load a firearm	*tlequiquiztlaltema*, "to fill a fire trumpet with earth"
Touch hole (*cebadero*)	*tlequiquizxictli*, "fire-trumpet vent"
Embrasure, gunhole	*tlequiquiztlacoyoctli*, "fire-trumpet cavity"

SOURCE: Molina.

ing of one of the Spaniards' more radical introductions, the wheel. Harnessed revolution was best known to preconquest central Mexicans through the spindle, the word for which, *malacatl*, had already been used to signify roundness in other contexts before the conquest.[9] Among the terms formed in this way was *temalacatl*, literally "stone spindle," in reference to a large round (but flat) stone used in ceremonies and sacrifices in preconquest temple complexes.[10] Although totally immobile, the object closely resembled an Old World wheel in appearance, so that the introduced wheel was identified as "temalacatl" rather than as "malacatl" itself. The wheel in general, however, had little immediate impact on America. Only in the form of the two huge wooden wheels that were the outstanding feature of the oxcart was it to become a prominent part of central Mexican life in the first generation or so after the conquest. Being of wood, a cartwheel was called a *quauhtemalacatl*, literally "wooden stone spindle" (though the etymological sense of "temalacatl" was clearly no longer felt). This secondary construction then became more important in the vocabulary than the form from which it derived.

With "quauhtemalacatl" established, an associated complex arose comparable to the one around "tlequiquiztli" (see Table 7.3). First the term was extended to mean the whole cart; naming something after its most essential or striking part has happened again and again in the history of human language.* Then the term was used in qualified identifications to name the most important appurtenances, actions, and personnel of carting. Whether because

*Practically the same construction occurs today in colloquial English's use of "wheels" for an automobile.

of its unwieldiness or because carts began to impinge on central Mexico later than firearms, leaving less time for the expression to get rooted before borrowing from Spanish began, "quauhtemalacatl" lacked the staying power of our first example. In Molina, it is something of an archaism, for Spanish *carreta* is already attested several times in the 1550's.[11]

Later we will see that in Stage 2 the grammatical characteristics of Spanish words were crucial to the process of borrowing them; nouns were easier to borrow than words in other categories. In Stage 1, this distinction did not yet obtain. Little or nothing was being borrowed; even more to the point, the Nahuas were mainly not reacting to Spanish linguistically at all, but denominating in their own language out of its own means certain phenomena that they had directly observed. When a Spanish introduction attracting the Nahuas' attention was an action, it could be treated in the same way as an object. The most widespread verbal neologism was a description: *quaatequia* (usually written with an *a* missing, *quatequia*), "to throw water on someone's head," for the act of baptizing a person.[12] The word is found on almost every page of the Cuernavaca census records and has survived as the definitive expression down to this day. It also gave rise to a modest complex of the usual type, including equivalents of baptismal font, baptistry, and baptismal register, as well as a noun "baptism."[13]

A similar construction, also denoting a Christian religious ceremony, was *tzonilpia*, "to tie one's head (hair)," to denote the rite of confirmation. The reference is to the bishop's act of tying a ribbon around a child's head as a token of the sacrament. No firm evidence exists that this descriptive neologism in fact originated during Stage 1. Molina has different equivalents for religious confirmation, and the earliest known attestation is a passage in Chimalpahin speaking of an event of 1592 and probably written even later.[14] Yet

TABLE 7.3

The Early Complex Around the Cart

English	Nahuatl equivalent
Wheel	*temalacatl*, "stone spindle, revolving thing of stone"
Cartwheel	*quauhtemalacatl*, "wooden wheel (stone spindle)"
Cartwheel axle	*quauhtemalacaelquauhyotl*, "wooden-wheel interior timber"; *quauhtemalacatl ic çotoc*, "what a wooden wheel is pierced with"; *quauhtemalacatl itic onoc*, "what lies inside wooden wheels"
Cart	*quauhtemalacatl* (i.e., the same as "cartwheel")
Cart bed	*quauhtemalacatlapechquauhyotl*, "wooden-wheel platform timber"
To transport by cart	*quauhtemalacahuia*, "to use a wooden wheel on something"
Cart driver	*quauhtemalacayacanqui*, "wooden-wheel guide"
Carter, cart builder	*quauhtemalacaxinqui*, "wooden-wheel carpenter"

SOURCE: Molina.

the expression has all the earmarks of the early stage and is so similar in every respect to "quatequia" that I think it must have been coined at the time of the first confirmations, which is to say, several years after the first baptisms of children. At any rate, "tzonilpia" like "quatequia" has remained in the language, rendering a loanword unnecessary.

Note that both expressions describe the visible act accompanying the rite, ignoring the words spoken or the intended purpose of the ceremony, both of which may well have been un-understood by the great majority of the Nahuas participating. The Nahuatl idiom "to see mass," using the verb *itta*, rather than "to hear mass" as in Spanish and English, probably also goes far back, if not actually to Stage 1, and has the same rationale; like the other expressions, it survived into much later times.*

As we saw in the use of "wooden wheel" to mean cart, extension of meaning often took over where transparent description left off, employing standard worldwide linguistic processes, among them, as in this case, widening a part to the whole, or a member of a class to the whole class (we will see some further examples of synecdoche below). More generally, extensions broadened a meaning to include additional similar things. As mentioned above, under the special circumstances of the first meeting of Spaniards and Nahuas, such metaphorical extensions are logically indistinguishable from identifications, and two of the most important—"deer" for "horse" and "copper" for "iron"—are of this type.

The deer, *maçatl*, was the only large grazing animal known to the Nahuas; as a fleet, hoofed, grass-eating quadruped, it surely had a great deal in common with the horse. Furthermore, since the deer was unique as far as Nahua knowledge went, it was all the more likely to be viewed generically.[15] How, then, can we be sure that "maçatl" for horse was not indeed an identification, based on a perceived overwhelming similarity of the two creatures, despite some superficial idiosyncrasies such as a lack of horns and a tolerance for bearing human beings? Though the question may not be susceptible of rigorous proof, if we consider the Nahuas' elaborate botanical and biological nomenclature, their propensity for devising different names for a multitude

---

*I mentioned in Chapter 3 that I am not sure whether the term -*namic*, "spouse," and the verb derived from it, *namictia*, "to marry," are postconquest innovations or not, although in postconquest times the -*namic* complex referred for the most part exclusively to marriage sanctioned by Christian sacrament. If the marriage meaning was new, and I increasingly suspect that it was, it could be considered a description, since the relevant sense of -*namic* here is "match, mate." The expression would differ from the examples just discussed in fastening on abstract characteristics rather than visible motions. In this, it is like a term such as *yolcuitia*, "to declare one's heart," for "to confess" to a priest. Here, too, there may have been a preconquest precedent. In any case, words like these imply greater communication between the two sides and greater comprehension on the part of the Nahuas, whenever it was that they became accepted among Nahuatl speakers with the postconquest meanings.

(see Table 7.4)

TABLE 7.4

Early Compound Words Based on the Extension of Maçatl ("Deer") to "Horse"

English (Spanish)	Nahuatl equivalent
Stable	_maçacalli,_ "deer house"
Stall	_maçatlaqualtiloyan,_ "place where deer are fed"
Fodder	_maçatlaqualli,_ "deer food"
Green fodders (_alcacer, herrén_)	_xoxouhqui maçatlaqualli,_ "green deer food"
To graze or feed horses	_maçatlaqualtia,_ "to feed deer"
Pasture, grazing grounds	_maçatlatlaqualtiloyan,_ "place where deer are made to nibble (graze)"; _mamaça intlaquaquayan,_ "the deer's nibbling place"
To shoe horses	_maçacactia,_ "to put footwear on deer"
Horseshoer	_maçacacti,_ "one who puts footwear on deer"
To put a packsaddle on a beast of burden	_maçatlamamalpechtia,_ "to make a base for a deer's load"
To hobble a horse	_maçamailpia,_ "to tie a deer's hands"
To brand livestock	_maçamachiotia,_ "to put identifying marks on deer"
To tame colts	_maçamachtia,_ "to teach deer"; _maçatlatlacahuiloa,_ "to cajole and persuade deer with kind words and gifts"
Colt trainer	_maçamachtiani,_ "teacher of deer"; _maçatlatlacahuiloani,_ "cajoler and persuader of deer"
Balky horse (_harón_)	_tlatzihuini maçatl,_ "lazy deer"
Horse comb, curry-comb	_maçatepoztziquahuaztli,_ "metal comb for deer"
Mouth disease of horses (_haba_)	_maçaquetolcocoliztli,_ "deer gum disease"

SOURCE: Molina.

of closely related varieties (as with their minute classification of what for the Spaniards were all merely ducks), then we must conclude that we are dealing with a conscious extension of the word to an animal recognized from the start as radically distinct.

Needless to say, a complex arose around "maçatl" as around the other expressions, of the same type but probably much more extensive in view of the pervasiveness of the horse in early postconquest Spanish life in Mexico. Even though a Spanish loan had taken over by the time of Molina's dictionary, one still finds there a large number of "deer" compounds for equine phenomena (see Table 7.4); there must have been even more of them earlier. The extension had become so familiar that for a while it may have survived even after the advent of the loanword as an alternative expression, especially in compounds.[16] But it would soon be gone from everyday speech, lingering only in the collective memory by the later sixteenth century. Its quick demise after such a strong start is no doubt to be attributed partly to the unequaled dominance of the horse in the postconquest situation and the frequency with which the Spanish word must have been pronounced in Spanish-Nahua contact episodes. Yet we should not forget that "maçatl" continued to refer to an important indigenous game animal, which was also prominent in Nahuatl idioms as a symbol of bestiality; ultimately, two terms were needed, not one.

Comparable in many ways to "maçatl" was *tepoztli*, "copper," which became the word for iron and metals in general.[17] It is hardly accidental that the two great identification/extensions of Stage 1 had to do with iron and the horse, the two features of Old World culture that made the conquest of America possible. Nevertheless, the corpus of expressions referring to them is not strongly martial in tone, for both played crucial roles in the establishment of Hispanic civil life in the country of the Nahuas, a process already beginning to gather strength during the first generation of occupation. Iron, perhaps generally the more important of the two items, surely affected more aspects of life, and the complex around the word designating it was correspondingly large. Moreover, the Nahuatl word in its extended meaning persisted well past Stage 1; though the complex surrounding it would gradually shrink, yielding to loans, the basic term and certain derivations have remained current through the centuries until our days.

At first the expression seems to have been a qualified identification, since under iron Molina gives *tliltic tepoztli*, "black copper," and under steel we find *tlaquahuac tliltic tepoztli*, "hard black copper."[18] Yet "tliltic" does not accompany "tepoztli" in any of Molina's many complex constructions based on the word and does not appear in attestations of "tepoztli" in texts of various kinds. My surmise is that the modification served as a transitional device justifying and explaining the identification but was dropped as unwieldy as soon as the equation began to take hold, leaving what looks like a simple extension. Thus the result after a few years resembled "maçatl" but was attained through a somewhat different avenue.[19] That a color designation should have been used was in keeping with Nahuatl metal nomenclature. *Teocuitlatl*, for example, was precious metal in general; when modified by *iztac*, "white," it meant silver, and when modified by *coztic*, "yellow," it meant gold (since gold was the more common in preconquest days, the unmodified form was usually taken to refer to that metal, even after the conquest when silver gradually took over).

Copper was a natural choice as an item to equate with iron; the role of iron among the Europeans as the premier workable, nonprecious metal for the manufacture of useful objects had an exact parallel in copper among the Nahuas. Yet though the word tepoztli did specifically mean copper as opposed to such other known nonprecious metals as lead and tin, which had their own names (*temetztli* and *amochitl*, respectively), it was inclined to a generic sense even more than the words for iron in European languages.[20] Indeed, though the vast majority of postconquest expressions using "tepoztli" refer to iron, the word continued to designate copper at times, as well as such

TABLE 7.5

Early Compound Words Based on the Extension of "Tepoztli"
("Copper, Metal for Useful Objects") to "Iron" and Other New Metals

English	Nahuatl equivalent
Blacksmith	*tepozpitzqui*, "copperworker, forger of metal"
Anvil	*tepoztlatzotzonaloni*, "metal instrument for pounding something"
Hammer	*tepoztlatetzotzonaloni*, "metal instrument for pounding something with a stone"
Saw	*tepozchichiquillateconi*, "metal instrument for cutting by scraping"
Woodcutting axe	*tepozquauhxexeloni*, "metal instrument for splitting wood"
Chisel	*tepoztlacuicuihuani*, "metal instrument for chipping at something"
File	*tepozichiconi*, "instrument for scraping metal"
Nail, spur	*tepozhuitztli*, "metal spine or thorn"
Horseshoe	*tepozcactli*, "metal footwear"
Fishhook	*tepozcololli*, "a bent thing of metal"
Wire	*tepozicpatl*, "metal thread"
Chain	*tepozmecatl*, "metal rope"
Pin	*tepoztlatlatzicoltiloni*, "metal instrument for sticking things together"
To brand livestock	*tepozmachiotia*, "to make an identifying mark with metal"
Rust	*tepozpoxcauhcayotl*, "metal mold"
To print	*tepoztlacuiloa*, "to write (paint) with metal"
Printer	*tepoztlacuilo*, "metal writer"
Manacles	*tepozmailpiloni*, "metal instrument for tying someone's hands"
Coat of mail	*tepozmatlahuipilli*, "metal net blouse"
Lance	*tepoztopilli*, "metal staff"
Sword	*tepozmacquahuitl*, "metal hand-stick (club with obsidian inserts)"
Dagger	*tepozteixilihuaniton*, "little metal instrument for stabbing people"

SOURCE: Molina.

introduced nonferrous metallic substances as bell metal.[21] Nahuatl expressions containing the term also fail to distinguish between iron and steel. Thus though associated with iron, postconquest "tepoztli" essentially meant all nonprecious, usable metal, and "metal" is often the best translation. This versatility, making it more useful than the Spanish word *hierro*, helps account for the longevity of "tepoztli"; the fact that the use of copper soon faded to insignificance after the conquest may have been a contributing factor.

Not only was the complex surrounding "tepoztli" larger than any other we have seen, it was of a somewhat different kind (see Table 7.5). Previous complexes have concentrated on items ancillary to the central item designated by the neologism, thus returning tightly upon themselves. With "tepoztli," only a few words are of that nature, such as the equivalents of blacksmith and anvil. The great bulk, of which Table 7.5 gives only a small selection, name an introduced metal artifact by prefixing "tepoz-" to an identification or description.[22] Since such artifacts were among the most numerous and striking of all Spanish introductions, the complex spreads in many directions, showing immense variety. Here the Nahuas had hit on something like a gen-

TABLE 7.6

Uses of "Tepoztli" as "Iron" in the Meaning "Metal Device"

English	Nahuatl equivalent
Hoe, mattock	*tlaltepoztli,* "earth iron"
Axe for dressing wood	*tlaximaltepoztli,* "(wood) shaving iron"
Adze	*matepoztli,* "hand iron"
To frizz cloth	*tepoztica ixpochina,* "to fluff, tease with an iron"
To stab with a dagger	*tepoztica ixili,* "to stab with an iron"
Bell	*miccatepoztli,* "dead-person iron"
Striking clock	*tlapohualtepoztli,* "count iron"
Belfry, campanile	*tepoztli ipilcayan,* "place where an iron hangs"

SOURCE: Molina; TCB, p. 9; TA, p. 70.

eral qualifier, limited it is true to things of metal, but nevertheless a significant fraction of all introductions.

Another way in which "tepoztli" produced words to designate new artifacts was through the figure of speech, found in many languages, naming an object after the material of which it is made (see Table 7.6), so that any tool of metal could be a tepoztli. Exactly the same construction occurs with "iron" in English, as in "shooting iron," "branding iron," or "iron" for clothes, and also with *hierro* in Spanish. It is unlikely, however, that the Nahuatl usage is a direct imitation of Spanish phrases, not only because in general the Spanish linguistic aspect played such a small role in Stage 1, but because for the most part the items to which this kind of extension was applied were different in the two languages.[23] It is entirely possible that "tepoztli" already named tools of copper in the preconquest period; the glyph of Tepoztlan includes a (copper) axe which, if the rebus writing is to produce the desired result, must have had the value "tepoztli."[24]

When the rush of Spanish loanwords began in Stage 2, terms for metal objects were an important category among them, cutting deeply into the use of "tepoz-" compounds. Even the relatively few that survived for a time were often streamlined by dropping the "tepoz-." Remember that "tliltic," "black," at first modified "tepoztli" to identify iron, then was dropped when the meaning was established and the introduction became familiar, in order to achieve the necessary compactness; the process repeated itself with "tepoz-" (and we will see it yet again in other contexts). Thus Molina has *tepoztlateconi,* "metal instrument for cutting something," in the meaning "axe," but in Stage 2 texts, one finds simple *tlateconi,* "instrument for cutting."[25] Most of the words in Table 7.5 fell by the wayside before the end of the sixteenth century.[26] An important exception is *tepozpitzqui,* "blacksmith," which indefinitely remained the undisputed term in use, as did tepoztli itself for iron and metal.* The expressions in which "tepoztli" means a metal device (Table 7.6) also hung on well into Stage 2 and in some cases longer.[27]

Up to this point I have been speaking as though Stage 1 involved no incorporation of Spanish words at all, but it did include the borrowing of some proper names. Indeed, one class of these was numerous: the Christian names (Spanish in form) that the ecclesiastics gave to all the Nahuas they baptized, and that the baptized Nahuas thereafter used as their own, together with their indigenous names, in everyday life. The censuses of the Cuernavaca region are full of examples. The core consists of common or reasonably common Spanish first names, with others taken from the Bible and religious history in accordance with the tastes of the ecclesiastics, who at first were virtually the sole determiners of the repertoire of names and probably in most instances of the names given to specific individuals.[28]

Presumably, Nahuas in various places also spoke the names of any Spanish layman or ecclesiastic with whom they had frequent dealings, or of any person who became famous or notorious in a certain area, though no direct contemporary record of such borrowing seems to remain. Somewhat posterior attestations do strongly hint that Cortés's indigenous interpreter doña Marina was called Malintzin or doña (tonan, tona, tonna) Malintzin.[29] As we see in this example, Spanish names were assimilated to Nahuatl in pronunciation, and when it was felt appropriate, Nahuatl elements could be added, here the reverential syllable -*tzin*. These facets of borrowing were to continue in Stage 2, under which they will be discussed more fully.

Among the Spanish appellations incorporated in Stage 1 were some elements that were strictly speaking titles rather than names. "Don" and "doña" occur regularly in the Cuernavaca census records attached to the baptismal names of people of high degree.[30] I take it, however, that they were construed simply as parts of certain names; the line between title and name was not sharply drawn in preconquest Nahuatl in any case. The same applies to the title Marqués, which, written "Malquex," appears frequently by itself in the census records from Tepoztlan.[31] Since Cortés was the only marqués in evidence in Mexico at that time and after about 1530 was generally called by the title alone by local Spaniards, the word was functioning just like a name in both languages.

One Spanish place-name found its way into Nahuatl in Stage 1, and a

---

* *Tepozpitzqui* differs in important ways from the other compounds in Table 7.5. First, in most of the others, *tepoz-* is simply a modifier; here it is the object of an action, the compound meaning "one who smelts iron or metal." Second, it fits a preconquest model in which the name for a worker in a certain metal consisted of the word for that metal plus -*pitzqui*, "forger, smelter." The entire word existed in preconquest times (the only one on the list of which that can be said), then meaning "copperworker," and it continues to figure with that now secondary meaning in Molina (f. 104).

TABLE 7.7

Some Early Uses of "Caxtillan," "Castile," to Describe Spanish Introductions

English (Spanish)	Nahuatl equivalent
Ship	*Caxtillan acalli,* "Castile boat"
Paper	*iztac Caxtillan amatl,* "white Castile paper"
Glass (container)	*Caxtillan tehuilocaxitl,* "Castile crystal bowl"
Spanish (language)	*Caxtillan tlatolli,* "Castile speech"
Clogs (*zuecos*)	*Caxtillan cactli,* "Castile sandals"
Balsam	*Caxtillan copalli,* "Castile copal"
Chicken	*Caxtillan totolin,* "Castile turkey hen"
Peacock	*Caxtillan quetzaltototl,* "Castile quetzal bird"
Sardine	*Caxtillan michhuatzaltepiton,* "little dried fish of Castile"
Wheat	*Caxtillan tlaolli,* "Castile maize (the grain)"; *Caxtillan centli,* "Castile maize (the ear)"
Miller	*Caxtillantlaoltezqui,* "Castile-maize grinder"
Wheat bread	*Caxtillan tlaxcalli,* "Castile bread"
Muffin	*Caxtillan tlaxcalçonectli,* "soft, crumbly bread of Castile"
Sugar	*Caxtillan chiancaca,* "sweet substance (made from chía) of Castile"
Garlic	*Caxtillan xonacatl,* "Castile onion"
Leek	*huey Caxtillan xonacatl,* "big Castile onion"
Pepper	*Caxtillan chilli,* "Castile chile" [a]
Carrot	*Caxtillan camotli,* "Castile camote"
Lentil	*Caxtillan pitzahuac etl,* "slender bean of Castile"
Broad bean (*haba*)	*Caxtillan ayecotli,* "fat bean of Castile"
Mint	*Caxtillan epaçotl,* "Castile epazote"
Rose	*Caxtillan xochitl,* "Castile flower" [b]

SOURCE: Molina.
[a] Also used for cloves and spices of the East Indies generally.
[b] Also for any introduced flower.

very significant introduction it was. Early attempts at communication between indigenous people and the outsiders must have frequently touched on the topic of where the outsiders came from, with the newcomers as interested in telling as the Nahuas were in knowing. Though the Spaniards usually referred to themselves as *españoles*, when asked about their homeland their reply was nearly always Castilla, "Castile," which in Nahuatl became Caxtillan.[32] Once current, the word proved useful not primarily as a way to talk about Spain the place (though it was indeed so used) but as the most all-inclusive of the modifiers of names and descriptions of introduced phenomena. (See Table 7.7, which gives only a sample.) While it could be added to longish descriptive expressions when desired, it served above all to form simple, compact qualified identifications, deploying a Nahuatl noun to draw the parallel and the modifying "Caxtillan" to make the distinction.[33] "Tepoztli" acted in much the same way, but its range was restricted to objects of metal. These two great modifiers seem to have been in roughly complementary distribution; "Caxtillan" was hardly used in connection with metal objects.[34] Nor does it seem to have modified words referring to human beings, as useful as it might have been in naming Spanish tradesmen and functionaries; *Caxtillantlaoltezqui* in Table 7.7 for "miller" means not "Castile maize–grinder" but "grinder of Castile maize" (i.e., wheat). Caxtillan was apparently employed primarily to qualify expressions referring to introduced species, foods, and artifacts (not forgetting, however, Caxtillan tlatolli, "Castile speech," for "Spanish").

The added *n* at the end of the word is not there by accident, or even because it was required by Nahuatl pronunciation (that being the reason for most Nahuatl alterations of Spanish loans). Rather Nahuatl speakers, or at least enough of them to set the tone, took it that Spanish "Castilla" not only was structured like one of their own place-names but actually ended in a common Nahuatl locative element. As illogical as such a belief may appear (since if the Spaniards had been cognizant of Nahuatl grammar and vocabulary there would have been no trouble in communicating with them), it is of a piece with the general lack of relation of Stage 1 developments to Spanish linguistic phenomena. In any case, many Nahuatl names for settlements ended in an element *-tlan*, which for simplicity may be considered to mean "(at) the place of"; thus the toponym Coatlan, *coa-* meaning "snake," signifies "(at) the place of snakes." If the nominal stem ended in *l*, the locative element assimilated to it, becoming *-lan*, as in Tlaxcallan (Tlaxcala), "(at) the place of bread." Caxtillan would then be a normal Nahuatl toponym, "(at) the place of *caxtil*," the only peculiarity being that the meaning of the stem was unknown.[35]

That Nahuatl speakers actually construed the word in this fashion might remain in doubt were it not for a popular derivation from it. For as little as "Caxtillan" itself was associated with words denoting people, it served as the basis for a term meaning Spaniard that even in Stages 2 and 3 was to continue to compete with the loanword *español*.[36] In Nahuatl, whenever a place-name ends in "-tlan" or "-lan,"* the word for an inhabitant there replaces the locative element with *-tecatl*; thus a citizen of Tlaxcallan was a *tlaxcaltecatl*. Just so from Caxtillan arose *caxtiltecatl*, "inhabitant of Castile" (that is, Spain).[37] The element "-tecatl" has no other origin than "-tlan/-lan," proving definitely that Caxtillan was considered, by many at least, to have the same structure as Tlaxcallan.[38]

Yet another neologism seems to betray the Nahuas' suppositions about the meaning of the supposed nominal root of Caxtillan. In one of the earliest Nahuatl texts we find the word *caxtil*, signifying "chicken."[39] Molina confirms this sense, and traces of it remain in the language to this day.[40] The

*Strictly speaking these are names of settlements or sociopolitical units rather than toponyms.

nominal root of a Nahuatl -*lan* word pointed to some striking aspect of the region, and nothing was more striking about the Spaniards than the animals they brought from their homeland. It would be a not unnatural deduction to conclude that Spain might have been named after them, or after some one of them. Perhaps the Nahuas never really thought of Spain as the "land of chickens," but it is hard to find any other explanation of how they arrived at the meaning (and in records that have reached us, the word has no other).[41]

Like the other modifiers we have seen, the role of Caxtillan was to be transitional. Many of the expressions using it, such as those for wheat, garlic, and broad beans, were to cede to Spanish loanwords early in Stage 2. But even when the Nahuatl word persisted, precluding a loan, Caxtillan was dropped in due course as the Spanish introduction became familiar, or in many cases predominant over the parallel indigenous phenomenon. There was no longer any point in modifying *amatl* in the meaning "Spanish-style paper" at a time, and it came quickly, when Spanish paper was virtually the only type in common use. The same thing tended to happen, however, even when the indigenous variant remained current along with the introduced item. Thus *Caxtillan totolin* generally gave way to simple *totolin* in reference to the chicken, that animal for which the Nahuas invented so many names, even though the same word designated the still popular turkey. In the long run, avoiding an awkward expression was more important than avoiding a possible ambiguity.

"Caxtillan" survived into Stage 2 mainly restricted to actual references to Spain, though it could still be used as an ad hoc modifier to resolve ambiguities (rather than as an automatic part of an expression). An entry of 1610 in a Xochimilco cofradía account book, for example, speaks of a purchase of "Caxtilla tlapalli," "Spanish colors" for painting, as opposed to indigenous materials, which were also in use, both usually called simply "tlapalli."[42] Caxtillan as a toponym and caxtiltecatl for Spaniard also continued in use indefinitely.* "Tepoztli" and "Caxtillan," then, each enjoyed great vogue as a Stage 1 modifier, but that role was sharply reduced as Stage 2 began, leaving each word in use in its core meaning plus a few sturdy derivations.

It is tempting to think of Caxtillan and the borrowing or adoption of Spanish names generally as coming chronologically late in Stage 1.† Yet doña Marina's name seems to have become familiar during the conquest it-

---

*In later generations, *caxtiltecatl* like Spanish *español* referred not necessarily to someone actually born in Spain but to any ethnic Spaniard wherever he was born (this being the meaning of *español* in the Mexican Spanish of the time). Thus in a document of 1738 from Azcapotzalco the term is applied to a person who was of at least the second generation, since he had inherited locally from his father (BC, doc. 17, p. 100).

†A chronological lag could explain why Caxtillan was not used to modify *maçatl* and *tepoztli*.

self, along with the names of other key figures perhaps,[43] and it is precisely in the very first encounters that the Spaniards are likely to have uttered the word Castilla repeatedly. Here we encounter a problem basic to the nature of Stage 1 in general. Was there an initial Nahuatl resistance to borrowing Spanish nouns, or put more neutrally, a lack of propensity or ability, with proper nouns acting, after a time, as the entering wedge, leading to a breaking of the barrier in Stage 2? That was my initial view of the matter.[44] Now I tend to think that Nahuatl was never characterized by a resistance to incorporating Spanish nouns or an inability to do so; the main limiting factor, it seems to me, was the simple lack of opportunity to hear the Spanish words and learn what they meant.[45] The names borrowed at some point in Stage 1 behave exactly like the ordinary nouns of early Stage 2, that is, they accept indigenous affixes, they are assimilated to Nahuatl in pronunciation and sometimes in morphological interpretation, and the meaning too may go its own way.

Many of the developments of Stage 1 are summed up in two well-defined sets of expressions, one dealing with the new animals, and the other with the new musical instruments. The Old World domestic animals, very few of them with any close indigenous parallel, deeply engaged the Nahuas' attention from the first, and almost all generated one or more Stage 1 expressions (see Table 7.8). These include identification/extensions, most prominently "maçatl," already discussed, but also *coyametl*, "peccary," for pig.[46] Other names are qualified identifications: *mizton*, "little cougar," for cat, and some "Caxtillan" modifications, "Castile turkey" for chicken and "Castile wild duck" for domesticated duck. Descriptions also abound: *quaquauhe*, "one with horns," originally for any bovine animal, then later gradually restricted; *tentzone*, "bearded one," for goat; and *quanaca*, "head flesh," in reference to the rooster's comb and hence to the whole animal, then including the chicken as well. I have already mentioned the neologism "caxtil" for chicken, as well as its presumed origin. The name for sheep is perhaps the most unusual, but only because two common Stage 1 mechanisms both came into play to form the word. First *ichcatl*, "cotton," was extended by identification to include the new European material wool, and then by synecdoche the material of the animal's coat was taken for the animal.[47]

The animal names are thus a good sample of all the favorite techniques of Stage 1. If they appear especially whimsical or inventive, that is a quality marking the whole era. As a group, their most striking trait is their longevity. Nearly all survived, at least in compounds, into the early years of Stage 2, and several persisted until the end of the colonial period or until today, in some cases obviating any Spanish loan, in others continuing in use, at least in some regions or with some speakers, despite the existence of directly competing loans.[48] Applied first to all cattle, "quaquauhe" generally ceased to apply

TABLE 7.8

Terms for the Main European Domesticated Animals

Animal	Stage 1 (originating before 1540)	Stages 2 and 3 (after 1540–45)
Horse	*maçatl*, "deer"	*caballo* (*cahuallo*), "horse" (Sp.)
Mare	(probably *cihuamaçatl*, "female deer")	first *cihuacahuallo*, "female horse," then *yegua*, "mare" (Sp.)
Colt	(probably *maçaconetl*, "young of the deer")	first *cahualloconetl*, "young of the horse," then *potro*, "colt" (Sp.)
Mule	(probably subsumed under *maçatl*)	*mula*, *macho*, "female and male mule" (Sp.)
Donkey	(probably subsumed under *maçatl*)	*asno*, "donkey" (Sp.)
Sheep	*ichcatl*, "cotton"	still *ichcatl*; also *carnero*, "sheep, mutton" (Sp.), especially for the meat
Cow, bull, ox	*quaquauhe*, "one with horns"	*vaca(s)*, "cow" (Sp.); first *quaquauhe* for both bull and ox, then *toro*, "bull" (Sp.) and *quaquauhe* or *buey* (Sp.), "ox"
Calf	*quaquauheconetl*, "young of those with horns"	(probably *ternero*, *becerro*, "calf" [Sp.])
Yearling	*telpochtli quaquauhe*, "adolescent one with horns"	*novillo*, "yearling" (Sp.)
Goat	(*quaquauhe*)*tentzone*, "bearded one with horns"	*tentzone*
Pig	*pitzotl* (meaning not known); *coyametl*, "peccary"	*pitzotl* becomes predominant
Rooster	*Caxtillan huexolotl*, "Castile turkey cock"; *quanaca*, "(one with) head flesh"	*quanaca* continues to some extent; also a loan?
Chicken	*Caxtillan totolin*, "Castile turkey hen"; *caxtil*, back-formation from *Caxtillan*, "Castile"; also *quanaca* as for rooster	mainly *totolin* or *pollo*, "(young) chicken" (Sp.); *quanaca* continues to some extent
Cat	*mizton*, "little cougar"	still *mizton*
Duck (Eur. domestic)	*Caxtillan canauhtli*, "Castile wild duck"	*pato(s)*, "duck" (Sp.)

SOURCES: Molina; NMY, pp. 55–74.

to cows with the borrowing of Spanish *vaca* in the first wave of loans; *toro*, "bull," followed, leaving the Stage 1 expression with only oxen as its domain, and even there it vied with *buey*; yet it remains the normal word for ox in widely separated Tetelcingo (Morelos) and Zacapoaxtla (Sierra de Puebla) to this day.[49]

The special claim of the new animals on the Nahua mind is perhaps not entirely attributable to their admittedly great impact on the conquest and postconquest scene and their filling of a nearly empty niche in indigenous life. Although the parallel seems impossible to draw rigorously, one cannot help being struck with how much the centuries-long adaptation of Nahuatl to Spanish resembles the process by which a human being acquires language. A

TABLE 7.9

Early Terms for Spanish Musical Instruments and Their Operation

Category	Nahuatl equivalent
"Drums"	
Drum (*atabal*)	*huehuetl*,[a] drum of tightened skin over a cylinder
Six-course guitar (*vihuela*), harp, lute	*mecahuehuetl*, "rope drum, cord drum"
Monochord	*petlacalmecahuehuetl*, "box cord drum"[b]
Organ	*ehuatlapitzalhuehuetl*, "hide wind-instrument drum"
To play an organ or drum	*tzotzona*,[a] "to beat"
To play a plucked stringed instrument[c]	*mecahuehuetzotzona*, "to beat a cord drum"
Wind instruments	
Wind instrument in general	*tlapitzalli*,[a] "something blown"
Flute or *chirimía* (single-reed instr.)	*tlapitzalli*[d]
Fife, high flute	*huilacapitzalli*,[a] "blown [?]"[e]
Bagpipe	*ehuahuilacapitztli*, "hide fife"
Trumpet, trombone (sackbut)	*tepozquiquiztli*, "metal conch horn"
To play a wind instrument, including brass, but especially a flute or reed	*pitza*,[a] "to blow"[d]
To play a brass instrument	*tepozquiquizoa*, "to operate a metal conch horn"
Spanish jingles and rattles (*sonajas*)	*Caxtillan tetzilacatl*, "Castile tetzilacatl"; *tepozayacachtli*, "metal rattle"[f]

SOURCE: Molina.

NOTE: As explained more fully in the text, the Nahuas, having no strings, originally classified nearly all the new instruments under their two principal categories, drums and winds.

[a]These are unmodified preconquest musical terms.

[b]*Petlacalli* means "box" only by extension, referring originally to a chest made of mats.

[c]To my knowledge, neither Molina nor any other source of that time takes cognizance of bowed strings, unless Molina's reference to the monochord be so considered.

[d]With *tlapitzalli* and *pitza*, Molina often mentions brass only as an afterthought.

[e]I have not been able to identify the element *huilaca-*, but since it is associated with the fife (especially clear in Molina, Spanish f. 111v), I take it to have to do with highness.

[f]The *tetzilacatl* was of copper (Molina, Nahuatl, f. 111); the element *tzil-* is reminiscent of ringing. The terms for playing an ayacachtli were *ayacachoa*, "to operate an ayacachtli," and *ayacachquetza*, "to raise an ayacachtli" (Molina, Nahuatl, f. 3); presumably they would apply to the *tepoz-* form as well. Of the word for playing a tetzilacatl nothing is known.

preoccupation with animals plays a large role in a child's acquisition of a language, and the same phenomenon appeared in the early stages of the linguistic reaction of Nahuatl to the Spanish presence.

Coming to the set of expressions related to introduced musical instruments, we find the type of thing we have come to expect, namely, some identification/extensions and some descriptions, here all qualified identifications (see Table 7.9). The musical terms are notable for their clear demonstration of how fully the Nahuas continued to rely on their own established lexical categories. In this case, the results tend to seem quaint, if not bizarre, to those of us brought up in the European musical tradition, but the same principles were at work everywhere. Before the conquest, the Nahuas had placed a high value on music, employing song and dance at both public ceremonies and more private entertainments, and accompanying such performances with musical instruments.* Instrumentalists bordered on the professional, cared much about precision and effect, and had mastered many special techniques, including a drumbeat notation that has still to be fully deciphered.[50] Thus the Nahuas were immediately interested in the musical instruments of Europe, at which they were soon to become adept.[51] The problem in devising adequate expressions for the new introductions was that while the European system recognized three main types, winds, strings, and percussion, the indigenous system recognized only two, winds and percussion.

Actually, we have no indication that the Nahuas had a category percussion as such. Rattles and jingles, things one shakes, stood apart and were readily identified with their Spanish counterparts. Everything else had to be a wind instrument or a drum; the existence of these two categories is betrayed by distinct terms for playing them, essentially the same as the Europeans used: for winds, *pitza,* "to blow," and for drums *tzotzona,* "to beat." The word *tlapitzalli,* "something blown," usually referred to the Nahua wind instrument par excellence, the flute, but the *quiquiztli* or conch-shell horn could be subsumed under that term. With these words as tools, creating designations for European winds was a straightforward task. European drums could simply be called *huehuetl* like the Nahua instrument of taut deerskin over a cylinder.[52]

It was only the strings, then, that, from a European perspective at least, would have presented a challenge for the Nahuas. Since bowed strings were rare among the Spaniards in Mexico in the conquest period, they could be ignored for the moment. This left the plucked stringed instruments, which the Nahuas settled on calling drums while recognizing the role of the strings; hence they resorted to the qualified identification *mecahuehuetl,* "cord drum." The term applied equally to guitar (*vihuela*), lute, and harp, the main Spanish plucked strings. All did have some kind of resonating chamber and were

---

*Nahuatl generic terms in the area of music did not coincide closely with the approximate European counterparts. Since the observed phenomena could be named equally well in either system, the divergence apparently caused little or none of the innovation and borrowing that the specific introduced artifacts were to occasion. No general term equivalent to "music" has been identified. Molina's entry "musica" (Spanish, f. 88) is restricted to the art of singing, giving the word *cuicatl,* a close approximation of what is conveyed by the word "song" in the European languages, i.e., words issued by a person on a definite but varying pitch. The metaphor *in xochitl in cuicatl,* "flower and song," implies a formal composition with considerable attention to the niceties of language, much as in European poetry, but singing was the mode here as well. *Cuicatl* also seems to imply dancing, though special terms for that activity, with emphasis apparently on body movement rather than on footwork, did exist. Song was normally accompanied by instruments, above all the drums, but instrumental music was not *cuicatl.* In one instance, such music is referred to as *in huehuetl in ayacachtli,* "the drum and the rattle" (ANS, p. 152). (The nature of "song" is discussed in more detail in Chap. 9.)

struck, if not exactly beaten, to produce the sound. An oddity was the organ, a wind instrument not blown by a human being and struck with the hands in a percussive manner. Drawing on both typological analogies, the Nahuas came up with the mixed term *ehuatlapitzalhuehuetl*, "hide wind-instrument drum," "hide" referring to the bellows. To play a plucked string or an organ, corresponding to their status as drums, was "to beat" ("tzotzona").[53]

As ratiocinative or far-fetched as some of these terms may seem, they were not the arbitrary inventions of Molina's assistants. "Cord drum" for guitar is found in actual usage, specifically in a list of Mexico City market specialties dating from about mid-sixteenth century.[54] With Stage 2, the Nahuas would quickly begin to borrow the Spanish words for nearly all the current introduced instruments, although in various corners of the land the Stage 1 terms might still be heard.[55] "Tlapitzalli" remained the general word for wind instrument, and "to blow" and "to beat" continued to define the notion of musical performance more than in the European tradition. Looking under "music" in the two most complete dictionaries of local varieties of modern Nahuatl, we find that one has *tlapitzalli*, "blowing," and the other *tlatzotzonaliztli*, "beating."[56]

Generally speaking, the centuries-long three-stage process by which Nahuatl adapted to contact with Spanish drew no comment from Nahuatl speakers,[57] and as slowly and gradually as it took place, it is unlikely that they were conscious of change within their own lifetimes or had any perspective on the overall evolution. The change from Stage 1 to Stage 2, however, represents a partial exception. Stage 1 was so brief, and a myriad of simultaneous changes in the 1540's, in nearly all spheres of life, set the new era so sharply apart from the preceding years, that for a time an awareness existed of the difference, at least in certain circles. Analytical thought was not brought to bear on the problem, but among post-1550 Nahuas, there did grow up a legend of some of the characteristics of Stage 1 speech.

When the Nahua writers of book 12 of the Florentine Codex (concerning the conquest) speak as narrators, they generally use the loanword *caballo* (*cahuallo*) to designate the horse, but when they report Moteucçoma's speech, they have him, as well as his contemporaries, use "maçatl" ("deer," as we have repeatedly seen). This distinction is the symbol of an awareness that the Nahuas at the time of the conquest used no Spanish loanwords. Further, the conquest generation is reported as describing Spanish phenomena in rather extravagant and naïve terms. A symbol had also arisen for this whole side of conquest-period speech; the Florentine Codex writers have their predecessors using the term *teotl*, "god," for the Spaniards.[58]

That these two expressions conveyed the essence of Stage 1 speech to Nahuas of the late sixteenth century beyond the group of Florentine Codex writers can be seen by a passage in a set of annals of Mexico City dating from that time, purporting to quote an address by Moteucçoma to the people: "atle quiqua yn immaçavan yn teteo," "the deer of the gods have nothing to eat" (i.e., the Spaniards' horses need fodder). Actual set Stage 1 expressions of the types discussed above, beyond those that remained current in the later period, are not at all frequent in Florentine Codex quotes of first-generation Nahuas—perhaps the writers were already somewhat out of touch with them.*

Stage 2

By around 1545, when the Nahuas in some subregions were beginning to produce texts in their own language on a regular basis, the barrier to borrowing Spanish nouns, whether it had been an internal block or a lack of opportunity, had been removed. With the gates open, a hundred-year period of borrowing virtually only nouns began with a flood of basic loans in the second postconquest generation, perhaps around 1545–70.† Molina's first edition of his Nahuatl dictionary (1555) already shows most of the loans contained in the expanded, definitive edition of 1571.[59] The Molina dictionary by itself establishes that a solid core of Stage 2 vocabulary rushed into the language in the time of the second generation. Doubtless a great many more words of a similar nature came in at the same time, but it is hard to know how many or what proportion of the total of Stage 2 loans they represent.

Mundane Nahuatl texts contemporary with Molina (and even antedating him) expand our knowledge of the total loan vocabulary considerably and duplicate many of Molina's items. But they also fail to attest many of them. It is a matter of chance whether a specific loan turns up in a specific document, and some loans have much more reason to be mentioned than others. The upshot is that loans must have been more numerous than present attestations, and that some words first attested at a late time must in fact have been borrowed many years earlier. The general impression remains that an overwhelming input came in the second generation, followed by sustained if less spectacular borrowing through the late sixteenth century and on into the seventeenth.

Clearer than the precise quantity and rate of the borrowing is its nature,

---

*CA, p. 57. I will not discuss here the interesting possibility that certain Nahuas in close touch with Spaniards during Stage 1 may not only have used some Spanish words (perhaps the phenomenon is as much code switching as borrowing), but in the not yet regularized situation employed terms that Nahuatl would not borrow for centuries, if ever. The Cuernavaca-region censuses raise the question. See the brief discussion in NMY, pp. 40–41.

† Although the matter remains in the realm of speculation, it is entirely possible that the onset of Stage 2 (in all its dimensions, not merely the linguistic) is to be attributed not only to the growing Spanish presence, but also to the maturing of a generation of Nahuas who had lived through their formative years in the postconquest period.

which can be treated as a unit for the entire period, since all the categories emerge in the earliest mundane documents and in Molina. The principle remains the same as in Stage 1 to the extent that Stage 2 loans occur under the same conditions as Stage 1 neologisms, both responding to the stimulus of some striking introduction of importance to indigenous people. But now the Nahuas were hearing and reacting to the spoken Spanish words, not just watching what happened. One might naturally expect that loans for tangible, visible objects would precede those with more abstract referents. If that was the case, the interval can have been no more than two or three years at most, and in the sources remaining to us no interval is detectable at all. It appears that in one leap Nahuatl became equipped to incorporate almost any loan, with the single proviso that it be grammatically a noun.[60] Loans other than nouns are minimal during Stage 2, and in most cases even they can arguably be interpreted nominally.[61]

Spanish loans in Nahuatl not only reveal a fascinating autonomous process; they map Hispanic cultural impact on the indigenous world or, to look at it another way, they pinpoint that part of Spanish culture that the Nahuas had reached out to understand, incorporate, and make their own. Table 7.10 gives some notion of the broad range of the loans and where the greatest weight fell. One large block, which had received much attention in Stage 1 as well, had to do with the introduced plants, animals, and objects. Newer were the words designating individual functions and group identities. Interest in the special practices by which the Spaniards organized their world had begun in Stage 1, but now it flourished, attaining a precision before impossible. It is here, in the realms of religion, law, economics, measurement, and calendrics, that one finds loans of a high degree of abstraction, including such an item as *esencia*, the one "essence" of the Holy Trinity.[62] Quantitatively, within the major categories two subgroups stand out in listings of all kinds as the largest and fastest growing: artifacts and characterizations of individuals. Tables 7.11 and 7.12 detail the internal distribution of these subgroupings.

It will be well to give some consideration to the characteristics of the different columns and categories of Table 7.10. The columns based on loans found in individual texts draw on a larger number of attestations, coming from vastly more varied and widespread sources covering a much longer period of time than the columns based on the publications of Molina and Arenas. Yet those publications have the advantage that their authors had access to people with a comprehensive contemporary knowledge of the Nahuatl of their respective times and were not subject to the limitations of certain sources or the vagaries of archival preservation. Thus their listings may be more balanced in some ways; their larger percentages for loans related to introduced plants and animals may be closer to the true situation than the

TABLE 7.10

Proportions of Loan Nouns in Various Categories

(Percent)

Category	Molina, 1571 (N = 221)[b]	Arenas, 1611 (N = 57)	Texts[a]		
			Pre-1650 (N = 496)	1650 forward (N = 224)	Total (N = 720)[c]
I. Concrete					
Introduced biological species and their products					
Plants and fruits	24.9%	10.5%	1.8%	3.6%	2.4%
Animals	3.6	14.0	2.0	3.1	2.4
Derived products	3.6	8.8	2.4	2.2	2.4
Diseases	—	—	0.4	0.4	0.4
SUBTOTAL	32.1%	33.3%	6.6%	9.3%	7.6%
Inanimate objects					
Materials (incl. cloth types, dyes)	1.8	1.8	3.8	2.7	3.5
Artifacts based on new principles and/or material	25.8	31.6	20.2	27.7	22.5
Physical complexes, large stationary features	1.4	1.8	7.3	9.8	8.0
SUBTOTAL	29.0%	35.2%	31.3%	40.2%	34.0%
TOTAL	61.1%	68.5%	37.9%	49.5%	41.6%
II. Quasi-concrete[d]					
Characterizations of individuals	11.3	10.5	24.0	20.5	22.9
Organizations, corporations	0.9	1.8	4.6	3.6	4.3
Places	1.4	3.5	1.6	—	1.1
Other	3.2	—	4.2	1.3	3.3
TOTAL	16.8%	15.8%	34.4%	25.4%	31.6%
III. More abstract[e]					
Religious	8.6	3.5	7.7	2.7	6.1
Legal	1.8	1.8	7.7	7.6	7.6
Other cultural	0.9	—	3.6	8.9	5.3
Measurement, subdivision	10.8	10.5	8.7	5.8	7.8
TOTAL	22.1%	15.8%	27.7%	25.0%	26.8%
GRAND TOTAL	100.0%	100.1%	100.0%	99.9%	100.0%

SOURCE: NMY, p. 17.

NOTE: The table in NMY, p. 17, is essentially the same as this one except that it gives the findings in absolute numbers, not percentages. Columns in this and the following tables do not always total 100 because of rounding. "Molina" and "Arenas" are the publications referred to in the bibliography of this book.

[a] These columns are based on a complete list of loan nouns found in a survey of mundane texts available at the time of publication of NMY; that list is given in detail in Appendix I there.

[b] Twenty loans have been located in Molina since the publication of NMY, enlarging the base; these were classified by category and considered in the computation of percentages.

[c] This column simply presents percentages based on the total number of loan nouns in NMY and hence gives more weight to Stage 2 (from which more loans were first attested) than to Stage 3. Such a procedure is adopted because the time when a given loan was actually made is usually impossible to determine, and late-appearing instances may actually have been borrowed earlier.

[d] Nouns with a concrete referent distinguished by an abstract quality.

[e] Concepts, actions, procedures, imaginary individuals, measurement words.

TABLE 7.11

Proportions of Loan Nouns in Artifact Categories

(*Percent*)

Category	Molina, 1571 (N = 57)	Arenas, 1611 (N = 18)	Texts		
			Pre-1650 (N = 100)	1650 forward (N = 62)	Total (N = 162)
Metal artifacts					
Tools, machines, moving parts	19.3%	27.8%	27.0%	8.1%	19.7%
Weapons	3.5	—	4.0	11.3	6.8
Other	3.5	5.5	6.0	1.6	4.3
SUBTOTAL	26.3%	33.3%	37.0%	21.0%	30.8%
Artifacts not mainly or necessarily of metal					
Clothing or other items of cloth or leather for personal use	35.1	5.5	18.0	19.4	18.5
Religious necessaries	17.6	—	14.0	4.8	10.5
Building components or accessories	—	11.1	6.0	20.9	11.7
Appurtenances of horse and oxen	3.5	11.1	8.0	6.4	7.4
Vehicles	—	—	3.0	9.7	5.6
Furniture and other movable fixtures	1.7	11.1	5.0	4.8	4.9
Musical instruments	3.5[a]	—	4.0[a]	6.5	4.9
Means of illumination	5.3	5.5	3.0	1.6	2.5
Utensils	5.3	22.2	2.0	1.6	1.9
Other	1.7	—	—	3.2	1.2
SUBTOTAL	73.7%	66.5%	63.0%	78.9%	69.1%
TOTAL	100.0%	99.8%	100.0%	99.9%	99.9%

SOURCE: NMY, p. 18.

NOTE: On the data and their sources, see Table 7.10.

[a] Half of metal.

smaller figures compiled from mundane texts, for in the types preserved those categories have relatively little occasion to appear. Both sources have their own biases, however.

Molina was a Franciscan friar and intended his work above all for the use of clerics dealing with the indigenous population, so it is small wonder that religious terminology so outweighs legal among the loans he lists. Furthermore, Molina seems to have had an eye for botanical curiosities and lists some loans for exotic plants that probably never had wide currency (such as boxwood, cedar, oregano, rue, and sage).[63] Arenas sticks much closer to everyday Nahuatl usage, and we can be sure all his loans really were on the lips of Nahuas in the early seventeenth century, but his emphasis is on the practical needs of the secular Spaniard trying to communicate with indigenous people in travel and everyday life, so his range is quite restricted; his small list of loanwords for individuals includes not a single religious functionary

TABLE 7.12

Proportions of Loan Nouns in Categories to Designate Individuals

(Percent)

Category	Molina, 1571 (N = 25)	Arenas, 1611 (N = 6)	Texts		
			Pre-1650 (N = 119)	1650 forward (N = 46)	Total (N = 165)
Names for functionaries					
Legal-governmental	32.0%	50.0%	26.1%	19.6%	24.3%
Ecclesiastical	24.0	—	18.5	13.0	17.0
Other	—	—	3.4	2.2	4.2
High functionaries of religious legend	12.0	—	3.4	2.2	3.0
Persons carrying out temporary or special functions	—	16.7	5.0	6.5	5.5
SUBTOTAL	68.0%	66.7%	56.4%	47.8%	54.0%
Names for practitioners of trades and professions	4.0	16.7	21.8	10.9	8.8
Titles	8.0	—	5.9	—	4.2
Names for members of ethnic and religious groups	8.0	16.7	9.2	10.9	9.7
Indicators of marital and ritual status	12.0	—	4.2	4.3	4.2
Indicators of consanguineous relationships	—	—	0.8	13.0	4.2
Indicators of social status	—	—	0.8	2.2	1.2
Other	—	—	0.8	10.9	3.6
TOTAL	100.0%	100.1%	99.9%	100.0%	99.9%

SOURCE: NMY, p. 19.
NOTE: On the data and their sources, see Table 7.10.

(see Table 7.12). Despite the difference in emphasis of the various sources, they show that the overall corpus of loan nouns looked broadly similar seen from several points of view and across a substantial period of time.

In any case, the percentages and the absolute numbers behind them cannot be compared without taking into account the nature of the categories. As important as the introduced biological species were, their number was finite, whereas artifact types not only were more numerous from the beginning but continued to be introduced. The words for measurement and calendrical counting were of the utmost significance, and before long, the Nahuas had adopted all of them. They loom quite large in Molina and Arenas, but less so in the pre-1650 list from texts and still less in new loans listed after 1650, not because they were not in use or less important than before, but because there were no more terms left to borrow. The same tends to be true of the basic terminology of Christian religion. New legal and other cultural terms of an abstract nature, however, continued to be picked up, not so much because law and secular culture were now relatively more prominent as because of the multiplicity of those realms and the number of words involved.

Comparisons like those just made, drawing inferences from the pre- and post-1650 columns of the compilations from texts, are of great potential interest, but for now they must be carried out with caution and sparingly. As noted earlier, a word can make its first appearance in texts decades or centuries after it actually entered the language, so that an apparent Stage 3 loan may actually belong to Stage 2. Another tool needed in evaluating the relative weight, timing, and trajectory of loans is the technique of frequency counts, something that until now has seemed impractical, but may become feasible as more Nahuatl texts are published.

Many texts have been discovered and transcribed, and quite a few have been made available to the public, since the appearance of the compilations on which the "Texts" columns of Tables 7.10–12 are based.[64] No new general compilation has been made, but the additional loans coming to light seem to follow the established types and trends. Although the absolute numbers in these columns would be considerably larger if all now identified materials could be considered, I believe the proportions would still be roughly as shown.[65]

We now have a complete list of loanwords in the largest single collection of Stage 2 Nahuatl texts to be published since the earlier compilation, the testaments of late-sixteenth-century Culhuacan.[66] If one subjects this list to the same procedures as the earlier general list (see Table 7.13), a familiar picture emerges.[67] Words for artifacts and for individuals again stand out, the former somewhat more and the latter somewhat less than in the larger listing. The greatest apparent discrepancy is the large percentage in the more abstract categories, dominated by the measurement words (the rest of the abstract types are not far out of the general range of Table 7.10). In fact, the difference is only a product of the nature of the source. The measurement words are overwhelmingly names of months and days. Since each testament had to be dated, calendrical words necessarily become a startling proportion of the loans, even though they are only the same ones accounted for in Table 7.10, with its larger universe.[68]

Categorization can only go so far in helping us comprehend the nature and significance of the waves of Spanish loans during Stage 2. There is no substitute for a direct confrontation with the words themselves, especially those most used. Toward that end, in the absence of rigorous frequency counts, I provide in Table 7.14 a list of some of the loans I judge to appear most frequently in texts generally, indicating that they had become a basic part of the Nahuatl vocabulary of the time, uttered and understood by all. Most were probably well established in the language by 1575, and many long before that.

TABLE 7.13

*Proportions of Loan Nouns from the Testaments of Culhuacan
(ca. 1580) in Various Categories*

Category	Number	Percent
I. Concrete		
Introduced biological species and their products		
Plants and fruits	3	2.3%
Animals	3	2.3
Derived products	—	—
Diseases	—	—
SUBTOTAL	6	4.6%
Inanimate objects		
Materials	3	2.3
Artifacts	34	25.9
Physical complexes, etc.	2	1.5
SUBTOTAL	39	29.7%
TOTAL	45	34.3%
II. Quasi-concrete		
Characterizations of individuals	27	20.6
Organizations, etc.	0	0.0
Places	1	0.8
Other	2	1.5
TOTAL	30	22.9%
III. More abstract		
Religious	12	9.2
Legal	14	10.7
Other cultural	5	3.8
Measurement, subdivision	25	19.1
TOTAL	56	42.8%
GRAND TOTAL	131	100.0%

SOURCE: S. Cline 1986, pp. 177–81, which gives the exact TC references. The total number of loans is different here, primarily because some adjectives listed there as separate loans are treated here as part of inseparable noun phrases.

NOTE: The categories are the same as in Table 7.10, with which this table may be compared.

Let me pick out just a few of the most prominent. A surprising number of Nahua homes had *durazno* (peach) or *higo* (fig) trees on the property. Nahuas saw *caballos* or *cahuallos* (horses) and *mulas* (mules) every day, and many traders and nobles owned one. Hardly a household lacked an *hacha* (axe), *cuchillo* (knife), and *caja* (wooden chest with metal hinges);[69] many houses were equipped with a *puerta* (wooden door swinging on metal hinges). Every man wore a *camisatli* (shirt), and most *zaragüelles* (pants) as well. *Gobernador* and *alcalde* were among the most common words in the language of the time; most adults probably had a *comadre* and *compadre*. Everyone went to *misa* (mass) and adored the *cruz* (cross, often pronounced and sometimes written *coloz*) and *santos* (saints). Many people had served as

TABLE 7.14

Common Stage 2 Loans in Various Categories

Category	Loanwords
I. Concrete	
Biological	
Plants and fruits	*pera(s)*, pear; *durazno(s)*, peach; *higo(s)*, fig; *haba(s)*, broad beans; *ajo(s)*, garlic
Animals	*caballo*, horse; *mula*, mule; *vaca(s)*, cow
Derived products	*sebo*, grease, tallow; *tocino*, bacon, dried pork; *queso*, cheese; *vino*, wine
Inanimate	
Materials	*paño*, woolen cloth
Artifacts	*hacha*, axe; *cuchillo*, knife; *azadón*, hoe; *escoplo*, chisel; *cerrojo*, bolt, latch; *caja*, wooden chest; *puerta*, swinging door; *mesa*, table; *taza*, cup; *candela*, candle; *camisa(tli)*, shirt; *zaragüelles*, pants; *frezada*, heavy blanket; *silla*, saddle; *costal*, sack for transport; *trompeta*, trumpet; *chirimía*, reed instrument
Physical complexes	*hospital*, hospital; *mesón*, inn; *tienda*, shop; *coro*, choir loft; *corral*, animal pen
II. Quasi-concrete	
Individuals	*gobernador*, governor; *alcalde*; *regidor*; *fiscal*; *escribano*, notary-clerk; *alguacil*, constable; *testigo*, witness; *obispo*, bishop; *virrey*, viceroy; *compadre*, co-godfather; *comadre*, co-godmother; *español*, Spaniard; *señora*, (Spanish) lady; *mestizo*; *don*; *doña* (titles)
Organizations	*cofradía*
Places	*Perú*
Other	*cruz*, (holy) cross; *imagen*, image; *altar*; *libro*, book
III. More abstract	
Religious	*ánima*, soul; *misa*, mass; *vigilia*, vigil; *dios*, God; *Santísima Trinidad*, Holy Trinity; *espíritu santo*, Holy Spirit; *diezmo*, tithe; *santa iglesia*, the holy church; *santo, santa*, male and female saints
Legal	*juramento*, oath; *testamento*, testament; *firma*, signature; *justicia*, justice, law; *sentencia*, judgment; *licencia*, license; *pena*, fine, penalty; *posesión*, (act of legal) possession; *pleito*, lawsuit
Other cultural	*letra*, letter of the alphabet; *prenda*, pawn, security
Measurement, subdivision	the names of the days and months; *mes*, month; *año*, year; *peso* (the monetary unit); *tomín*, eighth of a peso; *medio*, half a tomín; *fanega*, a dry measure; *almud*, fraction of a fanega; *vara*, yard; *libra*, pound

NOTE: Except for the category "diseases," where there was no common loan at this time, the table is modeled on Table 7.10 and may be taken for an illustration of it. The loans are given in modern Spanish without consideration of Nahuatl phonological adjustments, though a few morphological adjustments are indicated in parentheses.

a *testigo* (witness) on some occasion and taken a *juramento* (oath), and all knew what it meant to receive *posesion* (legal possession) of their land. To function without Spanish names of the days and months would have been an impossibility; equally essential were *tomin* (real, eighth of a peso) and *medio* (half a real).

Loans that were less frequently on the tongues of the general populace were nevertheless a real part of the language. Those who dealt with the law knew the value of an *original* (original signed copy of a document). Builders knew of the *boveda* (vault), those connected with Spanish agriculture of *barbecho* (land lying in stubble), metalworkers of the *punzon* (punch)—in brief, the practitioners of each trade knew its special Spanish vocabulary for tools, materials, and techniques. It is clear that the generality heard and even when appropriate used such terms, perhaps without always understanding the last subtleties of their meaning (as happens with English speakers today in similar situations, even in their own language).

Stage 2 thus represented a cultural and linguistic revolution. Yet continuities from Stage 1 were not lacking. We have seen that the areas of innovation were broadly similar in the two succeeding stages, though extended in Stage 2, and that many Stage 1 expressions continued in use; but the connections go much further. Often when a loan was still in the process of coming into the language or was new to a particular speaker, it would be accompanied as a transitional device by an explanation or equivalent using indigenous vocabulary, and this accompanying language was usually an identification or description in the style of the preceding stage, if not actually an expression coined during that time. Two good examples come from the testaments of Culhuacan: "anzaron tlaltepoztli," "*azadón* [hoe], a land iron," and "xera quauhteconi," "*sierra* [saw], an instrument for cutting wood."[70] At other times, the indigenous expression comes first, and then, as though the speaker were not quite satisfied with it, the Spanish loanword as well to make absolutely sure what is meant.[71] The phrase (*in*) *quitocayotia*, "that they call," came to be a signal of such new or relatively unfamiliar loans. In Chimalpahin, we find "acalli yehuatl yn quitocayotia navio," "a boat, what they call a *navío* [ship]."[72] ("Quitocayotia" was to persist even in Stage 3 as an indication that the speaker felt his hearers might not be well acquainted with the loan he is about to use; the Stage 3 phrase does differ, however, in that sometimes no Nahuatl equivalent is given at all.[73])

Just as in Stage 1 what I have termed complexes formed around important neologisms to reduce the necessity of further innovation, so in Stage 2 such complexes formed around important Spanish loanwords. A prime example is the loanword *cahuallo*, "horse"; the complex built on it is illustrated in Table 7.15. Not only are the typical devices of Stage 1 used to extend the

TABLE 7.15

The Early Complex Around the Loanword "Cahuallo," "Horse"

English (Spanish)	Nahuatl equivalent
Stable	*cahuallocalli,* "horse house"; *cahuallo tlaqualtiloyan,* "where horses are fed"
Groom	*cahuallopixqui,* "horse keeper"
Horseshoe	*cahuallocactli,* "horse footwear"
Horseshoer	*cahuallocacti,* "one who provides footwear to horses"
Saddle	*cahualloicpalli,* "horse seat"; *cahuallo ipan icpalli,* "seat on a horse"
Stirrup	*tepoztlacçaloni,* "metal thing to bear down against with the feet" [a]
Spur	*tepozhuitztli,* "metal spine"; *cahuallo itzapiniloca,* "what a horse is punched or stuck with" [a]
Cinch	*cahuallo icuitlalpica,* "what a horse's back is tied with"
Halter	*cahuallomecatl,* "horse rope"
Bridle (with bit)	*itepoztemmecayo cahuallo,* "metal mouth roping of a horse"
Reins	*cahuallotemmecayotl,* "horse mouth roping"
Hobble	*cahualloxotemecatl,* "horse foot rope"
Stake to tie a horse to	*cahualloquahuitl,* "horse stick"
Trappings, horse blanket	*cahuallopachiuhcayotl,* "horse covering"
To mount	*cahuallo ipan tleco,* "to climb up on a horse"
To dismount	*ipan hualtemo in cahuallo,* "to come back down off a horse"
To ride	*cahuallo ipan yauh,* "to go on a horse"
To hobble	*cahuallomailpia,* "to tie a horse's hands"
Mane	*cahualloquechtzontli,* "horse neck hair" [b]
Fancy rider (*jinete,* with high stirrups)	*cototzyetiuh ipan cahuallo,* "one who goes curled up on a horse"
Muleteer	*oztomecacahuallopixqui,* "traveling-trader horse keeper"
Farrier, horse vet	*cahuallopati,* "horse curer"
To joust	*cahuallopan teixili,* "to stab someone on a horse"

SOURCE: Molina.

[a] In these cases *tepoz-,* "metal," is used instead of *cahuallo.* The two are sometimes nearly equivalent in effect, as in *tepozcactli* for "horseshoe" (see Table 7.5).

[b] Molina defines "quetzontli" (f. 89) as "long hair on the nape of the neck (of a person)," so the description is quite close.

application of the loanword, but many of the expressions go back to a Stage 1 original, merely having put "cahuallo" in place of the now passé "maçatl," as in *cahuallocalli,* "horse house," rather than *maçacalli,* "deer house," for stable (compare Table 7.4). The complex forming around *vino,* "wine," is illustrated in Table 7.16. The process did not necessarily stop at this point, however. As accessories to the main loan became more familiar, they too might be incorporated. *Silla,* "saddle," was borrowed on the heels of "cahuallo."[74] On the other hand, some of the expressions might be retained indefinitely—*vinonamacac* is found for tavernkeeper as late as Chimalpahin—and some, especially those of a verbal nature, became definitive.[75]

Above it was mentioned that the proper names taken into Nahuatl from Spanish during Stage 1 were pronounced in Nahuatl, that is, speakers made

TABLE 7.16

The Early Complex Around the Loanword "Vino," "Wine"

Spanish	Nahuatl equivalent
vino, wine	*vino*[a]
vino tinto, red wine	*tlapalvino*, "colored wine"; *chichiltic vino*, "red wine"
vino aloque, light red wine	*coztic vino*, "yellow-red wine"[b]
doncel vino, mild, mellow wine	*amo tecocoai vino*, "wine that doesn't bite when drunk"
vino de ciruelas o de limones, plum or lemon wine	*xocovino*, "fruit wine" (or "bitter wine")
vinagre, vinegar	*vino xococ*, "bitter wine"
vinagrera, vinegar cruet	*xocovinocomitl*, "bitter wine pot"
bota, small leather wine bag	*vinoxiquipilli*, "wine bag"
cuero, odre, wineskin	*huey vinoehuatl*, "big wine skin"
jarro de vino, winejar	*vinocontontli*, "little wine pot"
bodega, wine cellar, wine shop	*vinocalli*, "wine house"
bodegonero, tavernkeeper, wine seller	*vinonamacac*, "wine seller"
viña, vineyard	*vinomilli*, "wine field"
viñedo, place of vineyards	*vinomilla*, "place of abundance of wine fields"
lagar, wine press	*vinopatzcaloyan*, "place where wine is squeezed out"
viga de lagar, wine-pressing beam	*vinopatzconi huepantli*, "beam for squeezing out wine"
escanciar, to serve wine	*vinoteca*, "to pour wine"

SOURCE: Molina.

[a] Apparently pronounced *huino*, since though *v* is ambiguous, the other possibility, *pino*, never appears in Nahuatl texts to my knowledge. Molina at times writes *u*, as in "xocouino comitl," Nahuatl, f. 160v.

[b] For white wine, Molina gives only *iztac octli*, "white pulque," but I imagine *iztac vino* also occurred.

no changes in their usual pronunciation, but whenever a Spanish word contained a sound not existing in their own language replaced it with the closest familiar sound (as in Malquex for Marqués). The same principle continued to operate in Stage 2, and indeed, with so many more loans, came into full flower. The substitutions were not haphazard, but followed entirely regular patterns, as happens when any two languages meet. Table 7.17 compares the Spanish and Nahuatl sound inventories, specifies many of the most common substitutions, and gives examples.[76] The core of the substitution was caused by Nahuatl's lack of voiced stops, the fricative *f*, and the liquid *r*. For the voiced *b*, *d*, and *g*, Nahuatl speakers pronounced respectively the unvoiced *p*, *t*, and *c* [k], which differ from the first series in nothing but the voiced feature. Spanish *bodega*, "wine cellar, etc.," would have been pronounced *poteca(h)*.* P had to serve also for *f*, and Nahuatl's only liquid *l* for *r*, both illustrated in *pilma(h)* for *firma*, "signature."

Other aspects of Nahuatl phonology also affected the pronunciation of

---

* We know of such pronunciations largely through spellings written down by the Nahuas in the postconquest centuries, confirmed by the pronunciation of older loans in modern Nahuatl. But the spellings are not the same thing as the pronunciations, as we will see.

loans. Nahuatl had no consonant clusters except between vowels, whereas Spanish had many initial clusters, often involving the pesky letter *r*. One frequent solution was to insert a vowel, most likely the same vowel immediately following, between the two consonants: thus *cruz*, "cross," would become *coloz*; similarly Francisco, "Palacixco(h)." Or the second consonant might be omitted altogether, as in *quixtiano(h)* for *cristiano*, "Christian." [77]

In Nahuatl, syllable-final *n* was weak and volatile, often omitted, but also, apparently, frequently inserted instead of other weak segments. In Spanish loans as well, final *n* was often left out, and was also added, especially when the word already had other nasals in it; thus the most frequent form of Spanish *ánima*, "soul," was *animan*.[78] Some alterations go beyond the simple matter of pronunciation. Nahuatl speakers could pronounce words ending in two vowels, but in fact the only words in their language of that type were some verbs in the present tense.[79] With loan nouns ending in two vowels, the Nahuas tended to omit the second, as in *porcatori(h)* for Spanish *purgatorio*, "purgatory."[80] Further, for reasons not yet clear, a glottal stop was added after any loan ending in a vowel (even though many Nahuatl words, including substantives, are vowel-final); this is the *h* that I have been using in indicating pronunciations.

Once rendered pronounceable, a Spanish loan noun was used exactly like any indigenous noun, that is, it was wrapped in all manner of affixes and compounded with other words. *Nanimantzin*, the form found in scores or hundreds of testaments, is "my soul (reverential)." *Amotlaçoanimantzin* is "your dear (or precious) souls."[81] *Imanimantica* would be "in respect to their souls." In one respect, it is true, the majority of loan nouns differed from the majority of indigenous nouns. Most native nouns have a so-called absolutive ending when in the singular and not possessed; the most common such ending is *-tl/-tli/-li* (depending on the nature of the noun stem). Thus in *calli*, "house," *cal-* is the core of the word and *-li* is the absolutive. Most loan nouns did not receive an absolutive ending. A few did, such as the already mentioned "camixatli," "shirt," but this appears to have occurred in the very first decades of Stage 2, and it soon halted, though the words affected have retained the ending to this day.[82] At any rate, various kinds of indigenous nouns also lacked an absolutive singular ending, so loan nouns were not anomalous.

Nahuatl nouns show the unpossessed plural with a separate set of endings much like the plurals in many European languages, though inanimate nouns were mainly not pluralized in older Nahuatl. The plural endings, *-me* and *-tin*, were suffixed to loan nouns in just the same way and under the same conditions as with indigenous vocabulary. Again, however, there was a difference. The Spanish plural ending *(e)s*, pronounced *(e)x* in Nahuatl, also came

TABLE 7.17

The Spanish and Nahuatl Phonemic Inventories and Resulting Nahuatl Substitutions

	Spanish		Nahuatl	Result	Examples of sound substitutions	
					Spanish	Nahuatl[a]
Stops	Unvoiced	Voiced	Unvoiced only	Unvoiced unchanged; voiced replaced by corresponding unvoiced stops[b]		
Labial	p	b/v	p		bachiller	pachilel
Dental	t	d	t		don	ton
Velar	c/qu [k]	g	c/qu [k]		gobernador	copelnatol
Fricatives						
Labiodental	f		No equiv.	Replaced by labial unvoiced stop, p	firma	pilmah
Alveolar	c/z [s]		c/z [s]	Unchanged	—	—
	s (retroflex)		No equiv.	Replaced by x [š]	salero	xaleloh
Palatal	x [š][c]		x [š]	Unchanged	—	—
	j (?)		No equiv.	Replaced by x	Juan	X(i)huan
Affricates						
	ch		ch	Unchanged	—	—
	g (dzh)		No equiv.	Replaced by x	gentiles	xentilex
Liquids						
Lateral	l, ll [ḷ]		l	l unchanged, Sp. ll replaced by identically spelled double l, or sometimes by single l only	caballo	cahual-lo, cahualo
			No equiv.			
Apical	r, rr [ř]		No equivs.	Both replaced by l	regidor (first r is rr)	lexitol
Nasals						
Labial	m		m	Unchanged	—	—
Alveolar	n		n	Unchanged (though devoiced finally and often omitted)	—	—
Palatalized	ñ		No equiv.	Replaced by n or nn	doña	tona, tonna
Glides						
Labial	hu [w]		hu [w]	Unchanged (though respelled uh finally)	—	—
Palatal	y		y	Unchanged	—	—
Vowels						
Front	i		i	Unchanged	—	—
Mid-low	a		a	Unchanged	—	—
Mid-high	e		e	Unchanged (though often i for unstressed e)	Gómez	Comiz
Back-low	o		o	Unchanged	—	—
Back-high	u		No full equiv.	Replaced by o	mula	molah

into play. Sometimes it was used with loan nouns instead of the native ending, but often the endings from both languages appeared simultaneously; "horses" might be *cahuallome, cahuallos,* or *cahuallosme.*[83] Such double plurals are often seen in language contact situations, usually resting on an incomprehension of the function of the plural ending in the other language. Considerable evidence exists for Nahuatl reanalysis of Spanish plurals; with many items seen mainly in the plural, the form borrowed included the plural ending even when a singular was meant, thus *patox,* "duck," *huacax,* "cow," *çapatox,* "shoe," and so forth. Yet in other cases the Spanish plural ending was handled correctly by Spanish standards.*

As a by-product of the morphological integration of loan nouns, their external form was often altered, in an interesting if minor way, even further from the original. The Nahuatl article (with a thousand other grammatical uses) is *in,* of which the *n* was often omitted in speech. When a Spanish loan began *in-* or just *i-,* or even *en-* (given the Nahuatl tendency to interpret unstressed Spanish *e* as *i*), Nahuatl speakers were likely to take that element to be the article and omit it from the word. Spanish *imagen,* "image," can be found written *mage(n),* pronounced *maxe(n); interrogatorio,* "questionnaire," as *telocatolio; encomendero* without its *en-,* and so on.[84]

Although the very point of a loan was to use the word to express its meaning in the language from which it came, the Nahuas may not always have apprehended the Spanish meaning exactly, and in any case, once a loan was incorporated in Nahuatl, it was an independent entity whose significance was no longer directly connected with Spanish. Certain loans thus came to diverge semantically from the Spanish original, though some relation to the Spanish meaning always remained. The most central example is *tomín,* refer-

---

*Having used the *h* to make the point that the glottal stop was added to vowel-final loans, I now revert to the general practice in this book of not notating glottal stop. Notice, however, that when the Spanish plural ending was used with a vowel-final loan, the glottal stop cannot have been present, for the combination would have been unpronounceable.

NOTE TO TABLE 7.17: The table does not attempt to show sounds or distinctions present in Nahuatl and absent in Spanish, since these are largely irrelevant to substitutions in loan vocabulary. Nahuatl had *tl* [tˡ], *tz* [tˢ], *cu/qu* [kʷ], including in syllable-final position, and *h* (glottal stop), all of which were lacking in Spanish. It also differed from Spanish in distinguishing systematically between long and short vowels. Furthermore, all syllable-final consonants were weakened (voiced consonants including glides were devoiced). Actually, some of these sounds and features did affect the pronunciation of loanwords. The modern form of older loanwords in Tetelcingo Nahuatl suggests that Nahuatl speakers of the postconquest period identified Spanish stress with their own long vowels, that is, they pronounced the vowel stressed in Spanish long, no matter where they put the stress in the word, following their own system. Consider *comārehtli* from *comadre* (Brewer and Brewer 1971, p. 24). The Tetelcingo dictionary has many other examples. Nahuatl speakers also added the glottal stop to any vowel-final Spanish loan.

*ª*The Nahuatl forms are hypothetical; these very words are found in texts written with some letter substitutions, but rarely with entire consistency. Here the letters are being used to represent pronunciation.

*ᵇ*Sometimes Nahuatl retained the voiced quality, sacrificing the stop quality, thus replacing *b/v* with *hu* [w], as in *cahualloh* for *caballo,* and *d* with *l* as in *melioh* for *medioh.*

*ᶜ*In 16th-century Spanish, many words now with *j* had *x,* as *caja,* then *caxa,* which was pronounced *caxah* in Nahuatl.

ring to a coin worth one eighth of a peso and also meaning an eighth of a peso generally. Nahuatl quickly borrowed the word, sometimes with the Spanish plural, sometimes restricted to the singular, in the Spanish meaning. It became so ingrained that it was retained even when the most common coin in that value became the silver *real*, which was already happening in the mid-sixteenth century. Almost immediately, the Nahuas extended the meaning, naturally enough, to coin in general, in effect "cash"; the extended meaning was common as early as the 1550's. From that time to this, "tomin" has been the primary word in Nahuatl for money or cash, though it never meant that in Spanish. Spanish *dinero*, "money," was never borrowed.[85]

To take some other prominent examples, *quixtiano*, the Nahuatl rendition of *cristiano*, "Christian," came to mean a person of Spanish birth, *xinola* (*señora*), "lady," a Spanish woman.[86] In the Chalco region, by the late seventeenth century (doubtless earlier in fact), the above-mentioned *telocatolio* (*interrogatorio*), "questionnaire," had become the main term used for "true title" (to land, etc.).[87] Such divergences are exceptional in their sharpness but are representative of the general process. Looking back to Chapter 2 on the altepetl, consider what a different meaning the Nahuas gave to *gobernador*, *alcalde*, and *regidor* from the Spaniards' sense of the terms, even though both parties had the same referents in mind. Every loan differed, subtly or blatantly, in connotation, range of applicability, or other ways, from the original, arriving at that point through the same mechanisms that produced the meaning and usage properties of any Nahuatl word.

Assimilated phonologically, morphologically, and semantically, Spanish loan nouns after about 1550 were fully a part of Nahuatl as spoken. To be sure, they remained in some ways idiosyncratic and identifiable; even after the phonetic adjustments, the sound patterns of loanwords often differed from those of indigenous vocabulary. Although *lexitol* for "regidor" no longer sounds Spanish, no native Nahuatl root or word began with *l*, and no substantive in the absolute form ended in one.[88] But such peculiarities were not different in kind from those distinguishing various subclasses of Nahuatl vocabulary. I much doubt that the ordinary Nahuatl speaker, by 1560 or 1570 if not before, had any consciousness that the more common Spanish loans were new, from the outside, or otherwise different from Nahuatl core vocabulary.

Nor is there any indication that the Nahuas resisted or resented loans as in any way suspect, unpatriotic, or damaging to the integrity of their language. The conscious purism that figures in an ongoing dialectic of linguistic evolution in Nahuatl today seems to be the product of a later time.[89] Surely no attacks on the flood of loans are to be detected in the writings of the Nahuas; indeed, no direct discussion of the matter surfaces at all. All the different types of texts written by the Nahuas themselves drip loanwords from every page. Even the work of the cultural patriot Chimalpahin, written in the highest register, is shot through with them. Only in texts produced under the supervision of Spaniards can one divine any intention to limit the use of loans in favor of indigenous vocabulary; my impression is that the impetus in this direction came from the Spaniards rather than the Nahuas. The attitude toward Spanish words was that shown toward Spanish phenomena generally, a nonpolemical, pragmatic preparedness to adopt whatever seemed advantageous, making no point of what was Spanish and what was not, but seeking familiar elements in the new and soon making it one's own in two ways, by naturalizing it and by identifying with it.

Yet if no recognizable conscious resistance affected the borrowing process, the language itself seemed to resist some types of loans. The more abstract cultural matter referred to in section III of Table 7.10 was expressed in Spanish as much through verbs as through nouns. Although the Nahuas of Stage 2 must have heard those verbs, they did not borrow them, using the nominal cognates instead and, in case of necessity, creating Nahuatl verbs from noun loans instead of incorporating the Spanish verbs directly. Signatures and signing were at the core of Spanish legal authentication. *Firma*, "signature," came into the language very early, and a word "to sign" was also needed, but rather than adopt *firmar*, "to sign," Nahuatl used *firmayotia*, in which through a combination of derivational elements a verb is formed on the basis of the loan noun "firma," meaning "to provide a signature."[90]

Occasionally, one sees the infinitive of a Spanish verb borrowed as a noun, and this noun can then be the object of the Nahuatl verb *chihua*, "to make, do, perform," yielding an equivalent of the verb. Thus with the infinitive of *apelar*, "to appeal," one could say *quichihua apelar*, "he performs appealing" (i.e., he appeals).[91]

Through the sixteenth and early seventeenth centuries, however, even this nominal-infinitive use of Spanish verbs was rare. Spanish verbs had their main impact on Nahuatl during Stage 2 by affecting indigenous verbs in ways reminiscent of Stage 1. That is, indigenous vocabulary that had some point of contact with the Spanish concept was extended beyond its original meaning in the direction of that concept. The difference was that in these cases there was no visible action to describe; the innovation related directly to the meaning and use of a particular Spanish word. Actually, only two instances of this way of finding equivalents for Spanish verbs are presently authenticated for Stage 2, but they involve important, frequently used words in Spanish and equivalent expressions that came to be almost equally current in Nahuatl.

First came the development of the Nahuatl verb *pia*, "to have custody or charge of, to hold," as an at least partial equivalent of the Spanish verb *tener*,

"to have." A generalized verb "to have," indicating in the first instance possession and extending to an extraordinary number of types of relationships,
is characteristic of most European languages but was not usually to be found
in American Indian languages, including Nahuatl. Nahuatl did not lack ways
of indicating possession, above all the possessed form of the noun, which
was used much more liberally than in a European language; the suffix -*yo*
extended possession to the constituent parts of larger wholes, including inanimate complexes. *Axcaitl* and *tlatquitl* were much-used words meaning
"property" or "possession," and in addition there was a possessor suffix.

When it was necessary to say something on the order of "I have (a particular thing)," the phrase ordinarily used was "there exists my (particular
thing)," with the verbal construction *onca*, like *hay* in Spanish, *il y a* in
French, or *es gibt* in German. Other stative verbs, such as *mani*, "to spread
out," *onoc*, "to lie," or *icac*, "to stand," could replace *onca*. Molina gives a
phrase of this type under "tener" in the sense of "possess,"[92] and we find it in
the earliest Nahuatl documents. A text written in the Coyoacan region in
1548 expresses "I have two daughters" with the phrase "omen oncate noch-
pochhuan," "there exist two daughters of mine."[93] The early censuses of the
Cuernavaca region, with hundreds of entries saying the equivalent of "he has
so-and-so many children," never use "pia," which in its few occurrences in
the texts always means something like "to take care of animals" or "to guard
the house."[94]

But by the 1570's, "pia" begins to appear in Nahuatl documents with the
meaning "to have." In a testament issued in Xochimilco in 1572, a merchant
says "tilmatli nicpia equimilli," "I have [pia] sixty blankets," and "centetl
nicpia cavallo," "I have a horse."[95] Not that the new expression took over
entirely from indigenous phrases, or that "pia" lost its older sense of custody.
In the testaments of Culhuacan (ca. 1580), "pia" in the new sense is rarely to
be found. Possession of houses and lands is indicated exclusively in traditional
ways (which largely continued to be true throughout the colonial period). One
document that does use "pia" for "have" also uses it to mean "to keep for
someone else."[96] Still, "pia" as "have" steadily gained ground. The stock testamentary phrase about having no worldly possessions, in earlier documents
"nothing my property," later became "I have [pia] nothing whatever."[97]

By the early seventeenth century, "pia" began to represent "tener" in
calques, literal translations of Spanish idioms that would have yielded no
sense in preconquest Nahuatl. A person's age had been reported in Nahuatl
by phrases such as "ye matlactli xihuitl in nemi," "it is ten years that he is
alive," or "ye matlactli xihuitl otlacat," "he was born ten years ago."[98] The
Spanish equivalent is "tiene diez años," "he has ten years." In the first decades
of the seventeenth century, the Spanish-style phrase made its appearance in

Nahuatl texts, built on the plan "quipia matlactli xihuitl," literally "he keeps or guards ten years." Chimalpahin reports the age of the archbishop of Mexico City at the time of his death in 1612 as follows: "ye quin ompohuallonmatlactli ypan macuilxihuitl oquimo*pia*liaya," "he was just fifty-five years old."[99] This idiom became standard after about 1650, and other "tener" calques would be added to the repertoire, but the movement had its beginnings early in the seventeenth century, or perhaps very late in the sixteenth, since with an expression gradually evolving from obscurity to becoming the usual way of saying something, first appearance and first attestation can diverge widely.

The other Spanish verb to find a Nahuatl equivalent during Stage 2 was *deber*, "to owe (money)." This development was discussed in Chapter 5 in the context of postconquest Nahua economic concepts, but it will bear review here in the context of language. The first approach to "owe" was once again through the verb involved in translating "tener," namely "pia," this time retaining more of the traditional custodial sense. It is as though once some sort of cross-language breakthrough had been made with this verb, there was a tendency to try to use it for all purposes, thereby in a sense economizing, somewhat as with the complexes around neologisms and key loanwords. The meaning "to owe" was distinguished from "to have" by the addition of the applicative suffix -*lia*, signifying to perform an action for the benefit of someone, giving *pialia*, "to keep for someone," as the equivalent of "deber." Sometimes, however, "pia" itself had virtually the same meaning, as in one of the testaments of Culhuacan (1581), where "pia" is used in connection with the fifteen-peso debt of a certain don Alonso.[100]

Attestations of "pialia" for "to owe money" cluster in the last decades of the sixteenth century and the first decade of the seventeenth.[101] After that, a new verb, although with a very similar etymology and structure, takes over, and "pialia" is seen no more. The replacement, *huiquilia*, is also an applicative, and the basic verb, *huica*, means "to carry, accompany, take care of, be responsible for."[102] The train of thought is thus nearly identical to that leading to "pialia." If one wonders why a change should have occurred at all, the reason may have been the overloading of "pia," with consequent excessive ambiguities.

In both these cases, "to have" and "to owe," a common Nahuatl verb with some affinity to the Spanish concept came to function as the equivalent of the Spanish word while retaining its older meanings as well. Both cases left plenty of latitude for Nahuatl misapprehension or reinterpretation of the Spanish notion. Yet different impressions arise from observing the use of the two sets. "Pia" as a "have" equivalent seems to have been moving rapidly and straightforwardly toward Spanish "tener." The "owe" equivalents, on the other hand, show in their very construction an interpretation of owing markedly different from that prevalent among Europeans, and the way the terms were used underscores the divergence.[103]

By the first years of the seventeenth century, occasional echoes of Spanish conversation were heard in Nahuatl. For example, the Spanish phrase "como un loco," "like a crazy person," to describe extravagant, disorderly behavior, had entered the language, partly translated and partly borrowed. Chimalpahin says that some people parading in the streets of Mexico City "yuhquin çan locoti yc nenque," "went about like crazy people."[104] In Coyoacan in 1613, a plaintiff asserted that her daughter-in-law had hit her, torn her clothing, and generally acted "yuhqui ce loca," "like a crazy woman."[105] Sometimes a whole phrase in Spanish will appear in a Nahuatl text. In 1608, a woman of the Coyoacan region requested burial "ça bar amor de dios," "just for charity, gratis," a slightly garbled form of Spanish "por amor de dios," "for the love of God, for God's sake" (i.e., free).[106]

At this point we may ask, or speculate, for no one seems to have left us any direct testimony on the matter, who it was that was bringing such things as Spanish idioms and verbal meanings into Nahuatl. Once the expressions became current, they were understood by all, but clearly many Nahuas lacked the opportunity to hear much Spanish spoken or the ability to understand it when they did. The originators of the new Spanish equivalents, loan nouns as well as the more conversational phenomena, must have been either Nahuas who, if not exactly bilingual, had a certain exposure to and grasp of Spanish, or Spaniards speaking Nahuatl.

No doubt a Spaniard thrust into Nahuatl would tend to look about desperately for a "tener" equivalent and proceed to use it to translate Spanish idioms. Yet surveying the postconquest centuries as they appear in the documentary legacy, one cannot doubt that many more Nahuas attempted Spanish than Spaniards Nahuatl. By the second and third postconquest generations, even the majority of the professional translators acting as intermediaries between the two languages were native speakers of Nahuatl. On the other hand, most Spanish ecclesiastics and some lower-level labor supervisors habitually tried to converse with Nahuas in their own language. Many Mexican-born Spaniards could speak some Nahuatl in case of necessity, relying on what they must have learned from childhood playmates. Since the need existed, the actual originators of equivalents for Spanish expressions may have been a very small proportion of all speakers, so numbers were not necessarily decisive.

If we look to the expressions themselves for internal evidence pointing in one direction or the other, the case of "pia" and "tener" seems neutral. Either a Spaniard or a Nahuatl speaker would have been impelled to search out some indigenous verb offering a foothold for the "have" meaning. It may seem questionable that a Spaniard would have hit on the particular verb "pia," but this depends on how the word was being used in everyday speech, which is hard to get a handle on at this remove in time and with the sources we have. If, as some passages hint, one of the common meanings of "pia" was "to hold (have control over)," then the choice would have been a natural one for a speaker of either language.[107] From "hold" to "have" is a common step in the evolution of languages generally; "tener" itself meant "hold" before it displaced *haber* as the primary word in Spanish for "have." The "owe" equivalents, however, since both "pialia" and "huiquilia" show a train of thought foreign to the Spanish concept, look much more like they were conceived by Nahuatl speakers who knew some Spanish but were still not quite at home with the notion of "deber."

Loan nouns in general are also inconclusive. Once the Spaniards were well established in the country, many Nahuas must have had frequent opportunity to hear words like "caballo," "horse," and "candela," "candle." The process of seeking names for new phenomena had already gained momentum during Stage 1, before the Spaniards were participating in it even indirectly. On the other hand, nothing would be more natural than for a Spaniard, just learning Nahuatl perhaps, to be at a loss for an equivalent and simply blurt out the Spanish word. Most of the phonological and semantic alterations in Spanish loanwords in Nahuatl do not speak to this question, since they could have been made after the word's initial adoption.

A few changes, however, do point unequivocally toward Nahuatl speakers as the originators. The Spanish word *huerta*, "orchard, intensively cultivated garden," which was one of the core Stage 2 loans in Nahuatl, entered the language as *alahuerta*, "to the orchard," and it continued to appear sporadically in that form for the rest of the colonial period.[108] Clearly, Nahuatl speakers were hearing the word in Spanish sentences and, from the Spanish point of view, making an incorrect decision on which part of the sentence meant "orchard." The most common such sentence was doubtless "go to the orchard," and we can infer that the Nahua originators recognized and understood the verb, and then, presuming that in Spanish as in Nahuatl direction was indicated in the verbal component, took the rest to be the noun. None of this would have occurred to a Spaniard.

Perhaps the only Nahuatl speaker who has left us a large enough quantity and variety of samples of his language to get a good sense of the process is the frequently mentioned Chimalpahin. Along with older loans, Chimalpahin uses many newer ones, including quite a few that, as he is careful to make clear, he is adopting provisionally and perhaps for the first time; often he explains the name as he goes, and equally often he spells the words in such a way as to show that he pronounced them with typical Stage 2 sound substitutions. The only conclusion we can reach is that in originating loans, Chimalpahin, a resident of Mexico City and long-time employee of Spanish ecclesiastics, rather than relying on Nahuatl conversations with Spaniards, drew directly on the Spanish that he had so much occasion to hear and that he understood quite well, though not perfectly. Without discounting the possible role of Spaniards, I think that Nahuas in direct contact with Spanish carried the main burden of innovation at all levels.*

Stage 3

After a long period in which, despite a large lexical input and some impact on Nahuatl idiom, loans from Spanish were virtually all nouns, and Nahuatl pronunciation and grammar were hardly if at all affected, the dam broke, and a whole set of approximately simultaneous additional adjustments took place, constituting a well-defined new stage corresponding to an expanded bilingualism. Perhaps because of its complexity, involving so many dimensions, or perhaps because of the uneven geographical distribution of bilingual people, Stage 3 took shape far more gradually than Stage 2, with more hints of regional variation in timing. Some advance signs can be detected as early as the final decade of the sixteenth century; then the momentum increases after about 1620 or 1630, and by around 1650 one can speak of a fully formed Stage 3 Nahuatl. However indistinct the transition, the basic phenomena of the new stage are clear-cut and need to be enumerated succinctly before we proceed to a more detailed discussion. Briefly, Nahuatl now began to borrow Spanish verbs and particles (uninflected words, mainly prepositions and conjunctions in this case); idiom translation was expanded and systematized; grammar began to be affected, not only by the particles and idioms, but by a change in the principles of pluralization on the Spanish model; and Nahuatl speakers acquired the Spanish sounds missing in Nahuatl, pronouncing new loans as in Spanish. The closer contact between Spaniards and Nahuas, some of the effects of which have been seen in previous chapters, was reflected in language as well; indeed, language would seem to have been a medium carrying many of the other changes.

One of the most striking features of Stage 3 Nahuatl was the use of a set

---

*Ecclesiastical terminology is possibly somewhat different. Ricard and others have given the impression that Spanish ecclesiastics simply dictated (not so much by their own usage as by fiat) what theological concepts should be expressed with Spanish words. Such a view of the matter cannot be left unexamined and cannot be considered well documented, resting as it does on some public statements by friars, who invariably assigned themselves too large and too innovative a role in any development. Yet aside from the great common loans like *misa*, *cruz*, and *santo*, which I would imagine arose in the usual way, the logic of the situation speaks in favor of the sponsored introduction of some of the more recondite theological terms. Their use by ecclesiastics in sermons and catechisms could also have had an effect. Note, however, that the great 17th-century grammarian Carochi tends to treat Spanish religious terminology in Nahuatl as a given, simply the way the Nahuas talked, just like any other aspect of their language, rather than as something to be manipulated.

formula for borrowing Spanish verbs as needed, just as nouns had been borrowed all through Stage 2, in such a way that the new word could be inflected
like any indigenous Nahuatl verb, not merely used as a noun in the infinitive,
which had been the previous prevailing mode, to the extent that verbs were
borrowed at all. The method that won out, however, still fastened on the
Spanish infinitive, suffixing to it the indigenous verbal element -*oa*, one of the
most common endings of indigenous Nahuatl verbs and also a productive
device for creating verbs from nouns and other words, often with a meaning
on the order of "to activate."[109] In a sense, Nahuatl continued to treat the
Spanish verb like a noun, making the frozen nominal infinitive the stem, while
-*oa* carried the inflection. Thus Spanish *notificar*, "to notify," was borrowed
as *notificaroa*; "I notify him" would be *nicnotificaroa* ("I-him-notify"); "he
will be notified" *monotificaroz* (with reflexive prefix and future suffix); "they
notified him" *oquinotificaroque* (with preterit and object prefixes and preterit
plural suffix).

Loan verbs were relatively few in number compared with nouns even after
they became a regular feature of the language. The last (and to date only)
systematic compilation from Nahuatl texts yielded twenty-four attested loan
verbs (that is, inflected -*oa* verbs) compared with 720 loan nouns over the
whole colonial period.[110] I am now able to present a list of forty (see
Table 7.18), and quite a few more have been sighted, if not recorded, by
myself and others, but there can be no doubt that loan verbs were overwhelmingly outnumbered by loan nouns during the entire period treated here.[111] Nor
did they, for the most part, vastly outweigh their small number by constant
use and great importance in daily life, like for example the calendrical terms.
Many of them were decidedly technical, with an emphasis on the legal among
those presently attested. Of the forty verbs in Table 7.18, I judge eighteen to
be legal in nature, six economic, three religious, two historical, and two related to introduced technology; only nine refer to unspecialized everyday actions (although the economic and one or two of the legal terms must be
granted their place in daily life and speech). Since the sample is small, the
great predominance of legal and economic over religious terms may be the
result of chance, but it fits with the general pattern in which the finite number
of important religious concepts was covered very early in one way or another,
whereas the other two realms expanded indefinitely, generating new loans.
For the most part, the verbs in Table 7.18 correspond to the more abstract
nouns borrowed in Stage 2, and in fact several of the cognate nouns appear
on earlier loan lists; in those cases only grammatical flexibility was gained by
incorporating the verb.[112] Yet if the majority of the terms are somewhat abstract, technical, or recherché (one suspects that some were simply "borrowed" ad hoc by that particular speaker on that particular occasion), a few

TABLE 7.18

"Oa" Verbs Attested in Nahuatl Texts

Date	Spanish loan	Date	Spanish loan
1592	*trasuntar*, to translate	1707	*prendar*, to take or lend on pledge, hock
1614–20?	*pasear*, to stroll, parade about	1710	*valer*, to avail oneself of
1634	*confirmar*, to confirm (an order, appointment)	1717	*cruzar*, to cross (a street, etc.)
1637	*espoliar*, to spur, stick spurs into something	1726	*traspasar*, to transfer (debts, property)
1650	*notificar*, to notify	1728	*elegir*, to elect
ca. 1650?	*conquistar*, to conquer	1736	*firmar*, to sign
	fundar, to found	1737	*entregar*, to deliver, hand over
1652	*arrendar*, to lease out		*embargar*, to sequester, seize
1679	*cobrar*, to collect (money)	1738	*contradecir*, to contradict (in legal proceedings)
	estrenar, to inaugurate	1746	*citar*, to cite, notify
1687	*jurar*, to swear (in law)		*costar*, to cost
ca. 1680–	*canonizar*, to canonize		*fundir*, to found, melt, smelt (metal)
1700	*consagrar*, to consecrate		*montar*, to total, amount to
	coronar, to crown	1750	*presentar*, to present (a petition, witness, etc.)
	culpar, to blame, accuse		*mantener*, to support, maintain (a person)
	obligar, to oblige		*recibir*, to receive
	pregonar, to proclaim by crier	1760	*trasladar*, to translate, copy
	sustentar, to sustain, carry through	1786	*descargar*, to unburden (one's conscience)
	visitar, to inspect (officially)	1788	*cumplir*, to fulfill, carry out
17??	*desmandar*, to countermand		
1706	*constar*, to be evident, be recorded		

SOURCES: NMY, pp. 70, 71, 73, 77–79; AGN, Tierras 56, exp. 8, f. 2v, 1520, exp. 6, f. 12, 2541, exp. 11, f. 3, 2301, exp. 10, ff. 4, 9, 2539, exp. 4, f. 1, 2549, exp. 1, ff. 1, 1v, 2554, exp. 2, f. 3v; AGN, Hospital de Jesús, 59: 6, f. 16; AGN, Civil 1072, exp. 13, f. 1v; MNAH AH, GO 184, passim (incl. ff. 21, 24); Karttunen and Lockhart 1978, pp. 168, 174; CH, 2: 132; UCLA TC, folder 14, Oct. 7, 1687, folder 25, March 1, 1768; NAC, ms. 1477 B [1]; Bancroft Library M 84/116m, f. 662; TN, p. 228; UCLA Research Library, Special Collections, McAfee Collection, titles of Metepec, title page and f. 8v.

ªThe dates refer to the first known attestation; several of the verbs occur more than once and some many times.

others speak of normal quotidian matters, such as *cruzar*, "to cross (of roads and the like)."[113] And the repeatedly seen *pasear*, "to stroll, strut, or parade about," is so frequently attested that it must have been a part of the ordinary vocabulary of ordinary people on normal occasions.[114]

It is with verbs that the relatively long time of transition into Stage 3 is best demonstrated. The first now known example of an *-oa* loan verb dates from 1592, long before the 1640–50 at which I set the beginning of full Stage 3. The passage, written in Tlatelolco, involves *trasuntar*, "to translate," and reads: "caocmo motrassuntaroa yn ixquich notitulos," "for all my titles have not been translated yet."[115] In this example, the writer has clearly hit on the definitive solution for borrowing Spanish verbs, for the *-oa* formula is manipulated exactly as it would later. As a first occurrence and an indication of ferment, the "trasuntar" attestation has clear importance, yet just as clearly the -*oa* strategy did not catch on immediately, not even in the circle of literate Mexico City Nahuas versed in Spanish legal lore where it may have originated. Not until 1634 has another -*oa* verb been detected in mundane texts, this time in Huejotla, across the lake from Mexico City, and again it is a legal term, *confirmar*, "to confirm."[116] The date is close enough to mid-seventeenth century and coincides so well with other marks of the changing times (especially the end of the agricultural labor repartimiento in the Valley of Mexico) that we can readily take the example as marking the beginning of a continuous movement in a new direction.[117]

To get some sense of what may have been going on in the years between 1592 and 1634, our best recourse is again Chimalpahin. In his writings, we have a large corpus of utterances in which the author expresses himself freely on many topics and in several subgenres or registers, repeating phrases frequently enough that we can get a good notion of his normal usage and for once are somewhat freed from the lottery of random attestations. Searching through the hundreds of pages that Chimalpahin covered with beautiful Stage 2 Nahuatl, we do find one -*oa* loan verb, *pasear*, the first known attestation of what was to be a very popular loan.[118] The entry concerns the year 1614, when an Augustinian friar was awarded a chair of Latin grammar and theology over rivals, and the proud fellow members of his order took him about the streets of Mexico City in triumph: "ypan cauallo yn oquipasseal-oltique," "it was on a horse that they paraded him." In its spelling the verb betrays some sound substitutions typical of the time, and later too it was likely to appear as *paxialoa* or the like, indicative perhaps of its having been borrowed earlier than most other verbs, which are generally written with few substitutions in the normal manner of Stage 3 loans (as we will see).[119]

Exactly when Chimalpahin wrote the sentence containing the -*oa* verb is hard to determine. The bulk of his Mexico City reportage has the appearance of having originally been written very close to the time of the event, but we know that he added, revised, and recopied. Although most of this activity apparently took place by 1620, there are stray marginalia from as late as 1629. The strongest likelihood is that Chimalpahin first set down his -*oa* verb when he wrote the original entry in 1614, though it remains possible that he added it at a later time, conceivably even after 1620. More important than the exact date is, first, the fact that during his lifetime he did use the -*oa* formula, and, second, the fact that in all his voluminous writings he used it only once. It is not that there was no occasion. In his entries on the Mexico City of his time, Chimalpahin covers almost exactly the same range, in a very similar register, as one of his closest competitors as a writer of wide-ranging Nahuatl prose, the anonymous author of annals set in Puebla who wrote mainly during the last two or three decades of the seventeenth century and whose discourse is liberally sprinkled with -*oa* verbs.[120] In Chimalpahin's day, the -*oa* convention had germinated but not yet flowered.

As the reader will have noticed, both of the earliest attestations of -*oa* verbs are from Mexico City, Tlatelolco being in effect an attached suburb of the capital. It is entirely possible that -*oa* verb loans (and other innovations for which there is less evidence) originated in the country's largest city, where the most Spaniards encountered the most Nahuas, and enjoyed a limited local currency for a time before spreading to the rest of the Nahua world. Spread they did. To specify the exact numbers in such a small sample as is presently available would be illusory, but the loan verbs of Table 7.18 come from all over the Nahuatl-speaking region: from Puebla, Tlaxcala, Tulancingo, the Chalco region and other places in the Valley of Mexico, the Toluca Valley, the Cuernavaca basin, and apparently from areas outside central Mexico. As for their chronology, one first attestation falls in the last decade of the sixteenth century, three in the first half of the seventeenth, fifteen in the second half, and twenty-one in the eighteenth century.[121] My provisional inference from these data is that after gaining some currency in a fairly small circle in the time around 1590–1620, an explosive expansion of the convention took place starting in the 1630's, and that from 1650 on, although loan verbs made up a small proportion of the lexicon, they represented a normal resource of the language all over Nahua central Mexico and further.[122]

Along with -*oa* verbs, Spanish loan particles (uninflected words, as mentioned above) stand out as one of the most prominent features of the Nahuatl of Stage 3. The Spanish items in question here are prepositions and conjunctions. That they should be incorporated into Nahuatl late in the game is not surprising; Nahuatl had no prepositions at all, and its "conjunctions" were mainly the same words as its adverbs, behaving quite differently from Spanish clause-introductory conjunctions. The grammatical obstacles to be surmounted were thus even greater than with verbs. More surprising, on the face of it, is that words of this type should have been borrowed at all.

A large majority of the verbs that Nahuatl accepted embodied a notion or practice not fully covered by indigenous vocabulary. Spanish prepositions and conjunctions, on the other hand, conveyed little if anything, in purely semantic terms, that was not somehow being expressed in Nahuatl already. The reason for the loans lies in bilingualism. The two systems achieved much the same overall result with dissimilar means, dividing the spectrum of relations and connections very differently. To ease the mediation between the two languages constantly going on in the late colonial period, innovation was required. Thus in Stage 3, loans were motivated not only by Spanish objects, ideas, and procedures that struck the Nahuas as useful or impinged on their lives; the simple existence of a prominent linguistic difference between Span-

TABLE 7.19

Loan Particles Attested in Nahuatl Texts

Date	Spanish loan	Date	Spanish loan
1652	*sin*, without	1737	*por*, for, as
1653	*hasta*, as far as, until, even		*ni aun*, nor, not even
	para, (destined) for, toward,	1738	*fuera de*, aside from
	in order to	1760	*a*, to, at
1672	*sino*, but, rather	1782	*entre*, among
1710	*pues*, well then, so	1786	*desde*, from, beginning at
1736	*como*, as	1795	*pero*, but[a]

SOURCES: NMY, pp. 71, 78–80; BC, pp. 74, 80, 174; AGN, Tierras 1520, exp. 6, f. 12, 2539, exp. 12, f. 2v, 2549, exp. 1, ff. 1, 1v, 5, 2615, exp. 5, f. 1; AGN, Civil 1072, exp. 13, f. 1; NAC, ms. 1477 B (1).

NOTE: The dates refer to the first known attestation. *En*, "in," and especially *y*, "and," appear frequently in Nahuatl texts, and there can be little doubt that the writers understood their meaning, but they always appear in whole Spanish phrases (with *en* usually date formulas), or in the case of *y*, at least between two Spanish words, so that one is not justified, on the available evidence, in counting them as full-fledged loans.

[a]*Pero* also appears in an undated document, probably done in the 1780's: AGN, Tierras 2310, exp. 10, f. 20v.

ish and Nahuatl could bring on borrowing, and particles are the best illustration of the principle.*

A Spanish preposition precedes a word that is its "object" but is connected in no other way: *sobre el caballo*, "upon the horse." In Nahuatl, many of the relational notions for which Spanish uses prepositions are expressed in the verb (the applicative being the equivalent of "for" and "from," and the directional affixes conveying "to," "toward," "from," "away," etc.). Nahuatl's specifically relational words are nounlike and must either be possessed ("its-on the horse," *i-pan in cahuallo*) or placed after the noun "object" (*cahuallo-pan*, "horse-on, on a horse"). The two modes, Spanish and Nahuatl, could not be combined, or were so distinct that it did not occur to the Nahuas even to try, so that no true integration with Nahuatl grammatical principles was achieved, as it was with verbs. When the time came, prepositions were simply used as in Spanish, placed before their objects with no overt indication of the connection, thus introducing into Nahuatl not only some new words but a whole new type of relationship between words, as in the earliest known example of *para*, "for": "para ycabalyo," "for his horse."[123]

It is in the 1650's that some Spanish particles first appear in now known Nahuatl texts (Table 7.19). All of these attestations happen to be from the far west, but further compilation will doubtless establish that the distribution was actually wider at that time.[124] The words involved, as far as we now

*Similarly, in the early postconquest years, the Nahuas in general took to those Spanish cultural patterns that were enough like their own to be workable and desirable; by Stage 3, they were sometimes adopting precisely those that were most different, as a result of close contact with the Spanish world and the need to interact with it smoothly. The history of kinship is a good example.

know, were far fewer in number even than in the case of verbs. The repertoire of words on which to draw was of course relatively small to begin with, but even so, only a few seem to have been taken over, and some are attested only once. *Ni aun*, "nor, not even," and *por*, "for, as, etc.," occur often enough that we can consider them to have been within the framework of normal everyday speech, something anyone would be expected to understand readily.[125] In a class by themselves were two items, *hasta*, "as far as, until, etc.," and *para*, "destined for, in order to, etc." These words, "hasta" apparently first, became ingrained in the usage of some Nahuatl speakers, who surely uttered them many times each day. By the eighteenth century, it would be hard to imagine the language without them (something that remains true today).[126]

Both words were used in ways showing that all the subtleties of their meanings in Spanish were transferred to Nahuatl. The writer of the anonymous late-seventeenth-century annals of Puebla employs "hasta" in all three of its main senses in Spanish: "until (a certain time or specified condition)"; "as far as, up to (a place)"; and "even." [127] A document from Calimaya in the Toluca Valley, dated 1750, uses "para" seven times and in several different ways.[128] Four times it means "in order to" in infinitive-like constructions, as in "para quichtlahuas ytlatocatlacalaquiltzi," "in order to pay his royal tribute." [129] Once it means "in order that," with a clause involving a change of subject: "para amo aquin quemania quipies tlen quitos," "in order that no one should sometime have some objection to make." Once it is a preposition with a noun object: "pena para ycajatzin," "fine for the exchequer of (the king)." And once it means "toward": "para ycalaquian tonali," "toward where the sun goes down (the west)." [130] "Para" in the sense "toward" was particularly associated with the popular Spanish phrases "para arriba," "upward (from a certain point)" and "para abajo," "downward" (which could be rendered "para yc tlatzintla").[131]

Spanish nouns continued to be borrowed in Stage 3, and by all indications the loans were of much the same types as earlier, differing mainly because of the exhaustion of some categories and the continued evolution and change of Hispanic society. A certain number of post-1650 loans, however, belong to categories previously avoided, or at least left uninvolved. Outstanding among them are words for close blood relationships, above all those for siblings and cousins, which sharply reorganized the conceptualization of same-generation kin (see Chapter 3). In a sense, these loans can be thought of as comparable to those of Stage 2, since they were a reaction to strikingly different substantive notions the Spaniards brought with them. They belong to a new stage, first, because of the notorious slowness of any language to change its terminology for close kin, and, second, because, as with the particles, a large part of the reason for the innovation must have been the increased communication between Hispanics and Nahuas, with greater comprehension on the part of the latter and increased need to function within a common framework.

The same reasons explain another new type of noun loan, a word used not for its primary meaning but in a particular idiomatic sense. Nahuatl had its own highly developed way of speaking of location, which generally remained intact throughout the colonial period, and *lugar*, "place," is correspondingly not to be found in known Nahuatl texts in a locational sense. An eighteenth-century testator of Tlapitzahuayan in the jurisdiction of Chalco Atenco, however, asked his relatives to take "nolugar," "my place," in disciplining his children.[132] It was also in Stage 3 that the Spanish words for the cardinal directions were incorporated into Nahuatl as part of the normal way of describing the location of property (though the indigenous expressions did not entirely disappear).[133]

As with *-oa* verbs, we find harbingers of some of these types of noun loans well before they became characteristic, and again the anticipations come from the environs of Mexico City. In the early decades of the seventeenth century, Chimalpahin writes *oriente*, "east," and *norte*, "north," and also uses the term *hermano*, "brother."* Each occurs once only, and each is accompanied by an explanation or equivalent using indigenous vocabulary; two come in the course of discussion of matters from the Hispanic or outside world.[134]

Early examples come also from Tetzcoco, a proud altepetl and former imperial center that with much justice could resent being considered a suburb of Mexico City. But despite the intervening lake, Tetzcoco after the conquest was in Hispanic terms little more than an appendage of the colonial capital. A special affinity, affecting aspects of life from rhetorical style to dynastic politics, had apparently existed between the two altepetl in preconquest times, and traces of it were still visible in the late sixteenth century.[135] The Tetzcoco attestations also occur in circumstances having to do with the Hispanic world; they are in papers relating to Juan Bautista de Pomar, the well-educated mestizo who functioned both as a Spaniard and as a Tetzcocan noble. The 1596 example of a kinship loan, "primo hermano," "first cousin," actually is in reference to Pomar; as in the comparable passage in Chimalpahin, a Nahuatl equivalent is given as well. The direction words norte and sur

---

*Although the preconquest Nahuas acknowledged the same four cardinal directions as in the European scheme, even giving them far greater importance, it would seem, in their cosmology, religious rites, and orientation of political boundaries, so that the loans would be a mere renaming, in some sense a mental reorganization was involved, as with kinship terms. For the Nahuas, the four directions were points along an ordered, ongoing revolution, not four entirely separate, independent points of reference. Above all, east and west, the solar directions, were better defined than north and south. The classical sources do not always agree on the Nahuatl words for north and south, or on which terms meant which. In postconquest land documents, there were set expressions (solar oriented) only for east and west, north and south being conveyed by ad hoc expressions referring to nearby settlements or physical features.

occur in documents of the late sixteenth and early seventeenth centuries having to do with Pomar's acquisition of land but do not relate to him directly; it appears that Tetzcocan notaries, or at least the writers of these particular documents, may have borrowed the terms for normal use quite far in advance of Nahuatl speakers in central Mexico in general.[136]

As mentioned above, Stage 2 saw Spanish loan nouns taking Nahuatl plural endings, Spanish plural endings, or both. Now, in Stage 3, Spanish plurals came to dominate (though never to the exclusion of indigenous and, more often, of double plurals, which hung on tenaciously with many older loans). In the late colonial period, the influence of Spanish plural marking went beyond the morphology of loan nouns to affect, apparently, the way the plural was used with indigenous nouns as well. Through Stage 2, plural suffixes were rarely used with nouns referring to inanimate things. Some particular species of trees and some objects such as stars were the main exceptions, apparently because of motions characteristic of them; also, certain suffixes, especially the diminutive -*ton*, sometimes themselves acted like animate nouns even when attached to inanimates.[137] But words like "house," "land," and "tree" were normally not pluralized.[138]

Spanish, of course, like other European languages, indicated plurals on nouns in general. In Stage 3, Nahuatl began to do the same, not with entire consistency (nor has it attained such consistency to this day), but the plural marking of indigenous inanimates now began to be a normal feature of speech. In a 1746 Amecameca document, several of the people involved use plurals such as *caltin*, "houses," *quauhtin*, "trees," and *amame*, "papers."[139] With some speakers these new plurals functioned entirely like traditional animate plurals, that is, other words in the sentence followed them in indicating plurality.[140]

We cannot say with absolute certainty that this change in usage was caused by contact, since Nahuatl continued to evolve in ways having nothing to do with Spanish, and as already seen, some movement toward a broader indication of the nominal plural had taken place earlier.[141] Yet the Spanish model remains the most likely source of the development, which thus, as with so many other facets of Stage 3, would be related to increased bilingualism.

Another prominent feature of Stage 3 was the maturation of a number of important equivalences between Nahuatl and Spanish words. These "equivalence relationships" were crucial in translating Spanish idioms. The resulting expressions often look like calques (literal translations of foreign idiomatic expressions) and indeed may be considered such, but they did not usually occur in isolation. Rather they grouped around a key equivalence; we have already seen the "pia"/"tener" equivalence evolving in this direction. All such relationships known to me involve verbs and particles rather than nouns, in large part, no doubt, because Nahuatl had been so freely borrowing nouns for most of the previous hundred years.[142]

The Spanish words involved in the few equivalence pairs were very common, and the equivalents soon tended to become common in Nahuatl, too. We may ask if, despite the Stage 3 breakthrough in the direct borrowing of verbs and particles, some reluctance to borrow still obtained when it came to the most basic vocabulary in these categories. Or did the fact that certain equivalences, perhaps precisely because of their basic nature, got established in the course of Stage 2, when the time of verb and particle borrowing had not yet come, preclude a simple borrowing of these items at a later time?[143] To me the latter possibility seems more likely.

Just how many equivalence relationships existed in the late colonial period remains unknown, and the matter is difficult to investigate systematically, partly because older Nahuatl idiomatic usage is itself still poorly understood, and it is hard to be sure exactly what is Spanish-influenced and what is not. "Pia" continued to absorb all the senses of Spanish "tener": to have a certain length, width, or other type of measurement (the usual Spanish expression, rather than saying something is so-and-so long); to have children; to have something to ask or demand; to have a right to something; and so forth.[144] In Spanish, "to have to" is "tener que," and in such phrases the Nahuatl word *tle* or *tlein*, "what (interrogatory), that which," took the place of "que," "what (int.), that (relative)."[145] The end result, attained surely by the eighteenth century and perhaps before, was that "pia" could automatically be used for any technical or idiomatic sense that Spanish "tener" might have or develop.

Given the hit-and-miss nature of specific attestations, caution is necessary in determining the chronological progression of this equivalence. Judging by the bulk of the evidence we have, it appears that through the sixteenth century the main development was the evolution of the sense "to possess," that the early seventeenth century saw certain calques based on "pia/tener," especially the one having to do with specifying one's age, and that not until after 1650 did full, automatic equivalence obtain. It is only with some expressions used constantly in the sources, however, that we can be sure about the timing.

Thus we can be certain that "pia" was not normally used with land measurements before about 1650, and that after that it frequently was (though still not in the majority of cases). We know that idiomatic uses of "pia/tener" are more common and varied in Stage 3 sources than in comparable records of Stage 2, whether mundane documents or annals. Yet in the 1611 conversational manual of Pedro de Arenas a surprising array of "pia" idioms makes its appearance, not only to possess in general and for a vendor to "have" some item in stock, but an expression "to be troubled" based on "tener pena" and even "tlein ticpia?," "what's the matter with you?," based on Spanish "¿qué tienes?" Reading Arenas, who captures the register of everyday business dealings and the like in a way not matched in other sources, we could imagine that full equivalence had been attained in the first part of the second decade of the seventeenth century. If so, the phenomenon was perhaps restricted to the marketplace; many kinds of early-seventeenth-century Nahuatl speech remained unaffected.[146]

One other case of apparent full equivalence is documented for Stage 3, between the Spanish *pasar*, "to pass," a common verb with many idiomatic meanings, and the Nahuatl *pano*, "to cross over the surface of something (specifically water, according to Molina), to ford."[147] "Pano" is attested meaning "to go, to proceed" (a short distance from a given place to another, a common sense of pasar): "otipanoque ipan in itlaltzin caxtiltecatl," "we (the parties and officials involved in a land transaction) went (from the courthouse) to the Spaniard's land."[148] The temporal sense of "pasar" also surfaces in Nahuatl texts: "opanoc macuilli tonali," "five days passed."[149] "Pano" was also used to translate the participle *pasado*, "past."[150] It seems reasonable to assume that the equivalence included all the other common senses of "pasar," such as "to happen," as it does in modern Nahuatl, even though not all of them appear in the available sources.[151] No example of "pano/pasar" is attested in texts prior to the late seventeenth century, so to date we have no evidence that this pair went through a Stage 2 evolution comparable to "pia/tener." The possibility should not be ruled out, however. Still other verb equivalences probably existed during Stage 3, but at present they are more glimpsed and divined than established.[152]

Acting as the semantic and idiomatic equivalent of a Spanish word did not mean that the Nahuatl word bearing the equivalence ceased to have its earlier meanings as well. "Pia" continued to mean "to take care of"; "pano" continued to mean "to cross." The Nahuatl verbs were thus even richer than the Spanish words they represented. No line divided "Spanish" from "Nahuatl" idiom. New idioms often show vestiges of earlier phrase types. The Spanish-based expression for having children, for example, contained, from the Spanish or English point of view, a redundant possessive prefix. Instead of "I have children," Nahuatl said "I have my children" (*niquimpia nopilhuan*); the "my" was left over from older phrases such as "there are my children" (*oncate nopilhuan*) or "three my children" (*yeintin in nopilhuan*).[153] Likewise, the Spanish phrase "en el año pasado de," "in the past year of," could become in Nahuatl "yn ipan xihuitl otihualpanoque de," "in the year that we passed of," continuing the general Nahuatl practice of using the first-person plural when specifying dates.[154] As in cultural borrowings generally, then, here too the liberal admixture of indigenous elements erased any line between the intrusive and the native, the Spanish and the Nahuatl, helping render such expressions a normal, unselfconscious part of current Nahuatl idiom.[155]

That equivalences involving particles were common I cannot at present assert, for I have isolated only one frequently employed example, Nahuatl *quenami*, "how, in a certain manner," for Spanish *como*, "how, as, like." The relationship is perhaps less than a full-scale equivalence to the extent that it seems not to have involved the interrogatory sense of "como," but only the "as" sense, or occasionally "how" with dependent clauses.[156] But, so used, it was widespread by the time of Stage 3, introducing both nouns and whole clauses:[157]

quenami ce soldado	"as a soldier" (Puebla, late 17th century)
yn quenami nesi	"as appears" (Amecameca, 1746)
yn quenami quitohua	"as he says" (Amecameca, 1746)
nehual quenami jues	"I as judge" (Calimaya, 1750)
quenami mitlania se pe-daso tlali	"(it is seen) how (that) a piece of land is requested" (Calimaya, 1750)

Probably also an equivalence was *ica*, "by means of, etc." for Spanish *con*, "with."[158] The phrase *cihuahua ica* (literally, "person having a wife by means of") appears repeatedly in a 1746 text in place of *casado con*, "married with [i.e., to]."[159] Here a vestige of the traditional indigenous meaning remains as a bridge to the Spanish, but in some passages in a 1750 text that connection is gone, and "ica" means simply "in the company of," one of the many senses of Spanish "con," as it is of English "with."[160] The popularity of "quenami" explains why Spanish "como," as much as the Nahuas seem to have been impressed with it, is attested as a loanword only once; an "ica/con" equivalence would likewise explain the total absence to date of attestations of "con" as a loanword.

A further characteristic of Stage 3 was the acquisition of the sounds of Spanish that Nahuatl had lacked, making it possible to pronounce new loans as in the original language. Now Nahuatl speakers learned to produce the voiced stops *b*, *d*, and *g*, the fricative *f*, and the liquid *r*—in short all the items for which they had had no equivalent (see Table 7.17). The new accomplishments had little effect on the pronunciation of indigenous vocabulary.[161] Moreover, older loans tended to retain the sound substitutions of the time when they were first incorporated.[162] But loans in general were now a better approximation of Spanish, bringing the two languages and peoples closer together, as in so many other manifestations of Stage 3.

The developments in pronunciation, like the evolution of *-oa* verbs and the equivalences, took place over a relatively long period of time, beginning well in advance of full Stage 3. Furthermore, the problems of determining the timing of this aspect are especially great, making very precise dating unlikely in the best of cases. To state only a bare outline of the matter, Nahua writers in general spelled pronounced sounds rather than words. If a writer left out an *n* in his speech, he did so in writing too, or if he pronounced a glide between *o* and *a*, he wrote *ohua*, or if he said *x* for syllable-final *ch*, he would write "noxpox" for standard *nochpoch*, "my daughter," regardless of other considerations. The "word" is in any case a far less distinct and identifiable, more flexible entity in Nahuatl than in a European language.

When it came to Spanish words, however, usage varied. Some writers had learned the canonical, invariant spellings of Spanish words as Spaniards spelled them, and always wrote them that way regardless of their own pronunciation. Some wrote Spanish vocabulary the same as Nahuatl, however they pronounced it. Most did a little of both. The result is that we can deduce very little from a given "correct" spelling of a loanword, but we can confidently connect "incorrect" spellings corresponding to expectable sound substitutions with the writer's actual pronunciation. The assertion that Nahuatl acquired Spanish sounds rests on the broader observation that across the seventeenth century, spellings of loanwords in general became more standard, except for some older loans. Enough substitutions occur in the eighteenth century to indicate that some people still used them in speech, but it seems clear that by then the ability to pronounce the full range of Spanish sounds was widespread.[163]

At times the written record affords fuller information on certain aspects of the process, making us aware of transitional steps. Nahuatl had neither *d* nor *r*, both being voiced consonants with, in Spanish, a similar point of articulation and manner of pronunciation (in fact, Spaniards themselves occasionally used one for the other). In seventeenth-century Nahuatl texts (known examples stretch from 1634 to 1683), *d* is sometimes found written for *r*, and vice versa. The explanation seems to be that when Nahuatl reached the point of acquiring the Spanish sounds, it first developed a new common class representing both *d* and *r*, and only later distinguished between the two. From known attestations, it would appear that the two middle quarters of the seventeenth century were the heyday of the transitional common class, and that by the eighteenth century or some decades before, *r* and *d* had distinct pronunciations in Nahuatl generally.[164] Such timing would fit well within the general framework of the chronology proposed above.

A final aspect of Stage 3 that deserves mention, even though it has not yet been studied systematically (and at this point it is not clear how to do so with the rich but uneven materials available), is the virtual disappearance of certain kinds of vocabulary characteristic of Stages 1 and 2, over and above the displacement of older expressions by the innovations we have been discussing.

Though hard to pinpoint, it is the absence of these terms, in combination with the new modes and elements, that produces a distinct, recognizable Stage 3 style. Perhaps the clearest example of the kind of loss I mean is the abandonment of the elaborate traditional Nahuatl terminology of social/ political rank, which is hardly more than vestigial in Stage 3 texts, as we saw in a previous chapter (p. 117). In this case, the documents have much occasion to mention the topic, and one can draw conclusions with some confidence.

When it comes to the highly developed older language of polite discourse (of which social terminology was a part), it is hard to be sure whether its decline is apparent or real. The reader of documents of Stages 2 and 3 will not fail to come away with the impression that polite rhetoric had declined greatly by the later period. But, then, with no manual of fancy talk comparable to the late-sixteenth-century Bancroft dialogues or collections of speeches like those found in Sahagún for the time after 1650, we lack adequate sources for Stage 3 conversational style;[165] and though the old rhetoric is no longer so dominant in Stage 3 petitions and correspondence as earlier, it certainly is not absolutely missing. Consider the following preamble to a letter of dissent the officials of a town in the bishopric of Puebla sent to their priest; except perhaps for the loan phrase "señor cura," this passage, written in about 1740, could as well have been composed a century and a half earlier:

May the Most Holy Sacrament be praised. Oh our dear honored priestly father, lord curate, may God the Holy Spirit dwell happily within your dear person for many years. Oh our dear honored father, with humble obeisance we kiss your priestly hands, all of us together, we alcaldes and all of us holding office and all the town fathers and elders here in San Agustín Yacapitzactlan.[166]

Even two documents that I have used here as prime examples of Stage 3 Nahuatl, one from Amecameca (1746) and the other from Calimaya (1750), are not without echoes of this register. A petition included in the Amecameca papers begins matter-of-factly with the names and affiliation of the plaintiffs, but finally gets around to saying "amotlatocayxpantzinco tinesi," "we appear in your rulerly presence," and "rulerly presence" is sprinkled liberally across the page.[167] The Calimaya document, a land grant, is almost entirely businesslike, but does speak of the grantee's petition in the following traditional terms (despite modern "quenami" and "ica" equivalences): "onesi ytlaytlan-ilis ynin Dˢ yconetzi quenami mopechtecatihuis yca ychoquis yhuan yyelsisi-huilis," "there appeared the petition of this child of God, how he comes bowing down with tears and sighing."[168] Plainly, the time-honored way of talking had not entirely disappeared, and in more private circumstances, it may even have flourished.[169]

In general, the various aspects of Stage 3—loans in new grammatical and

semantic categories, the fuller development of equivalences and idiom translation, pronunciation of loans as in Spanish or nearly so, and de-emphasis of
certain facets of traditional rhetoric—were all roughly simultaneous, gathering momentum as the seventeenth century progressed and approaching definitive form around mid-century, although a firm establishment of some
parts of the complex may have come later, and quantitative growth along the
same lines continued indefinitely. The Stage 3 innovations had in common
that they brought Nahuatl closer to Spanish, each in its own way, as was
appropriate and inevitable with the now-ubiquitous presence of Spaniards
among the Nahuas. As a set, the new developments formed a rounded system
permitting the Nahuas to take anything from Spanish that they needed whenever they needed it and facilitating communication between the two groups
of speakers, so that new currents of all kinds could easily cross the language
barrier, creating for some purposes a single interacting social and cultural
entity containing both groups.

But this rapprochement, which we must remember was not deliberately
planned or consciously implemented by a single human being of either group
at any point, did not take place against the grain of the Nahuatl language.
We have seen that in a long process of gradual change, each innovation built
on precedents, some from indigenous grammar and lexicon, some from earlier stages of adaptation to Spanish. Moreover, the important features specific
to Nahuatl not only remained in the language in a general way but were
frequently incorporated into the innovations. The new words and devices
were soon as natural as anything else in Nahuatl, and indeed, apart from
some hints in the work of the Tlaxcalan annalist Zapata,[170] we have no evidence that speakers even thought of them as other than Nahuatl, or that any
Nahuatl/Spanish dichotomy was of concern to them (just as in political, religious, and economic life). The process of adaptation including Stage 3 is
comparable to the experience of English in contact with Norman French,
registering a vast impact but not thereby ceasing to be itself at root and surely
not becoming a carbon copy of the language of the new arrivals.

"Stage 4"

I have put the heading of this section in quotes because the development
involved does not stand in a strictly sequential relationship to its predecessor
like the other stages. That is, "Stage 4" postdated Stage 3 but did not supplant it. The Nahuatl speakers of our times are still in Stage 3; loan verbs and
particles are much more numerous than in the late colonial period, but verbs
are still borrowed using -*oa* plus infinitive, and the old items are still in place,
from "paxialoa" ("to stroll") to "hasta" and "para." In speaking of a

"Stage 4," I am addressing the bifurcation of linguistic development. The evolution of Nahuatl in the postconquest centuries is only one side of a coin whose other side is Spanish spoken by Nahuas. For the most part, Spanish conversation by Nahuatl speakers, as important as we have seen it to be as the source of the innovations of Stage 3 and even Stage 2, occurred between individual Nahuas and individual Spaniards outside the context of the indigenous world that is the subject of the present book, and so my research and my discussions up to this point have skirted the topic. Some Nahuatl speakers habitually spoke Spanish, well or badly, from doña Marina forward, not only interpreters as she was, but employees of Spaniards and traders in cross-cultural transactions. From the very nature of Stages 2 and 3, we can deduce a cumulative growth in their numbers and accomplishments. Not until the second half of the eighteenth century, however, did Spanish-speaking Nahuas produce a substantial amount of written texts in Spanish, texts that we can study to try to determine to what extent the writers brought Nahua speech and cultural patterns with them into the world of Spanish speakers.

A few hints are available of what the Spanish spoken by Nahuas of earlier times was like. Judging from Chimalpahin's writing of Spanish loans in his histories, he probably spoke with a very strong accent.[171] From the hand of his contemporary Tezozomoc, a professional interpreter, we have a whole book in Spanish, a history of Tenochtitlan that for the most part appears to be a free translation of an already existing text in Nahuatl, probably originally composed by another party. Tezozomoc often follows the turns of older Nahuatl rhetoric so closely that his work is far from being elegant, lucid, fully idiomatic Spanish, but he possessed a large vocabulary and a perfect mastery of the ordinary elements of grammar and usage.

An isolated individual in a contact situation, however, can make great advances in the other language without having a noticeable impact on his peers. Doubtless there were many cases over the centuries of Nahuas who spoke perfect or near-perfect Spanish. Tezozomoc around 1600 was far closer to standard Spanish than the bulk of the Nahuas writing Spanish mundane texts over a century and a half later. One looks for evidence of group idiosyncrasies of Nahuatl speakers in Spanish, but with the lack of sources we can only deduce, from such tidbits as the remarks of a priest of the early eighteenth century on some Nahuatlisms in Indians' Spanish, that a Nahua way of speaking the language was in gestation by that time.[172]

That Spanish texts by indigenous writers appear in bulk in the later eighteenth century, apparently mainly after 1760–70, seems to me to indicate the development of a critical mass of Spanish competence in the population, comparable at a new level to what the phenomena of Stage 3 tell us must have been happening around mid-seventeenth century, so I am moved to speak in terms of a new stage even if the analogy with the other three stages is only partial. If the chronology of one of the most significant developments in Mexican history, the transition from Stage 2 to Stage 3 in the middle of the seventeenth century, is hard to tie to exterior events, the timing of "Stage 4" is not at all surprising, since it was just around 1760–70 that Hispanic society, economy, and governmental activity were undergoing explosive growth, raising the intensity of contact once again.[173]

One way to get a sense of the advance of Spanish speaking in the Nahua world, at least among the upper group who held office and were often called upon as witnesses, is to observe the language in which testimony was given in Spanish courts and the remarks made on the witnesses' fluency (the testimony itself, alas, always appears written in Spanish whether originally given in Nahuatl or not). In the sixteenth and early seventeenth centuries (in other words, during Stage 2), Nahuas virtually always testified through an interpreter, and such a procedure was taken as a matter of course. From the late seventeenth century forward, an interpreter continued to be used in most cases, partly because of possible legal challenge to the validity of statements made in Spanish by Indians, and surely partly because interpreters wanted to practice their trade and keep their jobs. But now one not infrequently comes upon the remark that a witness spoke through an interpreter "sin embargo de ser ladino en la lengua castellana," as the formula ran, "despite being fluent in Spanish."[174] In the second half of the eighteenth century, although the just described pattern is still seen, more Nahuas begin to testify directly in Spanish, or, even as laymen, to translate for others.[175] In the last decades of the eighteenth century and the early decades of the nineteenth, indigenous people often gave testimony without any mention being made of an interpreter or what language they were employing. Apparently they were speaking Spanish, and by that time, it seems to have been the expectation that all indigenous officeholders would be able to do so.*

Granted that Spanish speaking by Nahuas was taking on new dimensions in the late eighteenth century, what can we say about the quality, flavor, or idiosyncrasies of the Spanish spoken? Spanish clerks seem to have rephrased the Spanish-language testimony of indigenous witnesses to conform to their own style, for these statements differ in no way from those made by native Spanish speakers. It is to texts written directly by Nahuas that we must turn, and they prove a rich and suggestive source. What I have to say in this respect,

---

*I speak only of the officeholding group because these are the people constantly called on to testify, so that one can form reliable impressions and find numerous informative examples, which with extensive compilation could be usefully quantified. Nevertheless, from various hints and deductions, I am satisfied that many other Nahuas were speaking good Spanish, especially those who were permanently employed by Spaniards and those who habitually migrated to work temporarily in cities or on Spanish estates.

however, is more provisional than my analyses of texts in Nahuatl, because it does not rest on the survey of a corpus of comparable size and variety. Throughout my work on the book, I have used sources written in Spanish, both those surrounding Nahuatl texts and others, but only late in the game did it occur to me that documents in Spanish would reward the type of close analysis of language and genre that I had routinely applied to documents in Nahuatl. My remarks on Nahuatl-speaker Spanish are based on an analysis of texts from the Toluca Valley, with a few from Mexico City to put them in perspective.[176] But my impressions from other documents less closely read and recorded lead me to hope that the regularities observed will be borne out by further research.

Judging by my sample of late-colonial Spanish written by Nahuatl speakers of the late eighteenth century, the Nahuas were reasonable masters of Spanish pronunciation and had few vocabulary problems in terms of individual words.[177] Their difficulties, or to put it more neutrally, special habits, had to do mainly with syntax, the art of putting words into strings, which in Spanish as in any language involves not only grammar in the narrower sense but the manipulation of the frozen larger structures we call idioms. In a word, the Nahuas at this point, expectably if not fully predictably, retained large elements of Nahuatl grammar and usage in their Spanish. Although quite competent and sophisticated in many respects, the Nahuatl-speaker Spanish of "Stage 4" is sometimes unintelligible without reference to the Nahuatl substratum.

By the late decades of the colonial period, most Nahuatl speakers using Spanish appear to have had a quite full mastery of the basic principles of word order as well as of number and gender agreement (with some slips in the last because Nahuatl lacked gender). Nor did they have problems in indicating the subjects of verbs. It was with the indication of the objects of verbs that the trouble, or divergence, arose. The Spanish system, distinguishing direct from indirect, masculine from feminine, and singular from plural objects through a welter of object pronouns, was far more complex than the Nahuatl equivalent, so Nahuatl speakers tended to simplify, sometimes going so far as to use *lo* (masculine singular direct object) to cover all cases.

Perhaps the strangest thing about Spanish object marking from the Nahuatl point of view was the use of the preposition *a* ("to") to indicate that a noun designating a person is functioning as an object of a verb (as in "veo a Juan," "I see Juan"). Nahuatl had no case and originally no prepositions, and noun objects stood in apposition or cross-reference to a verbal object prefix, rendering anything on the order of a preposition accompanying the noun object entirely inappropriate. The result was that Nahuas often simply omitted the puzzling "a." Once they became aware of its frequency and apparent importance in Spanish sentences, they (or a good many of them) construed the "a" as indicating persons without recognizing its connection with objects, using it with subjects as well, as in "a Vuesa merced puede mandarnos," "your grace can order us." [178]

Prepositions are often used unidiomatically or omitted in the texts of Nahuatl speakers, especially it seems when they deal with location or direction. Even though Nahuatl had borrowed some prepositions by this time, fully integrating "hasta" and "para" as we saw above, the great differences between the two languages are still frequently reflected in the retention of Nahuatl grammatical principles in this realm. Thus Nahuatl place-names ordinarily contain a locative within themselves; in Spanish, Nahuatl speakers accordingly sometimes omitted words like *en*, "in," when specifying places: "esta Santa Maria Asumpcion," "it is in Santa María de la Asunción." [179]

Nahuatl speakers seem to have been able to handle the Spanish tenses very well, even the subjunctive (which causes present-day English speakers such grief); though the two systems vary at every point, overall they in one way or another make nearly the same distinctions. Nahuatl, however, was the richer of the two in progressives and modals. As a result, by Spanish standards, Nahuatl speakers made too much use of the progressive, and one finds odd expressions like "fue dejando," "he went leaving," an attempt to reproduce a Nahuatl modal construction meaning "left (something to someone) on departure or death." [180]

Over and above such matters of grammatical structure, Spanish texts by Nahuas are distinctive because, whether from preference or necessity, they often bypass Spanish idiom and attempt to reproduce favorite Nahuatl idioms instead. An example common in the texts, many of which discuss land transactions, has to do with the manner of explaining that two pieces of land border on each other. A current Nahuatl phrase type mentioned the owners rather than the fields and after using the first-person plural specified only the name of the nonspeaking person, the speaker being taken for granted as in all such Nahuatl constructions, as if one were to say "we abut John" (i.e., the lands of John and myself abut). Thus we are not surprised to find in Spanish texts things like "nos lindamos señor San Miguel," "we border señor San Miguel" (i.e., the lands of the lord San Miguel and myself border on each other), even though the phrase as written is not grammatical in Spanish and would not be comprehensible except for the context. [181]

Other and more numerous expressions in the texts are odd not so much because they are ungrammatical or unidiomatic in Spanish (though sometimes they are that too) as because they are things not normally said in Spanish. All the formulas, often highly localized, that had grown up in Nahuatl public statements are retained, such as the repeated exhortations for commands to be carried out.[182] In many instances, Spanish vocabulary is put to the service of Nahuatl syntax, idiom, formula, and ways of thinking. If the Nahuas had become versed at Hispanizing calques in their own language, they now showed themselves equally prodigal with Nahuatlizing calques in Spanish.

As for the geographical spread of this Spanish in which the Nahuatl substratum often juts onto the surface, there is no doubt that documents written by Nahuatl speakers in "bad" Spanish issued in the final decades of the colonial period from a large assortment of subregions, though they remain to be collected and studied closely. Three documents of this type from the Cuernavaca region, dated 1766 to 1795, have been made available to me, and they share some characteristics both general and specific with the Toluca Valley texts.[183] It is most suggestive that the Nahuatlizing Spanish documents from the Toluca region are connected with a set from the Nahua community of Mexico City, which though more complex and at a higher level of fluency essentially fits the same description.[184]

Indeed, the Nahuas of the two regions were using this kind of Spanish to communicate not only with Spaniards but also with each other. It appears that a variety of Spanish, distinct from the standard among Hispanics but with some uniformities across a wide area, had arisen and could be put to various uses, much like the dialects of English spoken by various minority and immigrant communities in the United States today—and this despite the fact that Nahuatl remained the primary vehicle for spoken expression in the community at large and had by no means become extinct for written expression either. Presumably, Nahuatlizing Spanish as a community-wide feature was a transitional phenomenon on the way to a broader acquisition of the more standard form spoken by most bilingual Nahuas today, but the timing remains for now a mystery.

Looking back over three centuries of Nahuatl adaptation to Spanish, one sees constants (such as the operation in terms of complexes around a central innovation) and seamless continuities (such as the long-term extension of "pia" in the direction of "tener") that transcend any notion of stages, not to speak of the many long transitions and subtle changes that we have observed. Nevertheless, in its totality, the three-stage sequence of the postconquest central Mexican experience is reflected in the linguistic dimension more clearly than in any other aspect of culture. Figure 7.1 attempts to convey a notion of both the larger simultaneities and the subtleties. In granting language a certain priority in the three-stage process, I am not placing it at the beginning of a causal chain. Rather the subconscious patterns of thought resulting in the regularities of language evolution were clearly set in motion by contact oc-

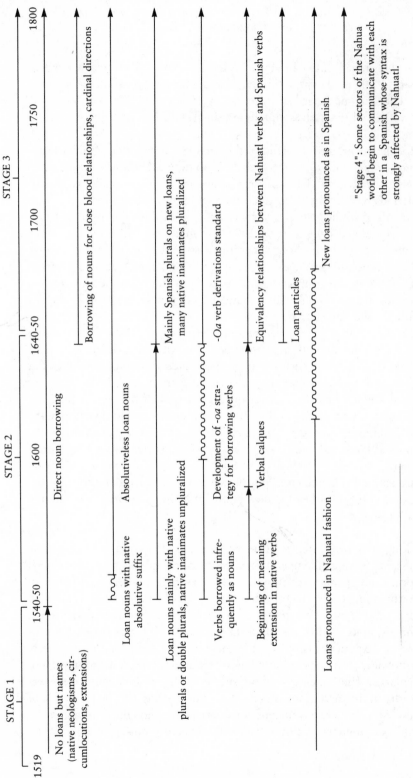

Fig. 7.1. The chronology of Spanish contact phenomena in Nahuatl. A wavy line indicates a period of transition. Source: An extended and revised version of a figure from Frances Karttunen, "Nahuatl Literacy," in George A. Collier et al, eds., *The Inca and Aztec States* (1982), p. 403.

curring for economic, social, political, and religious reasons. Yet the linguistic developments do have a greater generality and to some extent greater explanatory value as well as greater visibility, for the other aspects are in a sense included within language, and economic or political change in the Nahua world was also, perhaps even primarily, linguistic change, involving new words bearing altered concepts.

8

Ways of Writing

THAT THE SPANIARDS had paper and ink and used them for recordkeeping caused the Nahuas no surprise or puzzlement, for following a centuries-old Mesoamerican practice they had long been doing the same thing, and they quickly made the identification between the two traditions. The indigenous words for paper (*amatl*) and ink (*tlilli*) remained in use in postconquest Nahuatl and were applied to the Spanish variants, precluding the adoption of the relevant Spanish vocabulary.* Preconquest society also knew specially trained and quite honored functionaries charged with composing and preserving written records, so that the Nahuas, like all the other Mesoamericans and more than the paperless Andeans, were immediately ready to attempt writing in a new style and to step into the important role played in the Spanish system by notary-clerks.[1] The very word "to write" in Nahuatl, *icuiloa*, continued to be used instead of any Spanish-influenced term, and so for the most part did *pohua*, "to read."[2]

Yet as in other aspects of the two cultures, the convergence was not complete. That preconquest Nahua writing was pictographic-logographic rather than alphabetic was only the beginning of the differences. In line with the generous use of picture and color in indigenous writing, no strict demarcation existed between writing and painting. "Icuiloa" meant both to paint and to write, or at least to do what Europeans would tend to consider writing.[3] We have no firm evidence that preconquest Nahuas made any distinction of principle between the two activities. Likewise, *tlacuilo* (the agentive of "icuiloa") meant either painter or (by our lights) writer; sometimes, to make it clear what type of painter was in question, the material would be mentioned: *amatlacuilo*, "paper painter."[4] The Nahuas' concept of reading was also different from the Europeans'. "Pohua" had the additional, actually primary, meaning "to count," corresponding well to the very prominent numerical facets of

---

*"Amatl" apparently originally referred to the vegetable material used for the purpose (see also references to the word in Chap. 7, after n. 41, and in Table 7.7). "Tlilli" meant basically "black substance, soot," and was closely analogous to Spanish *tinta*.

preconquest records. The word also meant "to relate, recount, give an account of," hinting at the oral recital that accompanied a preconquest document, interpreting and expanding on it. The visible artifact was thus only a part of the total communication, which proceeded on two partially independent tracks. The pictorial part could convey some things that were beyond spoken words and had the ability to pass through time unchanged, but the oral part carried much of the burden of narration, formulation, and conceptualization, since whatever the inherent capacity of the preconquest central Mexican writing system, it was not ordinarily (or to our certain knowledge ever) used to capture complete utterances of running speech in the manner of some of the earlier Mayan writing.* For this and other reasons, the genres of Nahuatl documents before the conquest diverged substantially from their nearest Spanish equivalents.

This chapter addresses the process of the interaction of the two writing traditions as seen in Nahuatl documents of various kinds. It begins with the mechanics of writing, but gradually wanders further and further from a narrow interpretation of the topic, since for the Nahuas (and perhaps other peoples are not so different) writing always remained what it had been before the conquest, one part of a larger communication system from which we cannot separate it without great loss of insight. Moreover, the system varied immensely with genre, so that writing becomes bound up with form, convention, and even form-specific content, and soon one is discussing genre as much as writing per se. In Chapter 9, in a way an extension of the present one, the topic could still be called writing, but the emphasis shifts even more to the form and content of some genres of expression important to the Nahuas of postconquest times.

Preconquest Writing

Central Mexican writing at the time the Spaniards arrived employed three potentially distinct techniques: first, direct depiction, as in portraits of gods or priests showing every diagnostic detail of their accoutrements, or in maps of conquests; second, ideograms or logograms, as in the conventional signs (also originally pictures) meaning water, gold, sun, and the like; and third,

---

*I say central Mexican rather than Nahua because, although the Nahuas are the best-known practitioners of the system, there is little about it that is language-specific, and it seems to have existed with little or no difference among neighboring peoples. The Nahuas probably were not the originators of any of the system's main elements, although they had their own style. Even the name glyphs, which seem so peculiar to Nahuatl, would probably have been comprehensible to non-Nahuas, for many of the same names (that is, sounding very different and using roots native to each language, but meaning the same) were spread across the length and breadth of Mesoamerica. See Bricker 1986 for the early Mayan system. Charles Dibble recognized the double nature of Nahua expression (CA, pp. 9–10).

phonetic transcription, in which (usually conventionalized, ideogram-like) pictures were used to represent the various roots of a word by the sound regardless of whether or not the idea associated with the word-sign was relevant (see Fig. 8.1).[5] Actually, the vast majority of cases of the last type were still very near the ideogram, being representations of proper names (of individuals, altepetl, or altepetl constituents)[6] consisting of transparent words of the Nahuatl lexicon. Thus the glyph for someone named Mixcoatl, Cloud Serpent, would consist of conjoined pictures of a cloud and a serpent. Since on ordinary occasions people probably were not conscious of the original meaning of the elements of names, such transcriptions can in a sense be considered phonetic, but the moment one becomes aware of the original meanings, which are in no way obscured by the external form of the names, these name glyphs simply consist of more or less realistic ideograms. It is when the element depicted coincides in sound with the one intended but differs from it in meaning that we can be absolutely sure that phoneticism is at work. Such cases did occur. A notable example is the depiction of a person's buttocks, *tzin(tli)* in Nahuatl, to convey the diminutive -*tzin*- that is part of many altepetl and calpolli names (see Fig. 8.1).[7]

An extensive conventional syllabary on the order of that associated with the older Mayan script does not seem, however, to have been a feature of Nahua writing. Fluidity was the keynote. Though one can, as I say, detect three logically divergent methods in the Nahua repertoire, all begin with pictures and all involve some degree of convention. In actual documents, the modes are usually so intertwined that the distinctions between them seem artificial. Even "phonetic" elements may be drawn as recognizable pictures; the phonetic and ideographic usually coincide; and ideograms often convey the message through direct pictorial means in addition to convention, as in the burning temples to signify the defeat of an altepetl or a person's head with bleeding neck pierced through by a dart to signify an enemy king's death (Fig. 8.1). One part of the writing system, the numerical and calendrical, although it employed similar means, was so highly regularized that it escaped the usual flexibilities and ambiguities, reporting with great precision numbers of any magnitude and dates within a fifty-two-year cycle; in this dimension, one can speak of writing and reading in a sense hardly different from the European, for no interpretation or oral expansion was required.

This writing system, or rather communication system in which writing was one of two equally necessary components, provided the basis for records of several genres, including tribute lists, cadastrals, records of individual landholdings, historical annals of the altepetl, king lists and royal genealogies, works on gods and ritual, divinatory manuals, and probably other types of which notice is now lost.[8] It does not seem that any attempt was made to use

Direct depiction

The god Huitzilopochtli

Ideograms

"water"
atl

"stone"
tetl

"mountain"
tepetl

"sun, day"
tonatiuh

Phonetic transcription

Çoquitzinco
("little mud place")

Quauhnahuac
("next to the trees")

Huitztlan
("next to the spine")

Transparent ideograms

temple burning

leader pierced by dart

Fig. 8.1. Pictographic techniques. Sources: Sahagún 1905–7, vol. 6, cuaderno 2 ("Primeros Memoriales"); Codex Mendoza; Matrícula de Tributos; Historia Tolteca-Chichimeca.

writing in connection with the many set speeches that carried such a large proportion of Nahua lore. Book Six of the Florentine Codex, the greatest collection of such rhetoric (in alphabetic script), contains none of the relevant preconquest-style pictorial and glyphic material accompanying most of the other books in the work.[9] In any case, the writing as we know it could not have done justice to the subtleties of flowery phrasing that were the essence of Nahua formal talk.

The Introduction of Spanish-Style Writing

Let this glance at the traditional uses of Nahua writing suffice for now; before discussing the influence of preconquest on postconquest genres, I will examine the actual techniques of writing as they took shape in the postconquest period.

As usual, the earliest stage is poorly documented. Presumably, the Nahuas continued for some time to produce or at least use records in their traditional style with no change whatever, other than possibly an impact on the subject matter, but very little is preserved. (Even our most informative "preconquest" documents were mainly redone under Spanish auspices in the 1540's and later.[10]) During the 1530's, a number of Spaniards, who were overwhelmingly if not exclusively ecclesiastics, and within that category overwhelmingly friars, were on the one hand experimenting with pictorial communication themselves and on the other, reducing spoken Nahuatl to the Roman alphabet. In a few centers such as Mexico City and Tlaxcala, they were beginning to teach some of their Nahua student-aides how to write their own language in that fashion, as well as how to manipulate some of the Spanish-style documentary genres. That all this happened we know in a general way from the writings of the Franciscans (especially Sahagún, Olmos, and Motolinia and his successors). The extant writings by Nahuas in Nahuatl tend to confirm the Franciscan version indirectly, but we have virtually no direct evidence about the methods, content, and circumstances of instruction.

From the 1540's forward, however, documents of many types, in many styles, were produced, as alphabetic writing in Nahuatl spread with great rapidity. For the second half of the sixteenth century (Stage 2), the picture is extremely complex and varied. Although alphabetic literacy never became a majority phenomenon among the populace or even among the nobility, by 1570 or before even the smallest altepetl had a new-style notary or two attached to cabildo and church, and in the larger centers there was a whole corps of such figures, as well as a number of nobles able to write in Roman letters. Practitioners in this mode produced, on occasion, documents little different from Spanish models except in being in a different language, but most of them, most of the time, integrated the new writing into the indige-nous central Mexican tradition of recordkeeping, sometimes in subtle ways, sometimes in the most blatant fashion, drawing heavily on the oral tradition as well as the resources of the preconquest pictographic style. Still other Na-hua writers continued to hew to the pictographic method exclusively or at least primarily, adapting it of course to new subject matters and drawing additional symbols from new sources.

By the third quarter of the sixteenth century, the eclectic users of the al-phabet were the mainstream and the vast majority. The use of the picto-graphic system as the primary vehicle was at most a strong undercurrent, progressively fading with each decade and especially after 1600; in most places, it effectively disappeared before the onset of Stage 3.

Postconquest pictographic documents have received more than their proper share of attention, thanks in part to document collectors who mistakenly thought them of preconquest vintage and filled the European archives with them. As a result of their easy availability, many have been published, giving an inflated impression of their weight in the overall scheme of things. Actu-ally, their bulk is infinitesimal compared with the mass of Nahua-produced documentation existing in the Mexican national archives, where it is a great rarity to find anything originating after the 1540's that is mainly pictographic, and the known alphabetic Nahuatl corpus, already many, many times as large as the pictographic, is growing daily. All the same, the continuation of the nonalphabetic tradition has undeniable significance, and I will devote consid-erable attention to it here. It is after all not a topic fully separable from al-phabetic writing, for the two types were quite frequently practiced by the same people within a single overarching framework, and the two methods supported each other. Ultimately, however, they competed, and the alpha-betic method took over more and more of the functions of communication, to the point that the pictorial component became unnecessary and fell by the wayside.

Postconquest Pictographic Writing

In the second half of the sixteenth century, many Nahua writer-painters still mastered the form and sense of the basic repertoire of preconquest glyphs, though some showed an inclination to execute them in a style affected by European artistic conceptions. At the same time, they incorporated new European thematic material as needed, creating much the same kind of dy-namic amalgam of old and new as in other cultural realms, with the new assimilated to the old and adopted for its very familiarity. Pictographic writ-ing had long centered on names, and now it was presented with the challenge

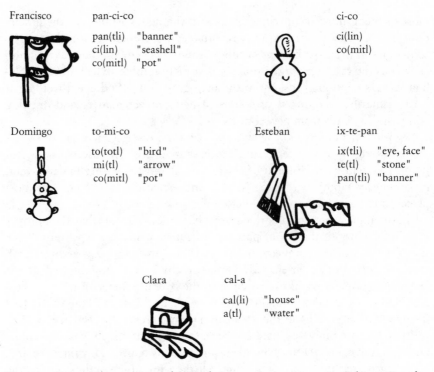

Fig. 8.2. Pictographic versions of Spanish names. Source: Joaquín Galarza, *Estudios de escritura indígena tradicional azteca-náhuatl* (1979), plates 2.7, 3.6, 3.10, 3.11.

of a host of Christian names, attached to both saints and the general population. One solution was to use the visual attributes of the saints (very similar in nature to those of preconquest deities) symbolically, as the basis of logograms for the respective names. A key stood for Pedro, a sword for Pablo, and so on.[11] Aside from the content, the method was entirely within the scope of the traditional writing system, and the new signs were mixed freely with the old as appropriate, in much the same way that indigenous vocabulary and loanwords mingled without distinction in spoken language.

Since in many cases no succinct and striking iconographic symbol emerged for a given name, the other solution was to reproduce it phonetically, at least enough of it for recognition, using the sound values of some of the stock of conventional preconquest ideograms. One of the most popular such renditions was of Francisco, consisting of the glyphs for "banner" (*pan[tli]*), "seashell" (*ci[lin]*), and "pot" (*co[mitl]*), adding up to "pan-ci-co"; see Figure 8.2. This may not seem a very close approximation, and the lack of a good equivalent for the *s* of Francisco is in fact a compromise. But "pan-"

for "fran-" is a perfect transcription of the normal sound substitutions in speech, involving the simplification of an unpermissible initial consonant cluster by the omission of the *r* so troublesome to Nahuatl speakers and the replacement of the nonexistent labiodental fricative *f* with the labial obstruent *p* (see Table 7.17). Later versions of the glyph often omit the first syllable, leaving "ci-co," which also probably corresponds to speech, since names all over the world are often reduced by dropping everything ahead of the stressed syllable.[12]

With both the symbolic and the phonetic aspects of postconquest pictographic writing, it is noteworthy that although ad hoc inventiveness and innovation by specific writers is much in evidence, a living broader tradition clearly still existed in the middle and later sixteenth century. Signs such as a chalice for Juan or the just-mentioned phonetic rendering of Francisco appear not in one document but repeatedly,[13] showing the existence of a stock of new signs generally accepted within a wide circle (available materials do not seem to tell us whether or not that circle extended beyond the Valley of Mexico).

An interesting question that seems beyond definite resolution at present is whether the widespread phoneticity of postconquest pictorial script is primarily a continuation of the preconquest tradition or primarily an adaptation caused directly or indirectly by the Spaniards and their phonetic alphabet. The more European in style and subject matter a pictorial document is, the higher its quotient of phoneticity is likely to be.[14] The preconquest-style tribute lists set down in the 1540's or earlier, the Codex Mendoza and the Matrícula de Tributos, contain a limited amount of unadulterated phoneticism; a document done at a greater remove from Spanish instigation, the Historia Tolteca-Chichimeca, contains less if any; and surviving preconquest glyphs on monuments are not demonstrably phonetic at all.[15] On the other hand, postconquest phonetic transcription in pictorial form operates in terms of syllables rather than in terms of sound segments, as it should have if influenced by European alphabeticism.[16] The syllable had been the unit in Mesoamerican phonetic writing ever since the Mayan script of many centuries previous, and in the Nahua system, as there, only the first consonant and vowel were generally intended to be pronounced (although sometimes the final consonant was included as well).[17] Note also that the great majority of signs used phonetically were taken from the conventional stock of the preconquest period. Moreover, the component signs of a phonetic transcription are to be read in various orders—left to right, bottom to top, top to bottom—or out of visual sequence, just like signs in the preconquest system.[18]

My own provisional, speculative conclusion is that pictorial phoneticism expanded in the postconquest period, but that the method already existed for use when needed; we have too little preconquest material to be able to tell much from the apparent absence of some trait. In preconquest times, however, since nearly all proper names consisted of readily intelligible roots, there must have been little occasion for a pure phoneticism that would use the sound value of a depicted root regardless of its meaning; even non-Nahuatl Mesoamerican names were translatable into familiar concepts and roots. Not so Spanish names, which seemed to consist of a series of nonsense syllables crying out for purely phonetic transcription. Thus it would have been primarily the opaqueness of the new subject material that caused one aspect of the indigenous system to be more practiced, not Spanish encouragement or conscious imitation bringing on an entirely new writing principle.[19]

A somewhat separate branch of pictorial expression were the comic-strip-like documents sometimes called Testerians, after a Franciscan friar associated with the style. They illustrate each episode and usually virtually each word of a Christian religious text such as the Lord's Prayer or the Ten Commandments.[20] Most seem to date from very early, centering on the 1530's, and all appear to have been composed under ecclesiastical auspices. Indeed, though we have little trustworthy direct evidence on the matter, the Testerian documents have the aura of having been produced directly by Spaniards. Beyond the use of visual material and the occasional presence of a Nahuatl translation of the text for oral presentation, there are few similarities with indigenous methods. The exemplars of this genre attempt to follow a spoken text far more closely and exhaustively than occurs in indigenous writing. Whereas in the latter tradition the pictorial aspect has its own life, veering from and sometimes taking precedence over the more discursive and explanatory spoken words, in the Testerians the spoken text has utter primacy, the pictures being nothing more than an attempt to reproduce or suggest it. The vocabulary of signs employed does not for the most part include the preconquest glyphs so frequent in ordinary Nahua postconquest pictorial documents, nor, in the main, are indigenous artistic conventions employed. Although the Testerian style did not take hold in indigenous pictorials generally, it may have had some impact. Thus a glyph for the assumption of Mary possibly had its origin in Testerian pictures showing two feet disappearing into the sky, the rest of the body cut off by the upper border of the picture.[21] Spanish ecclesiastical interest in pictorials appears to have been strong, not only in the early years when the friars' lack of knowledge of indigenous languages almost dictated it, but later as well, perhaps motivated by a feeling that this method would convey messages directly to a populace in the majority illiterate. Such attitudes on the part of ecclesiastics may have contributed to the creation of some late pictorials done when the tradition was generally receding quickly in favor of alphabeticism.[22]

Alphabetic Writing

But let there be no doubt: as early as the middle of the sixteenth century, alphabeticism was gaining the upper hand over pictorial treatment, and the balance continued to shift with every passing decade.[23] Not that it was a question of pure displacement. The products of the preconquest pictorial tradition have much in common with the items called "handouts" that play such a role in academic and business presentations today. The handout contains some diagrams, numbers, and key words or concepts, useful both to the audience, who thereby get the core elements of the message in easily comprehensible form as a guide and reference, and to the speaker, who is reminded of the main points in sequence and, even if a polished prose statement has been prepared, may speak extemporaneously from the handout, reconstructing the largely memorized statement. In an alphabetically written text, the Nahuas had in the first instance not something to compete with the skeletal, handout-like pictorial document, but something able to complement it through a faithful record of the extensive accompanying oral statement. Paradoxical as it may seem, the primary original purpose of alphabetic writing in the Nahua system of communication was to reproduce the oral component, and though things would change with time, this orality would always adhere to Nahua alphabetic documents more than to most comparable European texts.

As to the technical characteristics of the Roman alphabetic script applied to Nahuatl, they need to be considered in two phases, first as shaped by the Spanish ecclesiastics who originated the orthographic system and then as reshaped by the Nahuas. It is not clear that any one of the early Spanish titans of Nahuatl language studies was primarily responsible for the definitive adaptation of the Roman script to Nahuatl. Molina and Sahagún are too late in time, and in any case Sahagún's practice deviates considerably from the standard.[24] Fray Andrés de Olmos, the earliest student of Nahuatl to have produced an extant grammar, is a likely candidate, but his script too varies from the usual canon in some details.[25] The earliest known corpus of alphabetic Nahuatl, the Cuernavaca-region census records of the late 1530's and/or early 1540's, was written by various indigenous persons, manipulating the script very much in their own way but betraying their schooling in a single orthographic canon, probably developed by a friar of the Franciscan monastery of Cuernavaca. The system is essentially the definitive one except that *tz* is missing, *c* (*ç*) and *z* being used instead.[26]

In all probability, the standard orthography had several inventors; in any event, it operated primarily by using the Spanish values of the Roman alphabet for similar sounds in Nahuatl and is what one would expect any literate

TABLE 8.1

The Roman Alphabetic Orthography of Nahuatl

Sound	Ordinary Spanish symbols	Special symbols or different values	Changes by first half of 17th century	Stage 3 changes
a	a			
k	c (with a & o), qu (with e & i)			
kʷ	qu (with a), cu (with e & i)[a]	cuh, cu, uc, for unvoiced final [kʷ]	cu for all prevocalic cases in some usage	
č	ch			
e	e			
i	i			
l	l			
ll		ll		often l, with ll having value [y]
m	m			
n	n			
o	o	u, especially for long o		
p	p			
s	ç, z (final)			s
š	x			
t	t			
tˡ		tl		
tˢ		tz		
w	v, hu, u[b]	uh for unvoiced final [w]	hu predominant prevocalically	
y	y			sometimes ll
glottal stop		h (sporadically)		

[a] In Spanish, these did not represent a unitary segment, although the pronunciation was close to identical.
[b] The use of *u* with this value in Spanish writing would have to be considered quite a rarity.

Spaniard to have done (see Table 8.1). Because Spanish had close equivalents of a large proportion of the repertoire of sound segments in Nahuatl, this simple expedient went a long way, accomplishing much more than the reverse procedure would have done, since Nahuatl lacked more of the sounds of Spanish than vice versa (see Table 8.2). Even so, Spanish was without the equivalents of several important Nahuatl segments and distinctions.

The two most urgent needs were filled by straightforward digraphs, that is, two letters (representing familiar Spanish sounds) used as a unit to represent what in Nahuatl was a unitary segment: *tz* for [tˢ] and *tl* for [tˡ]. Faced with the true double [ll] of Nahuatl, which Spanish lacked (using written *ll* for a different sound), the friars who were developing the system drew on their training in Latin, which had geminate *l*, and used *ll* with that value. In Nahuatl, any voiced consonant was devoiced at the end of a syllable. Although Spanish had no equivalent phenomenon, the Spanish orthographers were aware of at least some aspects of the process and notated it in the case of [w] by writing *-uh* instead of the prevocalic *hu-* (or *u* or *v*); *-cuh* and *-uc* instead of *cu-/qu-* for [kʷ] had the same intention.[27] But Nahuatl's distinction between long and short vowels, which served to differentiate many roots from each other, went entirely unnotated, and although ways were devised to write the glottal stop, most usage ignored that important Nahuatl consonant, in both cases because of foreignness not only to Spanish orthography but to Spanish speech.[28]

Thus the system the friars taught the Nahuas was far from a perfect vehicle for recording the spoken language, but as practical orthographies go, it was nothing to be ashamed of. After all, vowel quantity, a basic feature of Latin, did not figure in Roman orthography either, and the glottal stop, too, has often been undernotated in the world's writing systems (remember that preconquest syllabic phoneticism also seems to have left vowel length and glottal stop out of account). The Spanish-based Nahuatl orthography was perfectly serviceable, and it surely captured speech far more easily, fully, and

TABLE 8.2

Comparison of the Spanish Alphabet and the Spanish-Based Nahuatl Alphabet, 16th Century

Spanish	Nahuatl	Spanish	Nahuatl
a	a	m	m
b	–	n	n
c, ç ([s] before vowels)	c, ç	ñ	–
		o	o
c ([k] before back vowels)	c	p	p
ch	ch	qu ([k] before front vowels)	qu
d	–	qu ([kw])	qu ([kʷ] before [a])
e	e	r	–
f	–	s[d]	–
g	–	t	t
h[a]	–	–	tl
hu [w]	hu, uh (syllable-finally)	–	tz
		u[e]	–
i	i	v	–
j	–	v ([u], [w])	v
–[b]	–[b]	x ([š])	x
l	l	y ([i] and [y])	y
ll ([l̄])[c]	–	z (syllable-final [s])	z

[a]Prevocalic, often silent. Not included on the Nahuatl side is the occasional practice of using *h* for glottal stop, always syllable-final.

[b]Though sometimes used by the highly educated in words of Greek origin, and very rarely appearing in the same way in Nahuatl texts, *k* was not part of the normal alphabet of either language.

[c]Nahuatl *ll*, a true double [l], does not correspond to this unitary sound.

[d]Some Nahuatl writers used *s* as equivalent to *x*.

[e]Some writers of Nahuatl used *u* for *o*; it was also used by some for prevocalic [w] instead of *hu* or *v*.

unambiguously than anything the Nahuas had known before. They took to the system immediately, and though as we will see they used it in their own way, they did not alter or attempt to tamper with the value of the symbols, nor did they try to add any.[29]

The primary innovation that indigenous writers made in the system, technically speaking, was to apply the introduced symbols to a different object. Spaniards used letters to spell words; the Nahuas used them to reproduce pronunciation. For the Spaniards, each word had a set spelling known to all, and for most writers at least, that spelling did not vary appreciably no matter how the writer happened to pronounce the word (this is the basic principle of all modern European standard orthographies).[30] Writing consisted of the spelling of a sequence of separate words (separate to the mind even though often written with no space between them).

For the Nahuas, each sound uttered was recorded by the corresponding letter in an ongoing string that took little if any cognizance of an entity "word" or its uniform spelling; rather each labial stop that the writer pronounced was written *p*, each palatal glide *y*, and so on. If the writer happened to pronounce the word for maiden "ichpochitl" rather than the standard *ichpochtli*, he would so write it. If he pronounced an extra glide between vowels, he would tend to write it in (though rarely with full consistency), as in "ohuacico" instead of standard *oacico*, "he arrived here." In much Nahuatl speech, it appears that any intervocalic consonant was likely to be pronounced double, and was consequently often so written whether the root involved contained a double consonant or not. Such gemination was especially common in tying a particle into a phrase, as in "huell anquimocuitlahuizque" instead of standard *huel anquimocuitlahuizque*, "you are to take good care of it" (see Fig. 8.3, which has two examples). Though incapable of yielding detail the orthography was not equipped to represent, this philosophy of writing automatically left a good record of dialectal and individual variation usually lost in texts done on European principles.

If there were units larger than the letter/sound segment in alphabetic writing as practiced by the Nahuas, they were not the word but the syllable and the phonological phrase. A few writers placed a discernible space between each pronounced syllable (morphology was ignored), and inadvertent repetition and omission took place mainly in terms of syllables. Whether or not this trait was influenced by the emphasis on the syllable in preconquest Mesoamerican writing is a matter for speculation. It appears to me that the Nahuas were simply operating in terms of all the elements directly perceptible in speech: the segment, the syllable, and the phrase.

The phonological phrase, consisting of a nuclear nominal or verbal stem with its affixes and its adverbial or other modifiers, is a far more obvious, detectable entity in Nahuatl than either the "word" or the complete utterance (sentence); frequently the phrase in fact is a complete utterance.[31] In what often appears to be an uninterrupted flow of letters across the page, it is hard to demonstrate a concern with this unit, but subtle indications of its importance do exist. Though usage varied, many Nahua writers followed the common Spanish practice of writing *i* as *y* at the beginning of a unit (for the Spaniards a sentence or word), but for them the unit was the phrase. For example, one would write "yuh quitoa," "so he says, he says that," but "yn iuh quitoa," "as he says"; "yquac ohualla," "he came at that time," but "yn iquac ohualla," "when he came"; and so on.*

To my eye, many Nahuatl texts look as though the writer is putting a space between most phonological phrases, but this is debatable, since the "space" was not a fixed category in the writing of the time, Spanish or Nahua. Occasional writers, however, like the one who produced the passage in Figure 8.3, placed a period (a dot, at least) between phrases, leaving no doubt about the matter. My present impression is that this type of notation is more characteristic of Stage 2 than of Stage 3, but even for the late period there are still many hints of the tendency of Nahua writers to think in terms of a phrase type quite foreign to European languages.

Spanish loanwords received somewhat different treatment in Nahuatl texts than did native vocabulary. Although sometimes they too entered into the flow of letters and were spelled according to the writer's pronunciation, sometimes they operated on the Spanish principle, being treated as distinct words with invariant canonical spellings.[32] Examples produced on the former principle are what allow us to deduce the pattern of Nahuatl sound substitutions in pronouncing loanwords (as treated in Chapter 7). Examples produced on the latter principle hint at a learning process in which Spaniards taught Nahuas the spelling of specific individual words, or the Nahuas in some other way saw the words written in lists or in Spanish texts.

Some items, however and wherever they were learned, spread in identical form through the entire literate Nahua world. Dios, "God," *santo*, "saint," *regidor*, and others are spelled standardly in the overwhelming majority of mundane Nahuatl texts, from the earliest forward.[33] The same invariant standard holds also for common Spanish abbreviations: for names such as Juan or Pedro ("ju⁰," "p⁰"), and for some terms like *justicia*, "justice, officer of the law," rendered as "justᵃ," and *alcalde*, rendered "allde." In fact, these

---

*Figure 8.3 contains three examples, "yn itlayecoltillocatzin" and "yn itlayecoltilloca" (both originally written solid), "the service of," and "yn itetzinco," "concerning, relating to." Throughout the text, whenever a phrase begins with a vocalic [i], the spelling *y* is used, whereas with two exceptions phrase-internal vocalic [i] is written *i*. In one of these cases, "auh yn," *auh* as an utterance marker is so separate that the following element may be thought of as initiating the phrase.

In iquac . quinmomaquilia topili . yn alcaldes . mexico . yn visorrey . quinmolhuilia .
yn amehuantin . alcaldes ye anmochihua yn axcan achtopa . cenca . ypan xitlatoca .
yn doctrina x̄piana . ma mochi tlacatl . quimati . yn itlayecoltillocatzin . yn totecuiyo . dios Auh çatepan . ypan antlatozque . yn itlayecoltilloca . yn totlatocauh . yn
Su magestad . yn tleyn quimonequiltia . yn itetzinco . monequi . ypan antlatozque .
huell anquimocuitlahuizque auh yn ixquich tlacatl . yn macehualtzintli . huell anquimocuitlahuizque . anquitlaçotlazque . ayac çan tlapictli . anquitlatzontequilizque .
yhuan . huell anquimocuitlahuizque . ynic mochi tlacatl . Elimiquiz . ayac tlatziuhti-
nemiz .

When / he gives the staff / to the alcaldes / of Mexico City, / the viceroy / says to
them: / "You / alcaldes who are being appointed / now for the first time, / greatly / see
to / the Christian doctrine; / let everyone / know / the service of / our lord / God. And
after that / see to / the service of / our ruler / His Majesty; / what he desires, / what by
him / is needed / you are to see to, / you are to take good care of. And as to all / the
commoners, / you are to take good care of them, / you are to treat them with
esteem; / no one without reason / you are to judge, / and / you are to take good care /
that everyone / cultivates (the land), / no one lives in idleness."

Fig. 8.3. Text from the Codex Osuna (1565), illustrating orthographic division into
phonological phrases. Source: Codex Osuna, f. 471v; also Charles Gibson, *The Aztecs Under Spanish Rule* (1964), plate 7.

NOTE: Since the particle *auh* indicates the beginning of a new utterance and implies a
full stop immediately preceding, the writer did not consider it necessary to put periods
before that element. In one or two cases, the period falls where one would not expect
it, probably because the writer was putting special emphasis on a word that would
ordinarily be included with the following phrase (as with *cenca*).

For easier comprehensibility, the transcription divides the letters into words by
modern principles, which as the reader can see is not true of the original. In the translation, the slashes correspond to the periods of the original; to retain the parallels,
I have at times departed from English idiom and syntax.

TABLE 8.3

Hypercorrect Letter Substitutions in Loanwords

Primary substitutions[a]	Examples	Hypercorrect substitutions	Examples
p for b, v	capilto (cabildo)	b for p	brigo (pregón, "proclamation")
p for f	Papia (Fabián)	f for p	forificacio (purificación, "purification")
t for d	totor (doctor)	d for t	desurello (tesorero, "treasurer")
c for g	clelico (clérigo, "priest")	g for c	Gremente (Clemente)
l for r	liplo (libro, "book")	r for l	morino (molino, "mill")
x for j, g, s	Xihuan (Juan), xolal (solar)	j, g for s[b]	julal (solar), gerencia (residencia)

[a]This list does not exhaust the primary substitutions (see Table 7.17), but the others do not lend themselves to hypercorrect merging. The use of *u* for Spanish *o* is not in this category because many Nahuas wrote *u* in native vocabulary either in free variation with *o* or to distinguish long *o*.

[b]No example of *j* or *g* for Spanish *x* is presently known to me. The frequent use of *s* for *x* in Stage 2 texts is not a hypercorrection but an alternate orthography occurring also, indeed primarily, in indigenous vocabulary.

and certain other words were nearly always abbreviated; furthermore, all except a very few abbreviations to be found in Nahuatl texts are normal Spanish renditions of originally Spanish words.[34]

That Nahua writers would have needed to rely on written help with loanwords is understandable, since these words contained sounds unfamiliar to them. Once introduced to the world of Spanish spellings, however, they encountered additional difficulties. The new sounds were represented by symbols not included in the orthography of indigenous Nahuatl vocabulary; moreover, coming from their particular phonological system, the Nahuas could often detect no difference in sounds distinct to the Spaniards. Thus, *b*, *f*, and *p* tended to sound the same to them; the only thing they could do was follow the Spanish spelling mechanically. But since all three of the letters just mentioned seemed to be pronounced *p*, it was easy to mix them up, or even to merge them generally, taking it that the Spaniards had three variant spellings of *p*; *b* and *f* were possibly the more elegant (as the rarer, from the Nahua point of view).

This led to not infrequent hypercorrection, the use of *b* or *f* even when the original was Nahuatl's own familiar *p*. Hypercorrection was perhaps most frequent when both the new and the familiar sound (and letter) were contained in the same word. Thus "Pablo" might appear as "Bablo," or the two letters might be switched to form "Baplo." But hypercorrect substitutions appear also without such contributing factors, as in "Biru" for Peru. Table 8.3 details the most common hypercorrect spellings, which are a mirror image of the sound substitutions (and hence primary letter substitutions) of Stages 1 and 2. The very fact of the use of the Spanish letters in this way tells us that the writers had not learned to pronounce the corresponding Spanish sounds. As Stage 3 progressed, both ordinary and hypercorrect letter substi-

tutions became rarer in Nahuatl texts, betraying changed pronunciation and
bringing Nahuatl writing a bit closer to the Spanish tradition (though the
manner of writing indigenous vocabulary was little affected).[35]

After a corps of Nahua notaries and nobles had learned alphabetic writing
and Spanish-style document production from Spanish friars (in the years
around 1535–45, and in smaller or more remote centers perhaps considerably later), the new tradition soon became self-perpetuating. We lack direct
reports on this process, just as we do for the original learning, but the Nahuatl documents preserved today contain much pertinent evidence. Several of
their general idiosyncrasies, things surely not imparted by Spanish instructors, have already been mentioned.

With few exceptions, texts produced by Nahuas, and especially mundane
texts, look different from those produced by Spaniards. Possibly the difference starts with the clear Italianate hand the Nahuas had first been taught, so
unlike the hasty, convoluted, abbreviation-ridden scrawl of Spanish clerks,
lay Spaniards, and even most ecclesiastics. But over and above the special
characteristics of the calligraphy that the Nahuas originally imbibed, their
writing, even as it varied and evolved over time, even when it was done flu-
ently by experts, always remained more rounded, clearer, and less cursive
than current Spanish practice.

Thus Nahua writing became a regionwide tradition of its own, evolving
similarly and quite contemporaneously in the many altepetl spread across
central Mexico. Within this framework, however, there were subregional traditions, traditions by genre or circle, and altepetl traditions. By the seventeenth century, the southern Toluca Valley, for example, had developed a style
of its own, and it would be possible to identify many documents as originating there even if no locality were specified.[36] Nahua annalists, each building
on predecessors and sharing with contemporary colleagues, maintained a
common style and vocabulary, at least within broad subregions.[37] The same
was even truer of the authors of the Stage 3 "titles," who in some subregions
at least shared not only content and style but had deviant orthographic traits
peculiar to themselves.[38]

Above all, each individual altepetl had its own style. Wills done in Coyoacan in the sixteenth and seventeenth centuries, for example, often mentioned specific offerings for tolling the bells at various churches, and might
include in the preamble the phrase "God omnipotent who created the visible
and the invisible."[39] In eighteenth-century Calimaya, the town granted people
land so that they could raise "a kernel of maize" for their sustenance.[40] Each
altepetl had its own conventions, extending beyond phrases like those just
cited to orthography and calligraphy. Consider the similar hands and pro-

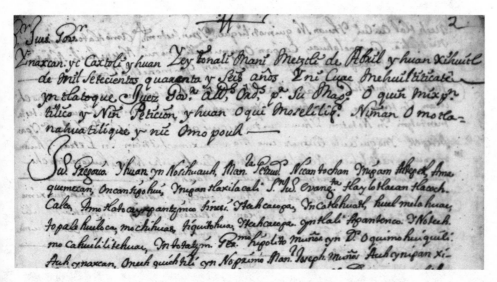

Fig. 8.4. A subregional writing tradition: lines by two different hands from Amaquemecan, 1746. Source: AGN, Tierras 1596, exp. 7, f. 2.

cedures of two writers from eighteenth-century Amaquemecan shown in
Figure 8.4. Altepetl-specific traits can only have been perpetuated by local
notaries handing the tradition down to their successors in a largely autonomous fashion. Surely the Spanish clergy, oriented toward the cities, rotating
about the country and preferring uniform practices, can have had little to do
with it.

Yet the world of writing in Nahuatl was not hermetically sealed. Evolution
took place not only in generally the same direction over the entire Nahua
sphere, but particularly in the direction of Spanish practice, and even following some of the same currents seen among Spaniards over the years. By the
mid-seventeenth century, spoken Mexican Spanish had apparently lost the
distinction between retroflex *s* and alveolar *c/z*; therefore the distinction soon
tended to disappear in writing as well as speech, with *s* being used for almost
all cases in many writers' usage. The same trend, the displacement of *c/z* by
s, occurred in the Nahuatl writing of Stage 3, even though the language did
not undergo any corresponding sound change. The difference in calligraphy
between sixteenth-century and eighteenth-century Nahuatl texts runs parallel
to changes in Spanish writing style, although as mentioned the two can always be distinguished. In some fashion, then, Spanish writing lore was reaching Nahua practitioners. Though tangible proof is lacking, it seems to me
that the most likely avenue was Spanish documents, for literate Nahuas, as

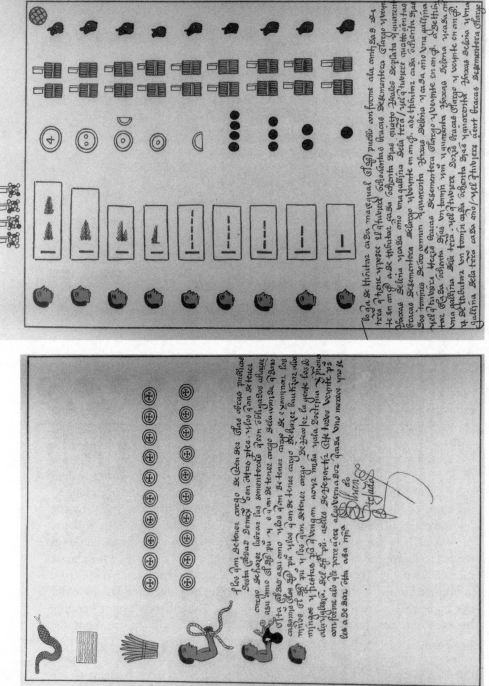

Fig. 8.5. Pages from the Otlazpan Codex. Source: Birgitta Leander, *Códice de Otlazpan* (1967), 2: 5, 6.

an effect of the ongoing expansion of the Hispanic world, increasingly had direct exposure to Spanish writing, and in line with their growing bilinguality they increasingly understood it.

From Pictographic to Alphabetic

The gradual transition from pictographic to alphabetic writing deserves some illustration. As late as the 1540's, some of the documents produced, though concerning current matters and incorporating new phenomena, were still being done entirely in the pictographic manner. An example is the so-called "Otlazpan Codex" of 1549, in which the emoluments of altepetl officials and the taxes and duties of the citizens are set forth in considerable detail.[41] Figure 8.5 shows two pages from the document. The first conveys that twenty pesos, signified by as many double circles containing crosses, were to be divided every year among the minor officials of the town, whose tasks are imparted by various symbols, some of them ad hoc, at the left of the page: a snake for those in charge of rotary draft labor on public works (*coatequitl*, which appears superficially to be analyzable as "snake work"); a conventional sign for a field to signify those in charge of working fields for the encomendero; a conventional sign for food (or fodder?) for those in charge of supplying that item to the same; a man with a rope for those in charge of binding people in marriage; a man pouring water for those in charge of baptisms (based on the Nahuatl word "to baptize," *quaatequia*, "to pour water on someone's head"); and a man's head by itself for those charged with other types of lower-level supervision, especially, apparently, gathering people to attend festivities and religious functions.

The second page shows the amount of money (or cacao for amounts below half a *real*) that each householder of Otlazpan was to pay as tribute every eighty days, based on a rate of one cacao bean for every *quahuitl* of land he possessed (assuming a uniform width of twenty quahuitl). Everyone also gave forty pieces of firewood every eighty days and a turkey annually; the items to be paid or contributed are conventionally depicted, and standard preconquest signs for twenty and four hundred, as well as for a day and a year, come into play.

The document was intended as much for Spanish eyes as for the locals. The alphabetic writing on the pages is done by a Spanish clerk in Spanish, and it seems that in this case, as in many similar ones, the original painter-writer left room specifically for that purpose. The Spanish text, being in the main a translation of the Nahuatl oral presentation accompanying the pictographs, contains a good deal of explanatory information not in the pictorial document itself.

Documents essentially no different from the Otlazpan Codex sometimes seem to contain a very considerable element of alphabetic Nahuatl; on examination this may be seen to be little more than the deciphering of the narrower meaning of the glyphs themselves. An example is the Codex Vergara, a cadastral manuscript from Tepetlaoztoc (Tetzcoco area), done perhaps in the 1540's.[42] The document falls entirely within the pictographic tradition; nevertheless, probably at the time of original composition or possibly a little later, alphabetic glosses were added (whether for the elucidation of the Nahuas or for the benefit of Spaniards is not clear). Many but not all the glyphs have alphabetic equivalents. In Figure 8.6, a page from the manuscript, a series of households are represented. A glyph identifies each household head; thus at the top left a three-part glyph consisting of obsidian blades (*itztli*), a pot (*comitl*), and water (*atl*) approximates in phonetic-syllabic fashion Itzcoatl, the name of the householder, and over the glyph is correspondingly written "yzcoatl." But the symbol "house," just to the right, has no alphabetic equivalent; neither does the line between the name glyph and the house glyph, signifying that the person named heads the household. Nor is there any explanation of the lines indicating kinship, or the positioning of the heads to distinguish blood ties from marriage ties. On the other hand, people are identified by only one name in glyph form, usually the indigenous name, but by two (if they had two) in the alphabetic version. Moreover, for the most part only the household head receives a name glyph, whereas in alphabetic form the names of the spouses and children are specified as well. Yet here alphabetic writing is at most an afterthought and minor supplement (serving as an easy alternative to devising and painting additional glyphs for secondary figures and secondary names of primary figures).

As late as the 1560's, documents much like the Codex Vergara were still being produced, and not only in minor altepetl such as Tepetlaoztoc. The Codex Osuna, a petition and complaint of the cabildo of Tenochtitlan to Spanish authorities in 1565, has many of the same characteristics. Indeed, in a sense it is at the even earlier stage of the Codex Oztlapan, for it required extensive supplementary oral communication to convey the overall message, and here too the pages are covered with Spanish paraphrases of the oral presentations made by the bearers of the document. Most of the alphabetic writing in Nahuatl merely identifies pictures and glyphs, as in the Codex Vergara. This mode of expression was not the simple result of a lack of competence in the new manner of writing, as may have been the case at least to some extent in Otlazpan and Tepetlaoztoc, for the Codex Osuna contains a few passages of extremely well-written Nahuatl prose (Fig. 8.3 was an example), moving in the direction of putting the complete, expanded oral explanation of the pictographic element on paper. In fact, full-fledged alpha-

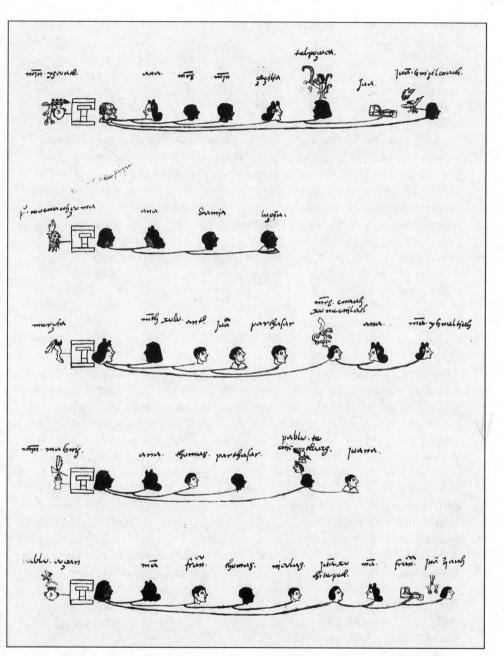

Fig. 8.6. Page from the Codex Vergara (1540's). Source: Codex Vergara, f. 38v; also in Barbara J. Williams, "Pictorial Representations of Soils in the Valley of Mexico," *Geoscience and Man*, 31 (1980): 53.

betic documents were already being regularly produced in Tenochtitlan in the previous decade.[43]

A further step in the evolution is represented by manuscripts that have a full, running alphabetic text but remain strongly pictographic at the same time. Of documents produced by Nahuas outside Spanish auspices, the most elaborate example is the so-called Historia Tolteca-Chichimeca, an account of the political and military history of certain ethnic groups connected with Cuauhtinchan (southeast of Puebla) from legendary times into the early post-conquest period, with overwhelming emphasis on the preconquest. Its modern editors date the work as we now know it between 1547 and 1560, and everything points to the correctness of their judgment.[44] Various composite pictographic-oral accounts, doubtless of preconquest vintage, were used as sources, for some events are reported twice, in a different way each time. The first thing that strikes the reader is the strength of the pictographic element. Glyphs, pictorial maps, and scenes, nearly all drawn in color and with only moderate European artistic influence in the main, are to be found on most pages, and several, including some facing pages done as a grand unit, are purely pictorial. Nevertheless, a copious alphabetic text, in a beautiful hand, is what holds the work together, and entirely alphabetic pages are no rarity.

In documents of the type to which this work belongs, the tendency is to treat every topic both pictorially and alphabetically. In the Historia Tolteca-Chichimeca, the relation between the two elements varies. Much of the time, as in the manuscripts considered above, the alphabetic text merely explains glyphs, though whenever appropriate it readily resorts to complete expanded utterances. Figure 8.7 shows such a page. Taking the right-hand column (for the one on the left presents some problems of interpretation), we see that the drawing toward the top represents an event, and the glyph just below it gives the year of its occurrence, 7 Reed, which is repeated in the alphabetic text as "vii Acatl xiuitl," "7 Reed year." The drawing includes an easily recognizable preconquest temple and a person seated before it, using a fire drill; the person is identified by a glyph consisting of a combined dart and bird, representing one of the ethnic groups playing an important role in the history, the Totomihuaque, for the name literally means "possessors of bird darts." The corresponding alphabetic text, after giving the date, says: "(in this year) the Totomihuaque inaugurated their temple in Chiquiuhtepec, in Chiauhtla." Since the Nahuatl verb "to drill, set a fire," also meant "to inaugurate,"[45] the only thing in the text not given in the drawing is the place of occurrence, which can be deduced from context.

At the bottom is another drawing followed by a year glyph. In the main drawing, to the left is a mountain (the conventional symbol of an altepetl)

Fig. 8.7. Pictorial and alphabetic elements in the Historia Tolteca-Chichimeca.
Source: Paul Kirchhoff, Lina Odena Güemes, and Luis Reyes García, eds., *Historia tolteca-chichimeca* (1976), f. 41r.

surmounted by a basket. To the right is a water symbol, strongly curved, and inside it a decapitated and bleeding person, with a dart entering his neck (the symbol of defeat); the bird dart again identifies the Totomihuaque. The text, after giving the year, reads: "(in this year) the settlement of the Totomihuaque at Chiquiuhtepec [literally, Basket Mountain] was destroyed. At this time they settled at Axomolco [literally, Water Corner]." Here, though the text is very close to the picture, one can sense the impact of an accompanying oral component.

The major portions of text on this page, then, do little more than reproduce pictographic material. Note, however, that several years intervening between events are given alphabetically only. In the source, these years of which no particular tradition remains must have been identified by glyphs that are omitted in the Historia Tolteca-Chichimeca; only the glyphs of noteworthy years are drawn. This principle is at times carried very far. A page giving the places marking the borders of the Nonoalca (f. 4v) contains an explanatory sentence, seventy-six names of places, and only one glyph, although in the source there must have been a glyph for each place. In the many sections and passages of this nature in the document, the pictographic element is still present as a determinant even though it is invisible.[46]

Still other passages, including long stories and conversations, would not have been represented by pictographic means in the preconquest sources, and the pictorial element in such cases is usually weaker, confined to a year glyph, a single large drawing giving the setting, or nothing at all. For example, a page about events at Tula (f. 5v) bears no glyphs and includes speeches such as the following, uttered by the Tolteca Chichimeca when the Nonoalca had already departed: "How are we to act? What are we to do? The Nonoalca have already left us and gone. Let us go too, then. What will those who live here next to us say [if we don't]? Let us go, let us leave the land." Though not pictorially oriented, passages like this go back to the oral component of the combined oral-pictographic medium.

With its different sources and its different types of materials, then, the Historia Tolteca-Chichimeca is something of a hodgepodge. It approaches but never systematically carries out a principle exemplified in certain manuscripts of the second half of the sixteenth century: to use the pictographic component as it was employed in preconquest times (allowing for changes in style and subject matter) and to use the alphabetic text as the equivalent of the preconquest oral component.[47] Few documents could be said to function in this fashion with utter consistency, but a set of annals known as the Codex Aubin, written in the second half of the sixteenth century by an anonymous citizen of the San Juan district of Tenochtitlan, comes very close indeed.[48] In places the early portions, put together retrospectively, have a good deal in common with the modes of the Historia Tolteca-Chichimeca. But for the author's own time (he may have started in 1562,[49] and he kept writing current accounts into the 1590's), the entries follow a set pattern. Each year has its own page, probably laid out in advance; on the left is the year glyph, in the middle the news items in alphabetic form, and on the right glyphs or pictures corresponding (usually) to each item of text.

Figure 8.8, reproducing the page for 1573, can serve as an example. At mid-page on the left is a glyph for 3 House, the year in the indigenous count equivalent to 1573, which is also given, with arabic numerals and letters, at the top of the page. The first item reports that don Francisco Jiménez died on Friday at midnight; the messengers arrived to tell of it on the 4th of January.[50] To the right is a horizontal, shrouded figure, the usual manner of representing someone's death, and a glyph for "Francisco" (see Fig. 8.2 and the discussion of it above). The next item reports that Antonio Valeriano, here called Anton Vareliano, came to be judge (of Tenochtitlan) and began his term on a specified day. To the right is a figure on a throne, depicted in the manner traditional for tlatoque of Tenochtitlan, except that he holds a Spanish staff of office. Above the figure is a glyph giving his first name as *a(tl)*, "water," and *to(totl)*, "bird," giving phonetically "a-to" for "Antón." In the third item, we are told that the Chalca were given possession (of what is not said) on a certain date. The accompanying drawing shows the traditional glyph for Chalco inside an overhead view of a plot marked out with stakes and ropes, as was the practice in Spanish acts of possession. The last item reports that ground was broken for shops in the San Hipólito market. The accompanying picture gives a blueprint-like view of some foundations.

Thus in the Codex Aubin, as in preconquest practice, the pictorial component identifies the topic and gives some basic information; the alphabetic text, assuming the role of the preconquest oral component, repeats the information and expands on it, giving many important details not portrayed pictographically. At times, the pictographs of the Codex Aubin provide some fact, connotation, or perspective not in the alphabetic text. But often, as in our examples, this is hardly the case, though one might say that the manner of depicting Antonio Valeriano shows, independently of the text, a tendency to identify the postconquest governorship with the preconquest rulership even when the dynastic connection had been lost. As the years progress, the pictorials in the manuscript seem to bear ever less of the load of communication.[51] They tend to become eye-catching topic indicators, used much in the manner of marginalia in older European writings, while the alphabetic text becomes the primary medium. The last entries in the work, concerning the early seventeenth century and apparently written by someone else, no longer have any pictorial component at all.

.1573. Años.

x Jnomie don fran ximenez axcan
viernes yoval nepantla ynacico ti
tlantli .a iij. de Enero.

x Jnovalla Juez anton varehiano axcan
domingo compevaltia ynitequh a xviij.
dias delmes de Enero.

x Jnoqn macaco posessi
o chalca axcan Jueves
a xxix. dias delmes de
Enero.

x Jnyemopevaltia motlallan a
dienta santy pohito tianqmz co ax

Fig. 8.8. Page from the Codex Aubin. Source: Codex Aubin, British Museum.

Postconquest pictographic expression was not spread evenly across the whole spectrum of things Nahuas put on paper, but was concentrated in certain genres. It is no accident that the discussion up to now has centered on historical writings, tribute lists, and cadastrals, all indigenous genres carried over from the preconquest period.[52] The situation with mundane documents based on Spanish genres is very different. From the very beginning of alphabetic writing, many items of this type completely lacked a pictorial component. There is not one picture in the entire volume of the Tlaxcalan cabildo minutes, beginning in 1547, with a fragment from 1545. Testaments, from the first known examples in the late 1540's, ordinarily lack any hint of a drawing or glyph.* The lack is important, considering the sheer preponderance of wills in the corpus of older Nahuatl writing. Likewise, letters and petitions in the Spanish manner, even when they first begin to appear in the 1550's, are usually without any pictographic dimension.

But (leaving testaments aside) wherever mundane alphabetic documents touch on questions of land and houses, there the pictographic element is likely to come to the fore, diminishing it is true with time, yet remaining common for the whole of Stage 2, and not disappearing altogether even after that. Alphabetic land-transfer documents in Tetzcoco, though complete in themselves, were standardly accompanied by a line map with measurements given in the preconquest manner, often placed in the center of the page. Or since the map was apparently done first, it might be better to say that the text accompanied the pictorial. This tradition continued into the early seventeenth century.[53] Property transfers of the same time in Tenochtitlan and Tlatelolco usually involved a detailed pictorial of house and land as well as an alphabetic record of sometimes elaborate Spanish-style proceedings (recall the examples in Figs. 3.1 and 3.2).

In composite documents of this type, the alphabetic text as usual repeats most if not all of the data contained in the pictorial and gives additional essential information, such as date, place, price, and terms of grant or payment. Rarely indeed does one find the pictorial alone attempting to give the bulk of the necessary information, as in an example from Xochimilco dated 1567.[54] Here we are dealing not with a pictorial made for the specific purpose of accompanying an alphabetic text but with an extract from a fully preconquest-style oral-pictographic land register still kept current.

Some examples from Coyoacan, where roughly the same trends can be observed as in Tenochtitlan and Tetzcoco, can give a further notion of the type and range of postconquest land pictorials.[55] Figure 8.9 reproduces three

*I do not say that no picture ever appeared in a will, but if so I am at present unaware of it. And this despite the prominence in testaments of questions of land, which as we will shortly see is precisely where one expects pictorials in mundane documentation.

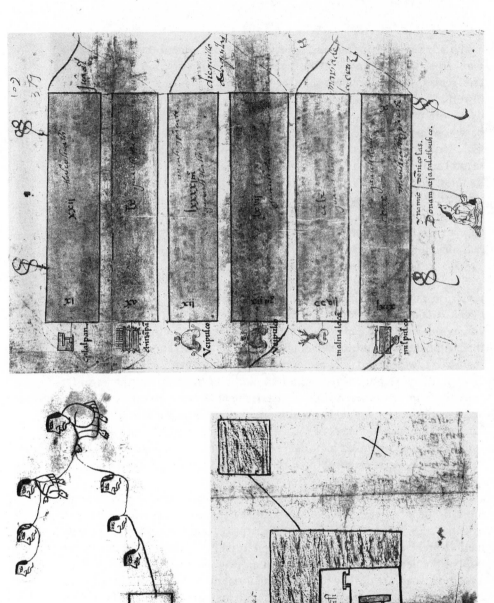

Fig. 8.9. Land-related pictorials, Coyoacan, 1550's–60's. Source: AGN, Tierras 1735,
exp. 2, cuaderno 2, ff. 108, 108v, 114.

items. The first occurs in loose association with a testament, though there is no cross-reference between the two items; the original purpose of the pictorial was apparently to document the inheritance of doña María de la Cruz, and only later does it seem to have been pressed into service to help indicate the division of lands among her children.[56] The plots are shown in preconquest style as uniform rectangles and located by glyphs, and doña María's ownership is asserted by a female figure representing her, but the measurements of the plots, the land categories, and doña María's name are given alphabetically.

Unlike the first example, which is at least indirectly related to Spanish-style legal proceedings, the others go back to the practice of the preconquest tlatoani sitting in audience on certain days to make ad hoc judgments on matters brought to him. In the second one, the alphabetic text (not shown) tells us that the governor divided a deceased man's land at Copilco equally between his niece Francisca and his daughter Ana (who seemed to want it all), and that a constable went to measure the boundaries.[57] The pictorial merely shows the two portions, with (veiled) genealogical information on previous holders, not specifying the location or any other detail. The location and the size of the two subplots are given alphabetically, apparently after the fact.

In the third example, the text reports that the governor affirmed the rights of María, a recent widow, to the property left by her late husband in Hueite-titlan, making María's uncles, whose names are given, custodians or guardians to assure her ownership. The text describes the house and land in some detail.[58] The pictorial is quite elaborate but is limited to representing the property, with no reference to place, owner, or the guardians. The text is actually more precise on measurements than the pictorial, but the latter gives perspectives on the physical layout not emerging from the text.

Like most sixteenth-century land pictorials, the Coyoacan examples, despite some alphabeticism here and there and enough realism in the drawing that many aspects are immediately recognizable, belong to the preconquest pictographic tradition, following its conventions, and are not merely attempts to draw likenesses or make diagrams corresponding to the actuality. With time, because of European influence or a weakening of the preconquest pictographic tradition, or both, portrayals of property became more realistic and less conventional. Figure 8.10 shows a page of a land document from Tulancingo in the mid-seventeenth century with a diagram of the property in question. No preconquest symbols are in evidence, not even for giving the measurements (and in fact, as in many late documents, the measurements are never given in either the alphabetic or the pictorial portion). There is apparently an attempt to portray the properties and the relative size of the two

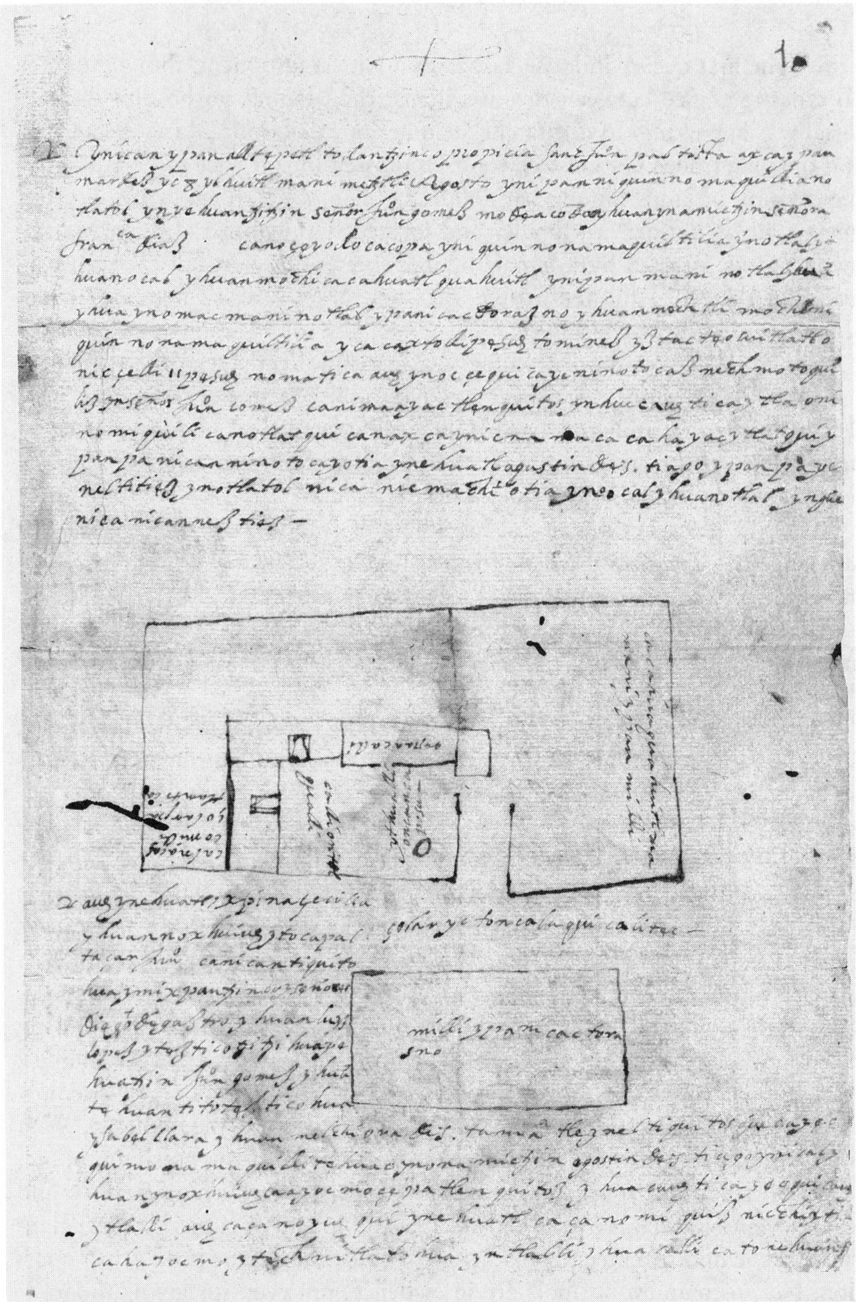

Fig. 8.10. Page from a Tulancingo land document, 1645. Source: UCLA TC, folder 14. Transcribed and translated in James Lockhart, *Nahuas and Spaniards* (1991), item 6.

plots directly, not the preconquest manner. The house and well are shown with simple realism, and features harder to draw are given alphabetically.* The only specific points of contact with the earlier tradition are the drawing's very existence and possibly its location toward the middle of the page; before the conquest, Tulancingo was in the political and cultural orbit of Tetzcoco, and the influence probably still made itself felt through the sixteenth century, if not longer.

The pictorial component, then, had disappeared in many genres of written expression by the early seventeenth century (not to speak of those in which it had never appeared at all), and the land-related diagrams and maps still to be found were hardly different from those often accompanying purely Spanish documentation of a similar kind. Even in the traditionally pictographically oriented genres there was a drastic falling off. Most late Nahuatl local censuses and tribute lists (which in any case are not abundant) are without illustration of any kind, as are the quite comparable baptismal registers. In the work of the greatest of the annalists, Chimalpahin, the epitome of mature Stage 2 Nahua high culture, there is hardly a picture; the same is true of the work of Chimalpahin's closest rival, don Juan Buenaventura Zapata, who wrote in the second half of the seventeenth century.[59] Other late annals do retain a pictorial aspect, including depictions of the four year signs (the related numbers usually being arabic, when given at all) and widely spaced topic emphasizers, among which a bishop's mitre is a favorite (some examples are shown in Fig. 8.11). No doubt such elements ultimately derived from a consistent double mode like that observed in the Codex Aubin, but they are so reduced or impoverished that despite their significance as authentic expressions of a long and continuous tradition, they appear vestigial or primarily decorative. They betray no hint of a retention of specific preconquest and early postconquest glyphic lore.[60] Their conventions, if one can use the term, are more European than anything else. Yet however secondary the pictorial component had become, it could still be done with verve, as may be seen in the whimsically varied rabbit year signs in Figure 8.12.[61]

A partial revival of pictorialism took place in the (in some ways peripheral) Stage 3 genre of "titles" compiled from various sources, including oral tradition and imagination, to authenticate a given altepetl's claim to legiti-

---

*The convention of combining overhead and frontal views (showing in this case the two residential buildings each as it would appear to a person standing in the middle of the patio, superimposed on a line drawing of the ground plan) was used by Spanish diagrammers of the time (see Robertson 1972, p. 257, n. 6). Whether it was also pre-Hispanic or not, I am not entirely sure. Robertson (ibid., n. 5) speaks of a preconquest "T-elevation" convention in which the different sides of a building were depicted in a straight line regardless of perspective, but does not specifically mention a preconquest manner of combining plan and elevation. Note that the much earlier example of María's property in Fig. 8.9, with a distinct preconquest aura, has the combination of plan and elevation as well as multiple perspective.

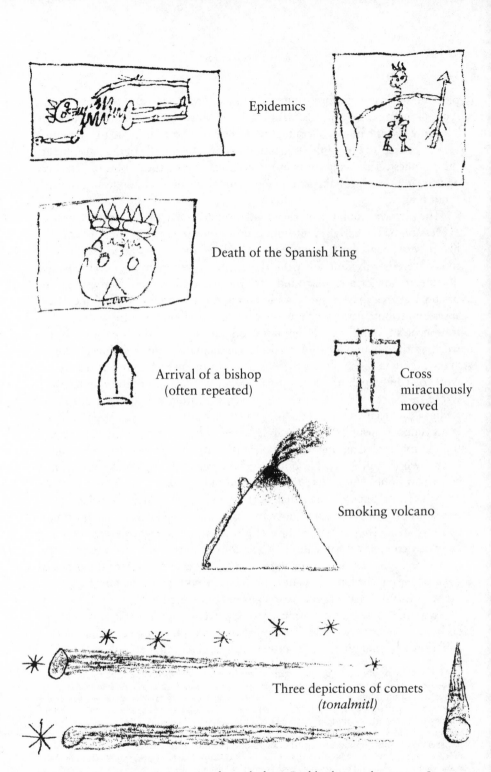

Epidemics

Death of the Spanish king

Arrival of a bishop
(often repeated)

Cross
miraculously
moved

Smoking volcano

Three depictions of comets
(*tonalmitl*)

Fig. 8.11. Some pictures in a set of annals from Puebla, late 17th century. Source: MNAH AH, GO 184, ff. 3–27 passim. The anonymous author or compiler of these annals used pictures primarily for earlier times, nearly abandoning them in the large part of the work recording contemporary events.

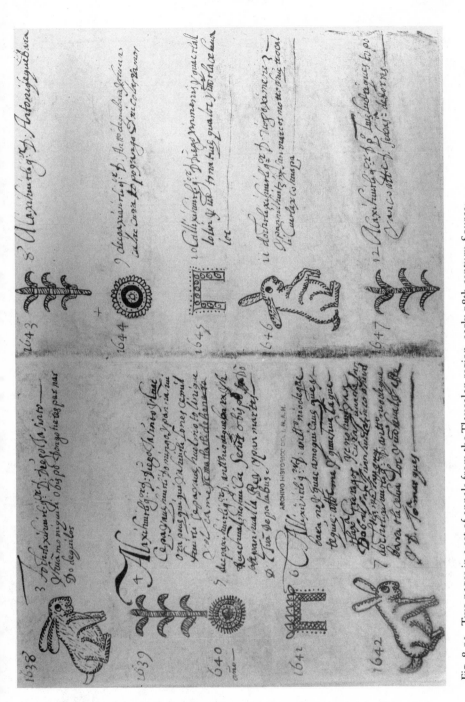

Fig. 8.12. Two pages in a set of annals from the Tlaxcalan region, early 18th century. Source: MNAH AH, Colección Antigua 872, ff. 21v–22.

Fig. 8.13. Illustration for a "title": mock(?) confrontation between representatives of Soyatzingo and neighbors over borders. Source: AGN, Tierras 1665, exp. 5, f. 178v.

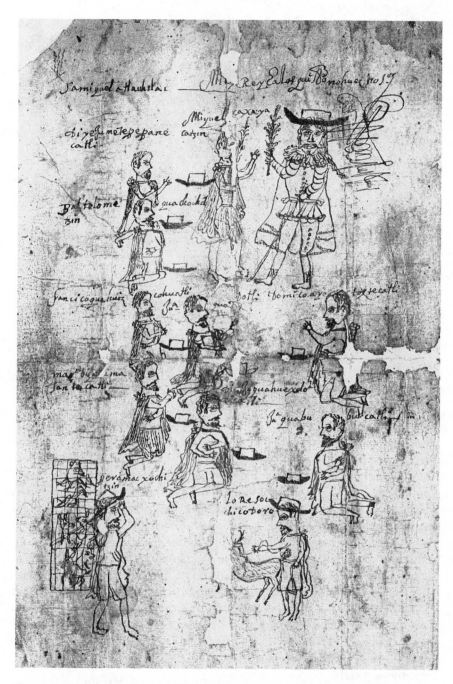

Fig. 8.14. Illustration for a "title": the leaders of Atlauhtla paying homage to Charles V. Source: AGN, Tierras 2674, exp. 1, f. 5v.

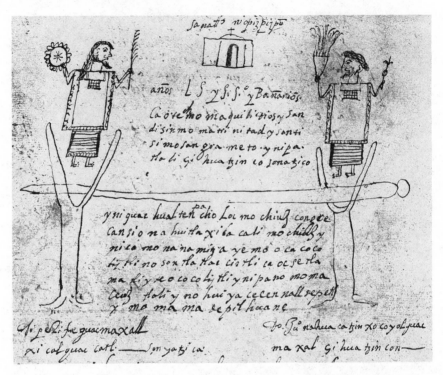

Fig. 8.15. Illustration for a "title": Early leaders of Soyatzingo/Cihuatzinco. Source: AGN, Tierras 1665, exp. 5, f. 179.

mate sway over its territory. Set in an indefinite past combining aspects of the preconquest and early postconquest period, these were archaizing documents, and pictures were often added, whether in the feeling that they were appropriate for that epoch or to give an air of authenticity. Some show signs of contact with older traditions and may have been attempts to copy or adapt existing materials. A schematic depiction of a border conflict between Soyatzingo (Chalco region) and its neighbors continues an earlier pictorial convention, well developed for example in the Historia Tolteca-Chichimeca, of showing the founding fathers of an altepetl as stereotyped Chichimecs with unkempt hair, beards, animal skins or less for attire, and bows and arrows for weapons (see Fig. 8.13).[62] The execution suffers greatly in comparison with the Historia Tolteca-Chichimeca, for the person responsible doubtless lacked any special artistic training, so it is hard to say whether he was trying to copy another picture or simply portraying the Chichimec stereotype in his own drawing style.

Nevertheless, there are some signs that if the illustrator did not have a specific antecedent in mind, he had at least seen documents in the older style. The preconquest war club is shown in a way approaching the old tradition. Several of the combatants, including all of the Soyatzingo contingent (on the right side of the line apparently representing the border) are accompanied by what appear to be name glyphs in addition to an alphabetic rendering of their names. The device at the left bottom can be deciphered; it uses a stream of small circles to represent spitting and at the same time gives a man's name (Chichichatzin, "Spitter").[63] On the right, however, the drawings do not seem to yield a name; two indeed, are the same, a bird (eagle?) over an arrow against a diagonal cross. Perhaps the person responsible for the picture knew that key figures should be accompanied by some device but did not know why. At any rate, this is as close to glyphic writing as the Soyatzingo titles come—closer than most such documents, for in general the titles as a genre are almost as innocent of glyphic writing as are the late annals.

Apparently nearer to following a specific model is the picture in the titles of Atlauhtla, also in the Chalco region, showing the leaders of the altepetl greeting and honoring Emperor Charles V (Fig. 8.14). Such an event never took place, of course, but the sixteenth-century hairstyles and dress and the gestures in the direction of three-dimensional figures point to the existence of an earlier drawing, done by an indigenous person influenced by Spanish style.[64] Still other illustrations in titles, though in some sense coming out of a combination of indigenous and Spanish modes and lore, are highly idiosyncratic, as though the maker were reconstructing traditions rather than operating fully within them. The Soyatzingo titles show the leaders of the two divisions during the conquest period (Fig. 8.15) in a garb surely not Spanish but not authentically indigenous either. Included in the Soyatzingo materials is also a strange item called a "map" ("maban") having nothing to do with delineating territory but picturing the altepetl church held within a giant hand, presumably that of God.[65] The concepts involved are familiar within either the Nahua or the Spanish tradition, and the drawing technique is primarily Spanish, but the design and nomenclature are entirely the writer's own, or at least belong to a new eclectic tradition, for a similar picture can be found illustrating another set of Nahuatl titles of the late period.[66]

In addition to their quasi-traditionlessness, an important trait of pictorialism in the titles is the relatively less close connection between picture and alphabetic text as compared with earlier practice, or even as compared with Stage 3 annals. Our examples range from the Atlauhtla picture, reflected fairly closely in the text, to the Soyatzingo "map," which lacks any relation to the text other than common concern with preserving the altepetl. Even the

Atlauhtla text, though it begins mentioning the people shown in the picture, immediately veers from the episode that forms the picture's topic. Nowhere in the titles do we see a meaningful consistent relation between the two components, whether it be the older relation of the text directly explaining the picture or the newer one of the picture closely illustrating the text.

Preconquest Modes in Alphabetic Texts

But if the pictorial component, earlier in some genres, later in others, lost significance, became Europeanized, or faded from view, that by no means meant the loss of influence of preconquest communication modes on postconquest Nahua writing. The oldest extant Nahuatl-language corpus, the Cuernavaca-region census or tax registers to which I have repeatedly referred, are a striking example. In the entire impressive mass, only the carefully done paragraph markers could be said to be at all directly pictorial; since each paragraph covers one household, the markers (resembling a "C") put one somewhat in mind of the house glyph at the head of each household section in preconquest-style cadasters. Yet the information given corresponds point for point with the content of typical pictorial census documents, and the great majority of it could easily have been rendered pictographically. Perhaps, in fact, a pictorial document actually existed, and the alphabetic text we know represents the oral explication of it. Each item, whether a person, a piece of property, or a tax obligation, is introduced by the expression *iz catqui*, "here is," as though one were pointing to a pictographic version while explaining it.

Whether a pictographic census existed or not is far less important than the indisputable fact that, as was already asserted, alphabetic writing in Nahuatl was cast from the first in the role of the oral component of preconquest communication genres. Nahuatl texts followed many of the conventions of preconquest oral communication modes regardless of the presence or absence of a pictographic component. The first thing one would expect in Nahuatl documents, then, would be evidences of orality, of untrammeled, spontaneous, colloquial speech. Such traits are in fact to be seen; the blow-by-blow tale of the turkey theft and mayhem in Tulancingo and the pleasantries accompanying Ana's land grant in Tocuillan, both of which the reader probably recognizes by now (they will be found in Appendix A in any case), are supreme examples from the late sixteenth century.[67]

Even in documents that in the main follow Spanish models closely, oral spontaneity may burst out at any moment. I will mention a few of my favorite examples. In the late-sixteenth-century testaments of Culhuacan, a woman is dictating her will and specifies that she is leaving her boat to her daughter, but at this point the daughter breaks into the proceedings to declare that she doesn't want the boat, that the person who uses it is her father, always going out on the lake to collect dried grass for tribute purposes, and that he should receive it, as then apparently happened. In another of these wills, a woman expresses concern about a debt contracted by one of her late husbands, feeling that his son, her stepson, should pay it. Someone is then sent to talk to the stepson, who with certain qualifications acknowledges his intention to pay, to the great satisfaction of the woman.[68]

Nor are all such cases early. In a set of lawsuit records from Amaquemecan in 1746, which follow Spanish procedures and observe the conventions with great nicety, when the defendant is cited—that is, informed of the action of the plaintiff, his cousin—he is not content merely to acknowledge the citation but goes on to declare in pithy words his own view of the situation, as a Spaniard in such circumstances would not have done (or if he had, it would not have been written down). The defendant says: "I placed my own petition in Tlalmanalco [seat of a higher court]; let us be heard there as to who has the rights to the land; if he does, let him take it and let's not have bad feelings about it. If he hadn't leased it out I would never have thrown him off; I threw him off because the people he leased it to were real idiots. Otherwise I would never have placed my petition in Tlalmanalco."[69]

A strong tendency of Nahuatl documents, seen in the items just mentioned but reaching its height in the written testimony of witnesses, is the apparently verbatim reproduction of long sections of dialogue. In Xochimilco in 1586, when the will of the noblewoman doña Juana de Guzmán was under challenge, her brother don Juan de Guzmán gave pages of testimony detailing their last conversation and repeating whole speeches just as they would have been given. The following excerpt can give the flavor:

Then she said to the person named Martín de Rojas, "Dear Martín, do please leave us, be so good as to go out for a while." And I, don Juan de Guzmán, changed my place and sat down at the edge of the bed where the lady my older sister was lying. Thereupon I said to her, "Oh my mistress, oh lady, I ask you, is it true that you have already made your testament? Let me hear a bit just in your words what you have ordered concerning the former palace of your late husband, señor don Pedro de Sotomayor whom our lord God took, what you have said and ordered in your testament." And then she answered me and said, "Why is it that you ask?" Then I said to her, "Just because I want to know if you have done something wrong about the ruler's lands, fields, and chinampas; let me hear a bit how it is." Then she said, "This house and everything that goes with it is all to be sold, and however much money is realized from what turns out to be its price will all be delivered to the church, and masses will be said with it for both of us, for me and for my dear late husband, señor don Pedro de Sotomayor whom God took, since no child of ours is alive, for if there were a niece or nephew of yours, certainly it would all belong to that person and I would leave it to him or her, but since there isn't anyone, because of that everything is to be sold."[70]

At this point, we begin to become aware that orality and spontaneity are not at all synonymous. Like many people relying primarily on oral discourse for communication, the Nahuas had long memories and with little effort were able to hold substantial oral texts in their minds, to be repeated later as the need arose. A Nahua asked to relate any human transaction he had witnessed or even heard about would normally respond with a mixture of detailed narrative, each thing as it happened, and realistic dialogue cast in the first person. The account would to all appearances not be compressed at all. When we compare elapsed time in the narrative with the length of such an account, however, we realize that in fact a great deal of selection has taken place.

Even so, the Nahua manner of oral narrative was to give a far more fleshed-out, dramatized version than the succinct third-person paraphrases preferred by Europeans for most nonliterary purposes, and this mode was faithfully reduced to writing in many alphabetic documents of the sixteenth century and later. Such material, both in its spoken form and on paper, although it is in a sense free and spontaneous and surely not the result of lengthy reflection, nevertheless obeyed a convention for reporting events no less fixed and sophisticated than the Spanish/European mode.[71]

Many of the often very precise conventions of Nahuatl oral genres were carried over into alphabetically written texts. Sometimes the origin can be pinpointed; in other cases, we must deduce some facet of preconquest oral convention because of the divergence from Spanish practice. The early letters and petitions of Nahua municipal councils to Spanish authorities were equated in the minds of those who set them down with preconquest oratory, public speeches to and by altepetl rulers and other high lords, of which the Florentine Codex gives us good examples.[72] Among the characteristics of this style were an elaborate obsequiousness, a special vocabulary for referring to the duties and attributes of the ruler, and a tendency to double if not triple or quadruple every noun, verb, and larger phrase; an often quite simple basic message was greatly elaborated in an attempt to impress, flatter, convince, and create an aesthetic effect.[73] This is neither more nor less than speechmaking in the grand manner, a primarily oral vehicle pressed into service for written expression. But the analogy between the Nahua oral form and the Spanish written one was very close in any case, for Spanish letters of this type had their own obsequious formulas and governmental vocabulary, and they too strove for eloquence, though they fell far short of the torrent of words and the intricacies of Nahua speeches.[74]

Much the same style was adopted in communications from one Nahua cabildo to another, but here one feels more strongly the presence of a somewhat distinct strain (already detectable in the first type, to be sure)—Nahuatl's highly developed conventions of polite conversation in everyday circumstances.[75] Most noticeable are elaborate inquiries about the other party's health and welfare. In the few fully private letters in Nahuatl we have, the rules and vocabulary of polite Nahuatl speech take over completely.[76] The bulk of known examples of Nahuatl correspondence of any kind are from Stage 2, when the styles and vocabulary of indigenous high speech were still flourishing. Perhaps letter writing faded in Stage 3 along with the tradition of speech that fed it. Yet a stray letter or two from the late period show less change than one might expect.[77]

What effect did preconquest oral modes have on testaments, the dominant genre of postconquest Nahuatl writing? Here we are unable to establish any one-to-one relationship as we can for correspondence because no samples of indigenous testamentary language have been preserved; indeed, it is not even certain that a form closely parallel to the European testament existed in preconquest times. The stunning success of the testament genre in the postconquest Nahua world, however, suggests a convergence with some significant indigenous antecedent.[78] We can approach the probable shape of this convention in two ways, first through analogy with known Nahua forms and second through systematic divergences of postconquest written testaments from the Spanish norm.

Taking the first tack, and considering the known body of preconquest Nahua oral forms for rites of passage both public and private (in the European way of looking at it), one would imagine that a dying person would make a rather elaborate speech quite rigidly conventional in its structure and vocabulary, full of rhetorical flourishes and admonitions. He or she would doubtless address the audience directly, exhorting them to carry out the requests made and to heed well all that was said, for their memory would in the future be the primary means of authenticating the proceedings. We can only speculate on the size of this audience, but it is well to remember the tendency of Nahuatl rhetoric to draw in a relatively large circle.

Only one possibly direct reflection of surviving preconquest practice is known to me, and it confirms at least part of this scenario. Among the testaments of Culhuacan is a fragment (ca. 1580) recording some of the dispositions of a man named Miguel Oçoma.[79] Miguel died before a formal testament could be written, and thus his final statement was not framed in the Spanish mode. A clerk subsequently wrote down his words, or rather the first part of his statement, very much in the manner of the first-person reportage of speech acts discussed above. Miguel begins with a call to two apparently high-ranking and trusted friends to approach: "Draw close, my lords, you, Miguel Iuhcatlatzin and you, Miguel Coatequitzin." He then immediately gets down to the details of his mass and burial and the division of his goods between his son and granddaughter. There is little that could not be in an ordinary testament except a direct appeal to Coatequitzin to take Miguel's son into his home. How Miguel's address ended we will never know; perhaps death broke into it. But the beginning alone implies the convention of a ceremonious convocation of people responsible for overseeing the fulfillment of the dying person's wishes.

Looking now for hints of preconquest antecedents in the large corpus of Spanish-style testaments in Nahuatl, we find first of all that they do in general follow very closely the structure and even in many respects the wording of the Spanish model; they nearly always obey the Spanish convention of having the testator make an absolute statement addressed to no one in particular and speaking of heirs, executors, and others in the third person, even when they are present.[80] But Nahuatl wills also tend to evince some peculiarities compared with Spanish equivalents. Taking a larger quotient of colloquial, speechlike remarks as something to be expected in all types of Nahuatl documentation, in wills a large proportion of such passages is admonitory.

The remarks are of two kinds, negative and positive. On the negative side, for negative admonitions are more nearly universal in the texts, the testator declares that his command must not be spoiled, vitiated, violated, or carried out wrong, the thrust of the verb pair *itlacahui/itlacoa*, forms of which were invariably used in such cases.[81] Or when he has bequeathed something to someone, the testator may add *ayac quicuiliz*, "no one is to take it from him," *ayac quichalaniliz*, "no one is to dispute with him about it," or *ayac quelehuiliz*, "no one is to covet it of him," or the like.[82] On the positive side, the testator will declare that his statement or order (*notlatol, notlanahuatil*) is to be carried out (the words employed are ordinarily *mochihuaz*, "is to be done," or *neltiz*, "is to be realized," or, most commonly, both).[83]

One is inclined to call these admonitions perorations, for they almost always come at the end of a section (often an item), and they are oratorical in character. Generally they are in the future tense, which in Nahuatl often (as sometimes in English) has the force of a very strong command. There may be only a single general exhortation or warning in the preamble or the ending or at some important juncture in the text, but often the urging becomes a formula automatically repeated after each item.[84] In Spanish wills, such additional commands are hardly found; adding nothing to the legal validity of the bequests, going beyond the purview of the testator, they would appear simply gratuitous. They make sense only if imagined as directed to an audience.

Thus for all that the Nahuatl will employed the Spanish testamentary form—an abstract first-person statement in which the words in writing, addressed to no one in particular, were primary, and a written signature lent validity—it remained residually a speech to a surrounding circle. An additional indication of that speechlike nature is the use of another element missing in Spanish testaments, the formula *ye ixquich,* "that is all," with which Nahuas customarily ended any longer utterance. Sometimes the notary changed to the third person at this point, writing "that is all of the sick person's statement," but more often the testator was permitted to speak for himself.[85] Once a Culhuacan notary allows the person issuing the will to come on stage in actual direct confrontation with the audience at this juncture, saying, "Oh my children, this is all I have said and what you who are present and will be named here have heard."[86]

Indeed, we must imagine that testators carried on in the old fashion much of the time, haranguing the audience rather than dictating to the notary, and that the notary partially abstracted from the proceedings to produce the versions that we read today. Even the perorations, though within an oral tradition, are probably abstractions to an extent. Testators doubtless uttered admonitions, but notaries standardized them. In general, admonitions and exhortations vary with the notary rather than with the individual testator.[87] Yet a Nahuatl will remained more a record of a speech act than a piece of paper, more like a courtroom transcript than a European bill of sale or testament.[88]

An evolution is involved here that I am not yet equipped to discuss systematically. My impression is that it may go somewhat as follows. The very earliest wills are often particularly close to the Spanish model, with little or no obvious oralisms and few deviations of any kind from the pattern originally set by the Spaniards.[89] The notary, with the new model still quite firmly in his consciousness, tended to abstract strongly from what was actually said. An autonomous tradition of Nahuatl testaments had not yet formed. After a generation or so, Nahua notaries ceased to think directly in terms of the original models and instead operated by precedents and their own evolving practice. Now more orality and other Nahua tradition crept in. It is at this time, with things still very fluid, that spontaneity was at a maximum, and more of what testators said was written down literally than at any other time. The next step was that certain aspects of orality and Nahua tradition were frozen as written formulas that represented but no longer so literally reproduced the testamentary speech act; the latter may have continued much as before or may have gradually assimilated to some degree to the now long-standing Spanish-Nahuatl formulas.[90]

These steps look a bit like my three stages of overall development but do not seem to coincide with them in most ways. They represent a quite purely internal evolution in the Nahua world rather than adjustment to an ever-increasing Spanish presence. The first two steps both took place in Stage 2, and though the third is indeed characteristic of Stage 3, wills were increasingly formulaic in the new style by the early seventeenth century.

Given the declamatory nature of the Nahuatl will, the audience was an integral part of the testamentary proceedings. In the Spanish genre, the closest thing to an audience was the body of witnesses (although their primary function was to observe the signing of the document), and that term (*testigos*) was quickly taken over and applied to the listeners present, or to some of them. In some early Nahuatl testaments there is, from the Spanish point of view, nothing special to note about the number or type of witnesses listed.[91] But two distinctive tendencies, not necessarily mutually exclusive, do characterize witnesses to Nahuatl wills across the sixteenth century and later, seen en masse. One was the use of altepetl officials—cabildo members, the fiscal of the church, and others—over and above the notary who wrote the will.[92] The other was the presence of a larger number and variety of witnesses than the Spaniards generally used.

Spanish wills, especially in the case of people of high rank, were sometimes attested to by a substantial number of witnesses, but rarely did they include females. Witnesses to Nahuatl wills were women as often as not. A convention even existed for listing them; after naming the male witnesses in one block, notaries would often write the heading *cihuatzitzintin,* "the women," and proceed to list them in turn. The body of witnesses often included close associates and neighbors of the testator, as well as those who were receiving bequests or who were debtors or creditors. Heads or elders of the immediate ward or subdistrict might be present. Married couples often made up a good proportion of the men and women witnesses.[93] Despite exceptions, it seems to me that the later sixteenth century was the great time of listing large numbers of ordinary people as witnesses, and that by Stage 3 the predominant pattern was to call on present or past governors and alcaldes and above all the fiscal of the church, supplemented by a few associates or relatives of the testator. Possibly women were less frequently represented among the witnesses of the eighteenth century, though this impression remains to be verified by systematic research as more wills become available in published form.

The apparent intention behind the use of both authorities and a cross section of the neighborhood as witnesses was to have valid representatives of the community hear the testator's statement. Likewise, it was apparently considered important to have people who were directly affected, and who might later be expected to raise objections, present at the proceedings. The nature of the witnesses, together with the nature of the statements of the testator, leads me to the conclusion (as earlier put forth elsewhere[94]) that the understood purpose of the witnesses' presence was much broader than in the Spanish system. It appears to me that the primary function of the body of witnesses was to give assent on behalf of and in the eyes of the community—assent not merely to the fact that a certain ceremony was properly carried out, but to the truth and validity of what the testator said. The Nahuatl wills in the archives were brought to the authorities not only to settle disputes among heirs, but to prove family possession in the first place, like a deed, something wills could not do in Spanish law. The audience by its silent presence was saying that the assets mentioned in fact belonged legitimately to the testator and that his allocation of his goods was also legitimate.

In this light, the testator's perorations take on the nature of the community's indirect statement that the will must be enforced. In this light, too, certain other assertions that seem to exceed the testator's proper scope can be understood. It was common for the testator to order items sold, and going beyond that, to order what price they were to fetch.[95] These apparently over-ambitious recommendations make more sense if we interpret them as implying the assent of the audience to the declared worth of certain items under current conditions. On the principle of "speak now or forever hold your peace," it is not strange that members of the audience sometimes did speak out. This was probably the expected course of action of audience members since preconquest times; thus some of the episodes I cited earlier as examples of oral spontaneity, though they do partake of that nature, involve purposeful, appropriate steps foreseen within the framework and are not spontaneous in the sense of being random departures from the norm. Likewise, apparently passionate outbursts on the part of the testator, lambasting deadbeat kinfolk, can be seen as a calculated and normal way of putting a case before the audience to justify actions against those relatives, leaving them out of the bequests or repudiating their debts.[96]

Because wills are so relatively abundant and so basic to Nahuatl documentation, I have used them to explicate the interplay between the pronouncements of the primary party and the usually implicit assent and legitimation of the witnesses as audience and representative of the community. Many of the same things can be said about most mundane Nahuatl documents that have any pretension to legal force, and especially land documents. The latter even show some of the characteristic phenomena more distinctly than the testaments, for as we saw from a different point of view in Chapter 5, the witnesses to acts of possession were often too numerous to name, being the bulk of the population of the neighborhood where the property was located. Furthermore, they were normally interrogated specifically about the validity of the transfer in question, and they gave their reply as a body, expressing the consensus.[97]

In many Nahuatl bills of sale, on the other hand, there is little noticeable orality and no special role for the witnesses that one can detect. The witnesses are often no more numerous than in a comparable Spanish document, and the Nahuatl notaries often follow the wording of the Spanish model even more closely than with wills, leaving the use of specific terminology as the primary way in which a strong indigenous residue shows through.[98]

The Evolution of the Spanish Documentary Genres in Nahuatl

The residual substratum of indigenous communication modes tends to be the most interesting and perhaps in some ways the most significant aspect of postconquest Nahuatl writing at all stages, in the sense that it gives it its special character. But we must not forget the enormous impact of various Spanish documentary genres, which became, in easily recognizable versions retaining the main lines of the original models, a basic component of Nahuatl writing practice. Very close reproductions of Spanish formats can be found at various time periods. Some of the closest are by well-instructed Nahua writers in major centers at a very early time. In the later sixteenth century, as alphabetic writing spread to smaller and more remote altepetl with less access to Spanish instruction, and as the Nahuas found ways to express traditional patterns within the new framework, Nahuatl documents in the Spanish genres tended to become rather less like the Spanish "originals." Then over the long haul into the middle and later eighteenth century, they again approached closer, never becoming identical but showing an impressive grasp of Spanish terminology, procedures, and formats.[99]

One would like to know much more about the details of this evolution. Just how did the Spanish formats reach Nahua writers in the first place? Were models in Nahuatl worked out in major centers by Spanish ecclesiastics with the help of Nahua aides, then diffused through the country? The variety of formulaic detail in early Stage 2 writing speaks prima facie for a multiplicity of models devised by different persons in different places. The prize exhibit at our disposal in trying to get a better notion of the process is a model will published by fray Alonso de Molina; the document and some of its implications are analyzed in considerable detail and in a rather technical fashion in Appendix B. Briefly, the Molina sample, which may have been a common product of the Mexico City–Tlatelolco Franciscan philologists, shares a good many formulations with actual Nahuatl wills both early and late. It may have had a significant influence, though in many cases the near-inevitability of translations of the general Spanish model makes this hard to prove. At the same time, actual Nahuatl wills vary from the Molina sample in a large number of ways, some because of Nahuatlisms and some probably because of other Spanish sources of inspiration. Only a tiny group of Nahuas directly instructed by the philologists in the capital appears to have made any attempt to follow the Molina model consistently. Consideration of Molina's sample testament thus strengthens the impression that multiple models were prepared on different occasions, making for individual and regional variation and favoring a gradual, semiautonomous evolution of style.

Though no outside explanatory information is available on the growing idiosyncrasy of late-sixteenth-century Nahuatl documents of Spanish type, the phenomenon tends to explain itself quite readily. It can only mean that the Nahuas soon became independent of their first mentors, and, left to their own devices, found ways of doing things appropriate to their own needs and traditions. The subsequent return in the direction of correct or standard Spanish-style formats and terms surely is in some way the artifact of the increasing Nahua-Spanish contact that defines the whole later period. As to the form that contact took, I tend to the same theory as with changes in orthography and calligraphy, that literate Nahuas were seeing and handling more Spanish documents in the course of their ordinary activities and because of their increased bilingualism were better able to understand and be influenced by them than in earlier times.

9

Forms of Expression

THE NAHUAS DID NOT lack for means of expressing themselves. All the matters talked about in the previous chapters were authentic, essential expressions of their way of life and manner of dealing with the changing reality about them. Other important vehicles of expression, such as the crafts, have largely escaped the net laid here to capture Nahua patterns. What the present chapter seeks to do is to separate out and examine the postconquest Nahuas' modes of more conscious self-expression, of the type often found in our civilization (at least in more recent times) in the arts, philosophy, scholarship, and journalism. We are restricted perforce to those aspects that have left tangible evidence behind; thus little can be said about dance, as well developed as we know it was both before and after the conquest.

Some genres, such as preconquest calendrical books of days and fates, were entirely lost after the Spaniards came, so far as we know, and others, if they did not disappear, at least largely went underground, including above all the set speeches that, as Sahagún recognized, contained philosophy as well as rhetoric.[1] But postconquest reduction and loss are not the only or even the main problem in the present endeavor. Although the Nahua mind and ours share vast reaches of the intellect and the emotions, they differ in their distribution over a spectrum. One is reminded indeed of the differences in the actual spectrum of colors; it is clear, for example, that Nahuatl *coztic*, generally translated "yellow," shaded into what we would consider orange and even light red, and the Nahuatl terms in the area of green and blue seem always to point in the direction of turquoise rather than sharply distinguishing the two colors that we see. In activities of the mind, though the Nahuas had well-defined genres, those genres did not divide the various functions as we would. Rarely will a text be found devoted to relatively pure self-expression or pure enjoyment; nor do I take this to be a new facet of postconquest life. Everything the Nahuas said or wrote seemed to have some immediate, pressing, practical, not to say ulterior, purpose;[2] for all their pride in themselves, the Nahuas were blessedly little inclined to narcissism. And no culture ever took more joy in words. Metaphor, order, elaboration, were everywhere, in practically every utterance, but one is hard put to find anything falling clearly into our category of belles lettres, with the possible exception of the song collections that have come down to us. Thus expression and aesthetics tended to be a part of all genres rather than rigorously compartmentalized, a state of things very common outside recent Western culture, and one to which perhaps it would be well to return.

Mundane Nahuatl documents, then, were an avenue of cultural expression second to none, but they will not be reconsidered here, for much of this book is devoted to their content, and Chapter 8 in discussing techniques of writing touched on their form. Instead, this chapter will treat four genres that in different ways stand aside from mundane documentation and that contain a large quotient of intellectual-cultural reflection or "expression": (1) histories, practically all in annals form; (2) songs; (3) drama, all religious or close to it; and (4) the late "titles" of altepetl, with overtones of history and legend. In addition, in view of recent advances in art historical research and the already mentioned affinities between writing and painting, I will briefly try to put some phenomena from the visual arts in the context of the other materials.

I approach the texts and genres I will be discussing with much diffidence. For well over a decade, I and others have been poring over the kinds of every-day Nahuatl documents so crucial to this book, and by now we are familiar with many of the paths they take. Only in the last five years or so has this New Philology, as I have called the movement,[3] begun to explore texts of the kinds traditionally more associated with what some think of as high culture. Though writings of this type entered the consciousness of the scholarly world ahead of mundane documents, they are at this point much less well understood. The process of producing the necessary high-quality editions and commentaries has only started. With some of the genres, especially the titles, only a fraction of the probably extant corpus is presently known.

Under the circumstances, it might seem that the enterprise of the present chapter is premature. Not entirely, I imagine. Enough has been learned about the materials to recognize in them some of the same patterns, emphases, and trends found in other aspects of the Nahua world, throwing light in both directions and making the overall evolution of the Nahuas more comprehensible. But the time for a comprehensive survey has not come, and what follows here does not mean to be one.[4] Rather, it makes a series of pertinent general points illustrated by selected outstanding or representative examples, some of them the same works used for a similar purpose in Chapter 8.

Annals

On several counts, a type of historical work that we can call annals, since the entries were normally ordered strictly by year, occupies a unique place among the kinds of writing practiced by the postconquest Nahuas. In general, annals were produced more independently of Spanish auspices than were extant Nahuatl songs and plays, and they continued to be written over a longer time period. "Titles" were equally autonomous Nahua productions, but they are confined to the late period, and their authors were often less than fully trained in the lore of Nahua government and literacy, whereas the authors of annals were well educated and well placed, usually cabildo members or functionaries in the local church establishment, in either case quite high ranking in society, centrally involved in altepetl affairs, and knowledgeable about both worlds, the Spanish and their own. The same sort of people wrote the annals as produced mundane Nahuatl documentation, but here they were freer to express personal or factional opinion in addition to representing the altepetl. Indeed, the annals form gave scope for a wider range of topics and attitudes than any other genre of the postconquest period.

Of the presently available examples, most are anonymous, possibly because of the accretive nature of the genre, but also because author attribution in general seems not to have been a very strong Nahua tradition. Where the author or authors are known, it is sometimes only because of chance remarks dropped in the body of the work, as in the case of the relatives named García who participated in the composition or revision of a set of annals of Huamantla (Tlaxcalan region).⁵ For the author to declare himself openly is quite rare; the main examples are Chimalpahin and Tezozomoc late in Stage 2, and the Tlaxcalan chronicler Zapata with his glossator Santos y Salazar in Stage 3.⁶

As became clear in the preceding chapter, this kind of history followed a preconquest tradition, but as so often, we must mainly deduce the nature of that tradition from postconquest evidence and are left with many uncertainties. The name of the genre was apparently *xiuhpohualli*, "year count, year relation," a term used by its greatest exponent Chimalpahin, *xiuhtlacuilolli*, "year writing," or *(ce)xiuhamatl*, "(each) year paper"; all three contain the word *xihuitl*, "year."⁷ Another possibility, however, is *altepetlacuilolli*, "altepetl writing," which rather than describing the structure of the genre succinctly expresses its central focus.⁸ In this connection, an important unanswered question concerns the sponsorship of preconquest annals. All known postconquest annals, whether the author is named or not, are personal, unofficial enterprises even though the altepetl is their primary topic, and they are correspondingly full of partisanship. Was this the case in preconquest times too, or were there not official altepetl historians, guardians of the canonical version of the truth? At present it seems impossible to say.

A near universal of Nahua historical writing is the inclusion of each event under its corresponding year reckoned by the indigenous calendar, creating a work in which the equivalents of chapters are the successive year units. The year is prominently marked and serves as a heading. Inside the year, the subunit is the separate event, signaled in the earlier annals by a glyph or picture and in the later ones at least by a paragraph marker or the introductory comment "also in this year," or the like. The year-chapter is thus a miscellany of distinct topics having in common only the fact of having occurred in the same year. Many annals, it is true, have only one or two events for most years. In those portions written contemporaneously by the author as observer, there is usually a chronological progression through the year, lending greater continuity and unity. But the form is very different from the type of history most practiced by the Spaniards in the Indies. Even though Spanish histories were also more often than not straightforwardly chronological (hence the name *crónica*, "chronicle"), each work had a special topic announced in its title and consisted of chapters, however episodic, which carried the story further along that thread, also usually titled, in the fashion of "How the Captain Escaped from His Enemies," or "How the Expedition Arrived at the Indian Town and Was Peacefully Received."

Annals organization is another example of the Nahuas' tendency to build larger units by the arrangement of discrete parts retaining their distinctness. In this case, since the number and size of the topics were bound to vary with the year, the often accompanying features of numerical symmetry and rotation are not present at the level of the subunits, the events, but they are prominent in the calendrical ordering of the years, with the four repeating year signs and the thirteen repeating numerical coordinates. Perhaps this is why Nahua annalists stuck so tenaciously to the indigenous system (as well as the Christian year in nearly all cases) when it so soon faded from all other kinds of Nahuatl writing, mundane and otherwise.

Aside from the persisting indigenous structure, postconquest Nahuatl annals early and late have certain common characteristics that in all probability go back to the preconquest genre. Practically all are written by a citizen of the local altepetl, and often a specific subdivision of it, and the home unit becomes not only the main topic but the vantage point from which anything else that comes up is viewed. Changes of altepetl office, above all in the governorship but also in the other cabildo posts, are the single most common type of annals fare, in some histories representing the bulk of the entries. If the work has a preconquest section, changes of tlatoani are reported in the same spirit and with much of the same vocabulary. The term often employed in the preconquest passages in reference to taking office, *tlatocatlalia*, "to place as tlatoani, as ruler," occurs also with the postconquest governorship.[9] Other major events affecting the altepetl as a corporation are also reported: for the preconquest period, migrations, foundations, wars, dynastic conflicts; for the postconquest, election disputes, changes in tributes, jurisdictional strife and rearrangements including *congregaciones*, and any other striking or controversial developments.

Over and above strictly altepetl-related news, annals concentrate on noteworthy events in general, the sort of thing that the populace would tend to become excited or concerned about and long remember. Even here the altepetl is still the viewing point and often the arena. More or less natural phenomena, most but not all bringing disaster, are prominent among such items. Comets and solar eclipses are copiously reported, as are earthquakes, snow and hail storms, downpours, floods, visitations of locusts, dry years with famine, and outbreaks of epidemic disease. Spectacles and scandals are not neglected: parades, consecrations of new buildings or images, celebrations, and notable theatrical productions (much of this kind of thing has directly to do with the corporate image of the altepetl), but also public hangings, disturbances of the peace, and notorious murders. In this vein, miraculously moving images of saints and the arrival of papal bulls were likely to find their place among the entries. In brief, much of the content of annals, though distributed over a longer time period, was a great deal like what goes into newspapers today, and to tell the truth, perhaps not into our most distinguished and analytical newspapers.

All of the above topics, mutatis mutandis, I take to have been characteristic of preconquest annals as well, as the preconquest sections of certain sixteenth-century histories tend to confirm.[10] In at least some sense new was the interest of postconquest annalists in the appointment and some of the activities of Spanish officials, primarily viceroys and bishops, but at times descending to corregidores and priors of monasteries or parish priests. This facet was an extension of the altepetl emphasis, in two ways. First, the information reported was for the most part of the same type as given for the local governor and cabildo and before that, for the tlatoani. Second, the Spanish officials were of interest first and foremost because of their direct interaction with the home altepetl; the only lesser functionaries mentioned, whether administrators or clerics, were those who served in the annalist's altepetl. High officials are noted when they assume or leave office, when they take actions with repercussions on the local altepetl, and when they pass through or come to visit, on which occasion, it is hoped, they will spend a long time and praise all they see. A seventeenth-century annalist of Puebla wrote approvingly of a viceroy's visit that "he admired things absolutely all over Puebla before he left." [11] Possibly annals of preconquest altepetl gave somewhat similar attention to the lords of Tenochtitlan and Tetzcoco, forming some sort of precedent, but this is not known for sure.

Despite their emphasis on the corporate and publicly known side of things, postconquest annals as unofficial productions often contain personal items as well. This is a bit ironic considering that so many annals early and late are anonymous. Yet the unnamed sixteenth-century author of the Codex Aubin put down, as we saw in Chapter 6, the start of construction on a house for a saint's image at his home, and he also recorded the birth over the years of Juana López, "Bastiana" (Sebastiana), and "Mariaton" (Little María), perhaps his daughters, as well as, unfortunately, a requiem mass for Juana López in 1584, seventeen years after she was born. [12] The work of the late-seventeenth-century Tlaxcalan annalist don Juan Buenaventura de Zapata is full of personal tidbits, of which the following is one of the juiciest:

In the night before the day of San Juan Papa Mártir, today Tuesday the 27th of May in the same year of 1675, thieves entered our house. There were six of them; two came in a window. One came in ahead of the others, and the very first thing he did was grab me; when I was about to get loose, he called his companion so that both of them took me on together. And when I grabbed his knife, he gave me some good cuts on the arms. The other four kept guard outside my house with swords and a musket. They took away a hundred pesos in cash, but they didn't take our clothing. Not a rag did they remove, nor did they do us bodily harm. [13]

In some cases, however, the personal goes far beyond adding life and color to become a basic part of the motivation for the whole work and hence an important criterion in the author's selection of material. This is easiest to see when we know the author's name and background. Thus Tezozomoc not only wrote of his own altepetl, but emphasized Mexica royal genealogies and dynastic marriages both before and after the conquest because he himself was connected with the Mexica royal lineage. [14] With Chimalpahin the case is even clearer. He had strictly speaking no position in the society of his own Amaquemecan at all, for he lived his whole adult life in Mexico City, and his parents seem to have been on the distant margins of the nobility of Tzaqualtitlan Tenanco, the subkingdom in which he was born. Chimalpahin had some more illustrious grandparents and more distant forebears, however, and was ultimately a descendant of the kings of the subkingdom. His work on Chalco, therefore, emphasizing, detailing, and extolling the line of kings of Tzaqualtitlan Tenanco at the expense of many other things he could have told us, has the double effect of raising up (one side of) his lineage and making the most of his own connections with it. [15] We saw in Chapter 5 that in matters of Nahua landholding, our categories public and private are not really appropriate, and in Chapter 6, the religion of the saints proved to be simultaneously personal and corporate. Here we have another piece of the same cloth, the fact that for annals writers corporate pride and personal lineage pride coincided.

Many annals, from all time periods, divide sharply into two distinct parts, though the division is never explicitly announced. A first portion deals with the time before the author-compiler's life, or at least the time before he started writing. The entries are usually brief, often confined to the barest essential facts, and few per year, with many years missing entirely. Clearly, beginning annalists usually went searching for historical writings left by their predecessors and copied out entries, at times eclectically, at times practically duplicating an entire earlier text.[16] Rare is the annalist who says a word about the origin of his material. Chimalpahin, who tells of exploring among old histories, apparently both pictographic and alphabetic, and interviewing some of their possessors, is an exception.[17] He is no exception, however, in his manner of operation, other than in the extent of his searches. Although in a few cases succeeding members of a family may have kept making additions to the same document for a while, and Zapata's work came into the hands of Santos y Salazar, who glossed it and made a few additions, annals seem to have typically terminated with a writer's life or period of activity, remaining in the hands of his descendants, most often doubtless to be lost in the long run. Each new annalist had to start from scratch.

Thus though the annals corpus is cumulative over the generations in specific regions, the transmittal was often disjunctive, the new writer at times mechanically copying items whose broader context and significance he no longer understood, and perhaps garbling the original beyond recognition as a result.[18] Transmittal seems to have followed along the lines of the genre quite rigorously. As well as one can tell, annalists did not generally consult old mundane documentation in Nahuatl or draw on purely oral tradition preserved among local people (both of which the authors of the "titles" to be discussed later apparently often did), but adhered to what they could find in other annals.

In the late Tlaxcala-Puebla annals, the same restricted corpus of rather threadbare entries on the sixteenth century appears again and again.[19] Chimalpahin, for all his advantages and resources, seems to have followed the same method. Though close to high-ranking Spaniards who could easily have given him all the information he wanted about past viceroys, he did not consult them on the date of the death of the first Viceroy Velasco, merely noting that the Tenochca and Tlatelolca (i.e., the annalists of those groups) disagreed on the point.[20] For all these reasons, entries on earlier periods tend to be highly unreliable as sources of hard facts on the time they purport to record, but all the more interesting as the tradition of the writer's own time.

From the date when the writer begins work, everything changes, creating a second section with quite different characteristics. Most annalists seem to have recorded current events as they occurred, year in, year out, using their own observations and public knowledge as the source. The author of the Codex Aubin apparently laid out blank pages with the year sign decades in advance, a year per page, to be filled in with entries later.[21] His plan would not have met the needs of some writers, however, for as they warmed to their work, they increased the number of entries per year and at times expanded them until they were vivid, detailed accounts filling long paragraphs and spilling over the page, the opposite of the terse manner one associates with annals in general. Some of these works became in effect journals, not written perhaps literally day by day, but accounting for all the high points of the year in a given altepetl. Some writers retain brevity even for contemporary events, but in either case these sections are far closer to the objective facts than the more historical parts. They are not, of course, to be taken entirely at face value.

Let us take a sample of a contemporary event reported in a set of annals of late-seventeenth-century Puebla, with the double aim of showing how far it veers from "typical" annals style (in which a year's entry might run "don Gaspar de los Reyes was governor; a flood carried away many houses") and how it combines relative closeness to fact with strong partisan coloration. In 1682, the annalist reports, the Spaniards began to raise the price of grain, despite a good crop of both maize and wheat. In September, a consortium of fifty Spaniards applied to the alcalde mayor for a monopoly concession to make and sell (wheat) bread, and Indians were given a day's notice to stop their breadmaking. The account continues:

But they couldn't keep it up. It was done for only two days in the city, and in those two days people were already starving because of it. On Monday, the 21st day of September, the very day of San Mateo, Monday, and on Tuesday, people were starving. Neither wheat bread nor tortillas could be found, neither in the marketplace nor in shops. And if someone secretly made half a carrying frame full and took it to the marketplace, even if it was tortillas, the Spaniards just fought over it. Even though it was someone of very high standing, the commoners (i.e., "Indians") no longer paid them respect. Whoever was first got the bread. There was nothing but weeping. And then everyone became disturbed, priests and Spaniards as well as commoners, so that everyone took the commoners' side. The commoners personally gave a letter they wrote to the alcalde mayor. When the alcalde mayor was going up to his palace, all the children together with some adults shouted to him, telling him, "Bread, bread, bread, lord captain, we'll starve, we'll starve!" And when the alcalde mayor heard it, and they read him the letter saying that the service of our great ruler the king would perish, that if they were going to forbid us our trade of breadmaking, let the Spaniards do the different services and pay the tribute, when the alcalde mayor had heard it, he quickly ordered a decree to be prepared, and then it was quickly proclaimed that the commoners could make bread, and he ordered that the Spaniards be punished, and then the Spaniards who had made the offer fled.[22]

Such dramatization is not exclusively characteristic of the late period. The best-developed examples known to me are contained in a set of annals done in Mexico City in the 1560's by someone who was close to the Tenochtitlan cabildo and to the Franciscan friars of the city; by internal evidence, he may have been both a notary and an artist, a *tlacuilo* in a very broad sense.[23] The author makes barely a gesture toward a historical section, with less than a page and a half of scanty notes starting well after the conquest, before he wades into a journal-type treatment of the year 1564, giving the full Spanish-style date for each of the entries, some of which run to pages. One might be inclined to question whether the work belongs to the annals genre at all. After using the names of the year signs in the vestigial first section (a pictorial component is entirely lacking, at least in the copy preserved), the author abandons them, introducing each year with a heading like "DE 1564 AÑOS." Yet the organization is by year, and the topics (with a little weakness in the areas of the heavens and the weather) are those we expect annals to cover.

No annals entry has ever given me as full a sense of immediacy, of drawing the writer and the reader into the observed action, as what this author set down for May 28, 1564:

– Today, 28th of May of the year 64, was the festivity of the Trinity, and the decree of the father guardian fray Melchor de Benavente was proclaimed, with three items: about curing, and that no one should perform divination in the water, and the third item I didn't hear very well.[24]

He then writes that the father guardian (of the Franciscan monastery of Mexico City) proceeded to preach, saying that no one should make up medicines for others, and told his audience that "your father fray Alonso has come back," a reference to fray Alonso de Molina, who had gone on a trip to Michoacan. It was in 1564 that the Mexica, having performed a series of duties for the Spaniards ever since the conquest, were obliged to accept full-scale tribute payment like other indigenous corporations, over their strong protest, and the annalist evokes many scenes involving the populace, the cabildo, and Spanish officials.

With all his excellences, this writer's specialty—a general Nahua propensity, to be sure, but not so often seen in annals—is the quasi-verbatim reproduction of longish speeches. After the members of the Tenochca cabildo had delivered the first payment to the royal treasury, they returned to their own headquarters, and three or four of them spoke, on the verge of tears. One don Martín did in fact weep, then moved to the corner of the room and from there made an ironic speech in reply to the rest, beginning as follows:

Here you are, you Mexica and Tenochca, now you are satisfied, since you have personally gone to deliver your tribute that you stripped from the hands of the female sex, the pay for their spinning, or a little something they borrowed from someone. You officials, are you happy and content to have been scolded somewhere? Do we have lands and fields? We only work for a living. You elders, you men of prudence and experience, you have committed malfeasance against the altepetl, you have fought with it, you have offended it.[25]

Looked at in both aspects, the laconic and the discursive, annals project an image of the splendor, continuity, and centrality of the altepetl, sometimes attacked and sometimes successfully defended, in an atmosphere of spectacle and against a background of repeating natural and quasi-natural events over which no one has control. How this image arises in the mind of the reader, however, is a bit hard to explain, for the annals tend to be nonreflective and usually ostensibly noncommittal. The simple choice of some topics over others and the march of entries through typical sequences are the most basic and important means of conveying the general message. The one thing that does often draw the annalist's open commentary is spectacle. For any occasion, good or bad, the highest and most frequently seen accolade is "never was the like of it seen before," or "never since the arrival of the true faith had such a thing happened." The late-seventeenth-century Puebla annalist quoted before, in describing the commotion over English corsairs in Veracruz, says: "It was a marvelous thing that frightened people greatly and had never been seen since the coming of the faith."[26] Annals tend to present each eclipse as more fearful than the last, and each reception of a viceroy or consecration of a new church is an unparalleled marvel. Here is a portion of a maximal but characteristic account of a solar eclipse of 1691, again from our annalist of Puebla:

At nine o'clock it became entirely dark, like seven o'clock at night, and it was dark for a full quarter of an hour. Then the little birds and the crows and buzzards all fell to the ground and went fluttering about, crying out in distress, and something like yellow tassels of fire lay over the mountains, like the fire and smoke from the volcano, and it was as though people had lost their senses. Some ran to the church, some fell down in fright, and three simply died right away. There was nothing but weeping, and people no longer knew each other. . . . All day there were very cold windstorms, and from three to four o'clock it rained. It was fearful what the lord of the near and the close, our lord God, did on that Thursday afternoon.[27]

Beyond emphasizing spectacle, annalists generally avoid editorial remarks or expressions of emotion. *Omochiuh onotlahueliltic*, "Woe is me," or *iyoyahue*, "alas," can be found in songs, speeches, conversation, and correspondence, but not in annals (unless perchance in quoted speech). A scholar recently noted, in the specific case of Chimalpahin, the apparent flatness of

Nahuatl annals entries,[28] and on one level his observation is absolutely correct. Any overtly value-laden remarks tend to be put in the mouths of the actors themselves. Even when annalists take partisan stands, and they often do, they usually present the matter as if it were objective fact, without explicit reflection, analysis, or generalization.

Let us take as an example the way some annalists handle mestizos. In point of fact, some people who were biologically partly Spanish functioned usefully and successfully, at a high level, within the indigenous world, but the general Nahua stereotype "mestizo" had mainly pejorative connotations and was often used as a weapon to attack one's enemies, especially those who aspired to altepetl office.[29] The Puebla annalist devotes much space to the partially successful battle to keep a don Juan de Galicia, whom he calls a mestizo, out of the governorship. He has only bad things to say about don Juan, and he reports that the cabildo sent to Mexico City for confirmation of the rule that non-Indians, including mestizos, could not occupy office in an indigenous corporation. But he does not openly generalize.[30]

The Tlaxcalan Zapata also had a mestizo archenemy in the governorship in his time. He tells how his foe came into office illegally, reports what he considers his foolish and harmful actions, and even calls him a "mictlan mextiço," an "infernal mestizo," but he does not reflect or expand. His glossator Santos y Salazar on occasion does so, saying that the "champurros" (an insulting term referring to mestizos) were not good in public office, that their blood boiled too easily.[31] Yet though Santos y Salazar was a Tlaxcalan patriot and of fully indigenous descent, he was Spanish-educated and as one of the few indigenous persons to be ordained into the priesthood, completely at home in Spanish, in which language he wrote most of his glosses, including the one just mentioned. His remark, though pro-indigenous, was more Spanish than Nahua in form.

For open reflection by a true Nahua annalist on this topic (or indeed any other, to my knowledge) we must go to Chimalpahin. He too disapproves of mestizo governors but mainly simply reports their terms of office. On one occasion, though, he delivers himself of the following thoughtful statement:

And with these mestizos we do not know how their lineage is on the side of the Spaniards, whether their grandfathers and grandmothers back in Spain from whom the mestizos' fathers who came from there descended were nobles or commoners; they have come here and married daughters of people of New Spain, some high nobles, and the Spaniards have married some daughters of poor commoners, so that those who have been and continue to be born of these matches are always mestizos, male or female; and some are born just through concubinage and illegitimacy, so that mestizos male and female descend from us local people. The honorable mestizos, male and female, acknowledge that they come from us; but some misguided mestizos, male and female, do not want to acknowledge that part of the blood they have is ours, but rather imagine themselves fully Spaniards and mistreat us and deceive us the same way some Spaniards do. But some Spaniards whom our lord God created with honorable blood do honor and esteem us, although we do not have their blood; yet they recognize and remember that at the foundation and beginning of the world we had only one father Adam and one mother Eve, from whom we descended, although our bodies are divided into three kinds.*

The author goes on to give open, emotional praise to certain high-ranking mestizos who still acknowledge and revere their origin, despite their great success in the Spanish world. The greatest of the annalists, Chimalpahin is both typical and atypical. This reflective mode is his alone, possibly as a function of the fact that his work is more highly developed in general than any other. We should keep in mind that even he more often than not maintains the reserve of the annals genre.

To such an extent were annals the dominant and most inclusive form of individual-corporate written expression among the Nahuas that other types of documents might become assimilated to them. A good example is the manuscript of seventeenth- and eighteenth-century Tepemaxalco discussed in Chapter 6 (the de la Cruz family papers), which was primarily an account book of current income and expenditures related to religion but took on many annals-like characteristics. It is, naturally enough, organized by year. Over a long stretch, it records the governor for each year, and often other altepetl officials as well. It mentions some disputes and highlights some religious festivities, and its central topic—the renovation of saints, churches, and ecclesiastical trappings—would fit right into a set of annals. As is common with annals, a large part of the motivation of the Tepemaxalco document is to glorify a particular lineage, and it too sometimes veers into the purely personal, recording the marriage or departure of some otherwise insignificant family member or dependent. It even includes a rudimentary set of actual historical annals for a period of some decades before the current accounting began, covering in minimal fashion many of the usual topics.[32]

As strongly marked and relatively uniform as the annals genre was, it of course varied with the author and the time period. Some writers had a deep vocation, others were perfunctory. The individual writers' predilections put a stamp on their works. Some emphasized politics, others (probably church employees) Spanish ecclesiastical appointments, still others festivities or astronomy and meteorology; some were great gossips.[33] The differences had the potential of creating separate subgenres, but that potential was never realized.

More substantial, systematic distinctions can be made on the basis of time period, specifically by recognizing two large groups corresponding to Stages 2

*CH, 2: 22. The three bodily types Chimalpahin refers to are presumably Amerindian, European, and African.

and 3. Many subtle lines of evolution cross and ignore the periodization by stages, naturally, and temporal distinctions exist that would call for further subdivision of the stages. Certainly, there is a substantial difference between the earliest postconquest annals, for which the Historia Tolteca-Chichimeca can serve as model, with an overwhelming emphasis on the preconquest period, and annals of the late sixteenth and early seventeenth centuries, in which the postconquest era receives a large part of the writer's attention.

Two facts argue definitively for a distinction between Stage 2 and Stage 3 annals, two facts that in the last analysis are aspects of the same thing. First, despite great differences in emphasis, Stage 2 annals in general contain a substantial section devoted to the preconquest history of the altepetl and carry it as a unit, with its own identity and traditions, past the conquest into postconquest times.[34] Second, the material presented about the preconquest era, though always in some sense fragmentary and tailored to the purposes of the writer, and surely not to be confused with objective truth, is authentic preconquest lore handed down in a direct line to a writer who still has some understanding of it. Stage 3 annals, on the other hand, are often without any preconquest section at all; or if they have a few entries, these are likely to be in obvious error or presented in such a way that the writer clearly did not understand them.[35] Stage 3 annalists had by and large lost contact with the preconquest period. For them, the sixteenth century had itself become a distant, legendary period about which they knew relatively little, although they did have certain living traditions about it.

The first distinction leads to the second, which is perhaps more basic. The early postconquest annalists were in possession of earlier pictographic annals and in contact with people who could expound them (perhaps they could themselves); later Stage 2 annalists knew the work of their predecessors well, using it as source material. In this sense, all the Stage 2 annals belong to a single coherent corpus or tradition. With Stage 3 annals, the thread was broken. The late annalists of the Tlaxcala-Puebla region, with the possible exception of Zapata, show no sign of ever having heard of Chimalpahin or Tezozomoc, or even of the sixteenth-century Tlaxcalan historian Tadeo de Niza (whose work has now disappeared and must have been lost to consciousness as early as the second half of the seventeenth century). Perhaps these writers knew of one or two skeletal annals of an early time, whose entries influenced their equally skeletal lore on the sixteenth century. In general, however, they give the impression of having started all over again in the seventeenth century, mainly in the second half. They form a new coherent corpus and tradition, for within the group successors knew and used their predecessors. The annals of the two stages thus represent two partially closed bodies of material.

One is inclined to say that in Stage 3 annals, appointments of Spanish officials and general activities of the Spanish population occupy more space, are more integrated and understood, and that this corresponds to the broadening out of the Nahuas from the altepetl base into the wider Hispanic world in the late period. I think in fact that this will be found to be the case overall, but meanwhile it is best to remember that Chimalpahin and even the Codex Aubin are full of well-understood Spanish activity and that any temporal ordering along the suggested lines must take them into account.

In any case, the difference in flavor between the annals of the two periods, at least those of a more discursive nature, is striking. It is partially attributable to the distinctions I have been making, but perhaps it is above all a matter of language. The annals genre in the hands of its masters allowed for relatively free, wide-ranging expression; in Stage 2 annals, we see the classic Nahuatl style and vocabulary in its full development, whereas Stage 3 presents us with the extensive loss of that vocabulary and rhetoric, plus the addition of loan verbs and particles, calques, and other characteristic phenomena of the Nahuatl of the late period, more richly illustrated than in any other form that has come down to us.[36]

Without attempting a full-scale examination of their works, I will say a few words here about some outstanding annalists who, when we have adequate and accessible translations of their writings, are certain to have a large impact on our view of postconquest Nahua thought and history. The dominant figure of Stage 2 is don Domingo de San Antón Muñón Chimalpahin Quauhtlehuanitzin, whom modern scholars for some reason call Chimalpahin. Except for the Domingo, he apparently assumed all of this resplendent name over the years: San Antón from the Mexico City church where he worked, possibly as fiscal; Muñón from Spanish patrons; Chimalpahin and Quauhtlehuanitzin from kings of old he claimed as forebears; and "don" for the position his erudition must have won him. In everyday life, he was doubtless known as don Domingo de San Antón. Born in the Tzaqualtitlan Tenanco subkingdom (*tlayacatl*) of Amaquemecan, for obscure reasons Chimalpahin came or was brought to the capital very early, apparently as a child, and he seems to have spent the rest of his life there. Starting probably in the last years of the sixteenth century and continuing into the 1620's, he wrote the largest and most distinguished corpus of annalistic history known to have been produced by a Nahua of any time period.[37]

If Pedro Cieza de León is the prince of the Spanish chroniclers of the Indies, and he is, Chimalpahin is just as clearly the prince of the Nahua annalists. His work has all the characteristics of the genre, and often illustrates its qualities better than any other text, even though in many ways it goes beyond that form as usually practiced. Chimalpahin followed the organizational norm to the letter; nearly everything he wrote is in discrete entries arranged by year, scattered in several different sets of annals.[38] It was not until a modern scholar published a transcription rearranging everything into a single chronological scheme that we could see Chimalpahin's work for what it is.[39]

In one respect (other than the quality of his mind, that is) Chimalpahin is unique. All other annalists known to me were solidly based in a single altepetl, the primary focus of their whole work. Chimalpahin had the same intense micropatriotism; he tells of having seen some annals stored away concerning all Amaquemecan and having read and copied only the portion concerning his own Tzaqualtitlan Tenanco.[40] Yet living in Mexico City, he became involved in the capital's affairs and the history of Tenochtitlan, with which to a point he identified. Though his more historical writing, the part about times before his own and especially the preconquest period, is most voluminous and systematic on Amaquemecan, Chimalpahin ranks as at least a major if not the premier indigenous historian of his adopted home. His postconquest entries begin to emphasize the area of the capital more, and his large journal-like sections deal with Mexico City almost exclusively. Thus through circumstances, the great Chalco patriot, without ceasing to be such, became the most cosmopolitan of the annalists.

Let us briefly consider some of Chimalpahin's excellences. We have already seen his unusual reflectiveness, for the genre. He carried out more extensive researches than any other annalist, and told us more about them (still not very much, by modern standards). He collected and consolidated a whole series of annals of the capital, several of which still survive, and he did the same for Chalco, where all the earlier works are now lost. Not only did he unite the work of his predecessors by bringing much of it together; he unified it by developing a uniform terminology, particularly in the realm of political life, giving us an invaluable, translucent insider's view of Nahua modes of organization.[41] And he was a master of the language, willing and able to bring whole scenes to life when something struck him. The following is only one of the passages one could quote in this respect:

> Today, Friday the 26th of the month of August of 1611, before dawn as the clock struck three, there was a very strong earthquake such as had never happened before, so that the earth here in the city actually moved, and the water of the great lake at Tepetzinco, going toward Tetzcoco, made great noises as it boiled and stirred, and the other waters surrounding Mexico City all made noises as they boiled and flew up. The water slapping made a sound as though something were falling to the ground from a precipice; it cannot be said or expressed how wide the great stream became and how frightful the slapping of the water was. And all the wells in people's homes everywhere stirred as though someone were taking a bath in them, the way the water flew, boiled, and splashed, hitting and throwing itself against the cistern walls.
>
> And everyone was sleeping in bed. When they realized there was a strong earthquake, they all got up and ran out of the bedrooms where they were sleeping and

came outside. The Spanish men and women too all came out just as they had been sleeping. Some were just in shirts, some came out naked into the patios, some then went out into the road. It was as though we were all drunk, we were so afraid when we saw how houses were collapsing and falling to the ground, for in people's homes everywhere much stone and adobe came falling in all directions from the tops of the houses. The walls of houses were damaged everywhere, they all ripped open even if they were new houses just built; those especially were all damaged and cracked. . . . It was very frightening what happened, and it was pitiful to hear the cries over what was happening to us, for the earth went this way and that and we couldn't stand, we just kept falling down as we stood up, and people really thought that the world was ending. No one remembered what money and property each person had in his house, everything was left inside the house, no one looked at it or saw after it while fleeing; everyone fled outside into the road as long as the earthquake lasted, and many people were hurt running out in the night.[42]

Chimalpahin then tops this off with an almost equally quotable passage criticizing don fray García Guerra, archbishop and interim viceroy, for taking no measures to help and console the people, going ahead with his great passion of bullfighting as if nothing had happened.

Don Hernando de Alvarado Tezozomoc, annalist in Nahuatl and chronicler in Spanish, a close contemporary and acquaintance of Chimalpahin's, is better known today in the broader world than his colleague, because of his Spanish work. The same was true in his own time, for he held a more prestigious position as a high-level interpreter, and he was an authentic member of the royal dynastic clique of Tenochtitlan, called upon at times to be the public representative of the Mexica and the royal line on ceremonial occasions.[43] Unlike Chimalpahin, he got his high dynastic surname from close relatives, and he was well known by it. But as a Nahuatl annalist he is no equal of Chimalpahin, in breadth or in most other ways. It is thanks to Chimalpahin, in fact, that we know Tezozomoc's Nahuatl work at all, for as part of his tireless researches, Chimalpahin copied his "Chronica mexicayotl," adding his own comments and corrections parenthetically, and this is the only form that survives.[44]

As we would expect, Tezozomoc emphasizes the history of the Mexica altepetl and the genealogy of noble Mexica, leading in the direction of himself. Valuable as his material is, it is extraordinarily narrow; he eschews most of the range of standard annals topics, and even his Mexica governmental history is mainly confined to the preconquest period. For that epoch, he seems to be following one or two older sources very closely. The bulk of the rest of the work deals with descent and marriage among the high nobles of Valley of Mexico towns, centered on the Mexica, in postconquest times, apparently based on Tezozomoc's personal knowledge and experience. Despite its clear bias, it convincingly shows the persistence up to Tezozomoc's time of preconquest dynastic marriage patterns in the Valley, with a wide network in which the Mexica played a unifying role.

Although Tezozomoc's Nahuatl history entitles itself a chronicle and even mentions a "first chapter" with a typical Spanish descriptive heading ("Which Discusses the Coming and Arrival of the Mexica Here in New Spain"),[45] it in fact follows the usual year organization of Nahuatl annals, broken only by lists of children and marriages that cannot be fit into a single year (the same thing happens with Chimalpahin at times). The outstanding characteristics of the "Chronica mexicayotl" are the depth and coherence of its genealogical information and the well-developed dialogues used as a narrative device in the preconquest sections. These are sometimes more oratorical, sometimes more conversational, but in either case usually equipped with all the niceties of Nahuatl oral protocol.

We must not entirely neglect Tezozomoc's most famous work, the *Crónica mexicana*, even though it is in Spanish, especially since it is full of titles and terms left in Nahuatl, and it gives signs of being in large part a close translation of an earlier Nahuatl text or family of texts, called by some the "Crónica X," which circulated in the second half of the sixteenth century among those interested in Mexica antiquities.[46] This history was a magnification of Tenochtitlan's preconquest imperial accomplishments, suiting Tezozomoc's purposes very well. All that was left for him to do was to explain terms, concepts, and allusions that a Spanish reader might have found puzzling, add an orthodox Christian perspective (perhaps already in the original), and make some connections with the Mexico City of his own day.[47]

An outstanding feature of Tezozomoc's Spanish chronicle, just as of his Nahuatl annals, is the inclusion of a large number of elaborate speeches by the actors. These prove to follow Nahuatl conventions through the barrier of language and indeed at the expense of idiomatic Spanish. Tezozomoc wrote fluent if not elegant Spanish, but the speeches often have a strange ring because of the literal translation of Nahuatl idioms. Thus the polite inversions of Nahuatl are retained; superiors call their aides their fathers, inferiors call the king their grandchild, and whole addresses follow Nahuatl conventional forms.[48]

The *Crónica mexicana*, unlike its Nahuatl counterpart, is truly in the form of a Spanish chronicle, with topically or episodically organized chapters and very little attention to dates. The book makes one wonder about the nature of the Nahuatl original; fray Diego Durán's history of Tenochtitlan, based on some version of the same text, is also in chapters and not at all annals-like.[49] Was there a preconquest genre separate from annals that was more episodic and narrated through dialogue? I think it not likely. Durán's version is lavishly illustrated, often with a picture per chapter, clearly derived from drawings accompanying the original Nahuatl alphabetic text. These, I warrant, derived in turn from topic-indicating pictographs within an annals format, each one triggering in the trained preconquest annalist a recital of associated dialogues and narrative.[50] In a Spanish context, the topics became chapters and the years were neglected. On the other hand, in the postconquest annals genre, much of the oral recital must have been lost at some point, leaving successors to reconstruct from the pictorial component alone and leading to the terse postconquest annals style.[51]

In the late period, the outstanding figure is the Tlaxcalan don Juan Buenaventura Zapata y Mendoza,[52] who did his writing through several decades of the second half of the seventeenth century. Zapata exceeds other known Stage 3 annalists by as much as Chimalpahin surpasses those of Stage 2, and indeed more, for in Zapata's time the competition was far less formidable.[53] To begin with, unlike his contemporaries, Zapata has far more than vestigial, pro forma information on the time before 1600. True, the emphasis falls on the seventeenth century and above all his own time, but his entries for the sixteenth century proceed year by year, giving the best account known of the membership of the Tlaxcalan cabildo outside the cabildo minutes (of which hardly two decades are preserved). Moreover, Zapata includes several pages of preconquest history that surely pale in comparison to Chimalpahin or the Historia Tolteca-Chichimeca, but that seem to come directly from sources of a much earlier period; even the language differs markedly from the author's own. We need to know much more about Zapata's historical sources, but it is already clear that he made a serious effort to go beyond received tradition and was in much closer touch with the reality of earlier times than other writers of his era.

When Zapata gets to the seventeenth century, his entries begin to become more copious, and for several decades before he stopped writing in 1692, the work is journal-like, with full reports on several separate events for most years. The material falls entirely into the normal annals range as described above, but it is so much more voluminous that it often seems something quite different, and of course it has its own special emphases and tendencies. Zapata himself was a member of the Tlaxcalan officeholding group, often alcalde, once cabildo notary, and once even governor, so he writes of municipal government as an insider. Each year begins with a full and clearly reliable list of all cabildo officials high and low, almost as though the book were a set of cabildo minutes, but the author adds interesting details about the members' affiliations and at times, probably in the case of political enemies, makes snide remarks that they are of low social origin, currying favor with Spanish officials, or have bought their offices.

Municipal pride swells large in Zapata, or perhaps he simply loved pomp and display; at any rate, he gives us splendid portraits of all kinds of public ceremonies, from viceregal receptions and chapel consecrations to royal funeral rites. He especially loved bells, thanks to which we are told of the founding, hanging, moving, and repair of the bells of every church in Tlaxcala. All of the splendor (and disaster too) is closely associated with the altepetl and the cabildo. When a festivity occurs or a new chapel is built, Zapata is sure to say who was on the cabildo at that time, even if he has given the same names a page or two before, and he is inclined to do the same even with floods and earthquakes. But if a ceremony did not go well, Zapata did not hesitate to say so; in fact, he seems to have rather enjoyed saying so. In giving the schedule of a bishop's visit in 1682, he does not fail to mention that the bishop went away leaving many unhappy children unconfirmed.[54] When a new curate arrived in 1685 to take possession of his office, not many people came out to meet and honor him despite the casting of coins to the crowd, because he arrived at midday mealtime.[55]

In many ways, Zapata shows himself to be a man of his time, and that includes his use of language; on his pages we find characteristic phenomena of Stage 3, such as loan verbs and particles, calques, and the extensive use of plural endings with inanimate nouns.[56] Yet one also detects a conservatism in Zapata's language. The concept of "past" governors and alcaldes was important to him, just as it was to his contemporaries, but he uses the somewhat strained indigenous term *omochiuhque* ("who had been made") rather than the Spanish *pasados*.[57] His favorite bells he calls *coyolin*, not *campana*, and they are housed in a *coyolcalli*, not a *campanario*; for bridge, he avoids Spanish *puente* in favor of *quappantli*. It is conceivable that Tlaxcalan Nahuatl was somewhat more conservative than the language of some other regions; it is also possible that Zapata, who must have grown up before the mid-seventeenth century, retained some of the usage of his youth. I strongly suspect, however, that we have here the beginnings of a conscious linguistic purism and culturally motivated resistance to loans that was not characteristic of earlier times (and never became the dominant current). Zapata tends to fall back into the use of Spanish loans ("campana," "puente") in unguarded moments.[58] It is particularly revealing that he is entirely uninhibited in his use of nominal plurals, I believe because he did not realize that the blanket pluralizing of inanimates was foreign to the Nahuatl of earlier generations. At any rate, Zapata's work is a major resource for Nahuatl cultural history; in time, his name will be as familiar as Chimalpahin's or Tezozomoc's.[59]

Songs

Our next genre has a good deal of affinity with the annals we have been discussing in the sense that it too was well developed in preconquest times, and that it too was often concerned with history and the altepetl. It was very different in many ways, of course, and one of them was in its relation to writing. Although one source mentions books of songs before the conquest,[60] it is hard to imagine, given the nature of writing as practiced by the Nahuas of that time, what these books could have been other than glyphic inventories of compositions committed to memory and to be recited orally. In postconquest times, though as we will see there is much evidence of the continuing popularity of songs in the indigenous style, the Nahuas did not spontaneously put them on paper, as so many hastened to do with their annals. The precious, not insubstantial corpus of sixteenth-century Nahuatl song that has reached us owes its existence to deliberate attempts to preserve something that would in the normal course of events perhaps never have been written down at all.

Far the most important item in the corpus is the Cantares Mexicanos, a large collection compiled by Nahuas under the auspices of the Franciscan philologists of the capital.[61] The version we know was produced in the late sixteenth century, but compilation, copying, and recopying had clearly been going on for some time,[62] and there are specific references to earlier decades. A second, smaller and more specialized collection, set down possibly as late as the early seventeenth century but apparently deriving ultimately from much the same circles as the Cantares, is the Romances de los señores de la Nueva España, found in association with the Spanish chronicle or report of the Tetzcocan mestizo author Juan Bautista de Pomar.[63] A set of several religious songs or hymns in Sahagún's Florentine Codex completes the larger accumulations of Nahuatl song of the sixteenth and seventeenth centuries, though additional scattered bits are found quoted in some of the annals. The restricted body of material is adequate for some kinds of analysis but hardly for others. So complex and sometimes veiled is the language, as was noted at the time,[64] that interpretations of the meaning and basic nature of the songs tend to remain controversial.

Scholars have often used the word poetry to classify Nahuatl song. In many respects, the category is extremely appropriate: the compositions employ a special, artificial or refined language full of metaphor and allusion; they are rigorously structured in ways not found in ordinary speech or even in oratory; and their themes bear a close resemblance to those we associate with European poetry.[65] Yet I prefer the category song.[66] The traditional European notion of poetry is closely associated with such characteristics as regular meter, fixed line, rhyme, the primacy of the written form, and a relative divorce from music and dance, none of which apply to Nahuatl song. The songs refer repeatedly to the speakers' dancing, singing, and playing musical instruments. Many are provided with an elaborate drumbeat notation, which though it remains to be definitively deciphered is undeniable evidence of a rhythmic percussive accompaniment (and the Nahua drums were capable of producing several different pitches). They appear to have been performed before an audience (idealized as a noble company) and at times have a strong flavor of theater or pageant.[67]

Moreover, Nahuatl seems to have had no word closely analogous to "poetry." In the corpus itself, the songs are repeatedly called *cuicatl*, which is translated "song" much as in English and seems to refer to the production of musical notes with the voice.[68] Molina glosses the verb *cuica*, from which our noun is derived, as "for a singer to sing, or for the birds to chirp." It is true that the special term (*in*) *xochitl* (*in*) *cuicatl*, "flowers and song," or "flowery song," is also used throughout the main collections and has been taken to be equivalent to "poetry," but it seems to me that it simply refers to a finer, more artificial and highly organized type of song (a common use of *xochitl*) as opposed to ordinary extemporaneous singing.[69] If we look for "poetry" in the Spanish section of Molina, we find what appear to be ad hoc equivalents invented by aides, meaning "composing words," "arranging words."[70]

Modern translators and students of the classic body of Nahuatl song, who have been at work for several generations now, have tended to view the bulk of the compositions we know as primarily the direct product of preconquest times, with the merest Spanish-Christian overlay to conform to the sensibilities of ecclesiastical sponsors (for example, replacing the names of indigenous deities with Dios, "God").[71] To be sure, the principal personae of the majority of the songs preserved are kings and nobles of central Mexican altepetl of the preconquest period (mainly fifteenth and early sixteenth centuries), and events of that time form the background. But the matter is not as simple as it seems. One thing is clear: the genre itself must be a survival from before the conquest, for it has elaborate conventions implying a long period of evolution, and those conventions are sharply distinct from anything found in Spanish counterparts. Let us discuss these uncontroversial matters first, before proceeding to examine the question of what may be specifically postconquest about the body of song.

Nahuatl song shares some elements of vocabulary and rhetoric with oratory and polite conversation, notably double phrasing,* but it is recognizably different from either, with an unmistakable flavor of its own. A fairly restricted set of stock metaphors, phrases, sentences, and sentiments recurs constantly through the corpus, mixed and varied in kaleidoscopic fashion, going far toward defining the genre and identifying the register of speech. Even more essential to the form, however, differentiating it radically from any other kind of utterance, is its structure. In its manner of organization, Nahuatl song is one more example of the pervasive tendency to achieve coherent

---

*It is true that diphrasis, the employment of a pair of terms to suggest a third concept metaphorically, the pair then often becoming a fixed idiomatic expression, is rather less characteristic of song than of oratory and conversation.

wholes through the symmetrical arrangement of independent parts, and indeed it vies with the altepetl as the most fully developed example of all.

In a song, the cellular unit is an entity we may call the verse. Every song is a numerical and ideally symmetrical arrangement of verses.[72] Like the calpolli in an altepetl, each verse is independent of the others, self-contained, so that all are of equal status. A verse may be recognized as such not by its length, for length varies greatly, and the line of a certain number of feet as known in European poetry is not seen; indeed, no fixed metrical scheme in terms of syllables has yet been discovered. Nor does rhyme enter in. A verse is defined by ending in a coda of nonsense syllables or vocables, derived apparently from various exclamations and lamentations, but used in extant song in a great variety of combinations primarily for rhythmic and sonorous effect and as punctuation. No verse is without its nonlexical coda.* The body of the verse, the lexical portion, makes statements related to the overall theme of the song but does not openly refer to other verses. Nor do the verses proceed from one to the next in such a way that each is logically prior to the succeeding one, nor, in the examples that have reached us, do they tell a story. They may use a well-known story as essential background, but only discrete excerpts appear in the song itself. The strictly speaking narrative element is practically nil in the known body of older Nahuatl song.

If the verse is the atom, the verse pair is the molecule. In the whole song corpus, a single verse not part of some sort of pair is a rarity and anomaly, leading one to suspect loss or a copyist's error. The vast majority of songs have an even number of verses; when a song reached the compiler with an odd-numbered set, he might take heroic measures to try to rectify the situation.[73] In some cases, pairing is a matter of subtle parallels or complementarity, but the most common, most basic mode of pairing is the sharing of material between two verses. In the classic pattern, a unique statement is followed by a shared statement (not, however, found elsewhere in the song); the coda may also be shared in this fashion. The amount of material shared varies, making for stronger or weaker pairs. The following pair is very strong:[74]

> Do nothing but enjoy, each one enjoy, my friends. *Will you not enjoy, will you not be content, my friends? Where will I get fine flowers, fine songs? y ahua yya o ahua yia yiaa ohuaya ohuaya*†
> One never spends two springs here. I am afflicted, I Quaquauhtzin. *Will you not enjoy, will you not be content, my friends? Where will I get fine flowers, fine songs? y ahua yya o ahua yia yiaa ohuaya ohuaya*

---

*In written versions the most common coda, *ohuaya ohuaya*, is sometimes omitted, being taken for granted.

†Here and in the song below, shared material in a verse pair is italicized. The nonlexical coda material is left untranslated.

The pair has the same characteristics as the verse on a different level. It too is self-contained, and when verses are reordered in variants, the pairs are usually respected, being moved as entities.

Following the altepetl analogy, we might expect that a song would ideally consist of eight verses, and we would not be entirely disappointed. The most common scheme for a shorter composition indeed calls for four pairs, eight verses in all. Larger compositions or cycles are often in multiples of eight, each eight being a subdivision. Ten is also common in independent compositions, however, and six is much used for the parts of cycles. Whatever the number, it is in principle always even, and it is the numerical symmetry of the pairs that renders the composition a whole.

At this point we must observe a distinction between the organization of songs and the organization of political entities. Cellular-modular structure allows for two main ways of unifying a whole; one is the arrangement of similar independent parts in a satisfying symmetrical scheme, and the other is the establishment of a fixed order of rotation and succession among the parts. Since each pair of a song tends to bear the same relation to the theme as any other,[75] the order of succession of the pairs is a matter of relative indifference and can be changed without affecting the symmetry of the whole. And in fact, in the collections we find that the same compiler-copyists who were so inflexibly intent on achieving an even number of verses, and so careful that they sometimes went back to add or omit a single letter in a long sequence of nonsense syllables, often put the pairs in different sequences in variant versions of the same song.

Here is an example of an eight-verse song, as typical in its structure as in its residual translation problems:[76]

1. The flower-plumed quechol bird enjoys, *enjoys above the flowers. An ohuaya.*

2. Sipping the various flowers he enjoys, *enjoys above the flowers. An ohuaya.*

3. Covered with green leaves are your body and your heart, Chichimec lord Telitl; your heart is jade, it is flowers of cacao and fragrant white blooms. *Ahua yyao ayya yye. Let us enjoy! A ohuaya.*

4. You come intertwined with smiling flowers on the flower tree, on a mat of flowers, from paradise; the flowers swell, rootless flowers. From within flower plumes you sing, Tlailotlac;* you are fragrant, you are intertwined. *Ahua yyao ayya yye. Let us enjoy! A ohuaya.*

5. We are not twice on earth, noble Chichimecs; let us enjoy. Flowers can't be taken to the land of the dead, we only borrow them. *In truth, we must go. Ohuaya.*

*A ruler's title, also an ethnic group name.

6. Ah, in truth, we are going, we are leaving the flowers and the songs and the earth. *In truth, we must go. Ohuaya.*

7. Where do we go? Where we go when we die, do we still live? Is it a place of enjoyment? Does the Giver of Life still wish entertainment? Perhaps only here *on earth are* there *sweet flowers and songs. Enjoy, each one, our wealth and our garments (of flowers). Ohuaya.*

8. Enjoy, noble Chichimecs, for we must go to the home of Popocatzin, Tlailo-tlac Acolhuatzin.* You will (?); no one will remain. *On earth are sweet flowers and songs; enjoy, each one, our wealth and our garments (of flowers). Ohuaya.*

A variant version starts with what is here the second pair; the third pair, having perhaps been lost, is replaced by a different pair put second in order, followed by the first pair here, so that only the last pair is left in place.[77]

Given, then, that a complex, highly characteristic indigenous song genre survived, with all its subtleties, past the conquest well into Stage 2, what of the compositions themselves? Do they too stem from preconquest times, or are they new products in an old tradition, or does the answer lie somewhere between? In the example just quoted, there is nothing that could not have been composed before the arrival of the Spaniards; even "Giver of Life" (*ipal-nemoani*), although it became an epithet of the God of the Christians, was originally applied to powerful indigenous deities. Famous preconquest kings and lords of Tenochtitlan, and secondarily of Tetzcoco and other central Mexican altepetl, are the protagonists of a great number of the songs, setting the tone for the whole corpus.

Yet all the dates given in the Cantares for composition, arrangement, or performance are postconquest, centering on the 1550's and 1560's.[78] Even more importantly, the people named as composers or arrangers are not the protagonists or central figures celebrated in the songs involved, though the latter are often made to speak in the first person.[79] One of the main things leading to the long-held belief in the direct preconquest origin of the songs was the impression that the central, first-person speakers in them were their authors. This belief no longer seems valid as a general proposition. The un-named singer is clearly differentiated from the protagonist in a large number of songs, and even when he is not, the whole point of view of that main core of the corpus concerning famous men of the altepetl is retrospective, the no-tion being to perpetuate their memory and bewail their passing, thereby hon-oring both them and the group to which they belonged.[80]

Even if a song's date of original composition is normally posterior to the

---

*"The home of Popocatzin is explained by the copyist as "the land of the dead." Whether "Tlailotlac Acolhuatzin" is direct address or in the third person is not certain.

life of the hero, it could still fall equally well before or after the conquest. The same is true of many songs not featuring any well-known historical personage. The very notions "original composition" and "author" are probably rather out of place in this context. Nahuatl song belonged to oral tradition, and in such a tradition, though much can be preserved over considerable periods of time, the distinction between author and performer can be blurred or nonexistent. Each performer has some model or source from which he to a greater or lesser extent varies in style and content, within the framework of the genre.

Things are made little clearer by the fact that the Cantares give credit for certain songs in the postconquest period to specific named individuals on specifically dated occasions. Some of these attributions employ a verb that invites the translation "compose": *tecpana*, "to put in order, arrange in a line or sequence." (The same word often refers to the action of a testator in ordering his will.) Either of two meanings could equally well be intended: to give already existing material a somewhat new numerical verse arrangement and rhetorical clothing, or to make up the basic material in the first place. Perhaps the Nahuas were not attuned to making such a distinction, which can easily be seen as artificial or at least a matter of degree. Another word used in attributions, *tlalia*, is just as ambiguous, since it can mean "to set down, to provide, to issue under one's responsibility," and a host of related notions, as well as "to compose."[81]

At any rate, there is no reason that a very large part of the song corpus we know could not represent relatively slight reworkings of preconquest songs, very much in the manner of the preconquest sections of Stage 2 annals. The great idiosyncrasy of Nahuatl song, before and after the conquest, is surely the same: the combination of themes of ethnic pride, battle, martial glory, and the divine not with epic narrative but with an intricate lyricism of flowers, birds, music, friendship, the refinements of nobility, and the pathos of ephemerality.[82]

Again as with the annals, however, an important portion of the corpus represents new postconquest composition, concerning the conquest, the new religion, and personages of postconquest times. And as with the annals, some themes remain much the same, adjusted to the conditions. One cycle deals with the Mexica in the Spanish siege of Tenochtitlan, concentrating on their great old rivals the Tlaxcalans.[83] These frankly postconquest songs use basically the same vocabulary as the rest but add Spanish loans as appropriate, loans in no way distinct from those found in other types of Stage 2 sources.[84] Like other Nahuatl materials of the time, these portions are firmly Christian. They also show admiration or affection for the Franciscans of Mexico City, and indeed some of the songs may have been composed by their aides.[85] Toward other Spaniards they are noncommittal, leaving them largely unmentioned except for the conquest battles; in these, the Mexica regret their defeat but treat the conquerors simply as the other side.[86]

Leaving aside many other complexities, ambiguities, and dimensions in a corpus amazingly rich and varied for its size, we may ask whether such a rarefied art, known to us only through copies made by aides of Spaniards, really was part of general Nahua culture. The answer appears to be that it was indeed, at least in the Mexico City region. The painter-clerk annalist of Tenochtitlan in the 1560's several times reports the performance of songs in subgenres mentioned in the Cantares, as though these were grand public occasions.[87] Chimalpahin too has some such entries, the last being for 1593.[88] "Headflying" (*quapatlanaliztli*), descending on spiraling ropes from a high pole, was part and parcel of such celebrations.[89]

After 1600, such reports are heard no more, possibly because of the paucity of late Nahuatl annals from the Valley of Mexico region. Nor were any more collections of Nahuatl song compiled, to our knowledge. The reason could be simply the decline of Spanish philology, leaving the Nahuas to rely once more on the oral tradition that had always reigned in the world of song. Zapata reports that in Tlaxcala in 1677, for a procession honoring the coronation of the new Spanish king, each of the four sub-altepetl set up a platform where singers in the ancient manner (*huehuecuicani*) held forth.[90] No texts or other details are given. Perhaps one is justified in drawing the conclusion that the sixteenth-century style of song had been altered substantially and was revived only for special ceremonial occasions. We can only wonder whether a living, fully authentic tradition survived in some circles, or whether the style was reconstructed from later notions of what it had been, as with much sixteenth-century history in the late annals.

From the Spaniards we hear mainly reports of pole-flying and dancing, and the dance most often mentioned is the *tocotín*, a name derived from the drumbeat notation of the songs of the sixteenth century (and presumably earlier). The Jesuit historian Clavijero reports this dance as still going strong in his time, the late eighteenth century.[91] A tocotín could have words; some preserved in Spanish differ in no way from contemporary Spanish verse.[92]

As to song texts in Nahuatl, they are few indeed, and one must go all too far to find them, leaving much doubt about whether or not they reflect ordinary practice. The late-seventeenth-century Spanish nun sor Juana Inés de la Cruz wrote some occasional poems imitating the language of Indians and blacks in Mexico City in her time; among them is a tocotín in Nahuatl.[93] It is in praise of the Virgin and evinces none of the rhetoric of the old songs. Without verses defined by a coda of vocables, it is organized in the typical Spanish manner, with rhyming lines containing a prescribed number of syllables, and stanzas of no set numerical pattern. We cannot know, however, whether sor Juana Inés was following current Nahua custom or her own propensities, and were this the only example at our disposal, we might give the matter no further thought.

Another set of examples does exist, however; it also arises under rather unclear circumstances, but at least it seems to have been generated by some Nahuatl speaker. The Tlaxcalan don Manuel de los Santos y Salazar, the collector and editor of late annals, was also interested in plays.[94] In 1714, he wrote, copied, or revised (as will be discussed in more detail in the following section) a Nahuatl play about Santa Elena and the Holy Cross. Included are some short Nahuatl texts to be sung. As in the example of sor Juana, they consist of stanzas of four more or less rhymed lines (*a b a b* or *a b b a*), with eight syllables or thereabouts. Here is the longest, the only one of more than one stanza:[95]

Yn Constantino axictini	Constantine arriving,
quinmahuiztilia iteohuan	honors his gods.
Ica on huel huelitini	For that reason he was able
Oquinxico in iyaohuan.	to overcome his enemies.
Ma nohuian yectenehualo	May everywhere be praised
Yn Constantino tlapaltic	valiant Constantine,
Ylhuiltic ymacehualtic	deserving
Nohuian mauhcaittalo.	to be feared everywhere.
Huelitini in iteohuan	Powerful are his gods,
Ca icxitlan quintlalique	for they have put at his feet
Yn nepapan yaohuan	his various enemies,
Yn huel oquicocolique.	who greatly hated him.
Ye oquimixmachilitzino	Now he has recognized
Yn Dios itlazopiltzin	the precious child [son] of God;
Ye oquimocelitzino	Now he has received
Yni necuayatequiliztli.	baptism.

Even if this song were given a much less literal, more flowing, elegant, and rhythmic translation than it has received here, it is no masterpiece (aside from its strangely contradictory message about religion). The point is that the old metaphorical language is practically gone (a hint of it lingers in the double phrase for "deserving"); the dialogue characteristic of the older form is absent, and so is its indirection, yielding to straightforward declarations. As to structure, we might say that the four lines per stanza and the four stanzas fit well in the Nahua tradition, as do in a sense the eight syllables per line, but Spanish *coplas* can have the same arrangement, and the basic organizational principles of the composition are European.

The above does not amount to a great deal of evidence, but it is consonant with the shape that Nahuatl song composition has taken in the twentieth century, often employing rhyme, meter, stanzas, and themes much like those of Spanish poetry, though still with some relics of the older indigenous mode.[96] If songs like the one composed or preserved by Santos y Salazar were representative of Stage 3 style, then song evolution would correspond closely to other developments we have seen. As with noble terminology, kinship terms, oratory and refined conversation, and land registration, a special indigenous vocabulary in its own genre or other framework weathered the conquest, then survived or flourished, with some adjustments, on into Stage 2, but would have undergone drastic losses and reductions in Stage 3, when a new vocabulary and form emerged, much closer to Spanish modes than before, though still the heir of indigenous antecedents. Pending the discovery of further Stage 3 song samples, I provisionally believe that the scenario just outlined in fact describes the situation.

Theater

Several theatrical works written in Nahuatl during the postconquest centuries have survived, most as manuscripts dating from the late colonial period or as copies made from such manuscripts still later. Numerous reports make it evident that indigenous-language plays were being composed and performed from the 1530's forward, becoming a normal, prominent part of postconquest Nahua cultural life.[97] All have Christian religion as their theme; most are biblical or hagiographic, while a few emphasize Christian morality in everyday settings. So Hispanic are the compositions in many aspects—plot, characters, message, and dramatic conventions—that they have often and with much justification been assumed to be the products of Spanish authors, primarily the philologists among the Franciscan friars.

Now that we begin to understand better the extent to which Spanish ecclesiastics relied on indigenous aides in producing Nahuatl texts, even those to which they claimed authorship, it is natural to search for evidence of Nahua participation in the composition of the plays (generally not ascribed to any author in the original). One strong indication of a Nahua role is the naturalization of the material; the characters, as we will see, take on Nahua ranks and operate within the context of Nahua social and conversational conventions. Nevertheless, it remains at least conceivable that an astute and knowledgeable friar would have made such adaptations deliberately, the better to reach his audience. A less ambiguous trace of indigenous writers can be found in numerous nonstandard spellings of Spanish loans corresponding to the usual Nahua substitutions and hypercorrections.[98] But since the copies known until recently all seem to be posterior to the original compositions, the deviant spellings could have been introduced by the copyists. A third indication of some Nahua autonomy in the production of the final versions is the existence of occasional doctrinal irregularities in the plays, things the friars surely would not have tolerated had they been fully aware of them.

The most blatant example known to me is in a piece apparently finished in approximately its present form in the first decade of the seventeenth century and dedicated to fray Juan Bautista, a Franciscan philologist based mainly in Mexico City and active in the production of Nahuatl texts, including not only sermons and confessionals but plays. The Franciscan on one occasion openly acknowledged the aid of Agustín de la Fuente, a Nahua who had earlier worked with Sahagún, in the composition of all his Nahuatl productions, including three manuscript volumes of plays (now lost).[99] In the play in question, the Virgin expresses her gratitude to one of the Magi in the following terms: "I thank you, Baltasar, on behalf of my precious child; his precious honored father the Most Holy Trinity has sent you here."[100] That this rather basic misconception about the Trinity, identifying the term with God the father and excluding Jesus, is no mechanical slip can be confirmed by its repetition on a following page.[101]

Even things of this nature, presumably, could have been brought in at some point in the copying process. Although both the specific clues and the general nature of Spanish-Nahua writing collaboration point to Nahuas as the ones responsible for the actual wording of the plays preserved today, what has been needed for final confirmation is access to some sixteenth-century manuscripts of the works. One has now appeared, a playlet for the Wednesday of Holy Week included in a book of sermons and other materials collected by a still-unidentified Franciscan as he traveled about central Mexico in the late sixteenth century, perhaps the 1580's or 1590's.[102] Headed "miercoles santo,"[103] it is written in an entirely different hand from the bulk of the book. In the clear, round, chiseled characters, so different from the smaller, more cursive, more abbreviated Spanish scrawl of the friar, one immediately recognizes an indigenous writer. If any doubt should remain, numerous spellings betray the Nahuatl speaker, including among others "cochilo" for *cuchillo*, "knife."[104]

On the other hand, here as in other plays we find multiple evidence of Spanish intervention. The story, a single scene essentially, concerns the attempt of Jesus to get Mary's blessing before going into Jerusalem to be sacrificed for mankind's salvation. She is most reluctant, saying, "Don't you remember how I bore you in a manger? Don't you remember how I raised you with the milk of my breasts?," and goes on to remind him of the difficulties she had experienced getting him to safety in Egypt and the like.[105] To reinforce

Jesus's point that mankind must be saved, angels appear with letters from Adam and other Old Testament notables imploring Mary's consent so that they can finally be freed from limbo. Though the very human tone of the confrontation between mother and son might be attributed to a Nahua, and the smooth phrases of perfectly idiomatic elevated Nahuatl conversation surely must be, the stage directions and the machinery of angels and letters, not to speak of the at times complex theology and the Spanish terms that go with it (such as "original sin," "holy Catholic faith," both in Spanish), can only have been Spanish-inspired.[106]

There remain as usual many questions about just how direct the Spanish inspiration and supervision were, but the particular circumstances of this original manuscript allow us to deduce certain procedures that may have been widespread in the composition of plays. Assuming that Spanish ecclesiastics were in many cases ultimately responsible for the plot and much of the content, a question that comes to mind repeatedly is whether the Spaniard committed material to paper, to be used directly by an aide who perhaps had some grasp of Spanish, or whether he simply communicated with the amanuensis orally, in some mixture of Spanish and Nahuatl. The Holy Wednesday playlet contains a very revealing hint in this respect. In general, the stage directions and asides are in Nahuatl, but at one point the following Spanish appears (in the hand of the Nahua writer): "vee y lee nra senora la carta de Adan y diez," "Our Lady looks at and reads the letter of Adam and ten . . . "[107] The passage tells us that in this case the Spaniard had indeed put something on paper, and that the Nahua who copied it and left an unintelligible "and ten" hanging did not understand the Spanish well at all.

And yet the passage was left just as the Nahua writer set it down. The book's Spanish owner did not make one mark anywhere on the script of the play. None of the "incorrect" Nahuatl spellings of Spanish words are altered. Nor is one theological irregularity that the Nahua writer committed challenged in any way. The writer has Mary address an angel as "noteouh notlatocauh," "my god, my ruler,"[108] implying perhaps the inclination to multiply autonomous yet interpenetrating divine entities that we can detect in Nahua Christianity generally. It is as though the directing Spaniard, although in a sense probably deserving to be called the author of the play, never looked at it again once he had given it to a Nahua to translate and realize as he saw fit. Presumably, the Spanish friar would show the script in the same spirit to literate Nahuas wherever he might be stationed, expecting them to organize its performance. In a word, the Holy Wednesday script confirms ultimate Spanish authorship and sponsorship as well as a large field of Nahua discretion and independence in translation, extending to numerous adaptations and additions.

In their adaptations, we would expect the Nahua amanuenses or second-ary authors to follow established traditions of their culture and especially the conventions of any sort of theater or theater-like genre the preconquest Na-huas possessed. The problem of reconstructing such an earlier form is much more difficult than with annals and songs. There, too, our direct knowledge of preconquest models is minimal, but the postconquest writings contain so many references to preconquest times and so much in the way of distinctive material and modes that it is not hard to form a good notion of basic aspects of the traditional genres.

In the case of drama produced after the conquest, preconquest references are rare and peripheral,[109] and the general Spanish framework is so dominant as to obliterate the outlines of a specifically dramatic preconquest genre, if indeed such a thing existed. Nothing purporting to be a drama in preconquest style has survived. Spanish observers and antiquarians of the sixteenth cen-tury speak of various kinds of mimicry, pageantry, and representation, some-times using the vocabulary of the European theater, but the descriptions gen-erally emphasize song and dance.[110] One is left wondering if preconquest song, which was apparently also always dance and surely contained elements of costume and pageant as well, was not identical with the dramatic perfor-mances mentioned. Some modern scholars have, not without reason, identi-fied certain of the multivoice cycles in the extant corpus of Nahuatl song as dramas.[111]

The first step in attempting to clarify the preconquest precedent for the religious plays of the postconquest period, then, should be to see if there are significant affinities between the plays and the corpus of Nahuatl song. In fact, a close search through the plays reveals few affinities and many differ-ences. Exclamations and laments crop up here and there in the plays, but the vocables that are so crucial to song organization are entirely lacking. So are the symmetrical numerical arrangements of units that are the songs' basic organizational principle. Song and dance are no part of the ordinary trans-actions of the plays; at most, some Latin hymns are interspersed between action segments, and these are not even entered into the scripts. Beyond some metaphors and doublets that pervade all older Nahuatl expression, the plays evince none of the strongly marked rhetoric and vocabulary of the songs. Where the latter are highly allusive and indirect, the former, though elevated in style and full of complex constructions, are lucid and direct, immediately intelligible to an audience, following a straightforward line of thought and action from the beginning to the end. Each speech takes direct reference to the preceding, just the opposite of the norm in the songs. Nor do the plays contain any trace of the themes of the songs; the illustrious Nahua ancestors are missing, and so is the whole lyric-martial aura surrounding them, with all its paraphernalia.

One characteristic of the plays does put one in mind of the songs. The direct replies of one speaker to another often (by no means always) involve a combination of repetition and variation strongly reminiscent of the verse pairing at the root of the symmetrical arrangement of Nahuatl song. An analysis of the seeming similarities quickly becomes highly subjective, however. I tend to the opinion that the repeating and varying seen in succeeding speeches does not generally go beyond that inherent in any human discourse and therefore does not represent an affinity of genre. In any case, the dialectic involved in a statement and reply, aimed directly at each other, is vastly different from the parallelism in the verses of a pair, each aimed at the same outside target.

Yet in one extant play, the same possibly early-seventeenth-century version of the story of the Magi mentioned above, a type of pairing appears that seems to bear more than coincidental similarity to the song mode. To take one of the stronger examples, at the beginning of the play an emperor somewhere in the East sends out a captain and two vassals to look for the prophesied star. The captain observes that it is a mystery how they were sent by God to the mountaintop where they are on the lookout. Thereupon follow the speeches of the two vassals:

FIRST VASSAL: What you say is very true, my dear companion, it is a mystery how we arrived here; *may it be His will that He likewise returns us whence we were sent.*
SECOND VASSAL: Let us kneel, let us pray to God the father; as He has brought us here safely, *may it be His will that He likewise returns us whence we were sent.*[112]

Except for the lack of vocables, these two speeches are structured exactly like a verse pair, with unique material first, followed by shared material, and with the two statements running parallel rather than directed at each other. Many other pairs, and sometimes triplets, occur throughout the play, though none are quite as strong (in the sense defined in the section on song) as our example.[113] Furthermore, the bulk of the speeches in the piece are not obviously paired, and I have not discovered this kind of deliberate pairing in any other play.

If Nahuatl song is very weakly reflected in the plays, the influence of the interrelated realms of oratory, didactic speech, and polite conversation is pervasive. Rather than rapid dialogue, the discourse tends to consist of a series of rounded speeches in the Nahua manner, varying greatly in length, of course, but rarely reduced to a simple "yes," "no," or "very well." Consider the following exchange between Abraham and Isaac, in which Abraham uses conventional Nahua metaphors to show appreciation of children and proceeds to dispense fatherly advice in the style of the *huehuetlatolli* or "ancient wisdom, speech of the elders."[114] Following the polite convention, Isaac outdoes himself expressing gratitude for the wise words and apologizing for the trouble he causes:

ABRAHAM: You my golden necklace, my jade bracelet, my silver necklace, you my dear child, come; it is with great consolation that I embrace you, for All-Powerful God, who made everything on earth, the visible and the invisible, created you.

Listen, my dear honored child, beware lest sometime you besmirch your spirit and soul in some way. Always consider it a jade, a pearl, for God created it. Do not violate a single one of our lord God's precious honored lordly commandments. Write them on your heart and always remember them, for your Engenderer and Creator who made you exists, He to whom praise should always be given in heaven and on earth.

Now you are to know, my dear honored child, that your relatives are coming here to see you and to find out how much I love my precious child.

ISAAC: You my dear father who engendered me in an earthly sense, now your body has grown old with all the concern and trouble I have given you here on earth in raising me. You give me my daily sustenance, you clothe my body; you do everything in your great mercy. But I am making you ill, my precious father [by prattling on like this]. I have greatly profited from the precious honored words with which you have admonished me. [If I keep talking] I will give you headaches and stomach pains, my precious honored father. All that you command me I will do.[115]

Greetings are often textbook perfect by the Nahua code. Consider the following exchange between Herod and Melchior on the arrival of the three Magi.

HEROD: You who have arrived and come here have fatigued yourselves [i.e., welcome], you honorable ones, you lords, you rulers. May the divine ruler our lord God give you health. And is the All-Present God granting you a bit of good health?

MELCHIOR: Remain seated, oh lord, oh king, oh Herod, we greatly appreciate your hospitality; you have been most generous to us your slaves and vassals. Yes, we are enjoying a bit of good health. We warmly kiss your precious hands and feet.

HEROD: Come up into your home, your altepetl, do enter and eat, for it is at your home that you have arrived.[116]

Nahuatl formal speech, with its combination of preachiness, elevated tone, and clarity, was perfectly adapted to the purposes of the type of religious drama the Spanish ecclesiastics wished to generate, and it could also lend verisimilitude and accessibility to otherwise exotic material. That it was used for specifically dramatic purposes in preconquest times is not, however, necessarily indicated. It serves and colors the postconquest genre rather than defining it. Possibly religious plays, like some successful Spanish-style documentary genres, had no single preconquest precedent, instead drawing on various indigenous resources and meeting a combination of indigenous needs and expectations.

A strong aura of nobility marked elevated speech among the Nahuas, and it was natural if not inevitable that many of the biblical characters of the religious plays would be given high social rank and placed in the context of Nahua sociopolitical organization. In the story of the sacrifice of Isaac, for example, Abraham is tlatoani of an altepetl, surrounded by noblemen (pipiltin), whereas his concubine Agar and her son Ismael are *tetlan nenque*, a specific type of marginal dependent.[117] In one version of the story of the Magi, Mary in referring to Jesus's charge injects Nahua notions of rulership as a burden.[118] In another version of the Magi story, the Old Testament prophets and patriarchs are spoken of in terms used in the Florentine Codex and elsewhere for Nahua rulers of the past.[119]

Though thus strongly naturalized, the predominant themes of the plays remain Spanish, with emphasis on teaching the audience the principal personae, doctrines, and morality of Christianity. Apart from a relatively small doctrinal error here and there, the strong adaptive tendency hardly affects the content at this level. It may well be, however, that some of the topics were chosen for their special applicability to the Nahuas' situation. The story of Abraham and Isaac, in addition to teaching obedience to God and parents, contains a strong implicit message against human sacrifice, perhaps a reminder for sixteenth-century Nahuas who had not entirely forgotten preconquest practices. And a few plays set in the central Mexico of the time, teaching Christian conduct in executing testaments and carrying on business, are aimed specifically at certain Nahua behavioral tendencies.[120] Presumably it was the friars who chose such themes as a result of their local experiences, but in some cases the Nahuas themselves may have pressed for a given topic or emphasis or made it popular by their reaction to it. That would appear to be the case with the Magi, in whom the Nahuas seemingly saw a token that Christianity was not just for Europeans but also for the peoples of distant lands, who had their part to play too; indeed the friar-historian Motolinia said as much at an early time.[121]

In view of what we know of the postconquest religion and general outlook of the Nahuas, one would expect them to have clamored for plays on the patron saints of altepetl. Surely from a very early time they were inclined to reshape Spanish-organized pageantry in the direction of local patriotism.[122] Yet very few indeed are the extant examples of plays with a single saint as protagonist. Except for the Magi (who were not the patrons of any important altepetl to my knowledge), the central characters in the corpus in general are Jesus and Mary (with God the father prominent in the background), surrounded by the disciples as a group, and some Old Testament greats. The

emphasis, then, is the same as in the early body of confessionals and catechisms, on a purist, almost saint-less religion concentrating on the Trinity, the
Virgin, doctrine, and individual morality. Surely this direction was dictated
by the ecclesiastics as part of their general thrust in the early and middle
sixteenth century.

We are confronted, then, with the superficially paradoxical situation that
the vast majority of extant copies of the plays are very late, while their basic
anatomy and central message correspond to a very early time. Nor are other
indications lacking that the basic corpus came into being long before the
copies that have reached us. As I have already stated, traditional decorous
Nahuatl speech and traditional social categories pervade the corpus, and we
have seen elsewhere that both elements drastically declined or disappeared in
Stage 3. Spanish loans in the corpus are entirely compatible with Stage 2 as a
time of composition, and indeed the core of the loans consists of staple items
that could very well have been included as early as mid-sixteenth century.[123]
We even see some possible hints that the first versions of some of the plays
may go back into Stage 1, for in some cases one finds *tepozmacquahuitl,*
"metal hand club," instead of the Spanish *espada,* "sword," and *maçatl,*
"deer," instead of loanwords for horses and donkeys.[124] Motolinia, after all,
reports the performance of plays in Nahuatl in the 1530's.[125]

A great deal of systematic textual research remains to be done, but my
preliminary conclusion is that the extant versions of the plays, nearly all from
Stage 3 and some specifically written down as late as 1760,[126] are in the main
reasonably faithful copies of material originating in Stage 2, predominantly
well before the end of the sixteenth century. Even the lost collection of plays
put together by fray Juan Bautista in the first years of the seventeenth century
must have been essentially a compilation of pieces that had proved successful
in earlier decades. If the play about the Magi that can perhaps be ascribed to
the Nahua amanuensis Agustín de la Fuente is indeed to be dated 1607 (and
this is by no means sure), the work would have come at the end of de la
Fuente's long career of collaboration with several Franciscans, and in any case
it contains many hints of being based on an older version or versions.[127]

The basic chronology of the religious plays, then, would have much in
common with that of classic Nahuatl song, both reaching a height in Stage 2,
and primarily the early and middle portions of the period, after which new
production in that style declined steeply or halted. A large difference is that
the Nahuas spontaneously continued to write the plays down to preserve
them and perform them, whereas songs virtually ceased to be transcribed,
and though song continued as part of Nahua culture, from the hints we have,
the compositions bore little resemblance to those of an earlier day. In the
plays, a phenomenon essentially of Stage 2 jelled, became canonical, and projected without major change into a later time. Exactly why this was remains

to be explored. As noted in greater detail in Chapter 6, I do not believe that the Nahuas were excessively enamored of the basic message the friars were originally attempting to convey. To me the most likely explanation is that individual plays or versions of plays, though they were at first intended to be performed all over central Mexico (remember the playlet that our ambulatory friar carried with him wherever he went), and though they were not specifically tied to any altepetl by theme, nevertheless gradually became localized, representing an important yearly altepetl function, expected by the audience and doubtless performed by the same amateur actors year in and year out.

Such a process implies a certain amount of change over time, and though I have until now emphasized the overwhelming continuity and conservation, I do not mean to imply that no change at all took place. Even in those late copies that seem purest and that are the basis of our knowledge of the sixteenth-century genre, one finds bits of syntax and vocabulary that jar and seem to belong to a later time.[128] Perhaps they arose by a copyist unwittingly following his own usage, or perhaps they deliberately reflect the evolving tradition of local actors. An occasion especially propitious to minor change would arise when citizens of one altepetl chose to copy and appropriate a popular play associated with another altepetl; that this happened we have good reason to believe.[129]

In some cases, the changes go beyond orthography and occasional variant language to affect the tone of a whole piece. A passion play associated with Tepalcingo (and especially with a famous image of Jesús Nazareno housed there), known in an eighteenth-century version, is to a large extent in the language of its time and place, despite the fact that it contains no blatant late loan phenomena and does retain a great deal of the older dramatic rhetoric and vocabulary as well.[130] The speeches often approach everyday utilitarian conversation more closely than usual in the old style, and more of what transpires involves action.[131] Either a great deal of new material has been added to an older core, or the whole was newly composed in the eighteenth century, preserving much of what had by then long been established as the manner and stock material of religious plays.[132] Despite aspects of modernity and a good many Spanish loans, at times the script uses indigenous constructions of the type employed in Stage 1 for words of Spanish origin that had been in common use in Nahuatl since the mid-sixteenth century, including *tepozmecatl*, "metal rope," for *cadena*, "chain," and *pepechtli*, "underpinning," for *silla*, "saddle."[133] Again, this vocabulary could either be a relic of a very early play or be newly included in the belief that the style of plays so demands. I believe on balance that an accretive process led to late plays like this one, but I would not discount the ability of late practitioners to imitate some of the features of what was by now a familiar, hallowed style.

One extant late play, concerning the discovery of the true cross by Santa

Elena in the time of Constantine, stands apart from the rest.[134] The script is unusual in specifying a date, 1714, as well as an author (or arranger; the ambiguity is no different from that surrounding the "authors" of Nahuatl songs)—the same don Manuel de los Santos y Salazar of Tlaxcala whom we have met before.[135] Santos y Salazar apparently chose the topic because he was curate of the town of Santa Cruz Cozcaquauh Atlauhticpac. Like the passion play of Tepalcingo, the piece contains archaizing vocabulary, speeches in the old manner, and blocks of familiar material that could have been done new but were probably taken, at least in part, from older plays. But a further transformation has taken place; Santos y Salazar has adopted certain of the conventions of Golden Age Spanish theater. Some of the speeches have the air of soliloquies. Two buffoons (*graciosos*, though the script does not use the term) punctuate the serious action by chasing each other about the stage, brandishing weapons in mock heroics and uttering crude jokes. Instead of Latin hymns between acts, songs in the vernacular, *tocotines*, or as the Spaniards would call them, *villancicos*, intrude into the main discourse.[136] Santos y Salazar was such an exceptional figure, or at least ahead of his time in being both an indigenous patriot-antiquarian and an expert in the arts of Spanish literacy, that one must await further evidence before concluding that the interesting innovations in what is to date a unique play represent a broader trend in the Nahua cultural world.

Titles

In all likelihood, some more examples of the genres we have been discussing—annals, songs, and plays—will come to light in future years, and sophisticated analysis of the examples we already have, using recent advances in Nahua ethnohistory and philology, has just begun. Yet in each case a real corpus has emerged, and serious work of discovery, translation, and commentary has been going on for many years. The same cannot be said for the next documentary type to be examined, the so-called "titles" (*títulos*) purporting to authenticate an altepetl's right to its territory. Although an awareness of the genre goes back some decades, and some preliminary statements and partial analyses have been available,[137] they have not involved a close reading, or in most cases any reading at all, of the Nahuatl texts. Nahuatl scholars have now begun textual analysis, and some studies have appeared or are forthcoming, but it is all very much work in progress, first because only a small portion of the probably extant corpus has been discovered, and second because of the enormous difficulty of the texts. It seems fair to say that to date hardly a single one of these documents has been satisfactorily transcribed and translated, much less edited and published. Somewhat like Nahuatl songs, but to an even

higher degree, the titles are sui generis, and whereas the songs constitute a
highly unified body of material, the titles are far more individual in almost
every respect.[138] Having already declared the matter of this chapter to be more
than normally provisional, I must further assert that that caveat applies with
greatest force to this section. Indeed, I will abbreviate my remarks, for the
most part merely summarizing and making some deductions from a few recent or ongoing studies, fully expecting that more extensive and definitive
treatments will soon follow, whether from my pen or another's.[139]

In several ways, the titles genre stands out from any other type of Nahuatl
writing. As far as we now know, it is entirely a Stage 3 phenomenon; no
known example antedates 1650. At least, this is the conclusion one must
draw from many indications, such as the vocabulary and syntax, dates
stamped on the paper, dates of presentation and translation, the handwriting,
and the confusion about well-known figures and events of the sixteenth century, even though many titles purport to be dated in the mid-sixteenth century
or earlier. It is true that Nahuatl plays are also almost all known in copies of
Stage 3 vintage. But they give every sign of following relatively faithfully an
earlier written tradition, whereas the titles, or most of them, have the air of
being a first gathering together of relevant oral tradition and various bits of
older documentation that might have been preserved locally. The apparent
reason for collecting such lore and putting it on paper (nowhere do we find a
direct statement on the point) was a new need for the legal justification of
land occupancy.

In the late colonial period, as the non-Indian population increased rapidly
and the indigenous population itself began to stabilize and grow, pressures
on the land mounted, so that Indian corporations abandoned their long-
standing relative indifference to outside encroachments and to the legal status
of their land rights.[140] In the growing number of land disputes that characterized the period, Spanish-style documentation of title was at a premium. Indian towns often had little or nothing of this nature in their possession, and
hence some of their citizens wrote down something considered appropriate,
which might then be presented to Spanish authorities. The majority of such
documents now known seem to have been preserved as a by-product of their
presentation as evidence in legal disputes over territory. Though they gained
little credence in court, since they lacked the apparatus of Spanish-style au-
thentication, it was perhaps in this way that they became generally known as
"titles," a term that the authors of the original documents seem not to
have used.

Ironically, then, it may have ultimately been Spanish pressures that brought
about the creation of one of the most peculiarly indigenous of all the forms
of written expression in Nahuatl. Stories, speeches, and conceptualizations

concerning the altepetl-shaking events of the sixteenth century must have
been kept alive in many Nahua communities, handed down from one generation to the next, which might understand them differently or repeat them un-
understood. Stage 3 annals captured very little of the material, but it flooded
into the titles. Essentially intracommunity lore thus reached the outside, not
helping the Nahua legal cause very much, but providing students a potentially
rich source for cultural history.

To give the reader some feeling for the flavor of the titles genre, here is
what is written under the heading "Grant" (Spanish *merced*, rendered "me-
sed") in a set of documents presented to royal authorities in 1699 by indigenous officials from Soyatzingo in the Chalco area:

Alas, Oh lord God, we honored the moon and the stars, the property of God the ruler
of the universe. Oh my dear children, you must entirely understand that Cortés don
Luis de Velasco Marqués [*sic*] brought us the true faith. Let no one flee when he
arrives. He brought the true belief in the precious honored body of our lord Jesus
Christ, so that we would become Christians. We need to make a house of God where
we can attend mass and learn the four ways of knowing our lord Jesus Christ (in our
words or language?), so that there we can confess and prepare ourselves to receive the
precious honored body of God, and so we can be baptized there, and when we die we
will be buried there. Thus Cortés don Luis de Velasco Marqués ordered us. My dear
children, ask yourselves what saint we shall serve.[141]

It is apparent that the writer was not at all sure what the Spaniards meant by
"merced," except that it was a document important to land rights. Instead of
language appropriate to the conveyance of land from the general domain to
a specific entity or individual by a higher authority, we find a portion of the
kind of speech, smacking very much of huehuetlatolli, that elders no doubt
gave to the assembled young on occasion, telling them how things were in the
altepetl in the past.

Here we have a fragment about the abandonment of pagan beliefs and the
adoption of Christianity under the sponsorship of the early Spanish conquerors and governors. But the first conqueror Cortés, later known primarily by
his new title of Marqués, and the viceroy don Luis de Velasco, in office in the
1550's and 1560's, have been amalgamated into a single symbolic person.[142]
The reference point in time changes abruptly and without explanation, as do
speaker and audience, in ways it would be illusory to try to interpret exactly.
It is as though a body of lore about earlier times had become canonical in the
community but was not preserved in its entirety, and the present writer is
putting down those bits he can remember, as he remembers them, without
much attention to flow and lucidity. Even the early sections of Stage 3 annals
are much more sophisticated about Spanish phenomena and closer to the
historical facts than passages like this. Many prominent and well-educated

Nahuas, even at this late time, doubtless realized that Cortés and Velasco were distinct, and many certainly knew full well what a "merced" was.

In the matter of spelling as well, titles tend to fall outside the range of the expected, as wide as we have seen that range to be (Chapter 8). Many give the impression of having been written not by the professional or near-professional notaries, church employees, and altepetl officials who were responsible for annals, songs, plays, and mundane documentation, but by amateurs. In the present case, the writer had definitely been subjected to considerable instruction in the skills of Nahuatl literacy; his hand is legible, and it is not hard to recognize the roots and affixes he intends to convey. His missing and intruded *n*'s and his hypercorrections (*d* for *t*) are commonplace in Nahuatl writing. He even knows the abbreviation "tt⁰" for *totecuiyo*, "our Lord." But when it comes to the common abbreviation for Cristo ("Christ"), "x̄po" or "x̄pto," he falters badly, once putting "pxoto" and once "xopto." He sometimes places a cedilla under an *s*, a true oddity. The letter *c* has gone berserk in his usage, being employed also for *z* in addition to representing glottal stops and being frequently omitted and intruded. Readers of titles almost come to expect such vagaries, though the writing sometimes approaches the standard.[143]

If annals, songs, and plays represent high culture, and mundane documentation an efficient, up-to-date quotidian culture, titles seem to correspond to popular culture, in both surface and deeper aspects. Something insulated the titles genre from other kinds of writing. Annals could have been useful to their purpose but were clearly almost never consulted. In Chalco, some of the same towns that presented fanciful titles written in an outlandish fashion also produced notarial documents entirely free of such qualities.[144] On the other hand, there was some sort of underground network of the writers and custodians of titles, at least on a subregional basis. The titles of various altepetl of Chalco betray that their writers lifted idiosyncratic names, phrases, and "facts" from each other or from some common source. It seems that a few sets may have been pirated from other towns almost in their entirety. A common vocabulary, not found (to date, at least) in other forms of writing, ran through the Chalco titles, one example being the term "telocatolio" (or "terogatorio," etc.), from Spanish *interrogatorio*, "questionnaire," which in this sphere had come to mean "papers proving the true title of an altepetl to its territory."[145]

Reducing local lore to written form, integrating modified extracts from whatever sixteenth-century documentation local citizens might have, and predating the results comes very close to falsification, though as well as we can judge today that was not usually the intention. Rather the intention was to give an authentic altepetl-internal view of the corporation's rights, grounded in its history, adhering closely to what the citizenry had said and believed for as long as the oldest alive could remember. Under the pressures of the situation, and perhaps having lost touch with relevant local traditions, some towns did resort to deliberate fabrication.

It seems that somewhere in the orbit of Mexico City there existed what amounted to a factory or studio for false titles, where towns in need could have a document made to order, complete with pictures in a pseudo-sixteenth-century style, indigenous-style paper, and a final smoking to give the appearance of age. These are the so-called "Techialoyan codices" (a modern term), whose Nahuatl texts are now being studied for the first time.[146] The antiquing process extended to the (often rather skeletal) texts themselves; knowing somehow that the Nahuas of earlier times had not yet borrowed many of the Spanish terms now current, and that they pronounced what they did borrow in their own way,[147] the fabricators bent over backwards to use indigenous vocabulary, as well as letter substitutions in names and any loanwords they could not manage to avoid. Indeed, for those conversant with actual sixteenth-century texts, they went much too far, destroying credibility, for they invented indigenous equivalents of universally used loans and substituted letters in items always spelled standardly (even though pronounced just as the fabricators surmised).

Nor were such devices restricted to the Techialoyans proper. A brief and rudimentary titles document from Cuitlahuac south of Mexico City gives the date, the equivalent of 1561, only by the indigenous number and year sign, something absolutely unheard of in sixteenth-century Nahuatl documents outside the annals genre, and even there the Spanish-style date is always added as well.[148] The document runs along throughout with many unrealistic terms and substitutions, of which the ending can serve as an example: "ninotlilmachiotia notoca notonal. Ton Locax te xantiaco tlacuilo" ("I sign my name and rubric. Don Lucas de Santiago, notary").[149] Here the invention "tlilmachiotia," literally "to make an ink sign," has replaced the usual loan-based *firmayotia*,[150] and *tonalli*, "day, day-sign, fate," is made to serve for the usual loan *firma*, "signature, rubric." *Tlacuilo* instead of the loan *escribano*, "notary," is possible but improbable. "Ton" for *don* and even "te" for *de* are sometimes, if rarely, seen, but hardly Locax for Lucas and surely not Xantiaco for the well-known name Santiago, virtually always abbreviated. An authentic document done in 1561 would have read more or less as follows (perhaps with some letter substitutions in "firma" and "escribano"), although no real notary of 1561 would have borne the "don": "ninofirmayotia [*or* nictlalia notoca nofirma] don Lucas de S^tiago escribano [escriuano, escrivano, esc⁰, etc.]."

The Techialoyans and other titles affected by some of the same tendencies are of limited significance within the larger titles corpus, in which context they are a somewhat aberrant subset. But demonstrating as they do the communication of materials and styles across a broad area of the Toluca Valley and the western Valley of Mexico,[151] they reinforce the notion of something of a titles underground operating in central Mexico, surely part of the Nahua cultural world but quite isolated from its other principal written manifestations.

Since even the titles we have (doubtless only a fraction of those extant) vary so much, compiling a list of characteristics that would apply to all or even the bulk of them is a hopeless enterprise. Nevertheless, one can identify a set of diagnostic characteristics frequently appearing in the corpus, even if they may not all be present in any one document. The most nearly universal component is a survey of the boundaries of the altepetl jurisdiction; often the document describes how leading citizens, together with representatives of neighboring entities and perhaps Spanish officials as well, made their way around the borders, agreeing on the altepetl's rights, and it always gives numerous place-names and landmarks on a line circling the territory. This core feature is entirely germane to the question of title authentification and corresponds quite closely to Spanish procedures of investigation and granting possession, but it also seems to portray a traditional preconquest rite of border verification.[152] Preconquest pictorial altepetl maps, though not directly narrating such rites, may have accompanied them. It is quite possible that the rites included a recital of the altepetl origin legend. As far afield as the present southwestern United States, some groups had a story type in which the totemic spirits conducted the first founders around what was to be the group's territory, noting the landmarks.[153]

When the survey is dated, the date is likely to fall between the conquest and 1560. The transaction is likely to be associated with the foundation of a Spanish-style municipality, an investigation ordered by a viceroy, or a congregación, or all three (and the three could in fact have coincided). At the same time, the proceedings may be linked with the altepetl's original founding in preconquest times and the legitimation of boundaries that accompanied it. The two foundations may merge, partially or completely. Building a church and accepting some basic rites of Christianity are often seen as an integral part of the process (as in the Soyatzingo example above).

A great many titles are cast at least partly in the first person; an elder speaks to the young and future generations with essential information on the altepetl and advice on how to preserve it. The elder (sometimes elders, or a father and mother pair) may belong to the generation of founders, or be the principal ruler of the altepetl at an early time, or be a symbolic incarnation of the altepetl. His speeches have the admonishing tone of the old huehuetlatolli, and he often uses terms and phrases associated with that form of discourse. Rarely is it entirely clear whether he is speaking in the present (after 1650), in the sixteenth century, or in preconquest times, or shifting back and forth from passage to passage. As a result of this concentration on the elder/ founder, a few titles are in the form of a testament issued by that figure.[154] Whether founding fathers speak in the first person or not, they are often present as the protagonists of the transactions related in the document.

In what has already been said one can detect the relatively atemporal or at least nonchronological nature of the titles, the opposite of the annals genre. If certain brief and relatively uncomplex titles refer exclusively to a single set of events dated unambiguously in a specific year in the sixteenth century, the majority leave the impression of a morass of temporal vagueness and contradiction. Various partial explanations can be offered. Knowledge of dates a century and more back was sparse in the Nahua community at any level, and even sparser, no doubt, in popular oral tradition. A process of accretion may have contributed. As we have seen, most titles were not manufactured whole cloth but stitched together from disparate existing local sources, with the result that the same events can be dated differently in the same document. Some of the Nahua title-writers may have understandably thought that the Spaniards were date-crazy and thrown a kaleidoscopic array of venerable dates at them simply to impress them.

None of this touches the core of the matter, however. Essentially, most titles were written from a timeless perspective much like that found in myth, ordering the material in a topical way, not concerned with making distinctions between similar phenomena across time but rather merging them, making all altepetl leaders the same, as well as all new beginnings and all outside threats, for all had the same function. The effect, not consciously intended, was the strongest possible assertion of the unchanging unity and strength of the altepetl regardless of time, that is, from its foundation in an infinitely remote past, the equivalent of the imagined beginning of the civilized world, to the present.

Thus the titles, for all their historical ammunition, are not history like the annals, but some combination of corporate ideology, special pleading, oratory, and myth. They hardly ever simply tell random interesting facts, and they are distinctly not the place to go for relatively reliable data on this or that event. But to disregard the historicity of titles material totally is to go too far. Some of the names dropped in titles have been proved to be actual historical personages, some of the congregaciones mentioned actually took place, and so on.[155] In view of the genre's general utter unreliability in this respect, we still cannot use unsupported assertions found in titles as evidence on facts, but the factual dimension allows us to see better into the nature of the documents themselves.

Prima facie the genre presents a wholly corporate façade, the only apparent crack in which is some hint of tensions between the two parts in altepetl with dual organization.[156] When something more is known of the personages named, it may turn out that the ostensible founding father was a member of one faction, and the trouble-making mestizo from the outside, excoriated in the document, was actually the father of an altepetl governor belonging to an opposing faction.[157] Here, as in the annals genre and in so much else in the Nahua world, individual, faction, and corporation merge in a complex balance, in which, though it is not devoid of conflict, the corporate aspect is used for individual ends without making any distinction in principle between the two.[158] The corporation indeed occupies the forefront, yet the system totally transcends older notions of monolithic Indian communalism.

But granted the need for subtlety in interpretation, the titles genre does give us a fuller, more direct and untrammeled expression of the Nahua image of corporate self, for the later period at least, than any other written medium. Despite the role of Spanish pressure in stimulating their composition, titles are freer from direct Spanish influence than plays, less thematically restricted than songs, and at times more discursive than annals, which do have much the same basic theme. Mundane documentation implies and illustrates the centrality of the altepetl but has little occasion to discuss it. The relative amateurishness and lack of sophistication of the titles writers put them in all the closer touch with popular stereotypes and made them more uninhibited in expressing them.

For the most part, the image projected in the titles is no surprise. A composite of the picture presented (again, not all of it will be found in most individual examples) would run somewhat as follows.[159] The altepetl is an organized people different from any other, existing from a remote time until today as an independent entity in sovereign control of its territory and destined to remain so, assuming its citizens hold to their time-honored traditions and stand firm against outsiders. The traditions include originally indigenous as well as originally Spanish elements, so fully merged and integrated that there is no separating them. The saint and the church (the physical building) are prominent altepetl symbols. As to the hostile outsiders, they too can be either Spanish or indigenous; an outsider is an outsider, and broader ethnic awareness or solidarity is no more to be found in the titles than anywhere else. The altepetl feels loyal to distant Spanish governmental authorities, the king and the viceroy, hoping from them support in its conflicts with more local authorities, Spanish laymen, and rival altepetl. Likewise, the feeling expressed about religion is enthusiastically if often unorthodoxly Christian, but distant archbishops are given a large role, while local priests are ignored.

The titles thus express a bit more openly the view that pervades almost all manifestations of Nahua culture, and most Nahuas of the entire postconquest period could probably have readily subscribed to the essence of what the texts assert. Some aspects of their vision, however, belong specifically to the late period. Sixteenth-century Nahuas were beginning to see a saint as the embodiment of the altepetl, and they were inclined to take any useful introduced element for what it was without asking where it came from. But in the titles the interpenetration of elements from the two cultures has gone much further than it had in Stage 2. The authors of the titles had often lost nearly all sense of any distinction between things of Spanish origin and things of indigenous origin as long as they belonged to the local tradition. Lost, too, was an awareness of the difference between the pre- and postconquest periods. Christianity and Spanish legal procedures might be attributed to the preconquest Mexica, or preconquest wars projected onto postconquest congregaciones. And if the image of the altepetl as an autonomous people had not changed, some of the entities to which the concept is applied in the titles must have been sub-altepetl, calpolli, or less in the sixteenth century before the late-colonial wave of fragmentation set in.

Even as a Stage 3 phenomenon the titles have their peculiarities. Late annals share much of their vagueness about earlier times. But whereas the annals are largely unconcerned with the preconquest period and do not concentrate on the sixteenth century, in titles the sixteenth century is the primary time of reference, and preconquest material and modes are rife even if the authors do not fully recognize them for what they historically are. Although essentially written in Stage 3 vernacular, often complete with loan verbs and particles, the titles, frozen perhaps in set presentations handed down from one generation to the next, retain far more of the old-style rhetoric and vocabulary than do the annals. Late annals, in contrast, following the trend of the times, show a far wider and more perceptive vision of the world beyond the altepetl. It was not by accident that the assertive corporate ideology of the titles, traditionally shared by all Nahuas, found written expression when many altepetl citizens were making individual contacts and accommodations with Hispanic society and partially transcending the corporation. The titles genre remains an opening into a corner of the Nahua mind to which we have no other access and an evidence of cultural vitality and creativity generations after the confrontation with the Spaniards had begun.

A Glimpse at Art and Architecture

Not only is writing an art, but the visual arts often approach the function of writing, expressing specific symbolic meanings through conventions broadly understood in a given society. Like writing, the nonverbal arts are genre-bound, but there, too, important conventions and techniques can be common to distinct genres. Conventions and techniques can even be shared by writing and visual art, and this was markedly the case in preconquest Mesoamerica. We have seen that a single term denoted both writing and painting (sometimes sculpture was also included), and that "writing" was highly pictorial.[160] The other side of the coin was that painting and sculpture were a great deal like writing. Lacking European-style perspective, relatively nonrealistic for the most part, depictions of a great many objects relied partly on convention to make the reference clear. In other words, painted pictures were somewhat glyph-like. Many of the same signs appeared in sculpture as well. Architecture was a rather different matter, no doubt, but it had its symbolism. Its way of arranging ensembles ran parallel to modes of organization in many aspects of Nahua culture, and above all it was covered with sculpture and painting, which served at once to ornament and interpret it. Moreover, the visual arts were like writing in some of their functions, especially the function of serving the altepetl and its religion. After the conquest, comparable continuities and transformations are to be observed in both realms.

It would be very much to the point, then, to treat the visual arts here in the same way as annals or plays. Alas, to do the massive basic research required would take many years, not to speak of new training. And the art historical literature, which contains some distinguished work, has mainly approached its topics in ways that leave the ethnohistorian's questions unanswered. Even so, a few authors do speak to the topics relevant here, or give relevant evidence, and one recent study on a set of sixteenth-century frescoes provides precisely the kind of basis needed to put art in the framework developed here. Using these materials, I will briefly examine some phenomena of art with a view to discovering processes and timing parallel or otherwise analogous to what we have already seen. The necessarily fragmentary nature of these remarks will perhaps frustrate some students sufficiently that they will consider making a career of combining art historical and ethnohistorical-philological research, for nothing less will do justice to a whole realm of significant phenomena traditionally seen far too much in isolation.

Among the forms already discussed, the circumstances seen in connection with theater bear the closest resemblance to those of postconquest Nahua artistic expression, and not only because both are primarily religious in theme; both involve production under Spanish auspices and supervision, so that the larger plan is at least to appearances Spanish, and it is mainly in the execution of details that indigenous people have a freer hand and operate more obviously within their own traditions. In both realms, when there are larger congruities between the product and Nahua tendencies or needs, it is hard or impossible to know whether the rapprochement should be attributed to Nahua initiatives or to prudent adjustment on the part of the Spaniards.

The largest such question has to do with the rise of a monastery church

complex consisting entirely of European elements but as an ensemble without
known precedent in Spain or elsewhere. Remarkable enough was the large
stone single-nave church, with a cut-stone portal, flanked by a cloister, but
more idiosyncratic was the precinct itself. The church faced onto a huge
walled-in open space with its own impressive stone archway at the entrance.
Somewhere near or attached to the church was an "open chapel" where mass
could be said for multitudes standing in the great patio. In the four corners
of the patio were as many small chapels, left open on two sides for processions to pass through, and in the center, on a platform, stood a stone cross,
usually decorated with carved insignia of the Passion.[161]

Affinities between this system and that prevailing before the conquest have
often been noted.[162] To begin with, the new complex was not infrequently
erected over the ruins of the main altepetl temple. Preconquest temples faced
large enclosed spaces where the populace stood watching the rites and participating in the processions. In the center of the space was a sacrificial platform not too dissimilar from the base on which the cross was to stand after
the conquest. Above all, everything happened outdoors in open view under
both arrangements.[163]

Such similarities go beyond coincidence. But how did they come about?
The origins of the outdoor complex, which often preceded the church and
cloister, go back into the legendary decades just after the conquest and are
correspondingly obscure. In the early years, the parallels with the preconquest layout may have been even more striking. One of the first known open
chapels, if not the first, in Tlaxcala, dating from the late 1530's, was elevated
far above the audience like indigenous temples,[164] whereas with some exceptions altars in later chapels were near ground level. Nahua pressure and Spanish accommodation remain equally plausible explanations for the prevalence
of the open chapel, for it is hard to imagine how the hordes of the early and
middle sixteenth century, before the epidemics took their full toll, could have
been served in any other way. Well before the end of the century, though the
physical plant of the outdoor system remained, it appears that Sunday services were being held in the church as in Europe, very possibly more because
of the reduced population than because of a changed perspective on the part
of either Nahuas or Spaniards.[165] At all odds, church architecture is one more
realm where Spanish modes were transformed in the process of being applied
to the Nahuas.

My analogy between religious architecture and Nahuatl plays admittedly
has its limits. The plays met indigenous tastes and needs and hence long survived, but it is doubtful that the Nahuas would have clamored for them had
the Spanish ecclesiastics not taken the first step. Churches were a different
story. Indigenous religious architecture had been the arena of a crowded cal-

endar of sacred rites deemed essential to success and good order in every human endeavor; now the buildings had been destroyed and the rites abolished. The need for replacement buildings and rites was imperative.[166] Of equal importance was the role of the temple as the primary symbol of the main framework of Nahua life, the altepetl. It was predictable that the citizens of each altepetl, from high to low, would not rest content until they had built a new equivalent edifice, as splendid as possible, to represent their polity and enable them to hold up their heads in dealing with other towns.

Another difference between theater and architecture (all art, really) has to do with the Spaniards' relation to the product. Plays required the use of idiomatic Nahuatl dialogue. This, as non−native speakers, the Spaniards were simply not capable of producing unaided, so that, as we have seen, they perforce left the production of the polished version to their aides, and we have many hints that they did not fully understand what the aides had written. But in building and carving, the protective veil of language was absent; Spaniards could see directly what was done, compare it with their plans and canons, supervise more closely, and intervene directly in production when they felt it necessary.

The overall surface of religious art was thus more comparable to Spanish originals than was the case with plays, and indigenous independence was much restricted. Few indeed must have been the major building projects of the sixteenth century carried out without a Spanish designer, a Spanish overseer, and some non-Indian technical personnel (crew bosses and trained craftsmen)—although in truth the question of personnel in building and decorative campaigns must be answered largely by deduction from the work itself and parallels drawn with other postconquest craft activity. Nevertheless, zones of indigenous independence existed in this realm. So much needed to be done that, apparently, Spanish supervisors often left certain tasks they considered less important in the hands of indigenous craftsmen alone, and the decoration of already set designs (sometimes highly skeletal) was one such assignment.[167]

Such a mass of work was needed all across central Mexico in the sixteenth century that a very large proportion of it had to be done by Nahuas alone, and no matter how close the supervision they were under, they could do only what they had at any given point in time learned to do. Under these circumstances, nothing could prevent indigenous styles, techniques, and perceptions from affecting the end result. Some indigenous practitioners of the arts in European style were from an early time so thoroughly trained and adept that their works are difficult or impossible to distinguish from those of Spaniards. But in the sixteenth century, for every one of these there were many craftsmen less fully exposed to the European tradition.

With the buildings themselves and even the architectonic aspects of por-
tals closely designed by Spaniards, sculpture was one of the main areas where
the indigenous could manifest itself, primarily in relief carvings on church
entryways, patio chapels, crosses, baptismal fonts, and the like. These included representations of human figures and flora and fauna, as well as more
abstract decorative motifs. Some of the work could pass for Spanish, and very
little of it shows a carryover of preconquest symbols (in contrast, for example,
to the postconquest glyphic writing discussed in Chapter 8), but at times it
treats the topics and tasks dictated by Spaniards in a fashion clearly in the
indigenous tradition.

One is not surprised to find in such carving yet another reflection of the
general Nahua propensity toward cellular-modular organization, the symmetrical arrangement of independent parts of which we have seen so much in
previous chapters. Consider the familiar ring of an art historian's observations on indigenous-Spanish carved ornament:*

The many stressed episodes do not add up to an expression of continuous movement,
but remain separate shoves and swirls. . . . The movement is repetitive . . . rather than
flowing. . . . Such all-over, metronomic, never-ending repetition, as opposed to metrical scansion with phrased grouping of accents, is one of the fundamental differences
between the typical Indian and European expressions in ornament. . . . Coherence
comes not from any organic or sequential interrelation of parts, but from their insis-
tent repetition in tight and seemingly endless patterns, and from the incessant interaction of their outlines. Almost everything seems equally important because almost
nothing submits to subordination.[168]

Many of the same things could be said about Nahuatl song or about the
altepetl. Not mentioned, however, is the numerical symmetry, the manipulation of twos, fours, and eights to create larger coherent entities, that is so
important in those types of organization. Perhaps the predetermined Spanish
forms into which the ornament was crowded precluded the full development
of organizational symmetry. Or perhaps it is actually there in many cases, as
unnoticed as it was until recently in song structure, and future research can
find it.

A second major characteristic of postconquest sculpted ornament in Nahua hands has to do with the manner of showing figures and designs in relief.
Emphasized elements stand out sharply, even exaggeratedly, but rather than
being rounded against a flat surface, they tend to be, though deeply incised,
nearly as flat as the background, what has been called the "cookie cutter"
style.[169] Many Nahua craftsmen of the time simply were not familiar with the
European manner of simulating roundness in relief, but in any case their so-

---

*I cannot bring myself to use the infelicitous invented term *tequitqui* for this style (the
word's origin and problematics are discussed in McAndrew 1964, pp. 196–97).

lution had the effect of reducing realism, heightening stylization, and bringing the compositions more in line with preconquest tradition.[170]

Nahua sculptors must have interpreted for themselves the shapes they were directed to carve, and the meanings they attached to them did not always precisely match their meanings in the European tradition. In many cases we have no indication—at least no superficial indication—of divergence, but in others it shows through. Notably in the churchyard crosses carved by indigenous sculptors with the paraphernalia of the Passion, the cross seems personified, a saint or deity itself, merged with Jesus, whose face and sometimes arms are depicted embedded in it. The Passion symbols on it are like the insignia carved on preconquest statues of gods.[171] The implied concept agrees well with behavior reported in sixteenth-century central Mexico but best known in Yucatan.[172] Thus Nahua sculpture done in the sixteenth century in Spanish modes, or at least much of it, can be compared to the Spanish words coming into Nahuatl at the same time (Stage 2), which were given an indigenous pronunciation and often assumed a partially indigenous meaning as well.

Postconquest Nahua painting has seemed to some more thoroughly dominated by European techniques and conventions than the sculpture,[173] to the point that much of it could be (and has been) taken for the work of Spaniards or Flemings, and only the sheer bulk of it, in fresco murals covering large spaces in central Mexican monastic establishments in lieu of canvases or cut-stone ornament, convinces one that it must have been executed primarily by indigenous people.[174] Yet though a great deal of extant sixteenth-century painting seems to confirm this impression of overwhelmingly European-style workmanship, certain exceptions have long been known.[175] Moreover, a recent study, the most thorough and broadest yet done in terms of searching out specific European and indigenous antecedents, shows a very considerable impact of the preconquest tradition on a set of monastic frescoes.[176] The cloister murals of the Augustinian monastery of Malinalco (southwest of Mexico City), executed probably in the 1570's, at first glance look to be entirely European in theme, style, and content. The design, doubtless worked out by some Augustinian friar, represents a paradisiacal garden (Eden or heaven). Between borders of foliage and grotesquerie, great panels are dominated by medallions with standard Christian religious insignia; the remaining large space is filled with flowers and verdure, as well as animals, birds, and insects seeming to enjoy the delights of the garden.

It is primarily in these spaces that the indigenous tradition asserts itself.[177] Some of the exuberant flora and fauna are European, and some are common to both hemispheres or unidentified, but many are identifiably species native to Mexico. Moreover, though most of these species are portrayed quite real-

Fig. 9.1. Song scroll and stylized bee in the Malinalco frescoes. Source: Jeanette Favrot Peterson, "The Garden Frescoes of Malinalco," Ph.D. dissertation, UCLA, 1985, fig. 45.

istically, continuities with preconquest conventions of drawing them can be detected. There are even some preconquest glyphs, including for example song scrolls (see Fig. 9.1). Nor have the indigenous elements become pure decoration. Butterflies and stylized bees sip at the flowers (a preconquest convention for expressing the joys of especially meritorious souls in the afterlife), and the song scrolls are put in the mouths of creatures singing the praises of paradise.

The Nahua painters at Malinalco thus retained preconquest techniques, conventions, and concepts, still forming a coherent ensemble, and integrated them into the murals as a whole in a congruent fashion. At the same time, they had gained much skill in the European manner, although some inconsistencies or deviances can be observed, such as mixed perspectives or light coming from more than one source. Many of the indigenous elements in the murals also fit within a European style and conceptual vocabulary, giving the work added depth, for parts of it can be interpreted in two ways (or in different ways by the adherents of the two traditions). The Nahuas involved were all trained painters, but not all at the same level of competence in the European style; those most exposed to European instruction did the main panels, leaving subordinates or apprentices to do much of the more purely ornamental work, in which examination shows a greater preponderance of indigenous technique. Here, as with sculpture and plays, Spaniards at some point left the execution of detail to the Nahuas, and what emerges in each case is a partial assimilation of the European to the indigenous, a naturalization.

All the artistic phenomena we have been discussing belong to Stage 2, and mainly to the core of it, the last three or four decades of the sixteenth century. Like so many other manifestations of Stage 2, including the writings discussed earlier in this chapter,[178] the art of the time combines strong, still vital and understood preconquest elements with introduced elements that tend to dominate the surface and are in fact quite well understood, although often reinterpreted to bring them closer to the indigenous tradition. The chronology here is determined ultimately by the same factors as elsewhere, by the framework of contact bringing exposure to the new and setting up processes of learning and adjustment. The relevant contact in this case is with Spanish experts in art, and the learning is of a highly technical nature, but the evolution still fits within much the same temporal framework as in other branches of life.[179] Not until the 1560's and 1570's, for the most part, had Nahua craftsmen mastered the new skills sufficiently to produce complex images that would satisfy European eyes. This was not enough time, however, to forget the old skills, which contributed to products as uniquely charming, valuable, and informative as their analogues in other dimensions of life.

Did the parallels continue into later times? That is, was there a Stage 3 in art, in which the Nahuas opened up even more to Spanish currents, lost contact with much preconquest lore, and carried on Hispanic-style artistic activity more as independent individuals? Part of the question can be answered positively. Religious art and architecture executed by Nahuas definitely became more Hispanic in style, and indeed it seems to have experienced a watershed earlier than most other branches of life (perhaps another effect of the irrelevance of the linguistic factor in visual art). Works of a markedly indigenous character, in touch with the preconquest tradition, are not reported in central Mexico after about 1600.[180] Provincial and metropolitan manners can be distinguished, but hardly Spanish and Indian. Despite a widespread feeling that the indigenous tradition somehow contributed importantly to the extravagant Churrigueresque of the eighteenth century, one hesitates to call it "Indian," even in its more popular manifestations in small towns whose inhabitants were overwhelmingly Nahuas.[181]

After the apprenticeship of the sixteenth century, some Nahua practitioners of art shook off Spanish tutelage. An itinerant indigenous painter, one don Baltasar, who did a canvas of the virgin Mary for the Franciscan cloister of Tula in 1614 and was duly paid for his services, cannot have been the only such figure.[182] Given the great dearth of information, I will repeat in some detail an episode related in the late-seventeenth-century Puebla annals quoted several times in a section above. In 1688, the Nahua district of San Juan del Río was beautifying its church by the addition of a dome (for in Puebla a church had to have a dome). The builder in charge of this highly technical task was an indigenous craftsman named Josef Francisco. Whether he was a resident of the district or not is not mentioned, but at any rate he was a contractor working for pay, not someone doing duty for the altepetl. That an indigenous mason/architect and his crew should attempt such a task says a great deal. But so does the fact that he did not succeed. No sooner was the vault closed than the dome began to crack. Thereupon Spanish masters were summoned; the first said the whole church would have to be torn down, but others maintained that it was sufficient to remove the dome and build a new one, which was done in a month's time.[183] Even if the Nahuas were operating quite independently in their own sphere, the Spaniards were still better placed in respect to the ever-changing world of European technology and style, and when there was difficulty, they were needed. Yet the implication is that Nahuas and Spaniards were operating within a single system, sharing all the same goals and suppositions.

Much remains to be learned about the role of the Nahuas in Mexican art in the later period. Already clear, however, is an evolution from a stage when, as in language, much new vocabulary was treated by traditional principles to a stage when the syntax itself was deeply affected.

IO

Conclusion

WHEN I SET OUT to do the research and writing that eventuated in this book, I wanted in a very general way to help put the history of indigenous people in Spanish America on the same level as the more developed literature about Spaniards.* I did not mean to tie the work to any single theme. Perhaps I was especially interested in demonstrating the desirability or necessity, as well as the feasibility, of using Indian-language sources in writing the history of at least some major indigenous groups after European contact. I wished to show, and believe I have shown, that such groups long continued to constitute an immensely complex, partly autonomous sector that must be studied on its own terms, if only because its nature was vital to questions of postconquest continuity and change affecting early Spanish America as a whole—Indians, Spaniards, and their common arena, Spanish American society in general.
Then too, the book, as the result of the first broad pass through the Nahuatl sources, contains much that may illuminate indigenous life in some way without being closely related to any particular special theme; I meant to let no detectable new characteristic of Nahua culture and its postconquest evolution escape mention.

Nevertheless, as the study progressed it became surprisingly thematic; nor could this result be said to have been entirely accidental. Ever since my first archival experiences with them, I have had great respect for the degree of integrity of both Hispanic and indigenous spheres in early Spanish America. I have felt that each long retained its own center of balance, relatively imper-

*Around 1973–75, when I first began to attack Nahuatl studies seriously, it seemed self-evident that the historical literature was markedly imbalanced in favor of Spaniards. The time since then has seen a flood of high-quality ethnohistorical publications on Mesoamerica and the Andes, and one is tempted to say that we have redressed the imbalance or even perhaps gone overboard in the other direction, especially with research on Indians seen in isolation from other groups. Nevertheless, at the present writing, the corpus of scholarship on Spaniards remains far bulkier, more varied, and more comprehensive in coverage, and we continue to have a far subtler, fuller understanding of the workings of the Hispanic component of Spanish American society and culture.

TABLE 10.1

The Three Stages and Some of Their Implications

Category	Stage 1 (1519 to ca. 1545–50)	Stage 2 (ca. 1545–50 to ca. 1640–50)	Stage 3 (1640–50 to 1800 and after)
Language	Essentially no change	Noun borrowing; no other change	Full range of phenomena of bilingualism
Temporary labor mechanisms	Encomienda (whole indigenous state assigned long-term to one Spaniard)	Repartimiento (small parties divided among Spaniards for short periods of time)	Informal, individual arrangements between Spaniards and Indians
Government of the local states	Tlatoani (king) and nobles as always	Hispanic-style town council, cabildo (manned by tlatoani and nobles)	Fragmentation of local states and more idiosyncratic forms of officeholding
Terminology of noble rank	No change	Terms applied to members of the cabildo	Terms disappear, replaced by →
Naming patterns	Christian (first) names	Complex stepped naming system gradually develops	Mature naming system, precisely locating every individual in society by rank
Kinship	No change	Spanish marriage concepts and terminology adopted	Terms for siblings, cousins, nephews/nieces, and in-laws change to conform with Spanish
Songs	?	Genre mixed preconquest-postconquest in content, preconquest in form, with verses indicated by vocables, pairing of verses, and symmetrical arrangement of pairs	Rhyme, meter, line length, indefinitely continuing set of verses with no numerical pattern
History	?	Annals divided equally between pre- and postconquest	Annals almost exclusively postconquest: syncretizing, atemporal legends called "titles" appear in written form
Records	Pictorial/ideographic-oral	Pictorial/ideographic-alphabetic (latter dominant)	Primarily alphabetic
Art and architecture	?	Great idiosyncratic monastery complexes built; frescoes and decorative carving in mixed Hispanic-indigenous idiom	Small Spanish-style parish churches built; art mainly European in style
Religion	God, baptism	Saints proliferate, one per sociopolitical unit	One saint, Guadalupe, takes on national significance

vious to influence from the other side except as brought home by some form of prolonged everyday contact between the two—an interaction that took place at a different level than policy and formal institutional activity, though policy could reflect it and institutional activity could be one manifestation of it.[1] I expected an evolution within the indigenous world that on the one hand would correspond to indigenous imperatives and on the other would be driven and temporally patterned by the nature and amount of contact between the two populations. In the event, a three-step process emerged with startling clarity across a wide spectrum of Nahua social and cultural phenomena.

A second theme is the nature of Nahua culture in itself, as it was before the Europeans came and in many respects long after that, for the Spanish presence fell far short of changing everything. Here the message is less amenable to brief summary. In one branch of Nahua life after another, it has been seen that remarkable similarities to or points of contact with European patterns existed (not always emphasized in the body of the study, since the English reader already knows the European elements and will immediately recognize the similarities). But needless to say, hardly anything was exactly the same on both sides. Many of the peculiarities of Nahua organizing principles have been pointed out, primarily through the identification and definition of key concepts such as "altepetl" and "callalli" (house-land). As in any culture, such concepts and the accompanying mechanisms are too diverse to be subsumed under a single principle, but one particular mode, the creation of larger units of many kinds through the ordering of separate independent constituent parts, does emerge as a prime characteristic of Nahua culture.

The Stages

In brief, the three stages of the general postconquest evolution of the Nahuas run as follows: (1) a generation (1519 to ca. 1545–50) during which, despite great revolutions, reorientations, and catastrophes, little changed in Nahua concepts, techniques, or modes of organization; (2) about a hundred years (ca. 1545–50 to ca. 1640–50) during which Spanish elements came to pervade every aspect of Nahua life, but with limitations, often as discrete additions within a relatively unchanged indigenous framework; and (3) the time thereafter, extending forward to Mexican independence and in many respects until our time, in which the Nahuas adopted a new wave of Spanish elements, now often more strongly affecting the framework of organization and technique, leading in some cases to a true amalgamation of the two traditions. Table 10.1 specifies some of the more notable developments by stage in a series of categories of interest.

Stage 2 saw the flourishing of several corporate phenomena in which Hispanic influence coexisted with a strong preconquest substratum—the cabildo, the monastery complexes and their personnel, the repartimiento labor
system, the annals and songs; and one could include the writing system as
well. In Stage 3, new developments tended to center not on the original corporation, the large altepetl, but on smaller corporations arising out of it, or
on the individual. Though the elements the Nahuas successfully adopted in
Stage 2 were new in some senses, they tended to correspond closely to something in the already existing Nahua tradition. In Stage 3, as the rapprochement between the two cultures advanced, precisely that which was different
might be adopted, easing the smooth operation of a still dual but ever more
intertwined society.

In the body of the book, I have spelled out in some detail the specific manifestations of the process in various aspects of life, as outlined in Table 10.1;
in all departments except art and architecture, the evidence comes primarily
from Nahuatl records. One very important category that went through the
three-stage process, the mechanisms by which Spaniards procured temporary
Indian labor, has not been discussed above, for several reasons: the known
Nahuatl-language record says relatively little about the matter; the activity
took place in a Spanish context, whereas the focus here is on an internal view
of the indigenous world; and an adequate treatment of the topic, in broad
outlines, already exists.[2] As it turns out, the chronological correspondence of
the evolution of temporary labor mechanisms to the three stages is perhaps
sharper and clearer than in any other realm except language. The parallel is
all the more striking because it emerges from a different historical context
and was established through different methods applied to different sources.

Quickly summarizing some facts already well known to experts on the
early history of Mexico, as soon as the military phase of the conquest was
past, the more prominent of the Spaniards involved received the various altepetl of central Mexico as encomiendas.[3] During the conquest generation,
each altepetl provided its encomendero with draft labor as well as tribute in
kind. In the orbit of Mexico City, a decree of 1549 abolished the draft labor
monopoly of the encomienda, instituting in its place a system called the repartimiento. In this arrangement, the altepetl continued to supply parties of
temporary laborers, but now they were assembled before a Spanish official to
be allocated, for that stint only, to all Spaniards with enterprises needing
them, on the basis of their demonstrated need. (Since the encomenderos had
the largest estates and greatest need, not to speak of the greatest leverage, and
the initial procurement of the labor did not change, the new system did not
represent so sharp a break as one might think.) Then in the 1630's, still speaking of the same area around Mexico City, the repartimiento was formally

abolished for agriculture (but not for public works, or silver mining where applicable), and Spaniards who wanted temporary labor had to make individual arrangements (as many had already in fact been doing).

This sequence, since it involves Spaniards directly, is most enlightening on the contact aspect, which because of the present study's concentration on the indigenous side must otherwise largely be deduced from the nature of the various indigenous phenomena. In Stage 1, the time of encomienda labor, an altepetl under its existing ruler (tlatoani) was assigned to a single Spaniard. It is true that the encomendero would immediately start acquiring Spanish and African subordinates to help collect tribute and oversee Indian laborers. But this network took some time to establish, remained relatively small in the first generation for simple paucity of Spaniards, and was further limited by the initial lack of language skills on both sides. Under the encomienda, temporary workers went in large parties under the supervision of the authorities of their own units to perform tasks, many of which were of a type already familiar to them. Contact and change were minimal.

Under the repartimiento of Stage 2, the indigenous *coatequitl*, or rotary labor draft of the altepetl, still provided the workers, although now they would usually be channeled through the governor and indigenous cabildo rather than the tlatoani and other traditional officials as such. Once assembled under indigenous direction, the workers were divided into a larger number of smaller parties than before, often without supervision from home and in direct contact with a Hispanic employer or foreman; the tasks were by now likely to be more Hispanic in nature, more closely tied to market activity for the Spanish cities.

In the informal arrangements of Stage 3, the altepetl was no longer involved in procurement. A single indigenous person hired on directly, in a face-to-face situation, with a Spanish employer or his representative for the amount of time and under the conditions agreed upon. (It is true that in the case of larger Spanish enterprises, mediators and supervisors coming out of indigenous society, called *capitanes*, sometimes informally carried out the earlier functions of altepetl officials, procuring gangs, taking responsibility for their payment, and even helping direct them on the job.[4])

Here we see a greater degree of person-to-person contact with each successive stage. The indigenous corporation remains central through Stage 2, though in modified form, then fades from the picture. The content and conditions of the activity move progressively in the direction of Spanish modes. In the matter of remuneration, encomienda labor was performed entirely as a public duty to the altepetl; repartimiento labor continued to be an altepetl duty, but the employer now provided, or was supposed to provide, a small amount of monetary pay toward the worker's expenses; and in Stage 3 monetary pay (sometimes partly in goods) was the sole factor impelling the temporary worker to accept employment. And yet the workers' place in estate structure and in society during Stage 3 descended directly from preconquest patterns without which the entire evolution would have looked very different indeed.

As to timing, given the nature of Spanish law in the Indies, one does not wish to give overwhelming importance to the date of certain ordinances passed by the government in Mexico City. As Gibson has so correctly pointed out for this specific case, the decrees only gave the formal stamp of approval to developments which had largely already taken place, and on the other hand, meaningful vestiges of older systems survived long after they were issued. Yet in the context of the rough dating of social and cultural phenomena in which I have engaged here, decrees can be of some use. The abolition of the encomienda-based temporary labor system comes in 1549, agreeing entirely with the ca. 1545–50 postulated as the dividing point between Stage 1 and Stage 2. The abolition of the general repartimiento in 1633 comes somewhat earlier than my estimated 1640–50 as the beginning of Stage 3, but only by a few years. It will be remembered that I have emphasized the relative gradualness of the onset of Stage 3, stretching across much of the middle part of the seventeenth century, as opposed to the distinctness of the beginning of Stage 2. For example, in linguistic evolution, the 1630's are the time when attestations of -*oa* loan verbs from Spanish, one of the primary diagnostic characteristics of Stage 3, begin to pick up momentum.

Not all dimensions of Nahua life reflected the three-stage evolution with equal clarity. An undercurrent of preconquest shamanistic and medicinal practices survived virtually unchanged into the seventeenth century and has been found in recognizable form in our own times.[5] The whole sphere may have shrunk progressively as the Spanish presence became more pervasive, but no series of structural changes appears to have taken place. Nor do the core living and working arrangements of the Nahuas obey the three-stage rhythm in any obvious way. Although adjustments of the expected type are seen in kinship terminology and in the rationale and legitimation of land tenure, it is hard to show change in the household complex and the basic structure of the household's landholdings. Perhaps, however, more detailed information would show subtle corresponding trends here as well. At any rate, I expect further research and reflection to identify many meaningful patterns in the varying reactions in different sectors of Nahua culture.

The stages represent a major secular trend for indigenous life in central Mexico and by extension for the whole of postconquest central Mexican society, Hispanic as well as Indian. We must ask what relation this primarily cultural and social movement bears to another large-scale, long-term trend, the statistical population curve across the postconquest centuries.[6] That trend too is worked out primarily for Indians, with rougher estimates for the Hispanic sector. In briefest outline, indigenous population dropped precipitously from a controversial but surely very high figure at contact all through the sixteenth century and beyond, with especially devastating epidemics in the late 1540's and late 1570's. In the early seventeenth century, the population of persons labeled Indians was a disputed but quite small fraction of its former size; by some indefinite point in that century, the nadir was reached, after which the Indian population began to recover, a trend that accelerated during parts of the eighteenth century. Meanwhile, the rest of the population—persons labeled Spaniards, those in categories indicating racial mixture, and other non-Indians—had grown constantly, if not exactly steadily; by the late colonial period, that sector was increasing so fast that even though "Indian" numbers were on the rise, persons labeled Indians represented an ever-decreasing share of the general population. Nevertheless, they remained a majority in the central Mexico of the Nahuas even at independence.

Comparing this with the cultural stages, the increasing number of Hispanics and decreasing number of Indians was clearly much of the reason for the progressive increase in the amount of contact between the two populations that I have identified as the force behind the process, that is, the force impelling the Nahuas to react, though increased contact did not exclusively determine the nature of the reaction. The decrease on the Nahua side was fully as significant as the increase on the Spanish side. The absolute figures seem relatively unimportant to the process; it is the proportions that matter. The impact of a few thousand Spaniards among millions of Indians was inevitably heightened as the numbers of the Nahuas fell to half, then a quarter, then less than that. The relatively fixed amount of contact a given number of Spaniards could provide would be a larger proportion of the total experience of a reduced number of Indians and hence would represent "more" contact.

If we look for more precise temporal correspondences, one cannot fail to notice that the epidemic of the later 1540's coincides squarely with the break between Stages 1 and 2. I have already speculated that the beginning of Stage 2 may be closely connected with the maturation of the first generation of Nahuas whose formative years fell primarily in the postconquest period.[7] The 1540's epidemics probably hit especially hard those who were older and weaker, and those who had been born after the first wave of epidemic disease at the Spaniards' arrival, leaving somewhat less affected those in their early prime who had weathered that first wave, precisely the cohort of which I was just speaking. These people in youthful maturity not only would have been more likely to survive; they would have come to a dominant position earlier than normal and, in view of the doubtless heavy infant mortality of the

1540's, would have retained it longer. Such a scenario could help explain the floodlike nature of the onset of Stage 2, as well as the permanent stamp it put on many aspects of postconquest Nahua culture.

What of the other great epidemic wave, that taking place in the later 1570's? No striking, clear-cut parallel with the three-stage process offers itself even on a speculative basis. Yet a subtler correspondence is a possibility. The reader may have noticed that some of the documents I have used most as illustrations come from the 1580's.[8] I do not wish to multiply substages, particularly not until an even larger corpus is available and more groundwork is done, but I have the impression that the time around 1580–1610 represents an absolute peak in postconquest Nahuatl alphabetic writing in a great many respects—expressiveness, aesthetic quality, range. Perhaps much the same thing happened as before, that is, that the 1570's epidemics brought to the fore and long kept there a new generation. This time the new cohort not only had not lived before the conquest but had had no real experience of Stage 1; Stage 2 culture was second nature to it, the only thing it had ever known.

As to the transition from Stage 2 to Stage 3, it occurs in an era of relatively slow demographic movement. Perhaps it coincides roughly with the nadir of the indigenous population and the beginning of its recovery, but if so, that would not be the operative factor. The "demographic" change that brought on Stage 3 was a decisive increase in the number of bilingual people. Since neither tribute records, censuses, parish registers, nor population estimates made a distinction between bilinguals and monolinguals, the demographic record in the usual sense tells us nothing about the crucial factor, though it is indeed in some sense demographic, that is, a quantitative consideration relating to the numbers of people in a certain category. We are left to deduce the development primarily from the linguistic phenomena of the time. Overall, the onset of Stage 3 seems to bear no close relation to any short-term demographic trends, as usually conceived.

Three successive strategies in relation to Spanish introductions, representing a cumulative reaction of increasing rapprochement with Spanish things and modes, define the stages. Yet, as I hope I have made clear, the Spaniards did not simply dictate the process. Surely they did not dictate it deliberately, for they were hardly aware of it, and important parts of it remained permanently hidden from them. Nor did they dictate it by their presence alone, for indigenous culture was as important as intrusive culture in determining the form, sequence, and timing of adaptation.

Nor was influence exercised in one direction only. The Spaniards retained the basic settlement pattern the Nahuas had already established, their enterprises were permeated by Nahua labor mechanisms, they made increasing use of essentially indigenous markets for everyday items of all kinds, they gradually adopted significant elements of indigenous diet and material culture, and their language too was affected. It was affected, in fact, in much the same way as Nahuatl was affected by Spanish. Known early loans into Spanish are a mirror image of those in the other direction, emphasizing markedly different plants and animals, artifacts, and role definitions.[9] Later, the Spaniards began to borrow verbs, such as *pepenar*, "to glean, pick over," and *sacamolear*, "to clear land for cultivation."[10] That actual clear-cut linguistic stages could be worked out may be doubted, however. And though much subtle influence of Nahuatl on Mexican Spanish probably remains to be discovered, the impact was surely far less than in the other direction. Meaningful adjustments occurred on both sides, but the overall process was far from symmetrical. It was conditioned, it appears to me, by two factors above all: the general dominance of the Spaniards and the fact that they came in sufficient numbers to create a viable, partially self-contained society in no danger of being swallowed up by the local milieu.*

The causal chain leading to the three-stage process starts with substantial and sustained Spanish immigration brought on by the discovery of an indigenous society more populous—and more like that of Europe—than any yet seen, followed by the development of a major silver mining industry (combined with the relative ease of reaching Mexico from Spain). As to just what called the successive stages into existence, I repeat that increasing contact between the two populations was at the root of it, but the factors involved interacted to affect each other in a circular fashion. This is especially true with language. Although contact—the opportunity to hear Spaniards speaking—was crucial in exposing Nahuas to Spanish words, expressions, and notions, the level of Spanish competence in the Nahua population at any given time itself served to impede or facilitate contact. Stage 2 Nahuas, with some basic Spanish vocabulary and corresponding substantive expertise, were better able to handle the small-party assignments of repartimiento labor than their predecessors of Stage 1 would have been, which is one of the reasons why the system was implemented when it was.[11] But no sooner was the system

---

*This is not the place to analyze the overall Spanish dominance. It began with overwhelming military superiority and was deepened by the Spaniards' mastery of a large set of Old World techniques not possessed by the Nahuas. It was not an arbitrary or superficial phenomenon that could have been reversed by any conceivable set of actions by any conceivable set of the actors. The Nahuas had in fact themselves been in much the same position in respect to the peoples they had conquered in prior centuries. Note the comment of Muñoz Camargo (1984, p. 206) that Nahuatl was purer than other Indian languages because it borrowed no words from them, whereas they borrowed heavily from it. As far as my own sense of the matter reaches, Muñoz Camargo is correct. The presence of enough Spaniards to create a relatively self-contained society was an essential element of the postconquest situation. But it is also important to note that Nahua resources and structures were such that Nahua entities could initially deliver certain needed benefits to the Spaniards without the latter having to intervene very directly (unlike semisedentary peoples without fixed territorial jurisdictions, strong rulers, and tribute mechanisms).

in place than it further increased contact between the two populations. We will need a much better understanding of the details of what went on at the actual points of interaction between the two sectors in order to be able to weigh the factors properly.

Some Aspects of Organization in Nahua Culture

Nahuatl sources provide a basis for understanding some pervasive principles that helped make indigenous culture what it was, principles that because of their distinctness from early modern Spanish counterparts can only have evolved in preconquest times even when we can discover no direct evidence to that effect. Again I emphasize that these differences must be seen against a background of shared features as basic as territorial states, kingship, state religion, the noble-commoner distinction, tax obligations, permanent intensive agriculture and individual rights to land, markets and commerce, recordkeeping on paper, female inheritance and property rights, special intermediary status for merchants and craftsmen, and much else. Furthermore, it would by no means be impossible to find some parallels in Spanish and generally European culture for the Nahua characteristics I will be discussing—it is a matter of degree and emphasis—and particularly I imagine that these features were widespread in cultures of Mesoamerica and the Western Hemisphere more generally.

Outstanding is the Nahuas' tendency to create larger wholes by the aggregation of parts that remain relatively separate and self-contained, brought together by their common function and similarity, their place in some numerical or symmetrical arrangement, their rotational order, or all three. This may be called cellular or modular organization. Figure 10.1 schematically illustrates the most striking examples of it that have come to my attention.

Note the similarity of the two master entities of Nahua civilization, the altepetl or state and the household. Each consists of subentities that function relatively independently, are a microcosm of the whole, and could be the germ of a new entirely independent unit. Elaborate schemes of numerical symmetry and strict rotational order naturally characterize the long-continuing altepetl rather than the fleeting household (although in truth we are simply in the dark about household-internal rotational schemes, which could very well have existed). At both levels, yet larger entities could be created with relative ease: at the state level, complex altepetl and imperial arrangements such as the "Triple Alliance" of Tenochtitlan, Tetzcoco, and Tlacopan; at the household level, "patios" around which were arranged several compound households (usually composed of relatives) functioning as a unit for some purposes.[12]

Just as important at both levels was the ease of hiving off. For the house-

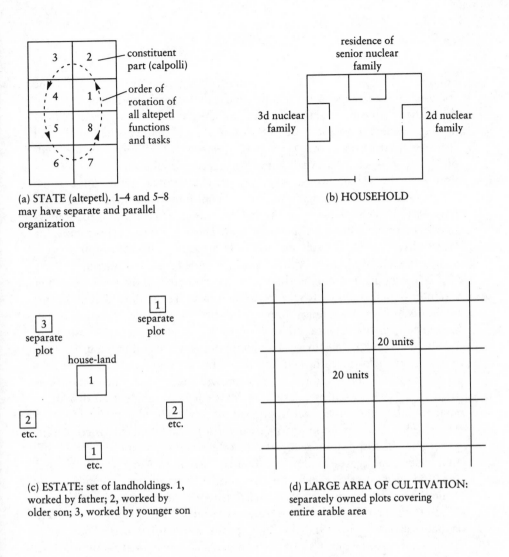

(a) STATE (altepetl). 1–4 and 5–8 may have separate and parallel organization

(b) HOUSEHOLD

(c) ESTATE: set of landholdings. 1, worked by father; 2, worked by older son; 3, worked by younger son

(d) LARGE AREA OF CULTIVATION: separately owned plots covering entire arable area

(e) SONG: discrete pairs of verses around a common theme

(f) HISTORY (annals)

(g) DECORATION: self-contained motifs tightly repeating in symmetrical sequence; no subordination

Fig. 10.1. Forms of cellular-modular organization in the Nahua world.

hold, this was the natural order of things, though also the source of some friction. For the altepetl, it was a perpetual threat; yet without the independence the scheme allowed to the proud and diverse subentities, it would have been impossible to persuade them to cooperate within the altepetl at all, and repeated splitting off from a parent entity was what had brought some complex altepetl, such as Tlaxcala, into existence.[13] Cellular-modular organization gave the Nahua world great resilience in postconquest times. Units seriously affected by demographic loss or Spanish reorganization always contained within themselves the means and the rationale to continue functioning. In the late colonial period, when times were becoming ever less propitious for larger altepetl units, the subunits not only made the adjustment but actively sought the independence to which they had tended from the beginning.

To bring out the common thread, let us compare various types of Nahua modular organization with Spanish counterparts. The Nahua altepetl invites comparison with the Spanish municipality-province. In the Spanish scheme, a juridically distinct central urban entity ruled and dominated the rest of the jurisdiction; ranking members of all hierarchies were based in the urban center, with tentacles reaching out and down to the hinterland; members of a single corporate council, the cabildo, exercised authority throughout the district. In the Nahua scheme, despite the existence of a single head of state, a common altepetl divinity, and an altepetl market, each subentity had its own separate head, its own nobility, its own version of all altepetl structures; no governmental corporation really existed other than the sum total of the subunit heads, who represented primarily their own units. Most general altepetl functions were carried out by the subunits in turn, and when common, simultaneous action was necessary, each was represented proportionally.

Both the Spanish and the Nahua house complex usually looked inward to a patio around which the dwelling spaces were distributed. The Nahua household was more radically self-contained and demarcated against the outside, with a single entry-exit in a solid enclosing wall. A Spanish residence usually consisted of a single contiguous if sprawling structure, with many of the rooms intercommunicating. In a Nahua household, the rooms, themselves called "calli," "houses," typically stood entirely separate, with their separate storerooms, and at any rate opened only onto the patio, each tending to contain a pair of adults with children or dependents.

The same sort of differences obtained between the household's lands in the two cultures. Scattering occurred in both, and in both there were small family holdings consisting of a single plot, but in the Nahua system, division into a larger number of smaller pieces, more widely separated, was normal. Moreover, in complex households, the individual nuclear families would each take primary responsibility for separate plots. A given plot was also often an element in a broader scheme dividing a whole large tract or basin into a large number of smaller pieces of relatively uniform dimensions, varying with the topography, of course, but based on a small standard unit. Even large plots held by high nobles tended to be multiples of the standard unit and were subject to subdivision at any time.[14] Apart from lots in the urban center, no such standard layout existed among Spaniards.

Turning to more specifically cultural manifestations, there too we find systematic contrasts. A Spanish song or poem, for example, often told a story in a linear fashion, or at least proceeded cumulatively, each succeeding element depending logically and aesthetically on those preceding. In extant Nahuatl song, pairing and numerical symmetry, together with a common theme, provide the unity; individual pairs of verses are self-contained, not referring to or implying each other, and in variants they often come in different sequences. A Spanish history or chronicle has a specific theme or title; it is organized into largish titled chapters, each of which carries the story one step further. A Nahua history or set of annals, though focused in a sense on the altepetl, covers a variety of topics; it is organized only by the cycle of the year signs, each year making a unit and each event within that again a separate unit. Spanish decoration in art and architecture tends to emphasize, centralize, and enlarge certain elements, subordinating the rest to them, whereas Nahua decoration creates panels and series in which self-contained like elements repeat to form some sort of symmetrical whole.

The indigenous and Spanish calendars could be compared in much the same way. So could the Spanish and Nahuatl languages. The topic would demand far more systematic demonstration than I can give it here, but I do want to sketch out in this connection what is perhaps one of the most basic manifestations of cellular-modular organization. In Nahuatl, not only every verb but also every noun bears a subject prefix and potentially constitutes a complete utterance. The language proceeds by a series of phonological/syntactic phrases consisting of a nuclear word (verb or noun), its affixes, and some half-attached particles; these conglomerate entities are larger than our words and often smaller than our sentences (some attention was given to these units in Chapter 8). Although Nahuatl can and does create supremely long and complex utterances, in such constructs the individual constituent phrases relate to each other primarily through cross-reference and parallelism; though many devices for unambiguous subordination exist, they are generally more subtle than their equivalents in European languages, and Nahuatl dependent clauses often seem less fully or unequivocally subordinated. The flow of language generally defies numerical symmetries and rotation schemes, but in Nahuatl double expressions are rife at all levels, bringing to mind the popularity of the 2, 4, 8 series in other domains.[15]

We have already seen that as pervasive as it was, cellular-modular organization was adapted in different ways to different purposes. It was no doubt the most general Nahua model for constructing anything whatever, but is not in itself a universal explanation. Without knowledge of the nature of the realm of the construction and of its purpose, one can predict little. Contradictions are found too—that is, principles other than cellular-modular organization may be admitted within the construct.[16] In altepetl organization, the site combining the residence of the tlatoani, the main temple, and the altepetl market could give rise to the semblance of a dominant central settlement, despite the lack of a unified conceptual framework for it and the rationale (and actuality) of separate rotating subdivisions. In landholding, the principle of a central dominant headquarters as opposed to scattered distant holdings was made explicit, even basic.

The numerical aspect varies greatly. On the basis of the altepetl and the songs, one is inclined to think of 2, 4, 8, etc., as the canonical scheme. But other schemes are found as well. In politics, the vagaries of confederation and splitting off could produce schemes of 3, 5, and other numbers. These seem to function as well as any, and indeed, the number 7 possibly constituted a competing canon.[17] Since 2 and 4 were also very important in preconquest religion and cosmology (which also obeyed the principles of cellular-modular organization, including rotation), I believe that these numbers were indeed the general ideal and point of departure. One might imagine that the altepetl's archetypal division into four parts, often oriented to the cardinal directions, had its origin in Mesoamerican religion. Without doubt these aspects of sociopolitical organization coincided with religious-cosmological notions and had corresponding connotations for the Nahuas, but one could say just as well that Mesoamericans projected their own organization onto the cosmos, or that the cosmic and the sociopolitical view coincided and interpenetrated. To me, organization in both these spheres, and in others, is the result of the principle of cellular symmetry operating in the context of a given numerical system.

Another notable aspect of Nahua organization is the general lack of clearly drawn polarities, seen above all in a disinclination to distinguish systematically between private and public, as with the shifting status of the teccalli or lordly houses, the interpenetration of social and political terminology, the land regime in general, the saints, and the combined individual-corporate expression often found in annals and titles. This tendency can be brought into connection with cellular-modular organization or even be seen as a facet or consequence of it.

Where the largest sociopolitical entities were divided into separate independent parts, those in turn into others, and those into still others, reaching straight down to the household as a constituent part and right on into the household's own constituent parts, each entity with its own rights and duties, there is no one place in the continuum where such rights and duties can be said to have been different in kind from those at the next level. A constant tug of war went on that could potentially lead either to greater emphasis on the overarching entity or to the hiving off of the smaller ones, but the process was at the same time the normal framework for the accommodation of diverse interests. Complex protocols and sliding scales, very hard to discern with the means available to us, helped to ward off chaos and arbitrary action. One such mechanism was the principle that the longer a given entity held certain land, the greater its claim and its discretion over use, and the fewer its duties to other entities.

Nevertheless, one major polarity did exist in Nahua culture at European contact, the sharp distinction between pilli or noble and macehualli or commoner. It is true that merchants and some skilled craftsmen may have shared characteristics of both, that formal and informal mechanisms existed for the rise of commoners to noble status, and that at the level of social reality, the difference between lesser nobles and wealthier commoners was sometimes virtually indiscernible. But in principle, at the level of rationale and ideology, the distinction was absolute and well developed, with a large associated vocabulary, well-defined roles, and stereotyped behavior expectations. From the perspective of the sixteenth century, the pilli-macehualli distinction seems to deserve to be called one of the three foundations of Nahua society and consciousness, along with the altepetl and the household. The last two survived better than the first: as we have seen, by the eighteenth century, upper and lower groups still existed in Nahua society, along familiar lines, but with more blurring and flexibility; the explicit polar distinction in terminology had fallen into disuse.[18]

A final pervasive feature of Nahua culture as seen through the window of Nahuatl documents is, despite the commonalities and parallels between sectors that I have been emphasizing, a high degree of compartmentalization, both between large domains and within them. Although a relation to the self-containedness of subunits in cellular-modular organization comes immediately to mind, I suspect that much the same picture would emerge for any culture examined in the same way, and particularly one in which massive contact with another culture brings the differential interaction between their varying corresponding systems into play. Above I briefly touched on some aspects of the differential.

Much of the best evidence concerns questions of genre and subgenre in written texts, where the entire concatenation is before our eyes in a way not equaled with other topics. Thus annals, plays, songs, titles, and incantations each have their own separate vocabulary, structure, conventions, and even orthography (especially notable with the titles and songs). The practitioners of each genre were in varying degrees in touch with one another and with their predecessors, and drew primarily on the tradition of that particular genre, ignoring potentially available and relevant material in other genres. Clearly, each of these forms corresponded to a somewhat different social circle, interest group, and situation relative to the Spanish presence. They are comparable to systems such as land tenure management or the household, which had their own constituency, their own vocabulary, and though we are a little less familiar with them, their own associated textual genres.

But as I say, compartmentalization does not stop with whole systems and social circles. Mundane postconquest documentation was a single system operated by the same people with the same training, yet distinct subgenres existed, those with closer preconquest precedent differing markedly from those without it. And we have seen one example of genre-internal compartmentalization, with a quite sharp distinction between the incantation-like testament preamble and the body in more vernacular language. One is inclined to think in terms of invisible boundaries or skins like those that in grammar contain words, phrases, and sentences and let them function as units in a larger context.

Some borders are more porous than others. The one around testament preambles was quite permeable; that around Stage 2 song considerably less so; and that around indigenous-style incantations almost impenetrable. Some boundaries permit continued evolution within them, whereas others lead to the fossilization and ritualization of their contents. The latter phenomenon may be associated with the drying up of the source, preconquest religious practice in the case of the incantations, and the abstract Christianity promulgated by the Spanish mendicants of the sixteenth century in the case of testament preambles. Boundaries can also open up or be erased. Something of this nature apparently happened with the system of kinship terminology at the onset of Stage 3, allowing the penetration of Spanish terms into a whole realm previously unaffected.

The Nature of Cultural Interaction

At the heart of this book is a three-stage process of interaction, over nearly three centuries, of two cultures, one indigenous and one intrusive, each borne by a substantial permanent local population, alike in many aspects of their basic profile yet with striking differences. If we seek to characterize that evolution at a yet more general level (still focusing, for now, on the effects on indigenous culture), we may begin by considering the viability of explanatory frameworks that have been used in the past.

The breadth and temporal extension of the regularities of the process, its subterranean aspect, with large parts of it quite hidden from Spaniards and even from the consciousness of Nahuas, put a severe limitation on any explanation that makes conscious policies, intentions, and attitudes the primary factor. There were, it is true, some things in Nahua culture so different from Spanish ways and in such direct conflict with them, such as human sacrifice and public non-Christian idolatry, that Spanish attitudes and policies led to their near-eradication in short order. But such spectacular cases have little to do with the overall movement. Notions of a planned and directed selective acculturation, conceived in the minds primarily of Spanish ecclesiastics, are inadequate, or, to put it more strongly, are false, for ecclesiastical policies and campaigns account for only a tiny proportion of what happened and cover an equally tiny proportion of the range of concepts and mental processes involved.[19]

Much the same objection attaches to explanations emphasizing indigenous resistance. One could no more have resisted Stage 2 or Stage 3 than one could have opposed the High German sound shift. At any rate, it is perfectly clear that the Nahuas, after an initial twenty-year period about which we know relatively little, were not for the most part in a mood of active resistance. The Spanish manner of using and building on the altepetl adequately met Nahua expectations and short-term interests. In one domain after another, we see that the Nahuas had no doctrinal distaste for Spanish introductions as such but related to them pragmatically as things they might make their own, according to criteria of familiarity, usability, and availability. If resistance is to be integrated meaningfully into the explanation of the broader process, it must be reconceptualized so as not to make a conscious decision to accept or reject something foreign the crucial factor. If a Spanish concept, practice, or organizational mode was too distinct from indigenous equivalents at a given time, the Nahuas would fail to understand it or see its utility, and in that sense would "resist" it. The advancing three-stage process could gradually change Nahua culture to the point of overcoming such "resistance." Seen in terms of compatibilities, boundaries, and changing thresholds, perhaps resistance can be salvaged as a theoretical tool, but it must be handled gingerly and remains problematic.[20]

As to the notion of isolation (from the Hispanic world) as a crucial variable in indigenous cultural history, the three stages in a way represent a resounding confirmation. What we now see, however, is a progressive breaking down of that isolation, starting at an early time, as part of a dynamic process of adaptation.

Recent anthropological and literary assessments of cultural contact situations often fasten on the mental worlds of the two cultures involved, which is all to the good, but they also often emphasize well-articulated, high-culture expressions of conscious attitudes and intentions, which is less apropos, bringing us back to the naïve perspectives of the institutional and intellectual historians of past generations. One also often sees the concept of "the other" given great prominence in this connection. To the concept itself I would have little objection, if it is taken as encouraging us to study the extent to which groups newly in contact view each other as sharing basic common traits or not—whether they identify each other as within the pale or without. But the approach seems to lead to the notion that the groups facing each other are absorbed with this question and furthermore that they generally view each other as radically distinct.

Not so with the Nahuas and Spaniards. Yes, it appears that the Nahuas may have called the Spaniards "gods" for a brief time,[21] and the Spaniards (though mainly in Spain, and mainly some years after first contact) may have debated the degree of humanity and rationality of the Indians. But their everyday actions and words (insofar as these can be traced) betray a very different conception on both sides, from the beginning. Each side remained essentially more concerned with its own internal affairs and conflicts than with understanding the other. Among the Spaniards, family, social status, regional origin, and time of arrival in the new country were only some of the factors bringing about a highly differentiated local Hispanic society, in which a multitude of factions struggled with each other for position and wealth. On the other side, the Spaniards saw simply "Indians," largely assimilated in their minds to the model they had already formed during their Caribbean experience.

Likewise, the Nahuas remained highly conscious of their altepetl and sub-altepetl, their calpolli and sub-calpolli, as well as of their social and microethnic distinctions, each entity and faction seeking, from the very moment the Spaniards arrived, to do the best for itself in the new situation. The Nahuas were concerned with the Spaniards only as they impinged on their particular subentity, and they were satisfied to lump the new arrivals under some blanket label, as *caxtilteca* (Castilians), *españoles* (Spaniards), or *quixtianotin* (Christians). The overall view of each side, then, was centered in its own society and culture, with a flat, one-dimensional, simplified view of the other side.[22]

The difference in the view the two societies took of each other lies, it seems to me, primarily in the realm of evaluation. Clearly, the Spaniards overall considered the Nahuas and their civilization (or more properly from their point of view, the "Indians" and Indian civilization[23]) to be markedly inferior, no surprise since they showed a somewhat less radical version of the same attitude toward non-Castilian Europeans (including peripheral Iberians) and other Old World peoples. The Nahuas had always had a similar attitude toward non-Nahuas, and more specifically, the people of each altepetl, calpolli, and subethnicity had always manifested it toward all outsiders. I suspect that there was more to the Nahuas' initial reaction to the Spaniards than their quick recognition of Spanish military and technological power, that an ethnocentric feeling of superiority was also an element. (In the Florentine Codex, we find a remaining hint of this; the Spaniards are said to babble, stutter, and speak in a barbarous tongue, the same expression used for non-Nahuatl indigenous languages.[24])

Nevertheless, in the long run, the fact of the conquest itself, the subsequent dominant position of Spaniards, and the consequent effectiveness of their modes gave high prestige to Spanish personnel, words, concepts, and methods. Nowhere can this be seen more clearly than in the way that in general Spanish surnames ranked higher in the Nahua world than indigenous names, and the closer a name approached to the characteristics of high rank among Spaniards, the higher ranking it was among Nahuas as well. Even so, the Nahuas did not therefore denigrate themselves. The situation might be compared with that among Francophile Americans and Englishmen in the late nineteenth and early twentieth centuries; the French were surely admired, and French culture was used as a ranking criterion, but always within an Anglo-Saxon context.

Aside from the question of rank, each society/culture approached the other in a similar fashion, manifesting relatively little interest in the other side's internal structure, apparently expecting it in some way to mirror its own. The unspoken presumption of sameness showed itself above all in the way each used its own categories in interpreting cultural phenomena of the other. Probably the same principle was at work, on both sides, with all the peoples the Spaniards encountered, but in this case, more perhaps than in any other, similarities between the two cultures reinforced the tendency.* At the root of cultural interaction between Nahuas and Spaniards was a process I have called Double Mistaken Identity,[25] whereby each side takes it that a given form or concept is essentially one already known to it, operating in much the same manner as in its own tradition, and hardly takes cognizance of the other side's interpretation. Each could view Indian town government, the monastery complexes, mural painting, land tenure, and many other phenomena of the postconquest Nahua world as falling within its own frame of reference. Under the unwitting truce thus created, Nahua patterns could continue indefinitely in a superficially Hispanic guise that was sometimes no more than

---

*To an extent, without much explicit comment, the Spaniards showed an awareness of the special affinities between the Nahuas and themselves by using them as auxiliaries everywhere they went in Mesoamerica and to the north, by attempting to remake the Indians of the north in the Nahuas' image, and by their particularly low and negative opinion of the northern Indians, an implicit comparison with the Indians of central Mexico.

a label. Then, over the centuries, without much obvious surface change, a rapprochement took place in many spheres, often leading to forms that cannot be securely attributed to either original parent culture, but that were accepted all along as familiar by both. Even when the end result looked more Hispanic than indigenous, the Nahuas, without second thoughts and with good reason, regarded the concept, pattern, or institution as their own.*

Perspectives

One would, of course, like to compare postconquest Nahua history with that of other indigenous cultures in Spanish America. Comparative scholarship, however, requires not only comparable structures and trends but similar sources and similar primary research on those sources. Otherwise, one is likely to repeat the errors of historians who once drew a series of contrasts between English and Spanish settlers in America on the basis of the supposed absence among the Spaniards of groups that actually were there, but had not yet been discovered because the sources with social content had not yet been opened up. No other group seems to have left us a legacy of indigenous-language documentation as large as that preserved in Nahuatl, and few have left any at all. Within Mesoamerica, where all the different regional cultures partook of the same general preconquest writing tradition, they also adopted alphabetic writing in much the same fashion as the Nahuas. In most cases, however, a bare start has been made on the kind of philological research done in the field of Nahuatl studies.

But one region, Yucatan, offers a foothold. Major research on both the indigenous and the Spanish sector has been done in recent years, a philological tradition dealing with postconquest Yucatecan Maya exists, and some work has even been done on Maya linguistic adaptations to Spanish in the postconquest centuries.[26] An extensive comparison, as rewarding as it would potentially be, would require much further study and research. Here I will only mention a few important points and their apparent implications. To begin with language, Yucatecan Maya at some undetermined point in the sixteenth century began to borrow Spanish nouns of the same types that came

---

*I have skirted the concept of "acculturation." In the past, it has often carried the implication that an individual or group is taking on a new culture, all of it, ignoring the possibility of cultural retention or the crucial question of convergences. When an isolated individual or small group is immersed in a new milieu and out of contact with the culture of origin, something like total absorption of the new without much relation to the old may indeed occur, including in Latin American history (as with Indians from peripheral areas brought to Spanish American central areas as slaves or dependents of Spaniards). But in general, acculturation needs to be understood as any meaningful interaction of cultures that leaves them or their adherents effectively different. In that sense, the patterns observed here surely belong to the history of acculturation.

into Nahuatl in Stage 2, with the same kind of phonological adjustments. (Of a Stage 1 and its timing little can as yet be said.) The outstanding difference lies in the length of the equivalent of Stage 2. It is not until mid-eighteenth century that one begins to see phenomena reminiscent of Nahuatl's Stage 3, and even then the movement is not as consistent or inclusive as with Nahuatl.[27] (Yucatecan Maya today, however, shows all the characteristics of Stage 3 in fully developed form.) The upshot, then, is that as far as can presently be determined, Yucatecan Maya went through an evolution very much like that of the Nahuatl language, but with the transition between Stages 2 and 3 retarded by at least a hundred years.

Because of the lack of comparable research, the same cannot be shown for all the branches of interest here. But it is known that the evolution of temporary labor mechanisms was similarly retarded, compared with central Mexico, and the greatest decrease of indigenous population seems to have fallen in a later time.[28] The books of Chilam Balam, the nearest equivalent to Nahuatl annals and titles, retained a great deal of authentic preconquest lore into the late eighteenth century, when they were still being copied and read, as was preconquest-style song.[29] The local tradition of writing in the indigenous language was still alive in Yucatan in the nineteenth century,[30] when to all appearances it was on the point of extinction in central Mexico. As late as the last decades of the eighteenth century, most of the Maya in Yucatan, including town council members and the like, still had indigenous surnames.[31] It is also known that far fewer Spanish immigrants went to Yucatan than to central Mexico, that the few Spanish cities long remained very small, and that the number of Hispanic people moving into the countryside was relatively tiny.[32]

The Yucatecan example, then, would seem to lead to the conclusion that something on the order of the three-stage process, in most or all of its dimensions, was general in Mesoamerica and probably in all areas of Spanish America where there were sedentary Indians, without doubt being colored by the idiosyncrasies of the local indigenous group, but varying most markedly in tempo, depending on the number of Spaniards entering the area and their distribution relative to the indigenous population. If we look about the area of sedentary Indian population including South America, many things are hidden for lack of sources, but one indicator of the trend in central Mexico, the evolution of temporary labor mechanisms from encomienda to repartimiento to informal arrangements, does vary from place to place according to the number of Spaniards present.[33] There is also some evidence of the progressive fragmentation of indigenous sociopolitical units as the Hispanic population increased.[34]

Nevertheless, I will not speculate about the general applicability of the central Mexican stages outside Mesoamerica, and not merely out of caution. Despite the great rarity of postconquest alphabetic writing in Quechua, certain evidence has recently turned up pointing to the existence of a mundane documentation comparable to that in Nahuatl. I would have expected, because of the greater separation of the Spanish and Indian populations, together with such indications as the tempo of the evolution of labor mechanisms and the very different situation in the two areas today, that the central Andean highlands would have remained in the equivalent of Stage 2 for a much longer time than central Mexico, at least as long as Yucatan, if not longer. Some Quechua texts from the central highlands in the 1670's, however, are written in a language fully comparable to Stage 3 Nahuatl.[35] Moreover, two well-known published sources from an even earlier time, approximately the first two decades of the seventeenth century and possibly going back as far as the last decade of the sixteenth, contain some Spanish loan verbs, particles, and other Stage 3 traits.[36]

I find it impossible to believe that the speech of the general highland Andean population included these innovations at that date, or that the broader social and cultural transformations accompanying them in central Mexico had taken place in the Andes at an even earlier time than there. The writers of both the early texts were primarily ecclesiastical aides, spending much of their lives within a Hispanic context. I provisionally theorize for the Andes an early bifurcation corresponding to the greater separation of the two societies, with only those indigenous people who were immersed in Spanish society or located in pockets of maximum contact going far along the process very early, the rest having long been less affected.

A tendency for Mexico City to lead was observed in central Mexico, too, but there the rest of the compact, well-integrated region quickly followed suit, maintaining a cultural unity and contemporaneity that I postulate as much less marked in the Andes. Indeed, I would expect not only great variation by region, rank, and occupation, but a different tempo in different realms of culture, so that well-defined, across-the-board "stages" may not have existed in the same sense as they did in central Mexico. Even so, the degree and nature of Spanish-Indian contact, along with the degree of convergence of the two cultures involved, would have been the ultimate determinants of a long process which when well understood will surely be seen to contain many elements familiar from the Nahua case.[37]

The attempt to compare has thus quickly turned into the highlighting of questions raised by the study—that is, likely directions for further related research, a subject to which I now turn by way of concluding remarks. As follows from the above, the investigation of the postconquest history of indigenous groups in Yucatan, the central Andes, and other regions endowed with adequate sources must be given a high priority, in order to sharpen our perception of what is general or specific about the structures and trends involved in the Nahua experience. Such research should fasten not only on the process of adaptation and interaction, but just as importantly, on the indigenous concepts and organizational modes that conditioned it, seen whenever possible in sources produced by indigenous people in their own language. With Yucatan, indigenous-language sources seem to be adequate for the purpose. It begins to appear that the Quechua region, too, may have more in the way of native-language texts than we once thought. Moreover, Spaniards and indigenous or mestizo translators in Peru often considered certain Quechua words so special that they retained them in Spanish translations of indigenous testimony, allowing one to identify and analyze some key terminology almost as well as if the entire source were in the original language.[38] For both regions, it is important not only that indigenous organizational principles be studied, as here, but that enough mapping of units and subunits be done to discover what the primary sociopolitical structures were; in this respect, Yucatan and Peru have not yet attained the level that Gibson reached for central Mexico in 1964 with his *Aztecs*.[39] It is a step that cannot be avoided, the indispensable background for further insight.

Closer to the Nahuas, puzzles and opportunities are located all along the edges of the present study. Temporally, both the beginning and the end are of special interest. Since alphabetic records in Nahuatl begin in any quantity only with the 1540's, I have had to approach Stage 1, the conquest generation, indirectly, through relics, survivals, and simple deduction. A good deal was achieved in this fashion, but the first of the stages remains by far the least well understood.[40] At the same time, it has great inherent significance as the starting point of the process and the earliest time for which strictly contemporary information can be gathered about Nahua culture. The outlook for the appearance of earlier alphabetic Nahuatl texts is dim, but the second-generation texts purporting to speak of the conquest period can be subjected to close internal analysis in order to determine what if anything of early provenience they contain; the earliest postconquest pictographic records can be examined; and above all, one could go back through the Spanish documentation of the conquest period, perhaps seeing much more than before, now that we understand Nahua patterns better.[41]

My original research plan for the present enterprise was to seek out central Mexican Nahuatl documentation of all time periods, early and late. The plan never changed, but eventually it became apparent that the quantity of Nahuatl records in known repositories drops off sharply after about 1770. What has been found after that time shows, it is true, a picture not yet drastically changed from the years immediately preceding. Consider the 1795 tes-

tament (already variously discussed) of Miguel Gerónimo in Metepec, in the
heart of the Toluca Valley.[42] He still identifies himself by altepetl and tlaxilacalli. He and all his family had quintessentially "Indian" names, no two with
the same surname. His lands were scattered, each measured by the traditional
quahuitl, and the measurements ran to the traditional 20's and 40's. In his
house were saints that he left to his children to serve. Each of his bequests is
followed by an admonition. The will could have been written any time in the
previous hundred and fifty years, and indeed, except for its late Stage 3 language, even somewhat earlier than that.

Despite the clear continuities, however, it is at this same time, around
1770, that I have found some Nahuas beginning to write their records and
communicate with each other for certain purposes in a Nahuatlized Spanish,
in connection with which phenomenon I have used the term "Stage 4." The
tendency to compose original records in Spanish is, of course, the obverse of
the diminution of the volume of Nahuatl texts.[43] I do not dismiss the possibility that 1770 or so is a watershed in other respects as well, marking another
major transition in the long history of cultural interaction in central Mexico.
If so, it would coincide closely with a series of economic, social, demographic,
and governmental changes that tend to divide Spanish American history generally into two periods at that point.[44] A large-scale research project on the
time from about 1770 to Mexican independence, along much the same lines
as the present book but relying of necessity more on Spanish-language
sources, could settle the question and should prove richly rewarding in other
ways as well.[45]

The invisible hero of the present study is the bilingual Indian, whose importance is seen only through a large imprint left on Nahua culture. The
group deserves more direct attention, although beyond professional interpreters the avenues of approach are anything but clear.[46] No less important, and
perhaps less hard to study, are the mainly humble Hispanics who bore the
brunt of Spanish contact with indigenous people.[47] We should not forget, of
course, that many of these marginal Hispanic people were in some sense the
descendants of bilingual Indians of previous generations. Given what I have
said about Mexico City as the possible point of origin of linguistic innovations (and perhaps of other new concepts and procedures as well), a head-on
study of the capital's indigenous community across the postconquest centuries, including its ties with other indigenous communities, would be a most
promising, if somewhat forbidding, research topic. I have already mentioned
the possibility (and the probable difficulty) of studying the adaptation of
Mexican Hispanic culture to the Nahuas, the mirror image of what is done
here. At least, we now have a somewhat better idea of what to look for. An
important consideration here is what one might call the post-Nahuas. By this

term I mean people who have made the language change and belong to the countrywide Hispanic society but have brought with them many things from the Nahua world. A final large task will be to study the culture of these slightly disguised descendants of the Nahuas, who have doubtless contributed to general Mexican culture in ways we as yet little understand.[48]

Appendixes

Appendix A

Four Nahuatl Documents

A growing number of increasingly accurate transcriptions and translations of mundane Nahuatl texts is available in published form, and students of Mexican ethnohistory will greatly profit from an acquaintance with them. The scraps presented here may help point the reader in their direction. I single out documents that are frequently quoted and cited in the body of the book in illustration of major themes. One is appearing in print for the first time, and two are retranslations of earlier efforts. All the texts are difficult and highly individual; future improvements in the translations are to be expected. The transcriptions follow the same conventions as the passages quoted in the body of the study (see Chapter 1, p. 11), except that here I retain overbars rather than resolving them.

1. Grant of a house site, San Miguel Tocuillan (Tetzcoco region), 1583[1]

[E?] onquimitalhui yn anatzin quimolhuili yn iatzin jua migeltzin notlaçoatzin ma quezquilhuitl mopaltzinco toyeca ca ça quilhuitzintli [sic] camo miactin niquipian nopilhua ca ça yehuatl y noxihuato ca

Ana spoke and said to her older brother Juan Miguel, "My dear older brother, let us be under your roof for a few days—only a few days. I don't have many children, only my little Juan, the only child.

1. AGN, Tierras 2338, exp. 1, ff. 8–9. A transcription and translation is in Lockhart 1980, along with commentary on substance, style, and technical detail (more on the last than in the present notes). A version with even more analysis and comment is in N&S, item 4. The original is not divided into paragraphs as here, though as will quickly be seen, it uses the particles *niman* and *auh* extensively to indicate the same units.

çan icelto ca çan i teyxtin y mote-
tzin y xihuatzin,

niman oquimitalhui yteatzin ma
yuhqui mochihua [no]tecauhtzinne
ma xiqualmoquanilica y tlen aqui-
p[ia] ma hualeco y tlen amotlatnqui,

niman otlananquili y çihuatl
quito hotinechmocnelili notlaçoatzin nictlaçocamati y motetlaçotlali-
tzin y manel nicnomaçehuia y mixitl
tlapatl auh ca niquitohua ca niman
ayc nitlamahuizpoloz yn ipa qui-
huatl [*sic*] ythuali ca nitlamahuiz-
tiliz Auh nica metztica y nonamic-
tzin y xihuatzin ytla quemania
ytla yc tlamahuizpoloz ca tel ocan
ametzticate ca ahmomactzinco ni-
cahua yn oquic aquimopialia yn
ibaratzin y Rein

ninman oquimitalhui y jua migeltzin quimolhuili yn ite[n?]catzin
yn anatzin notecauhtzinne Cuix
niquixnepehualtiz y notetzin ytla
quali yc mehuititaz

ca huel ipa hotobre yc çepohuali
tlapohua metztli yn iquac y nican
ometzticatca ça huel çe metztli yn
oquimochihuilique

niman oquimitalhui yn anatzin
macamo huel çenca miac netequi-
pacholi timitztomaquilica ma noço
tepitzin tictehuica ytlaçotlaltzin y
totlaçotatzin y santo sa migel ca
hoca ticquetzazque çetetl caltzintli
ytla ontemoc yn atzintli ytla ohuac
ca titemotazque

niman oquimitalhui ytextzin
mac niquinolhuili y jua francizco-
tzin nima yehuatz[in] juan migeltzin y pelaxtitla² nima yehuatzin y

There are only three of us with your
brother-in-law Juan."

Then her older brother said,
"Very well, my younger sister.
Move what you have, bring up all
your things."

Then the woman answered and
said, "Thank you very much, my
dear older brother, I appreciate
your generosity. Even if I should get
intoxicated, I declare that I will
never act badly in the household,
but will behave respectfully, and as
to my husband Juan here, if he
should ever lose respect, well, you
are all there, I leave it in your hands
as long as you hold the king's staff
[are members of the town govern-
ment]."

Then Juan Miguel spoke and
said to his younger sister Ana, "My
younger sister, am I going to pick
arguments with my brother-in-law,
if he goes along behaving himself?"

Now it is far into October, the
20th of the month, and they have
spent a whole month here now.

Then Ana said, "Don't let us
give you so much trouble; let us
take a bit of the precious land of
our precious father the saint San
Miguel, and there we will build a
little house. When the water has
gone down and things have dried
out, we'll move down."

Then her older brother said,
"Let me tell Juan Francisco, and
Juan Miguel of Pelaxtitlan,² and
also Francisco Baltasar, and also

2. I.e., Perastitlan, "next to the pears (pear trees)."

fraçizco bartesaltzin nima yehuatzin
Ato migeltzin teopaquiahuac amo
ximotequipachotzino notecauhtzinne [. . .]moqueme³ camo qui-
monequiltizque ma nima niquihual-
nanili ma çe tlaxcaltzintli xicmo-
manili tihuatzin amo mitzmotequi-
pachilhuiz ca oca y tlachictzintli
comitiquihue

niman ic omohuicac quimanilito

niman oquimolhuili yn iteca-
tzin ca ye hualhuilohuac tecatzinne
xihualmonochili

niman oquimitalhuique y na-
huiti tlaca ma dios amechmopiali-
tzinno quen ohuamoçemilhuitiltil-
que ca ye ontihualaque

niman oquito yn anatzin ma
ximocalaquica

niman ic ocalacolacohuac [*sic*]
onetlaliloc

niman oquimitalhui yn anatzin
quimolhuili yn iatzin ma xiquima-
quili y tlaxcaltzintli ma quimoma-
çehuitzinnoca

niman otlananquilique y huehuetque ma tictomaçehuica yn
amotetlaçotlalitzin cuix [ytla a]mo-
netequipacholtzin çihuapille

niman oquito yn anatzin ca axca
aquimocaquitizque y tonetequi-
pachol

auh in otlaqualoc niman ic ocalac yn anatzi quitlauhtia quimilhui
camo tlen ic onamechnonochili ca
yz catqui y titocnoytohua ma noço
tepitzin tictotlanica ytlaltzin y totlaçotatzin sato sa Migel ca oca ticnequi tictlalizque çetetl xacaltzintli ca

Antón Miguel of Teopanquiahuac.
Don't worry, younger sister, they
will not want . . . ³ Let me go get
them right away, and you be making a tortilla or two. There's nothing for you to worry about; there's
pulque for them to drink when they
come."

Then he went to get them.

Then he said to his younger sister, "We're already back, younger
sister; come greet us."

Then the four men said, "May
God keep you, and how have you
been today? Here we are."

Then Ana said, "Do come in."

Then they all came in and sat
down.

Then Ana spoke and said to her
older brother, "Give them some
tortillas, let them enjoy them."

Then the elders answered, "Let
us enjoy your hospitality. And is
there something that concerns you,
lady?"

Then Ana said, "In a moment
you will hear what it is that concerns us."

And when they had eaten, Ana
came in and addressed herself to
them, saying to them, "I have summoned you for a negligible matter.
Here is what we beg, that we might
apply for a bit of the land of our
precious father the saint San Mi-

---

3. I have not deciphered "moqueme." There may or may not be some letters missing to
the left.

tellamo miac nicpia noconeuh ca ça
niquixcahuia y noxihuato nochito⁴
cuix tihuelitizque

niman oquimitalhui y jua fran-
çizᶜᵒtzin ma tel momaca tlen aqui-
mitalhuia ma ticmacaca xihualmo-
huica jua migeltzin xocomanili
y mocaRochatzin ca no ticacaya
noxti⁵ yc motamachihuaz ma tihuia
çihuapille ma tiquitati cani ticme-
lehuilia

niman omohuicaque cani [tic]mo-
nequiltia cuix nica cuix noço nepa
capa ticmonequiltia ma xicmitalhui

niman oquito çihuatl ma nica

niman oquitoque y teteuhti ma
tel oca

niman oquimitalhui y jua fran-
çizcotzin aqui quihualtamachihuaz

niman oquitoque y teteuhti aqui-
nel amo yepa yehuatl y tlaocole y
juatze quitamachihuaz

niman oquilhuique y tlaocole
xihualauh juatze xocona [*sic*] y
caRocha momatica xictamachihua
nauhcap[a] chiquase caRocha
xictamachihua

Auh n oquitamachiuh nima
quilhuique ca [ç]a ixquichtzin y
timitzmaca y tlaltzi[ntli]

niman oquito yn anatzin ca
ohuatechmocnelili [*sic*] ca tictla-
[ço]camati yn amotetlaçotlalitzin

niman oquitoque y tla[to]que
ma niman opeuhtihuetzin macamo

guel, for we want to put up a hut
there. I don't have many children;
the only one I have is little Juan
alone.⁴ May we?"

Then Juan Francisco said, "Let
it be given them. What do you say?
Let's give it to them! Juan Miguel,
take your cattle prod . . . ⁵ to measure it with. Let's go, lady, and see
where you wish it to be."

Then they went. "Where do you
wish it to be? Here, or maybe over
there? Say where you wish it to be."

Then the woman said, "Let it be
here."

Then the lords said, "Then let it
be there."

Then Juan Francisco said,
"Who is going to measure it out?"

Then the lords said, "Who indeed? Other times, wasn't it good
old Juan? He'll measure it out."

Then they said to him, "Come,
good Juan, take the cattle prod in
your hands and measure it out.
Measure out six lengths on all four
sides."

And when he had measured it,
then they said, "That's how much
land we're giving you."

Then Ana said, "Thank you
very much; we appreciate your
generosity."

Then the rulers said, "Let it begin right away; don't let the stone

---

4. Possibly "nochito" is a variant diminutive of *mochi*, "everything."
5. I have not deciphered the string "canoticacayanoxti," nor am I sure how to divide it.

amechmotequipachilhuiz y tetzintli
ma ochitotihuetzi ynic opehua[z çi]-
mieto

niman oquito yn anatzin mac tihuia ca oc tepitzin atzintli aquimoma-
çehuitzinnozque

niman oquitoque y tlatoque
tlen oque ticnequi ca ye otictomaçe-
huiqu[e]

Auh yn anatzin mochoquili
yhua yn inamic mochoquili yn
iquac macoque y tlalli

niman oquimitalhui yn a[na]tzin
ca ye polihuiz cadelatzin yhua po-
potzintli nicnomaquilitaz y notlaçotatzin y santo sa Migel ypanpa ca
ytlalpatzinco y ninocaltia

niman oquimitalhui y jua Migeltzin ca oticmocnelili y motlaçota-
tzin ma mochipa yuhqui yez camo⁶

tenahuatecoc yn iquac yn otla-
tlatoli [*sic*] mochiti y macuilti
tetecuhti

axcan ipa ce[. . .]ilhui viernes
tlapohua metztli de otubre yhuan
ipa xih[uitl] de 1583 anos nehuatl
honitlacuilo nixpan omochiuh Do
jua bautista escrᵒ amaxocotitla
nica motecpana y tlatoque

Do jua Migel Regidor Do Bar-
tesal françizᶜᵒ Do juan Françizᶜᵒ
Do juan migel pelaxtitla Do Antᵒ
Migel teopaquiahuac

concern you, but let it quickly be
prepared to begin the foundation."

Then Ana said, "Let's go back
and you must enjoy a bit more
pulque."

Then the rulers said, "What
more do we wish? We've already
had [enough]."

And Ana wept, and her husband
wept, when they were given the
land.

Then Ana said, "Candles will be
burnt, and I will go along providing
incense for my precious father the
saint San Miguel, because it is on
his land that I am building my
house."

Then Juan Miguel said, "We
thank you on behalf of your precious father; let it always be so, not
[. . .]"⁶

When all five lords had spoken,
everyone embraced.

Today, Friday, the [20th?] day of
the month of October of the year
1583. I did the writing and it was
done before me, don Juan Bautista,
notary. The rulers convened here in
Amaxocotitlan.

Don Juan Miguel, regidor.
Don Baltasar Francisco. Don Juan
Francisco. Don Juan Miguel of
Pelaxtitlan. Don Antonio Miguel
of Teopanquiahuac.

---

6. Some words were apparently omitted after "camo," which I take to be "and (or for) not," though it could be "ca mo-" "for your."

2. Petition to altepetl authorities, Tulancingo, ca. 1584[7]

–totecuiyohuane tlatoquehe ca mix-
patzicō nitlacaquiztillia yn ipāpa
yn ilpitoc x̄poval ma ximocaquil-
ticā yn iquac mardes yohualticā yn
onechichtequilli nototol[8] yn iquac
ye quitzatzitia totolli niman oyçac
ȳ nonamic opa ocallactihuetz yn
opa mani totolti yn oquittac ye oqui-
quechcoto[9] yn totolli mano hual-
quiztihuetz yn x̄poval ca huel qui-
tac y nonamic cuezcomatitla quiztihuetz auh nima nechtzatzilia ȳ
nonamic quito tla xiça ye quihuicā
totolli x̄poval nima nineuhtiquiz
niya yn ichā ȳn ononaçito mozcoti-
cāte yn inamic çan ihuia niquilhui
catli nototol xinechmacā ça oquito
tle y mototol ca nica nomac tipo-
pollihuiz ac mopa tlatoz nima qui-
cuitehuac tepozhuictli[10] yc nech-
quatzaya niman tlalli yc nechmotlac
çan ixquich y nicac quilhuiya yn inamic xiqualcui cochillo opā onoco
[sic] cāxatitla yc nictoxahuilliz yn
icuitlaxcol yc nima quihualmacati-
huetz yn inamic ca o nopā motlalli
ayoc huel ninolliniya cā ça yeztitla
nactoc ȳnic onechquatzaya nima ye

Oh my lords, oh rulers, before you
I make an announcement about the
Cristóbal who is in jail; listen to it.
When Tuesday in the night he stole
a turkey[8] of mine from me, he made
the turkey cry out. Then my wife
woke up and quickly went in where
the turkeys are; when she saw him
he had already wrung the turkey's
neck.[9] Although Cristóbal came
running out quickly, my wife got a
good look at him as he rushed by
the grainbin. Then she shouted to
me, saying, "Wake up, Cristóbal is
carrying off a turkey!" Then I got
up and came out and went to his
house; when I got there he and his
wife were warming themselves by
the fire. I said to him in a peaceful
manner, "Where's my turkey? Give
it to me." But he said, "What turkey of yours? Here you are going to
perish at my hands; who is there to
speak in your favor?" Then he got
up and took an iron-tipped digging
stick[10] with which he cut open my
head, and then he threw me on the
ground. All I heard was him saying

7. Special Collections Department, library of the University of Texas at San Antonio. The
sheet containing the document, reversed, serves as a cover to some Spanish land litigation of
1584 and conceivably was composed a few years earlier than that. No specific statement indicates to whom the petition is addressed, but apparently it was to one or the other of the two
cabildos of Tulancingo, that of Tlatocan or Tlaixpan.

8. *Totolin* was used at times for "chicken." Given the time and place and the fact that the
word goes unmodified, I judge it more likely that the reference is to turkeys, but there is no way
of being sure.

9. *Quechcotona* is often translated as "decapitate" and without doubt can have that meaning, but by its parts it means "break the neck." See Tezozomoc 1975, pp. 387 and others, where
he seems to be translating this verb in that way (although in other cases he makes the other
decision, as on p. 386). Here the context favors the option taken in the present translation.

10. Although Molina gives "hoe or mattock" as one of the possible glosses of *tepozhuictli*
(f. 104v), other documents distinguish between a hoe and this item (see Chap. 5, last section).

nechcocoxixiliznequi oc ne nicma-
topehuā ynic ça nocuitlapa caqui
cochillo ye mo[. . .]ozquia[11] yc
niman itech nopillo nictzitzquilli
ȳtilma ca çā [. . .] ic nepiqui[12]
ayocmo no chicahuā nima quitza-
tzaya yn icamissaçol yhuā ymaxtla-
çol ça petlauhta ynic [. . .]llo[13]
nima callactihuetzicō y nochā yn
açicō quimictia y nōnamic quilhuia
xicana ȳ moquich onicpollo auh ca
niquitoā y nehuatl yni çihuatl ȳ
nonamic omictillo ca ninotlaytlaȳa
āmixpatzico yn atlatoque cāpa nic-
nocuilliz yn tomines ca nicnotlacatl
ça ye pacticā yn inamic x̄poval ma
huallauh ma quimocuitlahuiqui ȳn
itlamictil ma yxpā yntla patiz ytla
noço miquiz ma yehuatl mochi
quixtlahuaz y ye nictlallia tomines
ca ye ome pᵒs ca çan onicnotlane-
hui pochtecā ychā auh yn oquex-
quich quitlaniz espanor ca yc no-
tlaytlania yn amipatzico [sic] ma ça
yehuatl quimana yn tomines ca ça
mochipā yuh nemi yni ychtectinemi
yhuā ça mochipā temimictia yhua
tlatziuhcanemi ma yehuati tlatol-
mellahuacā y topilleq̄ santiago

to his wife, "Fetch the knife lying
there by the chest; with it I'll spill
his guts." Then his wife quickly
gave it to him; he threw himself on
me and I couldn't move, lying in the
blood from where he had cut my
head. Then he started trying to stab
me, but I pushed aside his hand so
the knife only entered my back. He
was about to [. . .],[11] then I hung
to him and seized his cloak, which
he was just wrapped in[12]—it was
no longer strong. Then he tore his
old shirt and his old loincloth, and
just went naked [. . .].[13] Then he
quickly came entering my home;
when he got there he beat my wife
and told her, "Get your husband;
I finished him." And I say as to this
woman my wife who was beaten,
I request in the presence of you rulers, where am I to get the money?
I am a poor person. But Cristóbal's
wife is healthy. Let her be brought,
let her come take care of the person
he beat, let her be present if she re-
covers. Or if she dies, let him pay
back all the money I have spent,
already two pesos that I have just
borrowed at merchants' houses,
and more that a Spaniard will be
demanding. Therefore in your presence I ask that he provide the
money, for he always lives like this,
going about stealing and always

11. Despite the missing letters, it is clear that something disastrous was about to happen to
Simón. The subject of the verb might be the knife rather than Cristóbal.
12. The meaning here is reasonably clear, but "nepiqui" appears an impossible form; perhaps the intention was *nepiquilo*, the passive.
13. The letters of the original are partially blotted at this point. Perhaps the intention is
"chollo," which would yield "and just went running off naked."

beating people and living in idleness. Let the officials of [the district
of] Santiago verify what I say.

nehuatl simo d. s.tiago nonamic   Simón de Santiago; my wife is
madallena[14]   Magdalena.[14]

3. Donation of houses and land to images, Coyoacan, 1621[15]

Sabato 7 dias de agusto 1621   Saturday, 7th day of August of the
año   year 1621.

yn yehuatzin s.tissima drinidat   I have been sweeping up here
yn nicā onicnotlachpaniliaya auh   for [the image of] the Most Holy
yn axcā ompa mohuicaz yn ichan-   Trinity, and now it is to be moved
tzinco s. ju⁰ bap^ta[16] yn onpa escuela   to the home of San Juan Bautista,[16]
ca umpa quimotlachpanililizque yn   to the school there, and the children
pipiltzitzinti yn ōpa mohuapahua   who are brought up there are to
yn ichantzinco yn notecuio dios auh   sweep for [the image] at the house
yhuā yn nocaltzin ca ychantzinco   of my lord God. And also my house
yez ynic cētetl huel ōcan ymmo-   is to be his [its] home; the first
yetztica tonatiuh ycalaquiyampa   [building] stands facing straight
ytzticac ynic otetl hueitepeccopa[17]   west, the second facing toward the
ytzticac yhuan yn icallalo çan mo-   big mountain [south],[17] together
cemmattimani[18] ayac tle quitoz on-   with its house-land. Everything is
can tlatoz ynic ocā mani milli yn   included[?];[18] no one is to make ob-
itechtzinco puhui yn dios notlaço-   jections or bring suit there. And a
tatzin ymiltitlan p⁰ comez yniquex-   second field that is dedicated to
can mani tlalli calpilco yhua ycalti-   God my dear father is near the field
tlantzinco mani aluar coca ypā ycac   of Pedro Gómez. And a third piece

---

14. These words are in the same hand as the rest of the document and thus do not represent a true signature by Simón.

15. UCLA Research Library, Special Collections, McAfee Collection. This translation and transcription supersede the ones in BC, pp. 112–13. The planned second edition of that work will contain extensive explanatory comment on the substance and language of this document and Document 4 here (as well as the other texts in that collection). The name of the donor, who speaks in the first person here, nowhere appears.

16. The Dominican monastery church of Coyoacan.

17. Rebecca Horn has found this term used to mean "south" in other documents of Coyoacan (1989, p. 146).

18. Or "it is known by all"?

yhuan yzquitlan mani ymiltitech
ju⁰ mateo

of land is at Calpilco and next to
the house of Alvar Coca, which
stands on it; and on all sides it is
next to the fields of Juan Mateo.

Auh yn yehuatzin yn notlaçotatzin s. fran^co yhua s. nicolas yhuan
yecce homo sta cricifixus [*sic*]
yhuan yehuatzin notepantlatocanan-
tzin asuptio maje yhuan s. jacinto
yhuan crucifixu maje yn intech-
tzinco puhuiz nocaltzin hueitepeccopa ytzticac çan itech çaliuhtica
tonatiuh yquiçayanpa ytzticac
yhuan xucotzintli mebrilo cēpantli
yhuan tzapuquahuitl yey matlactli
peso yc nicouh niccohuili m^a 4 p^os
nicmacac p⁰nila nicmacac 6 p^os

And to [the images of] my dear
father San Francisco, and San Nicolás, and Ecce Homo, the Holy Crucifix, and also to the image of my
intercessor and mother the Assumption [of Mary], and San Jacinto,
and the image of the Crucifix, to
them will belong my house [build-
ing] facing east that is attached to
the one facing south, with fruit
trees: a row of quince, and three zapote trees. I bought it for 10 pesos.
I bought it from María [and Petro-
nilla]; I gave [María] 4 pesos, and
I gave Petronilla 6 pesos.

4. Testament of Angelina, San Simón Pochtlan (Azcapotzalco), 1695[19]

Jesus Ma^a y Juceph
    y nehuatl angelina nican notla-
xilacaltian san simon pochtlan niquitohua yn axcan notech quimo-
tlalilia yn ijusticiatzin y noteotzin
notlatoca [*sic*] Dios cenca yetie[20]
y notlallo noçoquio auh y nanimantzin motlachieltitica auh yehica yn
axcan nocenyollocacopa notla-
neqliztica ynic nictlalia notesta-

Jesus, Mary, and Joseph.
    I, Angelina, my district being
here in San Simón Pochtlan, declare
that now God my divinity and ruler
has issued his sentence upon me.
My earthly body is very heavy,[20] yet
my spirit is aware; wherefore now
it is with all my heart and of my
own volition that I order my testament, and let no one go against

19. UCLA Research Library, Special Collections, McAfee Collection. This translation su-
persedes the one in BC, p. 113. See n. 15, above.
20. The final letter of what is transcribed here as "yetie" is a bit smudged. The intention
may have been *c*, which would yield the more standard *yetic* (*etic*).

mento auh yn tlein nocamatica ni-
quitoz macayac quitlacoz neltiz
mochihuaz

ynic çentlamantli niq̄tohua onca
çe noxhuiuhtzin ytoca tomas de los
santos auh niquitohua yn axcan
nicnomaquilitiuh y notlaçomahuiz-
nantzin candelaria quimotequipanilhuiz yntla quimochicahuiliz dios
ynin notlatol neltiz mochihuaz[21]

ynic ontlamantli niquitohua oncatqui tlaltzintli ompohualpa nican
mani ycampatzinco y notlaçoma-
huiztatzin s[to] domingo[22] auh yn
axcan niquitohua çano yehuatzin
nicnomaquilitiuh y notlaçomahuiz-
nantzin candelaria yc quimoteq̄pan-
ilhuiz y noxhuiuhtzin onicteneuh
ytoca tomas de los santos yntla quimochicahuiliz dios ynin notlatol
neltiz

yniquetlamātli niquitohua yn
yehuatzin ylhuicac ychpochtli s[ta]
catalina nicnomaquilitiuh ynic ome
noxhuiuhtzin yn itoca teresa de jesus quimotequipanilhuiz yn[tla]
quimochicahuiz [*sic*] dios ynin notlatol amo ytlacahuiz neltiz mochihuaz yhuan oncatqui tlaltzintli
yepohualli nicnomaquilitiuh y no-
tlaçonātzin s[ta] catalina yc quimotequipanilhuiz yn onicteneuh ytoca
noxhuiuhtzin teresa de jesus neltiz
mochihuaz

what I shall say with my mouth; it
is to be carried out and performed.

First, I declare that I have a
grandchild named Tomás de los
Santos, and I declare now that I am
giving to him [the image of] my
dear honored mother [of] Candelaria; he is to serve her if God gives
him health. This my statement is to
be carried out and performed.[21]

Second, I declare that there is a
piece of land of 40 [brazas] here behind [the church of] my dear honored father Santo Domingo,[22] and
now I declare that I am giving it
also to my dear honored mother
[of] Candelaria; my grandchild
whom I mentioned named Tomás
de los Santos will serve her with it if
God gives him health. This my
statement is to be carried out.

Third, I declare that as to [the
image of] the celestial virgin Santa
Catalina, I am giving it to a second
grandchild of mine named Teresa de
Jesús, who is to serve her if God
gives her health. This my statement
is not to be vitiated; it is to be carried out and performed. And there
is a piece of land of 60 [brazas]
that I am giving to my dear mother
Santa Catalina, with which my
grandchild whom I mentioned
named Teresa de Jesús will serve

21. Inserted before the next item is a notation in another hand: "yni tlalli motenehua mo-
namaca yc mopatla alahuerta tlaco," "this land mentioned is being sold; it is being exchanged
for half an orchard."

22. In an Azcapotzalco document of 1738 the districts (tlaxilacalli) of Santo Domingo
Huexotitlan and Pochtlan are mentioned in the same breath (BC, doc. 17, p. 104). The reference,
then, is to the church of that district and not to another saint's image.

her. This is to be carried out and performed.

Fourth, I declare that there are two small children, the first named Jacinto Ventura, the second named Josefa de la Encarnación; and I declare now that there is a piece of land here next to the house, 14 brazas long,[23] 11 wide, that I am giving to the aforementioned grandchildren of mine named Jacinto Ventura and Josefa de la Encarnación; it belongs to them. The two of them are to share it; no one may take it from them. This my statement is to be performed and carried out.

Fifth, I declare that there is a house looking toward Tacuba [south]; I give it to the one named Josefa de la Encarnación.[24] It belongs to her; no one may take it from her. This my statement is to be carried out and performed.

Sixth, I declare that there is a small [ruined shack or the like?] here.[25] And I declare that I am now giving it to my grandchild at Tianquiztenco, Nicolasa Jacinta; with it she is to serve [the image of] my dear honored mother [of the] Rosary. It belongs to her; no one may take it from her. This my statement is to be carried out and performed.

Seventh, I declare that the house is on land 10½ brazas long toward

y nauhtlamantli niquitohua oncate omentin pipiltzitzinti y ce tlacatl ytoca jacinto ventora ynic ome ytoca jucepa de la yncarnacion auh niquitohua yn axcan nica mani tlaltzintli caltitla matlactlo[23] yhuan nahui ynic huiyac auh ynic patlahuac matlactloce quahuitl niquinmacatiuh y noxhuihuan onicteneuh ytoca jacinto ventura yhuan jucepa de la yncarnacion yntech pouhqui concahuizque ayac huel quinquixtiliz ynin notlatol mochihuaz neltiz

ynic macuillamantli niquitohua oncatqui centetl caltzintli tlacopa[co]pa ytzticac nicmacatiuh yn itoca juceph[24] de la yncarnacion ytech pouhqui ayac huel quiquixtiliz ynin notlatol neltiz mochihuaz

ynic chiquacentlamantli niquitohua nican mani callatiltontli[25] tepiton auh niquitohua yn axcan nicmacatiuh y noxhuiuhtzin tianquiztēco ca nicolasa jacinta yc quimotequipanilhuiz y notlaçomahuiznātzin Rosario ytech pouhqui ayac huel quiquixtiliz ynin notlatol neltiz mo[chi]huaz

ynic 7 contlamantli niquitohua yn caltzintli ypan mani matlacqua-

23. The writer originally put "matlactloce," "eleven," then, realizing that that was the width, marked out "ce," leaving the anomalous "matlactlo."

24. The Nahuatl gives the masculine form of the name, but from the context, this seems to be an error, not a reference to a different person.

25. Under "callatelli," Molina gives "house site, where houses used to be" (f. 11v). Etymologically, the word means "house-mound."

huitl yhuan tlaco ynic huiyac inic
tlacopancopa auh ynic patlahuac
chicuequahuitl yhuan tlaco ynic
quauhtlacopa tlalpatlalli²⁶ auh yn
axcan oncan nicauhtia y nomontzin
yn itoca tomas peres yhuan inamic
francisca jacinta ayac huel quinquixtiliz yntech pouhqui ynin notlatol mochihuaz neltiz

ynic 8 tlamantli niquitohua yn
tlayxpan calli yn quauhtlacopa ytzticac çan oncan nicnocahuilitiuh yn
ilhuicac ychpochtli sᵗᵃ catalina çan
ichantzinco yez ayac huel quimo-
quixtiliz ynin notlatol mochihuaz
neltiz

ynic chicunauhtlamantli niquitohua yn ipanpatzinco sᵗᵒ san nicolas yn ompa quimopielia Domingo
Ramostzin quimochihuiliz centetl misa cantata yntech pohuiz mi-
micatzitzin²⁷ ynin notlatol mochihuaz neltiz

yc nictlamiltia y notlatol atle ma
ytla nicnopielia ca çan ixquich y nican onicteneuh ca nicnotlacatzintli
ymixpan testigos ynice tlacatl ytoca
juceph andres ynic ome tlacatl
ytoca juan matias yniquey tlacatl
ytoca pedro de los angeles ynic nahui tlacatl ytoca juan andres cihua-
tzitzinti ana de la cruz pedronila

yn tehuantin tonecuitlahuil sᵗᵃ
yglesia fiscal tixpan omochiuh in

Tacuba [north to south], and 8½
brazas wide toward the woods [east
to west]. It is [low or flat?]²⁶ land.
And now I leave there my son-in-
law named Tomás Pérez and his
wife Francisca Jacinta. No one may
take it from them; it belongs to
them. This my statement is to be
performed and carried out.

Eighth, I declare that as to the
house in front, facing toward the
woods [west?], I am just leaving
there [the image of] the celestial
virgin Santa Catalina. It will be her
home; no one may take it away
from her. This my statement is to
be performed and carried out.

Ninth, I declare, in regard to
[the church of] San Nicolás, where
they observe Palm Sunday, that they
are to perform a high mass dedicated to [the souls of] the dead.²⁷
This my statement is to be performed and carried out.

With this I end my statement.
Not another thing do I have; I have
mentioned everything here, for I am
a poor person. In the presence of
witnesses, the first named Josef
Andrés, the second named Juan
Matías, the third named Pedro de
los Angeles, the fourth named Juan
Andrés, and the women Ana de la
Cruz and Petronilla.

Before us in whose charge is the
holy church, [including the] fiscal,

---

26. *Tlalpan* is "(on) the floor, (on) the ground." Conceivably, the reference is to ground
stamped flat like a floor, since the land was doubtless primarily a patio. Other solutions, including the possibility that the term was used locally as a proper name of some sort, should not be
ruled out.

27. This passage is problematic on several counts, and the translation should be viewed as
especially provisional.

itestamento cocoxcatzintli otica-
quilique yn itlatol yc ticneltilia nican tictlalia totoca tofirma axcan
martes a 16 de agosto de 1695 años

Don Diego Juarez fiscal de la sta
yglesia juan domingo teopan topile

ante mi Don nicolas pelipe escrivano Real de la audiencia

the sick person's testament was
made; we heard her statement. To
attest to it we place here our names
and signatures, today, Tuesday,
on the 16th of August of the year
1695.

Don Diego Juárez, fiscal of the
holy church. Juan Domingo, church
constable.

Before me, don Nicolás Felipe,
royal notary of the court.

Appendix B

Molina's Model Testament

The sample testament contained in Molina's *Confessionario mayor*, ff. 61–63v of the 1569 edition, deserves close consideration, for it is the only known example of a model in Nahuatl specifically prepared to be shown to Nahua practitioners. Molina enjoyed great preeminence among Spaniards as well as indigenous people for his Nahuatl erudition, and if anyone's sample document is likely to have been widely diffused, it is surely his. The *Confessionario* was published in 1565, with new editions in 1569 and 1578,[1] a bit late to have been influential in the creation of the Nahuatl testament genre. But the sample is set in Tetzcoco, where we are told that Molina was stationed in 1555.[2] Molina doubtless possessed a similar text for practical use in his parish by that time or earlier; he had been active in generating Nahuatl materials since the later 1540's. The model could very well have circulated long in advance of its appearance in print, as often happened in sixteenth-century Mexico.

In examining Molina's text, we must ask whether or not his formulations became the general Nahua practice and at the same time whether or not they are closer to that practice than one would approach simply by direct translations, regardless of the translator, of the standard Spanish format into Nahuatl. Let us go over some of the opening passages of Molina's will in detail:

Yn ica ytocatzin, tetatzin, yuan tepiltzin, yuan spū sancto:	Through (in) the name of the Father and the Child and the Holy Spirit,

Something like this was the most frequent single beginning (there were others) for Nahuatl wills all across the postconquest centuries. Other ways to say "in the name of" could have been chosen and especially in early wills sometimes were.[3] Perhaps Molina or other Franciscans were responsible for making *ica* the standard form. Anyone in full command of Nahuatl would

1. Molina 1984, intro., p. 13.
2. Ibid., p. 11.
3. See for example BC, doc. 1, p. 44 (Tlaxcala, 1566).

have arrived at *tetatzin* for "the Father"; *tepiltzin* says "the Child" rather than "the Son," but the gender of children was not usually expressed in Nahuatl, so this is an equally uncontroversial, almost inevitable form. Espíritu Santo, "Holy Spirit," is left as in Spanish. It is so difficult to translate into Nahuatl that this, too, was nearly inevitable, but very possibly Molina or others in Franciscan circles are responsible for standardizing the use of the Spanish loan phrase.

Though all of the main words of Molina's opening entered the Nahua canon, some not insignificant differences can be observed in the generality of actual wills. The standard Nahuatl form included Dios, "God," at least once and usually with all three persons, and it did not include *ihuan*, "and." Here are examples, first one from the Culhuacan testaments, done around 1580, and then one from the Chalco region done in 1736.[4] The Culhuacan version is the classical form; the Chalco version varies slightly.

Culhuacan: In ica ytocatzin dios tetatzin dios tepiltzin dios Espū sancto
Chalco region: Yca yn itocatzin yn Dios tetatzin y Dios ypiltzin y Dios espirito santo

The inclusion of "Dios" in the phrase doubtless took place on the initiative of some Spanish ecclesiastic or ecclesiastics, but not Molina. Here alone we have good reason to believe that there was more than one model, or that a single model was varied to suit different preferences. The omission of *ihuan*, "and," which occurs twice in Molina's phrase, can be attributed with some confidence to Nahua taste, for it results in a more idiomatic Nahuatl utterance, since (though the use of *ihuan* is not absolutely incorrect) the normal way to handle a series in Nahuatl is simply to string the items together, very often punctuated by the particle *in*, as in the Chalco region example.

nicpehualtia yn notestamento.	I begin my testament.

Testamento is used as a loanword and quickly became common, perhaps because of the Franciscan model. The rest of the phrase is as anyone proceeding from Spanish practice would do it, and the whole phrase became normal if not de rigueur in Nahuatl testaments.

Ma quimatican in ixquichtin quittazque ynin amatl	Let all know who see this document

Here again is a nearly inevitable phrase coming from the Spanish format, and it became standard in Nahuatl testament writing.

ca in nehuatl notoca Francisco gomez; (anoço yn ni Juana sanchez:) nican	that I named Francisco Gómez (or I Juana Sánchez), whose home is here

4. TC, doc. 24, p. 74; NMY, doc. 10, p. 117.

nochan Tetzcuco, ytech nipoui in	in Tetzcoco, belonging to the parish
perrochia yn itoca sc̄ta Maria as-	called Santa María de la Asunción,
sumpcion: nicchihua notestamento	make my testament.

Most of this is again unremarkable and entered the canon, but there is an important exception. Nahuatl wills rarely (never, to my knowledge) mention the parish (in Molina's text, a Spanish loanword) but first name the altepetl as here, often using that term, omitted here, and then specify the altepetl district, using a classificatory term (*tlaxilacalli*, or later Spanish *barrio*) as well as a proper name. This is probably a Nahua innovation, an important and characteristic one. The same is probably true of another innovation, namely, that in Nahua wills one often loses sight of the object of Molina's "let all know"—"that I make my testament." Not infrequently, that phrase is entirely missing from Nahuatl preambles. The object then appears to be the statement that the testator belongs to a certain entity and/or that he is sick of body but sound of mind. Apparently there was originally some slippage here between Spanish instructors and Nahua students. Having (in many versions at least) just mentioned the beginning of the testament, Nahua writers may have judged it superfluous to announce again that one is making it, and emphasized pertinent new information within that framework.

The next section in Molina's version speaks of the testator being sound of mind although sick of body as death approaches, for which reason he issues his last will; the complex passage is too long to quote here. There might have been several ways to handle this part, but Molina's formulations correspond closely to those that became common coinage. It is especially noteworthy that one phrase, though it did not ultimately enter the canon, nevertheless is found literally repeated in many sixteenth-century wills: "in miquiztli, yn ayac vel ypampa yehua," "death, from which no one can flee." My conclusion is that Molina specifically or a family of Franciscan models of which his is representative exercised strong shaping influence on this section of the Nahuatl testamentary form. Missing from Molina, however, are certain items that are normally (though not universally) found in this part of the preamble, after the specification of the testator's affiliation and before the disposition of the soul: a declaration of belief in all the teachings of the holy mother church of Rome, and a request for the intercession of the Virgin, often along with other saints, in favor of the soul.

Molina's sections on the soul and body are very close to the later standard but also very close to the way anyone would translate the usual Spanish of these passages. The following part, on masses, emphasizes shortening the soul's stay in purgatory; the delivery of an offering to the church; and the use of that money for church ornaments and priests' necessities. Here the Nahua standard diverges widely from Molina; although almost always a mass is requested and the offering to the church is mentioned, purgatory is a rare item, and the offering is often specifically to be used to pay the church attendants (*teopantlaca*) for their services and to purchase candles and the like for the ceremony.

In the body of the will, dealing with bequests and the liquidation of debts, Molina takes a somewhat more general, hypothetical approach, at times giving instructions rather than examples. A good deal of what is said agrees with the Nahua norm, but an equal amount does not. Molina elaborately explains the system of separating out the property that husband and wife each brought into the marriage, designating the increase, and dividing it into two parts, one for the surviving spouse and the other for the children. No such rigid system is reflected in Nahua wills, which in any case give children strong preference over spouses. The section on debts, relying more on specific examples, is closer to the mark, but a succeeding passage ordering the payment of any unknown debts that might come to light, very common in Spanish wills, was little imitated in Nahuatl, and the same can be said of the donation to the local hospital that Molina includes. Only after this does Molina name the heirs and specify the equal division of goods among them, whereas in actual Nahuatl wills the heirs are named piecemeal along with the bequests, which though widely distributed are by no means always equal.

Then, in normal fashion Molina has the testator name two executors and urge that they do full justice to their charge, but he does not use the Spanish loanword for executor, *albacea*, which appears in the great majority of Nahuatl wills of all periods. A succeeding elaborate portion, usual in Spanish wills, revoking any previous testaments, is a rarity in the Nahuatl counterparts.

In the final section, Molina names witnesses, numbering them in the fashion current among the Nahuas, and describes the signing procedures somewhat more elaborately than usual in a Nahuatl will, but fairly close to the actual practice. The place, Tetzcoco, is again given (in actual wills generally "in the said altepetl"), but in a notable omission Molina leaves out any reference to the date, which is as close to a universal as anything in Nahuatl testamentary writing.

Although the witness list looks to be within the range of actual Nahua practice, Molina elsewhere explains that he has an entirely different view of witnesses from the Nahuas'.[5] He wants the notary to take charge of choosing them: they are not to be neighbors or relatives of the testator, but should live at some distance; there may be six to ten of them, but they are all to be male adults this side of senescence. Those who are close to the testator are not to be present at the proceedings, and the witnesses, as well as the notary, are to

5. Molina 1984, ff. 58v–60.

observe rigorous secrecy about the contents of the will until the testator has died. As already seen, except for the number of witnesses, this whole prescription goes against the grain of Nahua reality, for women were included, as well as all those directly involved, and rather than secrecy, the object was more a public consensus as a safeguard against nonfulfillment of the testament.

Looking over the whole sample, one notices that there is not a single oralism, no place where the testator talks directly to the listeners even by implication. In this respect the document belongs entirely to the Spanish tradition.

Yet the sample is not altogether out of touch with the Nahua tradition. Whether this is the result of the participation of Nahua aides or of Molina's own excellent command of Nahuatl and grasp of Nahua practice is impossible to say. That the will is not sharply divided into separate items, even though that was the Spanish procedure, is probably a concession to traditional Nahua modes. Ironically, the Nahuas not only immediately took to separate items but went the Spaniards one better by tending to number them (an important facet of Nahua will writing *a fortiori* not represented in Molina). Moreover, though the sample contains no perorations, the content of the two most basic such phrases does appear in the form of abstract recommendations.

At the end of the preamble, the testator says that he issues his testament "inic mochipa mopiyez ynic ayac quitlacoz," "so that it will always be observed, so that no one will violate it," using the ever popular *itlacahui/itlacoa* verb. Later, the testator asks that the executors see to his dispositions "ynic mochi neltiz," "so that all will be realized," using the key term *nelti*. These phrases are at once very similar to and very different from the direct appeals seen in so many actual Nahuatl wills. They contain the complete usual phrase, in the usual tense as well, the future, but here the phrase is subordinated through *inic*, "so that," reducing it to a recommendation within the convention of audienceless first-person discourse.

Definite evidence exists of the impact of Molina's testament model, or some antecedent or close relative of it, on the actual practice of at least one Nahua notary. Mateo Ceverino de Arellano, of Xochimilco, belonged to the team copying the Florentine Codex under the direction of Sahagún;[6] he also served as municipal notary in his home altepetl of Xochimilco. In 1572, he wrote the testament of Constantino de San Felipe, which has come down to us.[7] It is clear that he has memorized Molina's model or something like it as his basic format. Consider the two beginnings:

6. Sahagún 1975, p. 74 (prologue to book 2).
7. NMY, doc. 2, pp. 93–97.

Molina: Yn ica ytocatzin, tetatzin, yuan tepiltzin, yuan spū sancto: nicpehualtia yn
notestamento. Ma quimatican in ixquichtin quittazque ynin amatl, ca in nehuatl
notoca . . .

Mateo C.: yn ica ytocatzin te[ta]tçin tepiltçin yvan Espiritu santo ye nicpeoaltia yn
notestam^to ma quimatican yn isquichtin yn quittazque ynin amatl ca yn nehoatl
notoca . . .

And Mateo Ceverino's version continues in this vein throughout, with
greater detail than Molina, to be sure, and often varying significantly from
the model, but returning to it again and again, leaving no doubt of the close
connection. Perhaps the surest sign of a tie comes at the beginning of the core
section on bequests to heirs. Here Molina starts out with *iz catqui,* "here is,"
perhaps another hidden reflex of the preconquest oral explanatory style (see
the discussion of the Cuernavaca-region censuses in Chapter 8). In Molina's
version, the formulation fits very well into normal Spanish-style testamentary
discourse: "here is my property that I mention, belonging exclusively to me
as my own." At the same point, Mateo Ceverino says "iz catqui notlaçonamic
ytoca pedronilla teicuh," "here is my dear wife named Petronilla Teiuc,"
which is a very odd phrase in a Nahuatl testament. It appears that the notary
had the Molina model so firmly in mind that "iz catqui" was for him a sign-
post of the beginning of this particular section, and he used it even though it
was not fully appropriate to the following sentence by the norms of the decade and the evolving genre.

At the same time, even Mateo Ceverino departs from the Molina model
in the direction of general Nahua practice in several ways, of which I will list
some of the more striking. He specifies the testator's altepetl and altepetl
subdivision but not his parish as such. He consistently divides the testament
into separate items, which he begins numbering (though he does not finish).
The property arrangements do not follow Molina's prescriptions in the least,
either in format or in substance, nor does the allocation of funeral expenses.
There is an *ixquich* signaling the end of the testator's statement proper, lacking in Molina ("ysquichin ynic onictlalli notlatol notestam^to," "this is all of
the statement I have ordered as my testament").

Here, then, is the only presently known example of a Nahuatl testament
strongly and specifically influenced by the Molina model, and even it diverges
substantially. It is interesting that though Molina and Sahagún were aloof
from each other, possibly a bit touchy on the question of who was the greatest
practitioner of Nahuatl philology, here a protegé of Sahagún's (and using
Sahagún's orthography, not Molina's) is seen to be following Molina's sample
testament. Perhaps the two greats were not as distant as it sometimes seems.
Perhaps, too, it was not so much Molina's model as one evolved in the Mexico City–Tlatelolco Franciscan establishment as a whole. In any case, as far

as we can now make out, this model was not followed with any rigor by the Nahuas save for a few who had been aides to the Franciscans of that establishment. On the other hand, elements of it may have entered deeply into general Nahua practice through direct or indirect avenues, but a good many of these elements arise so straightforwardly from the usual Spanish formulations and the nature of the Nahuatl language that other origins cannot be precluded.

Notes

Notes

Chapter 1

1. The remainder of this section is adapted, with some changes, omissions, and additions, from Lockhart 1985, pp. 465–68.

2. Taylor 1979.

3. Ricard 1966 (1933).

4. As presented above all in Wolf 1959.

5. Gibson 1952, 1964. See the extensive discussion of both books in N&S, item 10.

6. See Lockhart 1968 and 1976; N&S, item 12; Szewczyk 1976; and Martin 1985.

7. Taylor 1979.

8. See Campbell and Clayton 1988, pp. 295–302.

9. See Bierhorst 1985, pp. 118–20; H. Cline 1973; and Nicholson 1973.

10. Garibay K. 1958, 1964–68, 1971; León-Portilla 1956, 1967, 1976, etc.

11. See his TN for further bibliography.

12. See N&S, items 10 and 11.

13. See the discussion in Chap. 4, as well as much of the contents of Chaps. 2 and 9. It is true that works in Spanish by Nahuatl speakers or people who knew Nahuatl well, using key Nahuatl terms in Spanish sentences, can serve the same function up to a point and at times even bring to light aspects of Nahua categorization that have little occasion to occur in the original-language documentation.

14. NMY.

15. Even a broad-gauged Spanish American ethnohistorian might find it useful to get an overview before turning to the individual substantive chapters, but I do not wish to burden the book with excessive introductory matter. One way to get a framework would be to read the conclusion first. In my opinion, however, the best introduction is a piece I wrote for a general audience, outlining in plain language and briefly illustrating many of the main themes and topics of the present book, which appears as item 1 of N&S.

16. See, respectively, AZ (a partial publication of the Cuernavaca-region censuses); TCB (unpublished); TA (a set of commentaries on, summaries of, and selections from the Tlaxcalan cabildo records); and CFP (unpublished).

17. As we come to understand older Nahuatl better and as the base of our knowl-

edge expands, the need is arising to re-edit some of these publications (quite aside from the issue of some going out of print). Many of the translations of BC need redoing (two are in fact retranslated in the Appendix to the present book), and considerable work toward a new edition has been done. The need with the documentary portion of NMY is not so urgent. TC, now out of print, will hopefully be republished in due course, with no great changes in its core, but with a different format. The different page numbers in the new editions will render a great many page references in this book obsolete, but the editors intend to keep the document numbers the same, so that the future reader will still be able to find the material without inordinate trouble.

Chapter 2

1. ANS, pp. 154–55; translated slightly differently there for a different purpose. Much the same phrase is found in anonymous annals of Tenochtitlan in the 1560's; for the marriage of don Luis de Santa María, governor and dynastic ruler (*tlatoani*) of Tenochtitlan, "nohuiyan huitza yn altepetl ypan tlatoque pipiltin," "rulers and nobles in all the altepetl around came" (MNAH AH, GO 14, p. 15). *Altepetl* has the first and third vowels long, and the second, on which stress falls, short. There are only three syllables, the final *tl* being a single voiceless consonant. The word is not easy to pronounce in English.

2. Anonymous annals of Tenochitlan, in CH, 2: 173, referring to events of 1575. *Altepetl* as an inanimate noun normally shows no plural in Nahuatl, and I use the same form for both singular and plural. The original phrase is "yn altepetl ypan tlaca."

3. Even so, Nahuas used *altepetl* and the names of individual altepetl to indicate location, as we might speak for example of traveling to the United Kingdom. Thus the rulers of Huexotzinco asserted in 1550 that "gold is not found in our altepetl" (BC, doc. 29, p. 186), and phrases such as "here in the altepetl of Amaquemecan" (Karttunen and Lockhart 1978, p. 166) head up many Nahuatl documents, from the beginning of the colonial period to the end.

4. CH, 2: 59; Schroeder 1984, p. 138.

5. Although the actual word hardly figures in Charles Gibson's *The Aztecs* (peripherally on pp. 169 and 267), the book is essentially about the altepetl. The core chapters one after another show how the altepetl was the basis for the major institutional arrangements the Spaniards introduced (and also what a departure the hacienda was in having an oblique rather than a direct relationship with indigenous polities at the altepetl level). Change is seen to consist very substantially of alterations in altepetl structure. See N&S, item 10.

6. In central Mexico (as in other parts of Spanish America), the terms *ciudad* and *villa* were mainly limited to Spanish foundations, each of which had a hinterland of partly subordinated altepetl or (Indian) pueblos. Only a very few altepetl received the title *ciudad* as an ornamental distinction, one not always respected in ordinary Spanish speech. Thus (aside from the question of the inherent appropriateness of the term), it confuses a basic distinction of the postconquest world to call an altepetl a

city. Since in the 16th century the great majority of the dependencies of a Spanish city were Indian "pueblos," the word *aldea* practically disappeared from the Spanish American vocabulary.

7. Not all of the elements of unity are necessarily strongly evident in any one form, but they do happen to be so in sociopolitical organization. For other manifestations of cellular-modular organization, see Chaps. 3, 5, and 9 especially, as well as the general discussion in Chap. 10.

8. See CH and Tezozomoc 1949, passim; and compare Schroeder 1984, pp. 140–47.

9. This view was still taken seriously by writers such as Vaillant (1944) and Soustelle (1955).

10. A document from Culhuacan, 1577, twice has an *h* before the *x*, implying the presence of a glottal stop (TC, doc. 71, p. 248), but aside from the apparent presence of *calli*, "house," in the compound, I have to date reached no satisfying etymological solution for the word. Nor am I sure whether the *l* after *i* should be single or double; Molina writes it single, and I incline to this form, but it is found written double more often than not in Nahuatl texts. Molina translates both *calpolli* and *tlaxilacalli* as "barrio."

In van Zantwijk 1985, pp. 249–66, *tlaxilacalli* is interpreted as a group associated with a small sanctuary dedicated to a 13-day period of the year, whereas *calpolli* is presumed to refer to a group (very often exactly the same people) associated with the god of that entity and with a particular day sign. For preconquest Tenochtitlan, van Zantwijk gives a plausible defense of his interpretation. Nothing in the sources for this study seems to speak to the issue; my own intuition is that the explanation is too pat and one-dimensional to have general validity. Van Zantwijk's etymology of *tlaxilacalli*—"structure of the flank, belly house"—is not acceptable. He apparently takes -*xila*- to be *xillan*, "womb, belly, etc.," but Molina, as just shown, gives a single *l*, the necessary -*n* never occurs in texts that I have seen, and the now-attested glottal stop would be incompatible with that derivation.

11. CH; Tezozomoc 1949; and see Schroeder 1984, pp. 173–74. One sometimes finds another term, *chinamitl*, "fence," referring to this unit, but it is most frequently seen south of central Mexico. It occurs to some extent in the early Cuernavaca-region censuses, for smaller units coming last in the list. See AZ, 1: xv, xxvii (table), 129, 134. See also Carrasco 1976b, p. 104.

12. See Schroeder 1984, pp. 178–79, with references to CH; and Tezozomoc 1949, pp. 26, 32.

13. See Schroeder 1984, pp. 246–52, with copious references to CH. *Teuctlatoani*, lit. "lord-speaker," contains the word *tlatoani* used for sovereign rulers.

14. The census-like surveys from the Cuernavaca, Tetzcoco, and Tlaxcalan regions (reproduced and/or analyzed in AZ; Carrasco 1971, 1972, 1976a, 1976b; Harvey and Prem 1984; Offner 1983; and Rojas et al. 1987), though not totally unambiguous, give a strong impression of generally contiguous subterritories.

15. See the works cited in n. 14. Though not much emphasized, widespread endogamy is the operating assumption of Carrasco, Offner, Hinz, and others in their writings on questions of family and community organization. In the Cuernavaca-region censuses (MNAH AH, CAN 549–51), though people from outside the unit

are not at all uncommon, the apparently routine mention of their provenience at every opportunity implies that the majority of the inhabitants were born within the unit.

16. See AZ; and Rojas et al. 1987. TC gives the impression of multitudinous shifting ward names inside the more stably named tlaxilacalli. Note that Cline and Offner tend to use "ward" for the entire tlaxilacalli, not for a subdivision as here.

17. Tlaxcala (originally), greater Chalco, and within Chalco, Amaquemecan, generally followed the historical principle in establishing rank. Tlaxcala and (more unequivocally) greater Chalco also proceeded generally from north to south. This could be the result of accident, but the rotation of the four parts of Tenochtitlan sweeps consistently in a counterclockwise direction, starting in the southwest. See below. See also the remarks in the conclusion (Chap. 10) relating four-part organization of this kind to general Nahua principles rather than specifically to religion.

18. CH has many such listings for Tzaqualtitlan Tenanco (see especially 2: 145–78), as does CFP for Tepemaxalco. A Tlaxcalan document of 1552 implies an order of rotation within Quiahuiztlan; see the mention in TA, p. 52, item 125, with exact reference to the location of the full original. The passage is in Celestino Solís et al. 1985, p. 131, item 443, but "ynic uiztaz tequitl" should be "yn icuixtaz tequitl," "how the tribute goes along being collected," so that the translation given in that edition on p. 327, item 443, is not correct.

19. CH, passim; Schroeder 1984, pp. 208–16, with many page references to CH. A specific example is the Çolteuctli or Quail Lord of Sula, i.e. Çollan, "place of the quail" (Lockhart 1982, p. 378; N&S, item 3).

20. See BC, doc. 25, pp. 138–49, for the fullest known example; compare Berdan 1982, p. 42.

21. See Parsons n. d.

22. See CH, 2: 61, which has both main expressions in *iyolloco in altepetl*, "at the heart of the altepetl," and *in altepeyotl Mexico* "the built-up part of Mexico Tenochtitlan (with houses and streets)." *Altepeyotl* consists of *altepetl* plus *-yo*, an abstract or collective nominal suffix.

23. Consider the negative and disdainful feelings of the Tenochca toward the splinter group that established Tlatelolco (Tezozomoc 1949, p. 76), their subsequent attempts to demote the Tlatelolco rulership, and the continuing resentment and denigration of the Tenochca by the Tlatelolca (FC, book 12, throughout). Van Zantwijk (1985) consistently views the Mexica as multiethnic from the beginning. In a sense, I can assent. No entity organized on altepetl principles was ever entirely unitary.

24. See Schroeder 1984, pp. 154–61, with many quotes from and specific references to CH. Chimalpahin's usage is most amply demonstrated with his native Amaquemecan, a composite state. He calls the whole unit *altepetl* and the constituent parts sometimes *altepetl*, sometimes *tlayacatl altepetl*, and sometimes just *tlayacatl*. In Nahuatl generally the word can mean a district of any size, including at the sub-calpolli level, and to date Chimalpahin's specific sense of *tlayacatl* has not been found in any other text, despite the frequency of similarly constituted entities.

25. See Gibson 1952, p. 105. In Amaquemecan, the Chichimeca teuctli of Itztlacoçauhcan held this position in general, which did not prevent the Teohua teuctli of second-ranked Tlailotlacan from becoming preeminent at times. See Schroeder 1984, pp. 49–56 (especially p. 52), 80–92.

26. Chalco's fate emerges from an overall reading of CH; compare Schroeder 1984, chap. 2.

27. See Schroeder 1984, chap. 2, especially pp. 69–72, 74, 88, with references to CH.

28. See Gibson 1952; TA, part 1 (especially pp. 3–5); and Anguiano and Chapa 1976, maps. Oddly enough, this spatial arrangement fails to emerge very clearly in Muñoz Camargo's *Descripción de la ciudad y provincia de Tlaxcala* (1984).

29. Muñoz Camargo 1984, pp. 163, 168–69, 172.

30. These settlements are Topoyanco (Ocotelolco); Atlihuetzyan (Tiçatla); Hueyotlipan (Quiahuiztlan), though at times Iztaccuixtlan took over the role; and Atlancatepec (Tepeticpac). See TA, pp. 12–13, 34, 125, and map.

31. For a highly ambiguous hint of the existence of tlatoque other than those presiding over the four altepetl, see Anguiano and Chapa, p. 139; Rojas et al. 1987, pp. 190–91, 312; and TA, p. 20. The census lists two important noblemen of Atlihuetzyan, belonging to Tiçatla, who were often on the cabildo. Though neither was the dynastic ruler of all Tiçatla, they are differentiated from all others by being called *tlatoque*. The uncertainty lies in the use of the plural for both rather than the singular twice, for the plural was often applied to groups of members of the cabildo who were not dynastic rulers (see n. 33).

32. The teccalli will be discussed in Chap. 4.

33. Nevertheless, nothing in either the later histories or the contemporaneous sixteenth-century records rules out the possibility that the four tlatoque merely occupied the senior positions in four sets of rulerships. The use of *tlatoani* in the Tlaxcalan Actas is ambiguous. The singular form always refers to one of the four main rulers, but the plural *tlatoque* is often used for the whole cabildo membership or some part of it (the broader use, however, may well be only a convention of courtesy, influenced by the Spanish word *señores*; see Chap. 4).

34. For more detail on many of the following points, see CH; and Schroeder 1984.

35. Chimalpahin is not informative enough on the other three parts of Chalco for the reconstruction of a reasonably full picture of organization, except to document the existence of tlayacatl. Were the reporting as full, they would no doubt prove closely comparable in complexity and organizational principles to Amaquemecan.

36. See HTC; and L. Reyes García 1977 (above all pp. 88, 104, 121–22 for a quick overview), 1978. It is likely that an extensive examination of all the original sources with the examples and specific terminology of Tlaxcala and Chalco in mind would reveal yet more similarities.

37. On the basis of a firsthand but not systematic examination of some of the materials with which Reyes worked, I accept his analysis in terms of the teccalli, but to bring this situation into line with others and to emphasize the possibility of multiple perspectives, it is important to note that a Nahua witness of 1553 considered each of the entities with a titled rulership to be an altepetl (L. Reyes García 1978, p. 85).

38. Other notable examples of complex altepetl are Xochimilco, with three rulerships and tlayacatl; Huexotzinco, with a four-part division in its core area plus two conquered areas or dependencies (the matter of rulerships and tlayacatl is not yet very clear); and Tulancingo, with two halves, each with a supreme ruler and each

divided into units not yet fully understood. See respectively Gibson 1964, pp. 41–42; Dyckerhoff 1976, especially pp. 158, 174–76; and N&S, item 2.

39. See, for example, the early portions of CA and Tezozomoc 1949; and CH, passim.

40. Van Zantwijk 1985, chap. 4, has a far more complex and partially conflicting version; he does not recognize the basic order of precedence and rotation. Most of the conflicting details are irrelevant; I am more interested in the mental organization of the unit than in facts of the foundation.

41. Tezozomoc 1949, pp. 74–75. Atzaqualco is a more common form of the name than Tzaqualco. For the sequence in postconquest times, see below.

42. Throughout van Zantwijk 1985 one will find much information on these points.

43. The line of the preconquest Cihuacoatl Tlacaellel, based in Acatla in the San Pablo Teopan tlayacatl, did not die out until 1610 (CH, 2: 91, 116). Don Diego de San Francisco Tehuetzquititzin, one of the postconquest governors of Tenochtitlan, who had borne the title Tlacochcalcatl, was also associated with Teopan (CH, 2: 13). So were the first two quauhtlatoque after the conquest (CH, 2: 8). Don Pedro de Moteucçoma Tlacahuepantzin and heirs were based in Atzaqualco (CH, 2: 117). See also van Zantwijk 1985, passim.

44. See Hicks 1984, p. 150; Ixtlilxochitl 1975–77, 1: 380; and Offner 1983, p. 111.

45. On Tulancingo, see Carrasco 1963 and N&S, item 2; on Azcapotzalco, Gibson 1964, pp. 38 (with notes), 189; for Acohuic and Tlalnahuac in Coyoacan, Horn 1989, pp. 53–62; and on Calimaya/Tepemaxalco, CFP, passim, AGN, Tierras 2441, exp. 1, f. 3 (statement of 1791 to the effect that they had separate governors but were substantially the same pueblo, divided only by the church, which was in the middle and shared by both); and Loera y Chávez 1977 (though not well explained there).

46. See Schroeder 1984, pp. 61, 64–65, 94–102 passim, with many references to CH, of which 1: 124 and 1: 152 are especially important.

47. Lockhart 1982, pp. 378–80 (also N&S, item 3).

48. Examples of splits in kingdoms, reductions, and attempted dominance in the Chalco region and particularly Amaquemecan will be found in Schroeder 1984, especially pp. 56–61, 87–92, 97–99, 105, with many references to CH; also L. Reyes García 1977 on Cuauhtinchan, which sometimes had a single general tlatoani and sometimes did not.

49. CH, 1: 143. Chimalpahin gives the phrase, a marvelous and characteristic Nahuatl utterance, as "nimexicatl camo nitlalle camo nimille."

50. See especially BC, doc. 29, pp. 180–83 (Huexotzinco), TA, selection 23, pp. 119–20 (Tlaxcala), and Archivo General de Indias, Seville, Patronato 184, ramo 50, Solicitud de los caciques de Suchimilco, 1563 (Xochimilco).

51. See Gibson 1964, maps of encomiendas, parishes, and towns, for these and other examples, and for a vast amount of jurisdictional information in general. See also Himmerich 1984. Gibson 1964, p. 42, shows that Cuitlahuac had no fewer than four tlatoque, but the whole was so small that the Spaniards succeeded in treating it as one undifferentiated unit.

52. Compare Lockhart 1968, p. 12.

53. See N&S, item 2; Carrasco 1963; and Gerhard 1972, pp. 335–38.

54. See Gerhard 1972, pp. 270–73.

55. See Gibson 1964, pp. 41–42, 103; and Horn 1989, pp. 53–62. Coyoacan's position as part of the extensive Marquesado del Valle had in many respects the same effects as being directly under the crown.

56. See above at nn. 28–33; TA, introduction; and Gibson 1952, passim. Tlaxcala avoided encomienda not only on the grounds of its size (and indeed any one of its four parts would still have been too large), but also on political grounds, taking advantage of its carefully cultivated reputation as the Spaniards' chief ally in the conquest.

57. See Gibson 1964, pp. 40–41, 43, 52, maps 3 and 6 (Tetzcoco); and Gibson 1964, pp. 42–44, Schroeder 1984 (Chalco).

58. See Gibson 1964, pp. 53–54.

59. See L. Reyes García 1977, pp. 86, 121; examples in Schroeder 1984, especially pp. 86, 87, 97, 218–19, with specific references to CH; and Zorita 1941, pp. 76, 85.

60. See Gibson 1952, pp. 12, 105.

61. Compare Horn 1989.

62. Gibson 1964, p. 167. It may be that the word *gobernador* as used in the early postconquest phase actually meant the same thing as *tlatoani*. In testimony given in 1553, don Juan de Guzmán, tlatoani and governor of Coyoacan, explained how he came to occupy his office. The recorded Spanish version uses words related to *gobernador* (*gobernar, gobernación*) in speaking of holders of the highest office from a very early time after the arrival of the Spaniards, with no awareness expressed of any difference between the first rulers and don Juan, who held a formal title as governor from the viceroy. In his original Nahuatl testimony, don Juan was doubtless using such words as *tlatoani, tlatocati,* and *tlatocayotl* throughout. (CDC, 1: 76.)

63. Gibson 1964, p. 167; for some examples of the phrases, see CDC, 2: 20, 93; and N&S, item 12. The 1574 Nahuatl will of the tlatoani of Tlacopan has all three primary terms in rare close conjunction: "tlatouani caçique gouernador por su magestad" (Zimmermann 1970, p. 12).

64. See Gibson 1964, pp. 167–72; and TA, pp. 19–21.

65. See TA, p. 8.

66. See Rounds 1982, pp. 75–78, and sources quoted there.

67. Well attested in both Tlaxcala (see TA, pp. 5–6, 12, 112) and the Cuernavaca region (Haskett 1985, pp. 69–77). See also Gibson 1964, pp. 176–77; and Tutino 1976, p. 186.

68. There are abundant examples throughout CH; Ixtlilxochitl; Rounds 1982; and Tezozomoc 1949.

69. As in the example from Coyoacan given in Gibson 1964, p. 159.

70. Schroeder 1984, pp. 236–38, with references to CH.

71. Gibson 1952, pp. 104–11; TA, pp. 2–3.

72. See Gibson 1964, pp. 37, 42, 168–69; and Schroeder 1984, pp. 239–46. Gibson, without a head-on discussion of the term, calls the quauhtlatoque military rulers. For some instances, this was not untrue, but quauhtlatoque were not ordinarily imposed from the outside as rulers by force alone or for military purposes alone. The

quauhtlatoque the Mexica set up in Chalco in the 15th century were not from their own ranks, but members of the Chalco dynasties holding the positions in lieu of the full tlatoque then in exile; and the quauhtlatoani of Tlatelolco before the conquest could be from Tenochtitlan because both altepetl were Mexica (see Gibson 1964, pp. 37, 42).

73. Gibson 1964, pp. 167–68.

74. See Gibson 1964, pp. 168–69; and Schroeder 1984, p. 245. The Mexica themselves must have taken the initiative in proposing quauhtlatoque, since the Spaniards were not familiar at that early point with the indigenous terminology and practice and surely would have been content with a dynastic ruler had the Mexica come up with a candidate.

75. CDC, 1: index entry Lucas García (judge from Tlaxcala in Coyoacan); CH, 1: 158 (judge from Xochimilco in Amaquemecan); CH, 2: 42 (judge from Tlaxcala in Tlacopan after death of its ruler, 1594); MNAH AH, GO 14, p. 158 (judge from Tenochtitlan in Chimalhuacan Chalco, 1569); TA, p. 140 (judge from Tlaxcala in [Chiauhtla?]).

76. CH, 2: 16; Gibson 1964, p. 169.

77. Most known examples of outside governors involve the Valley of Mexico.

78. CH, 2: 50.

79. Gibson 1952, p. 109; Gibson 1964, p. 172, n. 48.

80. CDC, 2: 93. See Horn 1989, chap. 3, on Coyoacan governmental history.

81. Most of this is common knowledge among historians of Spain and Spanish America, although many, taking the mayor-like alcalde of much later times as the norm, have tended to assume that alcalde was a higher-ranking post than regidor. That the opposite was the case, though not in doubt, remains to be documented fully. In Peru of the conquest period, some former tradesmen, nonencomenderos, and near-transients not likely to have become regidores did become alcaldes; for some examples, see Lockhart 1968, pp. 19, 67, 69, 124. On the use of the alcalde post as a step toward being regidor, see Offutt; and on Spanish trends, Altman.

It is true that in peripheral or dependent settlements where a full municipality had not evolved, an alcalde (often a single one) could be the primary official, and a couple of subordinates named to aid him would be called regidores, having little in common with the *regimiento* of a fully developed Spanish city (this was the case in Upper California in the late 18th century). Such a model may have been in the minds of Spanish officials at the time of the introduction of alcaldes and regidores, and if so, may have helped shape developments.

82. See Gibson 1964, p. 172; Offner 1983, pp. 55–66, 147–58; and Rounds 1982, pp. 76–78.

83. See Rounds 1982, pp. 75–76, with further references.

84. Gibson 1952, pp. 107–8; TA, pp. 3, 5–6. The exact size of the body in preconquest times is not known.

85. Gibson 1952, pp. 104–12; TA, pp. 3–14.

86. Partially tabulated in Gibson 1964, p. 175; much more information will be found in CH, 2, and MNAH AH, GO 14. See also Gibson 1953.

87. See CH, 2: 49, 89.

88. CDC, 2: 93–94. The petition, prepared by a lawyer and cast in Spanish,

says, typically, that a regidor should be chosen from each "sujeto," and the rest from the "cabecera," i.e., those units located near the seat of the main tlatoani.

89. CDC, 1: 74. Nevertheless, there is no other indication of tlatoque holding office perpetually ex officio in Coyoacan. As will be seen in Chap. 4, Spanish *principal* is generally equivalent to *pilli*, "nobleman," but is used more broadly and loosely, sometimes referring to plebeian ward heads and sometimes, as possibly here, to dynastic rulers.

90. Gibson 1964, pp. 188–89. The situation in Huexotzinco is not yet clarified. There were three larger regions, but two were subordinated to a core that was itself divided into four. Descriptions waver between emphasis on three and on four, and the cabildo seems not to have been analyzed closely. See Dyckerhoff 1976, pp. 158, 174–75. Doc. 29 of BC, a 1560 letter from the cabildo of Huexotzinco, is signed (among others; p. 190) by one governor and three alcaldes, but it is entirely possible that one alcalde was absent, or that his name was listed without his title.

91. This is one of the few points on which I find myself in direct disagreement with Gibson; see Gibson 1964, pp. 172–73.

92. BC, doc. 26, part 6, p. 162. The original phrase is "tehuatin in titecuhtla-toque ioan talgaldesme," "we teuctlatoque and alcaldes." The use of "ioan" ("and") is quite unusual in such a construction and raises some grammatical possibility that two distinct groups are meant, but from the context I feel confident that that is not the case.

93. BC, doc. 34, p. 212 (Tlaxcala, 1545).

94. BC, Appendix, p. 222. *Tlacateccatl* is a title found in polities all over central Mexico; the office is sometimes described as military or judicial (see FC; and Rounds 1982, p. 77), and I take it that some tlayacatl tlatoque were so designated (see the term's use in ANS, pp. 124–25, as the specific title of a tlatoani). Mixcoac was a subdivision of Coyoacan (Horn 1989), and *tlailotlac*, originally an ethnic name, was a title of some tlatoque and calpolli heads (see Schroeder 1984, p. 210). Because of the letter's linguistic difficulty, BC contains only paraphrases. A full translation by Luis Reyes García, still very literal and speculative, has appeared in CDC, 2: 201–2, and a slightly more advanced one is being prepared for a planned second edition of BC. In Culhuacan ca. 1580, preconquest titles for unit heads were still appearing as (apparently) surnames, either alone, as with Miguel Chimalteuctli or in conjunction with a Spanish surname, as with Miguel Sánchez Tlacateuctli (TC, doc. 12, p. 38, doc. 14, p. 46).

In the anonymous annals of Tenochtitlan in the 1560's (MNAH AH, GO 14, p. 36; 1564), one of the cabildo officials, referred to as "the tlacochcalcatl," makes a speech to the group. He is later identified as Tomás Vásquez, whose name elsewhere appears as Tomás Vásquez tlacochcalcatl (or Tlacochcalcatl, depending on one's interpretation; p. 3). One cannot categorically declare that the term is used as a title rather than as a name, but its use alone, preceded by the article, tends to give that impression.

95. These patterns are most amply demonstrated in TA (see especially the "Directory of Prominent Tlaxcalans"), but they can be seen in almost any 16th-century cabildo membership list.

96. Sullivan 1987, especially pp. 108–9. For Xochimilco examples, see AGN,

Vínculos 279, exp. 1. The one known case of a regidor acting as judge is Pedro de Paz, regidor of Coyoacan in the 1550's, who not only went by himself to adjudicate contested and unclaimed lands, but sat together with the governor-tlatoani deciding land cases (BC, docs. 9–10, pp. 84–91).

97. Gibson 1952, pp. 109–12; Gibson is not specific about the regidores being reduced in number, which can be deduced from TA, selection 25, pp. 125–26, and many entries for the time in Zapata (ZM).

98. These lists will be found scattered in prominent places through MNAH AH, GO 14, and CH, 2, under the relevant years.

99. BC, doc. 29, p. 178.

100. UCLA TC, folder 5, Sept. 15, 1582. The original phrase is "yhuan mochintin pipiltin tlayxpan."

101. For the first example, see N&S, item 13; for the second, from Coyoacan in 1553, see CDC, 1: 214. The accounts are translated into Spanish, so that in both examples the original word is "principales." In a document from Tula in 1606, there is the phrase "I the governor and we alcaldes and all the noblemen who live here in Tula and take care of justice" (AGN, Tierras 3548, exp. 3[?], f. 1v). Here the context shows that "all the noblemen" in fact are the regidores, but the broader phraseology is used anyway, indicative of how the ruling group was conceived, and how unprestigious the term regidor was among the Nahuas, at least by this time.

102. Nicholson 1971.

103. CDC, 2: 94.

104. See Horn 1989, pp. 110–12; NMY, doc. 1, p. 93; and TA, p. 9.

105. TA, pp. 9–11. TC shows the long-term notary of Culhuacan, Miguel Jacobo de Maldonado, becoming alcalde late in life, in 1603 (doc. 83, pp. 280–81). Compare also Cline 1986, p. 46. It is not clear whether other Nahua cabildos attempted to maintain minutes of meetings. Highly competent legal documents (petitions, decrees, litigation, and authentications of wills and sales, for example) issued by central Mexican municipalities from the 1550's forward indicate that many of them had the capability of keeping such records, but there is no definite proof that they ever kept minutes in the Spanish style and no apparent compelling reason why they should have done so.

106. It may be that the Nahua concept of nobility was rather broader in general, including more roles involving special skill and responsibility; thus practice of the fine crafts was compatible with nobility in preconquest central Mexico, which was not usually the case in Europe. See ANS, pp. 150–53; and Pomar 1941, pp. 26–31.

107. TA, pp. 12–14, 112. For more on the significance of names, see Chap. 4.

108. UCLA TC, folder 1; discussed more fully in N&S, item 2. The collectors are once called by the term *tlapachoani*, "one who governs"; Molina translated the word as "governor of one's property and family," hence possibly something on the order of a steward. I have not found the term in any other document. The four parts are referred to as *nauhcoco calpolli*. My impression is that these calpolli were themselves very complex units; as to *nauhcoco*, it contains "four," but I have yet to arrive at a satisfactory explanation of *-coco*. The final *-co* is presumably the locative suffix, as indirectly confirmed in the title "Nauhcocatl tecuhtli," where the *-catl* ending, meaning "inhabitant of," ordinarily corresponds to a toponym in *-co*.

109. CDC, 1: 74–75. Included among the title-surnames are Tlacateuctli (People-Lord); Huecamecatl (Inhabitant [or ruler] of Huecaman, Far-away-place); Hueiteuctli (Great Lord); Amiztlato (Master of the Hunt); Tlacochcalcatl (Person at the Armory). These and some examples harder to analyze can be seen in conjunction with the Christian names in Table 2.2. See also Horn 1989, pp. 115–20.

110. For example, one Miguel Josef was executor (of wills), diputado, and regidor (TC, docs. 60–62, pp. 221–25).

111. TA, pp. 12–14, 112; in Coyoacan, Miguel Huecamecatl as both majordomo and constable, CDC, 1: 74–75; S. Cline 1986, p. 45; TC, docs. 26, 82, pp. 85, 279, showing the same person as member of the church staff (*teopantlacatl*), constable, and diputado.

112. Or on occasion units defined in nonresidential terms, as in Coyoacan *tetzotzoncatopile*, "person in charge of stonemasons" (TC, doc. 29, p. 94).

113. See S. Cline 1986, p. 45; the best examples are from Culhuacan.

114. See AZ; Dyckerhoff 1976; Gibson 1964, p. 183; Prem 1974; and Rojas et al. 1987.

115. CDC, 1, consisting mainly of papers relating to a Spanish inspection tour of Coyoacan, is full of the testimony of small-unit leaders. See also BC, doc. 9, pp. 84–89.

116. One might compare TA, pp. 12–14, with Haskett 1985, chap. 6. See also Gibson 1964, pp. 182–83; and Horn 1989, pp. 115–20. A term used frequently by Spaniards for officials at the lowest level was *mandón*, "boss." Haskett finds that officers called *merinos* in Nahuatl might be referred to as mandones in Spanish, though *mandón* does occur in Nahuatl texts too (1985, pp. 321–25, especially p. 322). Molina does not have *tlayacanqui* or *tepixqui*. He glosses *tequitlato* as "mandón or merino, or one in charge of assigning the tribute and duties to the *macehuales* (Indian commoners)." *Teyacanani*, a variant of *teyacanqui*, is glossed as "guide of others, one who rules or governs."

117. See S. Cline 1984, p. 54.

118. AZ; Rojas et al. 1987. In CDC, 1, some ward heads have 60 brazas of land, others 40, not beyond the range for ordinary commoners. Gibson 1964, pp. 182–83, does not distinguish between intermediate and lower officials, and indeed it is often hard to do so.

119. In my experience, the singular *tlaxilacale* always means simple "district citizen," and it is only in the plural that the ambiguity arises. Instances in which the plural refers quite unambiguously to simple citizens may be seen in BC, docs. 14, 17, pp. 96, 100 (Azcapotzalco, 18th century); and CH, 2: 5, 125. Although *calpolli* occurs in some texts far into the postconquest period, I have not found *calpoleque* in the sense of "district officers" during this time.

120. See BC, doc. 9, pp. 84–89 (Coyoacan, 1554); and AGN, Tierras 165, exp. 4, f. 14v (Mexico City, 1600).

121. In AGN, Hospital de Jesús 298, exp. 4, ff. 5, 13 (Mexico City; 1593), *tlaxilacaleque* is translated as *mayorales*, another Spanish word for lowest-level indigenous officials.

122. In an instance from Culhuacan in 1583 (TC, doc. 60, p. 220), the first person listed among the *tlaxilacaleque huehuetque* is in fact the regidor from that district.

A problem endemic to the establishment of the identity of the tlaxilacaleque is that in the witness lists where they most frequently appear, further witnesses are appended with no indication of where the authorities leave off and the ordinary citizens begin.

123. This difference was not always so clear to later historians. Robert Ricard, who entirely lacked independent knowledge of indigenous society and put great credence in the self-magnifying reports of the early friars, gave the impression of virtually nomadic people being reorganized into entirely new units, and the Ricardian version formed the basis of many interpretations until the appearance of Gibson's *Aztecs* in 1964. In certain circles it still does.

124. Gibson 1964, pp. 282–85.

125. See Lockhart 1982, pp. 387–88 (also N&S, item 3); and Wood 1984, pp. 24–34. Better records of the mid-16th-century reorganizations may yet be discovered.

126. TA, selection 16, pp. 103–6. A similar impression arises from Chimalpahin's brief mention of relocation in Amaquemecan.

127. CH, 2: 57.

128. See Gibson 1964, pp. 54–55, for some examples.

129. See Wood 1984, pp. 212–34.

130. CH, 2: 57. For *sujeto*, he uses the actual Spanish word; for *cabecera*, he uses the close Nahuatl equivalent *tzontecomatl*, "head, skull."

131. For details of corregimiento development, see Gibson 1964, pp. 81–97; and Gerhard 1972 under individual jurisdictions. As Gibson makes clear (p. 82), the terminology actually used varied considerably, *alcalde mayor* for the official and *alcaldía mayor* for the district being the main alternate terms. Although the provincial administrators were sometimes referred to en masse as *corregidores de indios*, and a sharp distinction can be drawn between them and their approximate counterparts in Spanish settlements, the actual modifier *de indios* does not appear in documents concerning individual corregidores, not even in the decrees appointing them to office.

132. See Gibson 1964, especially pp. 11–12, 18, 90; and Offner 1983, especially pp. 60–61.

133. Celestino Solís et al. 1985; TA, throughout.

134. As in BC, doc. 17, p. 102 (Azcapotzalco, 1738); and UCLA TC, folder 19, July 30, 1720 (Tulancingo). For *oficiales* as limited to alcaldes and governors, see AGN Tierras 2338, exp. 1, f. 14 (San Miguel Tocuillan in the Tetzcoco area, 1722).

135. For example, BC, doc. 17, p. 102 (Azcapotzalco, 1738), "in senca mahuistililonime tlatoque," "the very honorable rulers."

136. AGN, Tierras 2554, exp. 4, f. 4 (Amaquemecan, some time between 1723 and 1764), "tlatocamahuispipiltin," "rulerly honorable nobles."

137. Ibid., 2554A, exp. 13, f. 11 (Toluca Valley), "alcalde pasado."

138. Examples in UCLA TC, folder 14, Oct. 7, Nov. 3, 1687 (Tulancingo).

139. Example in AGN, Tierras 2554, exp. 4, f. 23v (Tlapitzahuayan near Chalco Atenco, 1763).

140. Karttunen and Lockhart 1978. The example is from 1746.

141. AGN, Tierras 2549, exp. 1, f. 50.

142. Some examples will doubtless be found somewhere, but to date I have not seen a single occurrence of "regidor pasado."

143. As we saw above at n. 97, in the late 16th century Tlaxcala simultaneously dropped four regidores and added four provincial alcaldes.

144. TA, pp. 8, 127–39. The constant repetition in office and the small number of officeholders over a 20-year period are overwhelmingly documented; the continuing influence of nonincumbents is deduced partially from that very fact, and partially from such hints as the warnings of Spanish officials to incumbents not to reveal secrets to past cabildo members (selection 6, pp. 75–77) and the naming of nonincumbents to important delegations representing Tlaxcalan interests to the outside (pp. 140–43).

145. AGN, Tierras 1780, exp. 3. The exact date is not clear; although 1660 and 1680 are mentioned, the text may have been composed considerably later (although it at times purports to be from much earlier). See also Chap. 6 at n. 97.

146. For example, see Karttunen and Lockhart 1978. Witnesses to litigation in Coatlichan and Quauhtlalpan in 1762–64 were all past officials—governors, alcaldes, an alguacil mayor: no regidores (AGN, Tierras 2338, exp. 8). AGN, Tierras 2555, exp. 14, ff. 5–12 (Soyatzingo; 1734) is much the same, with the addition of fiscales.

147. AGN, Tierras 2541, exp. 11, f. 3 (also in N&S, item 7). The governor also asked "muchi comun," "all the commonality," but I take these to be little more than bystanders.

148. AGN, Tierras 2533, exp. 3, f. 22. A past notary also signed.

149. In Karttunen and Lockhart 1978, citizens of the full-scale altepetl Amaquemecan (1746) refer to the corregimiento cabecera as "totzonteconyocan," "our headplace" (p. 166).

150. NMY, doc. 10, p. 117.

151. In Azcapotzalco in 1738, the term used is -tlahuilanal, "something dragged along with something else" (BC, doc. 17, p. 100); in Acaxochitlan (Tulancingo) in 1768 (UCLA TC), the term is tlatilanalli, "something pulled."

152. See Gibson 1964, p. 54; and Wood 1984, pp. 222, 226, 278 (Toluca Valley, late 17th and 18th centuries). See also Chap. 6.

153. See N&S, item 12.

154. Gibson 1964, p. 285 and notes; Wood 1984, pp. 183–90.

155. As with Sula in the Tlalmanalco/Chalco region; see Lockhart 1982, p. 375 (also N&S, item 3).

156. Wood 1984, especially pp. 186–87. See also Wood's discussion (pp. 238–94) of how hacienda and mining settlements, though new, often partly non-Indian agglomerations, frequently attained recognition as Indian pueblos.

157. AGN, Tierras 2338, exp. 6.

158. An example is found in a late "título primordial" of Atlauhtlan (Chalco region); background in Lockhart 1982, p. 374 (also N&S, item 3).

159. AGN, Tierras 2338, exp. 1, f. 14.

160. UCLA TC, folder 25, March 1, 1768. That is, Santa María de la Natividad was the town's patron saint and also, as usual in such cases, gave it its Spanish name in addition to the indigenous name, which was not used in this text.

161. The latest example presently known to me is from Metepec in the Toluca Valley, 1795 (BC, doc. 6, p. 74).

162. In Azacapotzalco, 1703, San Simón is called a "Bario" but its inhabitants

are called "tlaxilacaleque" (BC, doc. 14, p. 96). In Calimaya, 1738, a district is given the double classification "tlaxilacali barrio" (NAC, ms. 1477B [1]). In Amaquemecan, 1746, a document has *barrio* seven times, *tlaxilacalli* twice (Karttunen and Lockhart 1978).

163. See Gibson 1964, pp. 41–44; and L. Reyes García 1978, p. 177 ("Tecpanecatle," Chichimecatecpan).

164. Karttunen and Lockhart 1978.

165. These include Tepanecapan and Mexicapan in Azcapotzalco and Calimaya/Tepemaxalco.

Chapter 3

1. My interpretation of *tlacamecayotl* is substantially concordant with that of Offner 1983, pp. 199–200. I do not agree with those who would interpret the word as meaning an organizational entity.

2. See Roys 1939 for constantly repeating indigenous surnames.

3. It is true that *calli* (without *cen-*) is the standard term for a household (and household head too, apparently) in the Cuernavaca-region padrones (see AZ; Carrasco 1972; and MNAH AH, CAN 549–51, throughout). *Cencaltin* occurs in the last source. For the rarer *cemithualtin*, see that collection, as well as AZ, 1: xvii, 27, 31, 41, 2: 10; and Carrasco 1976b, pp. 104, 114. *Cencale*, "householder, head of a household," built on *cencalli*, appears in an early Coyoacan land investigation (BC, doc. 9, p. 84; such seems at least to be the meaning). None of these terms appears in any testament that I have ever seen. I have not found *cenyeliztli* or *techan tlaca* in any text at all; to me both have the flavor of possible but rather ad hoc constructions offered by indigenous informants trying to satisfy Molina's insistence on getting a precise equivalent for the Spanish word *familia* where none in fact existed.

4. The expression is sometimes found with the element *ithualli* placed first (e.g., BC, doc. 1, p. 50), and it often appears in the locative, *quiahuac ithualcao* (see AGN, Tierras 2554, exp. 4, ff. 23–23v). *Quiahuatl* is frequently translated as "entryway," which is not incorrect, although the perspective on the aperture in the Nahuatl word is as a place through which to come out, not to go in. Note the speech of advice to the newlywed couple in the Tetzcoco Dialogues; although the desirability of having children is discussed, *quiahuatl ithualli* occurs in the speech, and any word referring more strictly to the personnel of a "family" is lacking (ANS, pp. 108–11).

5. See ANS, p. 110; and NMY, doc. 10, p. 118; examples from the 17th and 18th centuries are myriad.

6. *In oncan tictotlatolchialilia in totecuiyo Dios*; unfortunately, I did not save examples.

7. The form *chan-tli*, with the absolutive *-tli*, occurs in rare instances but is very much a secondary formation; in the overwhelming majority of cases, *-chan* appears with a possessive prefix: *nochan*, "(at) my home"; *mochan*, "(at) your home," etc.; see ANS, pp. 52–53. For *-chan* paired with *calli*, see AGN, Tierras 442, exp. 5, f. 10 (Tlatelolco; 1669).

8. In the will of don Julián de la Rosa, written in Tlaxcala in 1566 (BC, doc.

1), *-chanyo* (with *-yo* abstract and collective suffix) is used to mean "matters of (my) household" (p. 46), that is, what portions of the house complex are to go to the testator's brother, what portions to his wife. The testator then orders his wife at the time of her death to leave lands he is bequeathing her to his *-chan*, apparently meaning his lineage (p. 50). *-Chan* is also used in this text in its more frequent sense of "at the residence of" the testator (p. 52).

9. See ANS, pp. 52–53.

10. See TC, docs. 29, 30, pp. 92, 96, among many others, for *nican nochan*, the dominant formula in the Culhuacan of the late 16th century. *Nican nichane* is possibly even more common; examples from an assortment of times and places are in BC, docs. 1, 4, 6, pp. 44, 64, 74; and NMY, docs. 2, 10, pp. 94, 117.

11. See TC, doc. 52, pp. 188–91 (1581), where Ana Tlaco's *-chan* is distant Yecapixtla although she lives in a tlaxilacalli of Culhuacan ("ypan ninemi," "I live in . . . ") and has property and relatives there.

12. Many cases are on the borderline between the two senses. Since most Nahuatl altepetl names are in the locative, they already mean "in . . . "; *Tetzcoco ichan* could mean "his home is in Tetzcoco." When the Tlaxcalan cabildo threatens in 1547 to drive out outsiders, saying "yazque yn inchan," "they are to go (back) to their homes" (BC, doc. 22, p. 120), altepetl or regions are probably meant, but there is no way to be sure. For some cases in which the reference is unambiguously to the altepetl, see ANS, pp. 52–53.

13. See BC, doc. 2, p. 56. In a Nahuatl document of Tlatelolco, 1620, *aposento* is actually used as a loanword equivalent to *calli* (AGN, Tierras 442, exp. 5, f. 9v). By the 18th century, it is not unusual to find a plural suffix attached to *calli*. Thus a testator in Sacaquauhtla (in the northern part of the Tulancingo region) speaks of *nocalhuan,*"my houses" (UCLA TC, folder 25, March 1, 1768). See also Karttunen and Lockhart 1978, p. 170.

14. In fact, one occasionally finds turns of phrase such as *huel tonatiuh icalaquiampa itzticac,* "it faces straight west," which imply that directions given without such modifiers are to be taken as approximate only (there is an example in Appendix A, Doc. 3).

15. See AZ, 1: xix, xxix, xxxi; Carrasco 1964, pp. 190–93; Carrasco 1971, pp. 368–69; and Offner 1984, p. 138 (though the evidence concerns families more than buildings).

16. The classifier *tetl* (lit., "stone") is often used to enumerate the buildings rather than repeating "calli." *Nocal yetemani* is "my house which is in three parts" or "my houses, of which there are three"; *inic centetl* is "the first (house, building)"; etc. See TC, doc. 65, p. 236, for an example. *Caltontli* and *caltepiton* refer unambiguously to small structures. I have not been able to determine whether *caltzintli* is a diminutive, a relatively contentless reverential, or something else. The form is quite common; since it often comes first in the section of a will discussing buildings, I have thought at times that it might refer to the principal structure, if not the whole complex, but this has not been consistently borne out. In the Culhuacan testaments, it can hardly be a diminutive because it stands in contradistinction to *caltepiton, caltontli,* and *caltepitzin* (see TC, docs. 19, 24, 31, pp. 60, 74, 102). A document of Mexico City, 1639, also distinguishes three residential "caltzintli" from a "caltepitzin" (AGN,

Bienes Nacionales 339, item 9), and another from the same place, 1587, embodies the same distinction (AGN, Tierras 442, exp. 5, f. 7). Spanish translators of the time rendered *caltzintli* simply as *casa*.

17. See TC for many examples of house demolition around 1580 in Culhuacan, where the moist chinampa environment and frequent floods must have militated against the longevity of structures. The phenomenon is discussed in S. Cline 1986, pp. 101–2.

18. The standard phrase is *çan itech çaliuhtica*. See Appendix A, Doc. 3, for an example.

19. The usual wording is "las casas principales de mi morada," lit. "the main houses of my dwelling."

20. TC, doc. 48, p. 172. Juan calls the house a *telpochcalli*, "youth-house," and goes on to define the term, in effect, as a house built by a young man before marriage. See S. Cline 1986, p. 100, for a discussion and differentiation of this use of the word from the better-known meaning "preconquest establishment for the education of boys." The existence of a special term implies that it was a not uncommon practice for a youth to build a separate structure for himself prior to and perhaps preparatory to marriage. The custom may have applied to both genders, since Elena Angelina of Mexico City had in her house complex a small structure she called her *ichpochcalli*, "unmarried young woman–house" (NAC, ms. 1481, Jan. 6, 1581).

21. There is no definite indication that Bárbara's husband came to live with her in the new building. I have the impression, however, that he did.

22. The term used for the house's alleyway in both documents is *caltentli*, and the later one uses the loanword *corral* rather than the indigenous *tepancalli* for a corral or enclosure. An accompanying Spanish translation gives *callejón* for *caltentli*.

23. See BC, doc. 11, p. 90; and the discussion in Calnek 1974, pp. 45–46.

24. See, for example, AGN, Hospital de Jesús 298, exp. 4, ff. 5–6; and TC, doc. 19, p. 60, doc. 47, p. 166, doc. 50, p. 180 (the last two refer to the same structure), doc. 80, p. 270. These are also all the examples in which I am sure on which side of the patio the cihuacalli stands. No standard location emerges; two are on the west, one on the east, and one on the north.

25. TC, doc. 17, p. 58 (Culhuacan, 1580).

26. UCLA TC, folder 25, March 1, 1768 (Sacaquauhtla in the Tulancingo region).

27. Ibid. The house for the saints, and indeed the whole household layout, may have been the same in various parts of Mesoamerica. Houses built in the 16th century under Augustinian auspices at Tiripitío, in the Tarascan region to the west of the Nahuas, were "all on one level, following the custom of the country. Most of the houses had, however, besides the bedrooms, a common room, a kitchen, and a chapel where the holy images were kept." (Ricard 1966, p. 138, with references to contemporary chronicles.)

28. The building where the baking was done is referred to as a "tlachichih[ual]calin yhuan orno yhuan moch itlachichihualon." It is unclear to me at present whether *tlachichihualcalli* means "product-house" or "equipment house," in either case here a baking establishment, "with oven and all its equipment." The Spanish translation is *amasijo de pan*, with the *cosas necesarias para una panadería*. The sub-enclosure is called a *tepancalli*. (AGN, Bienes Nacionales 339, item 9.)

29. TC, doc. 34, p. 112, which contains an unambiguous use of both of the Nahuatl terms; *calnepanolli* is also seen in TC, doc. 20, p. 64, and BC, doc. 11, p. 90 (Coyoacan; 1568). The second is an example of two stories in modest circumstances. The term is derived from *calli*, "house," and *nepanoa* "to join, to put one thing on top of another." It is an entirely indigenous construction, doubtless preconquest. Prem (1967, p. 98; 1974, p. 546) is incorrect in presuming that the word is a Spanish-Nahuatl neologism, i.e., that it contains *calli* and *español*, "Spanish."

30. As in AGN, Hospital de Jesús 298, exp. 4, f. 4.

31. See BC, doc. 2, p. 56 (Coyoacan, 1588) for an example of the use of *tlapancalli* and its Spanish translation as *altos*.

32. There was a *chinancaltontli*, "little reed fence," together with small fruit trees around the place of Juan Miguel in Tezontla (Tetzcoco region) (AGN, Tierras 2238, exp. 6, April 28, 1689). A property in Mexico City, 1570, had an *acatzaqualli*, "reed enclosure" (AGN, Tierras 30, exp. 1, f. 37). See also S. Cline 1986, pp. 98–99. In TC (Culhuacan, ca. 1580) one does see some use of *tepancalli* (see just below) for the enclosure going all around the complex, implying a very solid structure (docs. 28, 49, pp. 86, 176), and in one case this is made explicit, with the specification that a *tepantlatzaqualli*, "wall enclosure," was made of adobe (doc. 82, p. 276). The last term also occurs in a Mexico City text of 1564 (AGN, Tierras 22, part 1, exp. 5, f. 123).

33. See TC, doc. 48, pp. 170–75; and AGN, Bienes Nacionales 339, item 9, for examples of use of the terms.

34. Examples in TC, docs. 26, 30, pp. 80, 96 (Culhuacan, 1580); NMY, doc. 2, p. 95 (Xochimilco, 1572).

35. Compare Calnek 1974, pp. 17 (map 1), 47–49.

36. See the 1567 Tlaxcalan reference to streets around churches (TA, selection 24, p. 124).

37. See BC, doc. 26, parts 4 and 5, pp. 154, 160 (Coyoacan, ca. 1550); and Celestino Solís et al. 1985, p. 65, item 129 (Tlaxcala, 1549). For the modern usage, see Karttunen and Lockhart 1978, p. 162, with further references.

38. Often written as *jolal* or *xolal*, the word also appears as *jollal* in NMY, p. 56, where the writer has apparently taken the form to consist of *jol-* and *-lal* (the assimilated form of *-tlal*, "land"). The root *-tlal* is seen even more clearly in the example *xotlal*, from Soyatzingo in the Chalco region, 1734 (AGN, Tierras 2555, exp. 14, f. ?).

39. See TC, docs. 12A, 14, pp. 38, 46 (Culhuacan, 1580), where substantial pieces of land are called the *-solaryo* (or *-jolaryo*) of a house in exactly the same way that *-callal* is used in other documents in the collection. The *-yo* in this context is a suffix of inalienable possession, as in *-atentlallo* (= *-atentlal-yo*), "(its) land at the edge of the water," another term used in the Culhuacan texts instead of *callalli* when chinampas are involved. The point can be seen even more clearly in a petition written in Tulancingo ca. 1570 (UCLA TC, folder 1, complaint about Martín Jacobo): "cequindi y macenvaltin atley yn ijolal . . . atley yn ijolal yvan anotley yn ivecanmil," "some commoners have no solar . . . they have neither a solar nor distant fields." *Huecamilli*, "distant fields," is the polar opposite and complement of "house-land" in the indigenous conceptual framework, so that in this passage *solar* and *callalli* are equated one to one. See also Chap. 5.

40. See, for example, BC, docs. 2, 4, pp. 54, 56, 68. It is not always possible to know whether an orchard accompanies a house or not, as in BC, docs. 3 (p. 60), 4 (p. 66), and 26, part 5 (p. 160). The one in doc. 4 had pears, figs, and avocados. All these examples are from Coyoacan between the mid-16th and the early 17th century.

41. See especially TC, again and again, for example, docs. 48, 67, pp. 172, 242. See also S. Cline 1986, pp. 101–2.

42. See TC, doc. 39, p. 128.

43. See NMY, doc. 2, p. 95 (Xochimilco, 1572); TC (Culhuacan, ca. 1580), doc. 69, p. 244; docs. 6, 31, 80, pp. 26, 102, 270 (all three of these grainbins were made of boards); NAC, ms. 1477 B [1] (Calimaya, Toluca Valley, 1738); AGN, Tierras 2533, exp. 5, ff. 1–2v (the wealthy sometime governor of Tepemaxalco, Calimaya region, in 1691 had one large cuezcomatl and at least six others). As it happens, references from the Toluca Valley in the 17th and 18th centuries could be multiplied.

44. TC, doc. 29, p. 94 (Culhuacan, 1580); see also Cline 1986, pp. 100, 102; and AGN, Tierras 22, part 1, exp. 4, f. 1v, a *temazcaltontli,* "little temazcalli," perhaps now collapsed (Mexico City, 1563).

45. L. Reyes García 1978, p. 176.

46. See the first reference in n. 44.

47. BC, doc. 2, p. 56 (Coyoacan, 1588); and TC (Culhuacan, early 1580's), docs. 38, 49, 56, pp. 126, 178, 202 (the last has the quote).

48. TC, doc. 47, p. 168 (Culhuacan, 1581). When and to what extent Nahuas took over Spanish-style raised beds is unclear.

49. TC, doc. 50, p. 182, and passim. In Nahuatl texts, the spelling is generally *caxa* (as it was in fact in Spanish texts of the time as well). I am uncertain when European-style tables and chairs became common household items. They occur in public or institutional settings as early as the 1550's (TA, p. 6; TC, doc. 13, p. 44), but I have not seen them listed in connection with 16th-century households and unfortunately did not note down the few occurrences I have seen for the later centuries. The relative absence is not conclusive, however; except for rare luxury products, tables and chairs were simple items with only a fraction of the monetary value of chests and do not appear very often in Spanish testaments either.

50. Appendix A, Doc. 2.

51. See NMY, docs. 2, 3, pp. 95, 99 (Xochimilco, 1572, Coyoacan region, 1608); and TC, docs. 39, 48, 67, 74, pp. 130, 172, 242, 256 (Culhuacan, ca. 1580).

52. AGN, Tierras 2338, exp. 6, June 4, 1713. The Nahuatl is "oncan cate platos ce docena yhuan tlaco ynon cuitlaxcohuapanecayo / escudillitas ome / huehhuey ayotecti ome."

53. This is true not only of politically oriented writings like Chimalpahin's annals and the *Historia tolteca-chichimeca,* but also of the encyclopedic Florentine Codex done under the eyes of Sahagún. Dana Leibsohn, a doctoral student in art history at UCLA, combed the Nahuatl text of FC for architectural detail and found very little that would distinguish one house type from another or define any house plan.

54. AGN, Tierras 104, exp. 8, June 27, 1721. The Spanish phrase used to locate a building is like an explanation of the traditional Nahuatl "facing": "que mira la puerta hacia el poniente," "with the door looking toward the west." The son's structure is called an "aposento," and the small house or room is a "casita o cuarto." The

complex was in the barrio of San Francisco Tepiton ("the Little"). The testator had another house in the barrio of Xocalpan, including a kitchen ("cocina"), and divided it in half without further specification between her two daughters.

55. Ibid., 2555, exp. 14, f. 2. For a brief description of a similar complex in Cuauhtinchan, 1707, see L. Reyes García 1978, p. 176.

56. The word is used mainly in the plural, and I have the impression that in that form it could include anyone in one's household or persons closely allied with one in other ways, but I have never seen a passage that would demonstrate this unambiguously. Under "pariente," Molina equates *tehuanyolqui* with "blood relative," giving a compound form with *cihua-*, "woman-," for "affinal relative." Under "teuayulqui," however, Molina gives "deudo o pariente," *deudo* being a broad term that includes not only in-laws but people with even vaguer ties. Regardless of the word's precise domain, the main point—that a primary category including blood relatives speaks of togetherness rather than of blood ties—remains untouched. For an example of *-huanyolque* used in an actual will, see TC, doc. 60, p. 220 (Culhuacan, 1583); in this case, the speaker seems to make a distinction between his *-huanyolque* and the people he has merely lived with. Another occurrence in a will comes from Mexico City, 1588 (AGN, Tierras 59, exp. 3, f. 17v). See also n. 58.

57. Many examples can be found in CH (and from CH but easier to locate, in Schroeder 1984) and Tezozomoc 1949.

58. I have seen *-tlacamecahuan* in texts only once (UCLA TC, folder 23, ff. 22–23; Acatlan, Tulancingo region, 1659) and not at all in dictionaries; the phrase runs "nopilhuan noxhuiuhan notlacamecahuan," "my children, my grandchildren, my descendants," with some question whether the last term describes the first two or, as is more likely, conveys "my descendants (beyond that)." The term *-tlacayohuan* occurs in TC, doc. 45A, p. 160 (Culhuacan, 1581) in a context where it seems to mean much the same thing as *-huanyolque*, and also in ANS, though in an unilluminating context (see p. 51 there). A passage from a Mexico City will of 1588 confirms the essential identity of the two terms, using *-tlacayohuan* at the beginning and *-huanyolque* in the same context at the end (AGN, Tierras 59, exp. 3, ff. 17, 17v).

59. BC, Doc. 4, p. 64. See n. 91, however, for an expression partly covering the lack of a general category.

60. Compare Offner's findings (1983, pp. 199, 200, 210), with which I agree, that the tlacamecayotl is not a descent group, and that descent groups did not exist in Tenochtitlan's households. Even to speak of "the" tlacamecayotl gives it too much of an independent existence. When it is unpossessed, it means lineal consanguineal kin relationships in general, and when it is possessed, it means the kindred in that sense of the particular possessor.

61. Such extensions are in fact not much seen in mundane texts, where *-col* and *-ci* are almost always the actual grandparents. I have seen no unambiguous use of the terms to refer to great-uncles and great-aunts.

62. See ANS, p. 162, for an example in which a man calls a boy his *-mach*, "nephew," hence must himself be considered the boy's *-tla*, and also calls his wife the boy's *-ahui*; there is no sure way of telling which of the two is the blood relative, but the principle is definitely established. It was possible when appropriate to disambiguate, however. One man refers to *cihuayotica notlatzin*, "my uncle through the female

side," that is, the husband of the sister of one of his parents (AGN, Tierras 55, exp. 5, f. 2; Mexico City, 1564).

63. Kin terms did add the absolutive suffix to make a rarely used citation form, as can be seen for many of them in Molina, but these are secondary formations. Several kin words end in a *-uh* that is by origin the possessive suffix: *-teachcauh*, *-teiccauh*, *-hueltiuh*, *-(i)xhuiuh*, *-oquichtiuh*, *-coneuh*. Ordinarily, the possessive *-uh* and the absolutive *-tl* replace each other as appropriate, using the same stem. But some of these words, being heard in effect in the possessive only, were reanalyzed in such a way that the *-uh* was considered part of the stem, and the absolutive form included it as well as the absolutive suffix, as in *hueltiuhtli* and *ixhuiuhtli* (for further evidence that this is so, see the discussion in ANS, pp. 97–98, with additional examples on pp. 47–51). In other words, the possessive form became the basis for the absolutive. The same thing has happened with a different form of the possessive ending in *-huezhui* and *huezhuatli*. On the other hand, *-coneuh* has the normal absolutive form *conetl*, which may show that the term came into use later than the others. Since *-teachcauh* and *-teiccauh* are doubly possessed, they do not show an absolutive form at all, although the related *achcauhtli* is based on reanalysis. As far as I know, no absolutive form of *-oquichtiuh* is attested. The obligatory possession of kinship terms seems to be common to Uto-Aztecan and Mesoamerican languages. Indeed, I presume that little if anything in the Nahua system as of about 1500 was idiosyncratic or new in the Mesoamerican context.

64. Offner (1983, p. 179) is on the right track on this point, and Gardner (1982, pp. 102–3) understands it completely. The original mistake was the misinterpretation by some (not by all) of Molina's reasons for appending "says a woman" or "says a man" to the gloss of certain terms. Since Molina's citation forms are in the first person, it is necessarily the possessor of the relationship who utters that particular form, and Molina never meant to say, nor would it indeed occur to a knowledgeable person that he might have meant to say, that that kin word would be uttered only by someone of a given gender regardless of possessor.

A problem has been that scholars working with kinship have tended to use lists and dictionaries as their source rather than actual texts, so they have lacked examples that would settle this question once and for all. I will give here three relevant examples. In Chimalpahin's annals (CH, 2: 16), the author, though a male, uses the term with female reference point, "yyachtzin," to mean "her older brother." In Mexico City in 1587, don Pedro Enrique de Moteucçoma, speaking of himself in the third person and addressing two female relatives, writes "amicuhtzin," the term with female reference point, for "your (pl.) younger sibling/cousin" (BC, doc. 32, p. 204). In Culhuacan in 1580, a woman speaking to two male relatives uses the term with male reference point, "amomach," "your (pl.) niece/nephew," for her daughter (TC, doc. 27, p. 86). Many more examples could be cited from unpublished documents.

65. The two terms are missing from the lists of Olmos and Sahagún (and hence from treatments that use those sources, such as Gardner 1982 and Offner 1983, pp. 177–200), an indication that they in fact were not a fully integrated part of kinship classification. Molina does include them, however (under "teichpuch" and "tetelpuch"). They are of high frequency in mundane documents of the postconquest period, from the earliest to the latest.

66. Nevertheless, the category sibling is in a sense recognized. The words covering brothers- and sisters-in-law imply a division of siblings by sex but regardless of age relative to ego; so do those for uncle and aunt. The terms for niece/nephew include the children of all one's siblings regardless of either age or sex. Nevertheless, no direct term for a sibling lacks reference to age; one of the few discrepancies in Offner's generally sophisticated discussion of Nahua kinship is that it somehow slipped him that -*hueltiuh* is "older sister of a male," not just "sister of a male." See Molina under "veltiuhtli" and "ermana mayor" (Molina has the age relationship but does not specify that the reference point is male.)

67. See above at n. 59.

68. See Offner 1983. Like Carrasco (1966, pp. 155–60) and Offner (1983, pp. 181–82), I see no way to be sure whether the modifiers *huecapan*, "distant," and -*tlamampan* with a number (from *tlamantli*, a numerical classifier) are of truly indigenous origin or not. -*Tlamampan* occurs occasionally in CH (2: 28, 136), but the general absence of the modifiers in texts outside Spanish-sponsored lists is suggestive. The one exception I know of is the relatively frequent use of *huecapan* in the early census records of the Cuernavaca region; the qualifier is applied to -*ci*, -*iuc*, -*iccauh*, -*teiccauh*, -*mach*, -*pillo*, and perhaps other terms (AZ, 1: 3, 10, 12, 15, 36, 2: 115, and others). MNAH AH, CAN 549, ff. 4v, 23v, has "vel iteycauh" and "vel ycava," with the modifier *huel*, "really, fully," applied to -*(te)iccauh*, "younger sibling/cousin of a male." In view of the generally untouched preconquest aura of this set of documents, even though they were doubtless done at Spanish instigation, I am inclined to believe, from these and other attestations, that *huecapan*, at least, was indeed part of the indigenous scheme, and that the lineal-collateral distinction was made at times in actual speech.

69. In Tlaxcala in 1566, don Julián de la Rosa used "niccauh," "my younger sibling," for Juan Jiménez, said in a Spanish text to be his cousin (*primo*) (BC, doc. 1, pp. 48–49). Don Pedro Enrique de Moteucçoma, in Mexico City in 1587, calls himself "amicuhtzin," "your younger sibling," in speaking to female cousins (BC, doc. 32, p. 204). Luis Tlauhpotonqui, in Culhuacan in 1581, calls his cousin María Tiacapan "noteicauh," "my younger sibling," and her husband "notex," "my brother-in-law," and she calls him "noquichtihuatzin," "my older brother," though in this case Luis's father had in effect adopted María and given her much of the inheritance (TC, docs. 41, 53, pp. 138, 192). In Tetzcoco in 1596, don Miguel de Carvajal calls Juan de Pomar "notiachcauh," "my older brother/cousin," which is then defined by the Spanish term for first cousin (López y Magaña 1980, doc. 4).

Returning to the first example, I have thought at times that there might be some distinction between -*teiccauh* and -*iccauh*, both forms of "one's younger sibling," beyond the fact that the former is much more common. Yet don Julián uses -*iccauh* both for a cousin and for Bautista Cuicuitlapan, who appears to be a brother. In AZ, 1: 21, 22, -*iccauh* and -*teiccauh* are both used for the same person and relationship. The form -*iccauh* can also be used in reference to a younger sister (TC, doc. 44, p. 154; Culhuacan, 1581), so there appears, as we would expect, to be no distinction by the referent's sex. -*Teachcauh*, "older brother/cousin of a male," is seen even less frequently without -*te*-, but that can occur (CH, 2: 6), and in one text "yachtzin" meaning "older brother of a male" lacks not only -*te*- but -*cauh* as well (AGN, Tierras

442, exp. 5, f. 9; Tlatelolco, 1620), thus becoming identical to the form for "older brother of a female." Also, "older brother of a female" appears once with -*te*-: "-tea-tzin" (Appendix A, Doc. 1). Furthermore, Molina (under "icuh. n.") asserts that males as well as females can call a younger sister -*iuc*. I have never seen this in a text or in any other description, however, and the sibling/cousin terminology is one of the very few things about Nahuatl that Molina seems not to have understood fully.

Despite the lack of complete consistency in usage, at some level the relationship between the terms for siblings of males and the terms for siblings of females was that they contained the same roots but, in principle, singled out the males' siblings with the prefix -*te*- and the suffix -*cauh*:

te-ach-cauh	-ach
te-ic-cauh	-iuc

The root *ach* is in some way related to *achto*, "first" (the length of the *a* is not yet established beyond doubt). The roots *ic* and *iuc* are probably identical in origin, since there is frequently a loss of rounding in *uc* [k^w] before a consonant in Nahuatl. The sense may be "thereupon" (i.e., "afterward"), as in -*icpac*, "on top of." The suffix -*cauh* is not related to *cahua*, "to leave," as Offner (1983, p. 184) speculates. As shown above (see n. 63), the -*uh* is originally the possessive suffix, leaving -*ca*-; since the *a* is long, this looks like the preterit combining form, implying that the roots were originally verbal. The -*te*- is the indefinite possessor prefix; the original rationale of the double possession is not clear to me, although in verbs too some indefinite prefixes have been absorbed into the stem.

70. I agree with Offner on this point (see Offner 1983, pp. 187–90). Proto-Uto-Aztecan *t* became *tl* before *a*, so that -*ta* (father) is merely the archaic equivalent of -*tla* (uncle), somehow unaffected by the broader sound change. Offner also understands the relationship between -*pil* and -*pillo* (ibid., p. 190).

71. See also -*huexiuh* in the text below, which is reciprocal but does not distinguish gender. English has a fully reciprocal term in "cousin"; if I am your cousin, then you are my cousin.

72. Compare Offner 1983, p. 185. The element -*ton(tli)* is a diminutive. The relationship of -*pi* and -*pipton* may not seem obvious and indeed is not fully established, but it is entirely plausible. The root -*pi* contains a final glottal stop that may correspond to the final *p* of *pip*-. Most older Nahuatl glottal stops whose origin is known come from *t*, but *c* [k] is also attested (see Molina's "colelectli" or "coleletli," "a certain demon"), and thus it seems that the glottal stop could be the reflex of any lost obstruent.

In a 1736 document from San Francisco Centlalpan in the Tlalmanalco jurisdiction (NMY, doc. 10, p. 118), -*achpil* is used for "great-grandmother" (there written "-achpillitzin"), as well as simple -*pil* (written "-pilitzin"). Given the rarity of these terms and the possibility of scribal error in one or both, I will not comment on them further, except to say that they conceivably represent variation or variation plus combination of the terms projected from sibling terminology. An alternate word for "great-grandfather" is -*achcocol* (with a glottal stop after the first *o*; see ANS, p. 45), which is based on -*col*, "grandfather." Here *ach*- probably means "first," "earlier" or "great-" directly rather than being taken from -*ach*, "older brother." -*Achcol* (found as "-ahcoltzin" in Azcapotzalco, 1738; BC, doc. 17, p. 102) presumably has the same meaning.

-*Achcol* cannot be taken as a cover term for "ancestors" as Offner asserts (1983, p. 186). The instances he uses as evidence (FC, book 6, pp. 47, 57) have -*achcocol* in the plural possessed form, not -*achcol* (-*col* does not reduplicate in the plural possessed form), and the word makes up only one half of a set formula including -*techiuhcauh*, "one's progenitor," which appears not only in FC but also in the Bancroft Dialogues (see ANS, p. 45). In other words, the expression "one's progenitors, one's great-grandfathers," is extended to "one's forebears." *Tocolhuan tachtonhuan*, "our grandfathers, our great-grandfathers," can be found with the same meaning (see ANS, p. 46), and other combinations of words for parents and grandparents (including grandmothers) are used in the same way on occasion. No single term for ancestor seems to have existed.

73. -*Huexiuh* does occur in actual texts: CH, 2: 6; TC, docs. 43, 64, pp. 150, 230 (Culhuacan, 1581, 1585). There is also the term -*ome*, used between two brothers-in-law who have married sisters (see CH, 2: 124, and Zimmermann's note on p. 199). The word occurs quite frequently in the Cuernavaca-region censuses, including AZ, 1: xvii, 17, 42, 49, 51; and MNAH AH, CAN 549, ff. 19v, 37, 38, 39v, 61, 61v. I have not seen enough examples to be certain how the term operates; possibly it is simply *ome*, the word "two," with a possessive prefix. At any rate, it is like other same-generation affinal terms in being reciprocal and ignoring the relative ages of ego and referent.

74. The situation with -*mon*, -*cihuamon*, -*telpoch*, and -*(i)chpoch* implies that at one time gender distinctions were made only with kin older than ego, but that at some point a conflicting principle was introduced, gender distinction for all kin past puberty.

75. Nevertheless, in one case -*tex* seems to mean the husband of ego's female cousin (though that cousin was functioning as a sister, sharing in the inheritance fully); see n. 69.

76. TC, doc. 46, p. 162.

77. UCLA TC, folder 23, ff. 22–23.

78. TC, doc. 74, p. 256.

79. López y Magaña 1980, doc. 3 (Tetzcoco, 1581).

80. CH, 2: 95, has "ymachcihuamon," "his niece/nephew–daughter-in-law."

81. AGN, Tierras 165, exp. 4, f. 14. In TC, doc. 31, p. 103 (Culhuacan, 1580), Miguel García calls his nephew and the latter's wife "nomachua."

82. TC, doc. 50A, p. 184 (Culhuacan, 1582).

83. See NMY, doc. 6, p. 105 (Coyoacan, 1613), "nomiccacihuamon," "my daughter-in-law, wife of my dead son."

84. Examples are in TC, doc. 43, p. 148 (Culhuacan, 1581), "nohuepol," "my brother-in-law" (where the sister is dead), and doc. 50, p. 182 (1581), "nohuezhuatzitzinhuan," "my sisters-in-law" (where the brother is dead). Offner (1983, p. 181) is thus wrong in contending that the absence of "-micca" in affinal terms referring to ego's generation or the adjacent generations necessarily meant that the consanguineal relative in question was still alive.

85. One example is CH, 2: 76.

86. For example, see AGN, Tierras 2584, exp. 3, ff. 6–7 (Amaquemecan, 1767), and Tierras 2550, exp. 8, f. 6 (Xocotitlan, Tlalmanalco jurisdiction, 1722). Both also have *-cetca* in the meaning wife (there appearing as "-setcatzin"). Molina has "cetca. no." "my relative [*deudo*], brother, or sister." I have yet to see the word in texts in Molina's meaning. I do not believe that it supplies the missing general term for sibling regardless of age or sex; my sense is that it is still more general, for any kind of kin, including probably affinal (at times an implication of Spanish *deudo*). Molina does not give the term again under "ermano" and "ermana," nor does he there present any term at all that is not differentiated by both age and sex. Etymologically, *-cetca* appears related to *ceti(a)*, "to be united."

87. AZ and MNAH AH, CAN 549–51, passim. AZ, 1: 36, has *-namic* in the case of a calpolli head married at the church; though I have not combed the entire set looking specifically for this word, after extensive reading I am aware of no other instance. AZ, 1: 42, has *-cihuauh* even though the couple was married in church.

88. FC, book 6, chap. 23; see especially pp. 127, 129, 131, 133 for uses of *-namic* or instances where another term is used when *-namic* would be expected. The word also occurs in book 6, chap. 29, pp. 161–62.

89. See, for example, BC, doc. 1, p. 46 (Tlaxcala, 1566); and doc. 2, p. 54 (Coyoacan, 1588).

90. Molina gives both "nenamictiliztli" and "teoyotica nenamictiliztli," glossing them as "marriage" and "marriage by the church."

91. But there is an expression, if not a category, that is susceptible of the "we" construction. *Nehuan ehua*, glossed by Molina as "brothers or sisters," means literally "they rise together," i.e., "they have the same parents." This in a sense covers the missing "sibling regardless of age or sex," but it is only a phrase, not a category as such, exists only in the plural, and except for some early litigation in which genealogy is in question, rarely figures in texts. A Tetzcoco document of 1589 (López y Magaña 1980, doc. 3) has a variant of the expression. After naming two uncles and an aunt, a person goes on to say "moch yeua" (*moch[intin] ehua*), "they are all brothers and sisters," or "they all have the same father and mother."

92. *Viuda* is attested as early as 1572 (AGN, Tierras 1735, exp. 2, f. 80).

93. "Widow or widower of . . ." was conveyed by *inamic catca*, "whose spouse was," or "who was the spouse of . . ." (there being no difference in Nahuatl): "Ana Juana inamic catca Francisco Lazaro" would be "Ana Juana, whose spouse was Francisco Lázaro," i.e., "Ana Juana, widow of Francisco Lázaro." The phrase is reminiscent of the Spanish expression, frequent in the 16th century, "mujer que fue de . . ." I have yet to see *viuda* or *viudo* in possessed form in a Nahuatl text.

94. CH, 2: 117; López y Magaña 1980, doc. 4. Otherwise, Chimalpahin uses *-tiachcauh* and *-teiccauh* even when speaking of Spaniards (CH, 2: 23). Chimalpahin's use of the loanword to say "their ecclesiastical brothers" (i.e., members of the same order) is not really related to kinship ("yn teoyotica ynhermanotzitzinhuan"; 2: 93.)

95. AGN, Tierras 1520, exp. 6, ff. 10r–10v (Huejotla, Tetzcoco region, 1672, "noermanotzin"); Tierras 2338, exp. 1, f. 2 (San Miguel Tocuillan, Tetzcoco area, 1691, "noermanatzin"); Tierras 2533, exp. 5, f. 1 (Tepemaxalco/Calimaya, Toluca Valley, 1691, "niquipie noyermanos noyermanas"). An unorthodox and rather incoherent document from the Sultepec region, with some qualities of the titles genre,

which seems to contain the dates 1660 and 1680 but could be from somewhat later, has "noermano" (AGN, Tierras 1780, exp. 3, f. 3v).

96. Karttunen and Lockhart 1978.

97. Looking at modern dictionaries, we find a word of indigenous origin, the equivalent of *-icniuh*, "one's friend," under "hermano" in Brewer and Brewer 1971 (Tetelcingo); it is like *hermano* in structure, however, in not distinguishing the sex of the reference point or the age of the referent relative to the reference point (the same word is used for both brothers and sisters, thus varying from both Spanish and older Nahuatl). The unpossessed construction "they are brothers" is possible. The words for cousin, listed under "primo," are fully Spanish in origin and structure: *-primo* and *-prima*. Key and Key 1953 (Zacapoaxtla) show exactly the same situation with *hermano*; under "primo" and "prima," the glosses use vocabulary of indigenous origin but make mainly the Spanish distinctions, being the equivalent of *-huecaicniuh* and *-huecacihuaicniuh*, "one's distant friend" and "one's distant female friend."

98. NMY, doc. 10, p. 118. The same text has the form "nohermanatzin," "my sister," with the reverential suffix *-tzin* frequently seen added to kin words taken from Spanish as well as to indigenous counterparts.

99. AGN, Tierras 2549, exp. 1, f. 1v (Tepetlixpan, south Chalco region).

100. CFP, f. 24v (Calimaya, 1746.) An isolated early example is somewhat like those mentioned above for sibling terms. "Ysuprina" in a text of 1598 (BC, doc. 33, p. 204) is not as in the other cases preceded by an indigenous term, but it does refer to Spaniards (the king and queen of Spain), and above all the text was written in Spain by a Nahua nobleman who had become a permanent resident there.

101. UCLA Research Library, Special Collections, McAfee Collection, Metepec, 1760 ("notiutzin"); UCLA TC, folder 25, March 1, 1768, Acaxochitlan near Tulancingo ("notio").

102. I have, however, seen *nieto*, "grandson," in a document from Calimaya in the Toluca Valley, 1718 (AGN, Tierras 2539, exp. 2, f. 13).

103. Since Nahuatl texts, as will be seen elsewhere, have a strong colloquial and spontaneous quality and vary greatly with locality, we can hope for new windfalls of this nature. Testimony in criminal cases concerning Indians that were appealed to Spanish courts may turn out to be a rich source, despite the translation into Spanish, now that Nahuatl texts have set a framework.

104. Appendix A, Doc. 1; see also N&S, item 4.

105. A Spaniard much experienced in the administration of justice among Indians of central Mexico maintained that Indian men of all ranks brought their wives to court and had the wife respond to anything the judge should ask, even an inquiry about the man's name (Gómez de Cervantes 1944, p. 135). The whole passage and further discussion will be found in N&S, item 4.

106. ANS; see the discussion of the origin of the text on pp. 2–13.

107. Kathleen Truman, in personal communications, has told me of the persistence of similar patterns among Mayan speakers of Chiapas whom she has observed; Hill and Hill 1986 have found the same persistence in part of the Nahua heartland, the Tlaxcalan region.

108. ANS, pp. 160–61.

109. ANS, pp. 140–43.

110. ANS, pp. 160–61.

111. See ANS, pp. 44–51, for a discussion of further same-generation extensions.

112. As far as is now known, inversions affect relative age (with a consequent ostensible reversal of roles) but not sex. Polite inversion was also applied to possession with the word -*chan*, "home," with my home being called yours and yours mine, both in the meaning of household and in the meaning of home altepetl. See ANS, pp. 45, 52–53.

113. NMY, doc. 1, p. 93.

114. TC, doc. 50A, p.184. The exact form used is "ticuiuhtzin," "our younger sibling." See text at n. 82 above.

115. I will not here discuss a document in AGN, Vínculos 279, exp. 1, ff. 126v–127v, written in Xochimilco in 1586 and using dialogue to describe a noblewoman's deathbed scene. Many aspects of language use and interaction shown there reinforce the patterns seen in the two documents discussed in the text. The text is reproduced and commented on in item 5 of N&S. An excerpt appears in Chap. 8 at n. 70.

116. FC, above all book 10, chaps. 1 and 2, but many of the speeches in book 6 bear on kinship norms.

117. BC, doc. 11, p. 90.

118. TC, docs. 30, 48 (pp. 98, 174, 176); doc. 40 (p. 132); doc. 60 (pp. 214–22). See also S. Cline 1986, pp. 72–75.

119. AGN, Tierras 3548, exp. 3 [?], f. 14.

120. Compare S. Cline 1984, p. 302, on Kellogg 1979. The same-sex inheritance preferences that Kellogg deduced from a relatively small sample of 16th-century Tenochtitlan testaments have no counterpart in the larger body of material from nearby Culhuacan in the same time period.

121. AGN, Tierras 30, exp. 1, ff. 5, 8, 32, 35 (Mexico City, 1569). Another testator ordered most of his house complex to be sold but left one structure to his wife, giving instructions that the new occupant was to close off his part (AGN, Tierras 38, exp. 2, f. 22; Mexico City, 1576).

122. TC, doc. 29, p. 94 (Culhuacan, 1580).

123. TC, doc. 50, p. 182 (Culhuacan, 1581).

124. Since the best and most numerous descriptions of households are from the early period, it might be thought that things had changed drastically by the 18th century, but the isolated descriptions extant still show elements of the same picture, as in the 1721 example from Tlatelolco (see text at n. 54).

125. See the case of Baltasar Bautista the baker above, at n. 28; Baltasar left one of the three residential buildings on his property to each of his three small children and only the bakery to his wife, to support them; yet clearly she was to be in charge of the residences too.

126. See NMY, doc. 2, pp. 94–97, with the typical statement, "although I give it to her, it is just so she will use it to raise my child." Compare S. Cline 1984, pp. 295–302, on these matters.

127. Cases of this kind are in BC, doc. 6, pp. 72–77 (Metepec in the Toluca Valley, 1795) and Appendix A, Doc. 4 (Azcapotzalco, 1695).

128. See the will of Juan Fabián, BC, doc. 4, pp. 64–69 (Coyoacan, 1617). In Tepetlixpan (Chalco region) in 1704, Francisca Ceverina left everything to her daugh-

ter-in-law instead of her son, whom she called lazy, negligent, and a drifter (AGN, Tierras 2549, exp. 1, ff. 53v–56v).

129. Some hints in this direction may be seen in S. Cline 1986, pp. 79–83.

130. See AZ throughout; and Offner 1984, p. 140. There are exceptions.

131. See the very congruent conclusions reached by Calnek (1974, p. 44) in relation to litigation over property in 16th-century Tenochtitlan. The article also reinforces much of the analysis of household layout contained in the first section of the present chapter.

132. See AGN, Tierras 2338, exp. 6, April 28, 1689 (Tezontla, near Tetzcoco) for the latest example I know of. The associations are doubtless preconquest in origin. See FC, book 6, p. 127 (chap. 23) for the axe associated with males; youths received axes when they were ready to marry and go out on their own. See also S. Cline 1986, pp. 112–13.

Chapter 4

1. The entire document in transcription and translation, with comment, constitutes selection 1 of TA (pp. 67–69).

2. The etymology of the word is not clear; *ma-* is the root "hand, arm," and *cehualli* by itself means "shade," not necessarily the original meaning here (*cehual/ cehui* is associated with various meanings having to do with coolness, resting, etc.). *Macehualli* is not derived from the etymologically equally puzzling *macehua*, "to do penance" and hence "to acquire that which one desires," since *macehualli* has a long *a* in the first syllable and *macehua* has a short vowel plus glottal stop; the two words could still be somehow related, since in Nahuatl long vowel and short vowel with glottal stop do sometimes alternate in the same roots in different contexts. My feeling is that the word at origin was some sort of polite metaphor for a human being in general and did not specify lower social rank.

3. NMY, doc. 6, p. 105.

4. As in the page of the Codex Osuna (Mexico City, mid-16th century) reproduced as Plate XI in Gibson 1964. This *-tzin* was often used in mock-humble meaning by people of very high degree, as when the members of the cabildo of Huexotzinco sign themselves "mocnomacevaltzitziva," "your poor humble vassals" (BC, doc. 29, p. 188).

5. Molina glosses the plural (under "maceualtin") as "pueblo menudo," "ordinary folk, little folk" (he also gives "vassal," which I consider not strictly correct for the unpossessed form).

6. CH, 2: 57. In FC, book 6, p. 93 (chap. 18), "timaceoalti" is close to meaning people in general. Most telling is what Molina gives in the Spanish-to-Nahuatl section under "man or woman" ("ombre o muger"; f. 90v): "tlacatl. maceualli." Likewise under "people or multitude" ("gente o gentio"; f. 65v), "tlaca. maceualtin."

7. See Lockhart 1982, p. 385 (also N&S, item 3).

8. Zorita 1941.

9. See the authors cited in Hicks 1976, p. 67. "Mayeque," the form used by Zorita and some other Spaniards, is a plural that they took for a singular, adding *s* to

form a Spanish plural. The Nahuatl word in the singular is *maye*, consisting of the root *mai-*, "arm, hand," and *-e*, "one who possesses something," so that the literal meaning of the construction is "possessor of hands and arms," and the thrust is much like that of English "hand," as in fieldhand or farmhand. The form was probably normally possessed, as it is in the only occurrences in Nahuatl texts I have seen (see n. 14).

10. Ramírez Cabañas 1941 contains an early comment on the rare occurrence of the word.

11. See especially Dyckerhoff 1976; Hicks 1976; and Olivera 1978. The analogous Andean *yana* seems to have been more distinct from the ordinary commoner.

12. See TA, p. 21, with more precise references in nn. 124 and 125; and BC, doc. 26, part 3, p. 152.

13. TA, pp. 21, 110; BC, doc. 26, part 7, p. 164. TA has the specific phrase "macevalli tlalmaytl" (selection 19, p. 110). In Coyoacan, "tepantlaca" also occurs (BC, doc. 26, part 2, p. 152); one wonders if there is not some confusion or merging with *tecpantlaca*, "palace people."

14. López y Magaña 1980, doc. 3. The other instance is from Mexico City, 1558; an indigenous witness, speaking of a time many years before and referring to another indigenous person, says, "we were his mayeque" (*timayecahuan*; AGN, Tierras 20, part 2, exp. 4, f. 6).

15. Carrasco 1976b, p. 110. Olivera 1978 (p. 196) finds that in 16th-century Tecali, dependents were called the macehualli of someone, or *-tech pohui*.

16. In 1566, the teuctli of a teccalli in Ocotelolco (Tlaxcala) refers once to the people who obey him as "teixhuiuh tepiltzin" (as well as calling them "teixuiuan" or "teixuivan"; BC, doc. 1, pp. 46, 48, 50). The indefinite possessed form of *pilli* (*tepiltzin*) frequently but not invariably refers to a person of noble birth; there is the further ambiguity that a noun doublet in Nahuatl can be either a list of two separate things or a complex term for one thing. In the Tetzcoco dialogues of ca. 1580, the phrase "tepilhuan teixhuihuan" seems to refer to prominent people distinguished from the macehualtin (ANS, pp. 40–41, 50–51).

17. TA, selection 19, p. 110.

18. BC, doc. 1, p. 47, n. 17, from a Tlaxcalan lawsuit of 1554.

19. The description of the *tecpanpouhque* ("those who belong to the palace") in the Tetzcoco region is reminiscent of the teixhuihuan. See Offner 1983, pp. 128–29, 135–37. See also Dyckerhoff 1976, p. 173, for examples from the Matrícula de Huexotzinco where the census takers found it so difficult to tell pipiltin from others that they first included some of them among macehualtin or dependents, and then erased the notations and counted them as pipiltin. Olivera (1978, p. 196) speaks of marriages between pipiltin and macehualtin in 16th-century Tecali.

20. Carrasco (1976b, p. 115) points out two cases in the Morelos records in which a teuctli's dependents coincide entirely or almost entirely with a unit that is called "calpolli."

21. See Dyckerhoff 1976, pp. 160–61; and L. Reyes García 1977, pp. 106, 112, 117–18.

22. See Hicks 1976; and Offner 1984.

23. Hicks 1976, p. 72. Hicks calculates dependents' holdings at an average

1,282 m², varying from 1,102 to 1,865, against 1,865 m² for ordinary commoners, with a range of 92 to 8,701. In view of the apparent tininess of the plots, Hicks surmises that the holders had additional plots or other means of livelihood. This seems likely, but we must remember that we have only the vaguest notion of the true equivalents of Nahuatl units of measure in any specific instance.

24. Carrasco 1976b, p. 113; MNAH AH, CAN 550.

25. Carrasco 1976a, p. 27; Carrasco 1976b, p. 113; Dyckerhoff 1976, p. 161.

26. Dyckerhoff 1976, pp. 160–61.

27. AZ, passim. See also Carrasco 1976b, pp. 107–8; Offner 1983, pp. 214–16; and Offner 1984, p. 139. The lords in the Cuernavaca-region documents, and therefore their establishments, are integrated into the altepetl-calpolli framework through the payment of tribute, but as discussed, this was probably the case for teccalli in general.

28. See, for examples of tlatlacotin, AZ, 1: xx, 2: 1, 3; and MNAH AH, CAN 549, f. 12, 550, ff. 5, 33v, 34v, 37v, 44v, 45, 47v. In the parlance of the early Cuernavaca region, -*tlan nemi* was often replaced by -*pal nemi*; for examples, see AZ, 1: 6, 9, 17, 23, 91, 2: 2; and MNAH AH, CAN 549, ff. 1v, 12. For the term -*tlan nemi*, see ANS, p. 43.

29. ANS, p. 146.

30. Some standard authorities on preconquest slavery are referred to in González Torres 1976. The material on slavery is mainly of the posterior oversystematizing and idealizing type on which little or nothing can be based.

31. Zorita (1941, p. 94) speaks of "los macehuales, que es la gente común y labradores"; Anguiano and Chapa (1976, p. 152) also equate macehualli and agriculturalist. All in all this equation seems justified in practice, but *macehualli* did not *mean* "agriculturalist." Molina has other words for *labrador*.

32. Zorita 1941, pp. 142, 144, 147.

33. CH, 1: 98, has an example of a commoner marrying the daughter of a tlatoani and succeeding; he is not specifically called a merchant, but his wealth is given as a prime reason for the match. Tezozomoc 1949 (p. 173) speaks of the eldest son of the tlatoani of Tlatelolco in the postconquest period marrying the daughter of a (preconquest) pochtecatl. The pochteca role in Tlatelolco, it is true, was extraordinary.

34. FC, Book 9. This account has the advantage and the disadvantage of having been composed (after the fact) by people close to the merchant group; jealous of their reputation, the informants tell more about merchants' social and political ambitions than about their business activity, doubtless enhancing the picture considerably.

35. ANS, p. 152. See also Pomar 1941, pp. 38–39.

36. Dyckerhoff 1976, pp. 165–66.

37. Anguiano and Chapa 1976, pp. 151–52.

38. L. Reyes García 1978, pp. 117–18.

39. See BC, doc. 25, pp. 138–49; Corona Sánchez 1976, pp. 96, 98; and Dyckerhoff 1976, p. 166.

40. See Dyckerhoff 1976, p. 166.

41. S. Cline 1986, pp. 90, 96; Dyckerhoff 1976, p. 167; NMY, docs. 2, 3, pp. 94–100.

42. See Olivera 1976, p. 196.

43. One of the most current among Spanish words for a nobleman, *hidalgo/hijodalgo*, "son of something," is closely parallel to "pilli" in its semantic origin.

44. Implied in Zorita 1941, pp. 86, 91. See also Carrasco 1976a, pp. 21, 22, 26.

45. The rounding of the final consonant of the stem *teuc-tli* was frequently omitted in combined forms, making *tec-*.

46. See Carrasco 1976a, p. 22; and TA, selection 9, pp. 85–86.

47. Carrasco 1976a, p. 20 and passim.

48. Ibid.

49. See Rojas et al. 1987, pp. 309–25.

50. In mid-16th century Tlaxcala, don Julián de la Rosa was reigning teuctli of the teccalli Ayapanco Tecpan, to which his cousin the high-ranking noble and cabildo member Juan Jiménez also belonged, so that one or the other was not the son of the previous teuctli. See Anguiano and Chapa 1976, p. 144; BC, doc. 1, pp. 44–53; and Rojas et al. 1987, p. 317.

51. Carrasco 1976a, p. 20; L. Reyes García 1978, pp. 112–13; TA, pp. 28 (n. 199), 56, items 144.2, 146.1.

52. CH, reported and analyzed in Schroeder 1984, pp. 220–23, with references. These cases refer to tlatoque, but as will be seen the tlatoani was at the same time a teuctli.

53. It is also true, nevertheless, that the word *teccalli* is based on *teuctli*, not the other way around. *Teuctli* has logical priority and must in some sense have had historical priority too. It seems to me that *teuctli* must originally have meant simply "person of high rank, one to whom people look up, person of influence." Indeed, in polite conversation, it retained this flavor; by no means everyone called "our lord" in this sense was actually head of a teccalli (ANS has apparent examples).

54. Anguiano and Chapa 1976, p. 147.

55. Compare Carrasco 1976a, p. 23.

56. Zorita, in particular, is associated with this position (see 1941, pp. 85–86), and much the same impression emerges from a reading of the preconquest sections of Ixtlilxochitl (1975–77).

57. See Carrasco 1984; Gibson 1964, p. 38; and Schroeder 1984, pp. 86, 87, 97, 218–19, 222–23, with references to CH.

58. See CH throughout; compare also Schroeder 1984. Except in royal titles, Chimalpahin mainly uses *teuctli* in the plural, paired with *pipiltin*, as a way of referring to the nobility collectively.

59. Carrasco 1976a, p. 21; Offner 1983, p. 132.

60. It does seem, however, that *tecpan* is used when the reference is to the king's court or to the social entity in general, while *tecpancalli* almost always means the buildings (though *tecpan* can refer to buildings as well). Compare Schroeder 1984, pp. 166–72. In the eastern sources, there are to my knowledge few implications that *teccalli* refers to an actual building (with the exception of a passage in Tlaxcalan records of 1548; see TA, p. 39, item 25). Molina, however (based it must be remembered in Mexico City), glosses "teccalli" as "royal (governmental) palace or court (building for litigation)" ("casa o audiencia real").

61. Anguiano and Chapa 1976, p. 144.

62. CH, passim; the second tecpan was ultimately extinguished (Schroeder 1984, pp. 97–99, with references to CH). Much the same impression arises from a

general reading of Tezozomoc 1975 and Ixtlilxochitl 1975–77. The seven tecpan of Teotihuacan (Corona Sánchez 1976, p. 93) seem to correspond to what Chimalpahin would call tlayacatl.

63. TC, docs. 36, 64, 71, pp. 118–19, 228, 232–33, 248–49; also doc. 17, pp. 56–57, though the term itself is not used. Even in the east, the statement by the Tlaxcalan teuctli don Julián de la Rosa that the buildings belonging (apparently) to the teccalli were *techan*, "someone else's home," could be interpreted in the same way (BC, doc. 1, p. 50).

64. Carrasco 1972. There are other examples in AZ and MNAH AH, CAN 549–51. In most cases, the term *pilli* does not come into play in descriptions of the establishments of the Cuernavaca-region teteuctin, leaving the parallel to the teccalli of the eastern region incomplete in one important respect. One could presume that the relatives of the teuctli were pipiltin, the nonrelatives commoners, but in many cases even relatives have such small land allotments as to cast doubt on their noble status.

65. Olivera 1976, pp. 196–97; L. Reyes García 1977, pp. 113, 122; L. Reyes García 1978, p. 83; TA, selection 9, pp. 85–86.

66. L. Reyes García 1977, pp. 104, 121. See also Chap. 2.

67. TA, especially pp. 43, 63 (items 58, 196). See also Celestino Solís et al. 1985, pp. 72, 211–12 (items 164, 831–33).

68. Dyckerhoff 1976, pp. 160–64.

69. See TA, pp. 25, 26, selection 1 (pp. 67–69). The very orders to the effect that nobles and commoners were to deliver their tributes at different places prove that both paid (see TA, p. 55, item 138.2).

70. Rojas et al. 1987.

71. Ibid., pp. 73, 76, 104, 317, 321, 323; Anguiano and Chapa 1976, p. 144; BC, doc. 1, pp. 44–53. In such cases, it is not possible to know for sure whether at a time more or less remote the lordly establishment took its name from the calpolli or vice versa. The important point here is that the two coincided.

72. Dyckerhoff 1976, pp. 164, 172.

73. See Ixtlilxochitl 1975–77, passim; and Offner 1983, pp. 124–39 (which among other things distills what Ixtlilxochitl says); also Corona Sánchez 1976, pp. 92–95. To the extent that the landholdings and land trading of nobles exist against the background of corporate lineage landholding, the distinction that Offner makes between individual holding by nobles and corporate holding by commoners would be illusory.

74. AGN, Hospital de Jesús 210. See Haskett 1985, pp. 494–97, 655–59 (document IV.A).

75. See Carrasco 1976a, p. 31. For a plethora of such titles and an analysis of them, see Schroeder 1984, pp. 208–16.

76. For some postconquest examples, the tlatoani of Tepoztlan ca. 1535–45 had dependents comparable in number to many a calpolli (MNAH AH, CAN 550, ff. 5–31v; see also Carrasco 1976b, pp. 112–13). In the late 16th century, the premier tlatoani and governor of Tecali seems to have had three times as many dependents as any other lord (Olivera 1976, p. 198). Also in Yecapixtla (eastern Cuernavaca region) in 1564, the governor held the largest number of dependents (Carrasco 1976b, p. 110).

77. The best example of a holder of dispersed lands is don Juan de Guzmán of

Coyoacan, in BC, doc. 26, pp. 150–65. The scattering of the holdings of other teteuctin should not be underestimated, however; Horn 1989 (chap. 5, part 3, especially pp. 240–41) gives examples for several other noblemen and noblewomen of Coyoacan. See also the case of don Julián de la Rosa of Tlaxcala (BC, doc. 1, pp. 44–53). Although the many locations of his lands and dependents cannot be mapped, they were surely not contiguous; they appear to have spread well beyond his own unit of San Pedro Tecpan and possibly even beyond the altepetl of Ocotelolco.

78. See Schroeder 1984, pp. 195–97; and CH, 1: 98, 151, 172 (excerpted in Schroeder).

79. Anguiano and Chapa 1976, p. 152; Dyckerhoff 1976, p. 173; Rojas et al. 1987, pp. 309–25.

80. See Lockhart 1968, pp. 200–201; and Lockhart and Schwartz 1983, pp. 71–72, 100–101. Although there was justified doubt even in the 16th century that the tlatlacotin should be equated with slaves as Europeans understood that term, the Nahuas did at times make the equation themselves, using *tlacotli* for black slaves in New Spain (TA, pp. 78–79).

81. Anguiano and Chapa 1976, p. 155; Rojas et al. 1987, p. 133.

82. See Gibson 1964, pp. 198–206.

83. See Zorita 1941, especially p. 154.

84. See ibid., especially pp. 72, 91–95. Zorita is full of scathing partisan statements against Indian municipal officials, including the untruth (taken from standard blanket accusations by the partially displaced tlatoque) that they were a pack of macehualtin (see p. 171 and elsewhere).

85. See Taylor 1979, chap. 2.

86. L. Reyes García 1978, pp. 108–9.

87. See Gibson 1964, pp. 154–64, 260–61, and especially 265–66.

88. BC, doc. 1, pp. 44–53, especially 46–47.

89. See Gibson 1964, pp. 154, 159.

90. López y Magaña 1980, doc. 3.

91. See the 1547 passage in the minutes of the Tlaxcalan cabildo (BC, doc. 22, pp. 118–21) specifying that drunks being forcibly hired out were to receive higher pay from Spanish than from Tlaxcalan employers.

92. Compare Lockhart and Schwartz 1983, pp. 138–42.

93. A good example of later lists is MNAH AH, GO 185, from Tepemaxalco (Calimaya, Toluca Valley) in the 1650's and 1660's. A section is transcribed and translated in NMY, doc. 8, pp. 108–11.

94. L. Reyes García 1978, pp. 219–20. The priest asserts, indeed, that macehualtin all over New Spain still give such payments to their caciques. He also presumes that in Cuauhtinchan in his time there was a "cacique" for each "barrio." Note that this secular cleric took the same view of things and adopted the same pro-teuctli stance as mendicant predecessors in the area a century and a half before.

95. NMY, doc. 7, pp. 106–7 ("cayanis"; Huexotla, Tetzcoco region, 1634); CFP, ff. 3v, 12 ("cayanis," "cayanixti"; Tepemaxalco/Calimaya, Toluca Valley, 1658, 1674); in the last instance a group of gañanes is mentioned. In all three instances, the word is written with substitutions characteristic of the time when Nahuatl had not yet made any substantial phonological adjustments to Spanish, indicating that the

term probably became current by the early 17th century at the latest. It is also seen each time with a reanalyzed plural; that is, the Spanish plural form was not recognized as such and was used as a singular, with another plural ending added when appropriate. This too is characteristic of relatively early loans. Haskett 1985 (p. 474) has an example of gañanes employed by an Indian noblewoman in 17th-century Yecapixtla.

96. See Tutino 1976; Konrad 1980; and Lockhart and Schwartz 1983, pp. 138–42.

97. *Español*, "Spaniard," appeared in Nahuatl before 1550 (BC, doc. 22, p. 118), though the doubtless even earlier *caxtiltecatl*, a folk-etymologizing construction meaning "inhabitant of Castile," never went entirely out of currency. See UCLA TC, folder 23 (Acatlan, Tulancingo area, 1659); and BC, doc. 17, p. 100 (Azcapotzalco, 1738). "Black" was almost as early, usually the literal Nahuatl translation *tliltic* rather than Spanish *negro*, though the latter does occur on occasion (for example, TA, selection 15, p. 103). Words for the ethnic mixtures appeared as the different terms at different times became prevalent in Mexican Spanish, which for *mestizo* and *mulato* was very early.

98. TA, selection 7, pp. 77–79; AGN, Tierras 39, part 2, exp. 1, f. 13 (translation of order of Audiencia judge, Mexico City, 1570).

99. Chimalpahin employs *indio* only once. The important Tlaxcalan annalist of the late 17th century, Zapata, does make regular, in my experience quite unparalleled use of the word (written "indio," "intio," "idio," "itio," or the same using *y*, often with *-tzin* added). "Tlaxcalan" (*tlaxcaltecatl*) is still his basic category for describing himself and members of his community, so that *indio* will not be found on most pages, but he readily resorts to the term when ethnic groups are being juxtaposed or when there is need to emphasize ethnicity. Some typical examples are "mochi tlacatl espanullestin yndiotzintzin," "everyone, Spaniards and Indians" (ZM, f. 99); "quixtianotzintzin mextisotzintzin ydiotzintzin moquixtianochichihuan," "Christians [i.e., Spaniards], mestizos, and Indians who dress like Spaniards" (the group to go fight the English pirates at Veracruz; f. 109v); "Juan Bauh^ta yntiotzin," "Juan Bautista, Indian" (who made a metal cross for the Virgin of Ocotlan; f. 110v). Zapata makes very little use of *macehualli*, plural or singular, in this sense (though it does occur: "caxtilteca yhuan maçehualtin," "Spaniards and macehualtin"; f. 84). Retaining as he did a strong sense of rank, the majority of his references go to that, in particular when he wants to denigrate altepetl officials he disapproves of, as in referring to a group of them as "çequitin pipiltin cequitin maçehualtin," "some nobles, some macehualtin" (f. 100). Perhaps it was his conservative reservation of the word for indicating rank that impelled him to use *indio*. This aspect of Zapata's usage will require systematic study.

100. TA, pp. 30, 76; TC, doc. 71, p. 250.

101. BC, doc. 29, p. 186 (Huexotzinco, 1560); CH, 2: 16, 17, 99, etc.; TA (selection 15, p. 79; in this instance *iz*, an alternate word for "here," is used instead of *nican*). Other examples will be found in early annals of Tenochtitlan and Tlatelolco.

102. Since *macehualtin* was already fairly close to the indicated meaning, it was a natural alternative, and isolated early examples can be found. Consider the phrase, apparently a translation of "los indios de Coyoacan" in a Spanish original, produced in 1557 (BC, doc. 35, p. 216): "i nican tlaca cuyuacan macevaltin," "the people here,

Coyoacan macehualtin," with the two terms in close association even though *mace-hualtin* is probably not conceived in quite the same way as later. See also below at n. 106.

103. CH 2: 45 (1595), 48 (1599), 86, 97, 112 (the last three pair the two terms). Although less frequently, Chimalpahin uses "macehualtin" without *ti*, "we," in the same meaning (2: 55, 60).

104. CH, 2: 45, 134, etc. (processions), 122 (Mixteca).

105. CH, 2: 142. The pairing of a Spanish term with its approximate Nahuatl equivalent is especially characteristic of a word or meaning that is relatively new and not yet entirely established in usage. CH, 2: 22, uses "Nueva España tlaca," "New Spain people," by itself in speaking of indigenous people both noble and plebeian of Chimalpahin's own time.

106. MNAH AH, GO 14. On p. 134 Audiencia judges, the archbishop, and "timacehualtin" are said to have gone to a consecration at the shrine of the Virgin of Guadalupe in Tepeyacac. The term thus already includes indigenous people of high rank. If there is any doubt about the meaning of this passage, there is none in a second case, p. 138: "micque omentin timacehualtin ce español yhuan ce tliltic," "two of us macehualtin, one Spaniard, and one black died."

107. CH, 2: 54, 56, 63.

108. As in CH, 2: 60, where I am not sure whether the macehualtin who were shipwrecked were specifically commoners or not. Likewise on p. 62, I am not sure of the intention of "incal macehualtin," "the houses of the commoners?/indigenous people?"; here I tend to view "commoners" as more likely, but it is quite possible that in such cases Chimalpahin was not really making a distinction himself, since in so many instances the two meanings would overlap, and they were only in the process of becoming fully differentiated. All questionable cases I have seen involve the third-person "macehualtin" (and also once the singular "macehualli"; 2: 145). "Timace-hualtin" with the first-person plural subject prefix *ti-* ("we") unambiguously means indigenous people. Even when *macehualli* means primarily commoner, the reference is to an Indian commoner. True, Chimalpahin does say at one point that some of the Spanish fathers of mestizos were pipiltin, and some macehualtin (2: 22), and on another occasion, he calls a person in France (about whom he has heard a story) "çan cuitlapilli atlapalli," "just tail and wing," a traditional metaphor meaning "mace-hualli" (2: 91). But apart from his work, I do not recollect ever having seen Spaniards called macehualtin or an individual Spaniard called a macehualli; the two categories were mutually exclusive.

109. BC, doc. 27, pp. 166–73, 226–29. The Spanish translation does not per se mean that the terms were actually equivalent. Spanish speakers were much more concerned with the general category Indian than with rank among Indians, and were entirely capable of translating any Nahuatl rank specification as "Indian"; they also frequently rendered Nahuatl *tlacatl*, "person," in the same way, as with this same translator (p. 277, "los yndios de mesquitique"). Note also this phrase in a mundane document of Tepechpan (northern Valley of Mexico) in 1652—"espanoles yhuan ma-çehualtin," "Spaniards and commoners," translated into Spanish at the time as "españoles y naturales" (AGN, Tierras 1662, exp. 5, ff. 1v, 3v).

110. MNAH AH, GO 184, ff. 17, 17v, 21, 22–24. As far as I am aware, all

attestations in this source are in the mock-reverential. The term also occurs in the singular (ff. 17v, 22v). As usual, this set of annals does not contain the word indio.

111. A further indication in this direction is the modern *macehualcopa*, "mace-hualli-fashion," one of the terms used to designate the Nahuatl language; I imagine it took on this meaning in the second half of the colonial period, though I have seen no definite evidence to that effect.

112. See Haskett 1985, pp. 171–73.

113. López y Magaña 1980, docs. 1–4. The latest example of such usage that I have seen is in a document of 1658 from Tulancingo, but it is in Spanish ("doña Francisca la soapile") and refers to a person who died many years before (UCLA TC, folder 14, Nov. 4, 1658).

114. For just a few examples, see Dyckerhoff 1976, p. 177; and Gibson 1964, pp. 153, 165.

115. For one complaint of the nobles, see BC, doc. 29, pp. 188–89 (Huexotzinco, 1560); for election rhetoric, see Haskett 1985, pp. 147–51, 163–84.

116. Compare HTC, introduction, p. 5.

117. See Schroeder 1984, p. 209; and CH on almost any page dealing with pre-conquest matters. With the Molotecatl teuctli of the Cuernavaca region, the title seems to have virtually displaced the name (Carrasco 1972).

118. See the genealogical tables in Schroeder 1984.

119. See FC, book 6, pp. 219–60.

120. The Dominican chronicler fray Diego Durán says (1967, 2: 252) that in preconquest times the priests did the naming shortly after birth, giving metaphorical or whimsical names to the sons of lords according to their physiognomy or the implications of their day sign but simply naming the commoners after the day of birth.

121. See especially AZ and TC throughout; and the discussion in S. Cline 1986, pp. 117–21. It may be that in other places women received a broader selection of names (women's names in the Huexotzinco census [Prem 1974] would so indicate), but the evidence in two such massive and well-separated sources is impressive. Ordinal names for women appear even among the gods. Four goddesses of lust and dissolution make a perfect set: Teyacapan, Teiuc, Tlaco, and Xoco (FC, book 1, chap. 12 [p. 23 in 2d ed.]).

122. See TC, doc. 71, p. 248.

123. CH, HTC, Tezozomoc 1949, passim.

124. BC, doc. 1, p. 46.

125. See AZ throughout and the as yet unpublished Cuernavaca-region census materials in MNAH AH, CAN 549–51. There is considerable change from the presumably earlier to the presumably later of these records.

126. See AZ 1: xxv, 1, 4, 5, and in many other places. An alternate though perhaps less used term with the same meaning was *nican itoca*, "one's here-name," "local name" (one example is in AZ, 1: 5). Observe the parallel between the set -*macehualtoca* and *nican* -*toca* for indigenous names and the set *macehualtin* and *nican tlaca* for indigenous people.

127. For examples of such alternation, see MNAH AH, GO 185, pp. 7, 15 (Tepemaxalco/Calimaya), where the same person is called Juan Miguel one year and Juan de San Miguel the next; and CFP (Tepemaxalco, 1658), where the same person ap-

pears as Nicolás de San Pedro and Nicolás Pedro. Similar examples abound in the archives. It appears that frequently the second name had no baptismal sanction at all, not being mentioned in the baptismal records. Exactly when and how it was then acquired is not known.

128. See the many María Salomés in TCB from the 1570's forward. It was possible for a woman to have a surname based on a masculine saint, as with doña Leonor de San Francisco (López y Magaña 1980, doc. 3; Tetzcoco 1589), but this could not be collapsed to the short form. I have rarely seen the converse, a man with a surname taken from a female saint, but it could happen, as with the don Pablo de Santa María mentioned in the footnote to p. 118.

129. Appendix A, Docs. 1, 4. With the Azcapotzalco example, a formal will, one might suspect that a commonly used additional name was omitted, and Barry David Sell and James Braun, exploring in UCLA's McAfee collection, have now discovered that this was the case. But the other text, though lengthy, highly colloquial, and done by a writer ignorant and insouciant in matters of Spanish norms, also fails to give a hint of any second name even though it was crucial in that instance to identify the person properly. I am confident that many Nahuas were called by only one Christian name in their daily comings and goings.

130. Appendix A, Doc. 2. Likewise, Lázaro de San Pablo, so called in Culhuacan in 1580, was no doubt just Lázaro when at home in the San Pablo section of Mexico City (TC, doc. 21, pp. 66–71).

131. BC, doc. 2, p. 54; AGN, Tierras 3663, exp. 3, f. 4; TA, index of names. Among the many don Nicolás de Tolentinos was one in Tepetlixpan in 1690 (Tierras 2549, exp. 1, f. 55v).

132. CH has many examples; others may be seen in BC, and they pervade mundane documentation.

133. Alvarado was the name of an important line of the royal family of Tetzcoco; see López y Magaña 1980.

134. N&S, item 12.

135. See CH, 2: 24, 25, 29. On p. 29, fray Juan Páez and don Felipe Páez de Mendoza are mentioned within a few lines of each other. "Mendoza" was doubtless from the viceroy.

136. TA contains a range of Spanish surnames of this type.

137. See N&S, item 2; and TA, p. 139.

138. I remain unsure whether the more prominent names were always taken from a specific Spaniard or Spanish family or not. That is, was don Juan de Guzmán, tlatoani of Coyoacan, so named after some Guzmán actually in Mexico at the time, or simply because "Guzmán" was a symbol of high nobility for Spaniards in general?

139. Especially frequent is the combination Mateo Juárez, perhaps after some Spanish holy man or ecclesiastical writer whom I have not yet identified.

140. See TA, part 4, sec. 2.

141. See TC, docs. 67, 71, pp. 240, 246–50.

142. See Haskett 1985, pp. 401, 405.

143. BC, doc. 6, pp. 74–77.   144. Appendix A, Doc. 4.

145. NMY, doc. 2, pp. 94–95.   146. BC, doc. 3, pp. 58–59.

147. See TA, selection 25, pp. 125–26. The annals of Zapata (ZM) carry the demonstration of the point into the late 17th century.

148. Gibson 1964, pp. 158–60 (I must mildly protest against the omission of the crucial "don" and "doña" here); Haskett 1985, pp. 140–46, 366–67, 374–75, 407–23; N&S, item 2; L. Reyes García 1978 (see Rojas in the index). Fragmentary indications suggest that prominent Nahua families, unlike the Spaniards, who often kept several surnames of allied families alive in a single set of siblings and cousins, ordinarily gave all the children the same surname.

149. See Lockhart 1968, pp. 35–37.

150. See BC, doc. 1, pp. 44–53; and TA, pp. 21–22, with n. 129. At a remote time, "don" in fact *had* been the equivalent of "teuctli."

151. See Haskett 1985, pp. 387–88; N&S, item 2; TA, pp. 135–36, entry "(don) Alonso Gómez"; and Chap. 2 tables.

152. Compare the name of teuctli don Julián de la Rosa (Tlaxcala, 1566) with that of his wife María Cozcapetlatzin, not only without the doña but still with an indigenous second name (BC, doc. 1, p. 46).

153. See N&S, item 2; and TA, p. 22. TC (Culhuacan, ca. 1580) has some cases of vacillation that we lack sufficient context to interpret; see docs. 13, 42 (pp. 42, 144, [don] Juan Téllez), 45A (pp. 158–60, [don] Lorenzo de San Francisco), and 63 (p. 226, [don] Pedro de Suero).

154. See TA, pp. 22, 112.

155. See N&S, item 2.

156. I will give just two examples of this frequently seen phenomenon. A Nahuatl will of 1692 from the south–central Toluca Valley is issued by "don Juan Alonso," but the summary of the case done a century or more later speaks simply of "Juan Alonso indio tributario" (AGN, Tierras 2533, exp. 3, introductory page and f. 1). Doña Felipa de Jesús made her Nahuatl will in Soyatzingo in 1734; just after her death the Spanish officials carrying out an inventory referred to her as "Felipa de Jesús india" (ibid. 2555, exp. 14, ff. 1, 3).

157. Ibid. 1810, exp. 1, f. 3v.

158. Ibid. 70, exp. 4, f. 13v. The writer characteristically ignored the gender distinction between masculine *fulano* and feminine *fulana*.

159. The background on these householders also comes from CFP.

160. In Coatlichan (southern Tetzcoco region) in 1762, a man known on all ordinary occasions as don Sebastián Ignacio, who had been governor of the altepetl, appeared on one occasion as don Sebastián Ignacio de Buendía, making the quite credible claim to be a descendant of the "cacique" family of that name (AGN, Tierras 2338, exp. 8).

161. See N&S, item 12, for evidence concerning the Toluca Valley in this period.

162. CH, 2: 117 (Juan Pérez de Monterrey, governor of Tenochtitlan); Wood 1984, pp. 66, 68 (Cristóbal de Rojas Cortés, governor of Toluca in 1623). On the other hand, mestizos of this time who used the don—like don Juan Martín (CH, 2: 46, 78), also governor of Tenochtitlan, and the historian don Fernando de Alva Ixtlilxochitl—were accepting indigenous identity.

163. See Haskett 1985, p. 426; examples are from the late 18th and early 19th

centuries. Later in the 19th century, this was to become even more common, as with the well-known Nahuatl translator Faustino Galicia Chimalpopoca.

164. I speak of such wills as in BC, doc. 1, pp. 44–53, and L. Reyes García 1978, pp. 109–19, and of Nahuatl historical writings such as CH and HTC.

165. See Carrasco 1963; and L. Reyes García 1978, pp. 149–50. Spanish lawyers probably had a hand in this manner of presentation.

166. Haskett 1985, pp. 69–77; Tutino 1976, p. 186.

167. See Anguiano and Chapa 1976, especially p. 126; Dyckerhoff 1976, p. 167; and Gibson 1964, p. 156.

168. CFP; additional detail on the family will be found in Chap. 6.

169. Haskett 1985, chaps. 8–9; Tutino 1976, pp. 182–87.

170. See Gibson 1964, pp. 156–65.

171. AGN, Tierras 2553, exp. 5, ff. 1–2.

172. Ibid. 2554, exp. 12, f. 11. I have not been able to determine just what part of the Toluca Valley this passage is from.

173. UCLA TC, folder 23, ff. 22–23.

174. See, for examples, CDC, 1: 97–142.

175. As in the López y Magaña 1980 documents.

176. See L. Reyes García 1978, passim; and compare Haskett 1985, pp. 381–84.

177. See examples in MNAH AH, Fondo Franciscano 49, and many other places.

178. AGN, Tierras 3663, exp. 3, ff. 4–6.

179. See ibid. 2554, exp. 4, ff. 2, 16a, 23–23v, from Tlapitzahuayan, near Chalco Atenco, where the marginally prominent (don) Josef de la Cruz (see Chap. 6) is called an "indio cacique," and he and his wife Dominga de Santiago "indios principales," terms that must have originated among the Nahuas carrying on the litigation. In the accompanying Nahuatl texts, no epithets are used. As far as I now know, *cacique* in the broader sense appears in Nahuatl only in election documents (see Haskett 1985, pp. 90–91).

180. AGN, Tierras 2549, exp. 1, f. 1v.

181. Ibid. 2338, exp. 8, ff. 16–18.

182. L. Reyes García 1978, pp. 81, 83, 109–19, 150, 167–69, 175–80.

183. AGN, Tierras 2549, exp. 1, ff. 1–1v, 6, 37, 41, 50, 53–56. On f. 55v, the Spanish version of the will of (don) Josef de Aguilar (1690) has the phrase "son ustedes mis padres" directed to the alcalde, fiscal, and alcaldes pasados. This may be a late example of the older inverted use of *-ta* in the possessed form by rulers to refer to their higher subordinates. See also Schroeder 1984, p. 129.

184. CFP; N&S, item 12, for Pablo de la Cruz; AGN, Tierras 1501, exp. 3, ff. 13–14v (1667 will of don Pedro de la Cruz in Spanish translation); Tierras 2533, exp. 5, ff. 1–2v (will of don Juan de la Cruz, 1691). I have seen one use of the word *tlatoani* in connection with the de la Cruzes; in CFP, f. 6 (1659), don Pedro as governor is referred to as "tlatohuani don p⁰e de la crus gō̄r."

185. See Haskett 1985, pp. 399–404; Rounds 1982, especially pp. 67–75, 80–83; and Schroeder 1984, pp. 86–91, 99, 221, 223. For evidence of a dynasty-like family in 18th-century San Francisco Centlalpan (Chalco region), see the will of don Nicolás de Silva in NMY, doc. 10, pp. 117–21 (though nothing emerges about the

family's political role). Another is the Larios family in 17th-century Acatlan (UCLA TC, folder 23).

186. See Haskett 1985, pp. 391–92.

187. López y Magaña 1980, doc. 3. The Nahuatl phrase is "ynic niçihuatl."

188. An example is in CFP, f. 18 (Calimaya/Tepemaxalco in the Toluca Valley, 1683).

189. TC, docs. 38, 41, 64, 65, 74, pp. 126, 140, 230, 238, 256; TCB (see Chap. 6 for the female cofradía officials who were like cihuatepixque); CFP. See also S. Cline 1986, p. 54.

190. Future publications by Stephanie Wood and Robert Haskett should shed more light on this topic.

191. See Appendix A, Doc. 1; N&S, item 4; and Taylor 1979, p. 116.

Chapter 5

1. Such is the common conclusion of Gibson 1964; Offner 1983; Harvey 1984; and S. Cline 1984, 1986.

2. The perhaps bewildering variety of land categories in older Nahuatl is quite simple from a linguistic standpoint, consisting in nearly every case of a noun compounded with the word *tlalli*, "land." However, since in Nahuatl [t'] assimilates to a preceding [l], becoming [l] itself, *tlalli* appears as *-lalli* whenever the preceding noun stem ends in *l*, as in *calpol-lalli*. That *calpollalli* is so much more often seen than *tlaxilacallalli* despite the general preference for *tlaxilacalli* over *calpolli* may indicate that *calpolli* was at some earlier time the predominant term. The only attestation of *tlaxilacallalli* I can presently produce is from Azcapotzalco in 1738 (BC, doc. 17, p. 104), but I have seen the term on a few other occasions over the years, including for the earlier time period.

3. BC, doc. 14, p. 94.

4. Of which a large portion is published in AZ.

5. Williams 1984.

6. It is also possible that in sources such as the Cuernavaca-region records where even numbers predominate, the figures were merely appoximations.

7. See AZ, 1: 76, 85, 86, 100, and 2: 114.

8. Motolinia, Zorita, etc., as mentioned in Harvey 1984 and Williams 1984.

9. AGN, Tierras 1525, exp. 5, ff. 3, 5v, 6.

10. López y Magaña 1980; BC, doc. 17, p. 106 (Azcapotzalco, 1738).

11. Williams 1984, pp. 105–7 (Tetzcoco); BC, doc. 16, part 4, p. 154 (Coyoacan, ca. 1550). TC seems to use the terms interchangeably.

12. Compare López y Magaña 1980, doc. 1, p. 63; and Haskett 1985, pp. 478–79.

13. BC, docs. 9, 26 (part 7), pp. 88, 164.

14. AGN, Tierras 1525, exp. 5, ff. 5, 6, 28. See additional examples and discussion in Castillo F. 1972, p. 212.

15. AGN, Tierras 2553, exp. 5, f. 1.

16. BC, doc. 17, p. 106. See Molina's entry "cennequetzalli," "un estado" (a measure of length sometimes given as equivalent to seven feet). *Cennequetzalli* also appears in a document dated in 1571 in Tenochtitlan (AGN, Tierras 35, exp. 1, f. 6).

17. Williams 1984, p. 107.

18. TC, doc. 47, p. 168 (Culhuacan, 1581). One possible interpretation of the Culhuacan example, and the one to which I incline, is that the mecatl here was a linear measure of 200 units. See Haskett 1985, pp. 479–80, for the mecatl in the Cuernavaca region as a measure of 20 units (or thereabouts), with continuing uncertainty whether a lineal or areal measure is meant.

19. See AZ; Williams 1984; and Offner 1984.

20. See Motolinia 1971, pp. 134–35; and Zorita 1941, pp. 87–88.

21. BC, docs. 10, 11, p. 90; CDC, 2: 147–51.

22. AZ, 1: xliv. That the word for "field" in these passages consistently appears in the singular (*imil*) in no way affects the present matter, since *milli* as an inanimate noun does not show an overt plural even when the referent is plural. When a person has both irrigated and unirrigated land, they are clearly in different places. Several times in these records (MNAH AH, CAN 549–51) it is specifically said that a person has two different fields. I see no way to tell whether this is to be interpreted as an exception or, as so often in Nahuatl documents, as a general phenomenon rarely put on paper.

23. See AZ, 1: xlii–xliii.

24. For an example see AZ, 1: 7.

25. BC, doc. 9, pp. 84–89. Rebecca Horn (1989) has located Hueipolco and identified Palpan as the same unit as San Agustín (Tlalpan).

26. The nobleman who left the vacant land was don Martín de Paz, possibly Pedro de Paz's relative.

27. In Mexico City in 1593, four tlaxilacaleque of San Hipólito Teopancaltitlan were asked about the status of a property owned by one Ana Justina; the contemporary Spanish translation calls them *mayorales* (lower officials; AGN, Hospital de Jesús 298, exp. 4, ff. 5, 13). In the San Sebastián district in 1571, those used as witnesses to a land matter were a merino, two tepixque, and four huehuetque (AGN, Tierras 2789, exp. 1, f. 10). See also AGN, Tierras 35, exp. 1, f. 5, a 1573 case in the San Sebastián Cotolco district of Mexico City, involving 12 tlaxilacaleque giving a single unanimous opinion.

28. In Mexico City's San Sebastián district in 1563, the same people first called "the householders there" are later called tlaxilacaleque (AGN, Tierras 20, part 2, exp. 4, f. 8v). In Tlatelolco in 1591, the unnamed group is called *in oncan chaneque in tlaxilacaleque*, a phrasing implying that "the householders there" and "the tlaxilacaleque" are the same people (AGN, Tierras 57, exp. 8, f. 4). In another example from Tlatelolco, dated 1599, the phrasing *in tlaxilacaleque ihuan in oncan chaneque*, with the added word *ihuan*, "and, along with," sounds more as if the two are conceived as separate groups (NAC, ms. 1481). The truth seems to be that no sharp line was drawn in these situations between district officials and ordinary neighbors, since the function of both was to register the community's consensus.

29. NAC, ms. 1481. "People next to the house" translates *calnahuac tlaca.*

30. BC, docs. 14, 17, pp. 96, 104 (Azcapotzalco, 1703, 1738).

31. See Lockhart 1982, p. 385 (N&S, item 3). The survival of these practices is discussed below at nn. 58–59 and after n. 111.

32. Humboldt Fragment, illustrated partially in Gibson 1964, plate X; Williams 1984, pp. 118–120 (Tepetlaoztoc).

33. Williams 1984, p. 120. Nevertheless, Williams seems to equate the term with the house site in the narrower sense, coming to the unnecessary and I believe erroneous conclusion that in certain cases where no space is indicated for a house lot, the "calli" glyph is not to be interpreted as *callalli*.

34. See examples illustrated in ibid., p. 119; and in the Atenantitlan investigation (BC, doc. 9, pp. 84–89). As noted in Chap. 3, Nahuas of the postconquest period sometimes equated Spanish *solar*, "houselot," with *callalli*, including agricultural land. TC, doc. 12A, p. 38 (Culhuacan, ca. 1580), contains an example in which the *-solaryo* of a house has the ideal callalli dimensions of 20 units square.

35. Generally in the Culhuacan testaments such holdings are referred to as the house's *-atentlallo*, its "land at the edge of the water," but once chinampas are specifically called *callalli* (TC, doc. 39, p. 130), and another time a house has its *-calchinanyo*, its "house-chinampas that go with it" (doc. 51, p. 186). The house itself usually stood on a strip of *tlalmantli*, built up and leveled land.

36. Examples are found throughout TC (see, for example, doc. 56, p. 200), and the circumstances mentioned by Williams 1984, p. 120 (callalli with no indication of a house on it) constitute further evidence.

37. BC, doc. 9, pp. 86, 88.

38. UCLA TC, folder 1, ca. 1570, complaint against (don) Martín Jacobo. Similarly, in Culhuacan (1581) *icalchinanyo calli*, "the house's house-chinampas," are contrasted with *in hueca chinampan*, "where the distant chinampas are" (TC, doc. 42, p. 144).

39. BC, doc. 26, part 5, p. 160. See also, among others, the holdings of don Julián de la Rosa of Tlaxcala (BC, doc. 1, pp. 44–53), and those of the larger holders in TC. The holdings of don Luis Cortés (Coyoacan 1557) were scattered, though there is no specific mention of callalli (BC, doc. 12, p. 92). See also Horn 1989, chap. 5, sec. 3.

40. For an example of the use of *cecni*, see BC, doc. 3, p. 58 (Coyoacan region, 1617). Commoners occasionally did hold land in different calpolli at the same time, possibly while in transition from one to the other; for an example, see AZ 1: 47–48.

41. Compare Williams 1984, p. 113. No equivalent Nahuatl term has yet come to my attention. The frequent *itocayocan*, which is generally found in Nahuatl texts where a Spanish translation has these terms, means simply "at the place named . . ." Nevertheless, it may have had the more specific connotation in these contexts, or it may be that a place with a name is exactly what a paraje was.

42. Ibid., p. 119.

43. AGN, Tierras 2554, exp. 4, f. 23. For some references to callalli at various times and places, see BC, doc. 3, p. 58 (Coyoacan region, 1617); AGN, Tierras 2338, exp. 6, April 28, 1689 (Tetzcoco region); and NMY, doc. 10, p. 118 (Chalco region, 1736).

44. As seen repeatedly in AZ and Carrasco 1972.

45. See the dependents and lands of don Juan de Guzmán of Coyoacan (BC, doc. 26, pp. 152–165). See also Horn 1989, pp. 224–30.

46. Categories can be found in Williams 1984. See also AZ 1: 2 (*amilli*, "irrigated field," and *tepecentli*, "mountain maize"), 2: 115 (*tlalhuactli*, "dry or unirrigated land"); and MNAH AH, CAN 549, f. 42 (*aquilitl*, lit. "watered greens"). The Cuernavaca-region census records contain still others.

47. See, for example, Spalding 1984, pp. 30–32, 37–39, 41.

48. See S. Cline 1984, p. 291; Ixtlilxochitl 1975–77, 1: 386; and FC, book 11, p. 251. Whereas in most words for land categories a noun is compounded with and hence modifies *tlalli*, "land," here the opposite occurs, and *tlalli* modifies the other term, *(tla)cohualli*, "something purchased," so that *tlalcohualli* actually means "land-purchase," but in effect it is used in the same places where English would use "purchased land."

49. MNAH AH, CAN 550, f. 55: "ymil napuali ytequiyocahv / ahv ymilcoval onpuali"; on f. 33v, the head of Tlacatecpan has 80 units of tribute fields ("ypa tequity") and 180 of purchased fields. The purchased fields are referred to as -*milcohual*, with *milli*, "field," taking the place occupied by *tlalli* in the more frequent term, as explained in n. 48.

50. Ibid., f. 2v.

51. BC, doc. 26, pp. 154–60. One of the oldest known Nahuatl notarial documents (1548) records don Juan de Guzmán's purchase of a house, doubtless with its land, from the widow of the ruler of San Agustín, a constituent or dependency of Coyoacan (NMY, doc. 1, p. 93).

52. BC, doc. 22, pp. 119–20.

53. As in the quote at n. 31 above.

54. The -*uh* of -*patiuh* is originally the singular possessive ending, leaving -*pati*-, which appears related to *patla* (applicative *patilia*), "to substitute one thing for another."

55. *Namaca* is a combination of *na*-, related to the reciprocal prefix *ne*-, and *maca*, "to give." *Cohua* is probably related to a series of words with *cu*- or *co*- having to do with turning, twisting, doubling, reciprocity, etc. (as in *cuepa*, "turn, return"; *coatl*, "twin, guest-host, snake"; *coatequitl*, "turn-work"; *cuel*-, "double"; *cuemitl*, "furrow, earth turned over"; and *cueitl*, "wrap-around skirt").

56. AGN, Tierras 17, exp. 4, ff. 144–46.

57. The wording is *ce quimilli quachtli in ipatiuh*, "its price was twenty quachtli."

58. See Berdan 1982, p. 44.

59. The procedure is reminiscent of that followed in the sometimes forbidden, sometimes countenanced sale of encomiendas in Peru and Mexico in the conquest period. See Lockhart 1968, pp. 20–21; and Himmerich 1984, pp. 98–100.

60. Magdalena Teyacapan was not from Tolpetlac, but from Tlocalpan (which I have not yet been able to identify more closely).

61. BC, doc. 20, pp. 112–15. In this document, *callalli* is used in a way suggesting, though ambiguously, that it refers to all the different lands the owner had accumulated.

62. See S. Cline 1984, pp. 291–93. But in a later work (1986, pp. 152–55), Cline does not make an association between purchased land and nobility.

63. The following discussion has specific reference to Gibson 1964, p. 257ff, the most basic and seminal discussion; Harvey 1984, p. 84 (with citations of others), and S. Cline 1984, which principally follows Gibson. Offner 1983, pp. 124–39 also shares the tendency.

64. For postconquest cases, see examples in AZ (1: 76, 84, 85, 86, 100) of tribute officials holding land from the pipiltin (the altepetl) for the governmental function, any other land presumably being inherited or allocated from the calpolli.

65. BC, doc. 26, parts 4, 6, pp. 154–57, 162–65. See also AGN, Tierras 3548, exp. 3 [?], ff. 3, 4, where in 1606 don Francisco Cornejo, tlatoani of Tepexi, is said to have tecpillalli, translated into Spanish as "his patrimonial lands" (which he proceeds to sell). In my opinion, the attempt of Ixtlilxochitl (and Offner 1983 following him) to make a firm distinction between tecpillalli and other pillalli is ill-advised.

66. L. Reyes García 1975, 1979. Harvey also affirms that the calpollalli "contained various tracts which were dedicated to the support of temple and government" (1984, p. 91).

67. Broda 1976, pp. 51–52.

68. *Tequimilli* is first seen in a document dated 1558 in Mexico City (AGN, Tierras 17, part 2, exp. 4, f. 244), and *tequitcamilli* in Tetzcoco in 1596 (López y Magaña 1980, doc. 4). These forms imply the more basic ones in -*tlalli*, but I have not seen any occurrences of those forms before the 17th century.

69. The earliest attestation of *tequio* is in the Cuernavaca-region censuses of the time around 1535 to the early 1540's (MNAH AH, CAN 550, f. 55); a person's -*tequiocauh* is listed separately from his purchased fields. Another instance is in TC, doc. 60, p. 216 (Culhuacan, 1583), equating *tequio* and *ipan tequitihua*.

70. The earliest attestation of *ipan tequiti* is in the same source as in the immediately preceding note (MNAH AH, CAN 550, f. 33v); as in that case, the piece of land so qualified is listed separately from purchased fields. (See also Haskett 1985, appendix document.)

Since *tequiti* also means "to work," the phrase could potentially refer to any workable land, but as the editors of TC have observed, a passage in doc. 26, p. 82, expanding on *ipan tequiti* by reference to the coatequitl and other public duties, removes all doubt that tribute is meant. The editors of AZ translate *ipan* in phrases of this type as "for," that is, "in return for." For example, on p. 3, *cempohualli amilli . . . ipan quitlalia* is translated as "twenty units of irrigated field . . . for which she delivers . . ." Although this makes good sense, *ic* rather than *ipan* would be the normal word if such a meaning were intended, and "in return for" is not an otherwise known meaning of -*pan*. I favor the rendering "on, on the basis of," as in TC. It is true that since both translations make adequate sense in all instances, it is hard to give definitive proof of the inappropriateness of "for." Consider, however, the following closely related phrase. In a document of Xochimilco dated 1567, it is said that the relatives of a person given certain land *ipan atlizque tlaquazque*, "will eat and drink on the basis of it," or "from it," but surely not "for it" (AGN, Tierras 1525, exp. 5, f. 6v). For *ipan moxtlahua itlacalaquiltzin in rey nuestro senor*, a Spanish translator of the 18th century has "donde pago yo los reales tributos de su majestad," "*where* (or on which) I pay his majesty's royal tributes" (AGN, Tierras 2550, exp. 8, ff. 7, 8v).

71. López y Magaña 1980, doc. 4.

72. For example, TC, doc. 21, p. 68.

73. AGN, Tierras 2550, exp. 8, ff. 7, 8v (Xocotitlan, Tlalmanalco jurisdiction, 1722); Tierras 2554, exp. 4, ff. 1, 18 (Tlapitzahuayan, near Chalco Atenco, 1723–64).

74. S. Cline 1984, p. 291.

75. AGN, Tierras 1525, exp. 5, f. 6v. S. Cline (1984, p. 290) also cites another instance in which a tecpan awarded a man huehuetlalli (Culhuacan, before 1580).

76. For one specific proof, in Culhuacan (1581) we find a holding called both "the house-chinampas" and "calpollalli" (TC, doc. 42, p. 144).

77. AGN, Tierras 17, part 2, exp. 4, f. 244: *in ya quimotlaltia amo quito nohuehuetlal çan quimotequimiltia.*

78. There are many examples in TC, including docs. 38, 46, 47, 53, pp. 126, 162, 166, 194. In doc. 64 (p. 232), however, a woman seems to apologize for having sold some huehuetlalli, saying all the proceeds were used for house repair, not on her personally, so that here huehuetlalli is viewed as the permanent support of a household, ordinarily to be maintained at the cost of personal sacrifice.

79. CH, 2: 125. The tlaxilacaleque were thereby saying that they could do whatever they felt like with the land, including keeping an old cross standing on it, no matter what anyone else wanted.

80. UCLA TC, folder 1, ca. 1570, complaint against (don) Martín Jacobo. The Nahuatl reads *in tocalpollal in tomil . . . huel tocolhuan totahuan inmil tohuehuemil.* It is in this sense that *huehuetlalli* is used for the lands of the various teccalli (tlayacatl, sub-altepetl) of Cuauhtinchan (see L. Reyes García 1978, p. 8; and S. Cline 1984, p. 291).

81. See the discussion in S. Cline 1984, pp. 290–91.

82. TC, doc. 64, p. 232 (Culhuacan, 1585).

83. In a text from Azcapotzalco in 1738 is the following passage: "for it is tlalcohualli and our -tlalnemac," "ca tlalcohualli ihuan totlalnemac" (BC, doc. 17, p. 102).

84. S. Cline 1984, p. 288.

85. For example, a couple in Coyoacan in 1575 based their right to sell a plot on the fact that it was the wife's cihuatlalli ("huel icihuatlal"), given to her by her father and mother (BC, doc. 21, p. 116). S. Cline 1984, p. 288, cites an example from Xochimilco (1582) in which *cihuatlalli* is translated into Spanish as land coming through the maternal line, considered property of the mother.

86. UCLA Research Library, Special Collections, McAfee Collection, will of Tomás Feliciano. See TC, doc. 71, p. 48, for *cihuatlalli* in the absolutive.

87. For some examples of lesser categories, see S. Cline 1984, pp. 288–90.

88. Harvey 1984, p. 84. Gibson also implicitly shares this opinion.

89. See S. Cline 1984, p. 286; and Gibson 1964, p. 261. Gibson tends to give the impression that the treating of tlatocatlalli and the like as "private" and the combining of lands of different original status in a single estate were postconquest phe-

nomena, whereas I imagine that exactly the same was characteristic of preconquest times.

90. Harvey 1984, p. 91.

91. *Calpollalli,* Haskett 1985, p. 483; *tlaxilacallalli,* BC, doc. 17, p. 104; *tequitlalli,* AGN, Tierras 2554, exp. 4, f. 1; *callalli,* AGN, Tierras 2554, exp. 4, f. 23; *huehuetlalli,* UCLA TC, folder 23, ff. 22–23; *tlalcohualli,* BC, doc. 17, p. 102. The last also contains an attestation of *-tlalnemac* for 1738, but as I say, I do not consider the term to be exactly a land category.

92. Haskett 1985, pp. 494–97.

93. See Wood 1984, 113–21 (Toluca Valley).

94. See the examples in BC, docs. 14, 17, pp. 96, 104 (Azcapotzalco, 1703, 1738). See also AGN, Tierras 2338, exp. 6, Sept. 11, 1721 (Tezontla, Tetzcoco region), where on being given possession of a piece of land, the new owner's claims to 10 more varas were rejected because of the opposition of "the witnesses and the whole town (pueblo)."

95. See, for example, the case of Juan Alvaro in Coyoacan (1575), where no documentary proof is offered of his many purchases in the indigenous community, although a bill of sale is drawn up for his transfer of the land to the Dominican monastery (BC, doc. 20, pp. 112–15).

96. See, for example, BC, doc. 17, pp. 100–109. The 17th-century will used as authentication had no clear connection with the testator's putative great-grandchildren now (in 1738) selling a piece of land that might or might not be the same as one mentioned in the will.

97. AGN, Tierras 2338, exp. 8.

98. Ibid. 1805, exp. 3.

99. Ibid. 165, exp. 4.

100. BC, doc. 6, p. 74 (Metepec, 1795). The latest example I presently have of *matl* is in a document of May 2, 1642, done in Tulancingo (UCLA TC, folder 12), but I feel that later attestations are likely to appear.

101. BC, doc. 17, pp. 100, 106.

102. AGN, Tierras 442, exp. 5, f. 12v (Mexico City, 1630); an alleyway is described as 9 matl long, 1 vara wide. The larger unit is specifically defined in terms of varas not only in the passage just referred to (at n. 101), but in Amecameca in 1661 (AGN, Tierras 2553, exp. 5, f. 1). Among the abundant examples of the vara's increasing currency, see AGN, Tierras 442, exp. 5, f. 9v (Tlatelolco, 1620); Tierras 1780, exp. 5, f. 18 (Coyoacan, 1654); and Tierras 104, exp. 8 (Tlatelolco, Nov. 1, 1712). It is true that nothing but intuition and the fact of its being used elsewhere as a fraction of the quahuitl/matl assure me that the intention of the Nahuatl varas is not the larger indigenous unit rather than the Spanish yard.

103. See Gibson 1964, pp. 309, 311; and Brading 1978, pp. xiv, 66–67. As Brading justly observes (p. 67), "any presumption of great precision in these matters is a delusion."

104. For examples, see NMY, doc. 10, pp. 118–19 (Centlalpan, near Tlalmanalco, 1736); AGN, Tierras 2554, exp. 2, ff. 3, 5v (Amecameca, 1726); UCLA TC, folder 14, Dec. 19, 1640 (Tulancingo area); and NAC, Ms. 1477B (1), (4) (Calimaya,

Toluca Valley, 1738 and 1751). Phrases such as (in the last cited source) *calaqui nahui almud tlaolli*, "four almudes of maize enter there" (i.e., can be planted there), usually obviate the necessity of borrowing *sembradura*, but it does appear at times (NMY, doc. 10, p. 119).

105. For examples, see UCLA TC, folder 14, July 1, 1656, Sept. 9, 1657, Nov. 25, 1668 (Tulancingo region); and AGN, Tierras 2552, exp. 3, f. 3 (Soyatzingo in the Chalco region, 1736). In all these, Spanish *yunta* is treated as a loanword.

106. BC, docs. 13, 26 (part 5), pp. 94–95, 160–63; NMY, doc. 1, pp. 92–93.

107. See, for example, BC, doc. 17, pp. 100–109 (Azcapotzalco, 1738).

108. For an extreme example, see Karttunen and Lockhart 1978 (Amecameca 1746).

109. BC, doc. 13, pp. 94–95. In some 16th-century documents from Mexico City, one sees a Nahuatl paraphrase of Spanish *posesión*, *tlamacehualiztli tlalquitzquiliztli*, lit. "deserving or attaining, land seizing" (examples in AGN, Tierras 2789, exp. 1, f. 10v, 1572, and Tierras 59, exp. 3, f. 15v, 1586). Despite the typically Nahuatl double construction and the fact that *macehua* was used in older expressions for the first occupation of land, the phrase seems subtly unidiomatic, a kind of calque, as can be seen especially in its use as the object of the verb *maca*, "to give," as in the Spanish formula.

110. AGN, Tierras 2541, exp. 11, f. 3 (N&S, item 7, text 1). See a very similar document from the same place in 1783, except that it is written in Spanish (Tierras 2541, exp. 11, f. 5; N&S, item 7, text 4).

111. See Gómez de Cervantes 1944, pp. 134–35, and below at n. 118 about fees for sales.

112. AGN, Tierras 442, exp. 5, ff. 9v, 12v.

113. Ibid. 2541, exp. 11, f. 3 (N&S, item 7, text 1). Despite the indigenous concept, the phrase contains a Spanish loanword for corner (*nahui esquinas*).

114. AGN, Tierras 442, exp. 5, f. 7v.

115. NMY, doc. 1, p. 93 (Coyoacan, 1548), is a bill of sale, though not yet following the standard formula, and BC, doc. 15, pp. 98–99, contains a full-fledged example from the early 17th century. Horn 1989 has a whole chapter (chap. 4) on the genre, with full texts in the appendix. The term carta de venta appears as a standard loan phrase in Nahuatl documents, but it was probably unanalyzed, that is, used without any awareness of the separate meaning of its constituent parts. *Venta*, "sale," did not displace the corresponding indigenous vocabulary and has yet to be found in a Nahuatl text by itself.

116. See the action against noblemen selling off teccalli lands in early Tlaxcala (TA, selection 9, pp. 85–86).

117. See, for example, AGN, Tierras 442, exp. 5, f. 12 (Mexico City, 1630: flooding, seller a poor old woman who needs the money to live); BC, doc. 15, p. 98 (Coyoacan, ca. 1610–20: to pay tribute and debts); and BC, doc. 17, p. 102 (Azcapotzalco, 1738: for masses). Horn 1989 (pp. 156–60 and appendix) has many examples (not tequitcatlalli, and other reasons).

118. AGN, Tierras 2548, exp. 3, ff. 4, 5, 9v, and unfoliated section. Note that both buyer and seller were apparently ordinary commoners. José Lázaro had only three pieces of land: the one he had bought, the one he already had next to it, called

in Spanish "de repartimiento," and a third said to be located very far from the district (barrio). The *l-tl* sequence in "notlaxilacaltlahuan" is unusual, though not entirely without parallel. Only once have I ever seen an open, formal statement of the payment of fees to altepetl officials. A land transfer in Mexico City in 1621 includes an affirmation by the purchaser that he paid the alcaldes and notary 5 pesos in costs for issuing a bill of sale and giving him possession, over and above the 15 pesos he paid for the property (AGN, Tierras 84, exp. 2, f. 3).

119. Examples will be found scattered through TC; compare S. Cline 1986, p. 154.

120. As in the above mentioned example of Juan Alvaro (Coyoacan, 1570's), who acquired several pieces of land from indigenous people through trade and purchase, then sold them at a high price (140 pesos) to the Dominican monastery. He had previously sold another piece to a neighbor (BC, doc. 20, pp. 112–17).

121. AGN, Tierras 442, exp. 5, ff. 9–10.

122. Ibid. 2338, exp. 6.

123. TC, doc. 4, p. 20. The same procedure of asking for money in return for bequests was applied to property other than real estate, as we will see in Chap. 6.

124. AGN, Tierras 1520, exp. 6, ff. 8–9v (Huejotla, 1632).

125. Horn 1989, pp. 264–68, demonstrates in detail the popularity of *patrimonio* and its equivalence with *huehuetlalli* in the Coyoacan region. A passage from Mexico City, 1563, shows the whole complex already in existence: *huel totlatqui in tlalli ca topatrimonio tohuehuetlal*, "the land is fully our property, for it is our patrimony, our huehuetlalli" (AGN, Tierras 22, part 1, exp. 4, f. 1). The term also occurs in the Cuernavaca region as early as 1579 (Haskett 1985, appendix doc. 5, p. 663).

126. See above at n. 92.

127. See Gibson 1964, pp. 265–67; Haskett 1985, pp. 574–79; and S. Cline 1986, pp. 155–56.

128. Compare Haskett 1985, chaps. 8–10; and Tutino 1976, pp. 182–86. It is true that Spanish haciendas also normally consisted of separate, often named and noncontiguous parts, but those parts (estancias, ranchos, and sets of caballerías) were themselves large consolidated holdings of a kind rarely found in the indigenous scheme of things.

129. Gibson 1964, especially chaps 6, 11–13. I believe that much more can be done on the basis of specific case material in the Civil and Criminal sections of the AGN, but such research would stand somewhat aside from the main thrust of the present project.

130. See Berdan 1982, p. 43.

131. Berdan 1982, p. 44.

132. BC, doc. 34, pp. 208–13.

133. See TA, pp. 23 (at n. 135), 25, 58 (item 157), and 79–84 (selection 8).

134. BC, doc. 25, pp. 138–49.

135. See S. Cline 1986, appendix 1, pp. 173–75.

136. NMY, pp. 54–55, 93 (doc. 1).

137. Compare Berdan 1982, p. 44, and Las Casas, quoted there.

138. Some passages, like this one in MNAH AH, CAN 551, f. 76v (79v alternate foliation), are set up in such a way that it is impossible to be sure whether *tlacoco-*

hualoni applies to the quachtli alone or also to some or all of a series of items like the following: "Here is the tlacocohualoni: 30 tribute quachtli, 20 hand cloths, 1,600 cacao beans, 200 turkey eggs, 10 turkeys, 1,200 chiles, 2,400 meals [*tlaqualli*]." Most passages, however, seem to equate the term specifically with tribute cloth, quachtli; see AZ, 1: 140; 2: 117; and MNAH AH, CAN 549, ff. 37v, 42.

139. NMY, pp. 42–43; Celestino Solís et al. 1985, pp. 44, 51. See the entry "dinero" in Brewer and Brewer 1971 and Key and Key 1953.

140. See NMY, p. 81. TA, selection 22, p. 118 (Tlaxcala 1562), has *pesos de oro común*.

141. See, for example, Gibson 1964, p. 357.

142. See ibid., pp. 202–5 and especially p. 209.

143. See Haskett 1985, pp. 504–7.

144. AGN, Tierras 2554, exp. 2, ff. 3–13.

145. TC, doc. 56, p. 200.

146. See Gibson 1964, pp. 76, 153 (with the references in n. 83). Part of the problem is that the word *rentero* used by 16th-century Spanish writers could refer to a dependent, but the passages have sometimes been interpreted differently by more recent scholars.

147. Examples in S. Cline 1986, p. 180.

148. AGN, Tierras 1780, exp. 5, ff. 17–18. The standard phrase for putting something in hock, used here among other places, is *(qui)tlalia prenda*, using the verb *tlalia*, "to place (down)," with the referent of the object prefix *qui-* being the goods hocked. In a 1581 example from Culhuacan, however, the verb appears to be *mana*, "offer" (or possibly by syllable omission the verb is *maca*, "give"; TC, doc. 41, p. 138). See also S. Cline 1986, p. 94.

149. In the cabildo records of Tlaxcala for the year 1547, *cohua*, "to buy," and *namaca*, "to sell," are used in connection with the forced hiring out of drunks as punishment (BC, doc. 22, pp. 118–19; on p. 118, last paragraph, "yeua macozque" should read "yc namacozque"). *Namaca* is also used in relation to a governor taking money for hiring out vagrants in Huejotla (Tetzcoco region) in 1634 (NMY, doc. 7, p. 107).

150. See TC, doc. 10, p. 35. Recall also the case of José Lázaro above at n. 118, with installment paying, confusion with pawning, and the original owner eventually claiming the land back.

151. Compare ANS, pp. 59–60, and TA, p. 40 (item 36 and n. 14). In early Tlaxcala, words of the *tlanehua* set are used in reference to real estate in a meaning verging on or including "to rent."

152. See TC (Culhuacan, ca. 1580), docs. 26, 41, pp. 82, 136, and others; and BC, doc. 15, p. 98 (Coyoacan, ca. 1620). *Tlanehuia* as "to borrow money" does occur as an exception (TA, selection 22, p. 118; Tlaxcala, 1562).

153. The causative *tlacuiltia*, "to lend (money)," is quite rare, but for an example see TC, doc. 41, p. 136 (Culhuacan, 1581). *Tlaneuhtia* may have become the usual term when *pialia*, "to owe," and *pialtia*, "to lend," faded out after the early 17th century (see below at n. 158). A will of April 28, 1689, from Tezontla (Tetzcoco region) has the passage *onictlaneuhtili nocompadre don Juan Andres 6 t^{o}s*, "I lent my compadre don Juan Andrés 6 tomines"; the word is used the same way in another will

from the same place dated Dec. 20, 1710 (AGN, Tierras 2338, exp. 6). Both times, repayment is specifically requested.

154. Molina, Spanish, f. 44v.

155. As in BC, doc. 3, pp. 60, 62 (Coyoacan region, 1617).

156. TC, doc. 56, p. 202. For some later examples of *pialia*, see BC, docs. 3, 4, pp. 60, 66; and NMY, doc. 3, pp. 98–99 (all from the Coyoacan region, first two decades of the 17th century).

157. See NMY, doc. 3, pp. 98–99, where "pia" is used for a whole list of people who owe small amounts of money to the testator; and BC, doc. 3, p. 61, where the debt of one Fabián is so described.

158. For examples, see BC, doc. 4, p. 66; and TC, doc. 81, p. 276 (the latter case is unambiguously a true loan). At the same time, *pialtia* could still refer to simple custodianship, either of money or of goods; see TC, docs. 36, 81, pp. 118, 274.

159. BC, doc. 27, p. 168. A Spanish translation specifically renders the word as *deber* (pp. 225, 227).

160. On Carochi, see Karttunen 1983, p. 90. For a later example of *huiquilia*, "owe," see AGN, Tierras 2338, exp. 6, will of Dec. 20, 1710 (from Tezontla, Tetzcoco region). Both Brewer and Brewer 1971 and Key and Key 1953 attest to the continuing use of the word in modern times.

161. For the "not yet paid" phrase, see TC, doc. 41, pp. 134–41; BC, doc. 4, pp. 66–67; and NMY, doc. 3, pp. 99–100. The last uses *pia* and *pialia* with money lent as opposed to purchase. Other common monetary terminology used by the Nahuas may also have varied subtly or not so subtly during a time of transition. From early texts forward, equivalents for "pay" and "spend" seem to be functioning much as in European practice, but the word for "pay," *ixtlahua*, originally (and apparently still at the conquest) meant "to restore to someone that which is his," and thus emphasized restitution or equivalence rather than paying out a certain amount of money. *Poloa*, which took over the function of "to spend," basically meant "to destroy, efface, make disappear." It may, however, have already had a relatively neutral meaning akin to "spend" in preconquest times. Consider Spanish *gastar*, which means both "spend" and "waste." Often in Nahuatl *-tech monequi*, "to be used for something or someone," appears where "spend" might be expected; but the same occurs in European languages.

162. TA, selection 22, pp. 118–19.

163. Examples in TC, doc. 41, p. 136; and Appendix A, Doc. 1. See also S. Cline 1986, p. 92.

164. NMY, doc. 3, pp. 98–100. The transactions appear to have been true loans of cash rather than debts for merchandise sold. In cases of the latter type in the document, the merchandise is specifically mentioned, and with the loans the verb *pia* is used, carrying an even stronger implication of the debtor having actually received the money than *pialia*. For evidence of moneylending by professional pochteca, see TC, doc. 41, pp. 134–41; Appendix A, Doc. 2; and the discussion in S. Cline 1986, pp. 91–93.

165. BC, doc. 3, pp. 58–63.

166. The play is extant in a typed copy made by J. H. Cornyn of another copy of 1912 (in Library of Congress, box "Aztec Dramas," MMC 2771 in the Library of

Congress, under the title "The Merchant"); it bears the heading "Neyxcuintilli yn-techpa tlantohua yn pochtecatl," "Exemplary play speaking of a merchant." The "original" was written out in Tulancingo in 1687 by a don Josef Gaspar (p. 21), but the text itself contains a reference (p. 39) to the date 1627 as a recent year. There is no reason, of course, why a yet earlier version could not have had another date.

167. See Gibson 1964, pp. 352–53; and BC, docs. 25, 26, pp. 138–149, 150–51 (the last contains an explicit statement that the market belongs to the tlatoani).

168. The Coyoacan lists, four of them (BC, doc. 25, pp. 138–49), are found among several documents that can be dated to a time close to the year 1550. Their purpose is to record taxes paid to the governor/tlatoani of the altepetl; each trade specialty is listed in turn, together with the amount paid by that group. The Mexico City market list is a copy of an earlier diagram of a market in the city (at exactly what site is not clear), with both glyphs and Nahuatl words indicating what was sold in spaces defined by lines forming rows of boxes. The document has been mentioned by Gibson (1964, p. 569, n. 132) and reproduced by Durand-Forest (1971, pp. 121–24). Aubin's belief that the market was in the capital may have been conjecture, but the amount of Spanish goods available at an early time confirms the attribution. Although the copy is a late one of unknown provenience, its careful reproduction of gaps in the original and its close agreement with other lists on obscure items (such as _cabezones_, "collars") help establish its authenticity, as do its Nahuatl spellings and vocabulary (as opposed to the patently posterior calligraphy). The product list agrees especially closely with the trade names in book 10 of FC. Indeed, some of the words used— "Castilla tlascalli" for wheat bread instead of _pan_ or _pan de trigo_, "mecahuehuetl" rather than _vihuela_ or _guitarra_—tend to indicate a time of composition in the 1540's and no later than the early 1550's. On the other hand, the document with its Spanish goods and what appears to be a Spanish-style fountain in the middle of the market does not represent the state of things at conquest or in the first few years thereafter. Since many of the spaces on the diagram are blank in the extant version, one can presume that yet more trade groups were functioning than are indicated.

The primary list for Tlaxcala is from 1545 (BC, doc. 34, pp. 208–13). Composed under the auspices of Spanish officials wanting to establish prices for travelers, it became in indigenous hands more a list of the main foods available in the market. Unlike the other lists, it proceeds by individual items for sale (e.g., different types of chiles) rather than by group or space. Nonfood items are hardly touched. A supplemental list of 1549, still made for the same purpose, adds a few more items (TA, p. 42, item 55). Other chance discussions in the Tlaxcalan cabildo minutes of regulations for or disputes with craftsmen, extending over the years to 1563, add the names of some trade groups (TA, calendar items 28, 179, 194, 204).

169. On the Coyoacan lists, no commodity seems to be listed for two separate groups of boat people (_acalpan tlaca_, "people on boats"). Conceivably, they actually sold boats, but it seems to me more probable that they simply sold certain merchandise from off their boats. Also, one trade group is listed only by its unit of origin (Iztacapan); probably its specialty was so well known that the list makers felt no need of being specific.

170. One may wonder whether the assessments reflect the value of goods and profitability for individual tradespeople or simply the bulk of business done. Most groups paid one-half, one, or two tomines. Those over two tomines stand out. The

lists tend to be organized from highest to lowest assessments, and list no. 3 follows that criterion quite strictly. At the top are the wood dealers with 22 tomines (probably representing several local trade groups) and the associated pine-torch splitters with four and split-oak sellers with three, all reflecting the area's greatest ecological specialty, but surely not its most lucrative business for given individuals. Others in the high range, however, were producers of more sophisticated items: candles (6 tomines), rabbit hair (5), and colors (4). Considering that such things as bells and Spanish-style collars are found at the half-tomín level, it seems all in all that the bulk of a trade rather than the specific value of wares was decisive. (The Spaniards, on the other hand, placed taxes primarily on items of high specific value.)

171. TC, doc. 21A, p. 40 (Baltasar León, *tlatzoncatopile*), doc. 29, p. 94 (Mateo Juárez Tecpanecatl, *tetzotzoncatopile*). See also S. Cline 1986, p. 90.

172. See TA, pp. 26–28, and the references there given.

173. See Gibson 1964, pp. 214, 356.

174. On the other hand, it is important to keep in mind that there was a whole range of imported or high-quality goods for which Spaniards went almost exclusively to Spanish merchants or artisans outside the marketplace proper (though their shops might be on it or in the case of Mexico City's famous Parián actually built in the middle of the square), and that this trade far outweighed the markets in money value.

175. MNAH AH, GO 184; the passage describing a specific episode is partially quoted and discussed in Chap. 9.

176. See Gibson 1964, pp. 354–57, 395; N&S, item 12; and Lockhart and Otte 1976, pp. 143–45.

177. Spaniards made a distinction between the *mercader*, the long-distance merchant involved in wholesale as well as retail, and the *tratante* or small trader, retailing goods usually locally produced and of less value. For the verb *pochtecati* (lit. "to act as a pochtecatl") Molina gives "to be a merchant or dealer ('mercader o tratante')," erasing the distinction. For *oztomecati*, "to act as an oztomecatl," he gives the nearly identical "to deal or sell merchandise ('tratar o mercadear')." But it is possible Molina understood "mercadear" as "to do business in a market," in which case the pochtecatl could be construed as higher ranking. In FC, book 9, the two terms apply to the same groups of people and on occasion appear as a pair, the only observable difference being that *pochtecatl* is used much more. In a passage in the Tlaxcalan cabildo minutes, *oztomecatl* refers to outsiders bringing wares in, *pochtecatl* to local merchants, but elsewhere in the document the terms are paired (see TA, p. 28, and references given there). The oztomeca of the Coyoacan market were, as seen above, mainly if not entirely people from inside the altepetl district. Chimalpahin on one occasion equates *pochtecatl* and *mercader*, speaking of "españoles mercaderes pochteca," "Spanish merchants (or) pochteca" (CH, 2: 92).

178. FC, book 9, p. 12. The passage speaks of six calpolli but gives seven names, headed by Pochtlan. This sort of discrepancy is seen not infrequently in Nahuatl texts, so there may have actually been seven groups, but another possibility is that Pochtlan is a general term including the others. The question also arises whether the merchants were organized into separate units called calpolli or simply had one unit within each of six altepetl calpolli (which that merchant group may have dominated), in the same fashion as various trade groups of the Coyoacan market.

179. See Gibson 1964, p. 398; and Codex Mendoza 1980, f. 70r.

180. BC, doc. 25, pp. 138–49; Dyckerhoff 1976.

181. TA, pp. 28, 50 (item 114). See also Berdan 1986; Gibson 1964, pp. 358–61; and Szewczyk 1976.

182. MNAH AH, GO 14, pp. 114, 135 (1565, 1566).

183. Berdan 1982, p. 176; Gibson 1964, pp. 271, 287–88; Szewczyk 1976, pp. 140, 142.

184. TC, doc. 41, pp. 134–41 (1581); see the discussion in S. Cline 1986, pp. 90–94. Even these two are not themselves called *pochtecatl*, but the nature of their dealings and the fact that the son gave merchandise to someone with which to *pochtecati*, "act as a pochtecatl," leaves no doubt.

185. TC, doc. 28, pp. 86–91. See also S. Cline 1986, p. 97.

186. NMY, doc. 2, pp. 94–97.

187. TC, docs. 44, 52, 53, 81, pp. 152–55, 188–91, 192–95, 272–77; see the discussion in S. Cline 1986, pp. 93–95.

188. Writing mainly in the first two decades of the 17th century, Chimalpahin still uses *pochtecatl*, but only in reference to Spanish and Japanese merchants (CH, 2: 92, 133, 141).

189. BC, doc. 3, pp. 58–63. See mentions of Juan Fabián in other contexts in BC, p. 3; and Lockhart and Schwartz 1983, p. 175. Accompanying Juan Fabián's will are two Nahuatl memoranda (*memorias*) explaining in considerable detail the obligations his son-in-law Diego Francisco had incurred for the loss of animals, other expenses mainly related to the packtrain, and fruit he had taken to sell. These documents raise the possibility that Juan kept written accounts of his business in the Spanish fashion. Yet since he was apparently illiterate, he could hardly have produced such clean and sophisticated documents himself. Some indigenous person did so, but the memoranda have the air of having been prepared at a single time after the fact, doubtless with information Juan Fabián supplied, rather than kept on a current basis. In some fashion, whether in his head or through some system of marks and signs (of preconquest provenience or not), Juan was keeping precise track of a number of miscellaneous items of expense across significant periods of time. The fruit Juan grew and sold is called in Nahuatl *tzapotl*, often translated as zapote or sapota fruit, but as used in some texts it seems possible that the meaning was broader.

190. NMY, doc. 3, pp. 98–100. Let me take this occasion to correct a probable error in translation. "Teoyotica noconeuh" (para. 26 of the will) is rendered as "my legitimate child." While *teoyotica* is found in just this meaning in many texts, it did not necessarily mean legitimate or by marriage, but referred to anything sanctioned by the church. One's offspring "through divinity" could also be one's godchild, as seen in the Culhuacan testaments (TC, docs. 20, 45, pp. 64, 156; see also S. Cline 1986, p. 220, n. 21). Since Bárbara Agustina gave her house to her daughter and only a turkey hen to Francisca, "teoyotica noconeuh," the translation should doubtless be "my godchild."

191. In FC, book 10, the illustrations from 119 through 148 show many women as sellers instead of men, and the Nahuatl texts take no position on the gender of the vendors. Yet the corresponding English translations speak of men, and so for the most part do the original Spanish renditions of Sahagún (Sahagún 1975, book 10); a note in FC, book 10 (p. 69, chap. 19), takes cognizance of the anomaly.

192. CH, 2: 39, 102, 124–25. The chocolate drink vendor is called a "chocola-namacac," the only occurrence of the word "chocolate" in a Nahuatl text of which I am presently aware. For the trade of Francisco the tailor Chimalpahin uses both the Nahuatl *tlatzonqui* and the Spanish *sastre*.

193. TC, doc. 53, pp. 192–95. See also S. Cline 1986, pp. 93–94.

194. TC, doc. 52, pp. 188–91. See also S. Cline 1986, p. 96.

195. See Haskett 1985, pp. 564–74, for the best-worked-out examples.

196. See Gibson 1964, pp. 349–52, 387, 397–402, and Szewczyk 1976, pp. 142–43, 146–47. One possible source of information lies in the lists of Indian witnesses who appeared before Spanish authorities, which sometimes give their occupations. For example, of five witnesses from Atocpan (Milpa Alta district, Xochimilco jurisdiction) in Mexico City in 1638, all with double first names and illiterate, aged 35 to 60, four are identified by trade. One was a butcher and three had trades related to wood—a woodcutter (*leñador*), a dresser of planks and shingles (*oficial de hacer tablas y tajamanil*), and a transporter of planks and beams (*trajinero de tablas y viguetas*; AGN, Criminal 234, ff. 83–96v). The systematic collection of such lists would no doubt result in a much better picture of Indian occupational specialties in various times and places, and of the type of people practicing them, than emerges from synthesizing statements of Spanish officials and other observers, or from census documents.

197. See BC, doc. 26, part 1, pp. 150–51, for the continuing duties of Coyoacan artisans to the tlatoani/governor as of ca. 1550.

198. TA, pp. 24, 49 (item 103); see also pp. 61, 63 (items 179, 194).

199. UCLA TC, folder 1, f. 8 (also in N&S, item 6, text 1). The painters are called *tlapallacuiloque*, "color painters," to distinguish them from writers (a *tlacuilo* could be either a writer or a painter; see Chap. 8). None of the 11 could sign. Seven of their surnames were either saint's names written out in full (e.g., Juan de San Francisco) or religious names (e.g., Gabriel de los Angeles); two were the quasi-Indian name Juárez, and two were full-fledged Spanish (Delgado and Alvarez). None of the 11 bore the "don," but none had a simple double-first-name appellation or an indigenous surname. They thus fall into the higher medium range of the naming scale of their time. The painters are not identified by any altepetl subunit or given any organizational definition other than "we painters." The cloths they were working on are as mysterious as they are interesting: six *tilmatli huehuey tlaixtlapachiuhcayotl* "large cloths for covering (the face?)." Perhaps they were awnings.

200. A volume in AGN, Tierras, has the story—from somewhere in the northern half of the Valley of Mexico in the 18th century, if my recollection is correct—about an indigenous man trained as a carpenter who came into the community from the outside, married a local woman, and stayed permanently. There were questions about his rights, so in his support his side argued that he had frequently volunteered to do repair work on the local church. Since I saw these records before the present project had taken shape, I took no notes and did not keep the reference.

201. AZ, throughout.

202. See especially TC, doc. 49, p. 178. For more examples of women weaving and related discussion, see S. Cline 1986, pp. 89–90, 113–14. TC is a mine of difficult technical terms having to do with spinning, weaving, dyeing, etc.

203. For example, see NMY, doc. 3, pp. 99–100, where the Bárbara Agustina in the text above (Coyoacan region, 1608) was weaving a *huipil* (a kind of blouse) for herself. *Onictetecac* is there incorrectly translated as "I spun"; it should read "I warped" or "set up on the handloom."

204. In 1587, Pedro Toçan had in his Mexico City house a loom and two lathes that his son had been operating (AGN, Tierras 442, exp. 5, f. 7). Around 1689 to 1710, Juan Miguel had in his house in Tezontla (Tetzcoco region) a small loom with its gear, two lathes, and two carding apparatuses (ibid. 2338, exp. 6). Spanish loan vocabulary is used for all these things in both instances: *telar, torno, carda.*

205. BC, doc. 1, pp. 44–45, 50–51. Later attestations, as in Chimalpahin, involve the wearing of archaic costume for purposes of pageantry (see CH, 2: 41, 49). In this limited form, however, traditional indigenous garb or what was thought to be such long persisted. When, in 1674, a new saint was honored in Puebla, the cabildo of Tlaxcala was invited; three members, including the annalist Zapata, accepted the invitation, and they went "dressed as Tlaxcalans" ("motlaxcaltecatlaquetique"; ZM, ff. 90–91v).

206. See NMY, p. 22; and Brewer and Brewer 1971, entry "camisa."

207. Gómez de Cervantes 1944, pp. 135–36. In this whole passage, the author is determined to show the humility and misery of Indian life to justify different regulations and legal officers for Spaniards and Indians. See Carrillo y Gariel 1959, pp. 44, 47, for opinions of contemporary outside observers that Indians generally wore shirts and pants (*zaragüelles*).

208. Appendix A, Doc. 2.

209. Gómez de Cervantes (1944) uses this word, but considers the ones the Indians wore to be short and tight-fitting (p. 136). See also NMY, p. 65; S. Cline 1986, pp. 114–15; and AGN, Hospital de Jesús 210, no. 67 (Cuernavaca, ca. 1605–10, "çarahueras"). A man in Mexico City in 1588 was outfitted with shirt (*camisa*), cloak (*tilmatli*), and *zaragüelles* (AGN, Tierras 59, exp. 3, f. 17).

210. TC, doc. 57, p. 206.

211. AGN, Bienes Nacionales 339, item 9. See also NMY, p. 68.

212. TC, docs. 13, 28, pp. 42, 88; NMY, pp. 62, 63, 71.

213. See TC, doc. 56, p. 200 (Culhuacan, ca. 1580), where Miguel Huantli mentions *notilma nofrezada*, "my tilmatli and frezada." In two cases, men seem to speak of wearing a frezada. Pedro Toçan (Mexico City, 1587; AGN, Tierras 442, exp. 5, f. 7), says *centetl frezada nicnoquentia*, "a frezada that I wear." *Quentia*, the verb used, means generally "to wear (clothing)," and more specifically (see Molina) "to put on or wear a cloak or cape." A similar example using *quemi*, a related verb of identical meaning, can be seen in TC, doc. 15, p. 52. Nevertheless, since the basic meaning is "to cover" and *tilmatli* in addition to meaning "a specific kind of male garment" meant "cloth" in general, ambiguities remain. In fact, in the second example here, the verb has the auxiliary *-toc*, which can imply a reclining position, hence use as a blanket.

214. AGN, Criminal 234, f. 128. An even more impressive outfit, including a *capote*, or Spanish cape, is recorded for 1652, but the example comes from the far west, outside central Mexico proper (BC, doc. 8, pp. 80–81).

215. AGN, Criminal 234, f. 128. Molina glosses *tlapachiuhcayotl* as "the cover of something, or a woman's veil and headdress ('toca')."

216. AGN, Tierras 2555, exp. 14, ff. 12, 14, 20v. In general, alas, Nahuatl documents so far seen are not informative on indigenous dress after about the middle of the 17th century.

217. A Culhuacan text of 1580 specifically equates *tlaltepoztli* and *azadón* (TC, doc. 15, p. 52). So do Molina (Spanish, f. 2v, under "açada o açadon") and Pedro de Arenas in his 1611 manual (1982, p. 142). The Spanish loanword sometimes replaces the indigenous word in Nahuatl texts; see L. Reyes García 1978, p. 140 (Cuauhtinchan, 1589).

218. TC, docs. 24, 28, pp. 74, 88, 91. See Rojas Rabiela 1984 for a documented discussion of preconquest tool types; see also S. Cline 1984, p. 140. There is apparently some possibility that the preconquest huictli already sometimes had a copper blade, but this is dubious if it rests on evidence like that of Francisco Clavijero, centuries removed, who was so out of the picture that he took Spanish *coa*, "digging stick," to come from Nahuatl *coatl*, "snake," rather than from an indigenous word of the Caribbean, as it actually did. Nahuatl *coatl* does not have the meaning "digging stick" in any text that I have seen. The Culhuacan texts also mention a *chicohuictli*, *chico-* being an element meaning "sideways, to one side, crooked," etc. (TC, doc. 75, p. 260). Whether this is different from the ordinary huictli I am not prepared to say.

Given Nahuatl's great tendency to create doublets, it might reasonably be imagined that *tlaltepoztli* and *tepozhuictli* were the same thing, the second term being merely a specification of what is said more generically in the first. A Culhuacan text of 1580 settles this matter definitively, establishing the two as distinct, with the passage "one azadón/tlaltepoztli and one tepozhuictli of mine" (TC, doc. 15, p. 52). See in addition TC, docs. 24, 45, pp. 74, 158, where the two also appear to be distinguished. In doc. 75, p. 260, the tlaltepoztli is distinguished from the chicohuictli. A list of tools from Cuauhtinchan in 1589 includes "one azadón, one tepozhuictli, and one *tlateconi tepoztli* (instrument for cutting things, made of metal/iron)" (L. Reyes García 1978, p. 140). Molina only partially confirms the distinction between tlaltepoztli and tepozhuictli. Under "coa de hierro," "digging stick of iron (i.e., with an iron blade)," he gives *tepozhuictli* as to be expected (Spanish, f. 26v), but under the Nahuatl word (f. 104v) he gives both possibilities: "hoe or mattock, or digging stick with iron blade."

Exactly what a *tlateconi* was is not entirely clear. I take the word to mean mainly "axe, hatchet." But there are three widely separated passages in which the tlateconi appears in tandem with tools of an agricultural nature, as though the three were the normal set. The example from Cuauhtinchan was just quoted; from Culhuacan, 1581, comes the series *in tlaltepoztli in tlateconi in tepozhuictli*, in which *tlateconi* is placed between the definitely agricultural tools (TC, doc. 45, p. 158). Speaking ostensibly of preconquest times, the Florentine Codex mentions in the same breath, as items sold in the market, a threesome of *huictli huitzoctli tlateconi* (FC, book 8, p. 68). Anderson and Dibble translate this as "digging sticks, pointed oaken poles, and hatchets," whereas Sahagún renders it as "digging sticks, levers, and shovels (*coas, y palancas, y palas*)"; Sahagún 1975, p. 476), so that one great authority votes for "shovel" as the meaning. It is possible that *tlateconi* was a broad word with many meanings. It is also possible that the axe was considered among other things an agricultural tool, or alternatively, that the underlying notion of the series involved sharp objects made of hard materials for heavy work, rather than agricultural tools specifically. In one case, the

Spanish loanword for axe appears in conjunction with *tepozhuictli: ce hachaton ihuan ce tepozhuictli*, "one little axe and one tepozhuictli" (Tezontla, Tetzcoco region, April 28, 1689; AGN, Tierras 2338, exp. 6). All in all, I tend to think that in the 16th century *tlateconi* was an axe, increasingly one in European style with a head of iron or steel, and that with time the word was displaced by the Spanish *hacha*.

219. AGN, Tierras 2338, exp. 6, April 28, 1689.

220. CFP, f. 3.

221. See AGN, Tierras 2533, exp. 5, ff. 1–2v (Calimaya in the Toluca Valley, 1691), will of don Juan de la Cruz, sometime governor of Tepemaxalco, leaving a total of 16 yoke of oxen to various relatives. At nearly the same time, also in the Tepemaxalco district, don Juan Alonso left eight oxen and two cows to various heirs (Tierras 2533, exp. 3, ff. 1–1v, Santa María de la Asunción, 1692).

222. TC, doc. 45, p. 158 (Culhuacan, 1581). See also S. Cline 1986, pp. 112–13.

223. TC, passim. See S. Cline 1984 for a valuable reconstruction of the chinampa regime of Culhuacan; and Gibson 1964, pp. 320–21, for a brief synthesis of chinampa agriculture across the colonial period. See also Rojas Rabiela 1988, passim.

224. As in BC, doc. 7, pp. 76–79.

225. See especially BC, doc. 4, pp. 64–68, and also docs. 2, 3, 26 (part 5), pp. 54, 56, 60–61, 160. See also Arenas 1982, p. 17.

226. UCLA TC, folder 23, ff. 22–23 (Acatlan, Tulancingo region, 1689).

227. For examples see BC, doc. 34, pp. 210–11; UCLA TC, folder 1, accounts for 1567; TC, docs. 16, 31, 38, pp. 54, 104, 126; and CH, 2: 44, 47. For the various names, see Chap. 7. Originally, *totolin* by itself unambiguously meant turkey (hen) and was used in contrast to chicken, as in the 1567 passage in UCLA TC, folder 1, but in time, as with Chimalpahin in the early 17th century (CH, 2: 44), it could be used also to mean hen or chicken, causing some confusion for the modern reader.

Chapter 6

1. BC, doc. 29, pp. 176–91.

2. Gibson 1952, pp. 29–37.

3. See AZ 1: 1, 10, 20, 32, 84, 98; Carrasco 1972; and MNAH AH, CAN 549, ff. 12, 25, 550, ff. 18v–19, 56v, 58, 64v, 551, ff. 82, 83v, 85. In most cases, the man with more than one wife is a tlatoani, teuctli, or calpolli leader, but a few seem to be ordinary calpolli members without large establishments or extensive land.

4. Sahagún 1986, especially pp. 146–55.

5. The facts of the above paragraph are extensively corroborated, though from a rather different perspective, in the chapter on religion in Gibson 1964, pp. 98–135. I am not sure at what point the term *visita* came to be applied to the town or the church rather than to the ecclesiastical tour, which was the original meaning. In account books of the Franciscan monastery of Tula in the second and third decades of the 17th century (MNAH AH, Fondo Franciscano 45), there is no instance in which the word unambiguously refers to the building, foundation, or settlement rather than the act of visiting. Whatever the terminology, the phenomenon of the dependent chapel based on a calpolli goes back at least to the 1540's (as can be deduced from

TA, pp. 14, 40 [item 36], 48 [item 93], 50 [item 112], and 60 [item 169]) and probably earlier. See Gibson 1964, p. 120, for a 1539 example (though it is somewhat dubious, since the record is contained in a posterior document with many of the characteristics of the "titles" genre). Muñoz Camargo, writing in the early 1580's, does use the word in the specific sense, but implies that the usage is a bit new or technical: "las iglesias, . . . las cuales llaman los ministros de doctrina visitas de los monasterios" (1984, p. 96).

6. See Ricard 1966, chap. 3.

7. TA, selection 15, pp. 97–103, especially p. 101, statement of Hernando de Salazar.

8. CH, 2: 11–12. The story is told under the year of 1537, but it seems to extend over both earlier and later years, and a section referring to the governorship may relate to the 1560's. Quetzalmaçatzin means Plumed Deer; Tequanxayactzin One with the Face of a Fierce Beast. See also Schroeder 1989, p. 26.

9. For one expression of this view, see Ricard 1966, p. 79.

10. CH, 2: 65. The matter was later settled (2: 67). Chimalpahin calls the church "ynhuehuechan," "their patrimonial home."

11. See Schwaller 1987, especially chap. 3; and Gibson 1964, pp. 102–10. The friars lost far less than they claimed they did.

12. It is in this light that I would interpret phenomena such as those reported in Gibson 1964, pp. 112, 120–21.

13. Example in BC, doc. 28, pp. 174–77. See Gibson 1964, pp. 54, 120–21. For related altepetl developments, see Chap. 2, section "The Evolution of Units and Unit Concepts."

14. Anales de Diego García, 1502–1601, MNAH AH, CAN 274, no. 24, pp. 986–87. My thanks to Frances M. Krug for access to these sections of the annals. The truth of what happened, of course, may be at considerable variance with the annalist's account.

15. CH, 2: 40, 41.

16. CH, 2: 121.

17. Robert Haskett has brought to my attention a passage in a Nahuatl petition directed to the Spanish governor of the Marquesado in Cuernavaca, ca. 1607, in which the writer, Pedro de Molina, claims that his grandfather don Francisco Cortés, active in the time of Hernando Cortés, was a "tecuihtlamacazqui," a "lordly priest," presumably an indigenous rank and function, who also in some way served the Christian church and even received what his grandson called "rations" for it. The grandson continued in the tradition, playing the organ and serving as secretary to the father guardian of the Franciscan monastery. (AGN, Hospital de Jesús 210, no. 38, included in Haskett 1985, appendix IIIA, p. 650.)

18. For some reason, despite Gibson's deep knowledge of altepetl officeholding, the nature and importance of the office of fiscal largely escaped him in *The Aztecs* (1964), as the religion chapter shows. The omission is all the stranger because Ricard before him had shown a very adequate grasp of the fiscal post and had given it quite prominent treatment (especially 1966, p. 98).

19. See Celestino Solís et al. 1985.

20. TCB, p. 11.

21. BC, docs. 20, 21, pp. 112–17.

22. TC, doc. 13, pp. 40–45. Don Juan seems to have made little distinction between church property and his own, nor did he always quickly put money received to the purpose intended. On his death, church debts exceeded assets.

23. CH, II, 32. The fiscal was don Esteban de la Cruz Mendoza, tlatoani of Tequanipan.

24. BC, doc. 3, p. 62.

25. BC, doc. 6, p. 76. In 1723, Santiago Chalco had a fiscal and a *fiscal teniente* (AGN, Tierras 2554, exp. 4, f. 1). Haskett 1985 gives further examples.

26. This is a rather frustrating situation considering that Chimalpahin was himself the next thing to a fiscal in a Mexico City church, and one suspects much the same of other ecclesiastically oriented Nahuatl annalists. Ricard's brief summary of the office's duties (1966, pp. 97–98) is accurate as far as I know, except that he somewhat confuses the titles of the fiscal and the lower-ranking *mandón*, a term in any case little used in Nahuatl. Ricard is aware that *mandón* is essentially restricted to Spanish but is under the misapprehension that the same is true of "fiscal." Moreover, Ricard had little notion of the fiscal's position within the indigenous community. Indeed, his picture of the fiscal's duties seems to come largely from modern sources, and its accuracy is a function of the fact that those duties are still the same as they have been ever since the late 16th century. Haskett (1985, pp. 329–34) gives additional but congruent details, drawn from documents of the time and place, about the fiscal's activities, including his responsibility for bell ringing.

27. The Tula monastery account book of the early 17th century (MNAH AH, Fondo Franciscano 45) is a storehouse of information on the fiscal's financial activities. During part of this time, Tula tried to maintain a distinction between the fiscal proper and the *síndico*, or treasurer, but the two posts showed a strong tendency over the years to collapse into one. The síndico Juan de Contreras became so active that the records hardly speak of a fiscal, until finally Contreras himself was given that title, without changing the nature of his activity (see records from 1608 to 1617).

28. AGN, Criminal 234, ff. 80–100.

29. The Spanish secular custodians of the property of the dead (*tenedores de los bienes de los difuntos*), however, did the same and worse, gaining well-deserved notoriety for using the funds for their own investments. Compare Lockhart 1972, pp. 290, 396.

30. AGN, Criminal 234, f. 83.

31. Some testators in the Culhuacan wills of ca. 1580 specifically set aside maize, beans, and chickens to be consumed by those taking part in the burial ceremonies (TC, docs. 31, 69, pp. 104, 244). Similar examples in later testaments are hard to find, but the explanation seems to be merely that, as so often, an action that had become routine was dropped from the written record, for similar practices survive among indigenous people to the present day.

32. The best laboratory for observing the Nahuas' use of the mass is, at present, the Culhuacan testament collection (TC; compare S. Cline 1986, chap. 3). Though there are not enough cases for a strictly statistical approach, the material is all from the same time and place, allowing one to make some well-founded analyses of the reasons for variation. The collection of Toluca Valley wills that Stephanie Wood is

forming, considerably more varied in provenience but including a greater number, should be an additional valuable resource for studying this topic. In the Culhuacan wills, it is more often than not women who ask for everything to be sold. Conceivably, a greater overall female religiosity, on the Spanish pattern, was forming. But even more relevant to the situation, I think, was the apparent fact that the heir of last resort, the place where the line stopped and remnant property was available, was more often a woman, perhaps because men left alone more quickly acquired additional dependents.

33. TC, doc. 44, p. 154: "yuhqui yn çan quimopatiotilliz."

34. The Culhuacan wills (TC) are full of such cases, many no doubt attributable to the then-raging epidemic, but in other cases years had passed; in the interval, remarriages had taken place and children had been born.

35. Examples in TC, as in doc. 31, pp. 100–107.

36. The extant copy of the Nahuatl bears the title "In animaztin ihuan albaceas" ("Souls and Executors"), which I can hardly believe was part of the original. The copy, a typescript by J. H. Cornyn, is the item "Souls and Testamentory Executors," Library of Congress, MMC 2771, "Aztec Dramas" box. See especially f. 3v.

37. AGN, Tierras 2338, exp. 6.

38. The only Spaniard I have seen so accused in Nahuatl materials is fray Gerónimo de Zárate, chaplain of San José in Mexico City in 1612, who according to Chimalpahin (2: 103–4, 109) took people's property and failed to say the masses due. Zárate is a bête noir for Chimalpahin and in his version was also detested by the Mexica, who suffered under his ministrations and were greatly relieved when he was replaced. He is said to have spent cofradía funds, insulted people in public, and had them whipped for resisting him, even if they were ill. Chimalpahin makes a point of saying that Zárate was a monstrous exception, and that no other friar at San José had ever behaved in such a manner.

Spanish ecclesiastics rarely served as witnesses to testaments, the whole proceedings taking place in the presence of Nahuas only. I have yet to see a priest named in connection with the testament of a commoner or even an ordinary noble. In the 16th century, one or more ecclesiastics sometimes (but by no means most of the time) appear when the testator was an important dynast. Even this faded out with time; the latest example I know is from 1622, when fray Alonso de Paredes witnessed the will of don Juan de Guzmán, a member of the tlatoani family of Coyoacán (BC, doc. 4, p. 68).

39. AGN, Tierras 3548, exp. 3 [?], f. 1. Similar concern by the cabildo, without the action of the fiscal, is seen extensively in TA (see pp. 17–18).

40. MNAH AH, Fondo Franciscano 45, ff. 117v-118. The loan had taken place during or before 1617; the fiscal was Juan de Contreras and the governor don Andrés Luis de Tapia.

41. AGN, Tierras 442, exp. 5, f. 9.

42. Ibid. 2338, exp. 1, f. 31 and unnumbered folio of May 1758.

43. Haskett (1985, pp. 328–30) resists the notion of rotation between the positions of fiscal and governor as a regular phenomenon, tending to see it instead as exceptional and emphasizing that the common run of fiscales in the Cuernavaca region never reached the governorship. As a statistical fact, this is probably generally

true. The same could be said of alcaldes. Haskett himself gives an impressive list of fiscal-governors in the Cuernavaca area, and instances occur from early-17th-century Tula to 18th-century Tlatelolco (AGN, Tierras 104, exp. 8, no. f., don Gregorio de San Buenaventura as fiscal Nov. 1, 1712, and governor June 27, 1721). In my view, regardless of exactly how common the officeholding sequence alcalde-fiscal-governor may have been in statistical terms, it ranks as a normal career pattern. See below at n. 97 for an example of this sequence, all the more meaningful because of its mythical-archetypal nature.

44. Whereas from the point of view of Spanish officials, the greatest responsibility of the indigenous functionaries was the collection and delivery of royal taxes and the procurement of draft labor.

45. As in BC, docs. 2, 4, pp. 54, 64 (Coyoacan 1588, 1622). The word *teopantlacatl* is virtually always in the plural, though it could if necessary occur in the singular with reference to a specific person .

46. UCLA TC, folder 1, entries for Dec. 11, 1567, Dec. 20, 1568, Dec. 16, 1569. Nahuatl noun doublets most often contain two words that mean the same thing or in conjunction metaphorically name a single thing, but *teopantlaca cuicanime* without further context could conceivably mean two separate groups or "those of the church people who are singers." A possibly slightly earlier attestation, from an entry for 1564 in anonymous annals of Tenochtitlan, has exactly the same phrase, "teopantlaca cuicanime" (MNAH AH, GO 14, p. 14). I have refrained from giving this as the earliest occurrence because we cannot be certain the entry was written in its present form at the same time as the events, but it probably was.

47. See NMY, doc. 2, p. 94 (Xochimilco 1572); and UCLA TC, folder 23, ff. 22–23 (San Miguel Acatlan, Tulancingo region, 1659). As the second example shows, *cantores* continues to appear occasionally in later texts, but in my experience it seems to become increasingly rare once *teopantlaca* had established itself.

48. The most straightforward evidence of the term's preconquest provenience that I have seen is Tezozomoc's reference to the servants of the preconquest god Huitzilopochtli as *teopantlaca*, all the more impressive because he inserts the Nahuatl word into a Spanish text (1975, p. 424). Another reason that can be adduced is that the word from which the term derives, *teopan*, appears to have referred to a sacred precinct in preconquest times.

Some have imagined that because of the implications of the word *teocalli* (lit., "god-house, divinity house")—the primary term for preconquest temples—a new word, *teopan*, "(Christian) church," was invented to refer specifically to Christian places of worship. Although *teopan* is in fact the standard postconquest term, and *teocalli* is less frequently seen except when there is some occasion to refer to preconquest temples, *teocalli* does occur in the meaning "house of Christian worship." The pious Chimalpahin uses it several times in this sense (CH, 2: 15, 31, 127), and it also occurs in mundane documentation (López y Magaña 1980, doc. 3; Tetzcoco, 1589) and "primordial titles" (AGN, Tierras 1780, exp. 3, f. 3v; Sultepec area, ca. 1680), not to speak of the Guadalupe story printed in the mid-17th century under the auspices of a Spanish priest (Lasso de la Vega 1926). Molina defines the word under "teucalli" as "church or temple" and under "teocalli" in even more strongly Christian terms as "house of God or church."

On the other hand, there is every indication that *teopan* (lit., "where a god is [or gods are], where divinity is") is not a postconquest formation. For example, the most common Nahuatl name for the San Pablo quarter of Tenochtitlan was Teopan. The term appears several times in the Florentine Codex in specific reference to preconquest temples, most impressively in FC, book 6, pp. 209–10, where *teopan* is twice used for indigenous non-Christian temples in general. See also book 2, chap. 20, f. 17, of Sahagún 1979; and FC, book 12, p. 96 (chap. 34).

The word would have been a strange choice indeed for Spanish clerics to have hit upon as a replacement for *teocalli*, since it repeats the very element that putatively gave them pause, *teotl*, "god," the use of which they apparently feared could imply too close an equation of preconquest deities with the Christian divinity. Regarding the preconquest status of *teopan* as proved, then, I believe that it simply evolved as post-conquest Nahua usage rather than being deliberately invented for a doctrinal purpose. And if it was in any sense a neologism, it was surely devised in the first instance by Nahuas, for it is utterly idiomatic. It was primarily used as a locative (i.e., it translates as "the church" less often than as "at or to the church"). The simple noun sense was a secondary development, and the form with the absolutive ending -*tli*, although it existed, was little used. *Teopancalli*, with the addition of *calli*, "house," was sometimes preferred for the structure, and I have often been left with the impression that *teopan* refers to the whole church precinct. Molina's definition of *teopan* is exactly the same as the principal one of *teocalli*, "church or temple." (I see no way of being sure just what Molina meant by "temple.") The two terms remind one very much of the set *teccalli* and *tecpan* (see Chap. 4, section "Nobles, Lords, and Rulers").

The Spanish word *iglesia* also frequently appears in Nahuatl texts, mostly in set loan phrases such as *santa iglesia romana* and with reference to the ecumenical organization rather than the physical plant, but occasionally with the latter meaning too. Since in my experience in the great majority of cases *teocalli* refers to a small church or chapel, it has occurred to me that a distinction of size might have existed between *teopan* and *teocalli*; yet Chimalpahin once calls the original cathedral of Mexico City a "teocalli" (CH, 2: 31). Because *teopan* mainly lacks an absolutive ending, one cannot be positive whether in the construction *teopantlacatl* it is bound to *tlacatl*, "person," or not. The form *teopan tlacatl*, with the elements as separate freestanding words, may be more correct than the form I have chosen.

49. BC, doc. 18, p. 110.

50. CH, 2: 18 (also pp. 11 and 12, possibly misplaced chronologically).

51. TC, doc. 60, p. 220.

52. Nineteen people received land; of these 13 are named, one without the size of the allotment. The distribution was as follows. The leader was allotted 100 units (doubtless the Coyoacan quahuitl, perhaps about 12 feet) by 60; two people got 80 by 60, four 60 square, and five possibly 60 by 40 or 40 by 40. The other seven presumably got less. Even the smallest of the amounts listed would have been substantial if good land was involved, and the largest are comparable to the tracts held by high nobles. (BC, doc. 18, p. 110; see also the detailed discussion of the document in Horn 1989, pp. 238–40.)

Nahuatl documents generally fail to mention the instruction in European music received from friars in the early time, giving instead the impression that the Nahuas perpetuated the skills among themselves. The only two references to Spanish instruction I have seen both mention fray Pedro de Gante in Mexico City. Chimalpahin (2: 25) speaks of fray Pedro as teacher of the Mexica cantors ("ynmaestro yn cantores mexica"). The anonymous annalist of the 1560's says (MNAH AH, GO 14, p. 150) that fray Pedro had the church singers learn a *pipilcuicatl* ("children's song") in 1567. The passage seems ambiguous and, as far as I can make out, does not quite say that fray Pedro actually taught them the song: "Septienbre 1567 ypan in mocuicamachtique teopantlaca pipilcuicatl in quimomachtique ompa teopan momachtiaya ytencopa in totatzin frai p⁰ de gante quito yevatl mevaz in iquac ylhuitzin quiçaz S. fran⁰." ("In September 1567, the teopantlaca learned [or were taught] songs. What they learned [or were taught] was a pipilcuicatl. It was being learned [or taught] at the church by order of our father fray Pedro de Gante. He said it was to be sung when the day of San Francisco is celebrated.")

53. See n. 46, above.

54. The musicians doubtless also received fees on other occasions less likely to appear in the documents, such as the parading of individuals' saints mentioned above (at n. 28); but it seems to me that funerals must have been their best business.

55. AGN, Tierras 2338, exp. 8, ff. 26–27.

56. See Haskett 1985, pp. 327–50, for lists of officers and duties in the Cuernavaca region over most of the colonial period. Haskett is aware of the interpenetration of functions. The same phenomenon is seen among lesser altepetl officials. See Chap. 2, section "Minor Officials"; and TA, pp. 13–14.

57. For example, BC, docs. 20, 21, pp. 112–17 (Coyoacan, 1575).

58. Ibid. Baltasar Pérez appears as "alguazil teopan" on p. 114 and as "teopan topile" on p. 116. Sometimes, as in this case, there were two church constables in the stricter sense, but in the records one preeminent figure is more common. Molina glosses *topile* as "alguacil" without giving any other alternative. The "teopan topile" mentioned in the Azcapotzalco region in 1695 (Appendix A, Doc. 4) also seems to have been a true alguacil de la iglesia.

59. TC, docs. 43, 55, pp. 150, 198. See also S. Cline 1986, pp. 9, 46. The Spanish word *coro* referred to the physical location in the church, not to the singers, who made up the *capilla* (though the singing did take place in the *coro*). Juan Bautista may have been the janitor for the choir rather than a person in charge of the singers.

60. TC, doc. 61, p. 222. Martín Jacobo never calls himself church notary, or cabildo notary either, but uses *escribano nombrado*, a term that in Spanish meant an interim notary named for the occasion. See the many indexed references to Martín Jacobo and notaries in S. Cline 1986.

61. This is not an exceptionless trend. Both examples and exceptions may be seen in the wills in BC and NMY.

62. See S. Cline 1986, pp. 44–46, 95–96. Notaries must have received a fee directly from the client for each document produced, as in the Spanish world, but I have seen no unequivocal direct evidence to that effect.

63. Ricard left the impression that cofradías sprang into existence immediately as part of a general plan of Christianization (see 1966, pp. 181–82). Gibson corrected the perspective, calling the cofradía a delayed phenomenon (1964, p. 127). He emphasizes the small number of sodalities founded in the 16th century, seeing the time

of vigor as coming after 1600. I would not deny this in terms of relative numbers, but without a firm statistical basis, I have begun to believe that important foundations in larger units were occurring regularly from the 1570's forward even though the wave of proliferation came later. Some of it may prove to bear a relation to late altepetl fragmentation.

For all that Gibson's multidimensional mapping did to increase the intelligibility of central Mexican history, it perforce stopped short of exhaustiveness. A great many constituent parts of altepetl and parishes remained unnamed and unlocated. The records may never permit us to fill in the picture entirely, but the resources for a very substantial thickening of the map do exist, and to improve our understanding of many topics affecting both the Hispanic and the indigenous world, it is imperative that further compilation be carried out. Robert Haskett and Stephanie Wood are doing valuable mapping beyond the Valley of Mexico, of the Cuernavaca region and the Toluca Valley respectively, but we also, and perhaps even more, require second-generation maps of yet greater detail. Intensive work on specific subregions may hold out the best hope; Rebecca Horn's research on Coyoacan (1989) has produced impressive results in this respect. Once we have a more detailed roster and map of sociopolitical units, comparing it with the process of cofradía formation should prove extremely fruitful, but there too large-scale, systematic work, not an easy task, is much needed.

64. Chance and Taylor 1985, pp. 8–12. Farriss 1984 shows the cofradía extremely well developed and integrated with other local mechanisms in colonial Yucatan. Perhaps this is one more indication, despite Yucatan's prominence in Mesoamerican culture history, of its relative peripherality by colonial times, and also of the difference in structure between its sociopolitical units and the central Mexican altepetl.

65. See, for example, BC, docs. 8, 27, 28, pp. 78–83, 168–69, 174–77.

66. What Gibson calls unofficial cofradías were, however, dedicated to such saints (1964, pp. 129–30). An example of such an arrangement comes from San Miguel Tocuillan (Tetzcoco region), dated 1722 (AGN, Tierras 2338, exp. 1, f. 14). A Spaniard (one of whose relatives married into the community) has rented a piece of land that a citizen of Tocuillan left to the patron saint San Miguel and has now paid two pesos, a year's rent, which is acknowledged by a group consisting of the alcalde (there was no governor), regidor mayor, fiscal, the "majordomo of the church," and "mochi tlacatl cofrandias," apparently meaning "all the people or members of the cofradía," although the writer of the Nahuatl may have been confused about the distinction between *cofradía*, the organization, and *cofrades*, the members. There was ordinarily no such position as "majordomo of the church," the title majordomo being reserved for the stewards of cofradías, and that is apparently what is intended here; I take the language not merely as a mistake but as indicative of the lack of differentiation between the cofradía and other organizations. Here the altepetl officials, the fiscal of the church, and the cofradía all act as one, with no concern for the last as a separate entity. This particular cofradía was doubtless an unofficial volunteer and booster group for the festivities of the patron saint, and "cofradía" was hardly more than a name for the more actively involved part of the whole congregation.

67. For an example, see BC, doc. 4, p. 68 (Coyoacan, 1622).

68. CH, 2: 33–34, 45.

69. CH, 2: 110, 120, 121. Diego López of Tlatelolco was a *quauhtlacuilo*; the word is defined by Molina as "woodcarver" despite its apparent etymological meaning "one who paints on wood." Chimalpahin is not specific, but I take it that Diego López, who was a good friend of his, was an indigenous person.

70. The Tula cofradía book (TCB) is in the section "Latin American Mss.— Mexico" in the manuscripts department of the Lilly Library, Indiana University. At one time, the book would probably have been far from unique; close counterparts may yet appear. Below (at n. 96) I will have some occasion to refer to fragments of a cofradía book, from 17th-century Xochimilco, which Gibson knew and used with much profit (1964, p. 128). The records I have seen correspond in most respects, including some small details, with what Gibson reports of them, but I found them in a place different from that specified in his reference. Gibson gives MNAH AH, CAN 339, ff. 1r et seq., 151r et seq. I found the same volume in the same repository, Fondo Franciscano 129; presumably some rearrangement took place between our visits. The volume is a superficially chaotic collection of disparate materials. Gibson, I believe, could not spend the great amount of time required to identify the various parts and construct an order or relationship. Neither could I, and the no doubt worthwhile task still faces us. It was not clear to me, nor I think to Gibson, which parts of the volume are from Xochimilco, and which from the Franciscan monastery in Cholula.

71. Although the constitution seems to envision a commingling of the two constituencies, that never happened, at least not on a large scale. The members listed are so overwhelmingly indigenous that it seems separate lists must have been kept for Spaniards; indeed, one such list is included in the volume. Two sets of officers were elected in 1590 (TCB, p. 40; my pagination; in the original the folios are not numbered); in 1591, *only* Spanish officers are mentioned. For the rest, all the officers seem indigenous. It appears to me that two separate organizations arose almost immediately, but that occasionally some of the affairs of the Spanish branch ended up in the indigenous book. When a Spanish person's entrance and fee payment are on rare occasions recorded in Nahuatl in the otherwise indigenous lists, conceivably that person in condescension or piety was lending his name to the indigenous branch, though I am by no means sure of this. (One sure case is that of the posthumous entrance of the alcalde mayor into the "cofradía de los naturales" in 1660: p. 75.)

72. TCB, p. 8, item 14 of the ordinances: "in teutlaçotlaliztli [*sic* for *tetlaçotlaliztli*] yn itoca Charidad." Another possibility, which I do not exclude even though it would not be characteristic, is that both the Spanish and the Nahuatl version (the Most Holy Sacrament being everywhere the premier cofradía) were so standard that they had circulated about the country for some time, which would explain the apparent archaism equally well. I must admit that Spanish-Nahuatl doublets do occur in much later texts also, but in general they are a sign of the newness of that particular Spanish concept to the writer.

73. TCB, p. 9, item 21 of the ordinances. *Miccatepoztli* is occasionally found also in later writings, including Chimalpahin.

74. TCB, p. 14.

75. The list covers pp. 55–63 of TCB.

76. TCB, pp. 11–17. The number is approximate because the records do not

always make a clear distinction between two people who entered as a couple and a woman (rarely man) who entered alone, with the spouse (probably dead without its being specifically said so, as it is in many cases) named only to identify the new member the better. The fee paid clears things up in some cases, but not all, since those entering on their deathbeds paid higher fees, and some people paid more than was required simply as a gesture. Some abbreviated notations commonly added to the entries may render their meaning clearer, if ever deciphered.

77. Nevertheless, the rate of entry of new members around 1579–81 did not differ substantially from the rate in the years just preceding and following.

78. Tepexic occurs seven times. I am not sure whether the entity meant is the major altepetl south of Tula, entirely out of the parish but closely associated with Tula's affairs in some ways, or a tlaxilacalli of Tula with the same name. An entry of 1607 (TCB, p. 63) refers to Tepexic as a member's tlaxilacalli ("ytlaxilacalco"). However, some of the surrounding altepetl are also sometimes so denominated (San Pedro and San Marcos, 1636, p. 73). Neither status would change the overall picture drastically. Over time, all the towns in the Tula parish appear at least once. Best represented is the largest, Tlahuelilpa (Tlaahuililpan), followed by the small entities located on the doorstep of Tula, San Lorenzo Xipacoyan, San Pedro, and San Marcos. I suspect that in preconquest times many or all of these entities were joined with Tula in some complex altepetl structure.

The fact that the remaining affiliations are tlaxilacalli of Tula proper is proved not only by the use of that term but by an occasional more specific phrase such as "chane nican tullan tzanpotla pohui," "citizen here in Tula, belonging to Tzapotla" (1634, p. 72). In the text, I speak of "twenty-odd" affiliations not merely because of the Tepexic question but because I am not sure whether some infrequently occurring words are personal names or affiliations. Moreover, the names seem to denote entities of different orders, some included within others, without the relationships ever being defined. Thus Tenexcalco appears in the 1570–73 list eight times, Panoayan three, and Panoayan Tenexcalco once, from which I deduce that Panoayan was very likely a subdivision of Tenexcalco. The tlaxilacalli named ten times or more in the list are Quanallan, 22; Tzapotla, 20; Tlacpac, 19; Quetzalhuacan, 17; Tepetlapan, 16; Acxotlan, 14; and Tlalcohualco, 12.

79. TCB, p. 90. It is possible, however, that for practical purposes the first ring of small altepetl around Tula had by this time been absorbed within the larger entity (seat of the alcalde mayor and a Spanish residential community) as barrios.

80. TCB, pp. 11, 17. Juan Damián's exact office in the cofradía is not given; it is only said that he and Juan García kept the entrance register from the beginning until May 1573. Thereafter, the newly elected diputados were to carry out that task with the help of the majordomo Juan García. Since Juan Damián's name precedes that of Juan García, it seems likely that he was majordomo; if not, he must have been diputado.

81. TCB, pp. 66 (for don Andrés Luis de Tapia as governor, see MNAH AH, Fondo Franciscano 45, ff. 117v–118), 68, 70.

82. TCB, pp. 40, 53, 54 (for Juan de Contreras as síndico/fiscal, see MNAH AH, Fondo Franciscano 45, accounts for the years 1608–17; see also n. 27, above).

83. TCB, p. 66. Because the names of many members are given without their

unit affiliation and many names with affiliations repeat so often that one cannot be sure which individual is involved in a given instance, I cannot document my strong presumption that officers were drawn from Tula proper, not the outlying altepetl.

84. TCB, pp. 68, 70, 76.

85. TCB, p. 17.

86. TCB, pp. 53–54. The governors and alcaldes of all the altepetl of the parish were informed of the action, showing again the provincewide aspect of the Most Holy Sacrament.

87. TCB, p. 68. The central passages of the Nahuatl run: "cenca huel ytlacauhtica huel poliuhtica yn cofradia atle cera ayac quimocuitlahuia yhuan ayc omopatlac yn mayordomo yhuan diputados ypanpa yn çan otlaxicauhque."

88. For the 1683 office, see TCB, p. 86.

89. TCB, pp. 68, 70.

90. TCB, pp. 86–87.

91. See n. 76.

92. TCB, p. 54: "yuan oc no nahuintin yllamatque yn tehuipanazque cenca mavizçotiyez teoyutl ynic atle çan [. . .] ventzintli vel no yehuantin quiqualitazque yn tleyn monequi yvan tenonotzazque teyxtlamachtizque." I suspect that the damaged portion contained something like "nenquiçaz." "Monequi" could be translated as "needed" rather than "used (spent)." The text continues "aço ittoz yntla aca motlapolololtitinemi ynic quixtiloz amo oncan pouiz confradia," "perhaps it will be seen if anyone is living senselessly so that he should be ejected and not belong to the cofradía." It is not clear to me whether or not this specifically meant that the old women were to involve themselves in such investigations and decisions.

93. TCB, p. 68: "yhuan nahuintin teoyotica tenantzitzinhuan ynic huel quimocuitlahuizque yn s^ta cofradia ynic huel mahuizyotiez yhuan ypan tlahtozque ynic calacohuaz yn cofradia yn aquique ayamo oncan mopohua yhuan quinmocuitlahuizque yn cocoxcatzitzinti yn motenehua hermanos yhuan yn icnotlacatzitzinti ypan tlahtozque yn tlein ytech monequiz yn ipanpa yAnima yhuan yn itech pohui ytlalnacayo."

94. TCB, pp. 86–87. It occurred to me that the diputados might be related to the diputadas in the ratio of four to one, and that some four-part sociopolitical division might still be at the root of the allocation, but 44 or 45 to 14 does not seem close enough.

95. TCB, p. 91.

96. MNAH AH, Fondo Franciscano 129, ff. 1–2. (On these records, see n. 70; and Gibson 1964, p. 128.) The word that in context seems to mean "contribution(s), that which was solicited" is *tlayehualli*. One presumes that later in the colonial period, cacao bean offerings became less common. The phrase relating to burial is *teanato*, "they went to get someone." The Cofradía de la Veracruz kept receipts and expenses in separate books; the Tula cofradía probably also kept such books, as implied in the 1604 inspection (TCB, p. 53). The extant Tula cofradía book is primarily a record of membership and elections, and the Xochimilco sodality likely had a similar one.

97. AGN, Tierras 1780, exp. 3, ff. 3v, 1, 5v–6 (Spanish translation); f. 1 continues f. 3v, but since the writer of the document probably patched it together from earlier materials, the church and the border parts may have been separate originally. I do not know whether Quatepec (Quauhtepec? Coatepec?) was an entirely indepen-

dent altepetl or a constituent part of Sultepec. Don Pedro speaks of himself and his son as having been governors, but does not specify the entity. The suit containing the document was brought by officials of Sultepec, who had it in their possession.

Since don Pedro mentions having been baptized (not a very newsworthy event for any time more than a generation or so after the conquest) and bears an indigenous surname, and since the exploits of two succeeding generations figure (however unclearly) in the narrative, I suspect that don Pedro was a quasi-legendary personage from the conquest period or not much later, and that he is here associated with actions, offices, and people of a later time by having the words put in his mouth. The date as given on f. 3 is "168 Años"; f. 1 has "166 Años." The Spanish translator omitted these as meaningless, but since the associated f. 2v gives a standard 1660, I believe the intention of the other two was 1680 and 1660. The Nahuatl contains the Spanish loanword *hasta* and other indications that it was written no earlier than mid-17th century.

98. See the discussion of the de la Cruz line in Chap. 4, section "The Persistence of an Upper Group."

99. CFP, f. 11: "Axca juebes a 21 de março 1669 años nica momachiotiz yn itoca jusepato otichuapanque nica yntic calli omohuapahua — axca omonamictique ytonca diego de s.tiago," "Today, Thursday, March 21, 1669, it will be manifested here that the one named Little Josefa, whom we raised, who was raised here inside the house, and one called Diego de Santiago were married."

100. Aside from those whose offices are given in Table 6.3, Matías de San Francisco, maestro, was a future governor (CFP, f. 11), and Gabriel de San Pedro a future alcalde (f. 3). Pedro Joaquín, who was one of the cantors in 1657 (f. 2v; likely already in 1647), was alguacil mayor in 1655 (f. 5v). Baltasar de Santiago was no doubt on the same level as Pedro Joaquín; given their low places on the list and their small contributions, we would not expect that they advanced much further. The two women were probably widows of former governors, alcaldes, maestros, or the like.

101. The "San Lucas people" ("Sa lucas tlacatl") must be the people of that constituent part as a unit. The *tlapaliuhque* (sometimes "tlapalique" in the text) were the equivalent of *macehualtin*, "commoners" (which occurs f. 17; 1683), but the term refers only to adult males (compare "tlapaliuhque yuan cinhuame," "tlapaliuhque and women," as witnesses in 1658; f. 17), especially in their capacity as cultivators of the soil (see also Chap. 4, section "The Persistence of an Upper Group"). What unit the tlapaliuhque were from is not said, but I think probably from the four Tepemaxalco districts clustered not far from the monastery (the ones listed in NMY, doc. 8, pp. 108–11; the fifth and last, Mexicapan, "where the Mexica are," does not figure in the de la Cruz book; otherwise the order in NMY is the standard one).

102. CFP, f. 1v: "timochti tictlalia tofirma amo quemania quitozque Aço mochi tlacatl oquicouhque organo ca ça quezqui tlacatl oquicouhque."

103. CFP, f. 2 (1656): "tlapalique ca ça otlapalehuique yc mitzoma cuezcomatl ça quezqui tlacatl oquauhhuilaque." Ibid., f. 3 (1655): "tlapaliuhque Acan amo quimopielia yotan: sa cemilhuitequitl sa yehuatl oquihuicaque huitzontli sa quezqui tlacatl otequipanoque." An entry of 1658 for once does acknowledge that the tlapaliuhque of San Pablo Tepemaxalco (the cluster near the monastery church) and the people of San Lucas and Santa María de la Asunción (outlying constituents) erected a

tequicalli, a tribute- or workhouse, for San Francisco (or for San Francisco Pochtlan?; see n. 109), in connection with the special field: "omoquez tequicalli sa fran^co oquiquesque tlapalique sa pablo tepemaxalcon — ynhua sa lucas tlacatl otlapalehuique — ynhua sancta maria Asupcio tlacatl otlapalehuique" (f. 3v).

104. CFP, f. 9v: "yhua calimaya tlacatl atley oquitemacaque tomi — san ixquich otetlaqualtique."

105. CFP, f. 2 (1647): "yn quemania amo acan quitos: Aço altepetl oquicouhque canmara"; "cuezcomatl amo quemania quitosque Aço altepetl oquichiuhque ca sa tehuati catores . . . oticchiuhque." *Altepetl*, though grammatically singular here, takes plural verbs. The writer seems to be thinking of the general population of the entity, or of the members of its governmental hierarchy, rather than of the entity itself. Consider a passage of 1667 (f. 9v): "amo quemania quitozque altepehuaque aço comonidad oquiz tomi," "the citizens of the altepetl [or town fathers] are not to say sometime that the money came from community funds."

106. CFP, f. 17: "amo quemania tlen quitozque y maçehualtin tehuantin ticmachiotia yni llibro tialtepepixcatzintzinhuan yn tt^o dioz."

107. CFP, f. 3v: "Amo quemania quitosque aço mochi yaxca altepetl oniquitlatlanili amo yaxca oconaque jurameton."

108. CFP, f. 16v. In March 1683, don Francisco Nicolás, alcalde pasado, and his wife Teresa Francisca donated a lot to Guadalupe and Jesús Nazareno on which to grow maguey for them, but it does not necessarily follow that they did so because the chapel had just been built.

109. San Francisco's church and field are never specifically tied to Pochtlan in the text, but I deduce the association from Pochtlan's advocation, seen in the phrase "Santo San Fran^co puxtla" (CFP, f. 21v).

110. From 1652, don Pedro was deeply involved in working San Juan's field, and he was majordomo in 1655 when a church (the first?) was built and consecrated (CFP, ff. 2, 5v). He became governor in 1657 (f. 6). See NMY, doc. 8, p. 109, for his affiliation. Paxiontitlan is based on Spanish *pasión*, "next to the (image of) the Passion."

111. See, for example, CFP, ff. 3v, 7.

112. CFP, f. 12. It is interesting that these district-specific chapels nevertheless drew some support from all over greater Tepemaxalco; see n. 103.

113. CFP, ff. 8, 8v, 10, 11, 11v.

114. CFP, f. 13, among others.

115. CFP, f. 24.

116. An entry of 1653 says that the "teonpatlacatl" (the Tepemaxalco book never has *tlacatl* in the plural) had the organ painted (CFP, f. 5), and an entry of 1660 speaks of the "tenopatlacatl [*sic*] cuicanime," "church people, singers," making a contribution from the cantors' maguey (f. 6v).

117. See CFP, ff. 1, 5, 6–6v, 7. The construction "ytequimil" (f. 1; see also Table 6.3), "their tribute field," appears to have a singular possessor, but in the Tepemaxalco book *i/y-* and *in/yn-* are used indistinguishably; compare "ytlaor catores," "the maize of the cantors" (f. 7; 1661).

118. A passage of 1659 shows the governor holding the cantors' money ("catonres ytomi nicpieya"; CFP, f. 6), but in 1666, when the governor and a notary checked the fund, the wording suggests the cantors themselves were holding it (f. 9).

119. CFP, f. 2 (1656).

120. The group that took care of San Juan's field from 1652 through 1654 consisted of cantors and former cantors (CFP, f. 1v).

121. CFP, f. 2v (apparently 1657). The names of the cantors, without "don" and in all but one case without "de San" between the two elements, in conjunction with the absence of any figures who are known to have held higher office previously, imply that retiring maestros and other persons attaining prominence did not rejoin the group as full participating members.

122. CFP, ff. 2v, 6v.

123. CFP, f. 6v.

124. CFP, ff. 1, 6v, 11. See Table 4.5 for their terms.

125. CFP, ff. 6, 6v, 7, 9. The exact forms of the names of the instruments are "tropeta" (and "tropeta mayor"), "sacabochi," "bajo," "quitaran," and "raber."

126. CFP, ff. 5v, 8v, 16v. *Fiscal* is twice written "fiscatl" because final [l] and [t¹] merged in the speech of many people of this region (see Lockhart 1981 [N&S, item 8]). Compare the predominance of an official called maestro rather than fiscal in Yucatan (Farriss 1984, p. 233 and elsewhere, as listed in index).

127. CFP, ff. 2v, 5v. Don Pedro specifically entitles himself "majordomo of the holy church."

128. In 1665, Miguel Serrano was both fiscal of Santa María de la Asunción and majordomo of the presumably unofficial cofradía of Santa María there (CFP, f. 8v), a pattern we saw in Tula as well.

129. CFP, ff. 13–13v. The passage is difficult paleographically and linguistically and doubtless would yield more useful information if fully deciphered.

130. TA, pp. 14, 40, 48, 50, 60 (items 36, 93, 112, 169).

131. See Lockhart 1982, pp. 378, 386–87, 391 (also N&S, item 3), and Chap. 9, section "Titles."

132. CH, 2: 41, 42. Tenochtitlan's patron saint situation was peculiar; as far as I can ascertain, the altepetl as a whole had no specific advocation; one hears much more of the saints of the four great parts. Though the indigenous chapel of San José preceded any other establishment and long remained the ceremonial center of the Mexica in matters of religion, it was obviously secondary to the much larger monastery church of Saint Francis to which the chapel was attached. Thus Saint Francis was indirectly the patron of Tenochtitlan. I am not sure whether the first representation referred to was a painting or a carving. Chimalpahin speaks of *tlacuiloque*, usually painters/ writers, but Molina defines *quauhtlacuiloque*, (lit., "wood-painters") as woodcarvers.

133. I will give two examples, which could be readily multiplied; "yn ichantzinco s. juᵒ bapᵗᵃ," "the home of San Juan Bautista" (BC, doc. 19, p. 112, Coyoacan, 1611); "ychantzinco Sancto Sa Juatzin," "the home of the saint San Juan" (CFP, f. 12; Tepemaxalco, 1674). Not until too late did it occur to me that I should have carried out a systematic count in a larger sample, but I believe that churches are more often called the home of a saint than the home of God, even where only one church is likely to be meant and there is no need to be specific.

134. Admittedly, hard proof of these assertions is scarce. But for example, in 1691 in Tocuillan (Tetzcoco region), Antonio de la Cruz asked to be buried at the feet of "my precious father Saint Michael Archangel" ("y notlaçotatzin San Miguel Arcan-

gel"), the town's patron saint. In the same place, in 1583, a woman referred to town land as "the precious land of our precious father the saint San Miguel" (AGN, Tierras 2338, exp. 1; Appendix A, Doc. 1; Chap. 2).

135. CA, p. 75: "a xxix mayo in lonestica nictlallan yn nocalton oncan onoc teisiptla."

136. UCLA TC, folder 25, March 1, 1768 (Sacaquauhtla in the Tulancingo region). See also Chap. 3, section "Terminology and Constitution of the Household Complex."

137. CH, 2: 48. The objects sold were "tlapopochhuilloni tlatemetzhuilli yn aço sancto anoço sancta." Clay candleholders in the form of angels ("çoquicamdelero angelesme") were also made and also forbidden.

138. Appendix A, Doc. 3. In BC, where this item was first published, we three editors as beginners did not realize that the reference was to images, even failing, alas, to recognize that "maje," which appears twice, is *imagen* (*i* having been taken by the writer to be the Nahuatl article *in* and final *n* having been omitted as it is so often).

139. As in TC, doc. 29, p. 94, "yn tt⁰ hixiptlatzin ynmase" (Culhuacan, 1580).

140. As in the example in n. 138 (Coyoacan, 1621).

141. For an example of a *lienzo* (canvas), see AGN, Criminal 234, f. 128 (San Pedro Atocpan, Milpa Alta district, ca. 1635). Physical attributes are more likely to be mentioned in accompanying Spanish notations than in Nahuatl wills. A testament of Soyatzingo, 1734, mentions only "yn Santos y Santas"; a Spanish inventory clarifies this as "cuatro santos de bulto y uno de lienzo de tres cuartas de alto" (AGN, Tierras 2555, exp. 14, ff. 2, 3). In the great majority of cases, Nahuatl texts do not specify the form of representation.

142. This is something we editors of BC obviously did not know in 1974 when we were doing the translations. I do not mean to say that the word "image" is *never* used in late colonial documents. See "yxiptlayotz[in] Dios" in a 1795 text from the Toluca Valley (BC, doc. 6, pp. 74–75), which even retains the Nahuatl *ixiptlatl*. By "image of God" is probably meant a Christ on the cross.

143. See below at n. 223.

144. See, for example TC, doc. 30, p. 98 (Culhuacan, 1580); and Appendix A, Docs. 3 (Coyoacan, 1621), 4 (Azcapotzalco region, 1695).

145. See Appendix A, Doc. 4; and NMY, doc. 3, p. 99 (Coyoacan region, 1608). *Tequipanoa* appears most frequently in the reverential form *motequipanilhuia*.

146. See Appendix A, Doc. 3 (Coyoacan, 1621); and AGN, Tierras 2552, exp. 3, f. 3 (Soyatzingo, 1736); the phrase in the latter instance is "quinmotlachpanililis santoti santati." See also Chap. 3 at n. 28.

147. See Christian 1981, p. 157. The notion of images in the home was also familiar to Spaniards (ibid., p. 147), but I do not know how far the parallels extend.

148. NMY, doc. 3, p. 99 (Coyoacan region, 1608): "catelan xochitzintli copaltzintli." The use of the word *copalli* gives such statements a more indigenous flavor, though by this time the meaning had clearly been extended from indigenous copal to any incense.

149. In Tulancingo in 1656, a married couple sold a Spaniard a piece of land belonging simultaneously to themselves and to San Miguel, using the money not for their own personal needs but for cleaning (restoring) the saint: "yn yehuatzin tlaço-santo san miguel yc omochipauhtzino" (UCLA TC, folder 14, July 11, 1656).

150. See n. 141 for an example in which the Nahuatl makes the gender distinction and a Spanish description of the same group of saints does not. See n. 146 for another example of gender distinction (here an indigenous plural ending is used).

151. Appendix A, Doc. 4. Angelina does bequeath another piece of land without reference to any saint. To the extent that transactions like the one described here were common, a special relationship may have existed between specific saints and specific household members, another reason to have several. (To anyone who should chance to see the version originally published in BC, let me repeat the apologies made in n. 138; the translation there has the whole process reversed, not speaking in terms of saints' images at all.)

152. NAC, ms. 1477 B [1]. "Two little Christs" is "ome christotzitzin"; the expression could be taken as reverential rather than diminutive.

153. NMY, doc. 3, p. 99. Bárbara Agustina mentions only one saint; a conceivable reason for the lack of more, although she was a reasonably well-off trading woman, was that she owned no land. She also had only one child.

154. AGN, Tierras 2554, exp. 4, ff. 1–27.

155. In a document of 1716, he is once titled "don," though his sons are not (ibid., f. 13). As we saw in Chap. 4, late-colonial Spanish documents often deny the "don" to people who bore it within the indigenous context.

156. *Doncellas* in the Spanish (ibid., f. 2v).

157. The term used is "altepetlatequitzintli," which contains the stems of *altepetl* and *tequitl*, "duty, tax, etc.," but has an intervening *tla-* that I have not seen elsewhere and do not know how to interpret.

158. So I deduce. The dating is problematical.

159. Let us look briefly at some additional, less-extended examples of the intertwining of household and altepetl interest in saints and their land. In a case that came to a head in 1762–63, one Nicolasa Agustina, citizen of Coatlichan in the central Valley of Mexico and member of a gubernatorial family there, had once had a very old San Agustín, in pieces and leaning against a wall, and around 1724 one of her married grandchildren had it renovated. In gratitude, Nicolasa (probably in her will) gave the couple a piece of land to sow in order to take care of the saint, and also, in some versions, to have a mass of San Agustín said every year. The then governor of Coatlichan confirmed their possession, and they planted the land in magueys. By 1763, altepetl officials (despite the current holder's demurral) considered the yearly mass obligatory and within community jurisdiction. In 1764, the town, with the permission of the Spanish alcalde mayor, harvested 12 magueys for the mass and fête of the saint. (AGN, Tierras 2338, exp. 8, ff. 10, 18, 20, 21, 30.)

In a document from Tulancingo, dated July 30, 1720, the altepetl officials confirm (or seek to confirm, for it remains highly ambiguous) the status of two pieces of land, planted in magueys, that belong to Santa Elena ("ytlatquitzin Sta Elena"). The land had been left to a María Agustina by her mother and before that by her grandfather, to serve the saint. The authorities in the end never do say that the land belongs to María Agustina even though they are confirming that it was left to her. The usual problems appear to be well on their way. (UCLA TC, folder 19; also N&S, item 6.) The very fact of the altepetl's confirmation of such personal arrangements was the entering wedge of altepetl appropriation.

In Santa María de la Concepción (Calimaya jurisdiction, Toluca Valley), a saint-

and-lands case developed across the 18th century, reaching its dénouement in the early 19th. In the usual fashion, a family claimed that lands supporting two images originally belonged to it and still did, while the altepetl claimed the holders were merely majordomos on community land belonging to the saints. The family, to establish its rights, apparently hired a transient rascal named Mateo, who had worked locally as both notary and image restorer (still in the tradition of the old *tlacuilo*), to fake an antique document giving the family ownership (using lime water and smoke to achieve the aging); he then pretended he had found it inside one of the images in the course of restoration. The fraud, however, was discovered. (AGN, Tierras 2533, exp. 2, especially ff. 3, 34, 54, 55.)

In another Toluca Valley case, from the same region and even from another Santa María, Santa María de la Asunción, belonging to Tepemaxalco, we find one don Juan Alonso referring in his will of 1692 to "another Our Dear Mother, Our Lady of the Assumption, whom I serve, who is in the large church" ("oc se tutlazonatzin Nra Sra de la Assump^{on} nicnotequipanilhuia opa meztica huey teopan"). He left her to his children, along with a large piece of land for her support, stoutly defending his personal property rights to both saint and land, though he foresaw that the altepetl might lay claim to them. The land had been given to him, he claimed, and as for the saint, "she is not the property of the altepetl; I bought her" ("amo yyaxca altepel Nehual onicnocohuili"). Nevertheless, in the late 18th century, the altepetl took the land away from don Juan Alonso's heirs and gave it to someone else, whom they made responsible for the image, now considered to belong to the community. Whatever the merits of the case, with a patron saint kept in the general church, it is hard to imagine any other final result. (AGN, Tierras 2533, exp. 3, especially ff. 1–1v, 22, 34.)

160. AGN, Tierras 1805, exp. 3, ff. 1, 21, 59, 104, 128, 130, 134. The elder nobles are called in Spanish "viejos principales," and Lorenciana Angelina appears also as a "principal" (f. 1); (don) Miguel Francisco is once called a cacique (f. 21).

161. A document of Mexico City, 1579, mentions within a house complex a little house where an image is, calling it "a little church," or *teopantonco* (AGN, Tierras 56, exp. 8, f. 3). A document from Tlamimilolpan in the Toluca Valley, 1695, uses the other word for a church or temple, *teocalli*, for a domestic saint-house (ibid. 2616, exp. 7, ff. 25–26). The document does not describe the structure, but I feel justified in presuming that it contained saints; the Spanish translator made the same presumption, speaking of the "oratorio de los santos."

162. See above, at n. 135; and Appendix A, Doc. 1. It is not clear whether the reference in the second example is to the altar in the altepetl church or to a household altar.

163. Occasional passages do occur that are compatible with honoring the saints but are too ambiguous to permit a definite interpretation in that sense. For example, don Julián de la Rosa of Tlaxcala in his 1566 will (BC, doc. 1, pp. 50–51) orders some of his accoutrements sold to buy candles to be used in the church of San Pedro, the saint of his own home district and lordly house. The candles could have been specifically for the saint, but they could equally well have been for burials, processions, or any use to which candles were put. The Mexico City document of 1579 referred to in n. 161 does mention an image (*tlaixiptlayotl*) and a structure, but no saint's name and no duties; possibly the image was a crucifix as in Culhuacan at around the same time.

164. TC, doc. 64, pp. 229–31.

165. TC, docs. 29, 30, pp. 94, 98. I take it that the "image of our lord" ("yn tt⁰ hixiptlatzin ynmase") was to be housed within the household complex, but the language is not very specific. The quoted sentence shows the testator's strong proprietary feeling about the image but at the same time can be read as implying fear of appropriation by the larger entity. It is by no means to be expected that saints will be mentioned in anything like a majority of testaments even where most householders can be presumed to have had them; even in later documents, they surface above all when they are divided among several heirs or where some complicated arrangement is required for their support. Yet not to find a single reference to saints (other than Christ on the cross) or to their service in such a large collection as the Culhuacan testaments must be viewed as significant.

166. See Christian 1981, pp. 186–96, for evidence of what he calls "the Christocentric nature of late sixteenth- and seventeenth-century Spanish devotion" (p. 190).

167. CH, 2: 78.

168. This is the burden of Christian 1981.

169. See Lafaye 1976, pp. 238–41; Ricard 1966, pp. 103, 189–90; Sahagún 1975, pp. 704–5 (addition on superstitions to book 11).

170. Nutini 1980–84, 1: chap. 10. This work and others by Nutini are of inestimable value as 20th-century ethnography, again and again confirming patterns detected in records of the colonial period. The concern to develop a diachronic approach is also highly praiseworthy, and much intelligence is shown in the analysis. Nevertheless, the documentary basis, which is not fully specified by the historian's standards, appears to be extraordinarily weak, and the grasp shown of the historical and historiographical context is rather inadequate. All of the historical matter in this volume will need reinvestigation.

A crucial piece of evidence is a document Nutini found in private hands (apparently it is no longer available) purporting to be a 1547 account of the apparition of the Virgin of Ocotlan. Nutini took his notes to Wigberto Jiménez Moreno, who recognized the document as some sort of forgery (which Nutini himself very honestly reports, although he continued to believe in its authenticity; pp. 448–49). The auspices under which it was found and its subject matter are entirely characteristic of posterior fabrications about saints. The original composition of the document might go back as far as the 17th century, when cross-regional saints began to come into their own, but that would still deprive the text of value for ascertaining the truth of events and policies of the 1540's. The document could hardly date before 1649, when the classic version of the Guadalupe story, on which this account is based, began to circulate. The person to whom the Virgin is said to have appeared is "Juan Diego Bernardino," not a credible name for an Indian of the colonial period. It is put together from Juan Diego, hero of the Guadalupe story, and his sick uncle Juan Bernardino (see Lasso de la Vega 1926, pp. 80–81). Some of Nutini's documentation, found in local parishes of Tlaxcala, appears to be far more authentic and in fact of the highest interest, but he does not locate it very exactly and above all does not describe it textually in enough detail for one to be able to judge its value or message. Nutini makes no distinction between the original patron saints of local units and the later cross-regional saints.

Although Nutini read widely in the traditional sources for Mexican ecclesiastical history, he remained quite naïvely Ricardian, readily believing in the near omniscience and omnipotence of the early friars. He also remained quite unaware of the civil organization of Indian towns (it is true that the Tlaxcala region presents special problems) and of the transitional contribution of cofradías to the practices seen in Mexican towns today. Despite his extensive archival and bibliographical work, for some reason he did not consult Gibson 1964, which could have done much to orient him on these matters.

Nutini does have valuable, suggestive evidence of syncretism in respect to saints (although little if any of it is from documentation of the colonial period). On pp. 293–94, he definitely establishes the perceived identity of San Bernardino of Contla with the preconquest god Camaxtli, who had a temple there, pointing to the fact that both are depicted holding a solar disk and the fact that like Camaxtli before him, the San Bernardino of modern lore is reported to be the lover of the female spirit possessing the Malintzin mountain. Yet as Nutini rightly says, in this case the syncretism can as reasonably be attributed to the Indians as to the friars.

In a more recent publication (1988) Nutini has modified his position on guided syncretism, or at least allowed for unguided syncretism as well; see my review (1989).

171. Christian (1981) observes that today Spanish priests who look disapprovingly on the importance the populace gives to saints in general will still talk warmly of the saint of their own hometown. Another possible mechanism for acquiring saints would have been to pick the name-saint of the ecclesiastic presiding in that parish at that time. One wonders if this happened at Xochimilco, where the patron is the name-saint of fray Bernardino de Sahagún, stationed there early in his career (see NMY, doc. 2, p. 94).

172. Christian 1981, p. 196.

173. CH, 2: 47. Those going to honor the Virgin were "in toquichtin yn cihua, yn caxtilteca, yn señoratin." For images to go to visit cathedrals or each other was already standard practice in Spain. See Christian 1981.

174. CH, 2: 50.

175. CH, 2: 101. The wording is "españoles yhuan tehuantin timacehualti Mexico."

176. CH, 2: 145.

177. CH, 2: 124–26. Chimalpahin calls the platform on which one of the crosses was raised a "momoztli," the same word used for a preconquest altar or sacrificial platform.

178. CH, 2: 92.

179. Still, according to the Lasso de la Vega publication of 1649 on Guadalupe, the Virgin of Totoltepec was especially helpful to Spaniards (1926, pp. 84–85).

180. In a somewhat related matter, when thousands of flagellants came out to show penitence in 1603, Chimalpahin reports that there were more Spaniards than indigenous people among them (CH, 2: 54).

181. Ricard 1966, pp. 56, 188–91.

182. Christian 1981, pp. 65, 73, 91.

183. Sahagún 1975, pp. 704–5 (addition on superstitions to book 11); see also Ricard 1966, p. 191, and Lafaye 1976, pp. 211–12, 216.

184. The Cantares Mexicanos, the great postconquest Nahuatl song collection,

written down in Mexico City in the late 16th century, lacks any reference to Guadalupe despite its in places markedly devotional character (see Bierhorst 1985, especially pp. 61–62). The same is true of the early religious plays, some of which were probably composed in the capital.

185. MNAH AH, GO 14, p. 1: "yn ipan xihuitl mill e qui⁰s 55 a⁰s yquac monextitzi⁰ in santa maria de guatalupe yn ompa tepeyacac."

186. Ibid., p. 134.

187. BC, doc. 2, p. 54. A Spanish-language version of the 1563 will of don Francisco Quetzalmamaliztzin calls for masses at the shrine of Guadalupe. However, the will was presented (and the translation apparently made) in the 17th century, under somewhat suspicious circumstances having to do with the claims of distant heirs. The Nahuatl original is said to exist, but I have not been able to examine it yet. (Ixtlilxochitl 1975–77, 2: 281–86; Munch 1976, pp. 44–46.)

188. CH, 2: 16.

189. CH, 2: 23, 44, 127.

190. Lasso de la Vega 1926, pp. 84–87. The Nahuatl is "oc quezquican altepepan."

191. The Virgin of Ocotlan not only is unmentioned in Lasso de la Vega, but appears to be little mentioned even in the late-17th- and 18th-century Nahuatl annals of the Puebla-Tlaxcala region, which do show a concern about Guadalupe. An exception is Zapata, based after all in Tlaxcala City almost in sight of the chapel, who makes frequent mention of the Virgin of Ocotlan and shows her taking over symbolic functions; thus in 1675, her image was brought in in connection with the blessing of a new bridge into Tlaxcala City (ZM, f. 94), and in 1682, when an eclipse was predicted, she went to the Franciscan monastery to be present at special masses (f. 108). Zapata's glossator, the Hispanizing priest Santos y Salazar, shares his interest in the Virgin of Ocotlan. On the other hand, Zapata is also aware of the Virgin of Guadalupe; he reports the building of a chapel for her in Tlaxcala in 1686 (f. 117v).

I have not seen any reference in Nahuatl texts to the Señor de Chalma, although it is true that any Christ or crucifix a person possessed *could* have had that association. Stephanie Wood reports references to the Lord of Chalma in Nahuatl documents from the Toluca Valley in the late colonial period. Some details about the early evolution of Sacromonte are given by Chimalpahin (CH, 2: 29; for further references and discussion, see Schroeder 1989, p. 25), but what he says seems to me to have the flavor of local boosterism. A large-scale sifting of all the sources relevant to these topics would lead to striking results (see Gibson's remarks in 1964, p. 498, n. 140).

192. See CFP, ff. 16v, 24; NAC, ms. 1477 B [1] (Toluca); AGN, Tierras 2554, exp. 4 (Chalco 1723); and MNAH AH, GO 184, ff. 1, 9v, CAN 872, f. 8v (Tlaxcala-Puebla annals). With this I merely document a few appearances in the broader region. The research has hardly begun; I am confident that scholars will find evidence of a massive growth of the cult in the whole Nahua world during the late 17th and early 18th centuries; perhaps even the sequence of expansion into different subregions of central Mexico can be worked out. Wood, "Adopted Saints" (n.d. [e]), has a massive tabulation of mentions of Guadalupe in Toluca Valley wills, primarily after the mid-17th century.

193. See Lafaye 1976, pp. 235, 237, 242–53, and Brading 1991, pp. 343–48.

194. Taylor 1987.

195. Lasso de la Vega 1926, pp. 20–21: "ma oncan quittacan in maçehualtzitzintin, ma intlàtoltica quimatican in ixquich in impampa oticmochihuili motetlaçòtlaliztzin, izçenca ic òpoliuhca in cahuitl in iuhcatiliz." More literally, "Let the commoners [i.e., 'Indians'] see there, let them know in their language all the love [or charity, charitable acts] you have performed on account of them, which had been very much erased by the nature of time."

196. Ibid., pp. 58–77. The two neutral miracles are the creation of a spring next to the shrine and the cessation of an epidemic, which though it was requested by the Franciscans must have redounded to the benefit of the indigenous population.

197. Ibid., pp. 72–75. See Christian 1981 for the Spanish background.

198. See Lafaye 1976, pp. 219–21, 227.

199. The 1648 Spanish publication by Miguel Sánchez is discussed in Brading 1991, p. 345. Brading makes the connection between the two versions, points to their overwhelming similarity, and demonstrates that Lasso de la Vega knew Sánchez's work and publicly praised it as a revelation.

200. Christian 1981, pp. 73–81, 121.

201. Lasso de la Vega 1926, p. 18.

202. Ibid., pp. 20–21. Though any translation from older Nahuatl on close examination will prove to have some misconstructions, Primo Feliciano Velázquez's 1926 translation of Lasso de la Vega is absolutely excellent, as good as any such work done to this day and far better than the efforts of his immediate successors.

203. See, for example, BC, docs. 3, 4, pp. 58–59, 64–65.

204. The sets written by different notaries in TC are the fullest illustration of this point.

205. BC, doc. 3, pp. 58–59 (Coyoacan region, 1617). More rarely, extensive personal outbreaks against relatives to be disinherited can come in the opening section, still without affecting the doctrinal language (as in TC, doc. 40, p. 132).

206. For example, NMY, doc. 3, pp. 98–99 (Coyoacan region, 1608), there "my precious father" ("notlaçotantzin dios"); or BC, doc. 3, pp. 58–59 (Coyoacan region, 1617), also "my precious father God" (probably a subregional formula). Though within the normal range of conventions, references to God as the father of humans are much rarer than the parallel phenomenon with Mary.

207. Sahagún 1975, p. 705 (addition on superstitions to book 11).

208. For its use in wills, see BC, doc. 2, pp. 54–55 (Coyoacan, 1588), at present my earliest attestation. On consideration, I tend to think that the function of *tlaço-* with religious concepts is to put them in a specifically Christian context. For Chimalpahin's use, see CH, 2: 16; and for Lasso de la Vega's, 1926, pp. 16–17, and passim in the appendix on miracles. The story proper seems to stick to "preamble terminology," though I have not surveyed every single line with this in mind.

209. That is, in Nahuatl testaments I have read to date. Exceptions do exist, in my experience very rare ones. A will done in Mexico City in 1587 has in the preamble *totlaçonantzin santa Maria yn mochipa ichpochtli*, "our precious mother Saint Mary, eternal virgin," combining both currents (AGN, Tierras 54, exp. 5, f. 4).

210. For example, BC, docs. 1, 4, pp. 44–45, 64–65.

211. NMY, doc. 3, pp. 98–101.

212. Ricard 1966, p. 56.

213. I am concerned not to mix genres and zones at this point, but at the level of "primordial titles," for some Nahuas at least, by the late colonial period, the generic term for a major protective supernatural being seems to have been *santo*. In a wonderful example found and discussed by Stephanie Wood (1984, p. 231), a version of the legend of Calpulhuac (Toluca Valley) recalls that in preconquest times the altepetl had "only a stone saint." Here "saint" could be construed as meaning "image" rather than "supernatural being," but for the Nahuas the two aspects were always tightly integrated.

214. Appendix A, Doc. 4; BC, doc. 6, pp. 74–75; NMY, doc. 10, pp. 118–19. The text of the 1695 example has "notlatoca Dios," which at first sight looks like "my ruler-God." Here "God" would seem to be generic as well as a name. That does in fact frequently happen, as in "çan uel ce nelli dios," "just (but) really one true God" (BC, doc. 1, pp. 44–45; Tlaxcala, 1566). But I feel that in this case one of the frequent inadvertent omissions has occurred, the intention having been "notlatocatzin Dios," so that the phrase would be as rendered in the body, "my god and ruler, God." The 1795 example runs as expected, "noteotzin notlahtocatzin Dios."

215. The earliest example of -*yolia* known to me (speaking of mundane Nahuatl texts) is in the 1549 will of don Pablo Çacancatl of Coyoacan (CDC, 2: 12). See also BC, docs. 3, 4, pp. 58–59 and 64–65. Scattered attestations are from much later; a document of 1763 contains the latest occurrence of -*yolia* I have seen (see n. 222 for the reference and the passage). A document of 1572 (NMY, doc. 2, pp. 94, 96) pairs -*yollo* rather than -*yolia* with -*anima*. -*Yollo* is "heart," but is used in many words and phrases having to do with volition, emotion, and mood, thus approaching "spirit." The approximate equivalent -*tonal* (see Molina under "anima o alma"), more literally "fate" (by way of "(birth)day" and before that "sun"), is never used in this context in mundane Nahuatl documentation to my knowledge. Probably it was felt to be too closely associated with preconquest religion and particularly with "sorcery."

216. Evidence of the penetration of the word into everyday life at least at the high society level can be seen in a private letter of 1587 written in Mexico City (BC, doc. 32, pp. 198–99), whose greeting formula consists of the hope that the Holy Spirit will dwell with the souls of the recipients ("amotlaçoanimantzin").

217. TC, doc. 41, p. 134.

218. An early example of the correct use of *personas* is BC, doc. 1, pp. 44–45 (Tlaxcala, 1566); more are in TC. A will of ca. 1730 from Jocotitlan in the Tlalmanalco jurisdiction (AGN, Tierras 2550, exp. 8, f. 6) and one of 1768 from the Tulancingo area (UCLA TC, folder 25, March 1, 1768) have exactly the same "yeintzitzin teotlacatzitzintin," "three god-persons." A will of 1712 from Mexico City (AGN, Tierras 104, exp. 8, Nov. 1, 1712) has "yn yeintintzitzin teotlacatzitzintin personas," almost the same but using the Spanish word as well; in a will of 1763 from Tlapitzahuayan near Chalco (AGN, Tierras 2554, exp. 4, f. 23), we find "imeixtintzin y teotlacatzitzinti yn personas," the same except saying "all three of . . . " Many preambles name the constituents of the Trinity but simply omit specific reference to the three

persons. Spanish *persona* did not supplant or supplement Nahuatl *tlacatl* in any context other than testament preambles, and then only with reference to the members of the Trinity.

219. AGN, Tierras 1805, exp. 3 (1686): "in yeintintzitzin teteo auh ca ça cetzin yn teotl Dios."

220. See NMY, doc. 2, pp. 94, 96 (Xochimilco, 1572); and TC, doc. 5, p. 24 (Culhuacan, ca. 1580).

221. AGN, Tierras 2550, exp. 8, f. 6v (Jocotitlan in the Tlalmanalco jurisdiction, ca. 1730).

222. At the moment I am aware of only one testament in which the testator seems to share the soul between God and the saints; in a 1763 will from Tlapitzahuayan near Chalco Atenco, the soul is left not only to God but also to Saint Mary and the town saint, San Juan Bautista (AGN, Tierras 2554, exp. 4, f. 23). The passage runs: "icenmactzico yn totecullo Dios niccahua nolloliatzin in toanimantzin [*sic*] yhuantzi in cenquiscaychipuchitli S^{n}ta maria yn totepachocatzin Sr S^n Juan Bap^{ta}."

223. An example is NMY, doc. 10, pp. 118, 120 (Centlalpan, Tlalmanalco area, 1736). Immediately after using the phrase, the testator goes on to say that his heirs are to serve San Diego there. See also Chap. 3, section "Terminology and Constitution of the Household Complex." One will occasionally meet with God as the possessor of land; a document from San Gerónimo Amanalco in the Toluca Valley, 1645, has "yaxca ytlalitzin [*sic*] dios Çatepa nehual nitlatlacohuani," "the property and the land of God, and after that of me a sinner" (AGN, Tierras 2554, exp. 13, f. 11). A question that I have not yet resolved is the meaning of the frequent formula *atle ma itla nicpialia in tt^o Dios*, "nothing whatever am I holding for our lord God (other than what I have declared in my testament)" (variants in TC, docs. 25, 29, 36, 39, pp. 78, 92, 116, 128, and elsewhere). Although the point is hard to demonstrate conclusively, I have the impression that this phrase refers primarily to cash, whether assets, credits, or debts. If so, it would appear that God owned money as well as households. I provisionally believe that God comes into this matter because of the general inculcated religious obligation to wipe the slate clean with the supreme deity at the time of death. The Spanish wills on which the Nahuatl ones were originally modeled carry a strong emphasis on the liquidation of debt for religious as well as economic reasons. The Spanish terminology concerning the relief of one's conscience, however, seems to have no counterpart in Nahuatl wills.

224. A few statements by 16th-century Nahua cabildos have some direct doctrinal significance. Outstanding is a long tirade against the cochineal trade, entered into the minutes of the cabildo of Tlaxcala in 1553 (TA, selection 8, pp. 79–86). It is highly unusual in demonstrating the effects of some of the Spanish ecclesiastics' moral teachings, condemning not only drunkenness and fornication but pride and excessive attachment to worldly wealth as detrimental to one's spiritual welfare, with whole phrases taken straight from the friars' sermons. This piety, however, is transparently motivated by the cabildo members' concern to justify, especially in the eyes of Spanish officials, a policy working to the social and economic advantage of themselves and their peers. A long letter from the cabildo of Huexotzinco to the crown, dated 1560 (BC, doc. 29, pp. 176–91), in its plea for favors emphasizes among other things the altepetl's allegedly immediate, total, and unanimous turning to Christianity (the usual

line among Indian towns), but has little doctrinal content (although it yields the phrase "yn icel teotl dios," "the only god God"; pp. 188–89). A similar letter from the cabildo of Tenochtitlan, dated 1554 (Zimmermann 1970, pp. 15–17), while showing a close alliance with the Franciscan friars, has even less of doctrinal interest. (It does contain the interesting formula of swearing "before God, Saint Mary, and all the saints".)

225. Nutini has shown that in a modern Tlaxcalan community, those not marrying find it hard to participate fully in the community's ritual life (Nutini 1980–84, 1: p. 74, 2: p. 479, n. 2). The unmarried then as now must have been mainly lower-ranking members of the community in all respects.

226. The only ecclesiastic of the pre-1650 period whom I consider at all likely to have written the texts appearing under his name unaided is fray Alonso de Molina.

227. As in Sahagún 1986, p. 75.

228. Burkhart 1989 has a multitude of examples. See also Klor de Alva 1988, 1991.

229. In the plays, one can find some occasional stumbling. In a drama of the Magi, written in the circle of the Franciscan fray Juan Bautista and dedicated to him, thus composed presumably around the beginning of the 17th century, the Holy Trinity is twice referred to as the father of Jesus (TN, pp. 314–16). See also Chap. 9, section "Theater."

230. Burkhart 1988.

231. Barry David Sell is now working on a doctoral dissertation which will systematically open up much of this literature. Burkhart 1989 is a major first step in the analysis of many facets of the corpus and contains a large number of brief excerpts in transcription and translation.

232. See ANS, pp. 35–36, for a list. *Tlalticpaque*, "possessor of the world," may have been employed more widely. Sahagún, the ANS texts, and the religious plays use these phrases heavily, as do some sermons; they are less prominent in the confessionals and catechisms that I have seen.

233. Recall the story of Santiago of Sula (above, at n. 131).

234. See Lockhart 1982, especially p. 382 (also N&S, item 3).

235. For examples of the Spanish reports, see Gibson 1964, pp. 101, 133–34. On the 20th-century evidence, see especially Taggart 1983; and Nutini 1988.

236. The Andrews and Hassig edition of Ruiz de Alarcón (RA) is a magnificent contribution to Mexican ethnohistory in several ways, but above all in its transcription and translation of the Nahuatl incantations and its commentary on them. It will richly reward anyone who gives it close and repeated study. As much as the edition accomplishes, its contents provide the raw material for many additional insights.

237. RA, pp. 49, 68.

238. Nevertheless, the texts were being treated as canonical (a major mechanism in the creation of separate zones of belief and practice), and some were on their way to meaninglessness for the speakers. Ruiz de Alarcón complains (RA, p. 152) that fortunetellers, when asked the meaning of their words, pleaded ignorance, saying they simply repeated what they had learned from their predecessors.

239. RA, pp. 54, 59, 72.

240. Andrews and Hassig understand this very well; see RA, introduction, p. 23.

241. RA, p. 94: "yxpantzinco tlatlaz yn tty⁰ Dios."

242. RA, p. 59. The saint-house was a general locus for spiritual business. Dough images of preconquest gods were eaten there, and there hallucinatory visions took place (pp. 53, 60).

243. RA, pp. 66–67, 184–87.

244. RA, pp. 189, 198, 199.

245. RA, pp. 146, 148, 149, 157.

246. The Ruiz de Alarcón incantations in general are geared to the individual within a household context; the altepetl and tlaxilacalli appear to play no role whatsoever. Yet some flavor of the corporate is seen in Ruiz de Alarcón's statement that one fortuneteller (and she was not the only one) claimed she could not get things right outside the limits of her own pueblo and never even tried unless importuned (RA, p. 152).

The way the spheres mix or fail to is of great interest and should receive more attention. In the modern stories collected by James Taggart (1983), preconquest cosmology and exemplary tales have mingled with the Trinity and sermon language, as well as with Spanish folklore, but absolutely not with the world of the saints, the rites of passage, and the altepetl. In the modern Tlaxcala region, the preconquest-style ritual specialists are held carefully apart from the Christian specialists and rites, even though the two complement each other within an overall system (Nutini 1980–84, 1: pp. 137–38; Nutini 1988, p. 338; and passim in Nutini's work).

247. Nutini 1980–84, 2: 371; 1988, p. 338.

248. As shown in Christian 1981.

Chapter 7

1. See Hill and Hill 1986 for the fullest study of modern Nahuatl and its relation to Spanish in a specific subregion.

2. For example, the Yaquis; see Spicer 1962, pp. 452–54. Nahuatl seems to have served as an intermediary in at least parts of the process; Yaqui uses -*oa* to borrow Spanish verbs.

3. A large sample is published in AZ, as well as an interesting excerpt in Carrasco 1972; S. L. Cline plans to publish another large portion. See the article by Hanns Prem in AZ, placing the documents late in the period 1535–45 on the basis of the chronology of epidemics and the demographic characteristics of the census population. I rather doubt that firm dating can be attained by such means when so little is known of the course of the epidemics, but I too would tend to date most of the corpus after 1540 rather than before. Quite a few Nahuatl documents have the reputation of having been composed in the 1520's, but without going into detail, I will say that it is my belief that all of these rest on later attributions made with the purpose of enhancing the document's value in the eyes of the reader.

4. In my discussion of the three stages, I use some of the materials in *Nahuatl in the Middle Years* (NMY; Karttunen and Lockhart 1976), and I both follow and expand on the analysis included there. In this chapter I will make specific reference to that publication only when it contains significantly more detail on a given topic than

I include here or when I wish to qualify its findings. Little would be gained by close referencing because the work, having appeared in a linguistic monograph series, does not normally give the source of specific examples. Colleagues and I have plans for a new, much larger and reorganized list of loanwords, to be fully documented. See also Karttunen's readable restatement of much of the core of the 1976 publication (Karttunen 1982). Pp. 40—42 of NMY are devoted especially to Stage 1.

5. *Acalli* means literally "water house" and is one of many examples demonstrating the breadth of meaning of *calli* in preconquest times.

6. The intention of Molina's Spanish-to-Nahuatl section, which in the first edition constituted the entire dictionary, was not, of course, to define Spanish words, but to inform a Spanish reader who already knew the meaning of those words how to say them in Nahuatl. Nevertheless, when Nahuatl lacked a ready equivalent of a Spanish word that Molina wanted to include, he and his aides often produced something akin to a definition (in Nahuatl) of the type normal in monolingual dictionaries.

7. Quaint as this description may seem, it states well the primary function of the artifact and coincides with the etymology of Spanish *sombrero*, based on *sombra*, "shade."

8. CH, 2: 39.

9. See the entries in Molina, f. 51v, beginning with *malaca-*. It seems likely that *malacatl* was originally not merely a chance, opaque designation of an artifact; the stem probably includes the element *ilaca-*, "to twist," and thus would inherently have had to do with revolving. (The *ma-* cannot be "hand," as one would half expect, because of a vowel-length discrepancy.) That the word became associated with flat round objects that did not revolve, such as a shield, must rest on the notion that the line defining the edge turns upon itself. Yet to my knowledge *malacatl* was never used in its unmodified form to refer to the Old World wheel. It did become the standard word for the mining whim, drawing on the similarity between the cable winding around the drum and yarn winding around a spindle. I presume, that is, that it was so used in Nahuatl, originating early and surviving into the later stages, because the Spaniards themselves took *malacate* as the primary designation for the whim, and the only place they could have learned the word was from the mine workers, who in the first generation or two were overwhelmingly Nahuas (see Bakewell 1971, pp. 132, 134, 135). Because of its etymological affinities, it is entirely possible that *malacatl* in preconquest times had a broader meaning than spindle, referring to other revolving objects as well, so that its use with round things would not have to have involved a direct comparison with the spindle. Yet "spindle" is the only meaning in Molina, and I have seen no other in texts.

10. See Tezozomoc 1975, p. 416, among others.

11. See NMY, p. 58. *Quauhtemalacatl* was not entirely limited to "cartwheel" and "cart." For "pulley," Molina gives "quauhtemalacatlatlecauiloni," "woodenwheel instrument for hoisting something" (Spanish, f. 24; Nahuatl, f. 87).

12. Molina gives both spellings (ff. 84, 86). An additional meaning, which Molina in fact presents first and which doubtless existed in the preconquest period, is "to wash one's head." *Teca* and its derivatives usually mean "pour" when the object is liquid, but for *atequia* (f. 7v) Molina's gloss is "to wet someone, throwing water on him." The intention of *quatequia* in reference to baptism may be "to sprinkle water

on someone's head." The expression may seem to go against the two-word tendency, since it contains *qua*-, "head," *a*-, "water," and *tequia*, "to pour or throw (liquid) on someone," but *atequia* was already an established unitary word in its own right. Moreover, the expression is compact and elegant.

13. See Molina, Spanish, f. 19.

14. CH, 2: 34. Molina (Spanish, f. 29) gives *confirmación* as a loanword, which it may have been in his circle; CA, p. 74, in an entry for 1563, has "omochiuh confirmacio," "confirmation was carried out," and Chimalpahin too once uses this (CH, 2: 67), though he uses *tzonilpia* as well. But in the long run, the word did not take with the Nahuatl-speaking community in general; later loans having to do with confirming were in the legal, not the religious sense. The same phenomenon occurs with baptism. Despite recognizing *quatequia*, Molina uses *bautismo* as a loanword (Spanish, f. 44v). Apparently it took some time for even the most popular indigenous neologisms to get established definitively; furthermore, some may have faced a challenge from a tentative loan in the great wave of borrowing early in Stage 2 before gaining definitive acceptance (many, indeed, lost out).

15. An entry in Molina (f. 82) hints that *maçatl* could easily serve as a generic term for large nonpredatory quadrupeds. "Ivory" is defined as the tusk of an elephant, conveyed by Spanish *elefante* plus an explanatory equation with *maçatl*: "maçatl elefante ycoatlan," "the snake-tooth (tusk) of an elephant deer." The aide who came up with this must have relied on a picture or on Molina's description, for he surely never saw an elephant.

16. All of the expressions in Molina equating "deer" and "horse" are complex; under simple "maçatl" (f. 50), nothing is said about the horse (and ironically, there is no Spanish entry for horse at all, despite the frequent use of "cauallo" in the Nahuatl). On the other hand, under "stable" (Spanish, f. 26) Molina gives *only* "maçacalli," "deer house."

17. *Tepoztli* consists of *te*-, "rock," and *poz*-, apparently the same root found in *poztequi*, "to break (in smaller pieces)." The original sense may have been "rock broken up in small pieces," in reference to metallic ore ready for smelting. In fact, under *metal* (Spanish, f. 84v) Molina gives *tepoztli* (as well as *tepoztlalli*, "tepoztli earth"). Spanish *metal* is somewhat ambiguous; today it means exclusively metal, but in the 16th century, it more often meant ore. See also Molina's entry *tepozpitza* (f. 104), "to smelt *metal*," here clearly ore. I speculate that the term at origin referred to any ore, was extended to the metal itself, and then for most purposes was restricted to the most prevalent utilitarian metal, copper (all this in preconquest times).

18. Molina, Spanish, ff. 18, 71.

19. I have seen little indication that *maçatl* was ever modified. It easily could have been, by a word referring to the animal's hornlessness, its use as a mount, its distant origin, or the like, but if so, the modification must have been abandoned almost immediately. I find no trace of such a thing in the dictionaries or in most Nahuatl histories and references. The one exception, which might or might not be meaningful, is in FC. Among the many passages in book 12 using the term, we find one where horses are indeed referred to as "mamaça in temamani," "people-carrying deer" (book 12, p. 73; chap. 25).

20. The word's probable origin in a generic term (see n. 17) goes far toward

explaining this fact. Another example of the generic propensity of *tepoztli* is Molina's entry for the new metal brass, for which the Nahuatl equivalent given is *coztic tepoztli*, "yellow tepoztli" (Spanish, f. 3v). I suspect that the expression was an ad hoc invention of a Molina aide, but if so, it illustrates the point equally well or better.

21. Consider *tepozcuarto*, a copper coin worth a fourth of a *real* (Molina, f. 104). *Tepoztli*, modified or unmodified, means "bell" in TCB, p. 9, CH, 2: 48, and Molina, Spanish, f. 23v, Nahuatl, f. 104v. Not all the items in Table 7.5 were of iron, at least not always, including pins, wire, and printer's type.

22. See Molina, Nahuatl, ff. 103–104v, for a large concentration of *tepoz-* constructions. Others will be found scattered through the book.

23. Spanish did tend to call a pointed weapon or the iron cutting portion of a tool with a wooden handle a *hierro*, which in principle approximates some of the usage in Table 7.6 even when the specific examples fail to coincide, but to use the word in this way with a bell or a clock would have been foreign to Spanish idiom.

24. Codex Mendoza 1980, f. 8; Matrícula de Tributos 1980, f. 4.

25. Molina, f. 104. For *tlateconi*, see TC, doc. 45, p. 158 (Culhuacan, 1581). Molina himself has the streamlined version as well (f. 134v). L. Reyes García 1978, p. 140 (Cuauhtinchan, 1589), has *tlateconi* with *tepoztli* following it, "of metal," but not incorporated into the noun. I deem it probable that *tlateconi* was already one of the terms for an axe or hatchet in the preconquest period.

26. *Tepozcactli* for "horseshoe," however, is attested for the 20th century (Brewer and Brewer 1971, p. 225).

27. *Tlaltepoztli* occurs frequently in TC (docs. 15, 24, 31, 39, 45, 75, pp. 52, 74, 102, 128, 158, 260; Culhuacan, ca. 1580), and *miccatepoztli* in CH, 2: 48, 104. New uses of *tepoztli* in this sense may have continued to evolve. In present-day Nahuatl, *tepoztli* can mean firearm (Brewer and Brewer 1971, p. 225; Key and Key 1953, p. 221).

28. For more on naming patterns, see Chap. 4. An important exception to ecclesiastical determination, as seen there, was that when the person baptized had a Spanish lay sponsor, he normally took the latter's name. The fact that in the early years, extending into Stage 2, certain names were especially popular in certain regions can be interpreted as reflecting the predilections of friars stationed there, but when we find siblings with the same name, it seems that the Nahuas must have had a hand in the choice, attaching at first a different value to the new names than in the Spanish system. See AZ, 1: 2 (Juan Acolnahuacatl and María Teiuc have two Pedros), 9, 46 (two Magdalenas in each); AZ, 2: 5–6 (two Domingos), 36 (two Vicentes); and MNAH AH, CAN 549, f. 1v (a pair with two Pedros and two Magdalenas). An example occurs in Culhuacan as late as 1585: TC, doc. 64, pp. 229, 230–31. In all cases, the siblings have different indigenous names. Before long, the Nahuas seem to have been primarily deciding their own names, retaining (and at the same time gradually expanding somewhat) the framework the ecclesiastics originally set.

29. In the Cantares Mexicanos, we find "tonan malintzin" (doña Marina, reverential; Bierhorst 1985, p. 318) attributed to speakers of the time; "Malintzin" occurs repeatedly in FC, book 12 (for example, p. 49, chap. 18; pp. 125–26, chap. 41) but is never actually put in the mouths of contemporaries.

30. MNAH AH, CAN 549, ff. 1v, 12; 550, f. 5; 551, f. 100.

31. Examples in ibid. 549, f. 6; 551, f. 82v; and too many to detail in 550.

32. Some Nahuatl writers preferred Castillan with an *s* (for an example see BC, doc. 34, p. 210); Molina himself used this form. In either case the pronunciation of the consonant in question was [š], which approximated the 16th-century Spanish retroflex *s*. Although the added final *n* may be missing in a few examples (any *n* was subject to optional omission), it is present in such a multitude, from so many authors, regions, and time periods, that there can be no doubt that the form with *n* was standard in Nahuatl. Even Molina, who rarely acknowledges Nahuatl adjustments in Spanish words, without exception includes this *n*. Moreover, the *n* is necessary for the morphological interpretation the Nahuas gave to the word, as we will shortly see.

33. Despite its principal function as a modifier, Caxtillan is not an adjective, nor does the *n* have anything to do with the Spanish adjectival form *castellano*. The word has the *n* even when used independently as a place-name. In Nahuatl grammar, one noun may modify another at need. Ordinary nouns are most often compounded with the noun they modify, as in the *tepoz-* expressions. Place-names also frequently modified nouns, in such phrases as *Tenochtitlan tlatoani*, "Tenochtitlan ruler, ruler of Tenochtitlan," but they were not susceptible of being bound to other words. Nahuatl place-names were complex constructions consisting of a nominal stem plus a quasi-nominal, relational suffix-word indicating location, so that in themselves they were locative. The Nahuas construed Caxtillan to be a word of this kind, as they continued to do later with Spanish place-names even when they could not identify any locative element in them. Consider how *Roma*, "Rome," and *Caxtillan* are treated identically in Molina (Spanish, f. 105v, entry "romance"); Latin is *Roma tlatolli*, "Rome speech," and Spanish *Caxtillan tlatolli*, "Castile speech." In both cases, as in the above example *Tenochtitlan tlatoani*, something of the locative sense remains: "speech in Rome," "speech in Castile," "ruler in Tenochtitlan." The effect is close to "of" in English: "speech of Rome," etc. The equation of Roma and Caxtillan here suffices alone to demonstrate that Caxtillan cannot be considered an adjective.

34. Of all the metal introductions dealt with in Molina, I have found only one using Caxtillan in the description; for "axe that cuts in two directions," Molina gives *Caxtillan tlaximaloni necoc tene*, "Castile instrument for carpentering with an edge on both sides." Even here, one modifier is used instead of the other, not with it. Caxtillan seems to have been avoided also in expressions where *maçatl* was the modifier; *maçatl* and *tepoztli*, however, competed and overlapped to a certain extent (see the items having to do with horseshoes and branding in Tables 7.4 and 7.5). Nor in my experience does Caxtillan ever modify either *maçatl* or *tepoztli*.

35. One phonological adjustment in Nahuatl Caxtillan is hidden by the spelling. *Ll* in Spanish is pronounced [ḽ], in 16th-century Spanish perhaps by some [ḽʸ]. Nahuatl had no [ḽ] and standardly assimilated [y] to preceding [l], giving geminate [ll], which is what the *ll* in Caxtillan represents. If one follows the morphological analysis through to the end in Nahuatl terms, one would expect that the mysterious stem *caxtil-* would be from a noun *caxtilli*, just as *tlaxcal-* in Tlaxcallan is from *tlaxcalli*. From Caxtillan itself there is no way of ascertaining what Nahuatl speakers imagined the root noun to have been, but the neologism *caxtil*, to be discussed just below, speaks in favor of that form over one with the absolutive *-li*. See also n. 41.

36. *Español* was borrowed as early as 1547 in Tlaxcala (BC, doc. 22, p. 118) and continued to appear frequently in texts during the following decades and centuries.

37. Everything about the word leads me to believe that *caxtiltecatl* is a Stage 1 formation, even though the first attestation known to me is from 1570 (NMY, p. 82, specific source not indicated). For a few of many subsequent occurrences, see CH, 2: 47; UCLA TC, folder 23, ff. 22–23 (San Miguel Acatlan, Tulancingo area, 1659); and BC, doc. 17, p. 100 (Azcapotzalco, 1738).

38. Had Caxtillan not been considered a -*lan* word, the most likely indigenous term for the Spaniards would have been *Caxtillan tlaca,* "Castile people." In fact, I have seen this term used (along with *españoles*) in some documents from the Tulancingo region around 1570 (UCLA TC, folder 1, document dated Oct. 27, 1570; also petition against Martín Jacobo), and in texts from Mexico City (AGN, Tierras 55, exp. 5, f. 2, 1564; CA, p. 54). The relative frequency of the two expressions, however, speaks for itself. In any case, a -*tlan/-lan* word is not excluded in theory (and occasional practice) from the construction with *tlacatl.*

39. BC, doc. 34, p. 210 (Tlaxcala, 1545).

40. Molina, f. 13 (several lines above this entry, there is another *caxtil* defined as "bowl"; this is a typographical error for *caxitl*). In present-day Zacapoaxtla, *caxtil* means "rooster" (Key and Key 1953, p. 145).

41. If in fact Nahuatl speakers had created a regularly inflected noun *caxtilli* as the supposed though un-understood root of *Caxtillan,* it could at least have been given the meaning "thing(s) characteristic of Spain." *Caxtil* could then conceivably be an apocopated form naming a particular animal (apocopation was among the devices Nahuatl used in creating names and specifically animal names, as can be seen with *quanaca* in Table 7.8). Yet in the total absence of any attestation of *caxtilli,* I consider it far more likely that *caxtil* is a direct back-formation from Caxtillan.

42. MNAH AH, Fondo Franciscano 129, entries for March, 1610. Since this writer frequently omits *n,* little or nothing can be deduced from its omission in "Caxtilla." It did happen not infrequently, however, that Nahuatl speakers of later generations, more cognizant of Spanish pronunciation, took it upon themselves to revise an earlier loan, bringing it closer to the original. In Molina, "color" in general is already *tlapalli.*

43. It is true that the main evidence is posterior by decades, but the Cantares Mexicanos put the name in the mouth of participants in the conquest battles (Bierhorst 1985, pp. 318, 328) and include other names as well, among them the well-known conqueror Castañeda ("Caxtañeta," p. 322). Cortés is referred to (same page) as "Genelal Capitan," which might be barely possible, but an indigenous woman is referred to as doña Isabel ("toya Ixapeltzin"), though she would not have received that name until later. Other words used must be posterior, including the loan "ixpayolme" (*españoles,* p. 320). Another conquest-related section has "Capitan," "Malia," and "caxtillan," but also "Amen" (pp. 328, 330). Under these conditions, any attestation can be no more than suggestive for times earlier than the date of the version preserved (well into Stage 2). Similarly, FC, book 12, has "Malintzin" (see n. 29) and "Castañeda xicotencatl" (p. 99, chap. 34); they are not spoken by contemporaries in the text, though with Castañeda at least such is strongly implied.

44. See NMY, p. 40.

45. The same is not true of the later stages and the borrowing of words of other parts of speech. We will see evidence that the Nahuas understood some Spanish verbs and found indigenous equivalents well before they took to borrowing them. Like-

wise, Spanish particles appeared in unanalyzed phrases used in Nahuatl before they were borrowed. In these cases, then, there was a significant lag between the time of comprehension (together with a demonstrated interest in the Spanish expressions) and the time of borrowing, so that one can speak with certainty of resistance or unpreparedness.

46. I have not been able to establish anything definite about the origin of *pitzotl*, the alternate word for "pig" and the one that won out in the long run. Molina's entry "pitziquiui," "to eat a great deal," suggests that the term might be descriptive of the animal's eating habits, but it could equally well be the name of some animal the Nahuas already knew.

47. *Ichcatl* was particularly apt for an extension to wool, and not only because of the whiteness wool shares with cotton. *Ichtli* means maguey fiber, the primary material from which clothing was made in central Mexico before cotton was imported from the south, and the compound *ichcatl* may be considered to have meant "high-quality textile fiber" in preconquest times. Yet in mundane Nahuatl texts, along with many cases where *ichcatl* means sheep and quite a few where it means cotton, I have yet to see an instance in which it means wool. Molina (Spanish, f. 76; Nahuatl, f. 32) gives *ichcatomitl* and *ichcatzomitl*, "sheep down, fur, or hair," for "wool," although some of the *ichca-* compounds on f. 32, such as *ichcatilmachiuhqui*, imply the direct meaning wool for the word. However fleeting and ultimately secondary the wool meaning was, it was logically necessary in order to arrive at the meaning sheep.

48. Regional variation is especially noticeable with the names of the European animals, at all time periods, today as during the postconquest centuries, as can be seen in modern dictionaries and word lists.

49. Brewer and Brewer 1971, p. 17; Key and Key 1953, p. 21. In Zacapoaxtla, *quaquauhe* is still the word for cow and bull as well (Key and Key 1953, pp. 124, 127, 147). Tetelcingo is more in the mainstream, using Spanish loans in these two cases. For a bull to bellow, however, is *quaquauhchoca* even in Tetelcingo (Brewer and Brewer 1971, pp. 98, 101, 122).

50. See Stevenson 1968, pp. 41–53; and Bierhorst 1985, pp. 72–79.

51. Much of the evidence for the early times comes from that suspect source, the Franciscan extollers of their own efforts. But though we may reserve judgment about the quality of the performance and about the transcendental enthusiasm the Nahuas are said to have shown, there is no question that within less than 20 years indigenous people in altepetl all over central Mexico were playing liturgical music on European instruments, not to speak of singing part songs.

52. Note that the huehuetl, not the *teponaztli*, the two-tongued log drum, was taken as representative of the type and bearer of the analogy.

53. In Tetelcingo, *tzotzona* is still to play musical instruments, though as expected *pitza* is used with the flute (and other winds). The Spanish loan *tocaroa* serves only to translate the idiom *le toca*, "it is his turn" or "it affects him" (Brewer and Brewer 1971, pp. 98, 198, 215, 234, 237). As to the bagpipe, another bellows-like instrument (see Table 7.9), the Nahuas would presumably have described playing it as *pitza*, since one does after all blow into the bag. Though the bagpipe was around in the early period, it was no everyday item, and I am not sure the expression in Molina is anything more than his assistants' solution to a task assigned them.

54. Durand-Forest 1971, p. 123.

55. In the modern Zacapoaxtla dictionary, the terms given for the main musical instruments have a Stage 1 ring: for guitar *tlatzotzonaloni*, "instrument to be beaten," and for flute *tlapitzaloni*, "instrument to be blown" (Key and Key 1953, pp. 60, 65).

56. Brewer and Brewer 1971, p. 67 ("blowing"); Key and Key 1953, p. 87 ("beating").

57. Spanish ecclesiastics did sometimes deplore the "corruption" of Nahuatl speech. Some of the mildest, and most insightful and least disapproving, comments on Spanish loanwords in Nahuatl are to be found in Molina's introductory remarks to his dictionary ("Auiso nono," in the prologue to the Nahuatl-to-Spanish section).

58. I am not yet prepared to take a firm position on whether or not the Nahuas of the conquest era in fact called the Spaniards gods. See Chap. 10, n. 21.

59. So a cursory examination of the 1555 edition convinced me. Barry David Sell has begun to do a systematic comparison of the two editions, and I expect the results to be published in due course.

60. A few types, such as nouns for close blood relationships, were generally excluded until Stage 3. The realms of general thought processes, emotions, actions, and the universal natural elements of the visible world were also unaffected as in Stage 1, but this seems more from lack of need than from any constraint or difficulty.

61. A few verbs appear in the sources, but in the infinitive, with the infinitive functioning as a noun and acting as the subject or more likely object of a verb (see below, at n. 91). More frequent are words that appear to be adjectives. In Spanish, adjectives not only have noun morphology, but can and do function as substantives; this accounts for many Spanish adjectives in Nahuatl. Others appear only attached to a Spanish noun, as in *alguacil mayor*, "chief constable," a combination best seen as a unitary or unanalyzed noun or noun phrase. There remain a few cases of words with an apparently truly adjectival interpretation in Nahuatl (see NMY, pp. 26–29). At one time I was convinced that there was no such thing in Nahuatl as an adjective, that all seeming adjectives were substantives. So-called Nahuatl adjectives still appear to me generally more nominal than their counterparts in English, but many words in *-tic* do have much the same characteristics as English adjectives, and a word that is acting as an adjective often (not always) behaves differently from a normal noun in remaining in the singular even when it modifies a noun in the plural.

62. S. Cline 1986, p. 178, with references to TC.

63. Molina, Spanish, ff. 21, 33v, 91, 105v, 107.

64. An expanded, updated, and reorganized compilation is planned.

65. I am reminded of how the results of a rough sampling of slave origins I did for early Peru (1968, p. 173) were later largely borne out by much more massive compilation.

66. S. Cline 1986, pp. 177–81.

67. Let it be clear that not all the loans in the TC list are new compared with the NMY list, though several are. TC does, however, present us with a distinct sampling based on a relatively large and coherent corpus.

68. Today probably all the month and day loans could be attested, but some had not yet been found when the NMY compilation was made, although it was already clear that they had all been borrowed early in Stage 2. Nor does Molina give them all.

These words are among the clearest examples of the distinction between loan time and first attestation.

69. Recall the case of the ne'er-do-well turkey thief Cristóbal in Tulancingo in the 1580's (Chap. 3, section "Terminology and Constitution of the Household Complex"; also Appendix A, Doc. 2).

70. TC, pp. 52, 104. The second example occurs another time, identical except for spelling: "siera quauhteconi." *Quauhteconi* in this phrase could be interpreted more adjectivally, giving a rendering "a saw for cutting wood," but I tend to think that the structure is the same as in the first example, with two cross-referent equivalent substantives.

71. This is one of Chimalpahin's favorite phrase types, as in "ycel yyoca nencatzitzinti mogestin," "those who live alone and by themselves, monks" (CH, 2: 140), or "quauhteocalli munomento," "wooden temple, the 'monument'" (2: 17). The opposite order also occurs: "campana yn miccatepoztli," "a bell, the dead-person iron" (2: 48).

72. CH, 2: 60. Chimalpahin's discussion of a shipwreck on pp. 60 and 61 gives us a good example of wavering usage where the speaker is unfamiliar with a loan or thinks his audience may be. After introducing the topic with the full phrase given in the body, Chimalpahin twice reverts to using the simple Nahuatl identification *acalli*, as in the first generation. Then he uses both terms together again, "acalli yn nabio," then just "acalli," then just "nabio."

73. Two examples in NMY, doc. 9, p. 114; also, from the same document, "yn quitocayotia mal pays," "what they call the Badlands" (MNAH AH, GO 184, f. 25v). Zapata also uses the phrase, as in "yn castila textl quitocayotia Blanquilio," "the Spanish flour that they call *blanquillo*" (ZM, f. 98), and also in an alternate form with *motenehua*: "cabildo yaxca motenehua probiyos," "the property of the cabildo, called *propios*" (f. 99v).

74. The loanword is already in Molina. Its nonstandard form *xile* (Spanish, f. 109), repeated in Arenas (see NMY, p. 89) and in later mundane texts, indicates a very early time of incorporation.

75. Chimalpahin's -*vinonamacayan* or -*huinonamacayan* (CH, 2: 115–16) for someone's tavern implies use of the agentive as well. As implied above, in specialist circles virtually the entire complex would eventually go over to loanwords.

76. For a detailed enumeration of substitutions, see NMY, pp. 1–8.

77. See NMY, p. 6. For examples of *quixtiano* see n. 86; for *coloz* and the like, see ZM, ff. 103v ("colostitla," *cruztitlan*, "next to the cross"), 110v ("iteposcolutzin," *itepozcru(z)tzin*, "her metal cross").

78. For some examples of *animan*, see NMY, pp. 98, 105; BC, docs. 2, 4, 5, 6, 32 (pp. 54, 64, 68, 74, 198); and TC, docs. 3, 9, 12A (pp. 20, 30, 38). See the discussion in NMY, pp. 8–14, especially p. 12. The final *n* in *animan* is actually not a simple addition, but a replacement for another weak segment, the glottal stop.

79. It is true that one can take the position that even here a glide was present between the vowels. On the other hand, nothing prevented Nahuatl speakers from pronouncing *ia* in Spanish loans as *iya*, etc.

80. TC has the spelling "purcatori" (S. Cline 1986, p. 180).

81. BC, doc. 32, p. 198 (Mexico City, 1587). The *ánima* was treated in the same manner as a body part and was never pluralized.

82. The most likely reason for the choice of a certain few words is that they were mainly personal items and quasi-kinship terms that were nearly always in the possessed form, so that speakers were not reminded of the lack of an absolutive and reconstructed it for the minority of occasions when the word was not possessed. There are some exceptions, however. See the discussion in NMY, pp. 21–22. Some modern loanwords retaining the ending are seen in Brewer and Brewer 1971 (*camīxahtli*, p. 113; *comārehtli* and *compārehtli*, p. 116; *pēxohtli*, p. 174).

83. See the discussion of the nominal plurals in NMY, pp. 23–24. I am no longer sure, however, of the temporal sequence of plural types there presented (except for the growing predominance of simple Spanish plurals in Stage 3). It may have been an illusion caused by the particular texts that chanced to be available at that time.

84. See Appendix A, doc. 3; Lockhart 1982, pp. 389–90 (also N&S, item 3); and NMY, p. 26.

85. See NMY, pp. 42–43. *Dinero* was in fact not a word much used in 16th-century Spanish; in any case, the Spanish word ultimately went back to a coin just like Nahuatl *tomin*.

86. NMY, doc. 9, p. 114 (*quixtiano*, twice); MNAH AH, GO 184, ff. 21, 23, 28v (*quixtiano*), 28v (*xinola*); ZM, ff. 109v, 112 (*quixtiano*), 85v, 118v (*xinola*); CFP (Tepemaxalco, Toluca Valley, second half of 17th century), f. 1v (*quixtiano*). The earliest example of *quixtiano* in this meaning that I have seen is in the anonymous annals of Tenochtitlan in the 1560's, in an entry for 1564: "xicihui yntlac° nimitzonnamacaz x͞piano ychan," "hurry up; if you don't, I'll sell your services in a Spaniard's house" (MNAH AH, GO 14, p. 55).

87. Lockhart 1982, pp. 389–90 (also N&S, item 3).

88. That Nahuatl speakers were immediately able to use *l* word-initially shows that although *l* had evolved medially in Nahuatl over the centuries, there was no constraint on initial *l* when the occasion arose, as opposed to the true constraint that existed on long vowels before a glottal stop, for long vowels occurring in front of a glottal stop were actually shortened. There is thus a basic difference between the historically determined absence of something and a constraint or inability.

89. For a great deal of insight into this purism, see Hill and Hill 1986. Antecedents can be seen in such a 19th-century figure as Faustino Galicia Chimalpopoca, but the only hint of puristic sentiment I have seen in colonial-period Nahuatl texts produced by Nahuas is some possibly conscious conservatism in the work of the late-17th-century Tlaxcalan annalist Zapata (see Chap. 9, section "Annals").

90. Example in NMY, doc. 6, p. 105. See also the discussion in NMY, pp. 29–30. A much used alternative to *firmayotia* was the circumlocution, though also a natural and succinct phrase, *quitlalia ifirma*, "to set down one's signature" (as in BC, doc. 3, p. 62, or NMY, doc. 2, p. 94).

91. An example in TA, selection 11, p. 89 (Tlaxcala, 1553); see also NMY, pp. 31–32. The anonymous annalist of Tenochtitlan in the 1560's made generous use of this convention: "desteral chihuililoc in gou°ʳ atlacuihuayan," "the governor of Tacubaya was exiled" (MNAH AH, GO 14, p. 48); "visitar quichiuh," "he carried out an inspection" (p. 119); "comulgar mochiuh," "communion was held" (p. 138); "notifical quinchihuilico," "he came to notify them" (p. 158). Note the use of the applicative form of *chihua* in two cases.

92. Molina, Spanish, f. 112v.

93. NMY, doc. 1, p. 93. The same construction appears in another phrase in the same text: "oncate ymecapilhuan yn nonamicatca," "my late husband had illegitimate children (who are still alive)." Other examples of this phrase type may be seen in the almost contemporaneous will of don Pablo Çacancatl, referring to possessions as well as children (CDC, 2: 12).

94. Although the censuses do use the *onca* construction at times (e.g., AZ, 1: 50, 73), the main phrase type is a verbless equative statement, such as "ce ypilçi" (MNAH AH, CAN 549, f. 13), "one his child," i.e., "he has one child." "He has no children" is "ayac ypilçi," "no one his child" (e.g., AZ, 1: 15, in this case "aocac ypilzi," "no longer anyone his child") or "amo pilhua," "he is not a child-possessor" (AZ, 1: 15; usually said of a couple as here). A pair of passages from these records can illustrate the occasional use in them of *pia*. "yz ca quitlapialli [*sic*] / y tlatovani / quipia ycuezco / yva totome quipia," "Here is the person who guards things for the tlatoani; he guards his granary and takes care of the birds" (MNAH AH, CAN 549, f. 12); "ça quixcaviya y xochipiya," "all he does is take care of flowers" (CAN 550, f. 82).

95. NMY, doc. 2, p. 95.

96. TC, doc. 44, p. 154. In "nicpia centetl nocahuallo," the sense is possession (the animal is not currently in the owner's hands), but in "quipia ytoca mīn cano," Martín Cano is only keeping it for the owner. It is of interest that the object of *pia* here again is a horse, and the person issuing the will is from Mexico City.

97. For the earlier phrase, TC, doc. 24, p. 74, "hatley y naxca y notlatqui." Compare, in Appendix A, Doc. 4, "atle ma ytla nicnopielia" (Azcapotzalco, 1695; earlier examples could be found).

98. These and similar phrases are seen repeatedly in the Cuernavaca-region censuses (AZ).

99. CH, 2: 107. Chimalpahin had not gone over to the *pia* phrase exclusively. At other times he uses ... *ye nemi tlalticpac*, "(so many years) he already lives on earth" (2: 2, 3). Another example of the *pia* calque, dating from 1611, "8 xihuitl quipia," "he is eight years old," is found in a text from Jalostotitlan in the Guadalajara region, well outside the area under study in this book (BC, doc. 27, p. 168). Yet for all the social, economic, and cultural differences to be observed in the peripheral areas, many of them seem to have kept in step with the Nahuatl of the center when it came to Spanish-language contact phenomena.

100. TC, doc. 41, p. 136 (Culhuacan, 1581). The most relevant phrase reads "quipia t^s (tomines) don a^{ol} xv p^{os}," "don Alonso has, keeps, owes 15 pesos of money." A few lines below is seen "ynn ompa mopia t^s," "the money owing there." The entire extremely complex and somewhat obscure passage will reward study. See also NMY, doc. 3, pp. 98–99, a will of 1608 from the Coyoacan region, where in addition to an instance of *pialia* ("nomonatzin nicpiellia 9 to," "I owe my mother-in-law 9 tomines"), *pia* is used with a whole list of people who owe the testator money. The document is a most instructive illustration of *pia* meaning "have," "keep," and "owe" under different circumstances. See further BC, doc. 3, p. 61 (Coyoacan region, 1617).

101. See preceding note; and BC, doc. 4, p. 66 (Coyoacan, 1622); TC, doc. 56, p. 202; and AGN, Tierras 54, exp. 5, f. 4 (Tlatelolco, 1587).

102. The earliest known attestation is in the 1611 Jalisco document cited in n. 99

(BC, doc. 27). Although from outside central Mexico, I think, in line with what I asserted there, that the example reflects and runs parallel with central Mexican usage.

103. See Chap. 5 at nn. 156ff.

104. CH, 2: 132.

105. NMY, doc. 6, p. 105.

106. NMY, doc. 3, p. 98.

107. See NMY, p. 44.

108. For example, "alahuertan" (BC, doc. 26, part 5, p. 160; Coyoacan, ca. 1550), "alahuerta" (BC, doc. 3, p. 60; Coyoacan region, 1617). Simple *huerta* can also be found (BC, doc. 2, p. 54, Coyoacan, 1588). NMY (p. 26) gives the impression that *alahuerta* disappeared in the later colonial period, but later examples have now been found. "Alahulta" occurs in a text of 1659 from San Miguel Acatlan in the Tulancingo region (UCLA TC, folder 23, ff. 22–23). Other common "a la" words were "Alachina," "China, the Philippines," and "Alaflorida," "Florida." "Alaela," *era*, "threshing floor," occurs in a 1632 text from Huejotla (AGN, Tierras 1520, exp. 6, ff. 8–9v), and "alaguna" (with elision of one *la*), *laguna*, "lake," in a 1645 text from San Gerónimo Amanalco in the Toluca Valley (Tierras 2554, exp. 13, f. 11). See also Chap. 5 at n. 225.

109. As in the verbs for playing certain musical instruments: *teponazoa*, "to play a log drum," from *teponaztli*, "log drum," or *quiquizoa*, "to play a trumpet," from *quiquiztli* (see also Table 7.9).

110. NMY, p. 18.

111. Loan verbs are still outweighed by loan nouns today, though they have become far more numerous and greatly extended their scope. See Brewer and Brewer 1971, passim. Among colonial-period loan verbs that I have seen but not specifically recorded is *tocar*, "to be someone's turn."

112. *Firmaroa*, "to sign," was practically identical in pragmatic meaning to the earlier noun-based *firmatia*.

113. *Cruzaroa* occurs in a text of 1717 from San Antonio la Isla near Calimaya (Toluca Valley): "canpa mocrusadohua otli yc quaxoxtenco," "where the roads cross at the border" (AGN, Tierras 2539, exp. 4, f. 1). I have seen this expression three or four times in Toluca Valley texts.

114. For just a sample of the attestations, see CH, 2: 132; AGN, Tierras 2541, exp. 11, f. 3 (Calimaya 1750); and BC, p. 106 (Azcapotzalco, 1738).

115. AGN, Tierras 56, exp. 8, f. 2v. It is possible that "trassuntaroa" should be read "trasjuntaroa," but this would change nothing of substance. The passage may mean "none of my titles is translated yet," since in Nahuatl "all are not" frequently has the meaning "none is," but there is not enough context to be sure this is the case.

116. NMY, doc. 7, p. 106. The form "quimocopirmalhui" is interesting: the use of the applicative of *-oa*, *-huia*, as a reverential implies that *-oa* was something well enough understood by the writer to be taken for granted and subjected to elaboration. It is true that the most common reverential for *-oa* verbs was to be the causative in *-oltia*; see, for example, BC, doc. 17, p. 106 (Azcapotzalco, 1738). But the *-huia* reverential continued to appear sporadically, as in the very same document from Azcapotzalco ("oquimofirmarhui," "he signed," p. 102). Another example ("camo oquimobalerhuique," "they did not take advantage of it, accept it") comes from Huejotla, the same place as the attestation of 1634; perhaps there was a local tradition (AGN, Tierras 1520, exp. 6, f. 12, 1710).

117. The 1637 example in Table 7.18, *espoliaroa* (UCLA Research Library, Spe-

cial Collections, McAfee Collection), is from a still unidentified settlement apparently located toward the west, possibly outside central Mexico altogether.

118. CH, 2: 132, line 6.

119. Chimalpahin's form is morphologically regular, containing the full infinitive as a stem and the usual *-ltia* causative of *-oa*. In the stem *-passeal-*, *l* for *r* is the normal substitution. The pronunciation of *ss* is hard to specify, but the spelling is sometimes found in Nahuatl texts where one would expect *x*. An example of a late attestation of *pasearoa* still with sound substitutions is "onicpaxaluchti," "I conducted him, caused him to stroll" (AGN, Tierras 2541, exp. 11, f. 3, also in N&S, item 7, text 1).

120. MNAH AH, GO 184. The verbs labeled "ca. 1680–1700" in Table 7.18 are those from this set. Internal evidence indicates that the work was recopied with some new commentary after 1700, but the primary time of composition clearly falls in the 1680's.

121. Subjecting the same corpus of verbs to numerical analysis by their semantic categories, as I did above, is not the same thing as analyzing their regional origin, because semantically they make one unified group of reasonable size, regardless of where they came from, whereas a larger sample will be required to make more of the vagaries of regional origin than that *-oa* was widespread (itself a most meaningful finding). The greatest concentration, eight new loans plus the use of some previously attested, is in a set of annals from Puebla (see n. 120), but this is clearly chance. It might turn out that Puebla as a second metropolitan area shares the role of Mexico City, but that remains to be seen. There is also a surprising concentration in the Calimaya region of the Toluca Valley, surely because it happens to be well endowed with late colonial Nahuatl documents and I have studied a good many of them. Limited temporal analysis of the sample is also more suggestive than the regional, because here too the whole group organizes around a single criterion and makes a pattern.

122. NMY, p. 32, puts forth the hypothesis that the pidginlike Nahuatl spoken by some in the far south of Mexico may have retained the older convention of *chihua* plus infinitive rather than *-oa*; p. 74 gives some examples. For full texts, see L. Reyes García 1961.

123. BC, doc. 28, p. 174 (San Martín, Guadalajara area, 1653). The situation with conjunctions was not so extreme (see the discussion in NMY, pp. 36–39). Perhaps this was the very reason why the emphasis in loans for a long time was mainly on prepositions (though *hasta* is often seen as a clause-introductory word, including in its earliest attestation, also BC, doc. 28, p. 174).

124. The 1653 examples of *hasta* and *para* (BC, doc. 28, p. 174) are from San Martín (Hidalgo), about 45 miles southwest of Guadalajara. The 1652 example of *sin* is from a place called Analcotitlan, and though it has not been firmly identified, internal evidence in the document points to the west. Despite these attestations, and the very early *-oa* verb attestation apparently from the west (see above, n. 117), I remain to be convinced that the periphery played a strong innovative role in Stage 3 Nahuatl, though it surely was au courant; until compilation is further advanced, we must keep an open mind. The apparently earliest attested particle in central Mexico proper is from Sultepec, 1660 (AGN, Tierras 1780, exp. 3, ff. 1–2v). The page that repeatedly uses "asta" actually gives "166" as the date, but an accompanying page specifying 1660 seems to clear up the matter.

125. *Ni aun* usually lost one of the vowels of its diphthong. The first attestation, in a document of 1737 from Tepetlixpan (Chalco region), has "nian" (AGN, Tierras 2549, exp. 1, f. 1). An Amecameca document of 1746 has "nion," "niun," and "nihon" (Karttunen and Lockhart 1978, pp. 158, 172, 174). In the Amecameca cases, as often, the meaning is close to simple "nor," but in the Tepetlixpan document, the term conveys the full original Spanish "not even": "amo quimacac aqui licencia nian se topile," "No one gave him permission, not even a topile (minor official)."

Por usually meant "as," since Nahuatl already had ready equivalents of the word's more basic senses in Spanish, especially "by (agency)" and "on behalf of." The Tepetlixpan document again has a good example (f. 5): "niquinnocahuilintehua por testigos," "I leave them behind as witnesses." Occasionally *por* does have other senses, however, as seen in another passage of the same document (f. 1): "amo . . . aqui . . . oquimacac yhuelitis por ytech omayauh yn tle altepetlali," "no one gave him his permission for having grabbed what is altepetl land."

126. Particles do not get their due in the modern dictionaries. Still, see, for Tetelcingo, Brewer and Brewer 1971, p. 73 (*¿para qué?: ¿para toni?*). Neither Brewer and Brewer 1971 nor Key and Key 1953 mentions the pervasive *hasta*, although it is found in the common phrase *hasta moztla*, "till tomorrow (*hasta mañana*)," and many others. Today several other particles have joined these two on the list of indispensable words, for example, *pero*, "but" (Brewer and Brewer 1971, pp. 76, 176).

127. See NMY, doc. 9, pp. 114, 115, for the temporal sense and the idiomatic "even"; and MNAH AH, GO 184, ff. 12, 14v, the complete original of the same text, for the spatial sense. NMY, p. 35, gives the full text and translation of three illustrative passages; pp. 38–39 discuss in some detail the indigenous equivalents of *hasta* and *para*.

128. AGN, Tierras 2541, exp. 11, f. 3; also text 1 in N&S, item 7.

129. The Nahuatl future tense used here has many affinities with the infinitive of European languages.

130. *Para* here replaces the indigenous *-pa* (or sometimes *-pahuic* or *-huic*), "toward"; the standard phrase in older Nahuatl was *icalaquiampa tonatiuh*.

131. NAC, ms. 1477 B [1]; Calimaya, 1738. *Ic* was used with positional phrases in a way quite similar but not identical to Spanish *para*. The speaker felt the necessity of both, continuing a long Nahuatl tradition of piling up particle-like words of related meaning. Standard spelling of the quoted passage would be *para ic tlatzintlan*.

132. AGN, Tierras 2554, exp. 4, f. 1 (1764). A similar loan comes from the Tulancingo region: "yhuan oc ome teztiguz yparte y tlalcoqui," "and two more witnesses on the part of the land purchaser" (UCLA TC, folder 14, Nov. 3, 1687).

133. In the NMY survey, the first attestation of *norte*, "north," was 1719 (p. 78), of *poniente*, "west," and *sur*, "south" 1738 (p. 79). *Oriente*, "east," is listed under ca. 1607–29 (p. 66); this attestation is from Chimalpahin. For a full sample of late colonial Hispanized directional vocabulary, see the 1738 Azcapotzalco document in BC, pp. 100–108.

134. For *hermano*, see Chap. 3 at nn. 94–95. The reference to *oriente* comes in a discussion of biblical history (Chimalpahin 1889, p. 31): "yn tonatiuh yquiçayampa motenehua Oriente," "toward where the sun rises, called East." Chimalpahin's use of *norte*, though not in a passage referring specifically to Spaniards, does occur in a news

item of general interest, the 1607 appearance of a comet (CH, 2: 63). Chimalpahin covers all the bases, giving the general Nahuatl term, the Spanish term, and a localized direction, toward Azcapotzalco: "mictlampa y norte yhuicpa yn Azcapotzalcopa."

135. See ANS, passim, a text originally set in 16th-century Tetzcoco, especially the royal wedding negotiations and the speeches of the old lady.

136. In López y Magaña 1980, doc. 2, dated 1587, *norte* is written on the accompanying pictorial but does not appear in the text proper. In doc. 4, dated 1596, *norte* and *sur* are both in the text, explained by the traditional local "ihuicpa yn chiyauhtla," "toward Chiauhtla [north]" and "chalcopahuic," "toward Chalco [south]." Doc. 5, dated 1605, uses Spanish loans for all four directions, without indigenous equivalents. This appears to be a meaningful progression (since north and south were the least developed cardinal directions in Nahuatl, it would be natural for them to be borrowed first), but the effect could arise from chance in a small sample. Tetzcoco, for all its importance, does not seem blessed with as large a legacy of Nahuatl documents as Coyoacan or Tlaxcala. Doc. 4, 1596, is where we find don Miguel de Carvajal calling Pomar both "notiachcauh," "my elder brother/cousin, and "noprimo hermano," "my first cousin." The two phrases occur at some distance from each other, in the order just given. See also Chap. 3 at n. 94.

137. In one of the testaments of Culhuacan, inanimates with *-ton* take the *-tin* plural suffix: "yn ichinanyo etetototi chichicueematototin onicnamaquilti," "I sold him the three little chinampas, eight brazas each, that go with it" (TC, doc. 74, p. 256, 1587; additional examples occur in TC). Note, however, that the verbal object prefix is singular nevertheless. *Tepetl*, "mountain," was among the inanimates sometimes pluralized, for reasons not yet clear (possibly their reputation as the home of spirits; see "tetepe" in CH, 2: 117).

138. A quasi-plural was sometimes attained by the use of the distributive (reduplication of the first syllable) without a plural suffix, as in *huehuei incacal*, "their houses (each of them) are large."

139. Karttunen and Lockhart 1978, pp. 160, 170, 174. The possessed plural was also used in this way: "icalhuan yn Geronimo Muños," "Gerónimo Muñoz's houses" (p. 170). Forms of these types are found all over central Mexico, for example "nocalhuan," "my houses," in the Tulancingo region (UCLA TC, folder 25, March 1, 1768).

140. In "niquipia nomehuan," "I have magueys" (AGN, Tierras 2555, exp. 14, f. 3; Soyatzingo in the Chalco region, 1736), "-qui-" is for *-quin-*, the plural verbal object prefix. In "yn omoteneuhque tlalti," "the aforementioned lands" (ibid., also Soyatzingo, 1734), both principal words have plural suffixes. The latter phrase seems to be influenced by the Spanish habit of almost always speaking of land as *tierras* in the plural.

141. See the discussion in Karttunen 1978. In the body of the study, I have not broached the question of the exact timing of the spread of nominal plural marking because not until late in the project did it occur to me to examine sources systematically for inanimate plurals. Most of the examples I have at present are from the 1730's and 40's, as in nn. 139 and 140. The Puebla annals in MNAH AH, GO 184, however, which I consider primarily written in the late 17th century, do attest the phenomenon with "imahuan," "his hands," and "ycxihuan," "his feet" (NMY, doc. 9, p. 115); body parts were not standardly pluralized in Stage 1 and 2 Nahuatl; GO 184, f. 25v,

shows an inanimate plural through the verb ("yey bobedas oquintzacuh," "he closed three vaults"). Zapata, writing in the second half of the 17th century, has a great many inanimate plurals (for a few examples, f. 22v, "Buertatin," "doors," "pilaltin," "pillars"; f. 28, "teocaltin," "churches," "caltin," "houses"). I expect that with further compilation examples will be attested yet closer to 1640–50. Also, though I am not yet prepared to present evidence, I have recently begun to suspect that inanimate plural marking was more common in the eastern part of the Nahua world than in the Valley of Mexico from the very beginning.

In some varieties of modern Nahuatl, *s* serves as a plural for certain indigenous words, especially preterit agentives, which may end in -*ques*; -*que(h)* is the indigenous plural of this word type, so that -*ques* is a partial double plural (for examples, see Horcasitas 1974a, p. 22, and others). I have yet to see the phenomenon in older Nahuatl texts, but it does occur in the Spanish of the Nahuatl speaker Tezozomoc, who flourished in the late 16th and early 17th centuries (1975, pp. 424, 451, 666: "cuauhhuehuetques," "tepixques," "tezozonques"). It seems quite plausible to me that the -*ques* plural originated during the colonial period in Nahuatl-speaker Spanish and then migrated back into Nahuatl.

142. Calques did exist with nouns. Examples would be *tlatecpanalli*, "something placed in order," used by Chimalpahin for Spanish *orden*, "regular order of the church" (2: 88), and -*tzonteconyocan*, "head or skull place," for Spanish *cabecera*, "capital, head town" (Karttunen and Lockhart 1978, pp. 159, 164). But to my knowledge such nouns do not figure in the translation of idioms.

143. By our own times, many basic and common Spanish verbs had been borrowed. See Brewer and Brewer 1971, passim.

144. Phrases illustrating these senses may be found in NMY, p. 45. The passages dated 1746 are from the document partially published in Karttunen and Lockhart 1978, and the one dated 1738 is in BC, doc. 17, p. 102. The exact provenience of the others is no longer available. NMY, p. 137, n. 13, points to an isolated example of *pia* with a measurement as early as 1576. As we would expect in view of other anticipations, the attestation is from Mexico City.

145. Example in BC, doc. 17, p. 102, quoted in NMY, p. 45. This kind of use was apparently the entering wedge for *tle(in)* as a generalized subordinator on the Spanish model, something characteristic of modern Nahuatl but not yet attested for the colonial period.

146. The Arenas examples are mentioned in NMY, p. 88 (Arenas 1982, pp. 41, 93, 94). At this remove, we are not in much of a position to judge whether or not a publication produced by a Spaniard, and one clearly without the accomplishments of a Molina or a Carochi, truly reproduces Nahuatl usage of the time. In my opinion, Arenas used indigenous informants or aides and gives us an authentic Nahuatl, very down-to-earth and colloquial. Perhaps it is particularly the Nahuatl of the market and the workplace; perhaps it even has something of the flavor of a subvariety used for communication between Spaniards and Nahuas (though it is no pidgin, nor is it the barbaric "Spaniards' Nahuatl" sometimes seen in proclamations prepared by Spanish officials, with -*cl* for -*tl* and the retention of the absolutive suffix on possessed nouns). All things considered, it is still possible that Arenas himself had something to do with the prominence of "pia" idioms in his text. In fact, Arenas can be used as an argument,

though hardly an unambiguous one, that Spaniards speaking Nahuatl were an important factor in Hispanizing innovations.

147. Here, as often, we are handicapped by a very incomplete knowledge of Nahuatl idiom. From "to ford" to "to pass" is an almost comically large leap, but I suspect that *pano* already had extended meanings closer to *pasar*. Consider the closely related *panahuia*, deeply built into traditional Nahuatl usage in the meaning "to exceed."

148. BC, doc. 17, p. 104 (Azcapotzalco, 1738). Also quoted in NMY, p. 46. A similar example is AGN, Tierras 2541, exp. 11, f. 3: "sa nima onipano yca nuReppᶜᵃ," "right away I went over there with my officials" (also in N&S, item 7, text 1).

149. MNAH AH, GO 184, f. 23v (Puebla, late 17th century). Also quoted in NMY, p. 45.

150. Karttunen and Lockhart 1978, pp. 159, 164 (Amecameca, 1746).

151. For a modern example of *pano* as a calque for *pasar* in the sense "to happen," see Horcasitas 1974a, p. 80.

152. For example, Nahuatl *quiça*, "to emerge (and many other senses)," at times seems to have taken on idiomatic meanings from Spanish *salir*, "to go out, leave, etc." In the late-17th-century Puebla annals (MNAH AH, GO 184), *quiça* is used in the sense "to turn out (as leader after a selection process)," in a section reporting Hispanic events and in which *salir* would no doubt originally have been used ("to turn out as" being a prominent meaning of the Spanish verb; see the passage and some discussion in NMY, doc. 9, pp. 113, 114). However, *quiça* has such a multitude of meanings and overlaps with such a large part of the semantic range of *salir* that I for one am not entirely sure that *quiça* could not have been used in a similar way even before the conquest. If this is an equivalence, it differs from the fully established ones in that the two verbs are a good semantic match from the beginning, without major adjustment in the Nahuatl term, although *quiça* is originally more "to come out (toward the speaker)" and *salir* more "to go out (away from the speaker)."

To date there are few relevant attestations of *quiça/salir*; for the equivalence of Nahuatl *neci*, "to appear," and Spanish *parecer*, also "to appear," many examples can be found in the meanings "to show up," "to seem," and even "to appear" from a text in the legalistic sense, as in "yn quename nesi ytech yn nonetlaytlanis," "as appears by my petition" (Karttunen and Lockhart 1978, p. 164; Amecameca 1746). Again the question is whether or not the Nahuatl verb already had these senses, that is, whether or not it was a natural equivalent of *parecer*. Molina glosses *neci* only as "to show up" (f. 64v; see also "parecer lo que se perdió" and "aparecer o manifestarse," Spanish, ff. 92v, 11v). The indigenous idiomatic sense "for a contribution of some kind to be raised, produced" also had to do with something physically manifesting itself. If the physical sense was the only one, then we are dealing with a typical equivalence pair. Yet *neci* has to do with light (see "nextia, nitla" in Molina, f. 71v), a likely semantic foothold for a verb of seeming (consider German *scheinen*, both "to shine" and "to seem"). Again, I suspect that the preconquest verb already had virtually all the senses of *parecer* and was automatically used in the same contexts, though of course such a state of things would not prevent Nahuatl awareness of *parecer* from reinforcing the equivalence and affecting certain specific turns of phrase. It is hard to believe that in the above-quoted legalistic phrase, where two of the other words are Spanish-influenced, *neci* does not stand for *parecer*.

153. The same structure obtained in *pia* possession phrases in general, as in "niquipia nomehuan," lit. "I have my magueys" (n. 140 above).

154. Karttunen and Lockhart 1978, pp. 159, 164 (Amecameca, 1746). The verbal directional prefix -*hual*-, so often used with past temporal expressions, also appears here, although the Spanish phrase has no comparable element. Its exact thrust in such phrases is not fully established. I think it means the same thing as in English "back in . . . , back when . . . " (compare ANS, p. 148, "in ìquāc nihuālnŏzcăli").

155. *Huiquilia/deber*, "to owe," which had come into existence as we have seen by the early years of the 17th century, differs from the equivalence relationships being discussed here in two ways: first, the Nahuatl verb is a derived form and thus externally something of a neologism, whereas the other equivalences involve common verbs in externally unchanged form, and second, *huiquilia* as far as is presently known never extended to cover the many idiomatic uses of *deber* (such as to indicate probability), but applied only to the economic sense.

156. *Quen* and *quenin* remained the primary interrogative words for this sense, as they always had been (*quenami* is a compound embodying *quen*). Their range is virtually identical to that of *cómo*, but this is the result of convergent evolution rather than an equivalence.

157. NMY, doc. 9, p. 113, 114; Karttunen and Lockhart 1978, pp. 164, 170; AGN, Tierras 2541, exp. 11, f. 3 (also N&S, item 7, text 1).

158. *I-ca* is the third-person singular possessed form of the instrumental relational word -*ca*; I doubt that any other inflection of the word was identified with Spanish *con*. Some relational words, despite their apparently different structure, have much in common with particles. The particle *ic*, "because of which, for which, with which, etc.," gives every sign of being a frozen form of a third-person singular relational word, possibly -*ca* itself, with which it shares several senses. *I-huan*, "in the company of, and," at some unknown time (apparently after the 18th century) lost the *i* and became a particle "and," at least for speakers in some regions.

159. Karttunen and Lockhart 1978, pp. 159, 171–73 (Amecameca, 1746).

160. AGN, Tierras 2541, exp. 11, f. 3 (Calimaya, 1750; also N&S, item 7, text 1). One of the phrases runs "nehual . . . yca nu s^res alcaldes," "I . . . with the lords my alcaldes," and another "onipano yca nuRepp^ca," "I went over with my officials." In these phrases, *ica* appears to have displaced indigenous -*huan*, "together with, in the company of, and." (In the first example, since those accompanying the speaker are plural, by strict grammar the form should be *inca*, which would have been written "ynca" here. That the plural is not indicated hints that *ica* has become an invariant particle. However, since *n* was so often omitted, we cannot be sure.) In another passage, *ica* appears at first to adhere more closely to its older meaning—"mocuaxuxhuia yca Calistro Joseph," "(the land) borders on (with) (that of) Calisto Josef"—since the sense appears somewhat connected with instrumentality. The usual indigenous phrase for bordering was structured quite differently, however, with the holders of the abutting entities as joint subjects of the verb. I believe that in the present case the entire Nahuatl phrase is a calque on a Spanish utterance like "linda con tierras de Calisto Josef." Here as so often, an aspect of traditional Nahuatl idiom is retained even in the

calque. In talking about borders, Nahuatl emphasized the holders, often not even mentioning the land itself, just as in this example.

Although I do not specifically remember having seen *ica/con* in documents beyond the two cited, I fear that without my realizing it the wider sense of *-ca* became so normal to me that it did not strike me as an innovation, as *quenami/como* always did. Further work will surely uncover more attestations.

Both *quenami* and *ica* differ from the verbs *pia* and *pano* in the manner of attaining the equivalence. With the verbs, an aspect of similarity of meaning provided the leverage for the extension, but there would have been few cases in which the Nahuatl and the Spanish word would have actually coincided in usage, and then more by coincidence than by virtue of meaning exactly the same thing. The particle equivalents, on the other hand, did fully share one well-defined meaning with the Spanish word involved (manner in the case of *quenami*, instrumentality in the case of *con*) and proceeded from there to take over other senses of the Spanish term. In this they possibly somewhat resembled the verbs *neci* and *quiça* (see n. 152).

161. Modern Tetelcingo Nahuatl does have some *r* in indigenous vocabulary (see Brewer and Brewer 1971, p. 178, for an *r* in the equivalent of *huilana*).

162. For example, the copyist of the late-17th-century Puebla annals, who writes most loans as in standard Spanish, nevertheless has "quixtiano" from *cristiano*, "Christian" (here meaning "Spaniard"), and "xinola" from *señora*, "lady" (here "Spanish woman"). (See n. 86.)

163. See the discussion in NMY, pp. 7–8; and Lockhart 1981 (also N&S, item 8).

164. See NMY, p. 8, for examples and more detailed discussion. It was Frances Karttunen specifically who had the insights leading to this section. One of the examples given in NMY, "gedencia," from a set of Tlaxcalan annals, ca. 1720 (MNAH AH, CAN 872, f. 15v), should not be counted. It is there presumed that the Nahuatl form was for Spanish *gerencia*, but on reflection I have come to the conclusion that it is most likely a garbled form of *residencia*, so that whatever truncations and substitutions have taken place, the *d* is standard. But another example of *d/r* merging is attested for 1717 (see n. 113).

165. ANS; FC, book 6. On the first, see the discussion and excerpts in Chap. 3, pp. 87–89. The lack of such materials could itself be indicative of a lack of need for them, of course.

166. AGN, Clero Regular y Secular 204, exp. 5, f. 248. I owe the reference and a copy of the document to William Taylor. The Nahuatl of the quoted passage runs: "Ma sequiscayectenehualo in Santisimo Sacramento = Thotlasomahuisteopixcatatzinne Sr Cura. Ma huel yehuatzin in D^s Espiritu Santo motlasomahuisnepantlantzinco mopacayetzinnotia [*sic*] Miec xihuitli. Totlasomahuisthatzinne. huel nepechtequilistica. ticontenamiqui in moteopixcamatzin tosepanniantzin [*sic*] tehuanti Alc^s timochintin tequihuaque yhuan mochinti Altepehuaque huehuetque nican San Aug^n yacapitzactlan." Compare the preambles in BC, docs. 29, 30, 31, 32 (pp. 176, 190, 196, 198). Some of these formulas are Spanish or Spanish-influenced, but they belong to an integrated Stage 2 high style.

167. Karttunen and Lockhart 1978, p. 164.

168. AGN, Tierras 2541, exp. 11, f. 3 (N&S, item 7, text 1).

169. Hill and Hill 1986 quote substantial relics of this type of speech in the present-day Tlaxcalan region.

170. See Chap. 9 at notes 57–59.

171. See above at pp. 303–4.

172. In his guide for priests, Manuel Pérez reports Nahuatl speakers saying such things as "lo llamo mi hermano," "I call my brother," that is, omitting Spanish object-marking *a*, essentially retaining the Nahuatl phrase structure (quoted in RA, p. 317, n. 32). A late-17th-century writer in the Tula cofradía book still had Stage 2 pronunciation (indicated by his writing *diputado* as "tiputado"), even though he wrote in Spanish and, in the limited sample we have, handled it competently (TCB, pp. 86–87; 1683).

173. See Lockhart and Schwartz 1983, pp. 305–8, 318–19, 321, 331. No doubt governmental decrees promoting the active participation of Spaniards in indigenous corporate affairs and favoring records in Spanish over Nahuatl documents (see Haskett 1985, pp. 102–17, 188–94) help explain the increasing production of Spanish and decreasing production of Nahuatl texts during this period, but part of the reason that the laws were passed and to some extent obeyed was precisely that Spaniards were already flooding into the Indian world. Equally important is the fact that the Nahuas were now well prepared for this development by the previous centuries of contact and linguistic adaptation we have been discussing, aside from needing to communicate more directly with the Spaniards, who were beginning to look over their shoulders on every occasion.

174. I cannot provide systematic proof but will give some illustrations. An example with the full "sin embargo" formula comes from Mexico City, 1697 (AGN, Tierras 165, exp. 4, f. 3); in this case, a whole group of Indians present are said to be fluent in Spanish. In the same year, the governor of Tenayuca used an interpreter despite knowing Spanish (AGN, Tierras 1805, exp. 3, f. 41), and in 1708, all the officials of Tenayuca spoke Spanish but were given a notification through an interpreter anyway (ibid., f. 127). In 1725, the town officials of Huejotla (Tetzcoco area) used an interpreter despite their fluency in Spanish, "which they speak and understand" (AGN, Tierras 1520, exp. 6, Oct. 4).

175. Again some illustrations. In 1764, a group of four officials of Tlapitzahuayan (Chalco Atenco jurisdiction) needed no interpreter "because they are sufficiently fluent in Spanish [*bastantemente ladinos*]"; in the same time and place, an Antonio Fermín spoke Spanish and did the interpreting for his father (AGN, Tierras 2554, exp. 4, ff. 3, 28v). In the Tulancingo region in 1768, a don Marcelo Simón Rosales received a notification in Spanish, "which he understands very well" (UCLA TC, folder 25, March 1, 1768). The transition was gradual, and everything occurs: in 1762–64, seven past governors of Coatlichan and Quauhtlalpan (central Valley of Mexico) testified, one speaking in Spanish, five using an interpreter although they were said to speak Spanish, and two using the interpreter without any remark being made, hence possibly not able to speak Spanish (AGN, Tierras 2338, exp. 8). I do not mean to give the impression that no Nahuas testified in Spanish before the 1760's. Forty years earlier, in Tezontla (Tetzcoco region) two former alcaldes, aged 31 and 50, gave their testimony in Spanish; another, aged 80, used an interpreter (AGN, Tierras 2338, exp. 6, May 23, 1720). Still earlier examples could be found.

176. For the most part, the following discussion briefly summarizes N&S, item 7, which contains more analytical detail and examples as well as complete illustrative texts.

177. Occasional letter substitutions in the texts do indicate the continuation of certain Nahuatl tendencies in pronunciation, such as the merging of *i* and unstressed *e*. See N&S, item 7.

178. This and several other examples can be found in AGN, Tierras 2541, exp. 9, ff. 1–4 (Mexico City, 1782–83).

179. Ibid. 1501, exp. 3, f. 8v (Santa María de la Asunción, Calimaya/Tepemaxalco district, 1772).

180. Ibid. 2541, exp. 11, f. 5 (Calimaya, 1783).

181. Ibid. 2533, exp. 2, ff. 21–22 (San Lucas Tepemaxalco, 1784).

182. For example, "esto a de ser fuerte mi palabra," lit. "this my word is to be strong" (ibid. 2541, exp. 9, f. 8; San Lucas Tepemaxalco, 1779).

183. I am very grateful to Robert Haskett for supplying me with transcriptions of these documents, which he unearthed and recorded in his own research. All three texts are in AGN, Hospital de Jesús 9: 1 (Amacuitlapilco, 1795); 59: 13, f. 35 (Yacapixtla, 1766); 55: 16 (Xoxocotla, 1784). The first contains a hypercorrect *a* ("salio electo Go^{or} a D^n Andres losiano"), an excess *el* ("para que el conste"), and a missing *de* corresponding to Nahuatl structure. The second contains an attempt to translate a Nahuatl idiom ("se le muestra madre la santa eglesia"; I have not been able to ascertain the exact Nahuatl phrase at the root of this language, but the meaning is "to look after local ecclesiastical matters"). The third has some even more opaque wording doubtless attributable to the Nahuatl substratum. In all three, the proportion of letter substitutions is such as to imply a greater deviance from normal Spanish pronunciation than appears to be the case with the Toluca texts.

184. N&S, item 7.

Chapter 8

1. Detailed studies of the preconquest recordkeeper-painters are not available, and perhaps the materials for such studies do not exist, but in general the roles in the two societies seem to have been much the same: prestigious, associated with nobility, influence, and wisdom but not with the very highest rank.

2. Occasionally, Spanish *leer* turns up, as it does (used as an infinitive-noun) in a Tlaxcalan will of 1566 (BC, doc. 1, p. 52). The indigenous terms *tlacuilo* or *amatlacuilo* to denote a trained writer can be found in some 16th-century texts (e.g., BC, docs. 12, 13, pp. 92, 94; Coyoacan, 1557, 1575), but Spanish *escribano* was far more common from the beginning (it occurs together with *amatlacuilo* in the examples just given), and the native words are hardly seen after 1600.

3. "To paint," "to spread or spatter liquid (colored) material on the surface of something," seems to be the basic meaning of the verb by the 16th century. Its etymology is not yet clear to me.

4. See UCLA TC, folder 1 (Tulancingo, 1570; also N&S, item 6, text 1), *tlapallacuiloque*, "color painters," for painters of houses, walls, and the like. See also, on *amatlacuilo*, n. 2.

5. See Sahagún 1905–7 for such god portraits; compare Nicholson 1971; and Galarza 1979. In most cases, I use the term ideogram rather than logogram (which

Bricker 1986 employs for something very similar in Yucatecan Maya writing) because although a given glyphic element can usually be equated with a specific Nahuatl word, it strikes me that in the central Mexican system the reference is more to the idea behind the word, or at least to an abstract and general semantic root, than to the lexical word. Nahua pictographic transcriptions tend to ignore grammar, not only omitting affixes but making no distinction between nouns and verbs. (The scroll or speech sign can apparently mean either "speech," *tlatolli*, or "he speaks," *tlatoa*, as in Quauhtlatoa, the Tlatelolcan ruler, represented by an eagle and the scroll; Codex Mendoza; Galarza 1979, plate 1.2, p. 17, items 11, 12.)

6. As I have insisted elsewhere, the names of the sociopolitical entities are far too often called "toponyms." The term is not entirely incorrect, but these words in Nahuatl do not directly name physical features (such as mountains or deserts), or even in the first instance denote areas as such, though they do shade into that sense.

7. See n. 15 below.

8. Berthold Riese (1986, part 2) has made a good beginning at defining the genres. I do have some reservations, though, about his too-confident use of terms such as "book" and "chapter," and his tendency to view the records as purely written communication.

9. See also Peterson 1988, pp. 288–89.

10. Such as the Codex Mendoza and Matrícula de Tributos. The former seems to have been put on paper in the late 1540's; about the latter there are various opinions, and it does seem the earlier of the two.

11. I here rely on a survey of the material reproduced, and carefully and skilfully analyzed, in Galarza 1979.

12. See ibid., p. 59, and plates 2.7, 3.6, 3.10–3.11. Galarza has laid the whole process bare, and he understands that the transcriptions involve substitutions for sounds missing in Nahuatl, but he is not fully aware of the systematic nature of the substitutions. A particularly fine example is the rendering of Esteban as "ix-te-pan" (depiction and analysis of the examples discussed here will be found in Fig. 8.2). Here we find not only the normal *x* for *s* and *p* for *b*, but also the common pattern in which unstressed Spanish *e* becomes *i* while stressed *e* remains the same. Another suggestive case is "cal-a" for Clara. One Nahua strategy for handling initial consonant clusters was epenthesis between the consonants, using the vowel of the adjacent syllable; the actual pronunciation may have been "calala(h)." It is true, however, that simply omitting the *l* in the cluster, plus the normal substitution of *l* for *r*, would give exactly the result produced by the glyph, "cala(h)." "Domingo" is also rendered with the expected substitutions, "to-mi-co," with unvoiced *t* and *c* for voiced *d* and *g*, plus the frequent omission of syllable-final *n*. Whereas the short form of Francisco omitted the first syllable, the abbreviated form of Domingo omits the last (Galarza 1979, plate 2.7, no. 12). In this case, we are probably not dealing with a speech phenomenon; possibly here -*co* was identified with the indigenous locative suffix of that shape, which was ignored in traditional glyphic transcription (even when other suffixes were rendered, as in the Matrícula de Tributos).

In the case of Francisco, I have taken it that the *l* of *cilin* is silent, as the final consonant for a syllable often was, but possibly the weak unvoiced final *l* could be taken as an equivalent of the Spanish retroflex *s* even though *x* was the normal substitute (the *l* here is part of the root, not of the absolutive suffix).

13. See Galarza 1979, pp. 55, 59, among others.

14. Though Galarza's interest is ultimately in the preconquest writing system, for this reason the great majority of his material is relatively late and shot through with European influence (as he fully realizes).

15. I do not mean to minimize the phonetic aspect in the tribute lists. The principle of phonetic transcription is definitely established in them, and a large number of glyphs are affected, but the elements used phonetically are few, and they are not used consistently (that is, for example, -*tlan* is represented only part of the time, often being ignored). While some suffixes are transcribed, equally important ones, especially the ubiquitous general locatives -*c*/-*co*, -*can*, and -*yan*, are not. The phonetic elements I have detected are the bottom half of a human, representing pictorially *tzin(tli)* (bottom, anus) and phonetically the diminutive -*tzin*-; some teeth embedded in gums or in a mouth to represent *tlan(tli)*, "tooth," and hence the locative suffix -*tlan*; an open mouth with a speech scroll to represent *nahua*, "to talk, make sounds," and hence -*nahuac*, "next to"; a stylized banner to represent *pan(tli)*, "banner," and hence -*pan*, "place of," etc.; a foot or feet to represent *o(tli)*, "road," and hence the element -*o*-/ -*yo*-, "covered with," as in the altepetl name Itzteyocan; and it may be, though I am not yet entirely sure, that an arm representing *ma(itl)*, "hand/arm," stands for phonetically similar elements, as in the altepetl name Cacalo*man*can. See Matrícula de Tributos 1980, ff. 3v, 5v, 7r, 9r, 10r, 11v, 13v, 15v, 16v; and the same or related items in the cognate Codex Mendoza 1980, ff. 2v, 3v, 16, 23, 33, 39, 54.

No sign in the early map at the beginning of the Historia Tolteca-Chichimeca (HTC) can be shown to signify anything other than the root it portrays (as far as I am aware the same is true for the other, more Europeanizing, pictographs in this work). Locative suffixes are ignored. See also Nicholson 1971.

Scharlau (1986) in her treatment of the Codex Xolotl, a document thought to have originated before 1542, referring to a preconquest historical-legendary episode and in no visible way connected with Spaniards, speaks of and gives several examples of the phonetic use of pictorial glyphs (pp. 68–77), but all are of the type that I consider to be simultaneously symbolic and phonetic, giving one after another pictures or ideograms corresponding to the constituent roots of a proper name, as in conventional depictions of an ant and a mound for Azcapotzalco (lit., "at the ant-hill"). It is true that some of the items depicted and words intended may not have been literally the same as the corresponding elements of the name, and indeed I think that systematic work on the whole corpus would show this state of things to be quite common, but I attribute it, generally and here, to folk etymology rather than to conscious phoneticism. (The Codex Xolotl, like most of the oldest pictorial documents, usually ignores suffixes whether derivational or inflectional.)

16. It is true that in notarial script especially, Spanish writing had some unitary signs for syllables (as for *ver*/*ber*), but they were a minor undercurrent in the Spanish system and much less used by alphabetic writers of Nahuatl than by writers of Spanish.

17. In the Matrícula de Tributos and Codex Mendoza, the tooth grapheme, *tlan(tli)*, represents -*tla* (-*tlah*) as well as -*tlan*. We find it in words like Coatlan primarily, but also in Ahuacatla and Xocotla (Matrícula de Tributos 1980, ff. 3v, 10r; Codex Mendoza 1980, ff. 3v, 39). The same principle continued to obtain later in the

century (see Galarza 1979, passim). Note that in the tribute lists the tooth grapheme can be used even when the locative morpheme *-tlan* through assimilation to the preceding syllable becomes *-lan*, as in Xallan or Quetzallan (Matrícula, ff. 9r, 10v; Codex Mendoza, f. 6).

18. Postconquest phonetic transcription leaves vowel length and glottal stop entirely out of account, as did (as well as we can tell) preconquest practice before it. This continuity, however, is not a very strong indication, since any arrangement inspired by the Spaniards, whose language lacked both features, would doubtless have done the same.

19. It is most improbable that the Spaniards would have hit on the syllable as the primary unit. Consider how the Yucatecan ecclesiastic Landa took some elements of a Mayan syllabary to be an alphabet. See Landa 1973, pp. 105–6 (chap. 41).

20. See Scharlau 1986, pp. 107–11.

21. Galarza 1979, plate 2.1; MNAH AH, CAN 776. See also Glass 1975, pp. 289 (item 802) and 290 (item 813).

22. As in the religious calendar studied in Galarza 1979, pp. 23–49.

23. When Scharlau composed her in many ways excellent treatment of early postconquest writing (1986, pp. 113–41), she was unaware of the volume, timing, and nature of mundane alphabetic documents in Nahuatl, a fact that renders several of her general conclusions and analytical perspectives unacceptable, without in any way detracting from the value of her contributions to the understanding of the pictorial side of things. One technical error I must call attention to; she speaks correctly of the growth of a mixed genre in which the pictorial and alphabetic exist side by side, but she at times gives as an illustration documents in which the pictorial component is accompanied by a text in Spanish written by Spaniards (being a translation of the document bearers' oral statements; see, for example, pp. 128–29). These documents, common enough from the 1540's to the 1560's, are not mixed but still entirely in the traditional pictorial-oral mode. At most one could say, given the amount of empty space one finds on the pages, that they show the composer's awareness that a translation of the oral component would later be written down alphabetically by someone else.

24. Especially in the use of *oa* and *hoa* for [wa] and the undifferentiated use of *i* for both [i] and [y].

25. Notably in the (laudable) use of *lh* for unvoiced final [l]. Olmos was conceivably the originator of the convention of *h* for glottal stop, in which most later practitioners followed him fitfully if at all; but then he himself was far from consistent in using the notation, and he had little if any awareness of the distinction between *h* for glottal stop and *h* to indicate devoiced final consonants. See Olmos 1972, pp. 199–201 (book 3, chap. 6).

26. See AZ, throughout. The orthography stopped short of consistently adding *h* to any voiced consonant in final position, though as mentioned in n. 25, Olmos wrote *lh*. Final *m* does not occur, becoming *n*, and final [n] was so weak that it often struck both Spaniards and Nahuas as absent rather than as devoiced. Final *y* coincided with *x* and was so written. The Spanish gestures toward recognizing syllable-final devoicing, though accurate and appropriate, hardly could be said to improve the usefulness of the orthography for Nahuatl speakers. The important thing from their point of

view was the identification of segments; once identified, they would automatically pronounce them correctly according to context. It is perhaps for this reason that some of the earliest Nahua writers of alphabetic texts were not faithful in writing the syllable-final form differently. Fabián Rodríguez, one of the first notaries of Tlaxcala, at times wrote [w] as *hv* regardless of context, as in "taltepehv" (TA, p. 118), and the writers of the early Cuernavaca-region censuses (AZ) repeatedly did the same.

27. In the texts of Sahagún and his circle, the circumflex accent sometimes indicates glottal stop, and later the Jesuit Carochi had a consistent system in which it is indicated by a grave accent; this convention is found not infrequently in ecclesiastical Nahuatl from the 1620's or 1630's on. But in documents done by unsupervised Nahuas, *h* was essentially the only convention, with an occasional peripheral writer using *c*. See Chap. 9 at n. 143; Lockhart 1982, n. 5 (also N&S, item 3; both Chalco region, late period); AGN, Tierras 2533, exp. 2, f. 31v (Santa María de la Concepción, Calimaya region of the Toluca Valley), "notlactol" for standard *notlatol*, "my statement"; UCLA TC, folder 23, ff. 22–23 (San Miguel Acatlan, Tulancingo region, 1659), "tetactzin" for standard *tetatzin*, "the father." Only once have I seen a mundane text by a Nahuatl speaker with a diacritic for glottal stop (N&S, item 6, text 1; Tulancingo, 1570).

28. See ANS, pp. 64–67, 93–100.

29. Representations of vowel quantity outside the framework of Spanish supervision are negligible. An undercurrent of *h* for glottal stop is perhaps more pronounced in mundane texts by Nahuatl speakers than in texts done by Spaniards or for them. It is noteworthy that the *h* was not written uniformly for all glottal stops called for by grammars, but primarily for root-internal instances, sometimes for root-final instances, and very rarely word-finally. Thus for the plural of *tlatoani*, "ruler," Chimalpahin often writes "tlahtoque," never "tlahtohqueh."

30. The uniform nature of Spanish spelling should not be obscured by the fact that in early modern times alternate conventions existed and might be used by the same writer; these orthographic variants (as in "iglesia, yglesia," or "saber, sauer") say nothing of the writer's pronunciation.

31. See Karttunen and Lockhart 1976a. Although the segments of such phrases were bound together in speech and the whole must have had a unitary speech inflection, and hence the unit is truly phonological, it is also a unit in syntax, constituting a minimal potentially complete statement.

32. I do not mean to say that native vocabulary was never treated on the invariant word principle at all. My impression is that many writers did have a stock of words, especially nouns, that they treated as units and always spelled the same, but this is very difficult to demonstrate, and it is still essentially the root or stem that is invariant. A few (and there are very, very few) common abbreviations of indigenous words, such as *tlpc* for *tlalticpac*, "the earth, on earth," unequivocally betray the principle of freezing the spelling of a given term. Even here, however, the unit abbreviated and frozen is likely to be a phrase, as in *tt⁰*, etc., for *totecuiyo*, "our Lord."

33. Texts outside the mainstream, such as the Bancroft dialogues and the Cantares Mexicanos (Bierhorst 1985), with more uninhibited letter substitutions, show us that despite the dominant spelling, these items must often have been pronounced *ti(y)ox, xantoh*, etc. See ANS, pp. 100–104.

34. So far as I know, the two abbreviations mentioned in n. 32, plus a super-scribed -*co* to indicate -*tzinco*, the reverential ending of a relational word, and *a⁰* for *amo*, "not," are the only widespread conventions for abbreviating native vocabulary, although individual writers often had additional conventions of their own, and some of these may have been traditional within specific altepetl.

35. Occasionally, hypercorrection appears in native vocabulary, as in "al*d*epetl" for *altepetl* (BC, doc. 24, p. 130), or "ab*ç*olco" for *apçolco* (BC, doc. 25, part 4, p. 146).

36. See N&S, item 8. A good deal of the effect, it is true, can be seen as the spontaneous result of phonetic writing across a subregion with strong dialectal speech idiosyncrasies. Yet I feel that there was also movement of writers and sharing of writing lore. Mateo, the scoundrel who forged a document and put it inside a saint's image (Chap. 6, n. 159) was not originally from the Toluca Valley town where he served as cabildo notary, Santa María de la Concepción in the Calimaya region, but from Metepec, not far away but in an entirely separate altepetl complex (AGN, Tierras 2533, exp. 2, f. 52v).

37. As demonstrated for the Tlaxcala-Puebla region in the 17th and 18th centuries in Krug n.d., passim.

38. The best documented example at the moment is the Chalco region; see N&S, item 3.

39. BC, docs. 2, 3, 4, pp. 54, 58, 64; NMY, doc. 3, p. 98.

40. N&S, item 7, texts 1, 4.

41. Leander 1967. The analyses of the editor, Birgitta Leander, have been very useful to me. She is correct in asserting that a Nahuatl alphabetic text placed together with the codex by its first editor, although somewhat related in date, place, and theme, is an entirely separate item, of different authorship. The writers of the alphabetic document appear to have been from outside Otlazpan, associated with larger centers. From the evidence of the pictographic document, totally innocent of alphabeticism, it would appear that alphabetic writing had not yet been introduced into Otlazpan in 1549–50. On the other hand, among the officials of the altepetl are depicted two persons, called notaries (*escribanos*) in the Spanish text, whose function is indicated by two unmistakably European-style books and stylized lines of cursive writing, in addition to a pen.

42. See Williams 1980. The document appears to have been maintained current for some time, rendering dating more difficult.

43. See the fully alphabetic letter of the cabildo, dated 1554, in Zimmermann 1970, pp. 15–17; and documents in AGN, Tierras, including Tierras 20, part 1, exp. 3, f. 260 (1551), 32, exp. 1, f. 10 (1555), and 20, part 2, exp 4, f. 5 (1558).

44. HTC, intro., p. 15. This edition, in which credit for much of the essential and difficult work with the language and with the meaning of Nahuatl concepts must go to Luis Reyes García, is one of the outstanding monuments of Nahuatl philology to date, and the work as presented deserves far more detailed and comprehensive study than it has received (few indeed are equipped to carry out such study).

45. The verb is *mamali*; although the relevant meaning is not given under the primary entry in Molina, see his entry "teocalmamali," "to dedicate or inaugurate a church."

46. For this reason, I think the editors of the HTC go much too far when they say (p. 9) that the glyphs are mere illustrations of the fundamental alphabetic text, although surely some of the pictorial material can be said to be primarily illustrative or even decorative.

47. The largest, richest, most varied corpus at the general level of the Historia Tolteca-Chichimeca is the body of documents produced under the direction of fray Bernardino de Sahagún, not only the Florentine Codex, but the earlier versions leading up to it. This material presents an enormous challenge, for several reasons: because of its mass and distinct subgenres, because it evolved over a long time, and because there is always the problem of just what stems from the Nahuas and what from Sahagún himself. At any rate, in the Sahaguntine corpus one will find portions in which the pictographic element is basic and the alphabetic text comments on it, others in which the pictographic is important but merely illustrative, and still others in which it is not important at all; there is also a frankly decorative purpose in some of the minor pictorials. Peterson 1988 represents an excellent beginning in analyzing the pictorial matter in the Sahaguntine corpus in relation to the text and from the perspective of the Nahua writers and painters.

48. I have used the Dibble edition (CA). An even fuller example of a two-channel document on the principle of obligatory pictographic plus alphabetic (= oral) components is the Códice Sierra, written in 1550–64 (León 1982), in which the pictographic portion is much fuller and more informative. It stands to the left, where it has more the aspect of being primary, with the alphabetic text a comment upon it. I have refrained from using it as my example because, although the text is in a Nahuatl not vastly different from that of central Mexico in general, it comes from slightly outside the Nahua culture area (the Mixteca). Nevertheless, I think there is little in it, aside from some archaisms and odd constructions in the language, that does not fit in perfectly with Nahua modes.

49. See CA, p. 13.

50. There is actually some question about which temporal expressions apply to the death and which to the arrival of the messengers, but that is irrelevant here.

51. Dibble noticed this; see CA, p. 12.

52. I am unsure at this point whether the Codex Osuna represents a preconquest genre, that is, whether or not there was an oral-pictographic convention for presenting major complaints to authorities.

53. See documents in López y Magaña 1980. It is true that the maps sometimes have their own alphabetic notations giving the cardinal directions, landmarks, the names of neighbors, and the like.

54. AGN, Tierras 1525, exp. 5, ff. 3, 6–6v.

55. See also S. Cline 1986, appendix 4, with transcription and translation of an extensive land document of Culhuacan dated 1581 (pp. 189–211), and a partial reproduction of the accompanying pictographic component (p. 128). In the pictorials, line maps and numerical symbols are in preconquest style, but soil types, locations, and ownership annotations are all alphabetic.

56. AGN, Tierras 1735, exp. 2, cuaderno 2, f. 108v. A reproduction, along with a transcription and Spanish translation of the associated alphabetic text, is in CDC, 2: 175–79.

57. AGN, Tierras 1735, exp. 2, cuaderno 2, f. 112. A reproduction, along with a transcription and Spanish translation of the associated alphabetic text, is in CDC, 2: 181–82. A transcription and English translation are in BC, doc. 10, pp. 90–91.

58. AGN, Tierras 1735, exp. 2, cuaderno 2, f. 108. A reproduction, along with a transcription and Spanish translation of the associated alphabetic text, is in CDC, 2: 174–75. A transcription and English translation are in BC, doc. 11, pp. 90–91.

59. A vestigial date-glyph or two is found in Chimalpahin. A few small drawings of year signs in the final part of ZM are at most an afterthought; they may well have been added long after the author's death; see Krug n.d., chap. 2, sec. 6. In any case, the glossator Santos y Salazar is responsible for a couple of inserted pages with illustrations in the manner of a European book.

60. One Stage 3 document showing such a hint is a book of local tribute records from Tepemaxalco (Toluca Valley), thoroughly alphabetic except for a series of yellow circles showing the number of pesos paid in tax each year (MNAH AH, GO 185).

61. In the last portion of the manuscript, however, the quality is not maintained, and the year signs become scrawls.

62. See Lockhart 1982 (N&S, item 3) for some more detail on the titles of Soyatzingo and Atlauhtla (discussed below).

63. HTC, ms. 54–58, pp. 1–2, the oldest part of the manuscript, has something similar in appearance, but there is no connotation of spitting.

64. The clearest example of following older pictures (16th-century Hispanizing portraits of indigenous persons, mainly) is the so-called Techialoyan tradition. See Wood n.d. (a).

65. AGN, Tierras 1665, exp. 5, unnumbered leaf between f. 169 and f. 172.

66. Titles of Cuixingo; illustrated in Archivo General de la Nación 1979, 5: 64. Stephanie Wood brought this item to my attention.

67. These two documents (Appendix A, Docs. 1, 2) are in lieu of, respectively, a Spanish-style municipal land grant and a written petition placed before a judge by the plaintiff's lawyer. The Tocuillan text bears no resemblance whatever to the Spanish genre; at first glance, the same appears to be true of the Tulancingo document as well, but though it has its own very distinct flavor and vocabulary, it does begin with polite formula, proceed to tell the facts of the case, and go on to make demands and ask for an investigation. It was also put in writing by some representative of the plaintiff and presented to court in his name, so that possibly there was a serious and quite knowledgeable attempt to duplicate a Spanish genre involved here.

68. TC, docs. 25, 29, pp. 78–79, 92–95. See also doc. 81, pp. 274–77, where a woman steps in to dispute the testator's version of the circumstances surrounding a borrowed shirt; and S. Cline 1986, pp. 30–32.

69. Karttunen and Lockhart 1978, p. 168.

70. AGN, Vínculos 279, exp. 1, f. 126v (also N&S, item 5).

71. Direct quoting of dialogue was built into Nahuatl speech in general almost as a rule of syntax, and certainly as a pattern of rhetoric. In my experience, the overwhelming majority of Nahuatl passages in which someone reports what someone else has said are put in the first person, with tense and all other speech variables expressed from the point of view of the original speaker at the time of the original statement. Although over the years I have seen what appear to be a few examples of indirect

quotes using third person and past tense, they are so few as to make me wonder if they were not Spanish influenced, or misunderstandings on my part. The archives contain a great deal of testimony given orally in Nahuatl by indigenous people, translated into Spanish orally by interpreters, and written down by Spanish clerks. Hardly any of this material has the usual characteristics of witnesses' statements in Nahuatl; rather it tends to be indistinguishable in style from testimony by Spaniards. The interpreters or the clerks, or both, not only used Spanish instead of Nahua conceptual equipment, but apparently paraphrased, compressed, and otherwise transformed the original utterances to meet Spanish expectations for this type of statement.

72. FC, book 6.

73. The best example preserved is the cabildo of Huexotzinco's 1560 letter to the crown, BC, doc. 29; some remarks on the style of the document will be found in Lockhart and Otte 1976, pp. 163–65. See also the 1554 letter of the cabildo of Tenochtitlan, in Zimmermann 1970, pp. 15–17. Some of the elements of the vocabulary having to do with rulership will be found analyzed in ANS, preliminary study, part 4.

74. A letter to the crown from the cabildo of Xochimilco, closely contemporaneous with the one from Huexotzinco (being dated 1563) but framed in Spanish by some lawyer or notary, is most instructive (Archivo General de Indias, Seville, Patronato 184, ramo 50). The concerns expressed are nearly the same, but hardly a hint of Nahua high rhetoric remains. The document is much more spare and to the point (though detailed in setting out pertinent facts), using familiar Spanish legal and governmental terminology instead of the indigenous equivalents. Though much meaning has been lost, this procedure was doubtless much more effective for the purpose.

75. See BC, doc. 31, pp. 196–99; the appendix there, pp. 221–24; and Karttunen 1982, pp. 415–16. A recent study of the genre of Nahuatl election reports shows them considerably affected by preconquest rhetorical devices and metaphorical governmental vocabulary (Haskett 1985, pp. 64–125).

76. See BC, docs. 32, 33, pp. 198–209, for examples of private letters. ANS has examples of conversational style, together with extensive analysis. Of course, Nahuatl letters were not entirely unaffected by Spanish epistolary conventions, but these are essentially restricted to the date, the signature, and sometimes a heading centered at the top of the page.

77. See the passage from the cabildo of Yacapitzactlan's letter (Tuxtla district, bishopric of Puebla) to the parish priest, dated 1740, in Chap. 7 at n. 166.

78. See the discussion of this and related questions in S. Cline 1986, chap. 3, especially pp. 16, 24–25.

79. TC, doc. 69, pp. 244–47.

80. There are some exceptions. In a will done in Mexico City in 1561, toward the beginning Marina Tiacapan says, "My children, you who are here next to me, I order you, do not forget me, always pray to our Lord for my soul" (*in nopilhuan in nican notlan anmoyetzticate namechnonahuatilia macamo annechmolcahuilizque ma mochipa ipampa anquimotlatlauhtilizque in totecuiyo in naniman*; AGN, Tierras 2729, exp. 20, f. 3).

81. Examples in BC, doc. 17, p. 108 (Azcapotzalco, second half of the 17th century); TC, doc. 3, p. 254, and many others (Culhuacan, ca. 1580); and AGN, Bienes Nacionales 339, item 9 (Mexico City, 1639), where "ynin notlatol amo ytlacahuiz,"

"this my statement is not to be violated," is repeated after each item. *Itlacoa*, the transitive counterpart of *itlacahui*, is often used instead, as in UCLA TC, folder 23, ff. 22–23 (San Miguel Acatlan, Tulancingo area, 1659), "acmo aquin quictlacoz ynin notlanahuatil," "no one is to violate my command," and NMY, doc. 3, p. 98 (Coyoacan region, 1608).

82. Examples of *cuilia* in BC, doc. 2, pp. 56–57 (Coyoacan, 1588); TC, docs. 11, 19, 21, pp. 36–37, 60–61, 68–69 (in the last repeatedly, mechanically); *ixtoquilia* in TC, doc. 30, pp. 148–51 (repeated as a formula); *elehuia* in TC, doc. 4, pp. 20–21; *chalanilia* in TC, doc. 30, p. 96. TC, doc. 31, p. 102, has the phrase, not so often seen used in this context, "macayac inca mocacayahuaz," "let no one trick them out of it."

83. For some examples, see TC, doc. 36, pp. 118–21 (Culhuacan, ca. 1580); Appendix A, Doc. 4 (Azcapotzalco, 1695; constantly repeated as a formula); AGN, Tierras 104, exp. 8, no f. (Tlatelolco 1700, 1712); NAC ms. 1477 B [4] (Calimaya, 1751; repeated); and BC, doc. 6, pp. 72–75 (Metepec, 1795). I am not sure whether the positive admonitions increase in frequency with time or whether I have saved more late examples by chance. Positive exhortations are rare in TC, negative ones rife.

84. See nn. 81–82 for instances of repeating after each item. An early example of formulaic repetition (with *ixtoquilia* and occasionally *cuilia*) is the will of don Luis Cortés, written in Coyoacan in 1556 (CDC, 2: 66–67).

85. TC has numerous examples of the notary speaking on behalf of the testator; in doc. 41, p. 140, a testator speaks: "ye ixquich y niquitohua notlatol," "This is all of my statement that I utter," and doc. 46, p. 162, is almost the same; other first-person statements are in BC, docs. 2, pp. 56–57 (Coyoacan, 1588), 3, pp. 62–63 (Coyoacan region, 1617), 4, pp. 68–69 (Coyoacan, 1622), 5, pp. 72–73 (Azcapotzalco, 1695, also and preferably Appendix A, Doc. 4), and 6, pp. 76–77 (Metepec, 1795). See also NMY, docs. 2 and 10.

86. TC, doc. 17, pp. 58–59.

87. A quick glance through TC with attention to the notaries and the formulas will provide some confirmation of this assertion.

88. Another difference between Nahuatl and Spanish testaments is that though both are divided into items (usually consisting of separate bequests), Spanish items are normally unnumbered, introduced only by the word *item* or a paragraph sign, whereas Nahuatl items have a strong (though by no means exceptionless) tendency to be numbered, an ordinal number being attached to *tlamantli*, "a separate thing," by way of introducing the statement. It is true that the numbers often peter out before the items end. The Culhuacan testaments (TC) rarely get past "first"; doc. 24 (p. 74) has a "second" in addition. For some examples of greater consistency, see BC, docs. 2, 3 (Coyoacan, 1588, Coyoacan region, 1617), and Appendix A, Doc. 4 (Azcapotzalco, 1695). I believe that this idiosyncrasy does not have to do with the oral nature of Nahuatl antecedents, but rather is an example of the general strong Nahua interest in ordering and numbering series of comparable entities. My intuition is that the presumed preconquest "testamentary" speech was not rigorously divided into separate bequests but was more flowing, like the indigenous speech forms known to us.

89. The will of don Julián de la Rosa (BC, doc. 1; Tlaxcala, 1566) can be taken as an example.

90. The testament of Angelina in Appendix A, Doc. 4, could serve as an example.

91. Except for some early wills that list none at all; see, for example, BC, doc. 2, pp. 56–57 (Coyoacan, 1588). This could suggest that the group in attendance was too large to name.

92. The witnesses to the 1566 will of don Julián de la Rosa in Tlaxcala were an alcalde and three regidores of the Tlaxcalan cabildo (BC, doc. 1, pp. 52–53). The same could occur with humbler testators as well. In 1572 in Xochimilco, a municipal constable accompanied the notary to witness the testament of Constantino (de San) Felipe, a middling pochtecatl with whom the constable seems to have had no personal connection (NMY, doc. 2, pp. 94–97). In San Francisco Centlalpan in the Chalco region in 1736, don Nicolás de Silva had six high officials and former officials witness his will in addition to five other witnesses (NMY, doc. 10, pp. 119, 121).

93. TC is full of examples of all these things. See the discussion in S. Cline 1986, pp. 28–32, and the references there given, which could be multiplied. For some examples from Mexico City, see AGN, Tierras 20, part 1, exp. 3, f. 260 (1551; many witnesses including women), 22, part 1, exp. 5, f. 123 (1564; 15 witnesses including women), 49, exp. 5, f. 122 (Tlatelolco, 1580; joint testimony of the elders of a district), and 70, exp. 4, f. 13 (1596; will in a woman's house *miec tlacatl ixpan*, "before many (unnamed) people").

94. Lockhart 1985, pp. 474–75.

95. See for one example the statement of Bárbara Agustina (Coyoacan region, 1608) that a partly finished blouse she was weaving was to be sold for six reales (NMY, doc. 3, pp. 99–100). In TC, see especially docs. 24 and 74, pp. 74–75 and 256–57. In AGN, Tierras 59, exp. 3, f. 18 (Mexico City, 1595), a woman says *onca nocue cuetlaxcueitl yancuic monamacaz ome pesos mocuiz*, "I have a skirt, a new leather skirt; it is to be sold for two pesos."

96. Compare S. Cline 1986, pp. 64–65, 72–73, with references to TC. Lest it appear that such statements were made only in Culhuacan and only by women, let me cite a will of 1587 done in Mexico City, in which Pedro Toçan disinherits his no-good daughter Francisca, complaining that she has not returned the many good deeds he has done her (AGN, Tierras 442, exp. 5, f. 7).

97. The indigenous characteristics of Nahuatl acts of possession are rather hard to detect and appreciate because the Spanish counterparts were themselves ongoing records of judicial rites rather than absolute statements on paper, and the Spanish proceedings also involved the interrogation of any and all interested parties. Although great value was always placed on a tangible written product, if possible original, as a source of validity, Spanish documentary genres varied greatly in the degree of primacy they gave to the written over the spoken word. Wills, sales, and most other notarial documents were written statements from the beginning, with at most flashes of the actual speech of the person issuing the document; petitions, appointments to office, and decrees of all kinds were much the same. But legal testimony did, with certain formalization and compressing, closely follow the actual statements of witnesses, and depended for its validity on the presumption that it was a faithful record of speech; yet judges never heard the spoken form, operating on the basis of the written testimony alone. Acts of possession went as far toward an open-ended reportage of words really spoken and actions really performed as Spanish documentation ever ap-

proached; even here, once the occasion was past, everything depended on the written version.

98. The reader should consult Rebecca Horn's detailed study of Nahuatl bills of sale as a genre in late-16th- and early-17th-century Coyoacan (Horn 1989, chap. 4).

99. Compare with the patterns in the evolution of orality in Spanish-genre documents discussed at nn. 89–90 above. The two trends show similarities in chronology and in other respects but are not quite identical. Here growing contact with Spaniards *does* come importantly into play.

Chapter 9

1. FC, book 6.

2. Karttunen 1982, pp. 413–15, shows a full awareness of this aspect of Nahuatl writing.

3. See N&S, items 10 and 11.

4. In due course, someone could and should do a book updating and broadening the work of Garibay, *Historia de la literatura náhuatl* (Garibay 1971), which rather than "History of Nahuatl Literature" should perhaps be entitled "History of Nahuatl Writing."

5. See Krug n.d., chap. 4.

6. I do not count the mestizo Spanish-language chroniclers Juan Bautista de Pomar of Tetzcoco and Diego Muñoz Camargo of Tlaxcala, or even don Fernando de Alva Ixtlilxochitl of Tetzcoco, who though he functioned as an "Indian" was as much Spanish as indigenous by descent and also wrote in Spanish using Spanish genres.

7. The second term is deduced from Molina's entry "xiuhtlacuilo," "chronicler"; the third appears in Molina with *ce-*, "one or each," prefixed, as "cexiuh amatl," glossed as "history from year to year." Chimalpahin uses "xiuhpohualli" in reference to a history of Amaquemecan done before his time, but not preconquest, since it spoke of events of 1540; it may well have been alphabetic (CH, 2: 12).

8. Under "coronista," Molina gives first "altepetlacuilo," "altepetl writer," second "xiuhtlacuilo," "year writer," and third "tenemilizicuiloani," "writer of people's lives," which I take to be an explanatory circumlocution made up for the occasion.

9. CA, p. 73 (1560 entry). Chimalpahin seems not to have *tlatocatlalia* but uses the verb *tlatocati*, "to be tlatoani, to rule," for judges and governors of Tenochtitlan as well as for viceroys of New Spain (CH, 2: 49, 79, and passim).

10. See, for example, CA, pp. 42–50, dealing with the 15th century and reporting, among other things, locusts, frost and famine, earthquakes, eclipses, breaking ground for a temple, the sighting of a specter, hail, and a flood.

11. MNAH AH, GO 184, f. 26: "hue[l] nohuiyan otlamahuisotehuac yn cuitlaxcoapan." On the other hand, the Tlaxcalan Zapata, though he had many triumphs to recount, complained that in 1680 one viceroy spent a much shorter time in Tlaxcala than in Puebla: "nican hocatca .5. tonali yn izquilhuitl huel quimahuiztilique = auh yn St franco teopan yexpan hoyluti yn quitlapaluto yn teopixcatzintzintin yhuan yn inamictzin nima yc yaqui cuitlaxcohuapan huel opa ohuecauh yn quichiuh 15 tonali = " ("He was here five days, and each day they greatly honored him; three times he

went back to the church of San Francisco with his wife to greet the friars. Thereupon he went to Puebla and was there a really long time; two weeks he spent"; ZM, f. 104v.)

12. CA, pp. 75, 78, 88, 91, 92.

13. ZM, ff. 92v–93: Axcan Ypan ylhuitzin hualathui ylhuitzin St Juan Papa martil martes a 27 de maya ça ya nu ypan xihuitl de 1675 anos — yn u topan calaque yn ichteque = 6 tlacatl yn umetin ocalaque Betana achtopa çe ocalac yn utlayecan huel achtopa onechquizqui yn iquac ye nicxicohua ynic oquinuz yn icniuh ynic ye nechocahuiaya = auh ynic onicquiquizquili yn icochilio huel onechmamatec y nahuin nechcaltepia yespada [for "yca espada"?] çe argapus quihualhuica yn tomitzin matlacpuhuali pesos = auh yn totilmatzintzinhuan Amo quihuicaque maçanel ce tzotzomatl amo quixtique [quiquixtique?] yhuan amo techcocotehuaque. The phrase "yn utlayecan" might refer to the leader, making the translation "the leader came in first." *Xicoa* is "to deceive, trick," but here it seems to mean "to evade" or possibly "to get the best of." The verb "quihualhuica" would seem to refer to the musket ("they had or brought a musket"), but a verb is needed in relation to the money. Perhaps Zapata was understandably a bit excited here.

I have refrained from quoting in full Zapata's next entry (f. 93), but I cannot refrain from summarizing it. Starting June 20, 1675, Zapata had Juan Gabriel, "an old man like me" ("nohuehueputzin") build him an oven (to make wheat bread for sale, probably); on July 11, it was first fired for purposes of tempering, and a priest came to bless it; two days later, on the eve of the author's saint's day, the first bread came out.

14. Tezozomoc 1949.

15. See the extensive treatment of these matters, with copious references, in Schroeder 1984, pp. 2–11.

16. Krug n.d. has many detailed, enlightening examples from the Tlaxcala-Puebla region. Anyone interested in Nahua annals, especially of the late period, should read this basic work, which has been very useful to me.

17. See the treatment of Chimalpahin's sources in Schroeder 1984, pp. 1–18.

18. Krug n.d. has a myriad of excerpts in transcription and translation that illustrate the point.

19. See Krug n.d., especially chap. 5, secs. 2 and 3.

20. CH, 2: 18. Zapata's researches may have included older documents beyond annals, especially the Tlaxcalan cabildo records, but the point is still in question.

21. See Dibble's intro., CA, p. 13. The main evidence that the pages were laid out in advance is that in some cases much less than a page turned out to be necessary, and two or more years could have been put on a page, as in the first, derivative part of the work.

22. MNAH AH, GO 184, ff. 17–18:

auh amo huel oquisustentaroque sann ica ome tonalli ynic omochiuh yn itec siudad ynin ome tonalli ye yc oapismicoaya ypan tonali lunes yc senpuali ose 21 tonali mani metztli septienbre huel ypan ylhuitzin san matheo lunes yhuan martes yn ohuapismicohuaya aocmo nesia ma pan ma tortillas yn tianquisco ma tienda auh yn aquin ychtaca oquimochihuili yn se mita caca[st?]li yn conaxitiaya yn tianquisco ma toltilla san ypan omomictiaya yn caxtilteca manel huel momahuis-

tilia aocan quipoaya masehualtzintli yn aquin achtoa [*sic*] sa yehuatl quihuicaya
yn tlaxcalli sa choquistli omania auh niman onca omacomanque ynic muchi tlacatl yuhqui teopixque yuh caxtilteca yuhqui masehualtzintzintin ynic mochi tlacatl ynpan omomanque ym masehualtzitzintin oquimacaque se amatl oquichiuhque masehualtzitzintin ymatica yn alcalde mayor yquac ye ontleco alcalde
mayor ypalasio niman muchin pipiltzitzintin yhuan sequintin huehuey tlaca
oquitzatzilique oquilhuique pan pan pa señor capitan ye tapismiquisque ye tapismiquisque auh in iuh oquicac yn alcalde mayor yhuan oquipohuilique yn amatl
yn iuhqui oquitotia ynic mochi polihuis yn itequipanolocatzin yn tohueytlatoca-
tzin Rey yntla techcahualtisque yn toofisio yn tlaxcalchihualistli ma yehuantin yn
caxtilteca quichihuacan yn quexquich tlatequipanolistli yhuan in tlacalaquili auh
yn iuhqui oquicac yn alcalde mayor niman isiuhca otlanahuati mochihuas yn acto
ynic niman omotlastihuetz pregon ynic quichihuasque yn masehualtzitzin yn
pantzin auh yn caxtilteca otlatequiuhti quintzatzaquasque auh yn yehuantin niman ocholoque yn caxtilteca yn omixquetzca

A somewhat similar selection from this set of annals can be found in NMY as doc. 9
(pp. 114–16).

23. MNAH AH, GO 14, a relatively recent, generally excellent but not error-
free copy; I have not seen and do not know the whereabouts of the original. The copy
bears the Spanish title "Anales de Juan Bautista." In my own far from exhaustive
examination of this more than ordinarily difficult text, I have seen no evidence confirming that attribution and prefer to consider the work, for now, anonymous. The
name Juan Bautista occurs once but with no indication it is that of the author, any
more than a great number of other names.

24. Ibid., p. 13: "axcan domingo a 28 de mayo 64 aᵒs yquac ylhuitzin quiz
trinidad. yquac yc tzatzihuac. ytlanahuatil in guardian frai melchior de venavente.
etlamantli ypampa in tiçayotl [*sic*, I read 'tiçiyotl']. yn ayac atlan teittaz. yniquetla-
mantli amo cenca huel niccac." The quote from fray Melchor just below runs: "ohual-
mohuicac yn amotatzin frai aᵒl." Instead of "I didn't hear very well," one could alternately translate, "I didn't understand very well."

25. Ibid., pp. 64–65 (note the repeated rhetorical use of the singular as a collective):

Ca nican ticah yn timexicatl in titenochcatl. ca onpachihuito / yn mix yn moyollo.
ca otoconyomahuito. yn otoconmocahuilito. yn motlacalaquiltzin. yn oticmatom-
ilti yn cueytl in huipilli. yn imalacapatiyouh. yn can [çan?] netlacuiltzintli ocon-
chiuh yn temac onmotlalli. cuix nel tahuia. cuix tihuellamati. yn timerino yc cana
otihualneauililoc cuix timilleque. cuix titlalleque ca çan iuh ca ni[?] yn titlayhi-
yohuitoque. yn tihuehue in tixtlamati. çan ca oticahuilquixti: yn altepetl ynic oti-
quixnamic. yn ixco ycpac otehuac.

The work contains many speeches even more packed with phrases and devices of the
old public rhetoric, but it would take prolonged and concentrated work on the text
as a whole to decipher them exhaustively enough to be able to quote them, and the
material here tends to be so sui generis that even then substantial gaps may be left. A
full-scale edition of these annals, taking advantage of the most recent advances in

Nahuatl philology and linguistics and searching for parallel forms in the Florentine Codex, the song collections, the Bancroft Dialogues (ANS), and other likely sources, is an imperative for Nahuatl studies. Given the nature of the text and the additional problems posed by the necessity of working from a late copy, the task will not be easy.

26. NMY, doc. 9, pp. 114, 116. There are similar examples in CH, 2: 41, 99 (also the quotation in the text below).

27. MNAH AH, GO 184, ff. 30–30v:

Oaçic yn chiucnahui hora niman OÇentlayuhtimoman [*sic*] Oquinenehuili yn chicome hora yohuac auh huel çe quarta ora ynic huecahuac yn otlayohuatimania auh y tototzitzintin yn cacalome y tzotzopi[. . .] niman muchin tlalpan huetzque Ça papatlacatinemia huel otlaocoltzatzique auh yn tetepeh yuhquin costic tlemiyahuatl ynpan motecaya yn popocatzin yuhqui yn tlepoctli yn ipan catca auh yn tlatlaca niman Çan yuhqui yn omotlapoltique teopan Çequintin omotlaloque Çequintin omauhcahuehuetzque auh Çan yey yn niman omomiquilique yn iquac Ça choquis [*sic*] omania aocmo omiximatia yn tlatlaca . . . auh yn Çemilhuitl yeyecapitzactli oquistoya ca huel çeçec auh ypan yey ora asta ypan nahui ora teotlac oquiauhticaya temamauhti yn oquimochihuili yn tloque nahuaque totecuiyo Dioz ypan on teotlactli jueues

This is the only occurrence of *tloque nahuaque* (an epithet of God) that I have seen in a fully indigenous Stage 3 text. For a typical statement of unprecedented splendor, see Zapata's description of the Tlaxcalan altepetl festivity of 1675: "huel omohueycachiuh yn aic yuhqui mochihuani yn umochiuh yn ixquich ica yn uc ocatca totahuan tonahuan" ("it was done in a really grand fashion; the like of what was done had never been done ever since the time of our fathers and mothers"; ZM, f. 93v).

28. Eric Van Young made this comment at a conference in December 1986, speaking of a series of passages of an ecclesiastical nature that Susan Schroeder had aptly translated and quoted.

29. See Haskett 1985, pp. 168–71. For discussion of mestizos or alleged mestizos who actually held high office, see pp. 388–90, 410–15.

30. MNAH AH, GO 184, ff. 23–23v.

31. ZM, ff. 88, 115.

32. CFP, ff. 4–4v.

33. Krug n.d. has many good examples of special tendencies among the Tlaxcala-Puebla annalists.

34. The so-called "Anales de Juan Bautista" discussed above at nn. 23–25 are an exception. They entirely lack a preconquest section, although the author is very much in touch with preconquest vocabulary and rhetoric.

35. Krug n.d. presents much evidence on these points (chap. 5, sec. 2, and passim).

36. For those who know Nahuatl, the passages quoted in nn. 22 (Stage 3) and 25 (Stage 2) can give some sense of the difference in flavor.

37. For systematic discussions of what is known of Chimalpahin's life and work, see CH, Zimmermann's notes; and Schroeder 1984, pp. 2–11, 18–27.

38. The "Eighth Relación" (CH, 1: 145–78), is a partial exception, being a unified political-genealogical history of Tzaqualtitlan Tenanco not specifically divided by years; it even uses the term Chronica toward the beginning (p. 146), although it is

not divided into titled chapters. A foreword in Spanish shows that Chimalpahin had an extensive vocabulary but was subject to slips in idiomatic usage.

39. This, the Zimmermann version, is the one I have used myself, with occasional reference to photocopies of the original manuscripts. Despite some occasional very minor problems of word division and the like, the publication is a truly major contribution to scholarship. Zimmermann's too often neglected endnotes are also most valuable. They do not, of course, replace the complete and up-to-date translation we so badly need. Zimmermann, though he had planned to publish a translation (which never came to pass), maintained at times that one was not needed, that those who knew Nahuatl could simply read the printed transcription. Actually, Chimalpahin uses too many rare words, idiosyncratic meanings, and unusual constructions for anyone to be able to read the more difficult passages without intensive study of the whole corpus, and even that does not always bring results. No modern scholar yet understands all of Chimalpahin, and some errors in Zimmermann's notes and transcriptions show that he did not either.

40. CH, 1: 157, described in Schroeder 1984, pp. 14, 17.

41. Schroeder (1984) has studied this aspect in detail.

42. CH, 2: 99–100. Other especially vivid passages concern the arrival of some Japanese in Mexico City (2: 92) and the funeral parade for Archbishop Guerra (2: 104–8).

43. Tezozomoc 1949, frontispiece; CH, 2: 49. By my orthographic principles I should write Teçoçomoc, the form that appears in his Nahuatl annals and that he doubtless used generally, but the name is now too well established with z.

44. See Tezozomoc 1949, p. 47, for only one, the most unmistakable, of Chimalpahin's comments; others are scattered throughout, sometimes identified by his name, other times by their content. Arthur Anderson is now working on a translation of a recently discovered manuscript of the "Chronica," apparently anterior to the copy from which León worked; when Anderson showed me a photocopy of some of it, it appeared to me to be in Chimalpahin's handwriting.

45. Tezozomoc 1949, pp. 11, 13.

46. See Barlow 1945; and Colston 1973, pp. 48–66 (which surveys the extensive literature).

47. Some parts of Tezozomoc's Nahuatl annals coincide quite closely with portions of his Spanish chronicle. Whether this material was generated by him and added to the chronicle, or lifted from the earlier Nahuatl history and put in the annals, is an interesting question I am not equipped to answer, though I incline toward the first possibility.

48. Tezozomoc 1975, pp. 227, 235. The speeches having to do with marriage negotiations on pp. 234–35 are highly reminiscent of ones in ANS, pp. 118–23. Other exact translations of Nahuatl phrases will be found on pp. 261, 273, 276, 288, 450, 457, 500, and many more.

49. Durán 1967. The disappearance of the original or set of originals on which these and other works were based is one of the greatest losses the Nahuatl-language corpus has ever suffered.

50. HTC and the preconquest section of CA have portions in dialogue in an annals framework.

51. It is possible that nonexpansive 16th-century annalists like the writer of CA were in a sense still in the first stage of alphabetic evolution (see Chap. 8)—that they were using the alphabetic component as little more than a translation of the pictorial component and were keeping a longer recital in their heads.

52. Although older Spanish usage demands "de" before the surname Zapata, the author in the many times he wrote and signed his name never seemed to use it, and one must respect his preference. Zapata's work is preserved as Mexican ms. 212, Bibliothèque Nationale, Paris.

53. The late-17th-century Puebla annalist whose work has been mentioned and quoted several times, the author of MNAH AH, GO 184, or of an earlier document on which it was based, is fully the equal of Zapata, if not at times superior, in evoking scenes during his own time, but his information is much less full and systematic, and when it comes to earlier times he falls far, far short of Zapata.

54. ZM, f. 108v.

55. ZM, f. 114v.

56. *Prendaroa* ("to hock") is on f. 35 of ZM, *presentaroa* ("to present") on f. 80, and there are other loan verbs; *hasta* ("until") is on f. 92v. Zapata standardly gives a person's age by using the calque *quipia . . . xihuitl* ("he has so-and-so many years"). Inanimate plurals will be found throughout the work; one is in the quote above, at n. 13.

57. In speaking of a procession in 1677, Zapata bends over backwards to find ways to avoid saying *pasados*. In rising order, we find "yn utequihuacatique Regidortin yhuan quimicahuique yn uhualcaldetique nima yn omochiuhque gubernadoreztin" ("the regidores who had held office, and behind them came those who had been alcalde, and then those who had been made governor"; ZM, f. 97).

58. A section on the repair of a bridge destroyed by flood uses primarily "puete" (ZM, ff. 91v–93); f. 113 has "quapatl" in the body of the text, "buete" in the margin; f. 22r has "campana" as well as the indigenous neologism "coyolcalli," "bell house" (bell tower).

59. I am not prepared at this time to make definitive comments on the potentially significant fact that the known Stage 3 annals are primarily from the Tlaxcala-Puebla region. It is quite possible that greater corporate and historical consciousness survived in that area, which may have been somewhat less overrun with Spaniards than the orbit of Mexico City. Yet in view of wide-ranging simultaneities, I am inclined to doubt the existence of a substantial difference. Important later histories from the western part of central Mexico may yet emerge, or they may have existed and be lost forever.

To return to Zapata, the Nahua secular priest don Manuel de los Santos y Salazar is considered by some to have been joint author of Zapata's annals, and with some reason, since on a title page he prepared he asserts that he finished the work. In fact, all Santos y Salazar did was to provide numerous marginal notes, mainly in Spanish. Most merely highlight the content, though he occasionally made an editorial comment or added a factual detail. He also added one or two pages in Spanish about the Virgin of Ocotlan and filled in some spaces left blank by Zapata with miscellaneous Nahuatl entries, often out of chronological sequence with the surrounding material. Thus Santos y Salazar has nothing to do with the nature and merit of Zapata's work.

He is, of course, a most interesting and significant figure in a different way. He was as great a Tlaxcalan patriot as Zapata, but he seems to have made the step over into the intellectual world of the Spaniards. He was more at home writing Spanish than Nahuatl, and his prose is indistinguishable in style and content from what a rural Spanish priest might write. He collected Tlaxcalan annals (see Krug n.d., chap. 2, secs. 5–6) almost in the same antiquarian spirit, it appears, as Spanish historians such as Sigüenza y Góngora or Clavijero. If he truly wrote a Nahuatl religious play (see below at nn. 94–95, 134–36), that would be something different, but I suspect that here too he was mainly collector, perhaps editor and reviser as well. As a priest and as a Spanish-Nahuatl intellectual, Santos y Salazar is an extremely early precursor of what was to become a major movement, the shift of portions of the Nahua upper rank over to operation within a Spanish context and tradition, bringing a good deal of indigenous culture and sentiment with them. The topic demands its own book, one perhaps even harder to research and write than this one.

60. Sahagún 1975, p. 214 (chap. 8 of the appendix to book 3).

61. Bierhorst 1985 contains a complete and reliable transcription of the collection.

62. See Karttunen and Lockhart 1980, pp. 34–35.

63. Nettie Lee Benson Latin American Library, University of Texas, Austin, ms. CDG-980 (G-59). Pomar himself did not necessarily write down the songs; indeed, many consider it unlikely.

64. Sahagún 1975, p. 582 (book 10, chap. 27); Durán 1967, 1: 195: Ixtlilxochitl 1975–77, 1: 525.

65. Compare León-Portilla 1983.

66. In this I coincide with Bierhorst 1985. Originally I did not question the category poetry, as can be seen in Karttunen and Lockhart 1980; but by the time the article appeared, I had decided in favor of "song."

67. These points emerge from almost any ten pages of the Cantares Mexicanos. See also the discussions in Bierhorst 1985, pp. 17, 42, 70–82.

68. See the many entries beginning *cuica-* in Molina, f. 26v.

69. León-Portilla has recently (1983) shown himself inclined to use *cuicatl* as the basic category. A preconquest glyph, still known and used far into the 16th century, divided the conventional "speech scroll" into segments (often eight, possibly corresponding to the eight parts of many songs); see Peterson 1985, pp. 101–2. I take the thrust of this device to be "song" rather than ordinary speech, so that it would add nothing to the question of poetry versus song as categories.

70. "Tlatollaliliztli," "tlatolchichiualiztli." The glosses for "poet" are based on the same roots. (Molina, Spanish, f. 97.) The noun *tlatolli*, in both constructions, can equally well be construed as "statement" rather than "word." It is particularly interesting that *tlatolli* was chosen for use in the gloss because in a sense it was the opposite of *cuicatl*, as León-Portilla has seen (1983).

71. The best-known and most assertive exponent of this school of thought was Angel María Garibay, who in his editions often omitted the word Dios from the transcription, leaving it only in the margin (Garibay K. 1964–68).

72. For a fuller discussion of the structure of Nahuatl song, see Karttunen and Lockhart 1980.

73. See Karttunen and Lockhart 1980, pp. 18–21.

74. Cantares Mexicanos, f. 26v. The Nahuatl is transcribed in Karttunen and Lockhart 1980, p. 44 (verses 7 and 8), and Bierhorst 1985, p. 218. The translation of the phrase "two springs" is especially speculative. Bierhorst (1985, p. 219) has "I'll pluck" instead of "Where will I get," which is an entirely possible interpretation and would fit the context rather better.

75. There are some exceptions to this tendency. See Karttunen and Lockhart 1980, p. 38.

76. Transcribed with marking of the structure, with considerable commentary, in Karttunen and Lockhart 1980, pp. 56–63. Also transcribed and translated in Bierhorst 1985, pp. 346–49. The "ghost-song" baggage and certain mannerisms aside, Bierhorst does offer some alternative translation possibilities that deserve the consideration of the reader who knows Nahuatl and cares to explore them. In the passage in verse 7, the Nahuatl verbal form, "ahuiltillano," perhaps consists of *ahuiltil-*, *-(t)lan(i)*, and a vocable *o*. In verse 8, though Bierhorst seems to think he has a solution to the queried phrase ("You will"), the meaning of the verb remains mysterious, even though a variant in the Romances has an apparently better version (see Karttunen and Lockhart 1980, p. 57).

77. Romances, ff. 11r–12r, transcribed and translated in Karttunen and Lockhart 1980, pp. 62–63. The structural comparison is represented graphically on p. 56.

78. See Bierhorst 1985, pp. 107–8.

79. See ibid., pp. 97–102, with copious specific examples.

80. I concur with Bierhorst in believing that the songs were primarily composed and set in a time subsequent to the lives of their protagonists. However, when they are made to speak, I take it that they are usually to be imagined as speaking in their own time perspective, whereas Bierhorst takes it that they are literally called back from the dead to do battle for the Mexica cause. The "ghost-song" interpretation, with which Bierhorst's edition is shot through, to the great detriment of what is in many ways a splendid publication, has met with general skepticism on the part of reviewers, but the unfortunate truth is that most of them do not know what they are talking about. The falsity of the interpretation as a blanket explanation of the Cantares hinges on matters of translation, and there are only five or six people in the world equipped to cope with the language of the songs, of whom only León-Portilla (1986) and I have made resounding and thorough rebuttals. See my review of the Bierhorst edition, N&S, item 9.

81. For *tecpana*, see Bierhorst 1985, pp. 254, 258, 268. For *tlalia*, see ibid., pp. 262, 272, 276, 324. Curiously, *tlalia* is often used in testaments as a synonym of *tecpana*. Another attribution in the Cantares speaks in terms of performance, using the verb *tzotzona*, "to beat (a drum)"; ibid., p. 152.

82. See my further related considerations in N&S, item 9.

83. Bierhorst 1985, pp. 318–23, 419–25.

84. The one unusual feature is that a large proportion of Spanish loans are spelled with typical Nahuatl sound substitutions, such as Luix for Luis, Palacizco for Francisco, and *coloz* for *cruz*, "cross." It is not that one would expect any different pronunciation from Nahuas at this time period, but that certain well-known words

and names, including those just mentioned, were practically always written with "correct" Spanish spellings no matter how they were pronounced. And surely the well-educated copyists knew the standard spellings. Whatever the reason for this phenomenon, it distinguishes the songs (the Cantares, at least) from other known Nahuatl writing except the Bancroft Dialogues (see ANS, pp. 100–104) and later the archaizing "Techialoyan" documents (see below; and also Wood 1984, 312–13, 318; Wood n.d. b).

85. See Bierhorst 1985, pp. 33–34, for a listing of specifically Christian or ecclesiastical songs and passages.

86. References to the conquest, direct and indirect, abound in the Cantares, but see especially Bierhorst 1985, songs 64 and 68, pp. 319–23, 327–31.

87. MNAH AH, GO 14, pp. 7, 14, 25, 53, 98, 118, 132, 134–35, 139–40, 150 (1564–67). The occasions were mainly saints' days, but included marriages of nobles, consecrations, and other celebrations.

88. CH, 2: 15, 41. The types mentioned are the *michcuicatl*, "fish song," and *chalcacihuacuicatl*, "Chalco woman's song."

89. Ibid.; MNAH AH, GO 14, pp. 5, 14, 58, 100, 139, 140 (1564–66). In the second source (p. 5), the annalist notes that don Pedro Tlacahuepan Moteucçoma bought the pole on one occasion. On another, after the four official fliers, dressed in their bird, butterfly, and monkey suits, had performed, four volunteers in only their cloaks followed suit, for which they were jailed (p. 58; 1564).

90. ZM, f. 97. Zapata also uses the verb *huehuecuicaque*, lit., "they old-sang, they elder-sang."

91. Bierhorst 1985, p. 90; also see his remarks in n. 23, p. 531.

92. An example is printed in ibid., p. 90.

93. De la Cruz 1975, p. 212.

94. See the discussion of Santos y Salazar in connection with annals in n. 59 above.

95. TN, p. 534. Others, all of one stanza, are on pp. 520, 522, and 526.

96. For examples, see Hernández Hernández 1986; Ramírez 1986; Xokoyotsi 1986; and Reyes García and Christensen 1976. See also Bierhorst 1985, p. 91.

97. See TN, passim. This basic work by Fernando Horcasitas, a vast contribution to Nahuatl philology, brings together a substantial amount of the existing theatrical corpus in transcription and Spanish translation, some of it published in the late 19th and early 20th centuries by Paso y Troncoso, and some of it discovered and published for the first time. In the library of Tulane University are many of the materials Horcasitas was amassing toward a second volume, which illness and premature death prevented him from completing. As Horcasitas realized, TN is far from definitive. The transcriptions mainly modernize the orthography, with consequent loss of distinctions, although some idiosyncrasies of the originals are retained; division into words is often highly inconsistent, punctuation is arbitrary, and typographical errors and misreadings are rife. Horcasitas' texts are sufficient for many purposes, and for the most part I have used them without further recourse to the originals (which are themselves nearly all posterior copies, some of them unreliable modern transcriptions). The translations improve on their predecessors and give a generally adequate

notion of the content, but errors abound, and much improvement is needed. In due course an updated, more complete, and much more critical edition of the corpus will be required.

98. A few examples from TN are "somprero" (*sombrero*), p. 258; "linpo" (*limbo*), p. 358; "prigonero" (*pregonero*), p. 368; "josticia" (*justicia*), p. 370; and "iburmasion" (*información*), "lasbenas" (*blasfemias*), both p. 394.

99. TN, p. 282. The play is reproduced on pp. 290–327.

100. TN, p. 314.

101. TN, p. 316, in the speech of "Capitan Reyes."

102. The manuscript is now at Princeton's Firestone Library and as I understand it, not available for consultation at this writing, but I read portions of it when I evaluated and described the Nahuatl text for Philadelphia Rare Books and Manuscripts, from whom Princeton made the acquisition. The Nahuatl runs over 18 pages, from f. 207 to f. 215v.

103. I was unable to determine whether the heading of this manuscript (hereafter referred to as Firestone ms.) was done by the Nahua amanuensis, my first impression, or by the friar writing more carefully than usual.

104. Firestone ms., f. 208v. F. 209 has "Herudes" for Herodes, Herod, f. 210v "peccato" for *pecado*, "sin," and "pe" for *fe*, "faith," f. 212v "jodio" for *judío*, Jew, and ff. 214v–215 "beticio" and "bedicio" for *bendición*, "blessing." Many other Spanish loans are written in the usual Spanish fashion.

105. Ibid., ff. 209–209v.

106. Horcasitas (TN, p. 237) mentions that a piece now lost, attributed to fray Luis de Fuensalida, one of the first 12 Franciscans in Mexico, is said to have had an angel presenting letters from inhabitants of limbo to Mary.

107. Firestone ms., f. 211v.

108. Ibid.

109. I have noted references to preconquest times only in the "Comedia de los Reyes" (TN, pp. 290–327; see Horcasitas' remarks on the question on p. 283) and in the late play on Santa Elena and the cross, copied, arranged, or written by the antiquarian Santos y Salazar (TN, pp. 520–54).

110. Horcasitas has brought together, quoted, and discussed much of this material in TN, pp. 36–46.

111. Notably, Garibay and León-Portilla; see TN, p. 45.

112. TN, p. 292.

113. Examples in TN, pp. 292 (in addition to the one quoted just above), 294, 296, 298, 300, 304, 308, 310, 312, 320, 322, 324. Of these, pairs on pp. 298 and 312, both involving the speeches of two Jews, are nearly as strong as the one quoted.

114. The huehuetlatolli may not have been so set a genre as previous scholars have imagined, and indeed the term may not have been so current among the Nahuas as has been thought, but the word does designate a pronounced characteristic of Nahuatl formal speech.

115. TN, p. 212. I have skipped past a puzzling word or two (probably related to transcription difficulties at some point in the transmission process), since they do not affect the passage for present purposes. The original contains several standard metaphors that do not translate well and are ignored here but can be seen in the Nahuatl

transcription in TN and to some extent in Horcasitas' translation. See ANS for close parallels of all these expressions. See also the speeches of two noblemen, TN, pp. 214–15, making much of the child Isaac in a way highly characteristic of Nahuatl polite speech. This too is found in ANS (pp. 138–45).

116. TN, p. 260. For parallels, see ANS, pp. 23–27; also Chap. 3 at nn. 107–13.

117. TN, pp. 214, 216. For the terms, see Chap. 4.

118. TN, p. 314.

119. TN, p. 272. See ANS, pp. 140–41; in places the passages run parallel word for word.

120. "Souls and Testamentary Executors" ("In animaztin ihuan albaceas") and "The Merchant" ("Neyxcuintilli yntechpa tlantohua yn pochtecatl"). The first is mentioned in Chap. 6 at n. 36, the second in Chap. 5 at n. 166. Both are in the Library of Congress, box "Aztec Dramas," MMC 2771. Only two such pieces seem to be preserved, but they imply a subgenre.

121. Horcasitas raises this point (TN, p. 135); see Motolinia 1971, p. 92.

122. See Motolinia 1971, pp. 106–14 (from *Historia de los indios de la Nueva España*, trat. 1, ch. 15), for a pageant of the late 1530's in several ways calculated to magnify the altepetl of Tlaxcala.

123. This is the impression that the reader of the plays receives, but Barry David Sell has done systematic research confirming the impression. He has compiled a list of all loans in the plays in TN and established that none are unambiguously of the type characteristic of Stage 3. Through a frequency count he has shown that some widespread early loans account for a huge percentage of all occurrences. He compares the loans in the plays with those in Molina's *Confessionario mayor* (1569, originally done some years earlier) and finds a close congruence. Sell's research will doubtless be published in due course.

124. See TN, pp. 222, 314, 322, 390.

125. See Motolinia 1971, pp. 101, 104–14 (from *Historia de los indios de la Nueva España*, trat. 1, ch. 15).

126. TN, p. 228.

127. This is also Horcasitas' conclusion. See TN, pp. 281–83.

128. For one small example, in the play about the sacrifice of Isaac, the word "eye" (*ixtelolotli*) is pluralized, which would be extremely rare in 16th-century Nahuatl; though perhaps barely possible in certain usage, it would definitely not be concordant with the high style of the play's speech in general.

129. Horcasitas (TN, p. 422) reports the existence of 18th-century play scripts, not identical in every respect but closely parallel over long sections, from the neighboring towns of Tepalcingo and Axochiapan in Morelos.

130. In TN, pp. 344–419. See Horcasitas' enlightening discussion of the Tepalcingo background and his convincing conclusions on the origin of this version of the play, p. 133.

131. The full demonstration of these assertions would require a long, detailed study, in fact an edition of this play and its relative from Axochiapan, which would be a most worthwhile enterprise.

132. For example, in one episode (TN, pp. 356–61) Mary in motherly concern attempts to dissuade Jesus from his sacrifice, as in the Holy Wednesday playlet men-

tioned above; the prophets in limbo are mentioned as there (though without letters and angels), and some of the same arguments are ventured on both sides.

133. TN, pp. 344, 390. P. 390 also has the ubiquitous *tepozmacquahuitl* for "sword."

134. In TN, pp. 514–51.

135. TN, p. 516.

136. Horcasitas has noticed these features; see TN, p. 516. The tocotines are discussed above at nn. 91–93.

137. Gibson 1964, pp. 271, 287–88; Gibson 1975, pp. 320–21. See also the substantial and acute work of Robertson (1959, 1975), though it largely concerns the peripheries of this genre and is done in the spirit of technical art history.

138. I here desist from putting "titles" in quotes, it being understood that the term is not to be taken literally and, appropriate or not, must be used because of its currency and for lack of an alternative.

139. I will primarily follow Lockhart 1982 (also N&S, item 3), which analyzes some Chalco titles and generalizes on that basis, adding some points from Wood 1984, chap. 8; Wood 1987; Wood n.d. (a)–(d); and Haskett n.d. Wood has made a large contribution to this field. My remarks here far from exhaust the potential of these publications, which will reward those who consult them.

140. Wood 1984, pp. 112–21, shows that the Indian towns of the Toluca Valley did not respond very enthusiastically to Spanish official offers of title adjustment for a fee (*composición*) in the early 17th century (compare Chap. 5, at n. 93).

141. AGN, Tierras 1665, exp. 5, f. 168:

> Yoyahue ttᵒʸᵉ Diosce ca odicmahuiçoque y metztli y citlali yn iaxcantzin y cem-anahua tladohuani Dios auh notlaçopilhuane ma xicancicamadica ca oncqui-hualmohuiquili y cordes y don luys de pelazcon marquez ynic titlaneldoncazque macanyac choloz ynic ticmochidic dᵒpan maxiticquiuh yn oquihualmohuiquili y tlaneltoquiliztli yn itlasomahuiznacayotzin ttᵒ jesoh pxoto yni tictochihuacque tichricticanoti yni monequi ticchihuazque yn ichatzinco Dios yn ocan micssan tiquitazque yhuan i ticmatisque y nauhtlamatli yn iximacholucatzin y ttᵒ jeşo xopto y totlatoli ynic onca titoyolcuiticque yn oca tocecahuazque y tictocen-lilizque yn itlasomahuiznacanyotzin ttᵒ dios ynic oca toquactequizque auh y to-micquilizque oca titococque auh ca yuhqui otechmonahuatili y curtez Dᵒ luys de pelazco marquez yn ac ye Şando ticdotequipanilhuizque ma ximotemolican notlasonpilhuane

Although I have put only one phrase of my translation in parentheses as particularly dubious, the text contains many uncertainties. I will not enter into them here except to say that although *iuhqui* most often refers backward, it is conceivable that the intention of the last part is "Cortés don Luis de Velasco Marqués told us, 'My dear children, ask yourselves what saint we shall serve,'" even though this too contains anomalies. The court translator at the time also had his problems, omitting some portions and making deductions about some of the rest that I am fairly sure are erroneous; his translation will be found at f. 184.

142. In the Spanish version, the court translator rationalized the string of names, recognizing that he was dealing with two people of different times, but this is unten-

able, for in the Nahuatl the entire string is treated grammatically as a singular subject. Moreover, Velasco is inserted between Cortés and the title he was mainly known by. Velasco was also a marqués, and though this fact was not very widely known, it doubtless contributed to the confusion; elsewhere in this set of documents, Velasco is called Marqués del Valle, the specific title of Cortés (ibid., f. 177A).

143. I have found deviant orthography the norm in titles of the Chalco region, and so has Wood for the Valley of Toluca (1984, p. 341), but Haskett has discovered some standard spelling in titles in the Cuernavaca jurisdiction (1990).

144. See Lockhart 1982, p. 392 (N&S, item 3).

145. The word is as close to a Nahuatl name for the titles genre as anything I have seen. This is one of the Spanish words beginning *in-* in which that element was taken to be the Nahuatl article and omitted. For further discussion and documentation of the sharing of elements of titles among altepetl, see Lockhart 1982, p. 392 (N&S, item 3).

146. Wood, on whom I rely: 1984, pp. 301–22; n.d. (a), (b).

147. Here is another piece of indirect evidence of a partial awareness on the part of Nahuatl speakers of the historical process of the linguistic stages of adaptation to Spanish (see Chap. 7, pp. 283–84).

148. MNAH AH, CAN 4. 273, no. 2, p. 995.

149. Ibid., pp. 1007–1008. The document I used is a copy by the mid-19th-century philologist, interpreter, and antiquarian Licenciado Faustino Galicia Chimalpopoca. I believe that Galicia Chimalpopoca reveled in letter substitutions and replacement vocabulary for loans, and though he produced many relatively faithful copies of Nahuatl texts, I rather suspected him of having done some embellishing here (although I do not believe that he ever altered the basic character of any document he copied). As this book was in press, Stephanie Wood brought to my attention an original in the Bancroft Library (Códice Nahuatl – A; M-M 468) that agrees in most details with Chimalpopoca's version, vindicating him of have changed anything other than very minor aspects of the orthography. Whoever created documents like this one had a good knowledge of actual colonial-period documentary practice and terminology, and deliberately translated term for term into an idiom reminiscent of Stage 1. It is quite possible that authentic documents of the 16th century were at times used as the pattern for this kind of doctored version. I had suspected that the original was more like a Techialoyan than is apparent in the copy; Wood informs me that it has indeed been listed among Techialoyans, but not being well illustrated, it lacks many of the normal characteristics.

150. Or *firmatia*. If we enter into technical details, the situation is a bit more complex than straightforward replacement. The statement in the titles document as it stands is redundant, even incorrect. If name and rubric are specified as here, the proper verb is *tlalia*, "to set down." The reflexive *firmayotia* ("to sign") and the replacement verb as used here are self-contained and not compatible with additional objects in the absence of an additional object prefix. Nothing should surprise the reader of titles, but this has the feel of a very late, unidiomatic improvisation. Nevertheless, Wood has shown (1984, p. 311) that *tlilmachiotia* is characteristic in the Techialoyan vocabulary.

151. See Wood 1984, pp. 304–22.

152. See Lockhart 1982, pp. 385–86 (also N&S, item 3). See also Chap. 5.

153. See Lamphere 1983, especially pp. 745, 752, 759, 763; and Heizer and El-sasser 1980, p. 204.

154. The titles of Capulhuac in the Toluca Valley, discovered and discussed by Wood, are in rambling testamentary form (see 1984, p. 325 and surrounding pages). A late-17th-century set of titles from the Sultepec region, though not formally in the shape of a will, bears a great resemblance to one (AGN, Tierras 1780, exp. 3, ff. 2–5).

155. Wood has taken the lead in ferreting out authentic facts in titles (for example, 1984, pp. 332–40). See also Lockhart 1982, pp. 387–88 (also N&S, item 3).

156. As in the examples of Sula and Soyatzingo/Cihuatzinco in Lockhart 1982, pp. 376–80 (N&S, item 3).

157. This is roughly the situation Wood (1984, pp. 329, 335, 338–39) discovered in relation to the titles of Capulhuac.

158. See Chap. 4 for the same point having to do with the teccalli/tecpan and calpolli, Chap. 5 in matters of land tenure, and Chap. 6 in religion.

159. The titles of Sula in the Chalco region come the closest of all the examples I have seen to illustrating the whole gamut of the standard themes of the genre. See Lockhart 1982 (N&S, item 3).

160. Molina glosses "quauhtlacuilo" (lit. "wood painter") as "wood carver," and under "esculpidor," "one who sculptures," there is also "tetlacuilo," (lit. "stone painter"). See also the other entries related to *esculpir*.

161. The complex has been described in Kubler 1948, pp. 314–41, and later, in much greater detail, in McAndrew 1964, especially in chap. 6. It is understood that not literally every foundation answered to the description in every respect. The term *posa* for the corner chapels is most likely posterior; indeed, no contemporary technical term for the "open chapel" itself has been established.

162. See Kubler 1948, p. 422; and McAndrew 1964, pp. 237–40.

163. For a sense of the preconquest situation, see Broda 1987.

164. Kubler 1948, p. 422.

165. See McAndrew 1964, p. 209. Direct evidence on the timing of the transition is extremely sparse.

166. On the need for new rites, see Kubler 1948, pp. 420–21.

167. On this point, see McAndrew 1964, p. 196.

168. Ibid., p. 199.

169. The cookie-cutter term is McAndrew's (ibid., p. 200). Weismann 1950, p. 63, prefers "cutouts." For McAndrew, flatness is one of the defining characteristics of "tequitqui" (pp. 200–201), and Weismann stresses it too (pp. 46–47, 63).

170. As McAndrew 1964, p. 200, notes.

171. Compare Weismann 1950, pp. 7–13, especially p. 11. See also the remarks and illustrations in McAndrew 1964, pp. 247–54. McAndrew sees the preconquest associations but also suggests (p. 250) that an anthropomorphic cross may have Spanish precedent.

172. On central Mexico, see Motolinia 1971, pp. 42, 84–85, 167; and McAndrew 1964, pp. 247–48. On Yucatan, see Farriss 1984, pp. 303, 315–16; and Bricker 1981, pp. 103–14, 155–61.

173. See Weismann 1950, p. 2. Donald Robertson has analyzed indigenous graphic style as emphasizing conventional forms that he calls "unitary," composed of separable parts, as opposed to the "unified" forms of European style. This is neither more nor less than yet another of the many manifestations of cellular-modular organization. (For a brief statement, see Robertson 1972, pp. 256–57.) It is often extremely difficult, however, to tell whether a part of an image is best imagined as separable or not; European images too seem to contain many elements which are at least potentially separable. To my eye, indigenous graphic images do partake of the general organizational tendency, but it is a tendency only, not to all appearances so full a manifestation as song structure or the organization of the altepetl and architectural ornament. Nevertheless, perhaps further research can put the tendency on a more systematic basis and identify traces of it in Stage 2 paintings done by Nahuas.

174. Reasons for fuller adjustment in painting are yet to be fully explored. One of the most likely, though it would not explain everything, would seem to be the use of prints and other graphics as models for both genres and the ease of copying effects from one flat surface to another, as opposed to trying to translate them into the round. See Weismann's discussion of a portal at Huaquechula (1950, p. 47).

175. The best-known exceptions are the frescoes of Xocoteco and the open chapel at Actopan; see Artigas 1979. But further detailed and subtle research may yet reveal an indigenous substratum in many other cases, as well.

176. Peterson 1985. The core chapters, and the ones on which the following discussion is based, are chaps. 3–6. This portion of the work should be read by all who are deeply interested in central Mexican ethnohistory.

177. Peterson also finds some indigenous materials being used (1985, p. 95), and doubtless they were prepared in traditional ways, but these things are not apparent to the eye.

178. Peterson (1985, pp. 107–13) shows many stylistic connections between the Malinalco muralists and the book illustrators of Sahagún's Florentine Codex; some of the latter may in turn have participated in copying the alphabetic text of the work. Here we see again how close writing and painting were, in every respect.

179. See Kubler 1948, pp. 425–26, on these points. It was a major intellectual accomplishment on Kubler's part that despite his immersion in Ricard, he saw that the rate of learning of the indigenous population determined the tempo. (Though he did not include the Spanish population as an element in the equation, it was logically implicated.)

180. Art historical research on the later period is not as distinguished, intensive, or oriented to ferreting out the specifically indigenous as the principal works on the 16th century. Much more in the way of indigenous survivals and substratum may yet be found. Such finds, however, could hardly alter the picture of a strong general Hispanizing trend after the 16th century.

181. Compare Weismann 1950, p. 125.

182. MNAH AH, Fondo Franciscano 45, f. 79v. He received 14 pesos. The "don" tells us of the artist's social standing and hints at the quite frequent phenomenon of a person of high rank being an artist or artisan, possibly in line with preconquest precedent.

183. MNAH AH, GO 184, f. 26. New personnel did the building; whether they were indigenous or not is unclear.

Chapter 10

1. See Lockhart 1972b, p. 10.
2. Gibson 1964, chap. 9.
3. The grants went far beyond the central Mexico of the Nahuas, of course. See Himmerich 1984.
4. See Tutino 1976, pp. 190–91.
5. RA; Nutini 1980–84, 1988. See also Chap. 6.
6. As established by Woodrow Borah and his colleagues in a series of publications; see, among others, Cook and Borah 1960 and 1971–79.
7. Chap. 7, footnote to p. 284.
8. Consider especially Docs. 1 and 2 in Appendix A; the originals of the dialogues of ANS must also date to around this time, and so does the extraordinary conversational testimony of don Juan de Guzmán excerpted in Chap. 8.
9. See Tuttle 1976 for a list that extends far beyond Spanish but still illustrates the point very well. What complicated the situation in Mexico was the store of borrowed words the Spaniards had already built up during their generation in the Caribbean. They usually retained the Arawak word for a New World phenomenon rather than adopting the Nahuatl equivalent, as with *cacique* instead of *tlatoani*, and *maíz* instead of *tlaolli* and *centli*. There were exceptions, however; *mitote*, from Nahuatl, for example, gradually replaced *areito*, the word from Arawak for indigenous dancing.
10. I give these examples as ones I have seen in late-colonial texts, but since I was not specifically doing research on this topic, I have had to pick them from memory and cannot provide exact dates or references.
11. Not the only reason, as already indicated. The measure went directly back to the numbers at the root of contact rather than to contact itself; more Spaniards and fewer Indians added up to the necessity of dividing up the Indians among a larger number of employers in smaller parties for shorter lengths of time.
12. See Carrasco 1976a, b; and AZ, 1: xvii.
13. See Muñoz Camargo 1984, pp. 163, 168–69, 172.
14. See Horn 1989, chap. 3.
15. William Bright (1990) calls the phonological/syntactic phrase a "line" and finds that in an example of Nahuatl oratory he has analyzed, it is systematically paired, pairs often being nested in larger pairs. See also, on graphic images in the two cultures, the analysis of Donald Robertson (1959, 1972, 1975), discussed briefly in Chap. 9, n. 173.
16. I refer here to eclecticism in principles, not the actual conflicts and opposing tendencies growing out of the consistent application of a single mode—of this, also, much has already been seen in the body of the book.
17. See L. Reyes García 1977, p. 88; and the discussion in Chap. 2, section "Basic Principles of Altepetl Organization."

18. I do not go so far as to say that the tension between a rigid polarity and other Nahua organizational modes was prominent among the reasons for the decay of the distinction. We have seen that it was part and parcel of the radical weakening of a complex older Nahuatl rhetoric across a broad spectrum.

A related area of interest, on which I am not prepared to make definitive statements, is the status of male-female polarity in Nahua culture. Very separate role definitions existed, both as social reality or unconscious ideology and as rationale or explicit ideology. Hints of the creation of two blocks exist, as with the separate *cihuatepixque*, female officers to keep order among women, or the separate listing of male and female witnesses to documents. *Cihuapilli*, "noblewoman," and *pilli*, "nobleman," were equivalent but mutually exclusive. Kinship terminology widely distinguished the gender of the reference point, far more than in English or Spanish. We have seen the special terms *cihuacalli*, "woman-house," and *cihuatlalli*, "woman-land" (though their exact meanings are not very well understood).

On the other hand, Nahuatl has no grammatical gender. One cannot tell whether the practitioners of a given market activity were women or men, and rarely is the gender made explicit. The general term *tlacatl*, "human being, person of either sex," was generously used in older Nahuatl. Both men and women were referred to as one's *-tecuiyo*, "lordship." In the household, the members of both sexes had similar if not totally equal rights and functioned primarily as individuals. If Nahuatl was strong on gender distinctions among kin by reference point, it was weak on such distinctions by referent, for they were not made with relatives younger than the reference point. The most common way of speaking of parenthood in 16th-century Nahuatl was to use the doublet "motherhood, fatherhood," which is found applied to a parent of either sex. Here we have duality rather than polarity.

The evidence thus points in both directions, and it will apparently not be easy to approach closer to the question (I by no means assert that it will be impossible). Meanwhile, my own impression is that on balance, there was less explicit male-female polarity in older Nahua culture than in Spanish culture. At any rate, a spectrogram of the phenomenon for one culture would look quite different from that for the other.

19. Originated by Ricard, this approach was developed further by anthropologists, including Foster (1960); for the north of Mexico, Spicer (1962); and looking back from the perspective of the 20th century, Nutini in his various works.

20. See my discussion in Chap. 7 of the applicability (and the lack thereof) of the notion of resistance to linguistic phenomena.

21. Much remains to be said on this topic, which I hope to take up systematically in a broader context in the future (Gillespie 1989 is an important recent contribution). For now, I will briefly point out some aspects that may help define the questions we need to answer. All of the texts saying that the Nahuas called the Spaniards gods were written at least 20 years after the fact, and most later than that; many are patently legendary or apologetic in nature, or both. With those in Spanish especially, one may reasonably suspect that the Spaniards themselves were fomenting a myth flattering to them. Yet a considerable number of Nahua texts, written under quite different auspices, do repeat the usage (that is, as something characteristic of the first years after contact). It is hard to doubt that the word did in fact circulate in the first generation in reference to Spaniards, though we may never know the contextual details and precise connotations.

Indeed, another major uncertainty concerns the range of meaning of the Nahuatl word *teotl*. It surely was the primary term for a pantheon of divinities whom one immediately recognizes as parallel to Old World gods, and it also served after the conquest as a generic description of the Christian God. It may be, however, that among the Nahuas the human and the divine interpenetrated even more than with, for example, the Greeks. Many if not most of their altepetl gods were also ancestors and former leaders of the group. Priests impersonated gods and took their names as titles, and ritual god impersonators, dressed in all the god's accoutrements, were first feted and then sacrificed. Furthermore, according to FC, book 10, p. 169 (chap. 29), in ancient Tula men (prominent men?) addressed each other as "teotl."

22. At the level of high culture, John Elliott (1970) has recognized the long-lasting initial lack of interest that Europeans showed in America.

23. The Nahuas took the same generic view of Spaniards; any European was a Spaniard. See Chimalpahin's "español . . . portugues" (CH, 2: 126). But then, the Spaniards themselves had a tendency to include non-Spanish Europeans among their number at a discount, i.e., to use the term *español* generically.

24. FC, book 12, pp. 31, 45. In ibid., p. 101 (chap. 34), during the siege of Tenochtitlan, one of the Mexica leaders called out, "aquique inin Tenime," "Who are these barbarians?" Also, in an early Spanish account based on indigenous sources (fragment appended to the Codex Ramírez 1975, p. 137), the mother of a ruler is said to have chidden her son for accepting the barbarians' religion so quickly.

25. Lockhart 1985, p. 477.

26. Among the important historical studies are Farriss 1984; Thompson 1978; and Hunt 1974, 1976. Some monuments of the Mayan philological literature are Roys 1933, 1939; Barrera Vásquez 1965; Edmonson 1982, 1986; and Bricker 1981. Karttunen 1985 contains pioneering work on Maya linguistic adaptations to Spanish.

27. See Karttunen 1985, pp. 59, 61, 65, 96, 103, 124.

28. See Hunt 1974, pp. 163–73, 367, 585–89; Farriss 1984, pp. 47, 58; Cook and Borah 1971–79, 2: chap. 1, especially pp. 96–120.

29. See Roys 1933; Edmonson 1982, 1986; and Barrera Vásquez 1965.

30. See Bricker 1981, pp. 185–218.

31. See Roys 1939. It may well be that the comparatively greater emphasis on named lineages in Yucatan impeded the widespread adoption of Spanish surnames (though some, belonging to the same types as among the Nahuas, are seen).

32. Hunt 1974, pp. 585–89; Farriss 1984, pp. 63–66.

33. A perusal of Lockhart and Schwartz 1983 will give some sense of this relationship; see also Stern 1982; and Bakewell 1984.

34. See Spalding 1984 and especially 1967.

35. Photocopies are in the possession of George Urioste. The archival provenience of the documents is not clear, but there can be no doubt of their authenticity. They consist of a complaint against a priest and an accounting of church and cofradía expenses, very similar to things often seen in Mexico. As this book was in press, I learned that Bruce Mannheim has also made some interesting finds.

36. Guaman Poma 1980; Urioste 1983. The Quechua in Huaman Poma consists only of fragments, but they are highly suggestive.

37. A special issue in the matter of convergences has to do with the grammars of languages. It is surely conceivable that two given unrelated languages might have more similar verb morphology than another two, and that verb borrowing could thus occur more quickly and easily in the first set than in the second, or that a given language might have very simple verb morphology, with the result of easier borrowing. This could lead to very different characteristics of the stages in different situations. Yet the case of Yucatecan Maya does not lead one to imagine morphology as the crucial variable. While Mayan verbs are no more similar than those of Nahuatl to Spanish verbs, they overlap more with nouns and are considerably less complex morphologically; their roots are more distinct and accessible. Nevertheless, verb borrowing comes late in the game with Yucatecan Maya, at approximately the same point in the overall process as with Nahuatl (and in terms of actual time elapsed, much later).

Both Nahuatl and Maya eventually fastened on the nounlike infinitive of the Spanish verb as a base, adding indigenous verbalizing elements. Quechua bypassed the infinitive, simply using the Spanish root (third-person singular form) as a Quechua verb. The simplicity of this mechanism perhaps facilitated verb borrowing. I do not know enough about Quechua at this point to understand where such a convention fits in the broader picture of Quechua grammar.

38. Mary Doyle (1988) is able to do this in her study of Andean religious survivals in the 17th century; some of the key terms are *malqui* (divine founding ancestor in mummified form), *machay* (ceremonial burial place of an ayllu), and *pacarina* (an ethnic group's mythical point of origin).

39. Yucatecan Maya sources such as the Titles of Ebtun (Roys 1939) and the books of Chilam Balam (Roys 1933; Edmonson 1982, 1986) make it abundantly clear that, though the term has received virtually no analysis, the equivalent of the altepetl is the constantly mentioned *cah*. Its constituent parts do not emerge clearly from the documentation so far seen, however. The matter of the cah's internal organization would seem to be the most urgent issue facing Yucatecan historiography.

In the Andes, it is the calpolli-like ayllu that leaps at us in the Spanish documentation, tending to obscure the larger altepetl-like units to which they belonged, but Andeanists are now beginning to make substantial progress toward identifying the larger units. There is every reason to think that cellular-modular organization was as well developed in central Andean sociopolitical entities as among the Nahuas, in a scarcely distinguishable form (and even with emphasis on the numbers 2 and 4, despite the decimal orientation of the Incas).

40. Much the same thing happened with the last major survey of central Mexican ethnohistory, Gibson 1964. The administrative records that were at the core of Gibson's sources also pick up markedly with the onset of Stage 2, so that here, too, the conquest period did not get as full a treatment as the rest. Once written about far more than any succeeding time period, the first generation is now well behind the later years, and serious, up-to-date research on it is called for to redress the balance.

41. This is in fact one of my current projects, and John Kicza is doing important relevant research.

42. BC, doc. 6.

43. I do believe, however, from the nature of the known late examples, which are

still polished and mature representatives of their genres, that the production of mundane Nahuatl texts continued for quite some time at a higher rate than the extent of their archival preservation might suggest.

44. See Lockhart and Schwartz 1983, pp. 306–8.

45. William Taylor's project on rural parishes and their priests in the 18th century will no doubt make a large contribution in this direction.

46. Rolena Adorno has spoken of a project of this kind embracing both Mexico and Peru.

47. Such study must go beyond demography and statistics to full-fledged research on large numbers of named individuals, seeking to establish career patterns, social networks, and cultural content.

48. Nutini's studies of 20th-century Tlaxcalan Spanish speakers are highly relevant here. The next step would be to go back over the same ground, carefully recording the elaborate speech acts that still accompany most socioreligious ritual and analyzing them for echoes of older concepts and rhetoric.

Glossary

Albacea (S). Executor of a testament

Alcalde (S). A first-instance judge who is at the same time member of a municipal council (cabildo)

Alcalde mayor (S). Chief magistrate in a given area, appointed from outside; in this book, generally the chief Spanish judicial and administrative official in a jurisdiction embracing several altepetl; often used interchangeably with corregidor

Almud (S). Unit of dry measure, one twelfth of a fanega

Altepetl (N). Any sovereign state; in central Mexico, generally the local ethnic states the Spaniards were to call pueblos. They became municipalities after the conquest and are sometimes called towns in this book.

Altepetlalli (N). "Altepetl land"; any land over which the altepetl has jurisdiction, in practice usually empty land that the corporation may redistribute, the same as calpollalli

Audiencia (Royal Audienca) (S). High court, here the one residing in Mexico City and with jurisdiction for all New Spain

Barrio (S). Subdistrict of a municipality; here subdistrict of an altepetl, equivalent to tlaxilacalli or calpolli

Braza (S). Among Spaniards, a unit of measure equal to a fathom; also used for the larger, regionally variable unit predominant among the indigenous population

Caballería (S). A land grant of moderate size intended for intensive agricultural use

Cabildo (S). Municipal council in the Spanish style

Cacicazgo (S, based on "cacique"). An indigenous rulership or the title and establishment going with it; a neologism on the model of "mayorazgo"

Cacique (S, from Arawak). Indian ruler, tlatoani; in late colonial Spanish, any prominent Indian

Callalli (N). "House-land"; a household's central agricultural plot, associated with its residence

Calpollalli (N). "Calpolli land"; land subject to redistribution by the calpolli

Calpolli (N). Constituent part, subdistrict of an altepetl

Calque. Translation of a foreign idiom by using equivalent native vocabulary for its constituent parts even though they would not have originally yielded that overall meaning in the native language

Chinampa (S, from N). Artificial raised plot for intensive agriculture built up in shallow water

Cihuapilli (N). Noblewoman, lady

Cihuatepixqui (N). "Woman-people-guard"; a lower-level official, herself female, in charge of keeping order among the women of a certain group

Cihuatlalli (N). "Woman-land"; land held by a woman in her own right, often brought with her into a marriage as her inheritance; perhaps in some cases the equivalent of dowry land

Coatequitl (N). Rotary draft labor for the altepetl

Cofradía (S). Sodality, lay religious brotherhood

Comadre (S). Female ritual coparent; refers to the relationship between the true parent and the godparent

Compadre (S). Male ritual coparent; refers to the relationship between the true parent and the godparent

Congregación (S). Resettlement (here of indigenous people) to achieve greater nucleation

Corregidor (S). Chief Spanish judicial and administrative officer of a given district, appointed from the outside; in this book, generally the officer presiding in a jurisdiction encompassing several altepetl, or sometimes one large one; at times used interchangeably with alcalde mayor

Corregimiento (S). The jurisdiction or office of a corregidor

Diputado (S). Deputy, person delegated; name of various secondary offices

Don, doña (S). High title attached to the first name; like "Sir" and "Lady" in English

Encomendero (S). Holder of an encomienda grant

Encomienda (S). Grant (nearly always to a Spaniard) of the right to receive tribute and originally labor from an altepetl through its existing mechanisms

Equivalence relationship. A relationship in which a Nahuatl word comes to be taken as the equivalent of a Spanish word and can automatically be used to represent it in any of its idiomatic meanings

Escribano (S). Notary, clerk

Fanega (S). Unit of dry measure; often considered equivalent to one and a half bushels

Fiscal (S). Here, church steward, the highest indigenous ecclesiastical official in a district

Gañán (S). Paid, resident, permanent employee, primarily among Spaniards, but in time also used in Nahuatl for the employees of high-ranking indigenous figures

Gobernador (S). Governor; here, an indigenous person filling the highest office of the altepetl, exercising many of the powers of the preconquest ruler (tlatoani)

Governor. Here, a gobernador

Huehuetlalli (N). "Old land"; patrimonial or inherited land

Huehuetlatolli (N). "Old words, elder words"; orations delivered by the older generation to the younger, full of cultural lore, advice on proper behavior, and elegant turns of speech

Huehuetque (N). "Old men"; elders, often referring to the authorities of a sociopolitical unit at any level; also often referring to ancestors, people of past generations

Huiquilia (N). "To carry for someone," later "to owe money to someone"

Huitzoctli (N). A heavy digging stick to break the ground by prying loose the sod

Indio (S). "Indian"; the cover term used constantly by Spaniards for all indigenous people, but little used by the people themselves

Macehualli, pl. macehualtin (N). Indigenous commoner

Macehualtocaitl (N). "Commoner name," "ordinary person name"; a designation for indigenous names as opposed to those given in baptism

Maestro de capilla (S). Choirmaster

Maguey (S, from Arawak). Agave; source of the drink pulque and of fibers for various uses

Matl (N). "Arm, hand"; one of the terms for the principal indigenous unit for measuring land; sometimes apparently equal to a quahuitl, sometimes a fraction of it

Maye, pl. mayeque (N). "One with hands"; a word little used in Nahuatl texts for a fieldworker dependent on a noble

Mayorazgo (S). Entail

Merced (S). (Land) grant (the document or act of giving it)

Merino (S). Name sometimes given to minor supervisory officials of an altepetl, at the calpolli or subcalpolli level; often synonymous with the more frequently seen tepixqui

Mesoamerica. Term used mainly among anthropologists for the area from central Mexico south to Guatemala containing "high" cultures with a great many common elements; used primarily of the preconquest period

Mestizo (S). Person of mixed Spanish and indigenous ancestry

Naboría (S, from Arawak). Permanent dependent of a noble or ruler, outside the framework of community rights and obligations; used by the Spaniards primarily for their own employees

New Spain. The large jurisdiction centered on Mexico City and embracing much of present-day Mexico; more broadly, the whole general Mexican region

Obraje (S). Any factory-like shop or works; here specifically an establishment for manufacturing textiles

Ololiuhqui (N). Ritual and hallucinogenic substance made from the seeds of a certain woody vine

Oztomecatl, pl. oztomeca (N). Indigenous merchant or trader; distinction from pochtecatl not clear

Paraje (S). Site, usually inhabited and with cultivated land, defined and separated from other sites by some natural feature

Parcialidad (S). Spanish term for each of the larger subdivisions of a complex altepetl

Peso (S). The primary unit in larger monetary transactions, consisting of eight reales or tomines

Pia (N). "To keep, guard, have custody of," a verb that gradually took over the meanings of Spanish *tener*, "to have"

Pialia (N). "To keep something for someone," a form of the Nahuatl verb "pia" that was used to mean to owe money until it was replaced in the 17th century by "huiquilia"

Pilcalli (N). "Nobleman-house"; the establishment of a noble who has set up independently but is not a teuctli or lord

Pillalli (N). "Nobleman-land"; land held under special conditions by a nobleman

Pilli, pl. pipiltin (N). Nobleman

Póchtecatl, pl. pochteca (N). Professional indigenous merchant active in interregional trade

Posesión (S). Proceedings giving someone formal possession of land

Principal (S). Spanish term for a prominent indigenous person; often equivalent to Nahuatl pilli

Prioste (S). Secondary official in a cofradía

Pueblo (S). Spanish term for an altepetl; also applied to any identifiable indigenous settlement

Quachtli (N). A length of cotton cloth used for tribute payment and also functioning as a standard of value or currency; quickly replaced by the peso after the conquest

Quahuitl (N). "Stick"; standard unit for measuring land, often in the range of seven to ten feet

Quauhpilli (N). "Eagle-noble"; nobleman by reason of war deeds or other personal merit rather than by inheritance

Quauhtlatoani (N). "Eagle-ruler"; interim ruler of an altepetl

Quetzal (N). A tropical bird with long, spectacular blue-green tailfeathers

Real (S). A silver coin worth one-eighth of a peso

Regidor (S). Councilman, one of the members of a cabildo

Stage 1. The time from 1519 to 1540–50 when Nahuatl did not yet borrow Spanish words other than names, and structures in general were little changed

Stage 2. The time from 1540–50 to about 1640–50 when Nahuatl borrowed Spanish nouns and the indigenous corporation underwent large adjustments

Stage 3. The time from about 1640–50 when Nahuatl began to borrow verbs and particles as well as nouns from Spanish and to be more deeply affected in idiom and grammar as bilingualism grew and the indigenous and Spanish populations were in greater daily contact

"Stage 4." Refers to an aspect of the time after about 1770 when some Nahuas began to write and even communicate with each other in a Spanish strongly affected by Nahuatl syntax and idiom

Teccalli (N). Lordly house, establishment, with a lord, related nobles, dependents, and lands; contains "teuctli" and "calli," "house"

-Tech pouhqui (N). "One who belongs to someone": a person dependent on another rather than performing obligations directly for the altepetl

Tecomate (S from N). Deep cup of various materials for beverages

Tecpan (N). "Where the lord is": palace, establishment of a ruler or lord; contains "teuctli"

Teixhuiuh (N). "Someone's grandchild"; a dependent inside a teccalli who though not a noble may in some cases have had some kinship ties with the lord

Temilti (N). "One who prepares someone's fields"; a dependent fieldworker

Teocalli (N). "God house"; a preconquest temple or a Christian church or chapel

Teopantlaca (N). "Church people"; the cantors and other church staff

Tepixqui, pl. tepixque (N). "Guarder or keeper of people"; name given to minor altepetl officials at the calpolli or subcalpolli level; often synonymous with "merino"; became a Spanish word, usually "tepisque"

Tequinanamiqui (N). "Tribute helper"; one who receives land from another and helps him with altepetl contributions rather than participating directly

Tequitlalli, tequitcatlalli (N). "Tribute land"; land subject to tribute and/or the performance of public duties

Terrazguero (S). Word for serf or dependent tenant used by the Spaniards to designate the various kinds of indigenous dependents

Teuctli, pl. teteuctin (N). Lord, titled head of a lordly house (teccalli) with lands and
  followers

Tilmatli (N). Man's cloak; cloth in general

"Titles." Documents purporting to establish an altepetl's right to its lands in Spanish
  times, usually done in Stage 3, containing in addition to accounts of a border survey
  various historical material, much of it legendary

Tlacotli (N). Slave

Tlacuilo (N). Painter or writer; sometimes synonym of "escribano"

Tlalcohualli (N). "Land purchase"; purchased land

Tlalli (N). Land

Tlalmaitl (N). "Land hand"; fieldworker dependent on someone else, usually a noble

-Tlalnemac (N). "Land given to one"; one's land inheritance or land allotment within
  a distribution

Tlalquahuitl (N). "Land stick"; same as the quahuitl

-Tlan nenqui (N). "One who lives with someone"; a lower-level household dependent

Tlapaliuhqui, pl. tlapaliuhque (N). "Vigorous person"; an adult male of marriageable
  age and fit for all work, generally applied to an ordinary person, commoner

Tlatoani, pl. tlatoque (N). Dynastic ruler of an altepetl

Tlaxilacaleque (N). Citizens of a tlaxilacalli; also its authorities

Tlaxilacalli (N). Altepetl constituent; more common than "calpolli," especially as a
  territorial unit

Tlayacatl (N). In this context, a sub-altepetl with its own tlatoani inside a complex
  altepetl that usually lacks a single dominant ruler

Tomín (S). A coin or value worth one-eighth of a peso; in Nahuatl, a term for coin,
  cash, or money generally

Topile (N). "One with a staff"; constable, official in any of various medium-level
  supervisory posts

Visita (S). Inspection tour, visit; by extension, a district church visited periodically by
  a priest from the main parish church

Vocales (S). The body of electors in an altepetl in postconquest times

Yaotequihuacacalli (N). "War leader–house"; an independent establishment set up
  by a person who has received recognition for achievement in war but is not a teuctli
  or lord

Bibliography

In all likelihood, well over half of all the older Nahuatl documents in existence are held by the Archivo General de la Nación in Mexico City (AGN). This repository is surely the first place to look for mundane Nahuatl records of all kinds, and it has been my mainstay. Among its holdings, the section Tierras stands out as the overwhelmingly predominant source, although a significant amount of material was found in Hospital de Jesús, Bienes Nacionales, and Vínculos as well. The documents tend to be wills and yet more wills, with a good sprinkling of land sales and transfers, petitions and other correspondence, lists of people or assets, local court proceedings, and records of cabildo actions.

But if the AGN has provided the basic archival landscape, other repositories have revealed salient features necessary to define it. With a few exceptions such as the great cache of documents concerning Coyoacan in Tierras 1735, or the collection of petitions and other papers from the Marquesado in Hospital de Jesús 210, the AGN seems at some past time to have been ransacked of spectacular materials in Nahuatl (or perhaps they were held back from the beginning and never entered the central governmental archives). The greatest single holder of such documents is the Archivo Histórico of the Museo Nacional de Antropología e Historia in Mexico City (MNAH AH). It contains, in its Colección Antigua and the Gómez de Orozco Collection, items as important for the present study as the early Cuernavaca-region censuses, the Tlaxcalan cabildo minutes, annals of Puebla and Tlaxcala, the sixteenth-century annals of Tenochtitlan associated (probably wrongly) with the name of Juan Bautista, and the de la Cruz family papers from Tepemaxalco (CFP). In the Archivo Histórico one will also find photocopies and microfilm of many Nahuatl documents whose originals are elsewhere, some of them now inaccessible or lost.

The Biblioteca Nacional in Mexico City holds the original of the Cantares Mexicanos, which I consulted (although I mainly used facsimiles and published transcriptions). The Biblioteca's holdings include a good share of mundane documentation, which I confess to not having explored systematically, since my allotted archival time was already being devoted to investigating virtually identical material in the AGN.

Repositories in the United States have been important for my project. At the top of the list are holdings of the Special Collections section of the UCLA Research Library, among which the Tulancingo collection (UCLA TC) was especially significant. The Nahuatl material is not very bulky (the whole collection is only a fraction of a much larger Tulancingo corpus thought to exist elsewhere), but it represents a typical range of mundane documentation spread across a wide time period and originating at the northeastern extreme of the Nahua world; thus it was invaluable for purposes of estimating the geographical and temporal scope of various phenomena. Also very useful at UCLA was the McAfee Collection, containing a concentration of mundane documents from Coyoacan, Azcapotzalco, and the far west (a good deal of this material entered into Anderson et al. 1976 [BC]).

The Bancroft Library at the University of California, Berkeley, holds the Tetzcoco dialogues, which were the basis of Karttunen and Lockhart 1987 (ANS) and thus added a dimension to the present study. After I had halted archival work, the Bancroft acquired a major collection of Nahuatl bills of sale from the Coyoacan region; although I did not use them directly, I profited from the study of them carried out by Rebecca Horn (1989). The Newberry Library's Ayer Collection contains older Nahuatl material both spectacular and mundane; most useful to me were some mundane records from the Toluca Valley in the late period. The Lilly Library at Indiana University holds the Tula cofradía book (TCB), and the Holy Wednesday playlet, so crucial to pinning down the original circumstances of theatrical production in Nahuatl, is now in Princeton's Firestone Library. In the Library of Congress I found some essential plays not included in the published collection of Fernando Horcasitas (TN). Many of the repositories just named have other related materials that I had no occasion to use, and they continue to make meaningful acquisitions of older Nahuatl documents.

Abroad, the Bibliothèque Nationale of Paris holds a well-known series of major Nahuatl writings. In the case of the Historia Tolteca-Chichimeca, I have used the excellent color facsimile published by Kirchhoff, Güemes, and Reyes García (HTC); with the writings of Chimalpahin, the Zimmermann edition (CH); and with the Tepetlaoztoc land documents, the writings of Williams and Harvey. Equally important, however, were the Bibliothèque's Zapata annals (ZM), of which to date no transcription or translation, and very little comment, has been published. The Codex Aubin is held by the British Museum; I used the Dibble edition (CA), which is satisfactory for many purposes. Late in the game, however, I became aware that the facsimile in the Dibble publication is a redrawing, not always accurate in every detail and by no means giving the esthetic impression of the original. A new facsimile publication would be very much called for, as well as a facsimile edition of Zapata's annals (a team presently plans to publish a transcription and translation) and of Chimalpahin's work.

Historical investigations based on Nahuatl texts continue to face major challenges at the level of locating the appropriate sources and preparing them for analysis, tasks which are far less at the forefront in research involving Spanish documentation. Texts are relatively numerous, but they are extremely dispersed, usually only one or two in a dossier with little outer indication of containing indigenous-language material (see also Chap. 1, pp. 8–9). When I first began working on the present project in the AGN, I would alert all the other scholars in attendance to inform me of the whereabouts of any document in Nahuatl, of whatever description, that they might chance upon. Today such primitive measures would hardly be necessary; a catalog of Nahuatl materials in the AGN (C. Reyes García et al., 1982) has been published, and various monographs and dissertations using Nahuatl texts provide excellent archival leads; yet these represent only a fraction of the AGN's Nahuatl holdings. Work at cataloging continues, but it is doubtful that the Nahuatl material can ever be as well indexed as the Spanish. Informal networking is still crucial to undertakings of this kind, and I have profited greatly from it.

Even when located, Nahuatl sources require special treatment. Spanish documentation is so relatively uniform that skeletal notes are normally adequate. Nahuatl documents vary a great deal more, and much of the message, particularly for the more cultural and intellectual analysis that now tends to absorb us, is precisely in the detail of the variation. With many texts, there is little alternative to a full transcription, in the original orthography. Adequate analysis of most topics of a sociocultural nature is hardly to be expected in advance of reviewing a substantial number of relevant transcriptions. In my case, I spent a prolonged period in philological endeavors, often together with others, in order to bring such a relevant corpus into existence. My own unpublished archival notes are also centered on full transcriptions, and students, friends, and colleagues have shared many similar ones of their own with me (for the names of these generous colleagues see Chap. 1, pp. 12–13).

Transcriptions being so crucial, studies based on older Nahuatl texts, whether historical, anthropological, linguistic, or literary, could profit greatly from the wide circulation among interested scholars of some of the relatively polished transcriptions being made in the course of research. Publication of texts has achieved much and in the future will doubtless achieve much more, but it is likely that many more texts are worthy of transcription and close analysis than will ever be formally published. Although informal networking, as in my own case, can help immensely, it has obvious limitations. Some sort of warehousing of transcribed texts in easily reproducible form is much to be desired, and indeed, some projects of the kind have been initiated.

To be useful, such transcriptions would have to respect the original orthography meticulously and in general be done with much care; if possible, they should be accompanied by a photocopy of the original. Research practices of many scholars in the field in fact make the fulfillment of these requirements quite realistic. The problem is how to protect the interests of the transcriber. A large amount of talent and skill is required to transcribe a Nahuatl document. Once an excellent transcription has been achieved, persons of very modest accomplishments can often translate and even interpret the text quite adequately; indeed, a good transcription contains very substantial elements of interpretation within itself, and rarely will the transcriber have completed the task without simultaneously having formed definite notions about the significance and context of the document. Thus it is unlikely that scholars will let their transcriptions roam free until they have made the fullest intellectual use of them. After that, however, perhaps such texts can contribute to easily accessible banks, greatly facilitating research of many kinds in the field.

The following list of relevant publications is perhaps not as extensive as one might expect in view of the scope of the present work. The reason is simple—Nahuatl studies and the writing of history have converged only very recently, and the corpus of directly relevant published items is relatively small. As made clear earlier (see Chap. 1, p. 13), I have relied above all on a small body of quite recently published philology, containing primarily precisely such transcriptions as those just discussed. Here I list in addition other items of interest for central Mexican ethnohistory, whether or not they feature indigenous-language materials, even when I have not directly referred to them in the body of the work. I have not, however, included other works important for the general history of central Mexico in the early period, although they have helped form my horizons and thus in some sense influenced the book, nor have I mentioned the standard documentary collections in Spanish.

Some of the items most cited in this book are dissertations based on Nahuatl materials; revised versions of two of them, Schroeder 1984 and Haskett 1985, have now been published as books (Schroeder 1991 and Haskett 1991), and although the page references will not match, the reader may find it useful to consult the published form of these works, which will be far more accessible than the original dissertations. The same is likely to happen in several additional cases. It is well to be aware, however, that the dissertations often contain precious transcriptions and extensive documentary quotes that do not find their way into the published books.

Altman, Ida, and James Lockhart, eds. 1976. *Provinces of Early Mexico: Variants of Spanish American Regional Evolution.* Los Angeles: UCLA Latin American Center.

Anderson, Arthur J. O., Frances Berdan, and James Lockhart. 1976. *Beyond the Codices* (BC). Berkeley and Los Angeles: University of California Press.

Andrews, J. Richard. 1975. *Introduction to Classical Nahuatl.* Austin: University of Texas Press.

Anguiano, Marina, and Matilde Chapa. 1976. "Estratificación social en Tlaxcala durante el siglo XVI." In Carrasco and Broda, listed below, pp. 118–56.

Archivo General de la Nación. 1979. *Catálogo de ilustraciones.* México: Centro de Información Gráfica del Archivo General de la Nación.

Arenas, Pedro de. 1982. *Vocabulario manual de las lenguas castellana y mexicana.* Facsimile of 1611 edition, with introduction by Ascensión H. de León-Portilla. México: Instituto de Investigaciones Filológicas, Instituto de Investigaciones Históricas, Universidad Nacional Autónoma de México.

Artigas H., Juan B. 1979. *La piel de la arquitectura: Murales de Santa María Xoxoteco.* México: Escuela Nacional de Arquitectura, Universidad Nacional Autónoma de México.

Bakewell, Peter J. 1971. *Silver Mining and Society in Colonial Mexico: Zacatecas, 1546–1700.* New York: Cambridge University Press.

———. 1984. *Miners of the Red Mountain.* Albuquerque: University of New Mexico Press.

Barlow, R. H. 1945. "La crónica 'X': Versiones coloniales de la historia de los Mexica Tenochca," *Revista Mexicana de Estudios Antropológicos,* 7: 65–81.

Barrera Vásquez, Alfredo. 1965. *El libro de los cantares de Dzitbalchi.* México: Instituto Nacional de Antropología e Historia.

Bautista, fray Juan. 1988. *Huehuetlahtolli.* Facsimile of 1600 edition, with introduction by Miguel León-Portilla and transcription and translation by Librado Silva Galeana. México: Comisión Nacional Conmemorativa del V Centenario del Encuentro de Dos Mundos.

Berdan, Frances. 1982. *The Aztecs of Central Mexico: An Imperial Society.* New York: Holt, Rinehart and Winston.

———. 1986. "Enterprise and Empire in Aztec and Early Colonial Mexico." In Barry

Isaac, ed., *Research in Economic Anthropology* (A Research Annual), *Supplement 2: Economic Aspects of Prehispanic Highland Mexico*, pp. 281–302. Greenwich, Conn.: Jai Press, Inc.

Bierhorst, John. 1985. *Cantares Mexicanos: Songs of the Aztecs*. Stanford, Calif.: Stanford University Press.

Borah, Woodrow. 1983. *Justice by Insurance: The General Indian Court of Colonial Mexico*. Berkeley and Los Angeles: University of California Press.

Brading, D. A. 1978. *Haciendas and Ranchos in the Mexican Bajío: León, 1700–1860*. Cambridge: Cambridge University Press.

———. 1991. *The First America: The Spanish Monarchy, Creole Patriots, and the Liberal State*. Cambridge: Cambridge University Press.

Brewer, Forrest, and Jean G. Brewer. 1971. *Vocabulario mexicano de Tetelcingo, Morelos*. 2d ed. México: Instituto Lingüístico de Verano.

Bricker, Victoria R. 1981. *The Indian Christ, the Indian King: The Historical Substrate of Maya Myth and Ritual*. Austin: University of Texas Press.

———. 1986. *A Grammar of Mayan Hieroglyphs*. Middle American Research Institute publication 56. New Orleans: Tulane University.

Bright, William. 1990. "'With One Lip, With Two Lips': Parallelism in Nahuatl," *Language*, 66: 437–52.

Broda, Johanna. 1976. "Los estamentos en el ceremonial mexica." In Carrasco and Broda, listed below, pp. 37–66.

———. 1987. "Templo Mayor as Ritual Space." In Johanna Broda, Davíd Carrasco, and Eduardo Matos Moctezuma, *The Great Temple of Tenochtitlan: Center and Periphery in the Aztec World*, pp. 61–123. Berkeley and Los Angeles: University of California Press.

Burkhart, Louise M. 1988. "The Solar Christ in Nahuatl Doctrinal Texts of Early Colonial Mexico," *Ethnohistory*, 35: 234–56.

———. 1989. *The Slippery Earth: Nahua-Christian Moral Dialogue in Sixteenth-Century Mexico*. Tucson: University of Arizona Press.

Calnek, Edward E. 1974. "Conjunto urbano y model residencial en Tenochtitlan." In Edward E. Calnek et al., *Ensayos sobre el desarrollo urbano de México*, pp. 11–65.

Campbell, R. Joe. 1985. *A Morphological Dictionary of Classical Nahuatl: A Morpheme Index to the 'Vocabulario en lengua mexicana y castellana' of fray Alonso de Molina*. Madison, Wis.: The Hispanic Seminary of Medieval Studies.

Campbell, R. Joe, and Mary L. Clayton. 1988. "Bernardino de Sahagún's Contributions to the Lexicon of Classical Nahuatl." In Klor de Alva, Nicholson, and Quiñones Keber, listed below, pp. 295–314.

Carochi, Horacio. 1983. *Arte de la lengua mexicana con la declaración de los adverbios della*. Facsimile of 1645 edition, with introduction by Miguel León-Portilla. México: Instituto de Investigaciones Filológicas, Instituto de Investigaciones Históricas, Universidad Nacional Autónoma de México.

Carrasco, Pedro. 1963. "Los caciques chichimecas de Tulancingo," *Estudios de Cultura Náhuatl*, 4: 85–91.

———. 1964. "Family Structure of Sixteenth-Century Tepoztlan." In Robert A. Manners, ed., *Process and Pattern in Culture: Essays in Honor of Julian H. Steward*, pp. 185–210. Chicago: Aldine.

————. 1966. "Sobre algunos términos de parentesco en el náhuatl clásico," *Estudios de Cultura Náhuatl*, 6: 149–66.

————. 1971. "Social Organization of Ancient Mexico." In Gordon F. Ekholm and Ignacio Bernal, eds., *Handbook of Middle American Indians*, 10: 349–75. Austin: University of Texas Press.

————. 1972. "La casa y hacienda de un señor tlalhuica," *Estudios de Cultura Náhuatl*, 10: 22–54.

————. 1976a. "Los linajes nobles del México antiguo." In Carrasco and Broda, listed below, pp. 19–36.

————. 1976b. "Estratificación social indígena en Morelos durante el siglo XVI." In Carrasco and Broda, listed below, pp. 102–17.

————. 1976c. "The Joint Family in Ancient Mexico: The Case of Molotla." In Hugo G. Nutini, Pedro Carrasco, and James M. Taggart, eds., *Essays on Mexican Kinship*, pp. 45–64. Pittsburgh: University of Pittsburgh Press.

————. 1984. "Royal Marriages in Ancient Mexico." In Harvey and Prem, listed below, pp. 41–81.

Carrasco, Pedro, and Johanna Broda, eds. 1976. *Estratificación social en la Mesoamérica prehispánica*. México: Centro de Investigaciones Superiores, Instituto Nacional de Antropología e Historia.

Carrasco, Pedro, and Jesús Monjarás-Ruiz, eds. 1976–78. *Colección de documentos sobre Coyoacán* (CDC). 2 vols. México: Centro de Investigaciones Superiores, Instituto Nacional de Antropología e Historia.

Carrillo y Gariel, Abelardo. 1959. *El traje en la Nueva España*. México: Instituto Nacional de Antropología e Historia.

Castillo F., Victor M. 1972. "Unidades nahuas de medida," *Estudios de Cultura Náhuatl*, 10: 195–223.

Celestino Solís, Eustaquio, Armando Valencia R., and Constantino Medina Lima, eds. 1985. *Actas de cabildo de Tlaxcala, 1547–1567*. México: Archivo General de la Nación.

Chance, John K., and William B. Taylor. 1985. "Cofradías and Cargos: An Historical Perspective on the Mesoamerican Civil-Religious Hierarchy," *American Ethnologist*, 12: 1–26.

Chimalpahin Quauhtlehuanitzin, don Domingo Francisco de San Antón Muñón. 1889. *Annales. Sixième et septième relations (1258–1612)*. Tr. and ed. by Rémi Siméon. Bibliothèque linguistique américaine, 12. Paris: Maisonneuve et Ch. Leclerc.

————. 1963–65. *Die Relationen Chimalpahin's zur Geschichte Mexico's* (CH). Ed. by Günter Zimmermann. 2 vols. Hamburg: Cram, De Gruyter.

————. 1983. *Octava relación: obra histórica de Domingo Francisco de San Antón Muñón Chimalpahin Cuauhtlehuanitzin*. Tr. and ed. by José Rubén Romero Galván. Instituto de Investigaciones Históricas, Universidad Nacional Autónoma de México.

Christian, William A., Jr. 1981. *Local Religion in Sixteenth-Century Spain*. Princeton, N.J.: Princeton University Press.

Clavigero, Francisco Javier. *Historia Antigua de México*. Ed. by Mariano Cuevas. 4 vols. México: Porrúa, 1958.

Cline, Howard F. 1973. "Selected Nineteenth-Century Mexican Writers on Ethnohistory." In Robert Wauchope, gen. ed., *Handbook of Middle American Indians*, 13 (*Guide to Ethnohistorical Sources*, part 2): 370–427.

Cline, S. L. 1984. "Land Tenure and Land Inheritance in Late Sixteenth-Century Culhuacan." In Harvey and Prem, listed below, pp. 277–309.

——. 1986. *Colonial Culhuacan, 1580–1600*. Albuquerque: University of New Mexico Press.

Cline, S. L., and Miguel León-Portilla, eds. 1984. *The Testaments of Culhuacan* (TC). Nahuatl Studies Series 1. Los Angeles: UCLA Latin American Center.

Codex Aubin, *see* Dibble

Codex Mendoza. 1980. *Colección de Mendoza o Códice Mendocino*. Facsimile by Francisco del Paso y Troncoso, commentary by Jesús Galindo y Villa. (Reprint of edition of 1925.) México: Editorial Innovación.

Codex Osuna. 1947. *Códice Osuna: Reproducción facsimilar de la obra del mismo título, editada en Madrid, 1878. Acompañada de 158 páginas inéditas en el Archivo General de la Nación (México) por el Prof. Luis Chávez Orozco*. México: Ediciones del Instituto Indigenista Interamericano.

Codex Ramírez. 1975. *Relación del origen de los indios que habitan esta Nueva España según sus historias* (together with Tezozomoc's *Crónica mexicana*, both introduced by Manuel Orozco y Berra). 2d ed. México: Porrúa.

Collier, George A., Renato I. Rosaldo, and John D. Wirth, eds. 1982. *The Inca and Aztec States, 1400–1800: Anthropology and History*. New York: Academic Press.

Colston, Stephen A. 1973. "Fray Diego Durán's *Historia de las Indias de Nueva España e Islas de la Tierra Firme*: A Historiographical Analysis." Ph.D. dissertation, UCLA.

Cook, Sherburne F., and Woodrow Borah. 1960. *The Indian Population of Central Mexico, 1531–1610*. Ibero-Americana, 44. Berkeley and Los Angeles: University of California Press.

——. 1971–79. *Essays in Population History*. 3 vols. Berkeley and Los Angeles: University of California Press.

Çorita, *see* Zorita

Corona Sánchez, Eduardo. 1976. "La estratificación social en el Acolhuacan." In Carrasco and Broda, listed above, pp. 88–101.

De la Cruz, sor Juana Inés. 1975. *Obras completas*. Ed. by Francisco Monterde. México: Porrúa.

Dibble, Charles E., ed. 1963. *Historia de la nación mexicana* (Codex Aubin). México: Ediciones José Porrúa Toranzas.

Doyle, Mary E. 1988. "The Ancestor Cult in Sixteenth- and Seventeenth-Century Central Peru." Ph.D. dissertation, UCLA.

Durán, fray Diego. 1967. *Historia de las Indias de Nueva España e Islas de la Tierra Firme*. Ed. by Angel María Garibay K. 2 vols. México: Porrúa.

Durand-Forest, Jacqueline de. 1971. "Cambios económicas y moneda entre los aztecas," *Estudios de Cultura Náhuatl*, 9: 105–24.

Dyckerhoff, Ursula. 1976. "Aspectos generales y regionales de la estratificación social (en Huexotzinco)." In Carrasco and Broda, listed above, pp. 157–77.

Edmonson, Munro S., ed. and tr. 1982. *The Ancient Future of the Itza: The Book of Chilam Balam of Tizimin.* Austin: University of Texas Press.

———. 1986. *Heaven Born Merida and Its Destiny: The Book of Chilam Balam of Chumayel.* Austin: University of Texas Press.

Elliott, J. H. 1970. *The Old World and the New, 1492–1650.* Cambridge: Cambridge University Press.

Farriss, Nancy M. 1984. *Maya Society Under Colonial Rule.* Princeton, N.J.: Princeton University Press.

Foster, George M. 1960. *Culture and Conquest: America's Spanish Heritage.* Chicago: Quadrangle Books.

Galarza, Joaquín. 1979. *Estudios de escritura indígena tradicional azteca-náhuatl.* México: Archivo General de la Nación.

García Martínez, Bernardo. 1987. *Los pueblos de la Sierra: El poder y el espacio entre los indios del norte de Puebla hasta 1700.* México: El Colegio de México.

Gardner, Brant. 1982. "A Structural and Semantic Analysis of Classical Nahuatl Kinship Terminology," *Estudios de Cultura Náhuatl,* 15: 89–124.

Garibay K., Angel María. 1970. *Llave del náhuatl.* 3d ed. México: Porrúa.

———. 1971. *Historia de la literatura náhuatl.* 2 vols. 2d. ed. México: Porrúa.

———, ed. 1958. *Veinte himnos sacros de los nahuas.* México: Instituto de Historia, Universidad Nacional Autónoma de México.

———. 1964–68. *Poesía náhuatl.* 3 vols. México: Instituto de Investigaciones Históricas, Universidad Nacional Autónoma de México.

Gerhard, Peter. 1972. *A Guide to the Historical Geography of New Spain.* Cambridge: Cambridge University Press.

Gibson, Charles. 1952. *Tlaxcala in the Sixteenth Century.* New Haven, Conn.: Yale University Press.

———. 1953. "Rotation of Alcaldes in the Indian Cabildo of Mexico City," *Hispanic American Historical Review,* 33: 212–23.

———. 1959–60. "The Aztec Aristocracy in Colonial Mexico," *Comparative Studies in Society and History,* 2: 169–96.

———. 1964. *The Aztecs Under Spanish Rule: A History of the Indians of the Valley of Mexico, 1519–1810.* Stanford, Calif.: Stanford University Press.

———. 1975. "Prose Sources in the Native Historical Tradition." In Robert Wauchope, gen. ed., *Handbook of Middle American Indians,* 15 (*Guide to Ethnohistorical Sources,* part 4, ed. by Howard F. Cline et al.): 311–21.

Gillespie, Susan D. 1989. *The Aztec Kings: The Construction of Rulership in Mexica History.* Tucson: University of Arizona Press.

Glass, John B. 1975. "A Census of Middle American Testerian Manuscripts." In Robert Wauchope, gen. ed., *Handbook of Middle American Indians,* 14 (*Guide to Ethnohistorical Sources,* part 3, ed. by Howard F. Cline et al.): 281–96.

Gómez de Cervantes, Gonzalo. 1944. *La vida económica y social de Nueva España al finalizar el siglo XVI.* Ed. by Alberto María Carreño. Biblioteca histórica mexicana de obras inéditas, series 1, 19. México: Antigua Librería Robredo.

González Torres, Yolotl. 1976. "La esclavitud entre los mexica." In Carrasco and Broda, listed above, pp. 78–87.

Gruzinski, Serge. 1989. *Man-Gods in the Mexican Highlands: Indian Power and Colonial Society, 1520–1800*. Stanford, Calif.: Stanford University Press.

Guaman Poma de Ayala, don Felipe. 1980. *El primer nueva coronica y buen gobierno* [1615]. Ed. by John V. Murra and Rolena Adorno. Translation and analysis of Quechua by George L. Urioste. 3 vols. México: Siglo Veintiuno.

Hanke, Lewis. 1949. *The Spanish Struggle for Justice in the Conquest of America*. Philadelphia: University of Pennsylvania Press.

Harvey, H. R. 1984. "Aspects of Land Tenure in Ancient Mexico." In Harvey and Prem, listed below, pp. 83–102.

Harvey, H. R., and Hanns J. Prem, eds. 1984. *Explorations in Ethnohistory: Indians of Central Mexico in the Sixteenth Century*. Albuquerque: University of New Mexico Press.

Haskett, Robert S. 1985. "A Social History of Indian Town Government in the Colonial Cuernavaca Jurisdiction, Mexico." Ph.D. dissertation, UCLA.

———. 1987. "Indian Town Government in Colonial Cuernavaca," *Hispanic American Historial Review*, 67: 203–31.

———. 1990. "Indian Community Land and Municipal Income in Colonial Cuernavaca: An Investigation Through Nahuatl Documents." In Arij Ouweneel and Simon Miller, eds. *The Indian Community of Colonial Mexico: Fifteen Essays*, pp. 130–41. Amsterdam: Center for Latin American Research and Documentation.

———. 1991. *Indigenous Rulers: An Ethnohistory of Town Government in Colonial Cuernavaca*. Albuquerque: University of New Mexico Press.

Hassig, Ross. 1985. *Trade, Tribute, and Transportation: The Sixteenth-Century Political Economy of the Valley of Mexico*. Norman: University of Oklahoma Press.

Heizer, Robert F., and Albert B. Elsasser. 1980. *The Natural World of the California Indians*. Berkeley and Los Angeles: University of California Press.

Hernández Hernández, Delfino. 1986. "Poemas nahuas de la Huasteca," *Estudios de Cultura Náhuatl*, 18: 99–107.

Hicks, Frederick. 1976. "Mayeque y calpuleque en el sistema de clases del México antiguo." In Carrasco and Broda, listed above, pp. 67–87.

———. 1984. "Rotational Labor and Urban Development in Prehispanic Tetzcoco." In Harvey and Prem, listed above, pp. 147–74.

Hill, Jane H., and Kenneth C. Hill. 1986. *Speaking Mexicano: Dynamics of Syncretic Language in Central Mexico*. Tucson: University of Arizona Press.

Himmerich, Robert T. 1984. "The Encomenderos of New Spain." Ph.D. dissertation, UCLA.

Hinz, Eike, Claudine Hartau, and Marie-Luise Heimann-Koenen, eds. 1983. *Aztekischer Zensus. Zur indianischen Wirtschaft und Gesellschaft im Marquesado um 1540: Aus dem "Libro de Tributos" (Col. Ant. Ms. 551) im Archivo Histórico, México (AZ)*. 2 vols. Hanover: Verlag für Ethnologie.

Horcasitas, Fernando. 1974. *El teatro náhuatl* (TN). México: Universidad Nacional Autónoma de México.

———, tr. and ed. 1974a. *De Porfirio Díaz a Zapata: Memoria náhuatl de Milpa Alta*. 2d ed. México: Instituto de Investigaciones Históricas, Universidad Nacional Autónoma de México.

Horcasitas, Fernando, and Bente Bittmann Simons, eds. 1974. "Anales jeroglíficos e históricos de Tepeaca," *Anales de Antropología*, 11: 225–93.

Horn, Rebecca. 1989. "Postconquest Coyoacan: Aspects of Indigenous Sociopolitical and Economic Organization in Central Mexico, 1550–1650." Ph.D. dissertation, UCLA.

———. 1991. "The Sociopolitical Organization of the Colonial Jurisdiction of Coyoacan." In Ricardo Sánchez, Eric Van Young, and Gisela von Wobeser, eds., *Ciudad y campo en la historia de México.* 2 vols. México: Instituto de Investigaciones Históricas, Universidad Nacional Autónoma de México.

Hunt, Marta Espejo-Ponce. 1974. "Colonial Yucatan: Town and Region in the Seventeenth Century." Ph.D. dissertation, UCLA.

———. 1976. "The Processes of the Development of Yucatan, 1600–1700." In Ida Altman and James Lockhart, eds., *Provinces of Early Mexico.* Los Angeles: UCLA Latin American Center.

Ixtlilxochitl, don Fernando de Alva. 1975–77. *Obras históricas.* Ed. by Edmundo O'Gorman. 2 vols. México: Instituto de Investigaciones Históricas, Universidad Nacional Autónoma de México.

Karttunen, Frances. 1978. "Development of Inanimate Plural Marking in Postconquest Nahuatl," *Texas Linguistic Forum,* 10: 21–29.

———. 1982. "Nahuatl Literacy." In George A. Collier et al., eds., *The Inca and Aztec States,* pp. 395–417. New York: Academic Press.

———. 1983. *An Analytical Dictionary of Nahuatl.* Austin: University of Texas Press.

———. 1985. *Nahuatl and Maya in Contact with Spanish.* Texas Linguistic Forum 26. Austin: Department of Linguistics, University of Texas.

———, ed. 1981. *Nahuatl Studies in Memory of Fernando Horcasitas.* Texas Linguistic Forum 18. Austin: Department of Linguistics, University of Texas.

Karttunen, Frances, and James Lockhart. 1976. *Nahuatl in the Middle Years: Language Contact Phenomena in Texts of the Colonial Period* (NMY). University of California Publications in Linguistics 85. Berkeley and Los Angeles: University of California Press.

———. 1976a. "Characteristics of Nahuatl Resonants." In Bates Hoffer and Betty Lou Dubois, eds., *Southwest Areal Linguistics Then and Now,* pp. 1–15. San Antonio, Tex.: Trinity University.

———. 1978. "Textos en náhuatl del siglo XVIII: Un documento de Amecameca, 1746," *Estudios de Cultura Náhuatl,* 13: 153–75.

———. 1980. "La estructura de la poesía náhuatl vista por sus variantes," *Estudios de Cultura Náhuatl,* 14: 15–65.

Karttunen, Frances, and James Lockhart, eds. 1987. *The Art of Nahuatl Speech: The Bancroft Dialogues* (ANS). Nahuatl Studies Series, 2. Los Angeles: UCLA Latin American Center.

Kellogg, Susan. 1979. "Social Organization in Early Colonial Tenochtitlan-Tlatelolco: An Ethnohistorical Study." Ph.D. dissertation, University of Rochester.

Key, Harold, and Mary Ritchie de Key. 1953. *Vocabulario mejicano de la Sierra de Zacapoaxtla, Puebla.* México: Instituto Lingüístico de Verano.

Kirchhoff, Paul, Lina Odena Güemes, and Luis Reyes García, eds. 1976. *Historia tolteca-chichimeca* (HTC). México: Instituto Nacional de Antropología e Historia.

Klor de Alva, J. Jorge. 1982. "La historicidad de los 'Coloquios' de Sahagún," *Estudios de Cultura Náhuatl,* 15: 147–184.

———. 1988. "Contar vidas: La autobiografía confesional y la reconstrucción de ser nahua," *Arbor*, 515–516: 49–78.

———. 1991. "Sin and Confession Among the Colonial Nahuas." In Ricardo Sánchez, Eric Van Young, and Gisela von Wobeser, eds., *Ciudad y campo en la historia de México*. 2 vols. México: Instituto de Investigaciones Históricas, Universidad Nacional Autónoma de México.

Klor de Alva, J. Jorge, H. B. Nicholson, and Eloise Quiñones Keber, eds. 1988. *The Work of Bernardino de Sahagún: Pioneer Ethnographer of Sixteenth-Century Aztec Mexico*. Albany, N.Y., and Austin: Institute for Mesoamerican Studies, State University of New York at Albany, University of Texas Press.

Konrad, Herman W. 1980. *A Jesuit Hacienda in Colonial Mexico: Santa Lucía, 1576–1767*. Stanford, Calif.: Stanford University Press.

Krug, Frances M. n.d. "The Nahuatl Annals of the Tlaxcala-Puebla Region, Seventeenth and Eighteenth Centuries." Ph.D. dissertation in progress, UCLA.

Kubler, George. 1948. *Mexican Architecture of the Sixteenth Century*. 2 vols. Yale Historical Publications, History of Art, 5. New Haven, Conn.: Yale University Press.

Lafaye, Jacques. 1976. *Quetzalcoatl and Guadalupe: The Formation of Mexican National Consciousness, 1532–1813*. Chicago: University of Chicago Press.

Lamphere, Louise. 1983. "Southwest Ceremonialism." In William C. Sturtevant, gen. ed., *Handbook of North American Indians*, 10 (*Southwest*, ed. by Alfonso Ortiz): 743–63.

Landa, fray Diego de. 1973. *Relación de las cosas de Yucatán*. Introduction by Angel María Garibay K. 10th ed. México: Porrúa.

Lasso de la Vega, Luis. 1926. *Huey tlamahuiçoltica* . . . Facsimile of 1649 edition, tr. by Primo Feliciano Velázquez. México: Carreño e Hijo.

Lastra de Suárez, Yolanda, and Fernando Horcasitas. 1978. "El náhuatl en el norte y occidente del Estado de México," *Anales de Antropología*, 15: 185–250.

Launey, Michel. 1979. *Introduction à la langue et a la littérature aztèques*, vol. 1: *Grammaire*. Paris: L'Harmattan.

Leander, Birgitta. 1967. *Códice de Otlazpan*. 2 vols, the second being a facsimile of the Nicolás León edition of "Códice Mariano Jiménez." México: Instituto Nacional de Antropología e Historia.

León, Nicolás, ed. 1982. *Códice Sierra*. México: Editorial Innovación.

León-Portilla, Miguel. 1956. *La filosofía náhuatl estudiada en sus fuentes*. México: Instituto Indigenista Interamericano.

———. 1967. *Trece poetas del mundo azteca*. México: Universidad Nacional Autónoma de México.

———. 1976. *Visión de los vencidos: Relaciones indígenas de la conquista*. With texts translated by Angel María Garibay K. 7th ed. México: Biblioteca del Estudiante Universitario, Universidad Nacional Autónoma de México.

———. 1983. "Cuicatl y tlahtolli: Las formas de expresión en náhuatl," *Estudios de Cultura Náhuatl*, 16: 13–108.

———. 1986. "¿Una nueva interpretación de los Cantares Mexicanos?," *Estudios de Cultura Náhuatl*, 18: 385–400.

Lockhart, James. 1968. *Spanish Peru, 1532–1560*. Madison: University of Wisconsin Press.

————. 1972a. *The Men of Cajamarca: A Social and Biographical Study of the First Conquerors of Peru*. Austin: University of Texas Press.

————. 1972b. "The Social History of Colonial Latin America: Evolution and Potential," *Latin American Research Review*, 7: 4–41.

————. 1976. "Capital and Province, Spaniard and Indian: The Example of Late Sixteenth-Century Toluca." In Ida Altman and James Lockhart, eds., *Provinces of Early Mexico*, pp. 99–123. Los Angeles: UCLA Latin American Center.

————. 1980. "Y la Ana lloró," *Tlalocan*, 8: 21–34.

————. 1981. "Toward Assessing the Phoneticity of Older Nahuatl Texts: Analysis of a Document from the Valley of Toluca, Eighteenth Century." In Frances Karttunen, ed., *Nahuatl Studies in Memory of Fernando Horcasitas*, pp. 151–69. Texas Linguistic Forum, 18. Austin: Department of Linguistics, University of Texas.

————. 1982. "Views of Corporate Self and History in Some Valley of Mexico Towns, Late Seventeenth and Eighteenth Centuries." In George A. Collier et al., eds., *The Inca and Aztec States*, pp. 367–93. New York: Academic Press.

————. 1985. "Some Nahua Concepts in Postconquest Guise," *History of European Ideas*, 6: 465–82.

————. 1989. Review of Hugo G. Nutini, *Todos Santos in Rural Tlaxcala*, *Hispanic American Historical Review*, 69: 571–72.

————. 1991a. *Nahuas and Spaniards: Postconquest Central Mexican History and Philology* (N&S). Stanford, Calif., and Los Angeles: Stanford University Press and UCLA Latin American Center.

————. 1991b. "Complex Municipalities: Tlaxcala and Tulancingo in the Sixteenth Century." In Ricardo Sánchez, Eric Van Young, and Gisela von Wobeser, eds., *Ciudad y campo en la historia de México*. México: Instituto de Investigaciones Históricas, Universidad Nacional Autónoma de México.

————, ed. n.d. *We People Here: Nahuatl Accounts of the Conquest of Mexico*. Forthcoming, University of California Press.

Lockhart, James, Frances Berdan, and Arthur J. O. Anderson. 1986. *The Tlaxcalan Actas: A Compendium of the Records of the Cabildo of Tlaxcala (1545–1627)* (TA). Salt Lake City: University of Utah Press.

Lockhart, James, and Enrique Otte, eds. 1976. *Letters and People of the Spanish Indies, Sixteenth Century*. New York: Cambridge University Press.

Lockhart, James, and Stuart B. Schwartz. 1983. *Early Latin America: A History of Colonial Spanish America and Brazil*. New York: Cambridge University Press.

Loera y Chávez (de Esteinou), Margarita. 1977. *Calimaya y Tepemaxalco: Tenencia y transmisión hereditaria de la tierra en dos comunidades indígenas (época colonial)*. México: Departamento de Investigaciones, Instituto Nacional de Antropología e Historia.

López Austin, Alfredo, ed. 1969. *Augurios y abusiones*. Instituto de Investigaciones Históricas, Universidad Nacional Autónoma de México.

————. 1984. *Cuerpo humano e ideología: Las concepciones de los antiguos nahuas*. 2d ed. 2 vols. Instituto de Investigaciones Antropológicas, Universidad Nacional Autónoma de México.

López y Magaña, Juan. 1980. "Aspects of the Nahuatl Heritage of Juan Bautista Pomar." MA paper in Latin American Studies, UCLA. (López y Magaña's UCLA doctoral dissertation, in progress, will also contain the Nahuatl documents referred to here.)

McAndrew, John. 1964. *The Open-Air Churches of Sixteenth-Century Mexico*. Cambridge, Mass.: Harvard University Press.

Martin, Cheryl E. 1985. *Rural Society in Colonial Morelos*. Albuquerque: University of New Mexico Press.

Martínez, Hildeberto. 1984. *Tepeaca en el siglo XVI: Tenencia de la tierra y organización de un señorío*. Ediciones de la Casa Chata. México: Centro de Investigaciones y Estudios Superiores en Antropología Social.

Matrícula de Tributos. 1980. *Matrícula de Tributos: (Códice de Moctezuma)*. With commentary by Frances F. Berdan and Jacqueline de Durand-Forest. Graz, Austria: Akademische Druck- u. Verlagsanstalt.

Maza, Francisco de la. 1981. *El guadalupanismo mexicano*. México: Fondo de Cultura Económica.

Mendieta, fray Gerónimo de. n.d. *Historia eclesiástica indiana*. 2d ed. 5 vols. México: Editorial Chávez Hayhoe.

Miranda, José. 1952. *El tributo indígena en la Nueva España durante el siglo XVI*. México: El Colegio de México.

Molina, fray Alonso de. 1970. *Vocabulario en lengua castellana y mexicana y mexicana y castellana (1571)*. México: Porrúa.

———. 1984. *Confessionario mayor en la lengua mexicana y castellana (1569)*. With introduction by Roberto Moreno. México: Instituto de Investigaciones Filológicas, Instituto de Investigaciones Históricas, Universidad Nacional Autónoma de México.

Motolinia (Benavente), fray Toribio de. 1971. *Memoriales o libro de las cosas de la Nueva España y de los naturales de ella*. Ed. by Edmundo O'Gorman. México: Instituto de Investigaciones Históricas, Universidad Nacional Autónoma de México.

Munch, Guido. 1976. *El cacicazgo de San Juan Teotihuacan durante la colonia*. Colección Científica, Historia, 32. México: Centro de Investigaciones Superiores, Instituto Nacional de Antropología e Historia.

Muñoz Camargo, Diego. 1978. *Historia de Tlaxcala*. Ed. by Alfredo Chavero. 2d ed. México: Editorial Innovación.

———. 1984. *Descripción de la ciudad y provincia de Tlaxcala*. Ed. by René Acuña. México: Instituto de Investigaciones Antropológicas, Universidad Nacional Autónoma de México.

Nicholson, H. B. 1971. "Phoneticism in the Late Pre-Hispanic Central Mexican Writing System." In Elizabeth P. Benson, ed., *Mesoamerican Writing Systems*, pp. 1–46. Washington, D.C.: Dumbarton Oaks.

———. 1973. "Eduard Georg Seler, 1849–1922." In Robert Wauchope, gen. ed., *Handbook of Middle American Indians*, 13 (*Guide to Ethnohistorical Sources*, part 2, ed. Howard F. Cline et al.): 348–69.

Nutini, Hugo G. 1980–84. *Ritual Kinship*, vol. 1 (coauthored with Betty Bell): *Ideological and Structural Integration of the Compadrazgo System in Rural Tlaxcala*; vol. 2, *The Structure and Historical Development of the Compadrazgo System in Rural Tlaxcala*. Princeton, N.J.: Princeton University Press.

———. 1988. *Todos Santos in Rural Tlaxcala: A Syncretic, Expressive, and Symbolic Analysis of the Cult of the Dead*. Princeton, N.J.: Princeton University Press.

Offner, Jerome A. 1983. *Law and Politics in Aztec Texcoco*. Cambridge: Cambridge University Press.

———. 1984. "Household Organization in the Texcocan Heartland." In Harvey and Prem, listed above, pp. 127–46.

Offutt, Leslie Scott. 1982. "Urban and Rural Society in the Mexican North: Saltillo in the Late Colonial Period." Ph.D. dissertation, UCLA.

Olivera, Mercedes. 1976. "El despotismo tributario en la región de Cuauhtinchan–Tepeaca." In Carrasco and Broda, listed above, pp. 181–206.

———. 1978. *Pillis y macehuales: Las formaciones sociales y los modos de producción de Tecali del siglo XII al XVI*. Ediciones de La Casa Chata. México: Centro de Investigaciones Superiores, Instituto Nacional de Antropología e Historia.

Olmos, fray Andrés de. 1972. *Arte para aprender la lengua mexicana*. Ed. by Rémi Siméon. Facsimile of 1875 Paris edition, with prologue by Miguel León-Portilla. Guadalajara: Edmundo Aviña Levy Editor.

Parsons, Jeffrey R. n.d. "Political Implications of Prehispanic Chinampa Agriculture in the Valley of Mexico." In H. R. Harvey, ed., *Land and Politics in the Valley of Mexico: A Two-Thousand Year Perspective*. Albuquerque: University of New Mexico Press. Forthcoming.

Paso y Troncoso, Francisco, ed. 1905–48. *Papeles de Nueva España*. 9 vols. Madrid: Sucs. de Rivadeneyra, and México: Vargas Rea.

———. 1939–42. *Espistolario de la Nueva España, 1505–1818*. 16 vols. Biblioteca histórica mexicana de obras inéditas, series 2. México: Antigua Librería Robredo.

Pastor, Rodolfo. 1987. *Campesinos y reformas: La mixteca, 1700–1856*. México: El Colegio de México.

Peterson, Jeanette Favrot. 1985. "The Garden Frescoes of Malinalco." Ph.D. dissertation, UCLA.

———. 1988. "The *Florentine Codex* Imagery and the Colonial *Tlacuilo*." In Klor de Alva, Nicholson, and Quiñones Keber, listed above, pp. 273–93.

Pomar, Juan Bautista. 1941. *Relación de Tezcoco*. In Joaquín García Icazbalceta, ed., *Nueva colección de documentos para la historia de México*. México: Editorial Chávez Hayhoe.

Prem, Hanns J. 1967. *Die Namenshieroglyphen der Matrícula von Huexotzinco*. Hamburg: Wittenborn Söhne.

———. 1976. "La propiedad rural como indicador de estratificación social (en Huexotzinco)." In Carrasco and Broda, listed above, pp. 178–80.

———, ed. 1974. *Matrícula de Huexotzinco*. Graz, Austria: Akademische Druck- u. Verlagsanstalt.

Ramírez, Alfredo. 1986. "Miltzintli Cualtzin y otros poemas," *Estudios de Cultura Náhuatl*, 18: 109–21.

Ramírez Cabañas, Joaquín. 1941. "Los macehuales," *Filosofía y letras*, 2: 112–24.

Reyes García, Cayetano, et al., comps. 1982. *Documentos mexicanos*. 2 vols. México: Archivo General de la Nación.

Reyes García, Luis. 1961. "Documentos nahoas sobre el Estado de Chiapas," *VII Mesa Redonda de la Sociedad Mexicana de Antropología*, pp. 167–93.

———. 1975. "El término calpulli en los documentos del centro de México." Paper presented at the Seminario de Verano sobre Organización Social del México Antiguo under the auspices of the Centro de Investigaciones Científicas, Instituto Nacional de Antropología e Historia.

———. 1977. *Cuauhtinchan del siglo XII al XVI: Formación y desarrollo histórico de un señorío prehispánico.* Wiesbaden: Franz Steiner Verlag.

———. 1979. "El término calpulli en documentos del siglo XVI." Paper presented at the International Congress of Americanists, Vancouver.

———, ed. 1978. *Documentos sobre tierras y señorío en Cuauhtinchan.* Colección Científica, Fuentes, Historia Social. México: Centro de Investigaciones Superiores, Instituto Nacional de Antropología e Historia.

Reyes García, Luis, and Dieter Christensen. 1976. *Der Ring aus Tlalocan/El anillo de Tlalocan: Mitos, oraciones, cantos y cuentos de los nawas actuales de los estados de Veracruz y Puebla, México.* Quellenwerke zur alten Geschichte Amerikas, vol. 12. Berlin: Gebr. Mann.

Ricard, Robert. 1966. *The Spiritual Conquest of Mexico.* Translation of *La "conquête spirituelle" du Mexique* (1933) by Lesley Byrd Simpson. Berkeley and Los Angeles: University of California Press.

Riese, Berthold Christoph. 1986. *Ethnographische Dokumente aus Neuspanien im Umfeld der Codex Magliabechi-Gruppe.* Acta Humboldtiana 10. Stuttgart: Franz Steiner Verlag.

Robertson, Donald. 1959. *Mexican Manuscript Painting of the Early Colonial Period: The Metropolitan Schools.* Yale Historical Publications, History of Art, 12. New Haven, Conn.: Yale University Press.

———. 1972. "The Pinturas (Maps) of the Relaciones Geográficas, with a Catalog." In Robert Wauchope, gen. ed., *Handbook of Middle American Indians,* 12 (*Guide to Ethnohistorical Sources,* part 1, ed. by Howard F. Cline): 243–78.

———. 1975. "Techialoyan Manuscripts and Paintings, with a Catalog." In Robert Wauchope, gen. ed., *Handbook of Middle American Indians,* 14 (*Guide to Ethnohistorical Sources,* part 3, ed. by Howard F. Cline): 253–80.

Rojas Rabiela, Teresa. 1984. "Agricultural implements in Mesoamerica." In Harvey and Prem, listed above, pp. 175–204.

———. 1988. *Las siembras de ayer: La agricultura indígena del siglo XVI.* México: Secretaría de Educación Pública/Centro de Investigaciones y Estudios Superiores en Antropología Social.

Rojas (Rabiela), Teresa, Marina Anguiano, Matilde Chapa, and Amelia Camacho, comps. 1987. *Padrones de Tlaxcala del siglo XVI y Padrón de Nobles de Ocotelolco.* Ediciones de la Casa Chata, Colección Documentos. México: Centro de Investigaciones y Estudios Superiores en Antropología Social.

Rounds, J. 1982. "Dynastic Succession and the Centralization of Power in Tenochtitlan." In George A. Collier et al., eds., *The Inca and Aztec States, 1400–1800,* pp. 63–89. New York: Academic Press.

Roys, Ralph, ed. and tr. 1933. *The Book of Chilam Balam of Chumayel.* Washington, D.C.: Carnegie Institution of Washington.

———. 1939. *The Titles of Ebtun.* Washington, D.C.: Carnegie Institution of Washington.

Ruiz de Alarcón, Hernando. 1953. *Tratado de las idolatrías . . .* Ed. by Francisco del Paso y Troncoso. 2d ed. México: Librería Navarro.

———. 1984. *Treatise on the Heathen Superstitions that Today Live Among the Indians Native to this New Spain, 1629* (RA). Tr. and ed. by J. Richard Andrews and Ross Hassig. Norman: University of Oklahoma Press.

Ruvalcaba Mercado, Jesús. 1985. *Agricultura india en Cempoala, Tepeapulco y Tulancingo, siglo XVI*. México: Departamento del Distrito Federal.

Sahagún, fray Bernardino de. 1905–7. *Historia de las cosas de la Nueva España. Edición parcial en fascimile de los Códices Matritenses . . .* 4 vols. Madrid: Hauser y Menet.

———. 1975. *Historia general de las cosas de Nueva España*. Ed. by Angel María Garibay K. 3d ed. México: Porrúa.

———. 1950–82. *Florentine Codex: General History of the Things of New Spain* (FC). Tr. by Arthur J. O. Anderson and Charles E. Dibble. 13 parts. Salt Lake City and Santa Fe, N.M.: University of Utah Press and School of American Research, Santa Fe.

———. 1979. *Códice Florentino*. El Manuscrito 218–220 de la colección Palatina de la Biblioteca Medicea Laurenziana. Facsimile edition. Florence: Giunti Barbera and the Archivo General de la Nación.

———. 1986. *Coloquios y doctrina cristiana*. Ed. by Miguel León-Portilla. México: Fundación de Investigaciones Sociales, Universidad Nacional Autónoma de México.

———. 1989. *Conquest of New Spain, 1585 Revision*. Tr. by Howard F. Cline and ed. by S. L. Cline. Salt Lake City: University of Utah Press.

Scharlau, Birgit. 1986. "Altindianische Oralkultur zwischen Bilderschrift und Alphabet." Part 1 of Birgit Scharlau and Mark Münzel, *Quellqay: Mündliche Kultur und Schrifttradition bei den Indianern Lateinamerikas*. Frankfurt: Campus Verlag.

Schroeder, Susan. 1984. "Chalco and Sociopolitical Concepts in Chimalpahin." Ph.D. dissertation, UCLA.

———. 1989. "Chimalpahin's View of Spanish Ecclesiastics in Colonial Mexico." In Susan E. Ramírez, ed., *Indian-Religious Relations in Colonial Spanish America*. Foreign and Comparative Studies/Latin American Series 9. Syracuse, N.Y.: Maxwell School of Citizenship and Public Affairs, Syracuse University.

———. 1991. *Chimalpahin and the Kingdoms of Chalco*. Tucson: University of Arizona Press.

———. n.d. "Indigenous Sociopolitical Organization in Chimalpahin." In H. R. Harvey, ed., *Land and Politics in the Valley of Mexico: A Two-Thousand Year Perspective*. Albuquerque: University of New Mexico Press. Forthcoming.

Schwaller, John Frederick. 1987. *The Church and Clergy in Sixteenth-Century Mexico*. Albuquerque: University of New Mexico Press.

Soustelle, Jacques. 1961. *Daily Life of the Aztecs on the Eve of the Spanish Conquest*. Translation of *La vie quotidienne des Aztèques à la veille de la conquête espagnole* (1955) by Patrick O'Brian. Stanford, Calif.: Stanford University Press.

Spalding, Karen. 1967. "Indian Rural Society in Colonial Peru: The Example of Huarochirí." Ph.D. dissertation, University of California, Berkeley.

———. 1984. *Huarochirí: An Andean Society Under Inca and Spanish Rule*. Stanford, Calif.: Stanford University Press.

Spicer, Edward H. 1962. *Cycles of Conquest: The Impact of Spain, Mexico, and the*

United States on the Indians of the Southwest, 1533–1960. Tucson: University of Arizona Press.

Spores, Ronald, and Ross Hassig. 1984. *Five Centuries of Law and Politics in Central Mexico.* Publications in Anthropology 30. Nashville, Tenn.: Vanderbilt University.

Stern, Steve J. 1982. *Peru's Indian Peoples and the Challenge of Spanish Conquest: Huamanga to 1640.* Madison: University of Wisconsin Press.

Stevenson, Robert. 1968. *Music in Aztec and Inca Territory.* Berkeley and Los Angeles: University of California Press.

Sullivan, Thelma D., ed. 1987. *Documentos tlaxcaltecas del siglo XVI en lengua náhuatl.* México: Instituto de Investigaciones Antropológicas, Universidad Nacional Autónoma de México.

Szewczyk, David M. 1976. "New Elements in the Society of Tlaxcala, 1519–1618." In Ida Altman and James Lockhart, eds., *Provinces of Early Mexico*, pp. 137–53. Los Angeles: UCLA Latin American Center.

Taggart, James M. 1983. *Nahuat Myth and Social Structure.* Austin: University of Texas Press.

Taylor, William B. 1972. *Landlord and Peasant in Colonial Oaxaca.* Stanford, Calif.: Stanford University Press.

———. 1979. *Drinking, Homicide, and Rebellion in Colonial Mexican Villages.* Stanford, Calif.: Stanford University Press.

———. 1987. "The Virgin of Guadalupe in New Spain: An Inquiry into the Social History of Marian Devotion," *American Ethnologist,* 14: 9–33.

Tezozomoc, don Hernando [Fernando] de Alvarado. 1949. *Crónica mexicayotl.* Tr. and ed. by Adrián León. Publicaciones del Instituto de Historia, series 1, no. 10. México.

———. 1975. *Crónica mexicana* (together with *Códice Ramírez*, both introduced by Manuel Orozco y Berra). 2d ed. México: Porrúa.

Thompson, Philip C. 1978. "Tekanto in the Eighteenth Century." Ph.D. dissertation, Tulane University.

Toussaint, Manuel. 1967. *Colonial Art in Mexico.* Tr. and ed. by Elizabeth Wilder Weismann. Austin: University of Texas Press.

Torquemada, fray Juan de. 1969. *Monarquía Indiana.* Facsimile of 1723 edition. Introduction by Miguel León-Portilla. 3 vols. México: Porrúa.

Tutino, John M. 1976. "Provincial Spaniards, Indian Towns, and Haciendas: Interrelated Agrarian Sectors in the Valleys of Mexico and Toluca, 1750–1810." In Ida Altman and James Lockhart, eds., *Provinces of Early Mexico*, pp. 177–94. Los Angeles: UCLA Latin American Center.

Tuttle, Edward F. 1976. "Borrowing Versus Semantic Shift: New World Nomenclature in Europe." In Fredi Chiappelli, ed., *First Images of America: The Impact of the New World on the Old.* Berkeley and Los Angeles: University of California Press.

Urioste, George L., tr. and ed. 1983. *Hijos de Pariya Qaqa: La tradición de Waru Chiri (Mitología, ritos y costumbres).* 2 vols. Syracuse, N.Y.: Maxwell School of Citizenship and Public Affairs, Syracuse University.

Vaillant, George C. 1941. *The Aztecs of Mexico: Origin, Rise, and Fall of the Aztec Nation.* Garden City, N.Y.: Doubleday, Doran.

Van Zantwijk, Rudolph. 1985. *The Aztec Arrangement: The Social History of Pre-Spanish Mexico.* Norman: University of Oklahoma Press.

Velázquez, Primo Feliciano, ed. 1975. *Códice Chimalpopoca: Anales de Cuauhtitlan y Leyenda de los soles.* México: Instituto de Investigaciones Históricas, Universidad Nacional Autónoma de México.

Vetancurt, fray Agustín de. 1974. *Teatro Mexicano: Descripción breve de los sucesos ejemplares, históricos y religiosos del Nuevo Mundo de las Indias.* Facsimile of 1697–98 edition. México: Porrúa.

Weismann, Elizabeth Wilder. 1950. *Mexico in Sculpture, 1521–1821.* Cambridge, Mass.: Harvard University Press.

Williams, Barbara J. 1980. "Pictorial Representation of Soils in the Valley of Mexico: Evidence from the Codex Vergara," *Geoscience and Man,* 31: 51–62.

———. 1984. "Mexican Pictorial Cadastral Registers." In Harvey and Prem, listed above, pp. 103–25.

———. 1989. "Contact Period Rural Overpopulation in the Basin of Mexico: Carrying-Capacity Models Tested with Documentary Data," *American Antiquity,* 54: 715–32.

Williams, Barbara J., and H. R. Harvey. 1988. "Content, Provenience, and Significance of the *Codex Vergara* and the *Códice de Santa María Asunción,*" *American Antiquity,* 53: 337–351.

Wolf, Eric. 1959. *Sons of the Shaking Earth.* Chicago: University of Chicago Press.

Wood, Stephanie G. 1984. "Corporate Adjustments in Colonial Mexican Indian Towns: Toluca Region." Ph.D. dissertation, UCLA.

———. 1987. "Pedro Villafranca y Juana Gertrudis Navarrete: falsificador de títulos y su viuda (Nueva España, siglo XVIII)." In David G. Sweet and Gary B. Nash, eds., *Lucha por la supervivencia en América colonial.* México: Fondo de Cultura Económica.

———. n.d. (a). "Don Diego García de Mendoza Moctezuma: A Techialoyan Mastermind?," *Estudios de Cultura Náhuatl,* 19. Forthcoming.

———. n.d. (b). "Comparing Notes: Techialoyan Texts and Other Colonial Nahuatl writings." Paper presented at the Latin American Indian Literatures Association meeting at Cornell University, 1987. Forthcoming in a volume edited by Monica Barnes.

———. n.d. (c). "Accepting the Sword and Cross? Views of Spanish Conquest in Indian *Títulos* of Colonial Mexico," *Ethnohistory.* Forthcoming.

———. n.d. (d). "The False Techialoyan Resurrected," *Tlalocan.* Forthcoming.

———. n.d. (e). "Adopted Saints: Christian Images in Nahua Testaments of Late Colonial Toluca," forthcoming in *The Americas.*

Xokoyotsi, José Antonio. 1986. "Sempoalxóchitl. Veinte flores: una sola flor," *Estudios de Cultura Náhuatl,* 18: 41–97.

Zimmermann, Günter. 1970. *Briefe der indianischen Nobilität aus Neuspanien an Karl V und Philipp II um die Mitte des 16. Jahrhunderts.* Beiträge zur mittelamerikanischen Völkerkunde 10. Hamburg: Hamburgisches Museum für Völkerkunde und Vorgeschichte.

Zorita (Çorita), Doctor Alonso de. 1941. *Breve y sumaria relación de los señores . . . de la Nueva España.* In Joaquín García Icazbalceta, ed., *Nueva colección de documentos para la historia de México.* México: Editorial Chávez Hayhoe.

Index

Many of the entries in this index are far from exhaustive. With frequently mentioned places and important themes, only the most salient page references have been included. For the places especially, much potentially useful additional information can be found in the notes.

DATE DUE

MAY 1 0 2007	

GAYLORD   PRINTED IN U.S.A.

... the conquest : a social and cultural history of
the Indians of central Mexico, sixteenth through
eighteenth centuries / James Lockhart.
    p.   cm.
  Includes bibliographical references and index.
  ISBN 0-8047-1927-6 (cloth):   ISBN 0-8047-2317-6 (pb)
  1. Nahuas—History.   2. Nahuas—Social life and customs.
3. Mexico—History—Spanish colony, 1519–1810.   I. Title.
F1221.N3L63   1992
972'.02—dc20   91-29972
                                                        CIP

♾ This book is printed on acid-free paper.